MACROECONOMICS
Principles and Policy
First Canadian Edition

MACROECONOMICS
Principles and Policy
First Canadian Edition

William J. Baumol

New York University and Princeton University

Alan S. Blinder

Princeton University

Marc Lavoie

University of Ottawa

Mario Seccareccia

University of Ottawa

NELSON / EDUCATION

NELSON / E D U C A T I O N

Macroeconomics: Principles and Policy, First Canadian Edition

by William J. Baumol, Alan S. Blinder, Marc Lavoie, and Mario Seccareccia

Associate Vice President, Editorial Director:
Evelyn Veitch

Editor-in-Chief:
Anne Williams

Senior Acquisitions Editor:
Craig Dyer

Executive Marketing Manager:
Dave Ward

Developmental Editor:
My Editor Inc.

Photo Researcher and Permissions Coordinator:
Indu Arora

Senior Content Production Manager:
Natalia Denesiuk Harris

Production Service:
Lachina Publishing Services

Copy Editor:
June Trusty

Proofreader:
Lachina Publishing Services

Indexer:
Lachina Publishing Services

Manufacturing Manager:
Joanne McNeil

Design Director:
Ken Phipps

Managing Designer:
Katherine Strain

Interior Design:
Lisa Albonetti

Cover Image and Design:
Jennifer Leung

Compositor:
Lachina Publishing Services

Printer:
Courier

Library and Archives Canada Cataloguing in Publication Data

Macroeconomics: principles and policy / William J. Baumol ... [et al.]. — 1st Canadian ed.

Includes bibliographical references and index.

ISBN 978-0-17-625255-7

1. Macroeconomics—Textbooks. I. Baumol, William J.

HB172.5.M33523 2008   339
C2008-906465-8

ISBN-13: 978-0-17-625255-7
ISBN-10: 0-17-625255-X

ABOUT THE AUTHORS

◼ WILLIAM J. BAUMOL

William J. Baumol was born in New York City and received his B.S.S. at the College of the City of New York and his Ph.D. at the University of London.

He is professor of economics at New York University, and senior research economist and professor emeritus at Princeton University. He is a frequent consultant to the management of major firms in a wide variety of industries in the United States and other countries, as well as to a number of governmental agencies. In several fields, including the telecommunications and electric utility industries, current regulatory policy is based on his explicit recommendations. Among his many contributions to economics are research on the theory of the firm, the contestability of markets, the economics of the arts and other services—the "cost disease of the services" is often referred to as "Baumol's disease"—and economic growth, entrepreneurship, and innovation. In addition to economics, he taught a course in wood sculpture at Princeton for about 20 years.

He has been president of the American Economic Association and three other professional societies. He is an elected member of the National Academy of Sciences, created by the U.S. Congress, and of the American Philosophical Society, founded by Benjamin Franklin. He is also on the board of trustees of the National Council on Economic Education and of the Theater Development Fund. He is the recipient of 10 honorary degrees.

Baumol is the author of more than 35 books and hundreds of journal and newspaper articles. His writings have been translated into more than a dozen languages.

◼ ALAN S. BLINDER

Alan S. Blinder was born in New York City and attended Princeton University, where one of his teachers was William Baumol. After earning a master's degree at the London School of Economics and a Ph.D. at MIT, Blinder returned to Princeton, where he has taught since 1971. He is currently the Gordon S. Rentschler Memorial Professor of Economics and co-director of Princeton's Center for Economic Policy Studies, which he founded.

In January 1993, Blinder went to Washington as part of President Clinton's first Council of Economic Advisers. Then, from June 1994 through January 1996, he served as vice chairman of the Federal Reserve Board. He thus played a role in formulating both the fiscal and monetary policies of the 1990s, topics discussed extensively in this book. Blinder is a partner in the Promontory Financial Group, a leading consulting and advisory company serving the financial industry. In that capacity, he has consulted for a number of the country's largest financial institutions.

For more than 10 years, Blinder wrote newspaper and magazine columns on economic policy, and his op-ed pieces still appear periodically in various newspapers. He also appears frequently on CNN and CNBC, and is a regular commentator on PBS's "Nightly Business Report."

Blinder has been vice president of the American Economic Association and is a member of both the American Philosophical Society and the American Academy of Arts and Sciences. He has two grown sons and two grandsons, and lives in Princeton with his wife, where he plays tennis as often as he can.

MARC LAVOIE

Marc Lavoie was born in Ottawa, Ontario. He attended Carleton University as an undergraduate and then moved on to the University of Paris I (Panthéon-Sorbonne) to do his master's studies and earn a Ph.D. He then returned to Canada in 1979 and joined the University of Ottawa, where he has taught ever since and where he is now full professor of economics.

Lavoie is the author and co-author or co-editor of nine books (two of which are on the economics of ice hockey), and has published over 50 book chapters and 100 articles in refereed journals. Besides sports economics, his main expertise is in pricing theories, monetary economics, and growth theories.

He has been named visiting professor at several French universities—Bordeaux, Nice, Rennes, Dijon, Limoges, Paris 1, Paris 13, and Lille—as well as at Curtin University in Perth, Australia. He has also been invited to give lectures at summer universities in Berlin, Dunkerque, and Kansas City.

Lavoie was a member of the Canadian national fencing team (in sabre) from 1973 to 1984, and took part in the Summer Olympic Games in Montreal (1976) and Los Angeles (1984). He won the Canadian national senior fencing championships seven times, in 1975–1979 and 1985–1986. He has three sons, plays soccer once a week in the summer months, and often plays tennis with his spouse.

MARIO SECCARECCIA

Mario Seccareccia was born in Galluccio, Caserta, Italy, and moved to Montreal at the age of seven. He attended McGill University, where he completed his Ph.D. Since 1978, he has been teaching at the University of Ottawa, where he is full professor of economics.

Seccareccia has authored or co-edited eight books or monographs and has published some 75 articles or chapters of books. He is also editor of the New York-based *International Journal of Political Economy*. His principal research interests are in the areas of monetary economics, labour economics, and history of economic thought.

Since 1988, he has taught economics regularly at the Labour College of Canada and, over the years, has been a consultant economist to a number of trade unions, including direct involvement in collective bargaining via the Association of Professors of the University of Ottawa. He has also been appointed visiting professor of economics at the Université de Paris-Sud and the Université de Bourgogne in France.

He has one daughter and two sons and, when time permits, enjoys squash, swimming, and bicycling along the Rideau Canal.

BRIEF CONTENTS

TABLE OF CONTENTS

■ PART II   THE MACROECONOMY: AGGREGATE SUPPLY AND DEMAND   89

CHAPTER 5   AN INTRODUCTION TO MACROECONOMICS   91

CHAPTER 14 THE DEBATE OVER MONETARY AND FISCAL POLICY 303

CHAPTER 15 BUDGET DEFICITS IN THE SHORT AND LONG RUN 325

◼ PART IV   CANADA IN THE WORLD ECONOMY   367

PREFACE

Seemingly defying the scarcity principle, students and teachers alike are struck by the abundance of first-year textbooks in economics. How is our book different from the others? When we were asked to write the Canadian edition of the Baumol and Blinder textbook, we quickly discovered why the latter has remained so popular over the last 30 years. William Baumol and Alan Blinder can be compared to Alfred Marshall, the author of the first truly comprehensive and successful textbook on the principles of economics: They enjoy applying economic theory, and they use algebra or formalization only when it is absolutely necessary, not as a deterrent to student understanding. More than a hundred years ago, Marshall thought that these were appropriate rules to follow when doing economic analysis; we are convinced that these are still good rules to follow in a principles of economics textbook.

The purpose of Baumol and Blinder is not to overwhelm students with a series of techniques, formulas, and diagrams; rather, they seek to have a conversation with their readers, encouraging them to think for themselves and to enjoy all of the facets of economic reasoning. Both Baumol and Blinder have been highly involved with policy making and economic counselling. Their textbook reflects this, constantly dealing with policy-oriented questions and issues, which should appeal to a vast majority of students interested in socially relevant questions about the real world. We have done our best to maintain and even strengthen this strong policy approach in the Canadian version.

Another feature of the Baumol and Blinder textbook that we find commendable is its eclectic approach. While being enthusiastic admirers of the capitalist system, Baumol and Blinder are not afraid to emphasize the fact that most markets do not function according to the standards of perfect competition. Unfettered markets, with no government intervention, often entail letting a few enterprises corner the marketplace. As a result, they pay more attention to the analysis of monopolistic competition than do most rival textbooks. Their analysis goes far beyond the standard introduction of imperfections and externalities in some otherwise ideal market setting. For them, the main accomplishment of the market system is not its static efficiency, which is traditionally emphasized in many competing textbooks but, rather, its historically unprecedented record of innovation and growth. The same kind of healthy skepticism transpires at the aggregate level when dealing with the macroeconomic problems of growth, employment, and inflation. Baumol and Blinder decline to assume the existence of perfect competition when dealing with all of these issues and point emphatically to the relevance of government intervention. Once again, we did our best to pursue this eclectic approach.

A further strength of the Baumol and Blinder approach that we sought to apply in the Canadian context is their emphasis on the institutional features of the economy. While economics students at an advanced level of study often know little about institutional details, we believe that knowledge of the institutions and structure of the economy helps you to understand how the economic system actually works, at both the microeconomic and macroeconomic levels. The emphasis on institutions and policy issues thus involved a sizable amount of work on our part to find their relevant equivalents in a Canadian setting. In some instances, this required a considerable number of changes and, at times, a total rewrite!

For a long time, we have considered writing a first-year textbook that would reflect our philosophy of economics and offer students some elements of an alternative vision, so we were truly excited to be offered the opportunity by Nelson Education Ltd. to do this first Canadian edition of the Baumol and Blinder textbook. As mentioned before, Baumol and Blinder are well aware that economics can provide only a framework for thinking out issues, and that the answers economists put forth depend on the assumptions being entertained. This is also our view. Pluralism, not dogmatism, should rule. Great effort therefore went into exploring the plurality of opinions that constitute the intellectual landscape of contemporary economics.

In keeping with this pluralistic bent, our efforts to present economics as a social science are quite clear in the very first chapter of the book, where we offer definitions of economics that are broader and that go beyond the usual "study of scarcity." Chapter 1 also provides a list of issues on which Canadian economists tend to agree and another on which they disagree. We extend the discussion to include the reasons that explain controversies among economists, which we relate to the new view of research in science and to political winds.

■ FEATURES OF THE FIRST CANADIAN EDITION

As mentioned earlier, one of the changes that we have made to the U.S. edition involves the Chapter 1 Canadianization of institutional features and the extension of the discussion of issues on which Canadian economists tend to agree and of ones on which they disagree. The following is a list of the other major changes we have made.

In Chapter 2, we have not only made an effort to describe the distinctiveness of the Canadian economy, such as its degree of openness to foreign trade, but we have also spent time discussing comparative economic systems and where the Canadian economy fits within that framework.

While a number of well-established concepts in economics regarding scarcity and choice are found in Chapter 3, a more elaborate discussion of the principle of comparative advantage has been included.

Chapter 4, which covers supply and demand analysis, provides a balanced appraisal of the rent control and agricultural supply management programs that have been set up in Canada, pointing out that the freely competitive market mechanisms are powerful indeed, while most markets are neither free nor fully competitive. The appendix to the chapter also presents the simple algebra of market equilibrium, a feature that was requested by many reviewers.

Macroeconomics as such starts with Chapter 5. In contrast to microeconomics, there is no standard way to introduce macroeconomics to students anymore. Nearly anything goes, as different authors try very different approaches. Baumol and Blinder have stuck to the familiar Keynesian cross diagrams, adding the price dimension through the well-known (and, perhaps some might say, well-worn) aggregate demand and aggregate supply framework that they were the first to introduce into first-year textbooks in 1978. After some agonizing reflection, we decided to keep both their outline and this framework. Notwithstanding the drawbacks of the aggregate demand and aggregate supply framework in the price level and output space, it is still widely used by instructors as it allows presentation of just about any puzzling macroeconomic issue using the simple and familiar demand-side and supply-side approach.

Various additions have been made to Chapters 5 through 7. There is a discussion of well-being indexes, a table with the monthly recession dates of the Canadian and American business cycles, and an extensive review of the various measures of inflation rates based on the Consumer Price Index. The data describing the evolution of labour productivity and real wages, as well as real wages based on education level, provided for two interesting paradoxes, giving us the opportunity to discuss the differentiated evolution of real labour compensation and real wages, as well as the famous Yule statistical paradox, which brings students' attention to the problems of aggregation in an intuitive way. The shift toward GDP-based national accounts is completed in Chapter 8.

In Chapter 9, which deals with the Keynesian cross diagram, we have reintroduced a discussion of the famous paradox of thrift, which in our view helps to explain the resilience of the American and Canadian economies over the last few years, despite the very low personal saving rates. We have seized the opportunity also to introduce Keynes's 1930 banana parable, which is another illustration of the possible effects of personal saving. Finally, Appendix A of Chapter 9 discusses the distinction between fixed investment and investment in inventories, clarifying why saving and investment are always equal to each other in a national accounting sense, while their equality, in a macroeconomic sense, turns out to be an equilibrium condition.

The aggregate demand and aggregate supply framework is open to criticism, as it often combines contradicting mechanisms that require "dirty pedagogy." We have tried to avoid this in Chapter 10 by building an aggregate supply curve based on imperfect competition and markup pricing, where the upward slope arises from the hypothesis of decreasing returns. The causality thus runs from the quantity decision of firms (based, say, on expected demand), that compute their unit cost at that level of output and then set prices on the basis of the estimated unit cost (in lieu of the standard construction based on market-determined prices, with firms being lured into producing more by the profitability arising from higher prices). Our suggested causality is most consistent with Chapter 9, which provides a derivation of the aggregate demand curve with the help of the Keynesian cross analysis, based on exogenously given prices and a mechanism of quantity adjustments. This approach also appeared to be most consistent with the rest of the book, with its predominant Keynesian take.

Chapter 10 also introduces the possibility of a flat aggregate supply curve, at least for some range of output or of capacity utilization—a feature that we relate to the analysis of oligopolistic features and constant marginal costs in Chapter 12 of our *Microeconomics: Principles and Policy*. Also introduced in Chapter 10 is the possibility of an *upward-sloping* aggregate demand curve, when the positive wealth effects of lower prices are overwhelmed by the negative effects arising from more real debt burden. This allows us to go beyond the slow and weak effects of self-stabilizing mechanisms, since self-stabilizing mechanisms are self-defeating in the case of the upward-sloping aggregate demand curve. This provides additional justification for active fiscal and monetary policies. Still, Chapter 11, which is devoted to an understanding of Keynesian fiscal policy, adds a discussion of surprising anti-Keynesian episodes, where reductions in government expenditures led to increases in GDP, as was the case in Canada after 1996.

Chapters 12 and 13, which deal with the banking system and the Bank of Canada, have been subjected to the greatest revision. In particular, we have entirely removed the analysis of the money multiplier. Reserve requirements have not existed in Canada since 1994, and we believe it is high time for textbooks to reflect this change. In addition, central bankers have stated on numerous occasions that, even when there were reserve requirements, reserves were being provided *on demand* in day-to-day operations as a way to stabilize interest rates at the level targeted by the monetary authorities. The power of central banks to set short-term interest rates depends on its key role in the settlement part of the payment system. As a consequence, instead of describing the money multiplier, Chapter 12 studies the clearing and settlement system, showing how banks interact with each other and pointing out why there are limits to credit creation, despite the nonexistence of reserves.

Chapter 13 continues this approach, showing how the Bank of Canada implements monetary policy and its target overnight rate, essentially through the use of a corridor system, with overdraft and deposit facilities, and with the help of cash-setting operations that move government deposits to banks or the central bank. Open-market operations, which are the traditional tool tied to the analysis of the now-demoted money multiplier, are used only sparingly, in the form of buyback operations, when the

Bank is unhappy about the evolution of the overnight rate. The monetary policy strategy of the Bank of Canada is studied in the first part of Chapter 13, so that students get the big picture right away and can be spared, if their instructors so wish, the technical details of policy implementation. The study of policy strategy includes a discussion of the goals being pursued by the Bank of Canada, the most important of which is inflation targeting. It also includes an explanation of the monetary transmission mechanism, as outlined by the Bank.

While previous chapters are constructed around an essentially Keynesian view, Baumol and Blinder present the alternative monetarist view in Chapter 14. In this chapter, we explain in addition why the Bank of Canada adopted monetary targeting in 1975 and why it was gradually abandoned, to be replaced by interest rate targeting. We also provide an assessment of inflation targeting, explaining why the Bank has not yet adopted a lower inflation band, despite some internal and academic pressures to do so. In this context, the Japanese experience with deflation is recalled.

Chapter 15 also required numerous changes, first because it includes lots of institutional details about fiscal policy and the public debt, but also because we needed to make its discussion of deficit monetization and crowding-out consistent with our Chapter 13 analysis of monetary policy strategy and implementation. We believe that we have provided a good summary of the arguments put forth by the two main sides regarding these important topics. The chapter also contains a short discussion of the distinction made between the public deficit and the primary deficit, as well as an appendix that goes over some of the differences between national accounting and public accounting measures of budgetary balance.

Chapter 16, which deals with the trade-off between inflation and unemployment (or, rather, the lack thereof) is written in the belief that students of introductory economics are able to understand some of the intricacies of the vertical Phillips curve and the nonaccelerating inflation rate of unemployment (NAIRU), which we also present here as the steady inflation rate of output (SIRO), provided they are explained in an intuitive way. The supply-side determinants of the NAIRU (for instance, labour market flexibility) are given special attention, as a means of explaining time-varying NAIRU. The chapter concludes with a look at alternative views of the NAIRU, based on persistence, hysteresis, and recent empirical evidence regarding flat Phillips curves. We believe that this chapter links well with Chapter 1, showing that economists can disagree even though they share a common framework of analysis, tied to the possible existence of a vertical long-run Phillips curve.

The last three chapters deal with the open economy. It should be pointed out, however, that the principle of comparative advantage is dealt with in Chapter 3, and that the effects of interest rates on the exchange rate, and hence on net exports and aggregate demand, have been treated as part of the transmission mechanism of monetary policy in Chapter 13. An instructor running out of time and unable to cover some of the last three chapters will thus still be in a position to discuss these two important topics from the standpoint of the Canadian economy. In relation to the international trade chapter, Chapter 17, the most noteworthy addition is probably the boxed feature that deals with the main objections that have been advanced against the application of the principle of comparative advantage to the current world trade situation (see "Objections to the Conclusions Drawn from the Principle of Comparative Advantage").

In Chapter 18, the main issue is why the Canadian dollar has reached parity with the U.S. dollar. The Bank of Canada equation, which claims that the Canada–U.S. exchange rate is determined by the prices of energy and non-energy commodities, along with the interest rate differential, is given a good deal of attention, because this equation constitutes the main framework of analysis in Chapter 19. Chapter 18 also contains a discussion of a possible North American monetary union, as well as an appendix that presents the Canadian balance of payments accounts.

Chapter 19 contains two important additions. The first deals with the exchange rate pass-through—a crucial issue, as consumer associations complain that the lower import prices that should accompany a stronger Canadian dollar have not translated into lower retail prices. The second addition is the distinction between exchange rate movements induced by capital flows and movements induced by changes in the demand for Canadian products (in particular, oil and primary commodities) and their implications for aggregate demand and aggregate supply analysis. This distinction helps to explain why the Bank of Canada finds flexible exchange rates to be a stabilizing mechanism, rather than a destabilizing one, and why it believes that it does not need to do anything to help the Canadian manufacturing industry, which has been suffering a great deal from the rising Canadian dollar.

■ SUPPLEMENTS

■ Instructor's Complete Resource CD

Instructor supplements are available on the Instructor's Resource CD for easy access:

- **Instructor's Manual:** The Instructor's Manual contains resources designed to streamline and maximize the effectiveness of your course preparation. Every chapter includes detailed chapter outlines, teaching tips and suggestions, answers to end-of-chapter questions in the main text, questions for classroom discussion, and suggested in-class activities.

- **Computerized Test Bank:** The ExamView® computerized test bank consists of more than 200 questions per chapter, including true/false, multiple-choice, and short-answer questions that assess students' critical-thinking skills.

- **Test Bank:** Word files extracted from the ExamView® computerized test are also available to instructors for easy access to questions.

- **Microsoft PowerPoint® Lecture slides:** A comprehensive and user-friendly lecture presentation for use in the classroom. This presentation covers the chapter objectives and points and is accompanied by graphs and tables from the main text.

- **Microsoft PowerPoint® Graphs and Figures:** These art and graphic resource slides provide the instructor with all of the tables and figures from the main text.

TurningPoint® Kit: Nelson Education Limited is now pleased to offer instructors book-specific JoinIn™ content for Response Systems, allowing you to transform your classroom and assess your students' progress with instant in-class quizzes and polls. Our exclusive agreement to offer TurningPoint software lets you pose book-specific questions and display students' answers seamlessly within the PowerPoint® slides of your own lecture, in conjunction with the "clicker" hardware of your choice. Contact your local Nelson representative to learn more.

Aplia: Available bundled with the text or as a digital solution, Aplia is fully updated for the first Canadian edition. The comprehensive, interactive online problem sets, analyses, tutorials, experiments, and critical-thinking exercises give students hands-on application without adding to instructors' workloads. Based on discovery learning, Aplia requires students to take an active role in the learning process—helping them to improve their economic understanding and ability to relate to the economic concepts presented. Instructors can assign homework that is automatically graded and recorded.

Baumol Website: To assist students in preparing for exams, the text-specific website contains Test Yourself questions and links to various economics websites:

www.baumolmacro1e.nelson.com

■ WALK THROUGH THE FEATURES . . .

The first Canadian edition of *Macroeconomics: Principles and Policy* is written in a way that doesn't overwhelm students. With a straightforward approach, the text provides the necessities required for optimal learning and encourages students to think for themselves. With a good balance of theory to application, *Macroeconomics* achieves the right level of rigour and detail and presents complicated concepts in an uncomplicated manner.

■ Issue-Driven Principles

To bring economics into the student's everyday living, chapters open with a real-life economic "puzzle" or issue to launch the material covered in the chapter. This chapter-opening economic problem is returned to within the body of the chapter to illustrate how it can be addressed with the theoretical tools and concepts being presented.

? ISSUE: *Should the Canadian Government Try to Stop the Canadian Dollar from Rising?*

The United States is Canada's major trading partner. As we already observed in the previous chapter, the Canadian dollar reached its lowest value ever relative to the U.S. dollar in February 2002, when one Canadian dollar was worth only US$0.618. At the time of writing this book, the Canadian dollar is trading nearly at par with the U.S. dollar—an appreciation of about 60 percent over five years. While most Canadian snowbirds who spend their winters in the southern regions of the United States welcome the rise of the Canadian dollar, Canadian manufacturers and producers of wood, paper, and pulp products have been complaining that such rapid changes in the exchange rate have damaged their businesses; they have lost export and domestic markets to their American rivals, and they are unable to adapt to the overly rapid appreciation of our domestic currency.

Some of the affected trade organizations have urged the Canadian government and the Bank of Canada to stop, or at least to slow down, the rise of the Canadian dollar. But the Bank of Canada has not intervened on foreign exchange markets to affect the value of the Canadian dollar since September 1998, and it has repeatedly insisted that currency values should be "flexible," that they should be determined in the world markets by the forces of supply and demand that we studied in the previous chapter.

PUZZLE: *Why Did Inflation Fall While the Economy Boomed?*

For years, economists have talked about the agonizing trade-off between inflation and unemployment—a notion that we will develop in more detail in Chapter 16. Very low unemployment is supposed to make the inflation rate rise. Yet the high growth in both Canada and the United States during the latter half of the 1990s and early in the 2000s seemed to belie this idea. The unemployment rate fell below 4 percent in the United States and to about 6 percent in Canada, the lowest rates in 30 years. But inflation did not rise; in fact, it *fell* for part of this period. How can we explain this exceptional conjunction of events—relatively low unemployment coupled with falling inflation? Does it mean—as many pundits said at the time—that standard economic theory does not apply to the "New Economy"? Before this chapter is over, we will have some answers.

In earlier chapters, we noted that aggregate demand is ... The same point applies to *aggregate supply*: The conce... refer to a schedule, but rather to a schedule (an ag... The exact relationship between the overall price leve... is being supplied depends on wages and other produc... on the state of technology, among other things. Figure... ply curve. It slopes upward, meaning that there us... between the price level and aggregate output, *other thin*...

■ Why the Aggregate Supply Curve Slopes U...

There are several reasons why one could argue that the... slopes upward. The main reason is the *principle of incr*...

? ISSUE: *How Can Canadians Compete with "Cheap Foreign Labour"?*

Canadians (and the citizens of many other nations) often want their government to limit or prevent import competition. Why? One major reason is the common belief that imports take bread out of Canadian workers' mouths. According to this view, "cheap foreign labour" steals jobs from Canadians and pressures Canadian businesses to lower wages. Such worries were prominently voiced, for example, by Canadian labour organizations when the North American Free Trade Agreement (NAFTA)—the free trade pact between Canada, the United States, and Mexico—came into effect in January 1994.

Oddly enough, the facts are somewhat inconsistent with this story. For one thing, wages in most countries that export to Canada have risen dramatically in recent decades—much faster than wages here. The biggest merchandise exporters to Canada are the United States, China, Mexico, Japan, Germany, and Algeria (because of oil) are also large exporters to Canada. Table 1 shows hourly compensation rates in nine of these countries, each expressed as a percentage of hourly compensation in Canada, in 1975 and 2006. Only workers in Mexico, one of our NAFTA partners, lost ground to Canadian workers over this 30-year period. Labour in Europe gained substantially on its Canadian counterparts—rising in Britain, for example, from just above half the Canadian standard to near parity. And the wage gains in Asian countries were nothing short of spectacular. Labour compensation in South Korea, for example, soared from just 5 percent of Canadian levels to more than half.[1] Yet, while all this was going on, Canadian imports of automobiles from Japan, electronics from Taiwan, and textiles from Korea expanded rapidly.

[1] China would surely be an even more extreme example, but we lack Chinese and German data dating back to 1975.

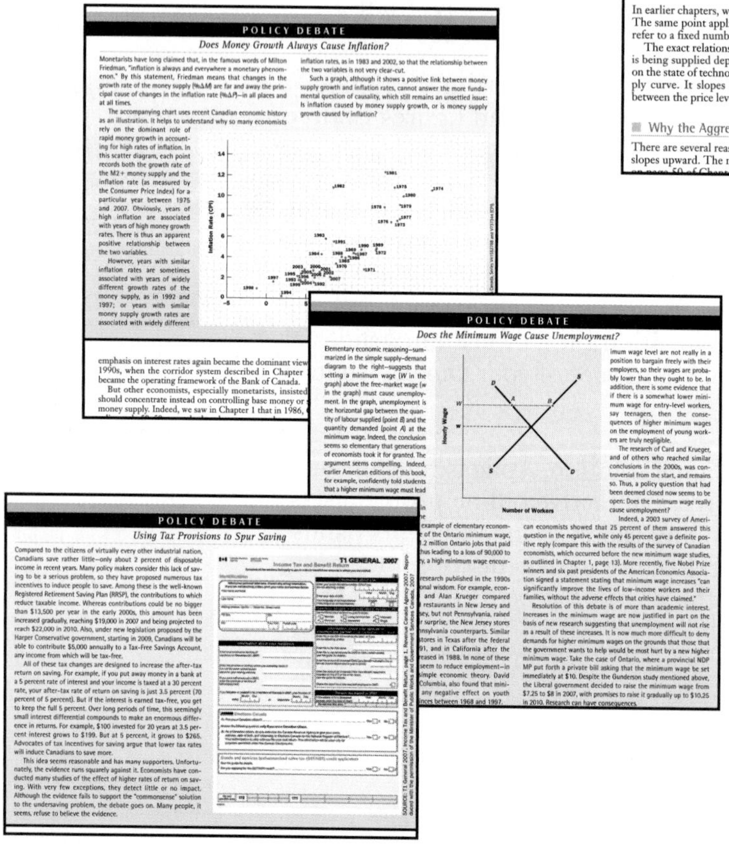

■ Policy Debate

Macroeconomics: Principles and Policy is known for being one of the most policy-driven texts on the market. Policy Debate boxes within the chapters are bound to spark discussion in the classroom!

POLICY DEBATE
Does Money Growth Always Cause Inflation?

Monetarists have long claimed that, in the famous words of Milton Friedman, "inflation is always and everywhere a monetary phenomenon." By this statement, Friedman means that changes in the growth rate of the money supply (M&M are far and away the principal cause of changes in the inflation rate (%ΔP)—in all places and at all times.

The accompanying chart uses recent Canadian economic history as an illustration. It helps to understand why so many economists rely on the dominant role of rapid money growth in accounting for high rates of inflation. In this scatter diagram, each point records both the growth rate of the inflation rate (as measured by the Consumer Price Index) for a particular year between 1975 and 2007. Obviously, years of high inflation are associated with years of high money growth rates. There is thus an apparent positive relationship between the two variables.

However, years with similar inflation rates are sometimes associated with years of widely different growth rates of the money supply, as in 1982 and 1997; or years with similar money supply growth rates are associated with widely different

inflation rates, as in 1983 and 2002, so that the relationship between the two variables is not very clear-cut.

Such a graph, although it shows a positive link between money growth and inflation rates, cannot answer the more fundamental question of causality, which still remains an unsettled issue: Is inflation caused by money supply growth, or is money growth caused by inflation?

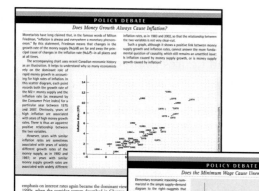

emphasis on interest rates again became the dominant view ... 1990s, when the corridor system described in Chapter ... became the operating framework of the Bank of Canada.

But other economists, especially monetarists, insisted ... should concentrate instead on controlling base money or ... money supply. Indeed, we saw in Chapter 1 that in 1986, ...

POLICY DEBATE
Does the Minimum Wage Cause Unemployment?

Elementary economic reasoning—summarized in the simple supply–demand diagram to the right—suggests that setting a minimum wage (W in the graph) above the free-market wage (in the graph) must cause unemployment. In the graph, unemployment is the horizontal gap between the quantity of labour supplied (point B) and the quantity demanded (point A) at the minimum wage. Indeed, the conclusion seems so elementary that generations of economists took it for granted. The argument seems compelling. Indeed, earlier American editions of this book, for example, confidently told students that a higher minimum wage must lead ...

imum wage level are not really in a position to bargain freely with their employers, so their wages are probably lower than they ought to be. In addition, there is some evidence that if there is a somewhat lower minimum wage for entry-level workers, say teenagers, then the consequences of higher minimum wages on the employment of young workers are truly negligible.

The research of Card and Krueger, and of others who reached similar conclusions in the 2000s, was controversial from the start, and remains so. Thus, a policy question that had been deemed closed now seems to be open: Does the minimum wage really cause unemployment?

Indeed, a 2000 survey of Ameri-

can economists showed that 25 percent of them answered this question in the negative, while only 45 percent gave a definite positive reply (compare this with the results of the survey of Canadian economists, which occurred before the new minimum wage studies, as outlined in Chapter 1, page 13). More recently, five Nobel Prize winners and six past presidents of the American Economics Association signed a statement positing that minimum wage increases "can significantly improve the lives of low-income workers and their families, without the adverse effects that critics have claimed."

Resolution of this debate is of more than academic interest. Increases in the minimum wage are now justified in part on the basis of new research suggesting that unemployment will not rise as a result of these increases. It is now much more difficult to deny demands for higher minimum wages on the grounds that those that the government wants to help would be most hurt by a new higher minimum wage. Take the case of Ontario, where a provincial NDP MP put forth a private bill asking that the minimum wage be set immediately at $10. Despite the Gunderson study mentioned above, the Liberal government decided to raise the minimum wage from $7.25 to $8 in 2007, with promises to raise it gradually up to $10.25 in 2010. Research can have consequences.

POLICY DEBATE
Using Tax Provisions to Spur Saving

Compared to the citizens of virtually every other industrial nation, Canadians save rather little—only about 2 percent of disposable income in recent years. Many policy makers consider this lack of saving to be a serious problem, so they have proposed numerous tax incentives to induce people to save. Among these is the well-known Registered Retirement Saving Plan (RRSP), the contributions to which reduce taxable income. Whereas contributions could be no bigger than $13,500 per year in the early 2000s, this amount has been increased gradually, reaching $19,000 in 2007 and being projected to reach $22,000 in 2010. Also, under new legislation passed by the Harper Conservative government, starting in 2009, Canadians will be able to contribute $5,000 annually to a Tax-Free Savings Account, any income from which will be tax-free.

All of these tax changes are designed to increase the after-tax return on saving. For example, if you put every money in a bank at a 5 percent rate of interest and your income is taxed at a 30 percent rate, your after-tax rate of return on saving is just 3.5 percent (70 percent of 5 percent). But if the interest is earned tax-free, you get to keep the full 5 percent. Over long periods of time, this seemingly small interest differential compounds to make an enormous difference in returns. For example, $100 invested for 20 years at 3.5 percent interest grows to $199. But at 5 percent, it grows to $265. Advocates of tax incentives for saving argue that lower tax rates will induce Canadians to save more.

This idea seems reasonable and has many supporters. Unfortunately, the evidence runs squarely against it. Economists have conducted many studies of the effect of higher rates of return on saving. With very few exceptions, they detect little or no impact. Although the evidence fails to support the "commonsense" solution to the undersaving problem, the debate goes on. Many people, it seems, refuse to believe the evidence.

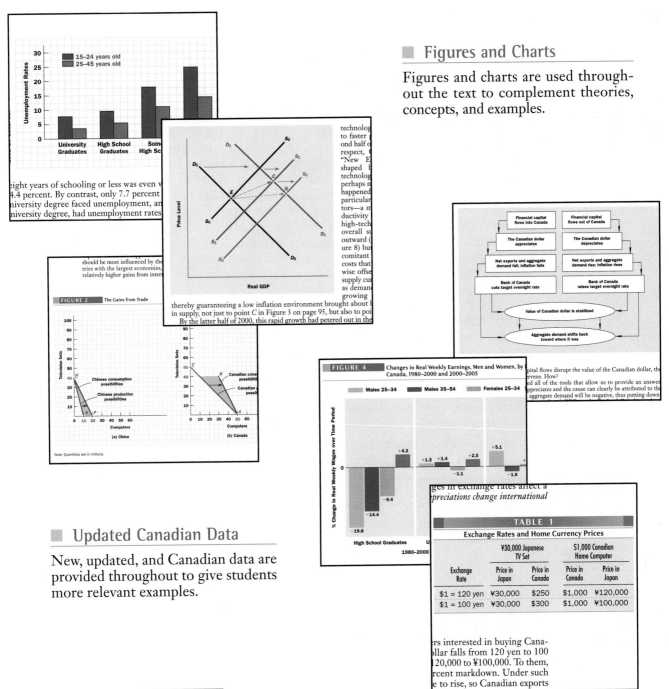

Figures and Charts

Figures and charts are used throughout the text to complement theories, concepts, and examples.

Updated Canadian Data

New, updated, and Canadian data are provided throughout to give students more relevant examples.

Chapter Summaries

Each chapter ends with a summary, a list of key terms, and questions and problems to help students complete their homework and prepare for exams.

■ IN GRATITUDE

We are pleased to acknowledge our indebtedness to four research assistants: Jung-Hoon Kim, Yong-Bok Lee, Peng Wang, and Jun Zhao. Without their help in collecting data and controlling for numerous details relating to the table of contents and the glossary, the book would not have so easily come to fruition. We also thank Peter Docherty at the University of Technology in Sydney, Australia, as well as Chuck Freedman, formerly with the Bank of Canada, for their very detailed and helpful comments on the two chapters dealing with banking and the central bank. Donna Howard at the Bank of Canada also graciously answered additional questions on the functioning of the large-value transfer system. Thanks also go to Andrew Sharpe, director of the Centre for the Study of Living Standards, who provided quick answers to our puzzles about the discrepancies between real wages and labour compensation growth rates, as well as to Marc Prudhomme from Statistics Canada, who cleared up some issues regarding the Consumer Price Index. A note of thanks must also go to Dean François Houle of the University of Ottawa's Faculty of Social Sciences for his special support of our six-month sabbatical leave during the winter–spring semester of 2007.

This first Canadian edition also benefitted from the input of numerous reviewers who read and contributed a substantial amount of relevant and valuable comments on the portions of the manuscript:

Morris Altman, *University of Saskatchewan*

Percy Christon-Quao, *Kwantlen University College*

Janice Compton, *University of Manitoba*

Fazal H. Dar, *University of Regina*

Helmar Drost, *York University*

Ergete Ferede, *Grant MacEwan College*

Robert Gateman, *University of British Columbia*

David Gray, *University of Ottawa*

Jorgen Hansen, *Concordia University*

Hanafiah Harvey, *Simon Fraser University*

Sunil Kaplash, *University of Victoria*

Eva Lau, *University of Waterloo*

Adian McFarlane, *University of Manitoba*

William Scarth, *McMaster University*

Peter Sinclair, *Wilfrid Laurier University*

Angela Trimarchi, *University of Waterloo*

Finally, we are grateful to Anthony Rezek, who originally contacted us, as well as publisher Rod Banister of Nelson Education Ltd. and Katherine Goodes of My Editor Inc. Indeed, the expert support provided by Katherine Goodes and by June Trusty, the latter for her patient editorial work, was crucial throughout the long process of bringing this book to press. Last but not least, we must thank our wives, Camille Lafortune and Giovanna Mazza, whose patience during our long struggle to complete the book was essential.

Marc Lavoie
Mario Seccareccia

GETTING ACQUAINTED WITH ECONOMICS

W elcome to economics! Some other students may have warned you that "Econ is boring." Don't believe them—or at least, don't believe them too much. It is true that studying economics is hardly pure fun. But a first course in economics can be an eye-opening experience. There is a vast and important world out there—the economic world—and this book is designed to help you understand it.

Have you ever wondered whether jobs will be plentiful or scarce when you graduate? Or why a university or college education becomes more and more expensive? Should the government be suspicious of big firms? Why can't pollution be eliminated? How did the Canadian economy manage to grow so rapidly in the second half of the1990s while Japan's economy stagnated? If any of these questions have piqued your curiosity, read on. You may find economics to be more interesting than you had thought!

The four chapters of Part I introduce you to both the subject matter of economics and some of the methods that economists use to study their subject.

WHAT IS ECONOMICS?

The purpose of studying economics is not to acquire a set of ready made answers to economic questions, but to avoid being deceived by economists.

JOAN ROBINSON (1903–1983), PROMINENT 20TH-CENTURY ECONOMIST, UNIVERSITY OF CAMBRIDGE, U.K., 1955

E conomics is a broad-ranging discipline, both in the questions it asks and the methods it uses to seek answers. Many of the world's most pressing problems are economic in nature. The first part of this chapter tells you how economists have defined their field through time. The second part briefly introduces the tools that economists use—tools you are likely to find useful in your career, personal life, and role as an informed citizen, long after this course is over. The third part will help you understand why economists disagree, or seemingly disagree, on a range of issues.

CONTENTS

■ THE RANGE OF ECONOMICS

Economics is a discipline that can tackle nearly every issue of public relevance and public concern. Reflecting its wide focus and strategic position in the social sciences, economists work in diverse milieus and are engaged in both quantitative and policy research. You find them employed in the financial and nonfinancial business sectors, the many agencies and departments of government, and numerous international agencies, as well as in organizations that transcend the traditional private/public divide, such as trade union and cooperative nonprofit associations.

Much like the domain in which economists work, students will discover in this book that the subject is incredibly vast and varied and that economics finds application in wide areas pertaining to individual and group behaviour. Its subject matter, however, cannot so easily be delineated and it has changed somewhat historically as the discipline has become professionalized and has embraced more sophisticated tools of analysis. Defining what economics is can be such a controversial task that some would rather say, "Economics is what economists do"!

■ Definitions of Economics

The origin of economics as a distinct discipline goes back to the eighteenth century. With the opening of markets to trade and commerce, early economic writers began to pose a question that remains crucial to social scientists and policy makers to this day: What makes nations grow and become wealthy? For Adam Smith (1723–1790), the father of classical economics, "political economy" was, therefore, concerned with what were "the causes of the wealth of nations." However, once certain nations did achieve economic growth and markets widened, the question of the distribution of output quickly came to occupy centre stage. Therefore, by the early nineteenth century, the scope of economic analysis began to expand somewhat with David Ricardo (1772–1823), for whom the principal problem of economics was to discover the mechanisms or "laws which regulate the distribution of the produce of the earth." Indeed, by the time one gets to the mid-nineteenth century, under Karl Marx (1818–1883), these two aspects converged and economics became simply the study of the "laws of motion of capitalism"—the study of how economies grow and stagnate as they undergo the social stresses and strains that accompany tremendous historical transformations.

Reflecting the major developments in economics since the 1870s, especially as it evolved as a professional discipline, the domain of economics has widened to include practically all aspects of social phenomena. Nowadays, economists are involved in researching market behaviour relating to traditional issues of pricing, production, exchange, consumption, and distribution, but they are also engaged in addressing less traditional questions of, say, why certain students choose to pursue a college or university degree or why high-level athletes take performance-enhancing drugs even though they know this may shorten their lives. For this reason, we rather like the definition proposed by Alfred Marshall (1842–1924), according to whom **economics** is the "study of mankind in the ordinary business of life" and for whom what distinguishes economists from noneconomists are the analytical tools and methods used to explain diverse aspects of social phenomena. This is why, to such celebrated twentieth-century economists as John Maynard Keynes (1883–1946), economics was seen merely as "a method rather than a doctrine, an apparatus of the mind, a technique of thinking" as it is applied to the study of human behaviour. This opinion is shared by Gary Becker (1930–), who is famous for having extended economics to the analysis of crime, illegal drugs, addiction, discrimination, fertility, marriage, and divorce, and according to whom what "distinguishes economics as a discipline from other disciplines in the social sciences is not its subject matter but its approach." Historically, numerous analytical tools and devices have been developed by economists to understand society in its

Economics is a method of analyzing individual and social behaviour, especially as it relates to market phenomena.

Galbraith on Galbraith

Jamie Galbraith, a professor at the University of Texas in Austin and also the son of Canadian-born economist John Kenneth Galbraith (see the feature "A Canadian-Born Economist Who Wrote a String of Bestsellers" on page 14), made the following comment on the definition of economics when he delivered the inaugural John Kenneth Galbraith Lecture at the annual meeting of the Canadian Economics Association in Halifax in June 2007. Clearly, Galbraith does not buy the definition of economics—the study of choice among scarcity—that is currently endorsed by a large majority of economists.

> Our economics should teach the great thinkers, notably Smith, Marx, Keynes, Veblen and Schumpeter—and John Kenneth Galbraith. We need not reinvent the field; nor should we abandon it. Economics over the sweep of history is not mainly about scarcity (which technology overcomes) nor about choice (which is generally neither free nor the defining characteristic of freedom). Rather, economics is about value, distribution, growth, stabilization, evolution, and limits. The great ideas in these areas, and the history in which they were embedded, are fundamental. They should be taught, not as dogma but rather as a sequence of explorations.

SOURCE: Jamie Galbraith, *The Abiding Economics of John Kenneth Galbraith*. Retrieved from http://progecon.wordpress.com/2007/06/04/the-inaugural-john-kenneth-galbraith-lecture

"ordinary business of life." In the next section, we will begin to explore some key constituents of contemporary economists' box of tools.

Before discussing these tools, however, there is one important subset of what constitutes the domain occupied by economics that is of special importance to most contemporary economists. Lionel Robbins (1898–1984) in his famous *Essay on the Nature and Significance of Economic Science*, originally published in 1932, defined economics as "a science which studies human behaviour as a relationship between ends and scarce means which have alternative uses." He later summed this up by saying that economics is the study of "behaviour conditioned by scarcity." Hence, among most present-day economists, scarcity is the focus of analysis. There is recognition that scarcity is a binding constraint on human activity that imposes trade-offs and forces individuals to make choices in allocating resources among alternative ends. Indeed, numerous concepts that will be presented in the following chapters flow from recognition of what is called the *scarcity principle*.

■ Microeconomics versus Macroeconomics

The variety of definitions that can be applied to the economics discipline has been reflected over the last 50 years or so by a division into two subdisciplines: microeconomics and macroeconomics.

Microeconomics   The issue of scarcity, which has become a defining characteristic of modern economics, is at the core of microeconomics. The definition provided by Lionel Robbins, but also the concerns of David Ricardo regarding the mechanisms that regulate the distribution of income, are at the heart of microeconomics. Microeconomists deal with questions related to individual agents—consumers, individual firms, agencies, governments—or to particular industries. In each and every case, such individuals must make hard choices. What should be produced? What quantity of resources should be allocated to a given activity or to a given consumption good? How much time should be allocated to a given project? Who should get the resources or the final products?

For all of these questions, prices play a key role, as they reflect the degree of scarcity. Things that are relatively scarce should carry a high price. If some of the materials that you are using to build a house are scarce, they should be expensive, and hence their high price should induce you to use alternative products, thus contributing to reducing the shortage of the scarce building materials. Similarly, if the prices of existing two-storey houses rise more briskly than condo prices, this should induce home builders to construct more houses and fewer condos, thus contributing to reduction of the relative scarcity of individual houses.

Also, for every one of the questions put above, any answer involves a trade-off. We can't do everything. We are facing time and financial constraints. What is our best choice? You have decided to go to university. As a result, most of you are forgoing the earnings that some of your friends might now be making by working full-time. You have given up these early earnings, you pay tuition fees, and you may also encounter additional lodging costs to acquire a university degree. These are your **opportunity costs** of going to university. In general, the opportunity cost is the value of what one must give up in order to acquire something else. The trade-off in this case is that you will learn quite a lot in university, and that, most likely, you will increase your future income. Economists have devised a computation method that allows them to conclude that, on average, even abstracting from the acquired knowledge, this is a good decision.

Everyone faces trade-offs and opportunity costs. Take the general manager of a National Hockey League (NHL) team. This person has a budget constraint. The team can spend only so many million dollars on the players' payroll. Indeed, with the new collective agreement that was signed in 2005 between the NHL players and owners, there is a payroll cap—a maximum amount that no general manager is allowed to surpass to pay players on the team roster; this amount was set at US$39 million for the 2005–2006 season and at US$50 million for the 2007–2008 season.

Even general managers who have the good fortune of having a team loaded with talented players must make hard choices. Should they hold on to their star defencemen, their star forwards, or their top goalie? To which ones of their best forwards should they make the best salary offer? After the Tampa Bay Lightning beat the Calgary Flames in the final of the 2004 Stanley Cup, the team's management made substantial salary offers (US$6 million per season) to their Canadian-born star forwards Vincent Lecavalier and Martin St-Louis, deciding in the process to let go their starting goalie, Nicolai Khabibulin, without whose heroics they could not have won the Stanley Cup. Obviously, the Lightning would have liked to retain the services of Khabibulin (who also ended up getting over US$6 million per year) but the Tampa Bay Lightning management faced a payroll constraint. The opportunity cost of keeping Lecavalier and St-Louis, the trade-off of that decision, was losing the services of Khabibulin. The Lightning management staff figured that losing Lecavalier or St-Louis would have been more detrimental to the team (performance-wise or revenue-wise). The Calgary Flames, the Edmonton Oilers, and the Ottawa Senators faced similar trade-offs after their nearly successful run at the Stanley Cup in 2004, 2006, and 2007.

Most of microeconomics, and even some macroeconomics, is based on a search for efficiency. Economists call this *constrained optimization*. Given the time and financial or resources constraints, what is the best that can be done? What is the optimal decision if the agent wishes to maximize some criterion (profits, growth, happiness, etc.)?

Macroeconomics   The definitions of economics provided by Adam Smith and Karl Marx are perhaps more relevant to macroeconomics. Macroeconomists ask questions such as: Why are some nations rich and others poor? How do the standards of living of an entire population rise? How can we avoid wasting the productive capabilities of unemployed labour? While such questions can also be given some answers at the microeconomic level, macroeconomists deal with aggregates: the production of an entire economy, such as that of Canada; the level of employment, or unemployment, in all of Canada or in a province or territory of Canada; the overall level of exports to foreign markets and imports from abroad; the average price level or the rate of growth of aggregate prices—that is, the rate of inflation. Macroeconomics also deals with government policies that affect the entire economy: monetary policy, as reflected in interest rates or the stock of money and possibly in the exchange rate of the Canadian dollar; and fiscal policy, as reflected in the overall level of government expenditures and the various tax rates.

> The **opportunity cost** of a decision is the value of the next best alternative that must be given up because of that decision.

The field of macroeconomics is said to have been created by John Maynard Keynes when he tried to explain the deep recession of the 1930s through arguments that were not connected to the malfunctioning of individual markets but rather to **paradoxical** effects that were arising when the intended behaviour of individuals led to exactly opposite aggregate results when all of these individuals acted in a similar way. Macroeconomics as a field separate from microeconomics owes its existence from the possible occurrence of what is called the **fallacy of composition.** One cannot assume that what is true of the parts will still be true of the whole. There might be a contradiction between what can be ascertained at the level of the individual and what can be said at the aggregate level. For instance, while each of us can get to work downtown more quickly if we drive our cars there instead of taking a bus or riding a bicycle, it will not be true anymore if all of us drive our cars to work, as streets will become overrun with traffic, resulting in traffic jams.

The paradox that Keynes himself underlined is called the *paradox of saving* or the *paradox of thrift*. While it is in the interest of every individual to save as much as possible instead of consuming, saving one's income instead of spending it will have detrimental consequences on the overall economy, at least when the economy is not fully employed. As individuals try to save more, less will be spent on consumer goods; therefore, firms will lose sales and make less profit and will be induced to hire fewer personnel. In the end, employees and owners will wind up with less income, and hence will not be able to save as much as intended. The intended increase in saving does not materialize and instead creates unemployment.

> Macroeconomists are interested in the economic system as a whole, while microeconomists are mainly concerned with the study of individual markets or agents in isolation.

While the principle of scarcity does not apply to all of macroeconomics—for instance, when the rate of unemployment is high, labour resources or at least some labour resources are idle and hence are not scarce—there still exist trade-offs that entail difficult choices. One of these is the trade-off between inflation and unemployment—meaning that low unemployment normally makes inflation rise and high unemployment normally makes inflation fall. Things need not always be that way; for instance, the Canadian economy has benefited from low rates of unemployment since the end of the 1990s without any increase in the inflation rate. In general, however, the trade-off between inflation and unemployment poses one of the fundamental dilemmas of national economic policy. The mechanisms underlying this trade-off are a key topic in macroeconomics.

Other such macroeconomic dilemmas may also exist. Should the government change the income distribution arising from the market even if such transfers weaken economic growth (this may also be considered a microeconomic question—the issue of equity versus efficiency)? Or should the size of the government sector be reduced, even though a larger public sector may be conducive to a more stable economy with fewer fluctuations? These are difficult questions that may go beyond the pure technical advice that economists can offer.

Sidebar:

A **paradox** is a contradiction between two principles that operate at different levels; it often involves an outcome that is contrary to intuition.

The **fallacy of composition** is the error of believing that what is true of each part of a system will also be true of the system as a whole.

■ INSIDE THE ECONOMIST'S TOOL KIT

Let us now look at some important analytical devices employed by economists to explain social phenomena.

■ Economics as a Discipline

Although economics is clearly the most rigorous of the social sciences, it nevertheless looks decidedly more "social" than "scientific" when compared with, say, physics. An economist must be a jack of several trades, borrowing modes of analysis from numerous fields. Mathematical reasoning is often used in economics, but so is historical study. And neither looks quite the same as when practised by a mathematician or a historian. Statistics play a major role in modern economic inquiry, although economists had to modify standard statistical procedures to fit their kinds of data.

The Need for Abstraction

Some students find economics unduly abstract and "unrealistic." The stylized world envisioned by economic theory seems only a distant cousin to the world they know. There is an old joke about three people—a chemist, a physicist, and an economist—stranded on a desert island with an ample supply of canned food but no tools to open the cans. The chemist thinks that lighting a fire under the cans would burst the cans. The physicist advocates building a catapult with which to smash the cans against some boulders. The economist's suggestion? "Assume we have a can opener."

Economic theory *does* make some unrealistic assumptions; you will encounter some of them in this book. But some abstraction from reality is necessary because of the incredible complexity of the economic world, not because economists like to sound absurd.

Compare the chemist's simple task of explaining the interactions of compounds in a chemical reaction with the economist's complex task of explaining the interactions of people in an economy. Are molecules motivated by greed or altruism, by envy or ambition? Do they ever imitate other molecules? Do forecasts about them influence their behaviour? People, of course, do all these things and many, many more. It is therefore vastly more difficult to predict human behaviour than to predict chemical reactions. If economists tried to keep track of every feature of human behaviour, they would never get anywhere. Thus:

Abstraction from unimportant details is necessary to understand the functioning of anything as complex as the economy.

Abstraction means ignoring many details so as to focus on the most important elements of a problem.

An analogy will make clear why economists **abstract** from details. Suppose you have just arrived for the first time in Toronto. You are now at Pearson Airport—the point marked *A* in Maps 1 and 2, which are alternative maps of part of Toronto. You want to

MAP 1		Detailed Road Map of Toronto

SOURCE: Map © by Rand McNally

Note: *A* indicates Pearson Airport and *B* indicates the Rogers Centre.

drive to the Rogers Centre, point *B* on each map. Which map would be more useful?

Map 1 has complete details of the Toronto road system. This makes it hard to read and hard to use as a way to find the Rogers Centre. For this purpose, Map 1 is far too detailed, although for some other purposes (for example, locating some small street downtown) it may be far better than Map 2.

In contrast, Map 2 omits many minor roads—you might say they are *assumed away*—so that the highways and major arteries stand out more clearly. As a result of this simplification, one route from Pearson Airport to the Rogers Centre clearly emerges. We can take Highway 427 heading south, then take the Gardiner Expressway. Although we *might* find a route by poring over the details in Map 1, most strangers to the city would be better off with Map 2. Similarly, economists try to *abstract* from a lot of confusing details while retaining the essentials.

Map 3, however, illustrates that simplification can go too far. It shows little more than the major highways that pass through the Oshawa–Toronto–Hamilton part of Ontario, and therefore will not help a visitor find the Rogers Centre. Of course, this map was never intended to be used as a detailed tourist guide, which brings us to an important point:

> There is no such thing as one "right" degree of abstraction and simplification for all analytic purposes. The proper degree of abstraction depends on the objective of the analysis. A model that is a gross oversimplification for one purpose may be needlessly complicated for another.

Economists are constantly seeking analogies to Map 2 rather than Map 3, treading the thin line between useful generalizations about complex issues and gross distortions of the pertinent facts. For example, suppose you want to learn why some people are fabulously

| MAP 2 | Major Toronto Arteries and Highways |

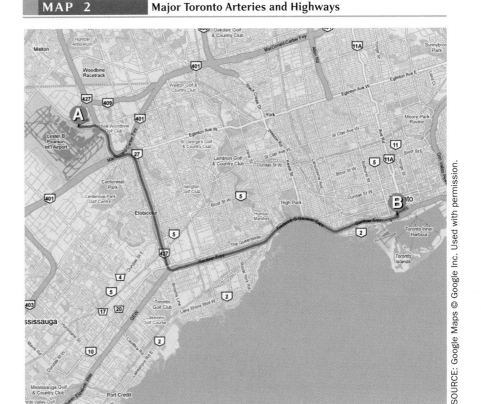

SOURCE: Google Maps © Google Inc. Used with permission.

| MAP 3 | Oshawa–Toronto–Hamilton Area |

SOURCE: © Queen's Printer for Ontario, 2006. Reproduced with permission.

rich while others are abjectly poor. People differ in many ways, too many to enumerate, much less to study. The economist must ignore most of these details to focus on the important ones. The colour of a person's hair or eyes is probably not important for the problem but, unfortunately, the colour of his or her skin probably is because racial discrimination can depress a person's income. Height and weight may not matter, but education probably does. Proceeding in this way, we can pare Map 1 down to the manageable dimensions of Map 2. But there is a danger of going too far, stripping away some of the crucial factors, so that we wind up with Map 3.

The Role of Economic Theory

Some students find economics "too theoretical." To see why we can't avoid it, let's consider what we mean by a **theory.**

A **theory** is a deliberate simplification of relationships used to explain how those relationships work.

To an economist or natural scientist, the word *theory* means something different from what it means in common speech. In science, a theory is *not* an untested assertion of alleged fact. The statement that aspirin provides protection against heart attacks is not a theory; it is a *hypothesis*, which will prove to be true or false once the right sorts of experiments have been completed. Instead, a theory is a deliberate simplification (abstraction) of reality that attempts to explain how some relationships work. It is an *explanation* of the mechanism behind observed phenomena. Thus, gravity forms the basis of theories that describe and explain the paths of the planets. Similarly, price theory (discussed in Parts II and III) seeks to describe and explain how buyers and sellers interact in markets to determine prices.

People who have never studied economics often draw a false distinction between *theory* and *practical policy*. Politicians and businesspeople, in particular, often reject abstract economic theory as something that is best ignored by "practical" people. The irony of these statements is that:

It is precisely the concern for policy that makes economic theory so necessary and important.

To analyze policy options, economists are forced to deal with *possibilities that have not actually occurred.* For example, to learn how to shorten periods of high unemployment, they must investigate whether a proposed new policy that has never been tried can help. Or to determine which environmental programs will be most effective, they must understand how and why a market economy produces pollution and what might happen if the government taxed industrial waste discharges and automobile emissions. Such questions require some *theorizing*, not just examination of the facts, because we need to consider possibilities that have never occurred.

Correlation and Causation

The facts, moreover, can sometimes be highly misleading. Data often indicate that two variables move up and down together. But this statistical **correlation** does not prove that either variable *causes* the other. A most famous example in economics, which led to vast changes in the way statistical research is conducted in macroeconomics, was provided in 1980 in the heyday of *monetarism*—the theory, based on the empirical observation that prices and the money supply grow in tandem, which claims that price inflation is primarily caused by an excessive growth rate of the money supply. A British researcher, D. F. Hendry, showed that he could find a nearly perfect fit (high correlation) between the price level in the United Kingdom and another variable, which until then had been ignored by economists but which was closely monitored by a government agency and the entire population. He further showed that this other variable was very good at predicting future values of the inflation rate. Unfortunately, this new, apparently highly useful variable was the amount of cumulative rainfall in the United Kingdom!

Two variables are said to be **correlated** if they tend to go up or down together. Correlation need not imply causation.

Further in relation to rainy days, we can offer another illuminating example of possible spurious correlation. When it rains, people drive their cars more slowly and there are also more traffic accidents. But no one thinks that it is the slower driving that causes more accidents when it's raining. Rather, we understand that both phenomena are caused by a common underlying factor—more rain. How do we know this? Not just by looking at the correlation between data on accidents and driving speeds. Data alone tell us little about cause and effect. We must use some simple *theory* as part of our analysis. In this case, the theory might explain that drivers are more apt to have accidents on rain-slicked roads.

Similarly, we must use theoretical analysis, and not just data alone, to understand *how*, if at all, different government policies will lead to lower unemployment or *how* a tax on emissions will reduce pollution.

Statistical correlation need not imply causation. Some theory is usually needed to interpret data.

Even if we are persuaded that statistical correlation in a given instance implies correlation, causality may go one way or another. One of the best-known relationships in economics is the positive relationship between the stock of money and the price level. Although all economists would agree that such a relationship does exist, two different causal stories, based on two different theories, have been put forward for more than 200 years. In one story, based on monetarism (the modern incarnation of the old *quantity theory of money*), the amount of money in the economy explains, or causes, the price level. In the alternative story, nearly just as old—the *Banking school of economics* view—it is the price level that explains, or causes, the amount of money. Two hundred years of studies have not allowed economists to know for sure which theory is the correct one. Indeed, the dominance of one or the other theory has moved in cycles. At times, as in the 1970s and 1980s, the quantity theory of money looked like the only serious contender, whereas in the 1950s and over the last few years, the Banking school view has been incorporated into several macroeconomic theories.

There are now statistical methods to assess causality but, unfortunately, even these sophisticated methods are usually unable to cut through the controversy and provide definite answers. In addition, taking into account the timing of events won't do. This is called, from Latin, the **post hoc, ergo propter hoc fallacy** (translation: *before this, therefore because of this*). For instance, consumers who are planning to purchase last-minute Christmas gifts or who wish to take advantage of Boxing Day sales and New Year's sales may decide to take out cash from the automatic teller machines a few days in advance (because they don't have, or don't want to use, credit cards). But can we say that sales around Christmas time went up because the amount of cash in the economy started to rise in the previous week (as shown in Table 1)? Or should we say instead that the amount of cash has risen because of the planned Christmas shopping spree? If the latter is more correct, then an event of the past (the increase in cash) is being caused by an event in the future (the Christmas sales), and hence the knowledge of timing will not be helpful in this case.

The *post hoc, ergo propter hoc* fallacy is the error of assuming that if some event occurred before another, then the first one must have caused the second.

Despite all of the difficulties involved, assessing causality is crucially important in economics. Theories based on the same facts will yield different predictions, because they rely on different causation mechanisms.

Having a causal story also allows the economist to know which policy should be put into place. For instance, if causality runs from the price level to the amount of money in the economy, then those who work in central banks and are responsible for keeping prices stable should not worry so much about the level of the money stock or the growth rate of the money stock. Instead, they should be concerned about other factors that might have an impact on the price level or on the growth rate of aggregate prices—particularly the inflation rate. But in order to assess these other factors, they need to *theorize*; they need an economic model.

TABLE 1	
More Cash Circulating around Christmas	
	Paper Cash in Circulation (millions of dollars)
December 5, 2007	$48,104
December 12, 2007	48,269
December 19, 2007	49,330
December 26, 2007	50,724
January 2, 2008	50,157
January 9, 2008	48,156

SOURCE: Bank of Canada, *Weekly Financial Statistics*, BFS Table B2, February 1, 2008.

■ What Is an Economic Model?

An **economic model** is a representation of a theory or a part of a theory, often used to gain insight into cause and effect. The notion of a "model" is familiar enough to children, and economists—like other scientists—use the term in much the same way that children do.

An economic model is a simplified, small-scale version of some aspect of the economy. Economic models are often expressed in equations, by graphs, or in words.

A child's model airplane looks and operates much like the real thing, but it is much smaller and simpler, so it is easier to manipulate and understand. Engineers for Bombardier also build models of planes. Although their models are far larger and much more elaborate than a child's toy, they use them for much the same purposes: to observe the workings of these aircraft "up close" and to experiment with them to see how the models behave under different circumstances. ("What happens if I do this?") From these experiments, they make educated guesses as to how the real-life version will perform.

Economists use models for similar purposes. The late A. W. Phillips, the famous engineer-turned-economist who discovered what is now called the *Phillips curve* was talented enough to construct a working model of the determination of national income in a simple economy by using coloured water flowing through pipes. For years, this contraption has graced the basement of the London School of Economics. Although we will explain the models with words and diagrams, Phillips's engineering background enabled him to depict the theory with tubes, valves, and pumps.

Because many of the models used in this book are depicted in diagrams, for those of you who need review, we explain the construction and use of various types of graphs in the appendix to this chapter. Don't be put off by seemingly abstract models. Think of them as useful road maps. And remember how hard it would be to find your way around Toronto without one.

SOURCE: Science Museum/Science & Society Picture Library

A. W. Phillips built this model in the early 1950s to illustrate Keynesian theory.

■ WHY ECONOMISTS (SOMETIMES) DISAGREE

"If all the earth's economists were laid end to end, they could not reach an agreement," the saying goes. Politicians and reporters are fond of pointing out that economists can be found on both sides of many public policy issues. If economics is a science, why do economists so often disagree? After all, astronomers do not debate whether the earth revolves around the sun or vice versa.

This question reflects a misunderstanding of the nature of science. Disputes are normal at the frontier of any science. For example, astronomers once did argue vociferously over whether the earth revolves around the sun. Nowadays, they argue about gamma-ray bursts, dark matter, the Big Bang, and other esoterica. These arguments go mostly unnoticed by the public because few of us understand what they are talking about. But economics is a *social* science, so its disputes are aired in public and all sorts of people feel competent to join economic debates.

■ Is There Consensus among Canadian Economists?

Economists actually agree on much more than popular opinion would have it. Surveys about the opinions of economists were first published in the United States in 1979 and such surveys were repeated in 1992 and 2003. Similar surveys were also conducted in European countries, and in Canada, a survey of members of the Canadian Economics Association was done in 1986 by Walter Block and Michael Walker, two researchers at the Fraser Institute, a think-tank located in Vancouver. Their results were published in 1988 in the journal *Canadian Public Policy*. The propositions that brought the highest degree of consensus are listed below. (*Note:* Responses such as

"No answer" and "Agree with provisions" were discarded, so the totals do not add up to 100 percent; clearly when a large percentage of economists "agree" with a proposition, this implies that the proposition receives even wider support, since there are also economists who approve of the proposition "with provisions.")

- A ceiling on rents reduces the quantity and quality of housing available. (80 percent agree, 4.7 percent disagree)
- Tariffs and import quotas reduce general economic welfare. (70 percent agree, 4 percent disagree)
- Flexible exchange rates offer an effective international monetary arrangement. (58 percent agree, 6 percent disagree)
- The redistribution of income in the developed industrial nations is a legitimate task for the government. (56 percent agree, 15 percent disagree)
- A minimum wage increases unemployment among young and unskilled workers. (68 percent agree, 15 percent disagree)
- Fiscal policy has a significant stimulative impact on a less than fully employed economy. (47 percent agree, 14 percent disagree)
- Taxes represent a better approach to pollution control than imposition of pollution ceilings. (49 percent agree, 17 percent disagree)
- Wage–price controls should be used to control inflation. (4 percent agree, 73 percent disagree)
- The fundamental cause of the rise in oil prices in the 1970s was the monopoly power of the large oil companies. (14 percent agree, 66 percent disagree)
- The government should be an employer of last resort and initiate a guaranteed job program. (14 percent agree, 61 percent disagree)

The above survey results are comforting: They disprove the saying that when asked about a given problem, ten different economists will give eleven different answers! There are issues, however, that clearly divide Canadian economists. Some of the most divisive issues, at least in 1988, but most probably still today, are the following:

- The distribution of income in the developed industrial nations should be more equal. (35 percent agree, 30 percent disagree)
- The economic power of labour unions should be significantly curtailed. (26 percent agree, 38 percent disagree)
- Antitrust laws should be used vigorously to reduce monopoly power from its current level. (33 percent agree, 27 percent disagree)
- The money supply is a more important target than interest rates for monetary policy. (32 percent agree, 40 percent disagree)
- Inflation is primarily a monetary phenomenon. (42 percent agree, 24 percent disagree)
- In the short run, unemployment can be reduced by increasing the rate of inflation. (30 percent agree, 26 percent disagree)
- The corporate state as depicted by John Kenneth Galbraith (see "A Canadian-Born Economist Who Wrote a String of Bestsellers" on the next page) accurately describes the context and structure of advanced economies (13 percent agree, 44 percent disagree).

Once again, all of these propositions give some indication of the sort of issues with which economists become intertwined. Note that nearly all of these nonconsensual propositions have clear and substantial policy implications. Yet, they are far from being settled. In that sense, economics is an evolutionary science. Amusingly, it should be pointed out that while American and Canadian economists do have closely resembling opinions on the above propositions, European economists have sometimes given a yes answer where a majority of Canadian economists would answer no, and vice versa, thus demonstrating that economics is indeed a social science that incorporates cultural traits, despite being based on mathematical reasoning and empirical analysis.

A Canadian-Born Economist Who Wrote a String of Bestsellers

John Kenneth Galbraith (1908–2006) is perhaps North America's most famous economist, but also a highly controversial one among his peers, as many of his ideas were thought to be either subversive to existing theory or just plain wrong. Born in Canada, Galbraith first studied at the Ontario Agricultural College (now the University of Guelph) and the University of Toronto. He then moved to California, where he completed a Ph.D. in agricultural economics. He was immediately hired by Harvard University, where he eventually became a professor. He was in charge of the administration of price controls during World War II, an experience that led to his peculiar description of the behaviour of large firms, in particular in his bestseller *The New Industrial State* (1967), where he claims that corporate planning supersedes market mechanisms. A prolific and witty writer, Galbraith was a left-leaning liberal economist who argued that the private sector has overextended, to the detriment of the public sector and the environment.

SOURCE: Hulton Archive/Getty Images

■ The Role of Assumptions

An important cause of disagreements among economists is that theorizing is based on assumptions. As we saw in the previous section, abstraction and theorizing require simplifying assumptions. In making such assumptions, economists may exclude variables that they judge to be irrelevant but they may also assume things that they know to be false in themselves. Fruitful assumptions are those that lead to a long string of deductions and to predictions that were not intuitively obvious from the start.

Assumptions play a key role in economic analysis. Changing the assumptions will lead to different results and most likely to different policy recommendations. Whatever the quality of the analysis, if the assumptions are wrong—if they do not adequately reflect stylized facts or the behaviour of people—the conclusions reached are most likely to be wrong as well. Keynes once said that it was preferable to be approximately right than precisely wrong. Economists who are using a different set of assumptions will most likely disagree on the implications of their theories or models.

Take the case of the National Hockey League (NHL). The collective agreement signed in 2005 contains a clause forcing the richest teams—high-revenue teams like the Toronto Maple Leafs and the Montreal Canadiens—to make equalization payments to the poorest teams—the teams with the lowest revenues. Will such an income redistribution toward low-revenue teams improve their performance on the ice? The answer depends on the motivations that drive the behaviour of the NHL owners. If the owners are assumed to maximize profits, as is usually alleged by economists, the prediction is that such equalization payments will have no impact whatsoever, as owners of low-revenue teams will simply pocket the additional money. However, if the owners are assumed to maximize winning, being constrained only by the fact that they want to avoid financial losses, they will use the additional funds to obtain or retain good players in an effort to improve the on-ice performance of their teams.

As another example of the importance of assumptions, think of the fiscal predictions of the Government of Canada. For many years now, the Department of Finance has been underpredicting the size of the federal budget surplus, while other economists, working for trade unions, banks, and forecasting agencies have been much closer to reality. Does that mean that the economists in the Department of Finance are just plain incompetent and are unable to assess and model the expenditures and revenues of the federal government? No. It simply means that the economists at the Department of Finance are using much more cautious and conservative assumptions when making their forecasts; for instance, assuming slightly too low future rates of economic growth, which decrease forecasted government revenues, or slightly too high interest rates, which increase forecasted government payments on debt servicing.

Different assumptions in economics will often lead to different conclusions, different predictions, and different policy recommendations. For this reason, it is important to clearly spell out our assumptions.

Why don't economists all accept the same assumptions? Besides the reasons that will be offered in the next section, it should be pointed out that an assumption may be quite appropriate in some circumstances and invalid in others. A problem that all economists face is ascertaining the domain of validity of an assumption. Does it apply to all agents, all industries, or all countries, or only to a subset of them? For instance, in the case of NHL hockey, could it be that some owners try to maximize profits (like the owners of the Toronto Maple Leafs?), while others try to maximize on-ice performance?

The Role of Value Judgments

Many disputes among economists are not scientific disputes at all. Sometimes the pertinent facts are simply unknown. For example, the appropriate financial penalty to levy on a polluter depends on quantitative estimates of the harm done by the pollutant. But good estimates of this damage may not be available. Similarly, although there is wide scientific agreement that the earth is slowly warming, there are disagreements over how costly global warming may be. Such disputes make it difficult to agree on a concrete policy proposal.

Another important source of disagreements is that economists, like other people, come in all political stripes: conservative, middle-of-the-road, liberal, radical. Each may have different values, and so each may hold a different view of the "right" solution to a public policy problem—even if they agree on the underlying analysis. Here are two examples:

1. We suggested earlier in this chapter that policies that lower inflation are likely to raise unemployment. Many economists believe they can measure the amount of unemployment that must be endured to reduce inflation by a given amount. But they disagree about whether it is worth having, say, 300,000 more people out of work for a year to cut the inflation rate by 1 percent.

2. In designing an income tax, society must decide how much of the burden to put on upper-income taxpayers. Some people believe the rich should pay a disproportionate share of the taxes. Others disagree, believing it is fairer to levy the same income tax rate on everyone.

While one would think that economists cannot answer questions like these any more than nuclear physicists could have determined whether dropping the atomic bomb on Hiroshima was a good idea, economists do engage in discussions on these issues on the basis of economic arguments. For instance, about the design of tax policies, some economists reason that the rich should not pay too much in taxes because economic growth and prosperity depend on how much the rich can afford to save. But then how much is too much? Ultimately, such decisions rest on moral judgments that can be made only by the citizens of a province or territory, or of the country, through their elected representatives.

Although economic science can contribute theoretical and factual knowledge on a particular issue, the final decision on policy questions often rests either on information that is not currently available or on social values and ethical opinions about which people differ, or on both.

◼ Two Views of Scientific Research

Value judgments permeate not just policy decisions, but the whole scientific process. There are two views of scientific research: the naive and the modern views, as illustrated in Figure 1. In the naive view, economists first collect objective statistical facts and observe agent behaviour; then, from this, they formulate grand theories and build models that represent a subset of these theories; third, they test the models, make predictions, and collect new facts. The models can thus either be rejected because statistical techniques or new facts falsify the theory and its model, or the model is found to be compatible with statistical analysis and new events, in which case, we can say that it is well corroborated. In the latter case, further work can be done to improve the model and its theory, and economic policies can be proposed in line with the lessons drawn from the model. Under this view, economics is a science where models get better and better, and where bad theories are progressively weeded out, to be forever abandoned. The naive view of science makes disagreements in economics nearly impossible to understand. Why wouldn't all economists finally agree on the improved, correct model?

The main two reasons for continuing disagreement among economists have already been spelled out: The facts may be uncertain and economists, like everyone in society, have opinions. Some economic "laws" may be verified in some countries or industries but not in others. In addition, statistical techniques rarely yield clear-cut results. Quite a lot of data massaging must be done to obtain statistics that correspond to the specification of the model or to obtain meaningful results. As the saying goes, the data must be tortured until they confess! The second reason is that economists have political opinions, feelings, cultural experiences, pecuniary interests, and vested interests from past research that will interfere at every stage of scientific enquiry. For instance, who would believe that economists working for tobacco producers, or whose research is being subsidized by tobacco associations, would not arrive at biased conclusions regarding the social costs of smoking? The way economic facts are collected, summarized, classified, organized, and interpreted depends to a large extent on the *a priori* opinions of the researcher. The stylized facts and the conclusions that arise from this exercise depend on ideology; they are not just the outcome of a detached quest for knowledge.

In addition, whether a given model will seem to be confirmed or disparaged by the test results will, to a large extent or at least to some extent, depend on the *a priori* opinions of the researcher. Researchers in social sciences tend to hold on tenaciously to ideas that took years of effort to develop, and will tend to find unconvincing any evidence that conflicts with their pet theories. In social sciences, the observer (the economist) has an influence on reality or at least on the perception of what reality is.

FIGURE 1

Research in Economics: Two Views

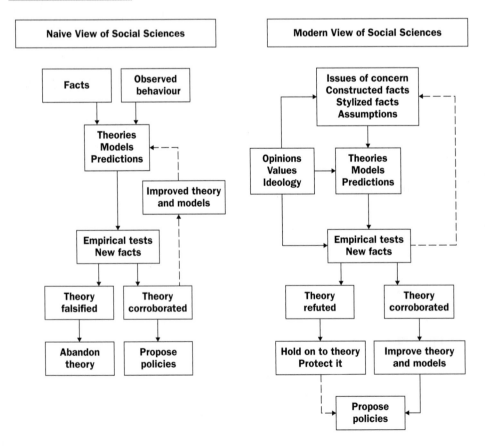

In other academic fields, this is called the *postmodern view*. Although we do not fully espouse this view of knowledge, the limits to objective research in economics must be recognized. Indeed, acknowledging these limits helps us to understand why well-trained economists can hold diverging views on a given economic topic, whatever the facts, and why highly intelligent researchers often cannot agree on a single model and a single policy proposition.

In the naive view of research in the social sciences, researchers are impervious to ideological or pecuniary influences. In the modern view, prior opinions and values have an impact at every stage of research.

Still, this does not mean that *anything goes*. When arguing a position, an economist puts forward assumptions, abstractions, models, a string of coherent implications, and historical or empirical evidence. Every stage of the argument needs to be justified.

The Influence of Political Winds

Figure 1 presented the modern view of scientific research. Philosophers who examine how research in the social sciences is being conducted claim that opinions and ideology do have an impact on the facts that are uncovered, the models and the theories that are put forward, and the policies that are recommended or advocated by researchers. This modern view of scientific research corresponds quite well with a comment made recently by Paul Samuelson, which appears at the bottom of this boxed feature. Samuelson (1915–) was the 1970 recipient of the Bank of Sweden Prize in Economic Sciences in Memory of Alfred Nobel. Samuelson received this prize—the equivalent of a Nobel Prize in Economics—the second year that it was awarded. Besides being an obviously bright and creative researcher, Samuelson is the author of the very first modern principles of economics textbook, *Economics,* first published in 1948. This textbook has been an inspiration for all first-year economics textbooks, including the one you are now reading. As you will see, Samuelson is rather sarcastic, but the main point is that research and theorizing are not done in a vacuum; these activities are influenced by society, our own beliefs, and even self-interest (money). This should help to explain why economists disagree on certain issues—even the most important ones. The difficulty of pursuing conclusive experiments, and hence the absence of absolute knowledge, makes it more likely that values and ideology will have some impact on the theories and the models that will be produced.

Political winds do have an influence on economists, just like important events, such as a deep recession or periods of high inflation, will have an impact on the agenda being pursued by economists.

In the foreword to his 2006 book with co-editor William A. Barnett, *Inside the Economist's Mind: Conversations with Eminent Economists,* Samuelson wrote:

I conclude with an unworthy hypothesis regarding past and present directions of economic research. Sherlock Holmes said, '*Cherchez la femme.*' . . . We economists do primarily work for our peers' esteem, which figures in our own self-esteem.

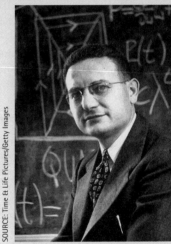

SOURCE: Time & Life Pictures/Getty Images

When post-Depression Roosevelt's New Deal provided exciting job opportunities, first the junior academic faculties moved leftward. To get back ahead of their followers, subsequently the senior academic faculties shoved ahead of them. As post-Reagan, post-Thatcher electorates turned rightward, follow the money pointed, alas, in only one direction. So to speak, we eat our own cooking.

We economists love to quote Keynes's final lines in his 1936 *General Theory* ["Practical men, who believe themselves to be quite exempt from any intellectual influences, are usually the slaves of some defunct economist. Madmen in authority, who hear voices in the air, are distilling their frenzy from some academic scribbler of a few years back."]—for the reason that they cater so well to our vanity and self-importance. But to admit the truth, madmen in authority can *self-generate* their own frenzies without needing help from either defunct or *avant-garde* economists. What establishment economists brew up is as often what the Prince and the Public are already wanting to imbibe. We guys don't stay in the best club by proffering the views of some past *academic* crank or academic sage.

SOURCES: Paul A. Samuelson, "Reflections on How Biographies of Individual Scholars Can Relate to a Science's Biography," in Paul A. Samuelson and William A. Barnett (eds.), *Inside the Economist's Mind: Conversations with Eminent Economists* (Boston: Blackwell Publishing, 2007), pp. ix–x; John Maynard Keynes, *The General Theory of Employment, Interest and Money* (London: Macmillan, 1936), p. 383.

SUMMARY

1. There are many possible definitions of economics. In the past, economics has been defined as being concerned with:

   a. The causes of the wealth of nations

   b. The laws that regulate income distribution

   c. The laws of motion of capitalism

2. Two further definitions could be offered today:

   a. Economics is a method of analyzing individual and social behaviour, especially as it relates to market phenomena.

   b. Economics is the study of behaviour conditioned by scarcity.

3. Microeconomics deals with consumers, firms, industries, or markets taken in isolation. Macroeconomics deals with economic systems taken as a whole, and thus confronts fallacies of composition.

4. Because of the great complexity of human behaviour, economists are forced to *abstract* from many details, to make generalizations that they know are not quite true, and to organize what knowledge they have in terms of some theoretical structure called a *model*.

5. Correlation need not imply causation, and the timing of events may not properly reflect what is the cause and what is the effect.

6. Economists use simplified models to understand the real world and predict its behaviour, much as a child uses a model railroad to learn how trains work.

7. Although these models, if skillfully constructed, can illuminate important economic problems, they rarely can answer the questions that confront policy makers. Value judgments are needed for this purpose, and the economist is no better equipped than anyone else to make them.

8. Economists agree among themselves on several fundamental issues, but as the reading of any newspaper will demonstrate, they disagree on some issues of doctrine and on many policy issues. There are several reasons that can explain such a situation.

   a. The facts are uncertain or statistics hard to come by.

   b. Different economists may start with different assumptions.

   c. Models or theories are hard to disprove, so different economic theories will be held and promoted concurrently by various schools of thought.

   d. Economists come in all political stripes.

9. There are two views of science, the naive and the modern view. In the naive view, all economists should end up accepting the same model. By contrast, the modern view says that value judgments, political opinions, and vested interests influence every step of scientific research, which helps to explain why there are disagreements among economists. Still, economists share the method of justifying every step of their arguments.

KEY TERMS

Economics   4

Opportunity cost   6

Paradox 7

Fallacy of compostion 7

Abstraction   8

Theory   10

Correlation   10

Post hoc, ergo propter hoc fallacy 11

Economic model   12

DISCUSSION QUESTIONS

1. Think about how you would construct a model of how your college or university is governed. Which officers and administrators would you include and exclude from your model if the objective was one of the following:

   a. To explain how decisions on financial aid are made

   b. To explain the quality of the faculty

   Relate this to the map example in the chapter.

2. Relate the process of abstraction to the way you take notes in a lecture. Why do you not try to transcribe every word uttered by the lecturer? Why don't you write down just the title of the lecture and stop there? How do you decide, roughly speaking, on the correct amount of detail?

3. Explain why a government policy maker cannot afford to ignore economic theory.

4. Provide another possible example of the *post hoc, ergo propter hoc* fallacy.

5. Provide an example where correlation may not entail causation, besides the examples mentioned in the chapter.

6. Provide different kinds of reasons as to why economists would disagree on whether the power of labour unions ought to be curtailed.

7. Describe in your own words the differences that you see between the old and the new views of social sciences.

APPENDIX *Using Graphs: A Review*

As noted in the chapter, economists often explain and analyze models with the help of graphs. Indeed, this book is full of them. But that is not the only reason for studying how graphs work. Most people will deal with graphs in the future, perhaps frequently. You will see them in newspapers. If you become a doctor, you will use graphs to keep track of your patients' progress. If you join a business firm, you will use them to check profit or performance at a glance. This appendix introduces some of the techniques of graphic analysis—tools you will use throughout the book and, more important, very likely throughout your working career. Students who have some acquaintance with geometry and feel quite comfortable with graphs can safely skip this appendix.

■ GRAPHS USED IN ECONOMIC ANALYSIS

Economic graphs are invaluable because they can display a large quantity of data quickly and because they facilitate data interpretation and analysis. They enable the eye to take in at a glance important statistical relationships that would be far less apparent from written descriptions or long lists of numbers.

■ TWO-VARIABLE DIAGRAMS

Much of the economic analysis found in this and other books requires that we keep track of two **variables** simultaneously.

> A **variable** is something measured by a number; it is used to analyze what happens to other things when the size of that number changes (varies).

For example, in studying how markets operate, we will want to keep one eye on the *price* of a commodity and the other on the *quantity* of that commodity that is bought and sold.

For this reason, economists frequently find it useful to display real or imaginary figures in a two-variable diagram, which simultaneously represents the behaviour of two economic variables. The numerical value of one variable is measured along the horizontal line at the bottom of the graph (called the *horizontal axis*), starting from the **origin** (the point labelled "0"), and the numerical value of the other variable is mea-

sured up the vertical line on the left side of the graph (called the *vertical axis*), also starting from the origin.

> The "0" point in the lower-left corner of a graph where the axes meet is called the **origin**. Both variables are equal to zero at the **origin**.

Figures 2(a) and 2(b) are typical graphs of economic analysis. They depict an imaginary *demand curve*, represented by the blue dots in Figure 2(a) and the heavy blue line in Figure 2(b). The graphs show the price of natural gas on their vertical axes and the quantity of gas people want to buy at each price on the horizontal axes. The dots in Figure 2(a) are connected by the continuous blue curve labelled *DD* in Figure 2(b).

Economic diagrams are generally read just as one would read latitudes and longitudes on a map. On the demand curve in Figure 2, the point marked *a* represents a hypothetical combination of price and quantity of natural gas demanded by customers in Calgary. By drawing a horizontal line leftward from that point to the vertical axis, we learn that at this point the average price for gas in Calgary is 30¢ per cubic metre. By dropping a line straight down to the horizontal axis, we find that consumers want 8 billion cubic metres per year at this price, just as the statistics in Table 2 show. The other points on the graph give similar information. For example, point *b* indicates that if natural gas in Calgary costs only 20¢ per cubic metre, quantity demanded would be higher—it would reach 12 billion cubic metres per year.

Notice that information about price and quantity is *all* we can learn from the diagram. The demand curve will not tell us what kinds of people live in Calgary, the sizes of their homes, or the condition of their furnaces. It tells us about the quantity demanded at each possible price—no more, no less.

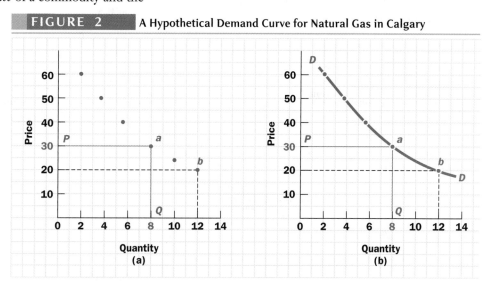

FIGURE 2 A Hypothetical Demand Curve for Natural Gas in Calgary

Note: Price is in cents per cubic metres; quantity is in billions of cubic metres per year.

TABLE 2				
Quantities of Natural Gas Demanded at Various Prices				
Price (per cubic metre)	20¢	30¢	40¢	50¢	60¢
Quantity demanded (billions of cubic metres per year)	12	8	5.6	3.8	2

A diagram abstracts from many details, some of which may be quite interesting, so as to focus on the two variables of primary interest—in this case, the price of natural gas and the amount of gas that is demanded at each price. All of the diagrams used in this book share this basic feature. They cannot tell the reader the "whole story," any more than a map's latitude and longitude figures for a particular city can make someone an authority on that city.

■ THE DEFINITION AND MEASUREMENT OF SLOPE

One of the most important features of economic diagrams is the rate at which the line or curve being sketched runs uphill or downhill as we move to the right. The demand curve in Figure 2 clearly slopes downhill (the price falls) as we follow it to the right (that is, as consumers demand more gas). In such instances, we say that *the curve has a negative slope, or is negatively sloped, because one variable falls as the other one rises.*

> The **slope of a straight line** is the ratio of the vertical change to the corresponding horizontal change as we move to the right along the line or, as it is often said, the ratio of the "rise" over the "run."

The four panels of Figure 3 show all possible types of slope for a straight-line relationship between two unnamed variables called Y (measured along the vertical axis) and X (measured along the horizontal axis). Figure 3(a) shows a *negative slope*, much like our demand curve in the previous graph. Figure 3(b) shows a *positive slope*, because variable Y rises (we go uphill) as variable X rises

(as we move to the right). Figure 3(c) shows a *zero slope*, where the value of Y is the same irrespective of the value of X. Figure 3(d) shows an *infinite slope*, meaning that the value of X is the same irrespective of the value of Y.

Slope is a numerical concept, not just a qualitative one. The two panels of Figure 4 show two positively sloped straight lines with different slopes. The line in Figure 4(b) is clearly steeper. But by how much? The labels should help you compute the answer. In Figure 4(a) a horizontal movement, AB, of 10 units ($13 - 3$) corresponds to a vertical movement, BC, of 1 unit ($9 - 8$). So the slope is $BC/AB = 1/10$. In Figure 4(b), the same horizontal movement of 10 units corresponds to a vertical movement of 3 units ($11 - 8$). So the slope is $3/10$, which is larger—the rise divided by the run is greater in Figure 4(b).

By definition, the slope of any particular straight line remains the same, no matter where on that line we choose to measure it. That is why we can pick any horizontal distance, AB, and the corresponding slope triangle, ABC, to measure slope. But this is not true for curved lines.

> Curved lines also have slopes, but the numerical value of the slope differs at every point along the curve as we move from left to right.

The four panels of Figure 5 provide some examples of *slopes of curved lines*. The curve in Figure 5(a) has a negative slope everywhere, and the curve in Figure 5(b) has a positive slope everywhere. But these are not the only possibilities. In Figure 5(c) we encounter a curve that has a positive slope at first but a negative slope later on. Figure 5(d) shows the opposite case: a negative slope followed by a positive slope.

We can measure the slope of a smooth curved line numerically *at any particular point* by drawing a *straight* line that *touches*, but does not *cut*, the curve at the point in question. Such a line is called a **tangent** to the curve.

> The **slope of a curved line** at a particular point is defined as the slope of the straight line that is tangent to the curve at that point.

Figure 6 shows tangents to the blue curve at two points. Line *tt* is tangent at point *T*, and line *rr* is tangent

---

FIGURE 3   Different Types of Slope of a Straight-Line Graph

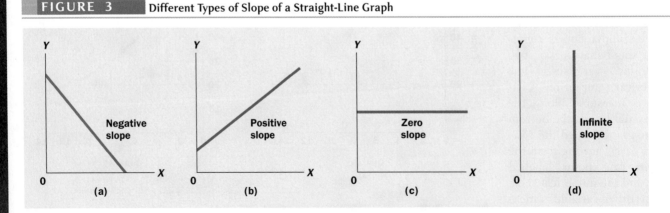

FIGURE 4   How to Measure Slope

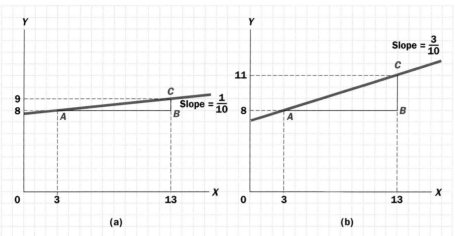

(a)   (b)

FIGURE 5   Behaviour of Slopes in Curved Graphs

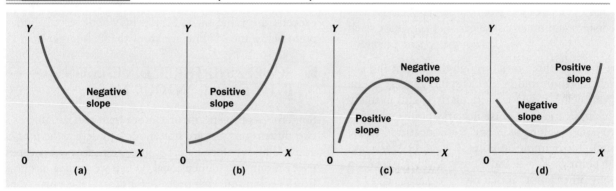

(a)   (b)   (c)   (d)

at point R. We can measure the slope of the curve at these two points by applying the definition. The calculation for point T, then, is the following:

Slope at point T = Slope of line tt

$$= \frac{\text{Distance BC}}{\text{Distance BA}}$$

$$= \frac{(1 - 5)}{(3 - 1)} = \frac{-4}{2} = -2$$

A similar calculation yields the slope of the curve at point R, which, as we can see from Figure 6, must be smaller numerically. That is, the tangent line rr is less steep than line tt:

Slope at point R = Slope of line rr

$$= \frac{(5 - 7)}{(8 - 6)} = \frac{-2}{2} = -1$$

EXERCISE Show that the slope of the curve at point G is about 1.

What would happen if we tried to apply this graphical technique to the high point in Figure 5(c) or to the low point in Figure 5(d)? Take a ruler and try it. The tangents that you construct should be horizontal, meaning that they should have a slope exactly equal to zero. It is always true that where the slope of a *smooth* curve

FIGURE 6   How to Measure Slope at a Point on a Curved Graph

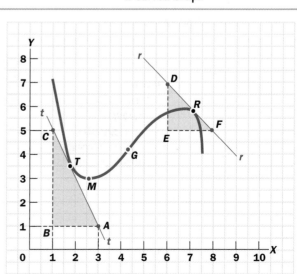

changes from positive to negative, or vice versa, there will be at least one point whose slope is zero.

Curves shaped like smooth hills, as in Figure 5(c), have a zero slope at their *highest* point. Curves shaped like valleys, as in Figure 5(d), have a zero slope at their *lowest* point.

■ RAYS THROUGH THE ORIGIN AND 45° LINES

The point at which a straight line cuts the vertical (Y) axis is called the **Y-intercept.**

The **Y-intercept** of a line or a curve is the point at which it touches the vertical axis (the Y-axis). The X-intercept is defined similarly.

For example, the Y-intercept of the line in Figure 4(a) is a bit less than 8.

Lines whose Y-intercept is zero have so many special uses in economics and other disciplines that they have been given a special name: a **ray through the origin, or a ray.**

Figure 7 shows three rays through the origin, and the slope of each is indicated in the diagram. The ray in the centre (whose slope is 1) is particularly useful in many economic applications because it marks points where X and Y are equal (as long as X and Y are measured in the same units). For example, at point A we have $X = 3$ and $Y = 3$; at point B, $X = 4$ and $Y = 4$. A similar relation holds at any other point on that ray.

How do we know that this is always true for a ray whose slope is 1? If we start from the origin (where both X and Y are zero) and the slope of the ray is 1, we know from the definition of slope that

$$\text{Slope} = \frac{\text{Vertical change}}{\text{Horizontal change}} = 1$$

This implies that the vertical change and the horizontal change are always equal, so the two variables must always remain equal. Any point along that ray (for example, point A) is exactly equal in distance from the horizontal and vertical axes (length DA = length CA)—the number on the X-axis (the abscissa) will be the same as the number on the Y-axis (the ordinate).

Rays through the origin with a slope of 1 are called 45° lines because they form an angle of 45° with the horizontal axis. A 45° line marks off points where the variables measured on each axis have equal values.[1]

If a point representing some data is above the 45° line, we know that the value of Y

---

[1]The definition assumes that both variables are measured in the same units.

FIGURE 7   Rays Through the Origin

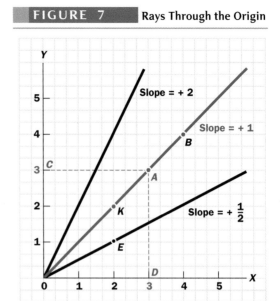

exceeds the value of X. Similarly, whenever we find a point below the 45° line, we know that X is larger than Y.

■ SQUEEZING THREE DIMENSIONS INTO TWO: CONTOUR MAPS

Sometimes problems involve more than two variables, so two dimensions just are not enough to depict them on a graph. This is unfortunate, because the surface of a sheet of paper is only two-dimensional. When we study a business firm's decision-making process, for example, we may want to keep track simultaneously of three variables: how much labour it employs, how much raw material it imports from foreign countries, and how much output it creates.

Luckily, economists can use a well-known device for collapsing three dimensions into two—a *contour map.* Figure 8 is a contour map of the summit of the highest moutain in the world, Mt. Everest, on the border of Nepal and Tibet. On some of the irregularly shaped "rings" on

FIGURE 8   A Geographic Contour Map

SOURCE: Mount Everest. Alpenvereinskarte. Vienna: Kartographisce Anstalt Freytag-Berndt und Artaria, 1957,1988.

this map, we find numbers (like 8500) indicating the height (in metres) above sea level at that particular spot on the mountain. Thus, unlike the more usual sort of map, which gives only latitudes and longitudes, this contour map (also called a topographical map) exhibits *three* pieces of information about each point: latitude, longitude, and altitude.

Figure 9 looks more like the contour maps encountered in economics. It shows how some third variable, called Z (think of it as a firm's output, for example), varies as we change either variable X (think of it as a firm's employment of labour) or variable Y (think of it as the use of imported raw material). Just like the map of Mt. Everest, any point on the diagram conveys three pieces of data. At point A, we can read off the values of X and Y in the conventional way (X is 30 and Y is 40), and we can also note the value of Z by finding out on which contour line point A falls. (It is on the $Z = 20$ contour.) So point A is able to tell us that 30 hours of labour and 40 metres of cloth produce 20 units of output per day. The contour line that indicates 20 units of output shows the various combinations of labour and cloth a manufacturer can use to produce 20 units of output. Economists call such maps **production indifference maps.**

A **production indifference map** is a graph whose axes show the quantities of two inputs that are used to produce some output. A curve in the graph corresponds to some given quantity of that output, and the different points on that curve show the different quantities of the two inputs that are just enough to produce the given output.

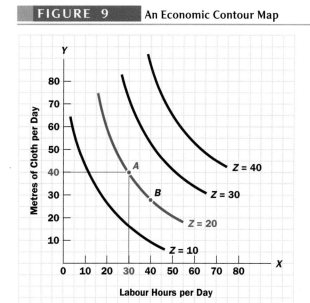

FIGURE 9 An Economic Contour Map

Although most of the analyses presented in this book rely on the simpler two-variable diagrams, contour maps will find their applications, especially in the appendixes to Chapters 5 and 7.

SUMMARY

1. Because graphs are used so often to portray economic models, it is important for students to acquire some understanding of their construction and use. Fortunately, the graphics used in economics are usually not very complex.

2. Most economic models are depicted in two-**variable** diagrams. We read data from these diagrams just as we read the latitude and longitude on a map: each point represents the values of two variables at the same time.

3. In some instances, three variables must be shown at once. In these cases, economists use contour maps, which, as the name suggests, show "latitude," "longitude," and "altitude" all at the same time.

4. Often, the most important property of a line or curve drawn on a diagram will be its **slope**, which is defined as the ratio of the "rise" over the "run," or the vertical change divided by the horizontal change. Curves that go uphill as we move to the right have positive slopes; curves that go downhill have negative slopes.

5. By definition, a straight line has the same slope wherever we choose to measure it. The slope of a curved line changes, but the slope at any point on the curve can be calculated by measuring the slope of a straight line tangent to the curve at that point.

KEY TERMS

Variable   19

Origin (of a graph)   19

Slope of a straight (or curved) line   20

Tangent to a curve   20

Y-intercept   22

Ray through the origin, or ray   22

45° line   22

Production indifference map   23

TEST YOURSELF

1. Portray the following hypothetical data on a two-variable diagram:

Academic Year	Total Enrollment	Enrollment in Economics Courses
2002–2003	3,000	300
2003–2004	3,100	325
2004–2005	3,200	350
2005–2006	3,300	375
2006–2007	3,400	400

Measure the slope of the resulting line, and explain what this number means.

2. From Figure 6, calculate the slope of the curve at point M.

3. Colin believes that the number of job offers he will get depends on the number of courses in which his grade is B+ or better. He concludes from observation that the following figures are typical:

Number of grades of B+ or better	0	1	2	3	4
Number of job offers	1	3	4	5	6

Put these numbers into a graph like Figure 2(a). Measure and interpret the slopes between adjacent dots.

4. In Figure 7, determine the values of X and Y at point K and at point E. What do you conclude about the slopes of the lines on which K and E are located?

5. In Figure 9, interpret the economic meaning of points A and B. What do the two points have in common? What is the difference in their economic interpretation?

THE ECONOMY: MYTH AND REALITY

When you cannot measure, your knowledge is meagre and unsatisfactory.

MAXIM ATTRIBUTED TO LORD KELVIN

I've come loaded with statistics, for I've noticed that a man can't prove anything without statistics.

MARK TWAIN

This chapter introduces you to the Canadian economy and its role in the world. It may seem that no such introduction is necessary, for you have probably lived your entire life in Canada. Every time you work at a summer or part-time job, pay your college or university bills, or buy a slice of pizza, you not only participate in the Canadian economy—you also observe something about it.

But the casual impressions we acquire in our everyday lives, though sometimes correct, are often misleading. We can see the trees but not necessarily the forest. We often harbour misconceptions about some very basic economic facts about the Canadian economy. There are many popular myths held by Canadians about the nature of the economy, such as the belief that we are inundated with imported goods, mostly from China, and that we produce very little in Canada today. The object of this chapter is to offer some important useful facts about the nature and evolution of the Canadian economy so as to dispel such misconceptions, and in the chapters that follow, to offer a framework for analyzing theories of how the economy works.

CONTENTS

THE CANADIAN ECONOMY: A THUMBNAIL SKETCH

Canada is a country that scores high on the United Nations *Human Development Index* (HDI)—an index that focuses on three measurable aspects of human welfare: life expectancy, literacy/school enrollment, and income level. While Canadian society performs very well in all three dimensions of human development, one cannot overlook Canada's relative success and maturity as an industrial economy. Yet, when analyzed from the perspective of the Group of Seven (G7) industrialized countries (Canada, France, Germany, Italy, Japan, the United Kingdom, and the United States), its population and, to a lesser extent, its economy appear comparatively small. With over 33 million inhabitants, Canada's population is slightly over one-tenth of that of the United States and one-third of that of Mexico, its two closest neighbours and trading partners on the North American continent. However, despite its relatively small demographic base, the Canadian economy produces a monetary value of its total output that exceeds that of, say, Mexico, when measured on the basis of a common currency unit. With a wide capacity in terms of human, physical, and natural resources, Canada places itself securely within the top tier of high-income countries internationally.

Why are some countries rich and others poor? As mentioned previously, that is one of the central questions facing economists. To try to answer this question, it is useful to think of the economic system as a machine that takes **inputs,** such as labour and other things we call **factors of production,** and transforms them into **outputs,** the things that people want to consume. On the basis of this relationship between inputs and outputs, the Canadian economic machine performs this task reasonably well. Of course, there are some countries, especially within the G7, that seem to accomplish this task even better, but there are many more that do not perform this function as well. Hence, a country like the United States holds the top rank when compared with other countries on the basis of such measures as output per person. Other less fortunate countries, such as Sierra Leone and Niger, are found at the bottom of the scale, with output per capita at less than one-fiftieth of that of Canada.

The 6.5 billion people in the world produced about US$45 trillion worth of goods and services in 2006. However, as Figure 1 shows, the G7 industrial economies, which accounted for just less than 12 percent of the earth's population, generated approximately 67 percent of world output. Given its low relative weight and the large gap between the United States and the other G7 countries, Canada's gross domestic product (GDP) per capita stood slightly below the G7 average in U.S. dollars, when adjusting for cost of living differences (at purchasing power parities) across the seven major industrialized countries.

Although Canada is a rich country and remains an important destination internationally for economic migrants seeking to improve their level of economic well-being, the ten provinces and three territories constituting Canada were not created equal. Population densities vary greatly among the regions of Canada, with enor-

Inputs or factors of production are the labour, machinery, buildings, and natural resources used to make outputs.

Outputs are the goods and services that consumers and others want to acquire.

SOURCE: Organisation for Economic Co-operation and Development (OECD), *OECD Statistics v. 4.4,* Dataset 1 (Gross Domestic Product), Dataset 3 (Total Population). www.oecd.org/statistics

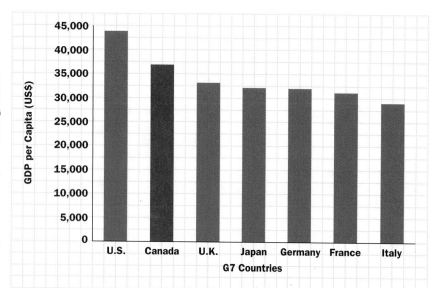

FIGURE 1   2006 Gross Domestic Product (GDP) per Capita in 7 Industrial Countries

Gross domestic product (GDP) per capita was obtained using current PPPs in U.S. dollars.

mous clustering in the south-central regions of the country. For example, while there are close to 12 inhabitants per square kilometre in the province of Ontario, there are only 0.01 people per square kilometre in the territory of Nunavut. Although much less pronounced, output per person also varies regionally. For instance, income per capita is now highest in Alberta, partly as a result of its vast oil wealth, while provinces such as Newfoundland and Labrador find themselves closer to the other extremity of the income scale, with their average provincial incomes being less than two-thirds of the Alberta average.

An Advanced Market Economy

Many economists would argue that part of the reason for the success of the Canadian economy in achieving a relatively high level of economic well-being relates to the fact that we have developed a sophisticated market economy with an appropriate balance of private and public ownership of property. While being a "land of opportunity" in creating incentives for private initiative, Canada has created a sophisticated social safety net that provides support, both financially and in kind, when the market fails for some of its citizens.

An economy with a mixture of private and public goods is sometimes referred to as a *mixed economy*, and all economies internationally could be said to be mixed. However, one can imagine on one end of the spectrum a pure market economy in which all goods are produced by private enterprises and sold in privately organized markets to individual consumers. In such a *free enterprise system*, all goods would be rationed on the basis of the prices that they fetch for their owners, and the decision to produce and sell one's products in the marketplace would be guided exclusively by the profit motive. Hence, in a pure *capitalist economy*, where individuals could hold and acquire ownership of capital goods so as to derive an income in excess of what they could get solely from their labour services, production and distribution would be purely in private hands. For example, the United States has one of the most "marketized" and "privatized" economies on earth, with even many of the public utilities being run by private companies.

At the other end of the spectrum, we have *command economies*, where decisions regarding the level and the composition of total output is set by a central authority, as in the former Soviet Union and, to a lesser extent, in such countries as China and Cuba today. While the actual ownership of the physical productive resources may or may not be in the hands of a central authority, the decision regarding what to produce is made by a central agency that normally sets specific objectives or plans for the respective public enterprises. This is why such economies have often been termed *planned economies*. This is not to suggest that no economic planning is actually undertaken in a market economy. Private enterprises, as much as public enterprises, must plan the combination of various inputs so as to fulfill orders and meet their commitments. However, in a *private enterprise economy*, it is the reaction to price signals arising from the marketplace that determines the amount of goods produced as well as who will get to consume these goods, based on an individual's ability to pay. Instead, in a command economy, the objective is set by a central authority, which decides what goods to be produced and who will get to consume them, sometimes regardless of an individual's income.

With the breakup of the Soviet Union in the late 1980s, many economies of Eastern Europe and Asia that constituted the former Soviet bloc moved away from the planned system and began to restructure their economies to fit more closely the market model prevailing in Western Europe and North America. Over the last two decades, these former socialist economies found themselves in a transitional phase as they moved from a planned to a market system and, for this reason, they are frequently referred to as *transition economies*. Although the terms *transition* and *emerging economies* are sometimes used broadly to describe any economy that is in the process of restructuring from a more regulated economy to a less regulated market economy (say, in the developing world), it is primarily the constellation of former socialist countries of Eastern Europe and parts of Asia that are most appropriately described as *transition economies*.

One should not, however, confuse a transition economy with a mixed economy. As was previously stated, all economies in the world today are mixed economies, regardless of whether they are market, socialist, or transition economies. All have a specific mixture of private/public production and consumption of goods and services. For instance, if you take the example of health care and compare the Canadian and American systems of delivery of medical services, you can easily distinguish how the two countries differ in terms of the private/public mix. In the American case, the market for health care services is dominated by private providers who ration these services largely on the basis of an individual's ability to pay (whether this is related to one's wealth or to how well endowed one is with private health insurance). In the Canadian case, as well as in many Western European countries, health care systems have features that are closer to the command economy model. In Canada, health care services are provided by provincial governments on the basis of the Canada Health Act to whoever needs medical services, without the intervention of the market and the price mechanism in allocating such services. A similar difference can be found in the area of higher education, where delivery is done largely through quasi-public institutions. The price mechanism (that is, tuition fees) plays a less important role in Canada and in many European countries than in the United States because of the varying degrees of direct government subsidies that are provided to Canada's and other countries' educational institutions.

The private/public composition of goods and services reflects policy preferences of governments that have been fashioned by the history of each country. Over time, the structure of output in an economy changes primarily because of political forces at work in reshaping those preferences. Hence, during the early post-World War II period, political forces internationally had moved in the direction that favoured more public sector involvement in the economy. During the 1970s and 1980s under the influence of Thatcherism in the United Kingdom and Reaganomics in the United States, the pendulum swung in the opposite direction, as governments sold off public assets and retreated somewhat from direct involvement in the provision of goods and services. Although the public sector share of production has declined somewhat from the earlier post-World War II period, Canada's uniqueness is its continued large public sector with close to one-quarter of total production flowing from public sector activities, thereby making it a mixed economy *par excellence*.

Gross domestic product (GDP) is a measure of the size of the economy—the total amount it produces in a year. *Real GDP* adjusts this measure for changes in the purchasing power of money, that is, it corrects for inflation.

The standard measure of the total output of an economy is called **gross domestic product** (or **GDP**), a term that appears frequently in the news media. In an advanced market economy such as ours, the share of GDP that passes through markets is enormous. Although government purchases of goods and services in Canada amount to about 22 percent of GDP, much of this is purchased from private businesses. Direct government production of commodities is rare, but the public sector supply of services is quite significant in Canada, with health care delivery and education subsidies being prime examples.

◾ A Relatively "Open" Economy

All nations trade with one another and, as one of Canada's most distinguished economists, Harold A. Innis, pointed out long ago, the economic history of Canada has been shaped very much by foreign trade. From the time of its first European contact, Canada was integrated into the world economy by establishing itself solidly as a producer of primary products and an importer of manufactured goods. While its share of primary commodities has declined significantly over time in this era of globalized product markets, exports now constitute a large and growing share of Canada's GDP. In 2007, our annual exports were about $535 billion and our imports about $503 billion. That's quite a significant amount of money transiting through the foreign sector. But, while very important, some may argue that Canada's international trade often gets a lot more attention than it deserves. The fact is that we still produce a large portion of what we consume and consume a great deal of what we produce, as Figure 2 shows. In 1959, the average of exports and imports was less than 20 percent of GDP. By 2000, this share had peaked at over 40 percent and then bottomed out at slightly less than 34 percent of

GDP by 2007. This was a hefty jump and turnaround in less than half a century, and the effect was to render the Canadian economy generally more dependent on foreign trade. However, these figures suggest that close to two-thirds of what Canadians buy annually is still made in Canada today.

Among the most serious misconceptions about the Canadian economy is the myth that this country no longer manufactures anything but, rather, imports everything from, say, low-wage countries such as China. Indeed, about 33 percent of Canada's GDP was imported in 2007. However, out of the total merchandise imports from the rest of the world, less than 10 percent came from China, thereby reflecting about 2.5 percent of GDP. It is true that Chinese goods constitute a growing share of our imports, but the fact still remains that two-thirds of all of our imports of goods and services originate from a relatively high-wage country and our principal trading partner—the United States.

Economists use the terms **open economy** and **closed economy** to indicate how important international trade is to a nation. A common measure of "openness" is the average of exports and imports, expressed as a share of GDP. Table 1, which lists the average of the exports and imports of commodities (excluding services) for nine countries, shows that Canada, together with such disparate countries as Germany and Mexico, could be classified as moderately open economies in 2006, but clearly not as open as the Netherlands, with over 50 percent of its GDP being dependent on foreign trade. On the other hand, the United States, together with countries such as Japan, are relatively closed economies with shares of GDP a bit less than 15 percent level. Despite its growing importance in world trade, China remains a highly closed economy.

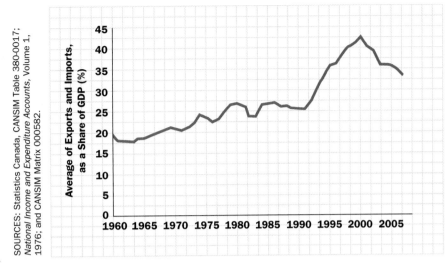

FIGURE 2   Share of Canada's Gross Domestic Product (GDP), Exported and Imported, 1959–2007

SOURCES: Statistics Canada. CANSIM Table 380-0017; *National Income and Expenditure Accounts, Volume 1, 1976*; and CANSIM Matrix 000582.

An economy is called relatively **open** if its exports and imports constitute a large share of its GDP.

An economy is considered relatively **closed** if they constitute a small share.

TABLE 1	
Openness of Various National Economies, 2006	
Country	Openness Ratio (%)
Netherlands	67
Germany	35
Mexico	31
Canada	30
Russian Federation	24
United Kingdom	22
Japan	14
United States	11
China	3

SOURCE: World Trade Organization (WTO), *Statistics Database;* and OECD, *OECD in Figures,* 2007 edition; China Statistical Yearbook 2007, The People's Bank of China. China's GDP was converted from Yuan to U.S. dollars at the exchange rate of December 2006 (1:7.8238).

SOURCE: University of Toronto Archives.

Harold Adams Innis (1894–1952) was a renowned Canadian economist and economic historian best known for his seminal contributions in developing the staples approach to understanding Canadian economic growth. In his numerous writings, he emphasized the role played by staple commodity exports in explaining the various phases of the economic development of Canada. His most celebrated work is The Fur Trade in Canada: An Introduction to Canadian Economic History *published in 1930 and reprinted many times since.*

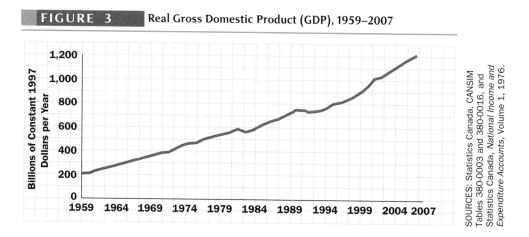

FIGURE 3   Real Gross Domestic Product (GDP), 1959–2007

SOURCES: Statistics Canada, CANSIM Tables 380-0003 and 380-0016, and Statistics Canada, *National Income and Expenditure Accounts*, Volume 1, 1976.

A Growing Economy . . .

The next salient fact about the Canadian economy is its growth—it gets bigger almost every year (see Figure 3). Gross domestic product in 2007 was around $1.5 trillion, which is about $45,000 per Canadian. Once adjusted for inflation, Canada's *real* GDP was about 5.5 times as large in 2007 as it was in 1959. Of course, there were many more people in Canada in 2007 than there were 48 years earlier, but even correcting for population growth, Canada's real GDP *per capita* was about three times higher in 2007 than in 1959. That's still not a bad performance: Living standards have tripled in less than half a century.

But with Bumps along the Growth Path

Although the cumulative growth performance depicted in Figure 3 is impressive, Canada's economic growth has been quite irregular. We have experienced alternating periods of good and bad times, which are called *economic fluctuations* or sometimes just *business cycles*. In some years—two major ones since 1980—GDP actually declined. Such periods of *declining* economic activity are called **recessions.**

A **recession** is a period of time during which the total output of the economy falls.

The bumps along the Canadian economy's historic growth path are barely visible in Figure 3, but they stand out more clearly in Figure 4, which displays the same data in a different way and extends them back further, to before the Great Depression. Instead of plotting the *level* of real GDP each year, Figure 4 plots its *growth rate*—the percentage change from one year to the next. Now the booms and busts that delight or distress people—and even swing elections—stand out clearly. For example, following periods of stunning decline during the Great Depression and then spectacular growth during the World War II era, we had fairly sustained growth from the mid-1950s to the mid-1970s. On the other hand, over the last quarter of a century, Canada went through two severe recessions—in both cases severe enough to have contributed to the defeat of the governments in power. In the early 1980s, Canada went through what some then dubbed as a "great recession"—an economic slump important enough to have helped in the defeat of John Turner's Liberals in 1984 by the Progressive Conservative Party led by Brian Mulroney. In much the same way, after a serious dip in GDP in the early 1990s, Canada's very weak performance at the time possibly contributed to the election of Jean Chrétien's Liberals in 1993.

One important consequence of these ups and downs in economic growth is that unemployment varies considerably from one year to the next (see Figure 5). During the Great Depression of the 1930s, unemployment peaked at about 20 percent of the labour force, but it fell to a mere 1 percent during World War II. Since the 1970s, Canada's unemployment rate showed a significant upward trend. Only during the last decade has the unemployment rate fallen to a low point of 6.0 percent by 2007—its lowest rate in 30 years. In human terms, the sustained high level of unemployment

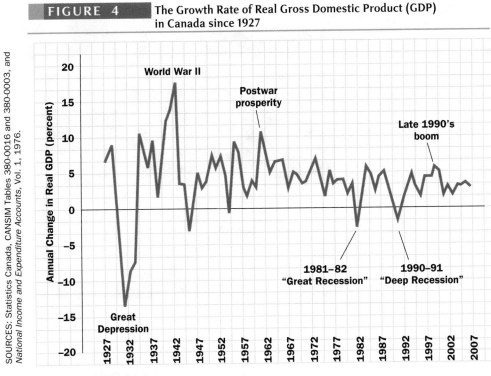

FIGURE 4   **The Growth Rate of Real Gross Domestic Product (GDP) in Canada since 1927**

SOURCES: Statistics Canada, CANSIM Tables 380-0016 and 380-0003, and *National Income and Expenditure Accounts, Vol. 1. 1976.*

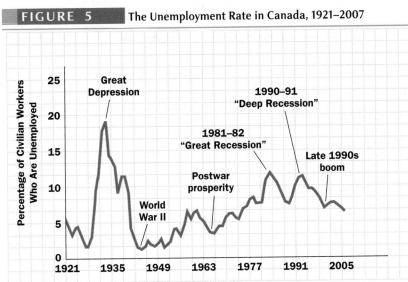

FIGURE 5   The Unemployment Rate in Canada, 1921–2007

SOURCES: Statistics Canada: CANSIM Table 282-0002; *Historical Labour Force Statistics, 1976–1977*; and *Historical Statistics of Canada, 1983*, Series D127, D132, and D143.

Note: Prior to 1976, Statistics Canada's definition of the working-age population included persons 14 years of age and over, rather than the present 15 years of age and over. This threshold age that defines who is included statistically in the potential labour force should not be confused with the legal working age, which varies between 12 and 17 among provinces.

since the 1970s has meant a "lost generation" of jobless workers, especially young ones, many of whom were excluded from standard labour market activity during the 1980s and the 1990s. Understanding why joblessness varies so dramatically and what can we do about it are major reasons for studying economics.

THE INPUTS: LABOUR AND CAPITAL

Let's now return to the analogy of an economy as a machine turning inputs into outputs. The most important input is human labour: the men and women who run the machines, work behind the desks, and serve you in stores.

Unemployment Rates in Europe

For roughly the first quarter-century after World War II, unemployment rates in the industrialized countries of Europe were significantly lower than those in North America. During the late 1970s, the situation reversed itself, as countries that had been used to full employment with unemployment rates in the range of 1–2 percent were often faced with double-digit unemployment rates. It is noteworthy that one important exception was the United Kingdom; unlike France, Germany, Italy, and Sweden, the United Kingdom did not join the euro zone in 1999. Put on a comparable basis by the U.S. Bureau of Labor Statistics, unemployment rates in the nine countries in 2007 were as shown in the accompanying table.

Country	Unemployment Rate
Canada	5.3%
United States	4.6
Australia	4.4
Japan	3.9
France	8.6
Germany	8.7
Italy	6.1
Sweden	6.1
United Kingdom	5.4

SOURCE: © Joel Stettenheim/Corbis

◼ The Canadian Workforce: Who Is in It?

Out of slightly over 33 million Canadians, about 17 million (or about half of the population) held jobs in 2007. Fifty-three percent of these workers were men; 47 percent were women. This ratio represents a drastic change from two generations ago, when most women worked only at home (see Figure 6). Indeed, the massive entrance of women into the paid labour force was one of the major social transformations of Canadian life during the second half of the twentieth century. In 1950, just 22 percent of women worked in the marketplace; now, about 63 percent do.

As Figure 7 shows, the percentage of women in the labour forces of other industrial countries has also been growing. The expanding role of women in the labour

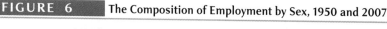

FIGURE 6 The Composition of Employment by Sex, 1950 and 2007

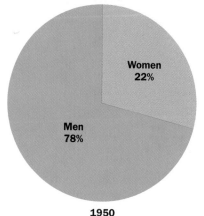

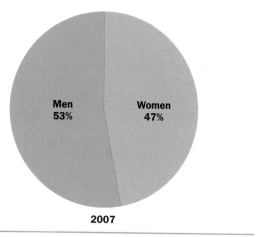

1950   2007

SOURCES: Statistics Canada, CANSIM Table 282-0002 and Statistics Canada publication *Historical Statistics of Canada*, 1983.

market has raised many controversial questions about how government should deal with gender discrimination in the workplace, who should bear the cost of maternity leave, and so on.

In contrast to women, the percentage of teenagers in the workforce has dropped significantly since its peak in the mid-1970s (see Figure 8). Young men and women aged 15 to 19 accounted for 10.9 percent of employment in 1974 but only 5.8 percent in 2006. As the baby boom gave way to the baby bust, people under 20 became scarce resources! Still, close to 900,000 teenagers hold jobs in the Canadian economy today—a number that has been pretty stable in the past few years. Most teenagers fill low-wage jobs at fast-food restaurants, retail outlets, and the like. Relatively few can be found holding full-time positions in the nation's factories and offices.

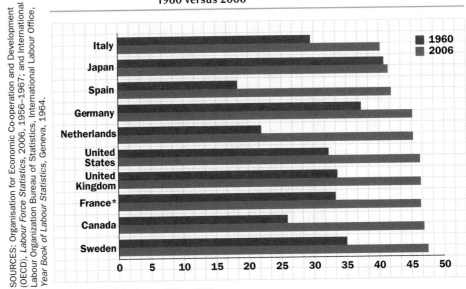

FIGURE 7 Working Women as a Percentage of the Labour Force, 1960 versus 2006*

* Data for France is for the years 1962 and 2006.

SOURCES: Organisation for Economic Co-operation and Development (OECD), *Labour Force Statistics*, 2006, 1956–1967; and International Labour Organization Bureau of Statistics, International Labour Office, *Year Book of Labour Statistics*, Geneva, 1964.

The Canadian Workforce: What Does It Do?

What do these 17 million working Canadians do? The only real answer is: almost anything you can imagine. At the end of 2006, there were 703,900 teachers and

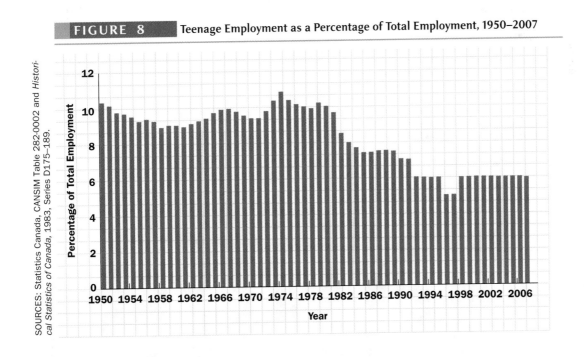

FIGURE 8 Teenage Employment as a Percentage of Total Employment, 1950–2007

SOURCES: Statistics Canada, CANSIM Table 282-0002 and *Historical Statistics of Canada*, 1983, Series D175–189.

professors employed; 480,500 nurses; 467,100 employed in art, culture, recreation, and sports; over a million employed in retail; 540,600 chefs, cooks, and related occupations in food and beverage service; 231,600 in protective services; 195,900 child care and home support workers; 372,800 in the construction trades; 810,000 machine operators and assemblers in manufacturing; and so on.

Figure 9 shows the breakdown by major sector. It holds some surprises for most people, because the majority of Canadian workers—like workers in all developed countries—produce services, not goods. In 2007, about 76 percent of all workers in Canada were employed in the service sector, with the vast majority in private service jobs. The remaining 24 percent were employed in the goods-producing sector, including agriculture. The once popular image of the typical worker as a blue-collar worker, often depicted on prime time television in both Canada and the United States—Homer Simpson, if you will—is really quite misleading.

Federal, provincial/territorial, and local governments employed over 3 million people in 2006 but, contrary to a popular misconception, few of these civil servants worked for the *federal* government. Federal employment (including reservists and full-time military personnel) was only about 393,000 or about 12.5 percent of total public sector employment in Canada, a number that declined significantly during the early and mid-1990s as successive federal governments sought to cut expenditures to combat their ballooning budget deficits. Finally, approximately 350,000 Canadians worked in agriculture and about 2.5 million were self-employed in 2006.

As Figure 10 shows, *all* industrialized countries have become "service economies." This shift toward the service sector can be attributed to at least two fundamental causes. As household real income has risen over time, a growing proportion of household spending has shifted toward consumer services and away especially from the primary sector's output that fulfills some of our most basic needs. Indeed, unlike even a half century ago when, for instance, relatively few ate at restaurants or travelled much, nowadays consumers rely on a vast variety of commercial services, such as

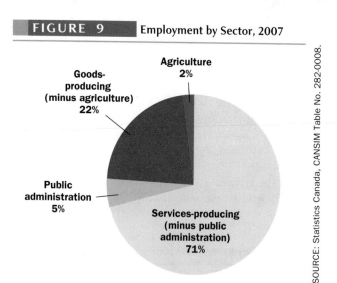

FIGURE 9   Employment by Sector, 2007

SOURCE: Statistics Canada, CANSIM Table No. 282-0008.

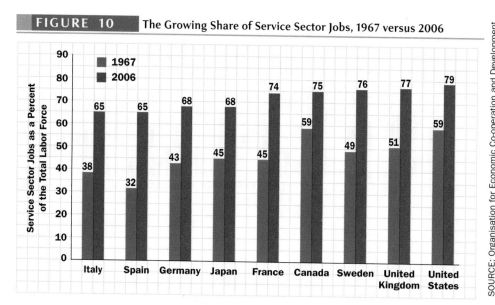

FIGURE 10   The Growing Share of Service Sector Jobs, 1967 versus 2006

SOURCE: Organisation for Economic Co-operation and Development (OECD), *Labour Force Statistics*, 2007, and 1956–1967. www.oecd.org/statistics

mobile phone and Internet services, day care services and the like, that fulfill needs often associated with a society that has attained a much higher level of affluence.

To a considerable degree, this historical shift to services has also been made possible by the growing efficiency of production resulting from the large-scale introduction of labour-saving technology in the goods-producing sector of the economy. With the production of more and more manufacturing products using fewer and fewer workers, it has been possible to free up labour from the primary and secondary sectors to meet this growing demand for services. If you look at the historical series on the sector shares of employment in Table 2, already by the late nineteenth century, these forces were at work in Canada as we moved from an agricultural-based society to a services economy. However, in more recent

TABLE 2			
Percentage Distribution of Employment by Major Sectors, Canada 1881–2006			
Year	Primary	Secondary	Tertiary
1881	51%	29%	20%
1891	50	26	24
1901	44	28	28
1911	40	27	33
1921	37	26	37
1931	33	16	51
1951	23	33	44
1961	14	30	56
1971	9	28	63
1981	7	25	68
1991	5	22	73
2001	5	20	75
2006	4	20	76

Note: The primary sector includes agriculture, fishing, logging, and mining and oil wells; the secondary sector includes manufacturing and construction; and the tertiary or services sector includes transportation, communications and other utilities, trade, finance, insurance and real estate, community, business and personal services, and public administration.

SOURCES: Statistics Canada, CANSIM Table 282-0008; Statistics Canada, *Historical Statistics of Canada*, 1983; Statistics Canada, *Historical Labour Force Statistics;* and various references; and W. L. Marr and D. G. Patterson, *Canada: An Economic History* (Toronto: Macmillan of Canada, 1980), Table 7:3.

decades, it may be argued that this "services revolution" has also occurred with the arrival of the "Information Age." Activities related to computers, to research, to the transmission of information by teaching and publication, and other information-related activities are providing many of the new jobs, notably in the public services. This means that, in the rich industrial countries, workers who moved out of both agriculture and manufacturing jobs into the services sectors have not gone predominantly into low-skill jobs such as dishwashing or housecleaning. Many have found employment in high-skill producers' service jobs in which education and experience provide a great advantage. However, there are also many who have found employment in relatively low-skill and low-wage consumers' service jobs, such as at McDonald's and Tim Hortons.

■ The Canadian Workforce: What It Earns

When taken together, these workers' wages account for over 60 percent of the total income that the production process generates in Canada. That adds up to an average hourly wage of over $20—plus fringe benefits like vacation, worker's disability, dental insurance, pensions and so on, which can contribute to as much as an additional 30 to 40 percent for some workers. With an average workweek of about 35 hours, a typical weekly paycheque in Canada is about $750 before taxes (but excluding the value of benefits). That is hardly a princely sum, and most university graduates can expect to earn substantially more. Indeed, according to the 2001 census of Canada, workers holding a university degree earned 91 percent more (on average) than those holding a high school certificate. Similarly wide differences in earnings according to the degree of schooling are also quite characteristic of the labour market in other industrial countries. It would thus appear that forgoing a few extra years of labour-market earnings would not be such a high price to pay for practically doubling your stream of earnings over your lifetime!

However, average wages throughout Northern Europe tend to exceed Canadian rates. Workers in a number of other industrial countries now receive higher compensation than either Canadian or American workers do—a big change from the situation a few decades ago. As illustrated in Figure 11, after converting into U.S. dollars, workers in Canadian manufacturing industries in 2006 made substantially less than those in Germany, Belgium, the Netherlands, Sweden, France, and the United

SOURCE: U.S. Department of Labor, Bureau of Labor Statistics, *International Comparisons of Hourly Compensation Costs for Production Workers in Manufacturing, 2006,* Table 2. USDL: 06-2020, November 2008. Retrieved from http://www.bls.gov/news.release/pdf/ichcc.pdf

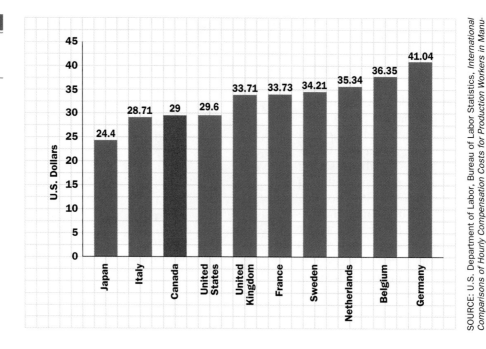

FIGURE 11

Average Hourly Compensation Rates in Manufacturing, 2006

Kingdom, and almost the same hourly compensation as workers in the United States. Canadian compensation levels did, however, exceed those of Japan and Italy. While this has rendered Canadian industry more competitive internationally, in our low inflation environment since the early 1990s, Canadian workers did not keep abreast of wage developments in a number of other industrial countries.

■ Capital and Its Earnings

The rest of national income (after deducting for the sliver of income that goes to the owners of land and natural resources) mainly accrues to the owners of *capital*—the machines and buildings that make up the nation's industrial plant.

The total market value of these business assets—a tough number to estimate—is believed to be in the neighbourhood of $3.5 trillion. With a rate of return to the ownership of capital of, say, about 7 percent before taxes, total capital earnings come to around $250 billion in Canada. Of this, corporate profits constitute approximately two-thirds of total earnings, while the rest is mainly interest income.

Public opinion polls routinely show that people are quite confused about the level of profits in our society. For instance, in polls conducted in the United States, it was found that the man and the woman on the street believe that profits account for about 30 percent of the price of a typical product. While the actual figure varies significantly across industries in Canada, corporate profits before taxes accounted for about 14 percent of the dollar value of total output in 2007. This figure (the share of profits in the value of a typical product) should not

FIGURE 12   Rate of Return on Capital (All-Industries Average), Canada, 1980–2006

SOURCE: Statistics Canada, CANSIM II, Series V219184 and V3871947.

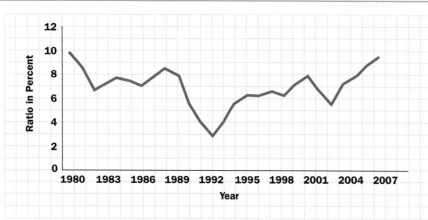

be confused, however, with the *rate* of profit, which is a ratio of the dollar value of profits in a given period to the value of the capital advanced. While we have assumed this rate to be about 7 percent on average, over the last quarter-century, this ratio has gone from as low as 3 percent annually for the all-industries average in some recession years (such as in 1992) to as high as 10 percent as the economy was approaching a business cycle peak in Canada (in 1980) (see Figure 12).

■ THE OUTPUTS: WHAT DOES CANADA PRODUCE?

What does all this labour and capital produce? Consumer spending accounts for about 60 percent of GDP. And what an amazing variety of goods and services it buys. Canadian households spend roughly 60 percent of their budgets on services, with housing commanding the largest share. For instance, in 2005, an average household with children spent $2,070 annually on health care, $2,420 on education, and, among many other services, $1,510 on personal care. The other 30 percent of Canadian budgets was spent on goods—ranging from food purchased from stores at $9,630 to clothing at $3,760 per household in 2005.

This leaves about 40 percent of GDP for all nonconsumption uses. That includes government services (hospital care, schooling for young people, and spending on national defence), business purchases of machinery and industrial structures, and consumer purchases of new houses.

■ THE CENTRAL ROLE OF BUSINESS FIRMS

When we peer inside the economic machine that turns inputs into outputs, we see primarily private companies whose principal objective is pecuniary gain. Astonishingly, we have about 2.5 million active business establishments in Canada—about one for every 13 people!

The owners and managers of these businesses hire people, acquire or rent capital goods, and arrange to produce things consumers want to buy. Sound simple? It isn't. Over 7,000 businesses fail every year. A few succeed spectacularly. Some do both. Indeed, it has been estimated that, on average, only one out of every five firms survives after only ten years of existence in Canada. Fortunately for the Canadian economy, the lure of riches induces thousands of people to start new businesses every year. Indeed, this high turnover of business enterprises in a market economy was long ago described as a process of "creative destruction" by a famous economist, Joseph A. Schumpeter (1883–1950).

A number of our larger firms do business all over the world, especially in the continental context of the North American Free Trade Agreement (NAFTA). However, there are perhaps still many more foreign-based *multinational corporations* doing business in this country. Historically, Canada has been primarily on the receiving end of *foreign direct investment*, with a high number of foreign-owned subsidiaries established here. The role played by multinationals has been a controversial one in Canada. However, some people would claim that, in this era of global markets, it has now become practically impossible to determine the true "nationality" of global corporations—which may have factories in ten or more countries, sell their wares all over the world, and have stockholders in dozens of nations. (See the boxed feature "What's the Nationality of a Global Corporation?" on the next page.) Most profits of large Canadian-based companies like Nortel are generated abroad, for example, and the Honda you drive was probably assembled in Alliston, Ontario.

Firms compete with other companies in their *industry*. Most economists believe that this *competition* is the key to industrial efficiency. A sole supplier of a commodity will find it easy to make money, and may therefore fail to innovate or control costs. Its management is liable to become relaxed and sloppy. But a company besieged by dozens of competitors eager to take its business away must constantly seek ways to innovate, to cut costs, and to build a better mousetrap. The rewards for business success can be magnificent. But the punishment for failure is severe.

What's the Nationality of a Global Corporation?

Have we entered a new era, with the inexorable convergence on a form of business organization that we now call the "global corporation"—an institution that is footloose, borderless, and capable of rendering national economic policies irrelevant? Or do multinational corporations continue to be shaped by the culture, institutions, and policies of their "home" countries? This remains a highly debated question of great concern to policy makers. For instance, Robert E. Reich, who was U.S. Secretary of Labour in the Clinton administration during the 1990s, was extremely concerned and, just before joining the government, argued that it was nearly impossible to define the nationality of a multinational corporation. In his 1991 book *The Work of Nations,* he wrote:

> What's the difference between an "American" corporation that makes or buys abroad much of what it sells around the world and a "foreign" corporation that makes or buys in the United States much of what it sells? . . . The mind struggles to keep the players straight. In 1990, Canada's Northern Telecom was selling to its American customers telecommunications equipment made by Japan's NTT at NTT's factory in North Carolina.

> If you found that one too easy, try this: Beginning in 1991, Japan's Mazda would be producing Ford Probes at Mazda's plant in Flat Rock, Michigan. Some of these cars would be exported to Japan and sold there under Ford's trademark.

> A Mazda-designed compact utility vehicle would be built at a Ford plant in Louisville, Kentucky, and then sold at Mazda dealerships in the United States. Nissan, meanwhile, was designing a new light truck at its San Diego, California, design center. The trucks would be assembled at Ford's Ohio truck plant, using panel parts fabricated by Nissan at its Tennessee factory, and then marketed by both Ford and Nissan in the United States and in Japan. Who is Ford? Nissan? Mazda?

The same can be said nowadays of a notable number of large "Canadian" corporations, such as Nortel and Bombardier, whose foreign activities often rival their operations here in Canada. However, although terms such as "global," "multinational," and "transnational" corporations are used quite loosely in the media, even economists

SOURCE: © AP / Wide World Photos

are not in general agreement about how to define a multinational corporation. Which dimensions of a corporation do we choose? Do we define it on the basis of its geographic structure of ownership, its management, the international distribution of its sales, or the geographical distribution of its production? Partly to shed light on this difficult issue, at about the same time that Robert Reich had raised his question in the early 1990s, the United Nations Conference on Trade and Development (UNCTAD) developed a *Transnationality Index* (TNI) to which the UN refers regularly in its annual *UN Investment Report.* The TNI is calculated as a weighted average of three key indicators of "transnationality" of corporations: the proportion of foreign sales to total sales, the proportion of foreign assets to total assets, and the proportion of foreign employment to total employment. When ranked on the basis of the TNI, some major Canadian-based companies, such as the Thomson Corporation, have tended to be placed very high on the UN list of highly globalized corporations.

SOURCE: Robert B. Reich, *The Work of Nations* (New York: Knopf, 1991), pp. 124, 131.

■ WHAT'S MISSING FROM THE PICTURE? GOVERNMENT

Thus far, we have the following capsule summary of how the Canadian. economy works: About 2.5 million private businesses, energized by the profit motive, employ about 17 million workers and about $3.5 trillion of capital. These firms bring their enormously diverse wares to market, where they try to sell them to over 33 million consumers.

Households and businesses are linked in a tight circle, depicted in Figure 13, a circular flow model that is discussed in greater detail in macroeconomics. For the time being, it will suffice to say that firms use their receipts from sales to pay wages to employees and interest and profits to the people who provide capital. These income flows, in turn, enable consumers to purchase the goods and services that companies produce. This circular flow of money and goods lies at the centre of the analysis of how the national economy works. All these activities are linked by a series of interconnected markets, some of which are highly competitive and others of which are less so.

| FIGURE 13 | The Circular Flow of Goods and Money |

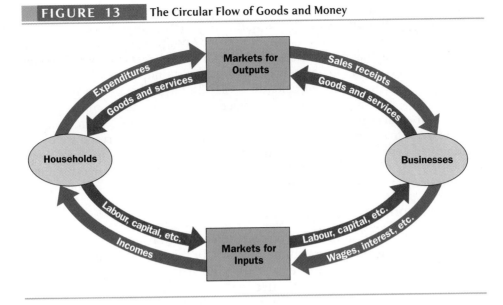

All very well and good. But the story leaves out something important: the role of *government*, which is pervasive even in our decidedly free-market economy. Just what does government do in the Canadian economy—and why?

Although an increasing number of tasks seem to get assigned to the state each year, the traditional role of government in a market economy revolves around five jobs:

- Making and enforcing the laws
- Regulating business
- Providing certain goods and services such as national defence
- Levying taxes to pay for these goods and services
- Redistributing income

Every one of these tasks is steeped in controversy and surrounded by intense political debate. We conclude this chapter with a brief look at each.

The Government as Referee

For the most part, power is diffused in our economy, and people "play by the rules." But, in the scramble for competitive advantage, disputes are bound to arise. Did Company A live up to its contract? Who owns that disputed piece of property? In addition, some unscrupulous businesses are liable to step over the line now and then. We saw some spectacular examples over the last decade with Bre-X, Nortel, and Hollinger, among others, that have rocked the corporate world in Canada and have necessitated government involvement, often as a regulatory referee. Also, we see major industrial strife, which can have significant consequences on the Canadian economy and which usually involves government mediation.

The government enters, therefore, as rule maker, referee, and arbitrator. The federal Parliament and provincial and local governments pass the laws that define the rules of the economic game. The executive branches of all three governmental levels share the responsibility for enforcing them. And the courts interpret the laws and adjudicate disputes.

The Government as Business Regulator

In market economies, governments must interfere with the workings of the marketplace in many ways and for myriad reasons—such as regulating the use of hazardous products and protecting the consumer against misleading advertising in the marketplace. Since market economies are vulnerable to abusive and detrimental market practices, governments have often introduced competition legislation in order to make markets work more efficiently. Given the small size of our domestic market, there is a greater tendency for industrial concentration. Canada's federal *anti-combines legislation* is there to protect competition against encroachment by monopoly, even though some critics would argue that it is not sufficiently strong. In much the same way, some government regulations seek to promote social objectives that unfettered markets do not foster—environmental regulations are a particularly obvious example. In general, it may be said that government regulations in the marketplace represent a response to what could be described generally as a problem of *market failure*. But there are some, especially from the business community, who would probably argue that "government failures" are sometimes a more serious problem than market failures in our economy.

Government Expenditures

The most contentious political issues often involve taxing and spending because those are the government's most prominent roles. In the federal House of Commons as well as in the various provincial legislatures, our major political parties have frequently battled fiercely over their respective budgets. Under the Chrétien and Martin Liberals, the federal government managed a significant turnaround in the state of the public finances, from huge deficits in 1993 to large surpluses at the end of their terms of office. But this turnaround had serious consequences, leading to, among other things, what nowadays are termed *fiscal imbalances* between the federal government and the provinces, which the Harper government sought to redress somewhat in 2007. During 2007, the federal government spent about $230 billion—an amount that is literally beyond comprehension for many of us, unless measured as a proportion of Canada's GDP. The first pie chart in Figure 14 shows where this money went. Over one-third went to social services and programs including *pensions and income security* programs funded by the federal government; 10 percent went largely in the form of *transfers for health care* administered by the provinces; and 11 percent went to *protection*, including national defence. Adding in *interest on the public debt*, these four functions alone accounted for about 70 percent of federal spending. The rest went for miscellaneous other purposes including education, transportation and communication, housing, environment, and foreign aid.

The consolidated government spending at the provincial, territorial and local levels was about $370 billion in 2007. As shown in the second pie chart in Figure 14, health care claimed the largest share of provincial budgets (28 percent), with education a close second (23 percent). Despite this vast outpouring of public funds, many observers

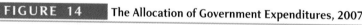

FIGURE 14   The Allocation of Government Expenditures, 2007

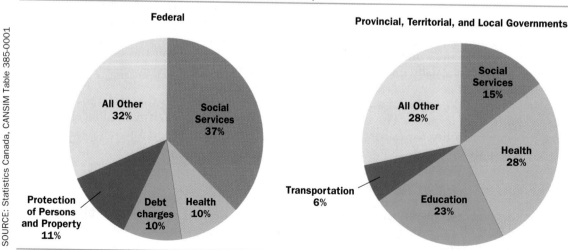

SOURCE: Statistics Canada, CANSIM Table 385-0001

Federal

- All Other 32%
- Social Services 37%
- Protection of Persons and Property 11%
- Debt charges 10%
- Health 10%

Provincial, Territorial, and Local Governments

- Social Services 15%
- All Other 28%
- Health 28%
- Education 23%
- Transportation 6%

believe that serious social needs still remain unmet. Critics argue that our health care system is poorly funded, our educational system is lacking, and our public infrastructures (such as bridges and roads) are inadequate, while there are others who feel that not enough is spent on the military or foreign aid.

Although the scale and scope of government activity in Canada is substantial, it remains on the low end when we compare it to other leading economies. Figure 15 is a bar graph showing government expenditure as a percentage of GDP for ten industrialized countries. We see that the share of government in the Canadian economy is the third-lowest in this group of countries.

Taxes in Canada

The government spends, thereby injecting money into the market system, but it also withdraws money from the economy when it collects taxes. The state of government finances is usually measured by its net spending—the difference between what the government spends and what it receives in tax revenues.

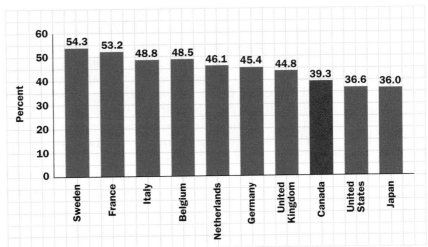

FIGURE 15 Government Spending as a Percentage of GDP in Selected Countries, 2006

SOURCE: OECD, *Annual National Accounts of OECD Countries*, Volume 2, 2008. www.oecd.org/statistics

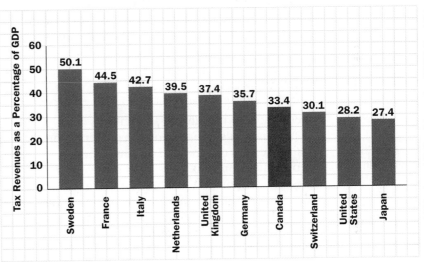

FIGURE 16 The Tax Burden in Selected Countries, 2006

SOURCE: OECD, *Annual National Accounts of OECD Countries*, Volume 2, 2008. www.oecd.org/statistics

When we consider taxes, the first thing that comes to mind is that there seems to be a tax on everything. Income and payroll taxes are withheld from our paycheques, the federal Goods and Services Tax and provincial sales taxes are added to our purchases, property taxes are levied on our homes—and then there are gasoline taxes, liquor and tobacco taxes, and even taxes on our telephone services.

When asked, not surprisingly, most Canadians would like to pay fewer taxes. However, while anti-tax sentiments have frequently been expressed by certain interest groups in Canada and sometimes also by certain politicians, we have not had the same kind of anti-tax movement that gripped the U.S. political scene during the 1980s and 1990s. For one thing, most Canadians tend to accept the fact that taxes are a necessary cost to ensure a greater role for a viable public sector in a mixed economy. Moreover, by international standards, one can hardly say that Canadians are overly taxed. Figure 16 compares the fraction of income paid in taxes in Canada with those paid by residents of other industrial countries. In fact, in terms of tax burden, we are just above the Swiss, who are the perhaps the least taxed in Western Europe. This is not to suggest that Canadians have not shown a growing preference for lower taxes. With rising budget surpluses since the late 1990s, the federal government, together with a number of provincial governments, has implemented policies in recent years to reduce taxes in Canada.

The Government as Redistributor

In a market economy, people earn incomes according to what they have to sell. Unfortunately, many people have nothing to sell but unskilled labour, which commands a paltry price. Others lack even that. Such people fare poorly in unfettered markets. In extreme cases, they are homeless, hungry, and ill. Robin Hood transferred money from the rich to the poor. Some think the government should do the same; others disagree.

If poverty amid riches offends your moral sensibilities—a personal judgment that each of us must make for ourselves—two basic remedial approaches are possible. The socialist idea is to force the distribution of income to be more equal by overriding the decisions of the market. "From each according to his ability, to each according to his needs" was Marx's ideal. In practice, things were not quite so noble under socialism. But there is little doubt that incomes in the old Soviet Union were more equally distributed than those in Canada.

Transfer payments are sums of money that certain individuals receive as outright grants from the government rather than as payments for services rendered.

A tax is **progressive** if the ratio of taxes to income rises as income rises.

For many economists, the idea is to let free markets determine the distribution of *before-tax* incomes, but then to use the tax system and **transfer payments** to reduce inequality—just as Robin Hood did. This is the rationale for, among other things, **progressive taxation** and the antipoverty programs colloquially known as *welfare.* Canadians who support redistribution line up solidly behind this approach. But which ways are the best, and how much is enough? No simple answers have emerged from debate on these highly contentious questions.

CONCLUSION: IT'S A MIXED ECONOMY

Ideology notwithstanding, all nations at all times blend public and private ownership of property in some proportions. All rely on markets for some purposes, but all also assign some role to government. Hence, people speak of the ubiquity of **mixed economies.** But mixing is not homogenization; different countries can and do blend the state and market sectors in different ways. Even today, the Russian economy is a far cry from the Italian economy, which is vastly different from that of Hong Kong.

A **mixed economy** is one with some public influence over the workings of free markets. There may also be some public ownership mixed in with private property.

With the collapse of the Berlin Wall in November of 1989, the formerly socialist economies of Eastern Europe and Russia went through and continue to undergo a painful transition from a system in which markets played a subsidiary role to one in which they have become dominant. These nations have changed the mix—dramatically—from a command economy to a system based on private property and the dominance of the marketplace. A central concern of this book is to help you to understand the essential workings of contemporary market economies and to answer the question: *What does the market do well, and what does it do poorly?* This task begins in the next chapter.

SUMMARY

1. The Canadian economy scores high when measured by international standards and as a member of the G7 industrial nations. Although being an advanced market economy, it is also a **mixed** and **open** economy.

2. The Canadian economy has grown dramatically over the years. But this growth has been interrupted by periodic **recessions,** during which unemployment rises.

3. Canada has a diverse workforce whose composition by age and sex has been changing substantially. Relatively few workers these days work in factories or on farms; most work in service industries.

4. Employees take home most of the nation's income. Most of the rest goes, in the forms of interest and profits, to those who provide the capital.

5. Governments at the federal, provincial/territorial, and local levels employ about 18 percent of the Canadian workforce (including the Armed Forces). Collectively, these governments both spend and take in taxes at the rate of about one-third of GDP. This percentage is higher than in the United States at about 27 percent but lower than most Western European countries, including the United Kingdom.

6. In addition to raising taxes and making expenditures, the government in a market economy serves as referee and enforcer of the rules, regulates business in a variety of ways, and redistributes income through taxes and **transfer payments.** For all these reasons, we say that we have a **mixed economy,** which blends private and public elements.

KEY TERMS

Inputs   26

Outputs   26

Factors of production, or Inputs   26

Gross domestic product (GDP)   28

Open economy   29

Closed economy   29

Recession   31

Transfer payments   42

Progressive tax   42

Mixed economy   42

DISCUSSION QUESTIONS

1. Which are the two biggest national economies on earth? Why are they so much bigger than the others?

2. What is meant by a *factor of production?* Have you ever sold any on a market?

3. Why do you think that per-capita income in Newfoundland is about two-thirds of that in Alberta?

4. Roughly speaking, what fraction of Canadian labour works in factories? In service businesses? In government?

5. Most Canadian businesses are small, but most of the output is produced by large businesses. That sounds paradoxical. How can it be true?

6. What is the role of government in a mixed economy?

A FUNDAMENTAL ECONOMIC PROBLEM: SCARCITY AND CHOICE

Our necessities are few but our wants are endless.

INSCRIPTION ON A FORTUNE COOKIE

Understanding what the market system does well and what it does badly is this book's central task. But to address this complex question, we must first answer a simpler one: What do economists expect the market to accomplish?

The most common answer is that the market mechanism resolves what is often called *the* fundamental economic problem: how best to manage the resources of society, doing as well as possible with them, despite their scarcity. All decisions are constrained by the scarcity of available resources, whether they are physical or financial. Since resources are scarce, all economic decisions involve *trade-offs*. Should you use that $10 bill to buy pizza or a new notebook for Econ class? Should General Motors Canada invest more money in assembly lines or in research? A well-functioning market system facilitates and guides such decisions, assigning each hour of labour and each kilowatt-hour of electricity to the task where, it is hoped, the input will best serve the public.

This chapter shows how economists analyze choices like these. The same basic principles, based on the concept of *opportunity cost*, apply to the decisions made by business firms, governments, and society as a whole. Many of the most basic ideas of economics, such as *efficiency, division of labour, comparative advantage, exchange,* and *the role of markets* appear here for the first time.

CONTENTS

ISSUE: *What to Do about the Federal Budget Balance?*

After the long era of deficit fighting in the 1980s and early 1990s and for over a decade since the late 1990s, Canada's federal governments (whether Liberal or Conservative) have targeted significant budget surpluses, which have regularly been vaunted at budget time as one of their most significant achievements, especially when compared to the performance of governments of other Western countries, such as the United States. Indeed, according to the *Public Accounts of Canada*, in the years between fiscal year 1997–1998 and fiscal year 2006–2007, the federal government achieved accumulated surpluses of about $85 billion.

This has meant that, over those ten years, the federal government reduced the federal public debt by roughly an equivalent amount. Yet, without failure, each year before budget time, federal government officials and politicians have agonized and debated over what to do with each annual forecasted budget *surplus*. Having revealed their strong political preference against budget deficits during the previous era, and given the predicted budget surplus, what should they do? Three choices face the federal fiscal authorities: (1) let the financial surplus materialize, thereby saving these funds and reducing the public debt by an equivalent amount; (2) spend the surplus by allocating the predicted funds to public expenditures, therefore choosing to run a balanced budget; or (3) spend the surplus through a cut in taxes, in which case the federal authorities would also be choosing a balanced budget scenario for the fiscal year. Over the last decade, successive federal governments have chosen a mixture of lower corporate and income taxes, greater spending in certain areas (such as on security), and targeted debt reduction.

On the basis of their spending *priorities*, choices were made by the successive federal ministers of Finance. However, everyone must make choices in an economy, particularly since the physical and financial resources that you face are never unlimited. An *optimal decision* is one that is the most desirable alternative *among the possibilities permitted by the available resources*, which are always scarce in this sense.

■ SCARCITY, CHOICE, AND OPPORTUNITY COST

Resources are the instruments provided by nature or by people that are used to create goods and services. Natural resources include minerals, soil, water, and air. Labour is a scarce resource because of time limitations and because skilled workers are rare. Factories and machines are man-made resources. These resources are often referred to as *land, labour,* and *capital*. They are also called *inputs* or *factors of production*.

One of the basic themes of economics is scarcity: the fact that **resources** are always limited. Ever since mercantilist times in the sixteenth and seventeenth centuries, when humans began generally to recognize that the earth was round and that the precious metal deposits it contained were finite, writers speculated on the limits of financial resources as measured by the limited stock of gold and silver. By the beginning of the nineteenth century, this concern was extended by classical economists to encompass a more important physical resource: good arable land. Nowadays, economists generally accept that this scarcity principle must be extended to all resources in our physical environment.

Indeed, the scarcity of *physical resources* is more fundamental than the scarcity of funds. Fuel supplies, for example, are not limitless, and some environmentalists claim that we should now be making some hard choices—such as keeping our homes cooler in winter and warmer in summer and living closer to our jobs. Although energy may be the most widely discussed scarcity, the general principle applies to all of the earth's resources—iron, copper, uranium, and so on. Even goods produced by human effort are in limited supply because they require fuel, labour, and other scarce resources as inputs. We can manufacture more cars, but the increased use of labour, steel, and fuel in auto production will mean that we must cut back on something else, perhaps the production of refrigerators. This all adds up to the following fundamental principle of economics, which we will encounter again and again in this text:

> Virtually all resources are *scarce*, meaning that humans have less of them than we would like. Therefore, choices must be made among a *limited* set of possibilities, in full recognition of the inescapable fact that a decision to have more of one thing means that we will have less of something else.

In fact, one popular definition of economics is the study of how best to use *limited* means to pursue *unlimited* ends. Although this definition, like any short statement, cannot possibly cover the sweep of the entire discipline, it does convey the flavour of a significant portion of the economist's stock in trade.

To illustrate the true cost of an item given limited resources, consider the decision to produce additional cars, and therefore to produce fewer refrigerators. Although the production of a car may cost $15,000 per vehicle, or some other money amount, *its real cost to society is the refrigerators that society must forgo to get an additional car*. If the labour, steel, and energy needed to manufacture a car are sufficient to make 30 refrigerators, the **opportunity cost** of a car is 30 refrigerators. The principle of opportunity cost is so important that we will spend most of this chapter elaborating on it in various ways.

The **opportunity cost** of any decision is the value of the next best alternative that the decision forces the decision maker to forgo.

▨ Opportunity Cost and Money Cost

Because we live in a market economy where (almost) everything has its price, students often wonder about the connection or difference between an item's *opportunity cost* and its *market price*. What we just said seems to divorce the two concepts: The true opportunity cost of a car is not its market price but the value of the other things (like refrigerators) that could have been made or purchased instead.

But isn't the opportunity cost of a car related to its money cost? The normal answer is yes. The two costs are usually closely tied because of the way in which a market economy sets prices. Steel, for example, is used to manufacture both automobiles and refrigerators. If consumers value items that can be made with steel (such as refrigerators) highly, then economists would say that the *opportunity cost* of making a car is high. But, under these circumstances, strong demand for this highly valued resource will bid up its market price. In this way, a well-functioning price system will assign a high price to steel, which will therefore make the *money cost* of manufacturing a car high as well. In summary:

> If the market functions well, goods that have high opportunity costs will also have high money costs. In turn, goods that have low opportunity costs will also have low money costs.

Yet it would be a mistake to treat opportunity costs and explicit monetary costs as identical. For one thing, the market does not always function well, and hence assigns prices that do not accurately reflect opportunity costs.

Moreover, some valuable items may not bear explicit price tags at all. We encountered one such example in Chapter 1, where we noted that the opportunity cost of a college or university education may differ sharply from its explicit money cost. Why? Because one important item is typically omitted from the money–cost calculation: the *market value of your time*, that is, the wages you could earn by working instead of attending school. Because you give up these potential wages, which can amount to $20,000 per year or more, so as to acquire an education, they must be counted as a major part of the opportunity cost of going to university.

Other common examples where money costs and opportunity costs diverge are goods and services that are given away "free." For example, some early settlers during colonial times destroyed natural amenities such as forests, beaver, and buffalo herds, which had no or very low market price, leaving later generations to pay the opportunity costs in terms of lost resources. Similarly, you incur no explicit monetary cost to acquire an item that is given away for free. But if you must wait in line to get the "free" commodity, you incur an opportunity cost equal to the value of the next best use of your time.

▣ *Optimal* Choice: Not Just *Any* Choice

How do people and firms make decisions? There are many ways, some of them based on hunches with little forethought; some are even based on superstition or the advice of a fortune teller. Often, when the required information is scarce and the necessary research and calculations are costly and difficult, the decision maker will settle on the first possibility that he can "live with"—a choice that promises to yield results that are not too bad, and that seem fairly safe. The decision maker may be willing to choose this course even though he recognizes that there might be other options that are better, but are unknown to him. This way of deciding is called *satisficing*.

In this book, like most books on traditional economic theory, we will assume that decision makers seek to do better than mere satisficing. Although sacrificing a certain degree of realism, we will assume that they seek to reach decisions that are optimal, in other words, decisions that do better in achieving the decision maker's goals than any other possible choice. We will assume that the required information is available to the decision maker and study the procedures that enable her to determine which of the possible choices is optimal to her.

An **optimal decision** is one that best serves the objectives of the decision maker, whatever those objectives may be. It is selected by explicit or implicit comparison with the possible alternative choices. The term *optimal* connotes neither approval nor disapproval of the objective itself.

> An **optimal decision** is one that is selected after implicit or explicit comparison of the consequences of each of the possible choices and that is shown by analysis to be the one that most effectively promotes her goals.

We will study optimal decision making by various parties: by consumers, by producers, and by sellers, in a variety of situations. The methods of analysis for determining what choice is optimal in each case will be remarkably similar. So, if you understand one of them, you will already be well on your way to understanding them all. A technique called *marginal analysis* will be used for this purpose. But one fundamental idea underlies any method used for optimal decision making: To determine whether a possible decision is or is not optimal, its consequences must be compared with those of each of the other possible choices.

▣ SCARCITY AND CHOICE FOR A SINGLE FIRM

The **outputs** of a firm or an economy are the goods and services it produces.

The **inputs** used by a firm or an economy are the labour, raw materials, electricity and other resources it uses to produce its outputs.

The nature of opportunity cost is perhaps clearest in the case of a single business firm that produces two **outputs** from a fixed supply of **inputs**. Given current technology and the limited resources at its disposal, the more of one good the firm produces, the less of the other it will be able to make. Unless managers explicitly weigh the desirability of each product against the other, they are unlikely to make rational production decisions.

Consider the example of Jones, a farmer whose available supplies of land, machinery, labour, and fertilizer are capable of producing the various combinations of soybeans and wheat listed in Table 1. Obviously, devoting more resources to soybean production means that Jones can produce less wheat.

Table 1 indicates, for example, that if Jones grows only soybeans, the harvest will be 40,000 bushels. But if he reduces his soybean production to 30,000 bushels, he can also grow 38,000 bushels of wheat. Thus, *the opportunity cost of obtaining 38,000 bushels of wheat is 10,000 fewer bushels of soybeans.* Put another way, the opportunity cost of 10,000 more bushels of soybeans is 38,000 bushels of wheat. The other numbers in Table 1 have similar interpretations.

TABLE 1		
Production Possibilities Open to a Farmer		
Bushels of Soybeans	Bushels of Wheat	Label in Figure 1
40,000	0	A
30,000	38,000	B
20,000	52,000	C
10,000	60,000	D
0	65,000	E

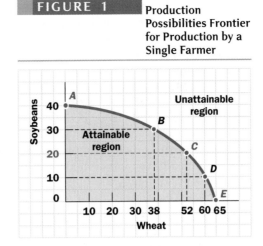

FIGURE 1 Production Possibilities Frontier for Production by a Single Farmer

Note: Quantities are in thousands of bushels per year.

The Production Possibilities Frontier

Figure 1 presents this same information graphically. Point *A* indicates that one of the options available to the farmer is to produce 40,000 bushels of soybeans and zero wheat. Thus, point *A* corresponds to the first line of Table 1, point *B* to the second line, and so on. Curves similar to *AE* appear frequently in this book; they are called **production possibilities frontiers.** Any point *on or inside* the production possibilities frontier is attainable. Points *outside* the frontier cannot be achieved with the available resources and technology.

Because resources are limited, the production possibilities frontier always slopes downward to the right. The farmer can *increase* wheat production (move to the right in Figure 1) only by devoting more land and labour to growing wheat. But this choice simultaneously *reduces* soybean production (the curve must move downward) because less land and labour remain available for growing soybeans.

Notice that, in addition to having a negative slope, our production possibilities frontier *AE* has another characteristic; it is "bowed outward." What does this curvature mean? In short, as larger and larger quantities of resources are transferred from the production of one output to the production of another, the additions to the second product decline.

Suppose farmer Jones initially produces only soybeans, using even land that is comparatively most productive in wheat cultivation (point *A*). Now he decides to switch some land from soybean production into wheat production. Which part of the land will he switch? If Jones is sensible, he will use the part relatively most productive in growing wheat. As he shifts to point *B*, soybean production falls from 40,000 bushels to 30,000 bushels as wheat production rises from zero to 38,000 bushels. A sacrifice of only 10,000 bushels of soybeans "buys" 38,000 bushels of wheat.

Imagine now that this farmer wants to produce still more wheat. Figure 1 tells us that the sacrifice of an additional 10,000 bushels of soybeans (from 30,000 bushels to 20,000 bushels) will yield only 14,000 more bushels of wheat (see point *C*). Why? The main reason is that *inputs tend to be specialized.* As we noted at point *A*, the farmer was using resources for soybean production that were relatively more productive in growing wheat. Consequently, their relative productivity in soybean production was low. When these resources are switched to wheat production, the yield is high.

But this trend cannot continue forever, of course. As more wheat is produced, the farmer must utilize land and machinery with a greater productivity advantage in growing soybeans and a smaller productivity advantage in growing wheat. This is why

A **production possibilities frontier** shows the different combinations of various goods that a producer can turn out, given the available resources and existing technology.

the first 10,000 bushels of soybeans forgone "buys" the farmer 38,000 bushels of wheat, whereas the second 10,000 bushels of soybeans "buys" only 14,000 bushels of wheat. Figure 1 and Table 1 show that these returns continue to decline as wheat production expands: The next 10,000-bushel reduction in soybean production yields only 8,000 bushels of additional wheat, and so on.

As we can see, the *slope* of the production possibilities frontier graphically represents the concept of *opportunity cost*. Between points *C* and *B*, for example, the opportunity cost of acquiring 10,000 additional bushels of soybeans is shown on the graph to be 14,000 bushels of forgone wheat; between points *B* and *A*, the opportunity cost of 10,000 bushels of soybeans is 38,000 bushels of forgone wheat. In general, as we move upward to the left along the production possibilities frontier (toward more soybeans and less wheat), the opportunity cost of soybeans in terms of wheat increases. Looking at the same thing the other way, as we move downward to the right, the opportunity cost of acquiring wheat by giving up soybeans increases—more and more soybeans must be forgone per added bushel of wheat and successive addition to wheat output occur.

■ The Principle of Increasing Costs

The **principle of increasing costs** states that as the production of a good expands, the opportunity cost of producing another unit generally increases.

We have just described a very general phenomenon with applications well beyond farming. The **principle of increasing costs** states that as the production of one good expands, the opportunity cost of producing another unit of this good generally increases.

This principle is not a universal fact—exceptions arise frequently. But it does seem to be a technological regularity that applies to a wide range of economic activities. As our farming example suggests, the principle of increasing costs is based on the fact that resources tend to be at least somewhat specialized. So we lose some of their productivity when those resources are transferred from doing what they are relatively *good* at to what they are relatively *bad* at. In terms of diagrams such as Figure 1, the principle simply asserts that the production possibilities frontier is bowed outward.

Perhaps the best way to understand this idea is to contrast it with a case in which no resources are specialized so costs do not increase as output proportion changes. Figure 2 depicts a production possibilities frontier for producing black shoes and brown shoes. Because the labour and machinery used to produce black shoes are just as good at producing brown shoes, the frontier is a straight line. If the firm cuts back its production of black shoes by 10,000 pairs, it can get 10,000 additional pairs of brown shoes, no matter how big the shift is between these two outputs. It loses no productivity in the switch because resources are not specialized.

More typically, however, as a firm concentrates more of its productive capacity on one commodity, it is forced to employ inputs that are better suited to making another commodity. The firm is forced to vary the proportions in which it uses inputs because of the limited quantities of some of those inputs. This fact also explains the typical curvature of the firm's production possibilities frontier.

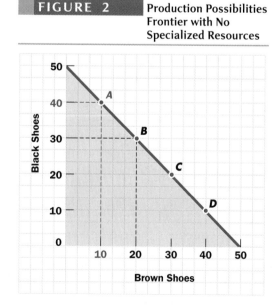

FIGURE 2   Production Possibilities Frontier with No Specialized Resources

Note: Quantities are in thousands of pairs per week.

SCARCITY AND CHOICE FOR THE ENTIRE SOCIETY

Like an individual firm, the entire economy is also constrained by its limited resources and technology. If the public wants more planes and helicopters, it will have to give up some boats and automobiles. If it wants to build more factories and stores, it will have to build fewer homes and sports arenas. In general:

> The position and shape of the production possibilities frontier that constrains society's choices are determined by the economy's physical resources, its skills and technology, its willingness to work, and how much it has devoted in the past to the construction of factories, research, and innovation.

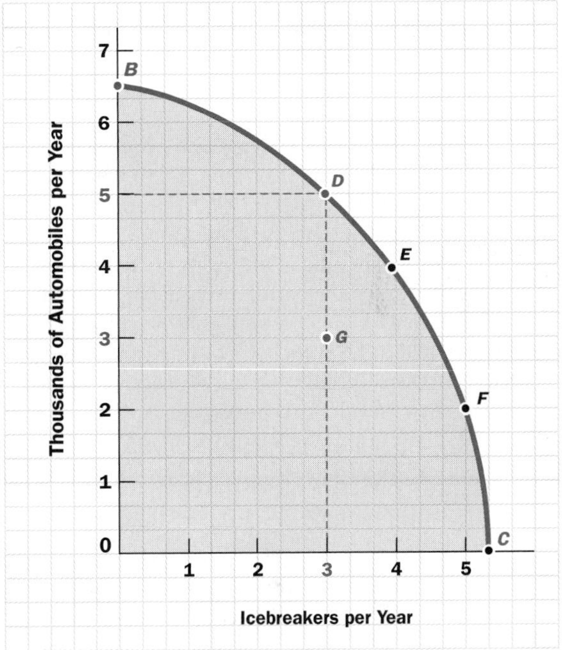

Let us illustrate the nature of society's choice by an example where we must decide between national defence and civilian consumption. There has long been public pressure on successive federal governments to protect our sovereignty in Canada's Arctic. Given the enormous cost of equipping the Canadian Navy with more icebreakers, we would have to forfeit a certain amount of civilian consumption, such as fewer automobiles. Indeed, just like a single firm, the economy as a whole in this example faces a production possibilities frontier for icebreakers and autos, determined by its technology and the available resources of land, labour, capital, and raw materials. This production possibilities frontier may look like curve *BC* in Figure 3. If most workers are employed in auto plants, car production will be large, but the output of icebreakers will be small (as at point *D*). If the economy transfers resources out of auto manufacturing when consumer demand declines, with the budget approval of the House of Commons, the government can alter the output mix toward the production of more icebreakers (the move from *D* to *E*). However, something is likely to be lost in the process because some physical resources may be specialized and not be easily transferable from one industry to another, thereby encountering some increasing costs as this transfer of resources is made. For instance, the rubber tires used in car manufacturing would not be of much use in the production of icebreakers nor would the existing car manufacturing plants. The principle of increasing costs strongly suggests that the production possibilities frontier curves downward toward the horizontal axis and explains its curvature.

FIGURE 3 Production Possibilities Frontier for the Entire Economy

We may even reach a point where the only resources left are not very useful outside of auto manufacturing. In that case, even a large sacrifice of automobiles will get the economy few additional icebreakers. That is the meaning of the steep segment, *FC*, on the frontier. At point *C*, there is little additional output of icebreakers as compared to point *F*, even though at *C* automobile production has been given up entirely.

> The downward slope of society's production possibilities frontier implies that hard choices must be made. Unless resources are not fully utilized, civilian consumption (automobiles) can be increased only by decreasing defence spending, not by rhetoric or wishing. The curvature of the production possibilities frontier implies that, as public spending increases, it becomes progressively more expensive to "buy" additional "defence" (icebreakers) in terms of the resulting sacrifice of civilian consumption.

Scarcity and Choice Elsewhere in the Economy

We have emphasized that limited resources force hard choices on business managers and society as a whole. But the same type of choices arises elsewhere—in households, universities, and other nonprofit organizations, as well as the government.

Hard Choices in the Real World

Commenting on the choices made by consumers over the last decade in Canada, which witnessed a growth in disposable income of high-income groups while that of low-income households stagnated, the 2006 report from Industry Canada's Office of Consumer Affairs clearly shows the link between changing household budgets (scarcity) and choice:

The changes in disposable income . . . have had repercussions on the marketplace. In the area of housing, for example, there is a general trend among high-income earners to acquire large homes with considerable amenities, such as improved storage areas, double garages and two or more bathrooms. . . .

At the other end of the income scale, the situation is markedly different. Approximately 6 percent of Canadian households faced overcrowded housing conditions in 2000, that is, the number of bedrooms in the home was insufficient for the size and make-up of the household.

Food is another area affected by substantial changes in consumers financial situations. . . . Statistics Canada reports that Canadian consumers' spent a higher proportion of their food dollars on meals outside the home (primarily in restaurants) in the 1990s than they did in the 1980s. . . . Not surprisingly, high-income earners led the growth in restaurant spending.

Low-income earners are in a different position: Statistics Canada's 1998–1999 *National Population Health Survey* reported that more than 10 percent of Canadians (an estimated 3 million people) were living in food-insecure households. In addition, the

SOURCE: Ronnie Comeau/iStockPhoto

Institute for Research on Public Policy reports that food banks opened between 1997 and 2002. . . . These developments suggest that, far from boosting restaurant and grocery store business, many low-income Canadians rely on charity for part of their food budget, or sometimes do without, as they are unable to fully participate in the market-based food retail sector.

SOURCE: Industry Canada, Office of Consumer Affairs, *Consumer Trends Report*, May 18, 2006. Retrieved from http://strategis.ic.gc.ca/epic/internet/inoca-bc.nsf/en/ca02093e.html

The nature of opportunity cost is perhaps most obvious for a household that must decide how to divide its income among the goods and services that compete for the family's attention. If a family buys an expensive new car, it may be forced to cut back sharply on some other purchases. This fact does not make it unwise to buy the car. But it does make it unwise to buy the car until the family considers the full implications for its overall budget. If the family members are to utilize their limited resources most effectively, they must recognize the opportunity costs of the car—the things they will forgo as a result—perhaps a vacation and an expensive new TV set.

? ISSUE REVISITED: *Coping with the Budget Balance*

As already noted, even a relatively wealthy country like Canada must cope with the limitations dictated by scarce resources. The necessity for choice imposed on the various levels of government by the limited amount they feel they can afford to spend is, in some ways, similar in character to the problem faced by business firms and households. For the goods and services that it buys from others, a government must prepare a budget similar to that of a very large household. For the items it produces itself (education, police protection, public transport, and so on) it faces a production possibilities frontier much like a business firm does. Even though all levels of government in Canada spent about $550 billion in 2007, some of the most acrimonious debates between the government in power and its critics over the last decade have been about how to allocate the federal budget surplus among competing ends. Even if unstated, the concept of opportunity cost is central to these debates.

THE CONCEPT OF EFFICIENCY

So far, our discussion of scarcity and choice has assumed that either the firm or the economy always operates on its production possibilities frontier rather than *below* it. In other words, we have tacitly assumed that, whatever the firm or economy decides to do, it does so **efficiently**.

> Economists define efficiency as the absence of waste. An efficient economy wastes none of its available resources and produces the maximum amount of output that its technology permits.

To see why any point on the economy's production possibilities frontier in Figure 3 represents an efficient decision, suppose for a moment that society has decided to produce three icebreakers. The production possibilities frontier tells us that if three icebreakers are to be produced, then the maximum number of automobiles that can be made is 5,000 (point *D* in Figure 3). The economy is therefore operating efficiently only if it produces 5,000 automobiles rather than some smaller amount such as 3,000 (as at point *G*).

Point *D* is efficient, but point *G* is not, because the economy is capable of moving from *G* to *D*, thereby producing 2,000 more automobiles without giving up any icebreakers (or anything else). Clearly, failure to take advantage of the option of choosing point *D* rather than point *G* constitutes a wasted opportunity—an inefficiency.

Note that the concept of efficiency does not tell us which point on the production possibilities frontier is *best*. Rather, it tells us only that any point *below* the frontier cannot be best, because any such point represents wasted resources. For example, should society ever find itself at a point such as *G*, the necessity of making hard choices would (temporarily) disappear. It would be possible to increase production of *both* icebreakers *and* automobiles by moving to a point such as *E*.

Why, then, would a society ever find itself at a point below its production possibilities frontier? Why are resources wasted in real life? The most important reason in today's economy is *unemployment*. When many workers are unemployed, the economy must be at a point such as *G*, below the frontier, because by putting the unemployed to work, some in each industry, the economy could produce both more icebreakers *and* more automobiles. The economy would then move from point *G* to the right (more icebreakers) and upward (more automobiles) toward a point such as *E* on the production possibilities frontier. Only when no resources are wasted is the economy operating on the frontier.

Inefficiency occurs in other ways, too. A prime example is assigning inputs to the wrong task—as when wheat is grown on land best suited to soybean cultivation. Another important type of inefficiency occurs when large firms produce goods that smaller enterprises could make better because they can pay closer attention to detail, or when small firms produce outputs best suited to large-scale production. Some other examples are the outright waste that occurs because of favouritism (for example, promotion of an incompetent brother-in-law to a job he cannot do very well) or restrictive labour practices (for example, requiring a railroad to keep a firefighter on a diesel-electric locomotive where there is no longer a fire to tend).

A particularly deplorable form of waste is caused by discrimination in the workplace against women, visible minorities, immigrants, or aboriginal people. When a job is given, for example, to a white male in preference to an immigrant woman who is more qualified, society sacrifices potential output and the entire community is apt to be affected adversely. Every one of these inefficiencies means that the community obtains less output than it could have, given the available inputs.

A set of outputs is said to be produced **efficiently** if, given current technological knowledge, there is no way one can produce larger amounts of any output without using larger input amounts or giving up some quantity of another output.

THE THREE COORDINATION TASKS OF ANY ECONOMY

In deciding how to **allocate its scarce resources**, every society must somehow make three sorts of decisions:

Allocation of resources refers to the society's decisions on how to divide up its scarce input resources among the different outputs produced in the economy and among the different firms or other organizations that produce those outputs.

- First, as we have emphasized, it must figure out *how to utilize its resources efficiently*; that is, it must find a way to reach its production possibilities frontier.
- Second, it must decide *which of the possible combinations of goods to produce*—how many icebreakers, automobiles, and so on; that is, it must select one specific point on the production possibilities frontier.
- Third, it must decide *how much of the total output of each good to distribute to each person*, doing so in a sensible way that does not assign meat to vegetarians and wine to teetotalers.

There are many ways in which societies can and do make each of these decisions—to which economists often refer as *how, what,* and *to whom?* For example, a central planner may tell people how to produce, what to produce, and what to consume, as the authorities used to do, at least to some extent, in the former Soviet Union. But in a market economy, no one group or individual makes all such resource allocation decisions explicitly. Rather, consumer demands and production costs allocate resources *automatically* and *anonymously* through a system of prices and markets. For our introduction to the ways in which markets do all this, let's consider each task in turn.

SPECIALIZATION FOSTERS EFFICIENT RESOURCE ALLOCATION

Production efficiency is one of the economy's three basic tasks, and societies pursue it in many ways. But one source of efficiency is so fundamental that we must single it out for special attention: the tremendous productivity gains that stem from *specialization*.

The Importance of the Division of Labour

Division of labour means breaking up a task into a number of smaller, more *specialized* tasks so that each worker can become more adept at a particular job.

Adam Smith (1723–1790), the founder of modern economics, first marvelled at how **division of labour** raises efficiency and productivity when he visited a pin factory. In a famous passage near the beginning of his monumental book, *The Wealth of Nations* (1776), he described what he saw:

> One man draws out the wire, another straightens it, a third cuts it, a fourth points it, a fifth grinds it at the top for receiving the head. To make the head requires two or three distinct operations; to put it on is a peculiar business, to whiten the pins is another; it is even a trade by itself to put them into the paper.[1]

Smith observed that by dividing the work to be done in this way, each worker became quite skilled in a particular specialty, and the productivity of the group of workers as a whole was greatly enhanced. As Smith related it:

SOURCE: ©Bettmann/Corbis

> I have seen a small manufactory of this kind where ten men only were employed. . . . Those ten persons . . . could make among them upwards of forty-eight thousand pins in a day. . . . But if they had all wrought separately and independently . . . they certainly could not each of them have made twenty, *perhaps not one pin in a day.*[2]

In other words, through the process of the division of labour and specialization, ten workers accomplished what might otherwise have required thousands. This was one of the secrets of the Industrial

---

[1] Adam Smith, *The Wealth of Nations* (New York: Random House, 1937), p. 4.
[2] Ibid., p. 5.

Revolution, which helped lift humanity out of the abject poverty that had been its lot for centuries.

The Principle of Comparative Advantage

But specialization in production fosters efficiency in an even more profound sense. Adam Smith noticed that *how* goods are produced can make a huge difference to productivity. But so can *which* goods are produced. The reason is that people (and businesses, and nations) have different abilities. Some can repair automobiles, whereas others are wizards with numbers. Some are handy with computers, and others can cook. An economy will be most efficient if people specialize in doing what they do best and then trade with one another, so that the accountant gets her car repaired and the computer programmer gets to eat tasty and nutritious meals.

This much is obvious. What is less obvious—and is one of the great ideas of economics—is that two people (or two businesses, or two countries) can generally gain from trade *even if one of them is more efficient than the other in producing everything*. A simple example will help explain why.

Some lawyers can type better than their administrative assistants. Should such a lawyer fire her assistant and do her own typing? Not likely. Even though the lawyer may type better than the assistant, good judgment tells her to concentrate on practising law and leave the typing to a lower-paid assistant. Why? Because the *opportunity cost* of an hour devoted to typing is an hour less time spent with clients, which is a far more lucrative activity.

This example illustrates the principle of **comparative advantage** at work. The lawyer specializes in arguing cases despite her advantage as a typist because she has a *still greater* advantage as an attorney. She suffers some direct loss by leaving the typing to a less efficient employee, but she more than makes up for that loss by the income she earns selling her legal services to clients.

Precisely the same principle applies to nations. The theory of comparative advantage is often used to analyze international trade patterns. A country that is particularly well endowed with a natural resource, because of the availability of a particular quality of land or other natural circumstance, or is simply better adept at producing certain items—such as wheat in Canada, coffee in Brazil, and cameras in Japan—should specialize in those items, producing more than it wants for its own use. The country can then take the money it earns from its exports and purchase from other nations the items that it does not make for itself. And this is still true if one of trading nations is the most efficient producer of almost everything.

The underlying logic is precisely the same as in our lawyer–typist example. Canada might, for example, be better than Mexico at manufacturing cars and textile fabrics. But if Canada is vastly more efficient at producing cars and only slightly more efficient at making fabrics, it pays for Canada to specialize in car manufacture, for Mexico to specialize in fabrics, and for the two countries to trade. This principle, sometimes also called the *law of comparative advantage*, was discovered by David Ricardo (1772–1823), one of the giants in the history of economic analysis, almost 200 years ago.

Even if one country (or one worker) is worse than another country (or another worker) in the production of *every* good, it is said to have a *comparative advantage* in making the good at which it is *least inefficient*—compared to the other country. Ricardo discovered that two countries can gain by trading even if one country is more efficient than another in the production of *every* commodity. Precisely the same logic applies to individual workers or to businesses.

In determining the most efficient patterns of production and trade, it is comparative advantage that matters. Thus, a country can gain by importing a good from abroad even if that good can be produced more efficiently at home. Such imports make sense if they enable the country to specialize in producing those goods at which it is *even more efficient*.

One country is said to have a **comparative advantage** over another in the production of a particular good *relative to other goods* if it produces that good less inefficiently than it **produces** other goods, as compared with the other country.

From an Isolated Island Economy to the International Economy

Let us consider a simple, although somewhat unrealistic, example of two individuals independently shipwrecked on a remote tropical island, named Robinson Crusoe and Friday, somewhat as in Daniel Defoe's classic 1719 English novel. To survive, each individual requires a daily intake of proteins (say, found in fish in the sea) and of vitamins (to be found in fruit growing on the island). Let us assume that Friday, having come originally from a far-off island, is highly skilled at fishing, while Robinson Crusoe does not know how to fish and is therefore less productive at acquiring fish. Let us suppose further that, if Friday dedicates half of his day to gathering fruit and the other half to fishing along the shoreline, at best he can gather two fruit and trap four fish daily. On the other hand, if Robinson Crusoe similarly dedicates half of his day to each of the two activities, he can harvest only two of each. This information is found in the table below, showing that Friday is a bit more productive than Robinson Crusoe with a total daily output of six and four food items, respectively—a daily joint output of ten food items.

Output per Day of Labour before Specialization

	Quantity of Fruit	Quantity of Fish	Daily Output of Food Items
Friday	2	4	6
Robinson Crusoe	2	2	4
Total joint output	4	6	10

The principle of comparative advantage states that, if instead of each going their separate ways and producing both goods in isola-tion for a daily maximum of ten items for the island economy, the two should cooperate by specializing in what they are relatively best at producing, which in the case of Friday is fishing (a more skilled activity) while for Robinson Crusoe it is gathering fruit (a less skilled activity). Indeed, Friday must give up twice as many fish as Robinson Crusoe in order to gather one additional fruit. Clearly, with specialization and the division of labour, both could *potentially* be better off. As shown in the following table, if each would specialize, the total daily number of items of output would rise by 20 percent— from ten to twelve food items daily.

Output per Day of Labour after Specialization

	Quantity of Fruit	Quantity of Fish	Daily Output of Food Items
Friday	0	8	8
Robinson Crusoe	4	0	4
Total joint output	4	8	12

This same principle also forms the basis of the theory of comparative advantage as applied to international trade, whereby our analogy of the tropical island is extended to our planet as a whole. If instead of Robinson Crusoe and Friday, we replace them with, say, Costa Rica, producing bananas, and Canada, producing fish, both countries could potentially enhance their welfare if, owing to different natural endowments, they specialize in what they are comparatively good at producing and then trade with each other.

■ SPECIALIZATION LEADS TO EXCHANGE

The gains from specialization are welcome, but they create a problem: With specialization, people no longer produce only what they want to consume themselves. The workers in Adam Smith's pin factory had no use for the thousands of pins they produced each day; they wanted to trade them for things like food, clothing, and shelter. Similarly, the administrative assistant has no personal use for the legal briefs she types. Thus, specialization requires some mechanism by which workers producing pins can *exchange* their wares with workers producing such things as cloth and potatoes, and office workers can turn their typing skills into things they want to consume.

Without a system of exchange, the enhanced productivity achieved by comparative advantage and the division of labour would do society little good. With it, standards of living have risen enormously. As we observed in Chapter 1, such exchange could benefit *all* participants.

Unless someone is deceived or misunderstands the facts, a *voluntary* exchange between two parties must make both parties better off—or else why would each party agree? Trading increases production by permitting specialization, as we have just seen. But even if no additional goods are produced as a result of the act of trading, the welfare of society is increased because each individual acquires goods that are more suited to his or her needs and tastes.

Although people can and do trade goods for other goods, a system of exchange works better when everyone agrees to use some common item (such as pieces of paper with unique markings printed on them) for buying and selling things. Enter *money*.

Then workers in pin factories, for example, can be paid in money rather than in pins, and they can use this money to purchase cloth and potatoes. Textile workers and farmers can do the same.

These two phenomena—specialization and exchange (assisted by money)—working in tandem led to vast improvements in humanity's well-being. But what forces induce workers to join together so that society can enjoy the fruits of the division of labour? And what forces establish a smoothly functioning system of exchange so that people can first exploit their comparative advantages and then acquire what they want to consume? One alternative is to have a central authority telling people what to do. Adam Smith explained and extolled yet another way of organizing and coordinating economic activity—markets and prices can coordinate those activities.

■ MARKETS, PRICES, AND THE THREE COORDINATION TASKS

Smith noted that people are adept at pursuing their own self-interests, and that a **market system** harnesses this self-interest remarkably well. As he put it—with clear religious overtones—in doing what is best for themselves, people are "led by an invisible hand" to promote the economic well-being of society as a whole.

Those of us who live in a well-functioning advanced market economy like that found in Canada tend to take the achievements of the market for granted, much like the daily rising and setting of the sun. Few bother to think about, say, what makes Costa Rican pineapples show up daily in Ontario supermarkets. Although the process by which the market guides the economy in such an orderly fashion is subtle and complex, the general principles are well known.

The market deals with efficiency in production through the profit motive, which discourages firms from using inputs wastefully. Valuable resources (such as energy) command high prices, giving producers strong incentives to use them efficiently. The market mechanism also guides firms' output decisions, matching quantities produced to consumer preferences. A rise in the price of wheat because of increased demand for bread, for example, will persuade farmers to produce more wheat and devote less of their land to soybeans.

Finally, a price system distributes goods among consumers in accord with their tastes and preferences, using voluntary exchange to determine who gets what. Consumers spend their incomes on the things they like best (among those they can

> A **market system** is a form of economic organization in which resource allocation decisions are left to individual producers and consumers acting in their own best interests without central direction.

afford). But the ability to buy goods is hardly divided equally. Workers with valuable skills and owners of scarce resources can sell what they have at attractive prices. With the incomes they earn, they can purchase generous amounts of goods and services. Those who are less successful in selling what they own receive lower incomes and so can afford to buy less. In extreme cases, they may suffer severe deprivation.

This, in broad terms, is how a market economy solves the three basic problems facing any society: how to produce any given combination of goods efficiently, how to select an appropriate combination of goods to produce, and how to distribute these goods sensibly among people. As we proceed through the following chapters, you will learn much more about these issues. You will see that they constitute the central theme that

SOURCE: ©Robert W. Ginn/PhotoEdit

permeates not only this text, but the work of economists in general. As you progress through this book, keep in mind two questions:

- What does the market do well?
- What does it do poorly?

There are numerous answers to both questions, as you will learn in subsequent chapters.

Society has many important goals. Some of them, such as producing goods and services with maximum efficiency (minimum waste), can be achieved extraordinarily well by letting markets operate more or less freely.

Free unregulated markets will not, however, achieve all of society's goals. For example, they often have trouble keeping unemployment low. In fact, the unfettered operations of markets may even run counter to some goals, such as protection of the environment. Many observers also believe that markets do not necessarily distribute income in accord with ethical or moral norms.

But even in cases in which markets do not perform well, there may be ways of harnessing the power of the market mechanism to remedy some of its deficiencies, as you will learn in later chapters.

LAST WORD: DON'T CONFUSE ENDS WITH MEANS

Economic debates often have political and ideological overtones. However, the central theme of this chapter should be construed as neither a *defence of* nor an *attack on* the capitalist system. Most of the formerly socialist countries of Europe and even countries such as the People's Republic of China and Cuba have recognized that the market mechanism can be a very helpful instrument in the pursuit of economic goals and, to varying degrees, have succeeded in marketizing their economies.

The point is not to confuse ends with means in deciding how much to rely on market forces. Those on the left and the right of the political spectrum surely have different goals. But the means chosen to pursue these goals should, for the most part, be chosen on the basis of how effective the selected means are, not on some ideological prejudgments.

Even Karl Marx emphasized that the market is remarkably efficient at producing an abundance of goods and services that had never been seen in precapitalist history. Such wealth can be used to promote conservative goals, such as reducing tax rates and increasing military spending, or to facilitate goals favoured by the left, such as providing more generous public aid for the poor through increased public spending.

Certainly, the market cannot deal with every economic problem. Indeed, we have just noted that the market is the *source* of a number of significant problems that are not handled well by market techniques. The analysis in this book is intended to help you identify both the objectives that the market mechanism can reliably achieve and those that it will fail to promote or, at least, not promote very effectively.

SUMMARY

1. Supplies of all **resources** are limited. Because resources are **scarce**, an **optimal decision** is one that chooses the best alternative among the options that are possible with the available resources.

2. With limited resources, a decision to obtain more of one item is also a decision to give up some of another. What we give up is called the **opportunity cost** of what we get. The opportunity cost is the true cost of any decision.

3. When markets function effectively, firms are led to use resources efficiently and to produce the things that consumers want most. In such cases, opportunity costs and money costs (prices) correspond closely. When the market performs poorly, or when important, socially costly items are provided without charging an appropriate price, or are given away free, opportunity costs and money costs can diverge.

4. A firm's **production possibilities frontier** shows the combinations of goods it can produce, given the current technology and the resources at its disposal. The frontier is usually bowed outward because resources tend to be specialized.

5. The **principle of increasing costs** states that as the production of one good expands, the opportunity cost of producing another unit of that good generally increases.

6. Like a firm, the economy as a whole has a production possibilities frontier whose position is determined by its technology and by the available resources of land, labour, capital, and raw materials.

7. A firm or an economy that ends up at a point below its production possibilities frontier is using its resources inefficiently or wastefully. This is what happens, for example, when there is unemployment.

8. Economists define **efficiency** as the absence of waste. It is achieved primarily by the gains in productivity brought about through **specialization** that exploits **division of labour** and **comparative advantage** and by a system of exchange.

9. Two countries (or two people) can gain by specializing in the activity in which each has a *comparative* advantage and then trading with one another. These gains from trade remain available even if one country is inferior at producing everything.

10. If an exchange is voluntary, both parties must benefit, even if no additional goods are produced.

11. Every economic system must find a way to answer three basic questions: How can goods be produced most efficiently? How much of each good should be produced? How should goods be distributed among users?

12. The **market system** works very well in solving some of society's basic problems, but it fails to remedy others and may, indeed, create some of its own. Where and how it succeeds and fails constitute the central theme of this book and characterize the work of economists in general.

KEY TERMS

Resources 46	Production possibilities frontier 49	Comparative advantage 55
Opportunity cost 47	Principle of increasing costs 50	Market system 57
Optimal decision 48	Efficiency 53	
Outputs 48	Allocation of resources 53	
Inputs 48	Division of labour 54	

TEST YOURSELF

1. A person rents a house for which she pays the landlord $12,000 per year. The house can be purchased for $100,000, and the tenant has this much money in a bank account that pays 4 percent interest per year. Is buying the house a good deal for the tenant? Where does opportunity cost enter the picture?

2. Graphically show the production possibilities frontier for the nation of Stromboli, using the data given in the following table. Does the principle of increasing cost hold in Stromboli?

Stromboli's 2007 Production Possibilities	
Pizzas per Year	Pizza Ovens per Year
75,000,000	0
60,000,000	6,000
45,000,000	11,000
30,000,000	15,000
15,000,000	18,000
0	20,000

3. Consider two alternatives for Stromboli in 2007. In case (a), its inhabitants eat 60 million pizzas and build 6,000 pizza ovens. In case (b), the population eats 15 million pizzas but builds 18,000 ovens. Which case will lead to a more generous production possibilities frontier for Stromboli in 2008?

4. Jasmine's Snack Shop sells two brands of potato chips. Brand X costs Jasmine 60 cents per bag, and Brand Y costs her $1. Draw Jasmine's production possibilities frontier if she has $60 budgeted to spend on potato chips. Why is it not "bowed out"?

DISCUSSION QUESTIONS

1. Discuss the resource limitations that affect:

    a. the poorest person on earth

    b. Bill Gates, one of the richest people on earth

    c. a farmer in Saskatchewan

    d. the government of Indonesia

2. If you were president of your college or university, what would you change if your budget was cut by 10 percent? By 25 percent? By 50 percent?

3. If you were to leave college or university, what things would change in your life? What, then, is the opportunity cost of your education?

4. Raising chickens requires several types of feed, such as corn and soy meal. Consider a farm in the former Soviet Union. Try to describe how decisions on the number of chickens to be raised, and the amount of each type of feed to use in raising them, were made under the old communist regime. If the farm is now privately owned, how does the market guide the decisions that used to be made by the central planning agency?

5. Canada is a relatively wealthy country. Think of a recent case in which the decisions of the Canadian government were severely constrained by scarcity. Describe the trade-offs that were involved. What were the opportunity costs of the decisions that were actually made?

4

SUPPLY AND DEMAND: AN INITIAL LOOK

The funny thing is that the sophisticated economist sometimes errs by assuming that every transaction marks the intersection of a demand curve and a supply curve, while the economically unsophisticated noneconomist forgets that most observed transactions are at the intersection of a demand curve and a supply curve.

ROBERT M. SOLOW (1924–), 1987 RECIPIENT OF THE SVERIGES RIKSBANK PRIZE IN ECONOMIC SCIENCES IN MEMORY OF ALFRED NOBEL, 1997

In this chapter, we study the economist's most basic investigative tool: the mechanism of supply and demand. Whether your Econ course concentrates on macroeconomics or microeconomics, you will find that the so-called law of supply and demand is a fundamental tool of economic analysis. Economists use supply and demand analysis to study issues as diverse as inflation and unemployment, the effects of taxes on prices, government regulation of business, and environmental protection. Supply and demand curves—graphs that relate price to quantity supplied and quantity demanded, respectively—show how prices and quantities are determined in a competitive market.[1]

A major theme of the chapter is that governments around the world and throughout recorded history have tampered with the price mechanism. As we will see, these bouts with Adam Smith's "invisible hand" have produced undesirable side effects that often surprised and dismayed the authorities. The invisible hand fights back!

CONTENTS

---

[1] This chapter, like much of the rest of this book, uses many graphs like those described in the appendix to Chapter 1. If you have difficulties with these graphs, we suggest that you review that material before proceeding.

PUZZLE: *What Happened to Oil Prices?*

Since 1949, the dollars of purchasing power that a buyer had to pay to buy a barrel of oil has remained remarkably steady, and gasoline has continued to be a bargain. But there were two exceptional time periods—one from about 1975 through 1985, and one beginning in August 2005—when oil prices exploded, and filling up the automobile gas tank became painful to consumers. Clearly, supply and demand changes must have been behind these developments. But what led them to change so much and so suddenly? Later in the chapter, we will provide excerpts from a newspaper story about the a recent oil crisis that describes some dramatic events behind suddenly shifting supply, and will help to bring the analysis of this chapter to life.

SOURCE: Image courtesy of Cdnauto.org

■ THE INVISIBLE HAND

The **invisible hand** is a phrase used by Adam Smith to describe how, by pursuing their own self-interests, people in a market system are "led by an invisible hand" to promote the well-being of the community.

Adam Smith, the father of modern economic analysis, greatly admired the price system. He marvelled at its accomplishments—both as an efficient producer of goods and as a guarantor that consumers' preferences are obeyed. Although many people since Smith's time have shared his enthusiasm for the concept of the **invisible hand,** many have not. In countless instances, the public was outraged by the prices charged on the open market, particularly in the case of housing rents, interest rates, and insurance rates and thought they could do better by legislative decree.

Attempts to control interest rates (which are the price of borrowing money) go back hundreds of years before the birth of Christ, at least to the code of laws compiled under the Babylonian king Hammurabi in about 1800 B.C. Our historical legacy also includes a rather long list of price ceilings on foods and other products imposed in the reign of Diocletian, emperor of the declining Roman Empire. More recently, Canadians have been offered the "protection" of a variety of price controls. Laws have placed ceilings on some prices (such as rents) to protect buyers, whereas legislation has placed floors under other prices (such as farm products) to protect sellers. Yet, somehow, everything such regulation touches seems to end up in even greater disarray than it was before. Despite rent controls, rents in Toronto have soared. Despite laws against "scalping," tickets for popular shows and sports events sell at tremendous premiums—tickets to the Stanley Cup, for example, often fetch hundreds or even thousands of dollars on the "grey" market. To understand what goes wrong when we tamper with markets, we must first learn how they operate unfettered. This chapter takes a first step in that direction by studying the machinery of supply and demand. Then, at the end of the chapter, we return to the issue of price controls.

Every market has both buyers and sellers. We begin our analysis on the consumers' side of the market.

■ DEMAND AND QUANTITY DEMANDED

People commonly think of consumer demands as fixed amounts. For example, when product designers propose a new computer model, management asks: "What is its market potential?" That is, just how many are likely to be sold? Similarly, government bureaus conduct studies to determine how many engineers or doctors the Canadian economy will require (demand) in subsequent years.

Economists respond that such questions are not well posed—that there is no single answer to such a question. Rather, they say, the "market potential" for computers or the number of engineers that will be "required" depends on a great number of influences, including the price charged for each.

The **quantity demanded** of any product normally depends on its price. Quantity demanded also depends on a number of other determinants, including population size, consumer incomes, tastes, and the prices of other products.

> The **quantity demanded** is the number of units of a good that consumers are willing and can afford to buy over a specified period of time.

Because prices play a central role in a market economy, we begin our study of demand by focusing on how quantity demanded depends on price. A little later, we will bring the other determinants of quantity demanded back into the picture. For now, we will consider all influences other than price to be fixed. This assumption, often expressed as "other things being equal," is used in much of economic analysis. As an example of the relationship between price and demand, let's think about the quantity of milk demanded. If the price of milk is very high, its "market potential" may be very small. People will find ways to get along with less milk, perhaps by switching to fruit juice or soda. If the price of milk declines, people will tend to drink more milk. They may give their children larger portions or switch away from juices and sodas. Thus:

> A **demand schedule** is a table showing how the quantity demanded of some product during a specified period of time changes as the price of that product changes, holding constant all other determinants of quantity demanded.

There is no one demand figure for milk, or for computers, or for engineers. Rather, there is a different quantity demanded at each possible price, all other influences being held constant.

■ The Demand Schedule

Table 1 shows how such information for milk can be recorded in a **demand schedule.** It indicates how much milk consumers in a particular area are willing and able to buy at different possible prices during a specified period of time, other things held equal. Specifically, the table shows the quantity of milk that will be demanded in a year at each possible price ranging from $1.50 to $0.90 per litre. At a relatively low price, such as $1 per litre, customers wish to purchase 7 billion litres per year. But if the price was to rise to, say, $1.40 per litre, quantity demanded would fall to 5 billion litres.

Common sense tells us why this happens. First, as prices rise, some customers will reduce the quantity of milk they consume. Second, higher prices will induce some customers to drop out of the market entirely—for example, by switching to soda or juice. On both counts, quantity demanded will decline as the price rises.

TABLE 1		
Demand Schedule for Milk		
Price per Litre	Quantity Demanded	Label in Figure 1
$1.50	4.5	A
1.40	**5.0**	**B**
1.30	5.5	C
1.20	6.0	E
1.10	6.5	F
1.00	**7.0**	**G**
0.90	7.5	H

Note: Quantity is in billions of litres per year.

As the price of an item rises, the quantity demanded normally falls. As the price falls, the quantity demanded normally rises, all other things held constant.

■ The Demand Curve

The information contained in Table 1 can be summarized in a graph like Figure 1, which is called a **demand curve.** Each point in the graph corresponds to a line in the table. This curve shows the relationship between price and quantity demanded. For example, it tells us that to sell 7 billion litres per year, the price must be $1.00. This relationship is shown at point *G* in Figure 1. If the price was $1.40, however, consumers would demand only 5 billion litres (point *B*). Because the quantity demanded declines as the price increases, the demand curve has a negative slope.[2]

> A **demand curve** is a graphical depiction of a demand schedule. It shows how the quantity demanded of some product will change as the price of that product changes during a specified period of time, holding constant all other determinants of quantity demanded.

[2] If you need to review the concept of slope, refer back to the appendix to Chapter 1.

FIGURE 1   Demand Curve for Milk

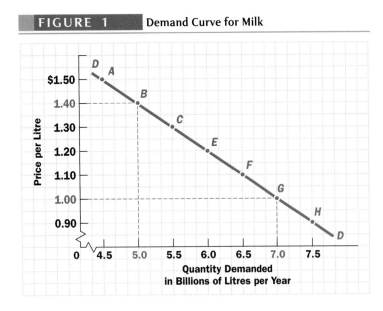

Quantity Demanded
in Billions of Litres per Year

Notice the last phrase in the definitions of the demand schedule and the demand curve: "holding constant all other determinants of quantity demanded constant." What are some of these "other things," and how do they affect the demand curve?

Shifts of the Demand Curve

The quantity of milk demanded is subject to a variety of influences other than the price of milk. Changes in population size and characteristics, consumer incomes and tastes, and the prices of alternative beverages such as soda and orange juice presumably change the quantity of milk demanded, even if the price of milk does not change.

Because the demand curve for milk depicts only the relationship between the quantity of milk demanded and the price of milk, holding constant all other factors, a change in milk price moves the market for milk from one point on the demand curve to another point on the same curve. However, a change in any of these other influences on demand causes a **shift of the entire demand curve.** More generally:

> A change in the price of a good produces a movement *along* a fixed demand curve. By contrast, a change in any other variable that influences quantity demanded produces a shift of the *entire* demand curve.

A **shift in a demand curve** occurs when any relevant variable other than price changes. If consumers want to buy *more* at any and all given prices than they wanted previously, the demand curve shifts to the right (or outward). If they desire *less* at any given price, the demand curve shifts to the left (or inward).

If consumers want to buy more milk at every given price than they wanted previously, the demand curve shifts to the right (or outward). If they desire less at every given price, the demand curve shifts to the left (or inward toward the origin).

Figure 2 shows this distinction graphically. If the price of milk falls from $1.30 to $1.10 per litre, and quantity demanded rises accordingly, we move along demand curve D_0D_0 from point C to point F, as shown by the red arrow. If, on the other hand, consumers suddenly decide that they like milk better than they did formerly, or if more children are born who need more milk, the entire demand curve shifts outward from D_0D_0 to D_1D_1, as indicated by the blue arrows, meaning that at *any* given price consumers are now willing to buy more milk than before. To make this general idea more concrete, and to show some of its many applications, let us consider some specific examples of those "other things" that can shift demand curves.

Consumer Incomes   If average incomes rise, consumers will purchase more of most goods, including milk, even if the prices of those goods remain the same. That is, increases in income normally shift demand curves outward to the right, as depicted in Figure 3(a), where the demand curve shifts outward from D_0D_0 to D_1D_1, establishing a new price and output quantity.

Population   Population growth affects quantity demanded in more or less the same way as increases in average incomes. For instance, a larger population

FIGURE 2

Movements along versus Shifts of a Demand Curve

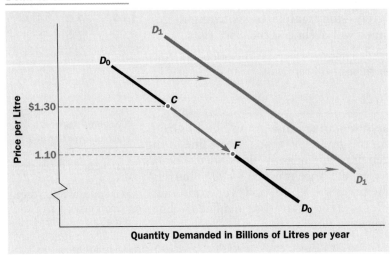

Quantity Demanded in Billions of Litres per year

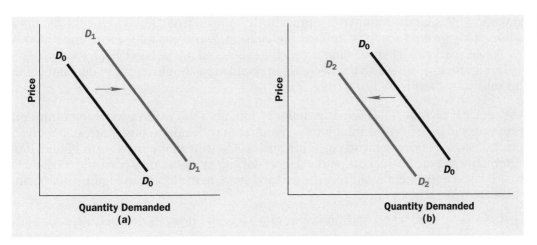

FIGURE 3

Shifts of the Demand Curve

will presumably want to consume more milk, even if the price of milk and average incomes do not change, thus shifting the entire demand curve to the right, as in Figure 3(a). Increases in particular population segments can also elicit shifts in demand—for example, Canada experienced a miniature population boom between the late 1970s

The Ups and Downs of Milk Consumption

The accompanying graph shows the evolution of per-capita milk consumption in Canada between 1986 and 2006. What is striking in the appearance of this graph is that the consumption of the various grades of milk does not change in sync. In fact, quite the contrary can be observed. While the per-capita consumption of whole milk (3.25%) and 2% milk has been cut approximately in half over the last 20 years, the consumption of 1% milk and skim milk has soared. This obviously is related to growing concerns among Canadians about the dangers of cholesterol, saturated fat, and calorie intake (and not much to changes in relative prices). But these concerns have not stopped the annual consumption of cream from rising by more than 60 percent over the last 20 years, from 5.0 to 8.6 litres per Canadian—thus creating doubt about this explanation. The overall per-capita consumption of fluid milk, including chocolate milk, decreased from 100 litres per year in 1986 to 83 litres per year in 2006—a 17 percent reduction. This decrease may be attributed to an aging and changing population, whose diet does not necessarily include dairy products, but also to competition from highly publicized beverages such as sodas and bottled water. In addition, although not shown in the graph, figures indicate that the consumption of ice cream has diminished over the last 20 years, being replaced by more yogurt consumption.

Canadians Consuming More Low-Fat Milk—*and* Cream (annual per-capita consumption in litres, 1986–2006)

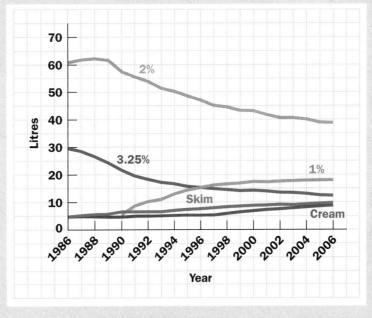

SOURCE: Data is based on Statistics Canada CANSIM database http://cansim2.statcan.ca, Tables 003-0012 and 051-000. (Calculations done by AAFC-AID, Dairy Section)

and mid-1990s, as the number of annual births jumped from 350,000 to 400,000 for a while. This group (which is dubbed Generation Y and includes most users of this book) has sparked higher demand for such items as cell phones and video games.

In Figure 3(b), we see that a decrease in population should shift the demand curve for milk to the left from D_0D_0 to D_2D_2.

Consumer Preferences   If the dairy industry mounts a successful advertising campaign extolling the benefits of drinking milk, families may decide to buy more at any given price. If so, the entire demand curve for milk would shift to the right, as in Figure 3(a). Alternatively, a medical report on the dangers of kidney stones may persuade consumers to drink less milk, thereby shifting the demand curve to the left, as in Figure 3(b). Again, these are general phenomena:

> If consumer preferences shift in favour of a particular item, its demand curve will shift outward to the right, as in Figure 3(a).

An example is the ever-shifting "rage" in children's toys—especially video game consoles such as PlayStation 3, Xbox 360, and PSP. These items become the object of desperate hunts as parents snap them up for their offspring, and stores are unable to keep up with the demand.

Prices and Availability of Related Goods   Because soda, orange juice, and coffee are popular drinks that compete with milk, a change in the price of any of these other beverages can be expected to shift the demand curve for milk. If any of these alternative drinks becomes cheaper, some consumers will switch away from milk. Thus, the demand curve for milk will shift to the left, as in Figure 3(b). Other price changes may shift the demand curve for milk in the opposite direction. For example, suppose that cookies, which are often consumed with milk, become less expensive. This may

Volatility in Gasoline Prices

The accompanying graph shows the volatility of gasoline prices in the Ottawa–Gatineau area. The upper curve shows the highest price observed during one day of each month from September 2005 to June 2007, the lower curve indicates the lowest price observed during the same day, and the middle line is an average of the two measures. The volatility from one day of one month to one day of another, as can be seen from all three curves, is remarkable, as is the volatility of gas prices between one retailer and another, as shown by the distance between the upper and the lower lines. Sometimes all gas stations offered nearly the same price, but on other days there was a large discrepancy. Gas prices also seemed to peak in the spring and summer, when presumably there is an increase in gas demand due to increased vehicular travel.

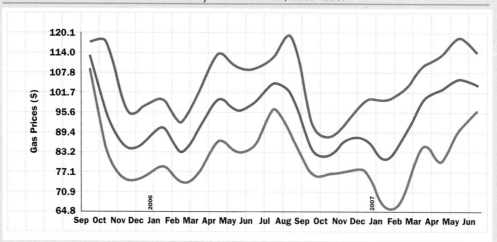

Ottawa–Gatineau Gas Prices on One Day in Each Month, 2005–2007

SOURCE: GasPricesInOttawa.com © 2007, Gas Prices in Ottawa. Retrieved from http://www.gaspricesinottawa.com/GasPriceStatistics.aspx

TABLE 2

The Demand for Milk in a Nutshell

There is a movement *along* the demand curve, and hence the quantity of milk demanded . . .	
. . . increases if . . .	. . . decreases if . . .
The price of milk falls	The price of milk rises

The *entire* demand curve for milk *shifts* . . .	
. . . up if	. . . down if
Consumers' incomes rise (in general).	Consumers' incomes fall (in general).
Population rises.	Population falls.
A milk advertising campaign is successful (preferences change favourably).	Medical reports emphasize health dangers related to milk (preferences change unfavourably).
The prices of alternative drinks rise.	The prices of alternative drinks fall.
The prices of goods normally consumed with milk decrease.	The prices of goods normally consumed with milk increase.

induce some consumers to drink more milk and thus shift the demand curve for milk to the right, as in Figure 3(a). In general:

> Increases in the prices of goods that are substitutes for the good in question (as soda is for milk) move the demand curve to the right. Increases in the prices of goods that are normally used together with the good in question (called *complements*, such as cookies and milk) shift the demand curve to the left.

This is just what happened when a frost wiped out almost half of Brazil's coffee bean harvest in 1995. The largest coffee producers raised their prices by 45 percent, and, as a result, the demand curve for alternative beverages such as tea shifted to the right. Then in 1998, coffee prices dropped about 34 percent, which in turn caused the demand curve for tea to shift toward the left (or toward the origin).

Although the preceding list does not exhaust the possible influences on quantity demanded, we have said enough to suggest the principles followed by demand and shifts of demand. These are summarized in Table 2, where, once again, the fundamental distinction between, on the one hand, a movement along the demand curve (and hence a change in the quantity demanded) and on the other hand, a move of the entire demand curve, is very noticeable. Let's turn now to the supply side of the market.

■ SUPPLY AND QUANTITY SUPPLIED

Like quantity demanded, the quantity of milk that is supplied by business firms such as dairy farms is not a fixed number; it also depends on many things. Obviously, we expect more milk to be supplied if there are more dairy farms or more cows per farm. Cows may give less milk if bad weather deprives them of their feed. As before, however, let's turn our attention first to the relationship between the price and quantity of milk supplied.

Economists generally suppose that a higher price calls forth a greater **quantity supplied.** Why? Remember our analysis of the principle of increasing cost in Chapter 3 (page 50). According to that principle, as more of any farmer's (or the nation's) resources are devoted to milk production, the opportunity cost of obtaining another litre of milk increases. Farmers will therefore find it profitable to increase milk production only if they can sell the milk at a higher price—high enough to cover the additional costs incurred to expand production.

The **quantity supplied** is the number of units that sellers want to sell over a specified period of time.

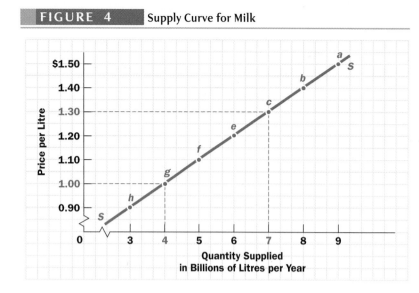

FIGURE 4   Supply Curve for Milk

TABLE 3

Supply Schedule for Milk

Price per Litre	Quantity Supplied	Label in Figure 4
$1.50	9	a
1.40	8	b
1.30	7	c
1.20	6	e
1.10	5	f
1.00	4	g
0.90	3	h

Note: Quantity is in billions of litres per year.

In other words, it normally will take higher prices to persuade farmers to raise milk production. This idea is quite general and applies to the supply of most goods and services.[3] As long as suppliers want to make profits and the principle of increasing costs holds:

> As the price of any commodity rises, the quantity supplied normally rises. As the price falls, the quantity supplied normally falls.

▣ The Supply Schedule and the Supply Curve

Table 3 shows the relationship between the price of milk and its quantity supplied (if the market for milk was a free competitive market, which it isn't in Canada, as we will see later on in this chapter). Tables such as this one are called **supply schedules;** they show how much sellers are willing to provide during a specified period at alternative possible prices. This particular supply schedule tells us that a low price like $1.00 per litre will induce suppliers to provide only 4 billion litres, whereas a higher price like $1.30 will induce them to provide much more—7 billion litres.

As you might have guessed, when such information is plotted on a graph, it is called a **supply curve.** Figure 4 is the supply curve corresponding to the supply schedule in Table 3, showing the relationship between the price of milk and the quantity supplied. It slopes upward—it has a positive slope—because quantity supplied is higher when price is higher. Notice again the same phrase in the definition: "holding constant all other determinants of quantity supplied." What are these "other determinants"?

A **supply schedule** is a table showing how the quantity supplied of some product changes as the price of that product changes during a specified period of time, holding constant all other determinants of quantity supplied.

A **supply curve** is a graphical depiction of a supply schedule. It shows how the quantity supplied of some product will change as the price of that product changes during a specified period of time, holding constant all other determinants of quantity supplied.

▣ Shifts of the Supply Curve

Like quantity demanded, the quantity supplied in a market typically responds to many influences other than price. The weather, the cost of feed, the number and size of dairy farms, and a variety of other factors all influence how much milk will be brought to market. Because the supply curve depicts only the relationship between the price of milk and the quantity of milk supplied, holding constant all other influences, a change in any of these other determinants of quantity supplied will cause the entire supply curve to shift. That is:

> A change in the price of the good causes a movement *along* a fixed supply curve. Price is not the only influence on quantity supplied, however. If any of these other influences change, the *entire* supply curve shifts.

---

[3] This analysis is carried out in much greater detail in later chapters.

Figure 5 depicts this distinction graphically. A rise in price from $1.10 to $1.30 will raise quantity supplied by moving along supply curve S_0S_0 from point f to point c. Any rise in quantity supplied attributable to an influence other than price, however, will shift the *entire* supply curve outward to the right from S_0S_0 to S_1S_1, as shown by the blue arrows. Let us consider what some of these other influences are and how they shift the supply curve.

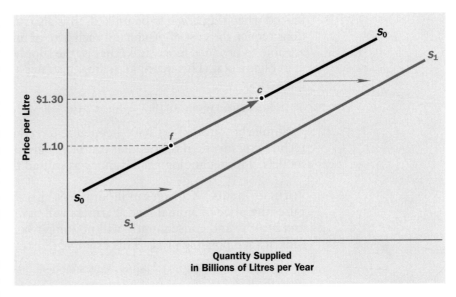

FIGURE 5

Movements along versus Shifts of a Supply Curve

Size of the Industry   We begin with the most obvious influence. If more farmers enter the milk industry, the quantity supplied at any given price will increase. For example, if each farm provides 600,000 litres of milk per year at a price of $1.10 per litre, then 10,000 farmers would provide 6 billion litres, but 13,000 farmers would provide 7.8 billion. Thus, when more farms are in the industry, the quantity of milk supplied will be greater at any given price—and hence the supply curve will move farther to the right.

Figure 6(a) illustrates the effect of an expansion of the industry from 10,000 farms to 13,000 farms—a rightward shift of the supply curve from S_0S_0 to S_1S_1. Figure 6(b) illustrates the opposite case: a contraction of the industry from 10,000 farms to 6,250 farms. The supply curve shifts inward to the left from S_0S_0 to S_2S_2. Even if no farmers enter or leave the industry, results like those depicted in Figure 6 can be produced by expansion or contraction of the *existing* farms.

Technological Progress   Agriculture, just like most industries, benefits from innovation and technological progress. As funny as it may sound, cows are now much more productive than they used to be. Farmers have discovered all sorts of ways to improve their milk production. For instance, some farmers have found that classical music helps cows to relax while being milked, thus increasing their milk production. Other farmers are using automatic milking machines with electronic devices that allow cows to be

FIGURE   6   Shifts of the Supply Curve

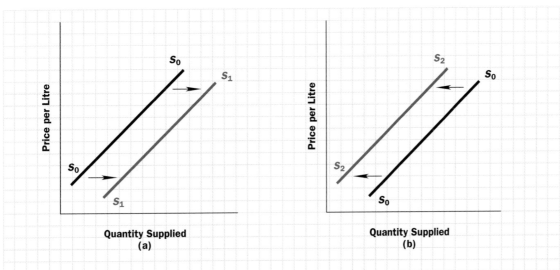

milked when they *want* to be milked, thus also raising milk production. These innovations reduce the cost of producing each litre of milk. Thus, for any given price, farmers are able to produce more milk; that is, the supply curve will shift outward to the right, as in Figure 6(a). This example, again, illustrates a general influence that applies to most industries:

> Technological progress that reduces costs will shift the supply curve outward to the right.

Similarly, automakers have been able to reduce production costs since industrial technology invented robots that can be programmed to work on several different car models. This technological advance has shifted the supply curve outward.

Prices of Inputs   Changes in input prices also shift supply curves. Suppose a drought raises the price of animal feed. Farmers will have to pay more to keep their cows alive and healthy and consequently will no longer be able to provide the same quantity of milk at each possible price. This example illustrates that:

> Increases in the prices of inputs that suppliers must buy will shift the supply curve inward to the left.

Prices of Related Outputs   Dairy farms sell products other than milk. If cheese prices rise sharply, farmers may decide to use some raw milk to make cheese, thereby reducing the quantity of milk supplied. On a supply–demand diagram, the supply curve would then shift inward, as in Figure 6(b).

Similar phenomena occur in other industries, and sometimes the effect goes the other way. For example, suppose that the price of beef goes up, which increases the quantity of meat supplied. That, in turn, will raise the number of cowhides supplied even if the price of leather does not change. Cowhides and meat are *joint* products. Thus, a rise in the price of beef will lead to a rightward shift in the supply curve of leather. In general:

> A change in the price of one good produced by a multiproduct industry may be expected to shift the supply curves of other goods produced by that industry.

The factors that cause a movement along the supply curve on the one hand (and hence in the quantity supplied) and that cause a move of the entire supply curve on the other hand, are summarized in Table 4.

TABLE 4	
The Supply of Milk in a Nutshell	
There is a movement *along* the supply curve, and hence . . .	
. . . the quantity of milk *supplied* . . .	
. . . increases if . . .	. . . decreases if . . .
The price of milk rises.	The price of milk falls.
The *entire* supply curve for milk *shifts* . . .	
. . . to the right (there is an increase in supply) if . . .	. . . to the left (there is a decrease in supply) if . . .
The number of milk producers rise.	The number of milk producers fall.
Technical progress occurs.	Technical regress occurs.
The prices of inputs fall.	The prices of inputs rise.
The price of cheese (alternative product outlets) falls.	The price of cheese (alternative product outlets) rises.

SUPPLY AND DEMAND EQUILIBRIUM

To analyze how an unfettered market determines price, we must compare the desires of consumers (demand) with the desires of producers (supply) to see whether the two plans are consistent. Table 5 and Figure 7 help us do this.

Table 5 brings together the demand schedule from Table 1 and the supply schedule from Table 3. Similarly, Figure 7 puts the demand curve from Figure 1 and the supply curve from Figure 4 on a single graph. Such graphs are called **supply–demand diagrams,** and you will encounter many of them in this book. Notice that, for reasons already discussed, the demand curve has a negative slope and the supply curve has a positive slope. That is generally true of supply–demand diagrams.

In a competitive market, price and quantity are determined by the intersection of the supply and demand curves. At only one point in Figure 7, point E, do the supply curve and the demand curve intersect. At the price corresponding to point E, which is $1.20 per litre, the quantity supplied and the quantity demanded are both 6 billion litres per year. This means that at a price of $1.20 per litre, consumers are willing to buy exactly what producers are willing to sell.

At a lower price, such as $1.00 per litre, only 4 billion litres of milk will be supplied (point g) whereas 7 billion litres will be demanded (point G). Thus, quantity demanded will exceed quantity supplied. There will be a **shortage** equal to 7 minus 4, or 3 billion litres. Price will thus be driven up by unsatisfied demand. Alternatively, at a higher price, such as $1.50 per litre, quantity supplied will be 9 billion litres (point a) and quantity demanded will be only 4.5 billion (point A). Quantity supplied will exceed quantity demanded—creating a **surplus** equal to 9 minus 4.5, or 4.5 billion litres.

Because $1.20 is the price at which quantity supplied and quantity demanded are equal, we say that $1.20 per litre is the equilibrium price (or the "market clearing" price) in this market. Similarly, 6 billion litres per year is the equilibrium quantity of milk. The term **equilibrium** merits a little explanation, because it arises so frequently in economic analysis.

An equilibrium is a situation in which there are no inherent forces that produce change. Think, for example, of a pendulum resting at its centre point. If no outside force (such as a person's hand) pushes it, the pendulum will remain exactly where it is; it is therefore in equilibrium.

If you give the pendulum a shove, however, its equilibrium will be disturbed and it will start to move. When it reaches the top of its arc, the pendulum will, for an

A **supply–demand diagram** graphs the supply and demand curves together. It also determines the equilibrium price and quantity.

A **shortage** is an excess of quantity demanded over quantity supplied. When there is a shortage, buyers cannot purchase the quantities they desire at the current price.

A **surplus** is an excess of quantity supplied over quantity demanded. When there is a surplus, sellers cannot sell the quantities they desire to supply at the current price.

An **equilibrium** is a situation in which there are no inherent forces that produce change. Changes away from an equilibrium position will occur only as a result of "outside events" that disturb the status quo.

FIGURE 7 Supply–Demand Equilibrium

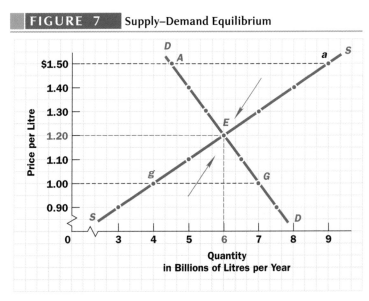

Quantity
in Billions of Litres per Year

TABLE 5				
Determination of the Equilibrium Price and Quantity of Milk				
Price per Litre	Quantity Demanded	Quantity Supplied	Surplus or Shortage?	Price Direction
$1.50	4.5	9	Surplus	Fall
1.40	5	8	Surplus	Fall
1.30	5.5	7	Surplus	Fall
1.20	6	6	Neither	Unchanged
1.10	6.5	5	Shortage	Rise
1.00	7	4	Shortage	Rise
0.90	7.5	3	Shortage	Rise

instant, be at rest again. This point is not an equilibrium position, for the force of gravity will pull the pendulum downward. Thereafter, gravity and friction will govern its motion from side to side. Eventually, the pendulum will return to its original position. The fact that the pendulum tends to return to its original position is described by saying that this position is a *stable* equilibrium. That position is also the only equilibrium position of the pendulum. At any other point, inherent forces will cause the pendulum to move.

The concept of equilibrium in economics is similar and can be illustrated by our supply-and-demand example. Why is no price other than $1.20 an equilibrium price in Table 5 or Figure 7? What forces will change any other price?

Consider first a low price such as $1.00, at which quantity demanded (7 billion litres) exceeds quantity supplied (4 billion litres). If the price was this low, many frustrated customers would be unable to purchase the quantities they desired. In their scramble for the available supply of milk, some would offer to pay more. As customers sought to outbid one another, the market price would be forced up. Thus, a price below the equilibrium price cannot persist in a free market because a shortage sets in motion powerful economic forces that push the price upward.

Similar forces operate if the market price exceeds the equilibrium price. If, for example, the price should somehow reach $1.50, Table 5 tells us that quantity supplied (9 billion litres) would far exceed the quantity demanded (4.5 billion litres). Producers would be unable to sell their desired quantities of milk at the prevailing price, and some would undercut their competitors by reducing the price. Such competitive price cutting would continue as long as the surplus remained—that is, as long as quantity supplied exceeded quantity demanded. Thus, a price above the equilibrium price cannot persist indefinitely.

We are left with a clear conclusion. The price of $1.20 per litre and the quantity of 6 billion litres per year constitute the only price–quantity combination that does not sow the seeds of its own destruction. It is thus the only equilibrium for this market. Any lower price must rise, and any higher price must fall. It is as if natural economic forces place a magnet at point E that attracts the market, just as gravity attracts a pendulum.

The pendulum analogy is worth pursuing further. Most pendulums are more frequently in motion than at rest. However, unless they are repeatedly buffeted by outside forces (which, of course, is exactly what happens to economic equilibria in reality), pendulums gradually return to their resting points. The same is true of price and quantity in a free market. They are moved about by shifts in the supply and demand curves that we have already described. As a consequence, markets are not always in equilibrium. But, if nothing interferes with them, experience shows that they normally move toward equilibrium.

The law of supply and demand states that in a free market the forces of supply and demand generally push the price toward the level at which quantity supplied and quantity demanded are equal.

■ The Law of Supply and Demand

In a free market, the forces of supply and demand generally push the price toward its equilibrium level, the price at which quantity supplied and quantity demanded are equal. Like most economic "laws," some markets will occasionally disobey the **law of supply and demand.** Markets sometimes display shortages or surpluses for long periods of time. Prices sometimes fail to move toward equilibrium. But the "law" is a fair generalization that is right far more often than it is wrong.

■ EFFECTS OF DEMAND SHIFTS ON SUPPLY–DEMAND EQUILIBRIUM

Figure 3 showed how developments other than changes in price—such as increases in consumer income—can shift the demand curve. We saw that a rise in income, for example, will shift the demand curve to the right, meaning that at any given price, consumers—with their increased purchasing power—will buy more of the good than before. This, in turn, will move the equilibrium point, changing both market price and quantity sold.

The Ups and Downs of Burqa Prices

Céline Galipeau is a Radio-Canada (French CBC) reporter who travelled through Afghanistan in March 2006 and then again in November 2006 disguised as an Afghan. In this interview about her latest trip, Galipeau coincidentally gives an illuminating example of the laws of supply and demand tied to the prices of burqas—an Afghan or Pakistani garment that covers the entire female body, with a net or grille over the eyes to allow the wearer to see.

I noticed that the situation of women has experienced a setback. In March 2006 I could see many women in the streets of Kabul without a headscarf, or with just a hidjab. Not so now. Women are

scared. The price of burqas is increasing because the demand for them is becoming extremely strong. Women fear the comeback of the Talibans, they fear the conservatives, who are more and more influential in the government and in the rest of the country. The barometer of all this is the price of burqas. Whenever it goes up, it implies that there is insecurity in the country, as all women want to purchase burqas again to protect themselves.

SOURCE: Translated from a transcript of the radio interview conducted by Christiane Charette, Radio-Canada, November 9, 2006. The transcript is available in French at http://www.radio-canada.ca/radio/christiane/modele-document.asp?docnumero=28107&numero=1880

This market adjustment is shown in Figure 8(a). It adds a supply curve to Figure 3(a) so that we can see what happens to the supply–demand equilibrium. In the example in the graph, the quantity demanded at the old equilibrium price of $1.20 increases from 6 billion litres per year (point E on the demand curve D_0D_0) to 7.5 billion litres per year (point R on the demand curve, D_1D_1). We know that $1.20 is no longer the equilibrium price, because at this price quantity demanded (7.5 billion litres) exceeds quantity supplied (6 billion litres). To restore equilibrium, the price must rise. The new equilibrium occurs at point T, where the price is $1.30 per litre and both quantities demanded and supplied are 7 billion litres per year. This example illustrates a general result, which is true when the supply curve slopes upward:

Any influence that makes the demand curve shift outward to the right, and does not affect the supply curve, will raise the equilibrium price and the equilibrium quantity.[4]

Everything works in reverse if consumer incomes fall. Figure 8(b) depicts a leftward (inward) shift of the demand curve that results from a decline in consumer

FIGURE 8   The Effects of Shifts of the Demand Curve

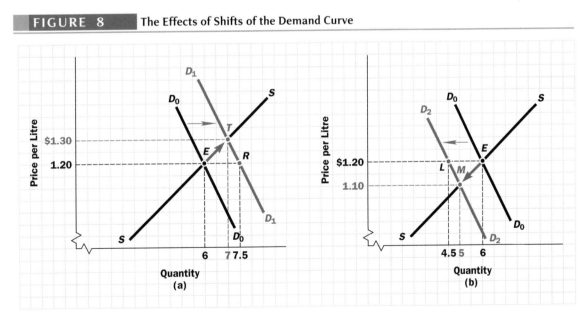

Note: Quantity is in billions of litres per year.

---

[4] For example, when incomes rise rapidly, in many developing countries the demand curves for a variety of consumer goods shift rapidly outward to the right. In Japan, for example, the demand for used Levi's jeans and Nike running shoes from the United States skyrocketed in the early 1990s as status-conscious Japanese consumers searched for outlets for their then-rising incomes.

incomes. For example, the quantity demanded at the previous equilibrium price ($1.20) falls from 6 billion litres (point E) to 4.5 billion litres (point L on the demand curve $D_2 D_2$). The initial price is now too high and must fall. The new equilibrium will eventually be established at point M, where the price is $1.10 and both quantity demanded and quantity supplied are 5 billion litres. In general:

> Any influence that shifts the demand curve inward to the left, and that does not affect the supply curve, will lower both the equilibrium price and the equilibrium quantity.

SUPPLY SHIFTS AND SUPPLY–DEMAND EQUILIBRIUM

A story precisely analogous to that of the effects of a demand shift on equilibrium price and quantity applies to supply shifts. Figure 6 described the effects on the supply curve of milk if the number of farms increases. Figure 9(a) now adds a demand curve to the supply curves of Figure 6 so that we can see the supply–demand equilibrium. Notice that at the initial price of $1.20, the quantity supplied after the shift is 7.8 billion litres (point I on the supply curve $S_1 S_1$), which is 30 percent more than the original quantity demanded of 6 billion litres (point E on the supply curve $S_0 S_0$). We can see from the graph that the price of $1.20 is too high to be the equilibrium price; the price must fall. The new equilibrium point is J, where the price is $1.10 per litre and the quantity is 6.5 billion litres per year. In general:

> Any change that shifts the supply curve outward to the right, and does not affect the demand curve, will lower the equilibrium price and raise the equilibrium quantity.

This must always be true if the industry's demand curve has a negative slope, because the greater quantity supplied can be sold only if the price is decreased so as to induce customers to buy more.[5] The cellular phone industry is a case in point. As more providers have entered the industry, the cost of cellular service has plummeted. Some cellular carriers have even given away telephones as sign-up bonuses.

Figure 9(b) illustrates the opposite case: a contraction of the industry. The supply curve shifts inward to the left and equilibrium moves from point E to point V, where the price is $1.40 and quantity is 5 billion litres per year. In general:

> Any influence that shifts the supply curve to the left, and does not affect the demand curve, will raise the equilibrium price and reduce the equilibrium quantity.

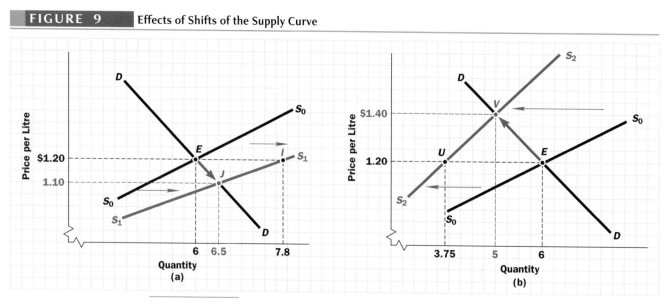

FIGURE 9   **Effects of Shifts of the Supply Curve**

[5] Graphically, whenever a positively sloped curve shifts to the right, its intersection point with a negatively sloping curve must always move lower. Just try drawing it yourself.

Many outside forces can disturb equilibrium in a market by shifting the demand curve or the supply curve, either temporarily or permanently. In 1998, for example, gasoline prices dropped because recession in Asia reduced demand, and a reduction in use of petroleum resulted from a mild winter. Often these outside influences

---

PUZZLE RESOLVED: *Those Leaping Oil Prices*

The disturbing recent behaviour of the price of gasoline, and of the oil from which it is made, is attributable to large shifts in both demand and supply conditions. North Americans are, for example, driving more and are buying gas-guzzling vehicles, and the resulting upward shift in the demand curve raises price. The rapid development of China over the last decade is also said to have led to rising demand pressures on oil and gasoline.

On the supply side, instability in the Middle East and in Russia has undermined the production and distribution of oil. For instance, in 2004, the price of crude oil rose briskly when Iraqi oil lines were blasted and when it was announced that the largest Russian oil producer was on the brink of bankruptcy. Also the price of crude oil doubled, reaching $78 a barrel in the summer of 2006 when market participants started to fear that the war between Lebanon and Israel might lead to oil supply cuts, only to fall later when the war ended. But it all looks like small change now with the price of crude oil reaching $145 in July 2008.

High oil prices have become the norm since August 2005 as a consequence of the devastation brought about by Hurricane Katrina. The following newspaper story describes the impact of this natural disaster on Canadian gasoline prices.

Canadian Gasoline Prices Soar

Motorists in Canada's biggest cities were jolted awake Wednesday by a stunning jump in gas prices—in some centres costs rose as much as 20 cents a litre—in the wake of the devastating impact of Hurricane Katrina on the U.S. energy sector. In Toronto, prices were running around the $1.19 a litre mark at some stations. Overnight in Vancouver, gas prices jumped 12 cents to about $1.13 a litre. In Fredericton, prices at some stations went up to $1.19, an increase of about eight cents a litre. Lineups were reported at places still offering regular unleaded for $1.11. According to Torontogasprices.com, the highest per-litre price reported over the past 24 hours was in Newmarket, Ont., where costs hit $1.29.

The price hikes come on the heels of reports of extensive damage to oil platforms in the Gulf of Mexico that sent crude oil prices surging above $70 (U.S.) overseas for a second consecutive day on Wednesday in what some analysts described as an "evolving energy crisis" as a result of the hurricane. Hurricane Katrina touched land just east of New Orleans on Monday, leaving as much as 80 per cent of that historic city underwater. "Besides the human tragedy unfolding in Louisiana, Mississippi and Alabama—replete with looting, shootings and dramatic rescues—there is an evolving crisis in the Gulf of Mexico's oil and gas industry," BMO Nesbitt Burns chief economist Sherry Cooper said. "Oil futures hit a record settlement of $70 per barrel as traders awaited damage reports from U.S. oil and gas refineries in the Gulf."

The U.S. Coast Guard said at least seven rigs were adrift, while eight refineries have shut down because of the damage caused by the hurricane. According to some estimates, about 95 per cent of the daily oil output from the Gulf of Mexico is out of commission, resulting in soaring commodity prices and surging gasoline costs across much of North America.

"Given that the United States produces 7.75 million barrels of oil per day including natural gas liquids, Hurricane Katrina has knocked out roughly one-fifth of all domestic production," Ms. Cooper said. "To put this in perspective, the U.S. would need to find either a new Canada, Venezuela, Mexico, or Saudi Arabia to replace this loss based on what these countries sell to the United States."

Source: Terry Weber, "Canadian Gasoline Prices Soar," *The Globe and Mail*, August 31, 2005. Reprinted with permission of *The Globe and Mail*.

change the equilibrium price and quantity by shifting either the supply curve or the demand curve. If you look again at Figures 8 and 9, you can see clearly that any event that causes either the demand curve or the supply curve to shift will also change the equilibrium price and quantity.

■ Application: Who Really Pays That Tax?

Supply and demand analysis offers insights that may not be readily apparent. Here is an example. Suppose your provincial government raises the gasoline tax by 10 cents per litre. Service station operators will then have to collect 10 additional cents in taxes on every litre they pump. They will consider this higher tax as an addition to their costs and will shift it to you and other consumers by raising the price of gas by 10 cents per litre. Right? No, wrong—or rather, partly wrong.

The gas station owners would certainly *like* to shift the entire tax to buyers, but the market mechanism will allow them to shift only *part* of it—perhaps 6 cents per litre. They will then be stuck with the remainder—4 cents in our example. Figure 10, which is just another supply–demand graph, shows why.

The demand curve is the red curve DD. The supply curve before the tax is the black curve S_0S_0. Before the new tax, the equilibrium point is E_0 and the price is $1.00. We can interpret the supply curve as telling us at what price sellers are willing to provide any given quantity. For example, they are willing to supply quantity $Q_1 = 50$ million litres per year if the price is $1.00 per litre.

So what happens as a result of the new tax? Because they must now turn 10 cents per litre over to the government, gas station owners will be willing to supply any given quantity only if they get 10 cents more per litre than they did before. Therefore, to get them to supply quantity $Q_1 = 50$ million litres, a price of $1.00 per litre will no longer suffice. Only a price of $1.10 per litre will now induce them to supply 5 million litres. Thus, at quantity $Q_1 = 50$, the point on the supply curve will move up by 10 cents, from point E_0 to point M. Because firms will insist on the same 10-cent price increase for any other quantity they supply, the *entire* supply curve will shift up by the 10-cent tax—from the black curve S_0S_0 to the new blue supply curve S_1S_1. And, as a result, the supply–demand equilibrium point will move from E_0 to E_1 and the price will increase from $1.00 to $1.06.

The supply curve shift may give the impression that gas station owners have succeeded in passing the entire 10-cent increase on to consumers—the distance from E_0 to M—but look again. The *equilibrium* price has only gone up from $1.00 to $1.06. That is, the price has risen by only 6 cents, not by the full 10-cent amount of the tax. The gas station will have to absorb the remaining 4 cents of the tax.

Now this really *looks* as though we have pulled a fast one on you—a magician's sleight of hand. After all, the supply curve has shifted upward by the full amount of the tax, and yet the resulting price increase has covered only part of the tax rise. However, a second look reveals that, like most apparent acts of magic, this one has a simple explanation. The explanation arises from the *demand* side of the supply–demand mechanism. The negative slope of the demand curve means that when prices rise, at least some consumers will reduce the quantity of gasoline they demand by reducing their car usage. Others will replace gas-guzzling older cars with ones that provide reduced fuel consumption. That will force sellers to give up part of the price increase. In other words, firms must absorb the part of the tax—4 cents—that consumers are unwilling to pay.

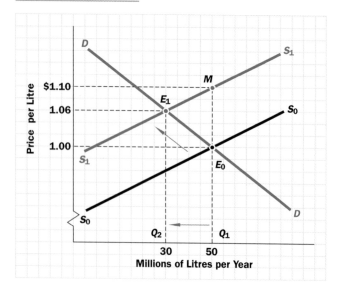

FIGURE 10

Who Pays for a New Tax on Products?

POLICY DEBATE

Economic Aspects of the War on Drugs

For years now, governments have engaged in a highly publicized "war on drugs." Billions of dollars have been spent on trying to stop illegal drugs at countries' borders. In some sense, interdiction has succeeded: Police officers have seized literally tons of cocaine and other drugs. Yet these efforts have made barely a dent in the flow of drugs to European and North American city streets. Simple economic reasoning explains why.

When drug interdiction works, it shifts the supply curve of drugs to the left, thereby driving up street prices. But that, in turn, raises the rewards for potential smugglers and attracts more criminals into the "industry," which shifts the supply curve back to the right. The net result is that increased shipments of drugs to Montreal or Vancouver docks replace much of what the authorities confiscate. This is why many economists believe that any successful antidrug program must concentrate on reducing demand, which would lower the street price of drugs, not on reducing supply, which can only raise it.

Some people suggest that the government should go even further and legalize many drugs. Although this idea remains a highly controversial position that few are ready to endorse, the reasoning behind it is straightforward.

How would things differ if drugs were legal? Because South American farmers earn pennies for drugs that sell for hundreds of dollars on the streets of Vancouver and Toronto, we may safely assume that legalized drugs would be vastly cheaper. In fact, according to one estimate, a dose of cocaine would cost less than 50 cents. That, proponents point out, would reduce drug-related crimes dramatically. When, for example, was the last time you heard of a gang killing connected with the distribution of cigarettes or alcoholic beverages?

Some specialists, such as University of Ottawa criminologist Line Beauchesne, argue that legalization should be accompanied by reg-ulation. Drugs would be freely accessed in standardized form from Crown corporations, as is now the case for alcohol and the Liquor Control Board of Ontario, for instance. This would improve the quality of these currently illegal drugs, just as adulterated alcohol was eliminated when alcohol was once more legalized, thus reducing health risks for consumers.

The argument against legalization of drugs is largely moral: Should the state sanction potentially lethal substances? But there is an economic aspect to this position as well: The vastly lower street prices of drugs that would surely follow legalization would increase drug use. Thus, while legalization would almost certainly reduce crime, it may also produce more addicts. If you think the increase in quantity demanded would be large, you are unlikely to find legalization an attractive option.

SOURCE: Nick Procaylo/Canadian Press.

But note that the equilibrium quantity Q_1 has fallen from 50 million litres to $Q_2 = 30$ million litres—so both consumers and suppliers lose out in some sense.

This example is not an oddball case. Indeed, the result is almost always true. The cost of any increase in a tax on any commodity will usually be paid partly by the consumer and partly by the seller. This is so no matter whether the government says that it is imposing the tax on the sellers or on the buyers. Whichever way it is phrased, the economics are the same: The supply–demand mechanism ensures that the tax will be shared by both of the parties.

■ BATTLING THE INVISIBLE HAND: THE MARKET FIGHTS BACK

Lawmakers and rulers have often been dissatisfied with the outcomes of free markets. From biblical times to the space age, they have battled the invisible hand. Sometimes, rather than trying to adjust the workings of the market, governments have tried to raise or lower the prices of specific commodities by decree. In many such cases, the authorities felt that market prices were, in some sense, immorally low or immorally high. Penalties were therefore imposed on anyone offering the commodities in question at prices above or below those established by the authorities. Such legally imposed constraints on prices are called *price ceilings* and *price floors*. To see their result, we will focus on the use of price ceilings.

Restraining the Market Mechanism: Price Ceilings

A **price ceiling** is a maximum that the price charged for a commodity cannot legally exceed.

The market has proven itself a formidable foe that strongly resists attempts to get around its decisions. In case after case where legal **price ceilings** are imposed, virtually the same series of consequences ensues:

1. *A persistent shortage develops because quantity demanded exceeds quantity supplied.* Queuing (people waiting in lines), direct rationing (with everyone getting a fixed allotment), or any of a variety of other devices, usually inefficient and unpleasant, must substitute for the distribution process provided by the price mechanism. Example: Rampant shortages in Eastern Europe and the former Soviet Union helped precipitate the revolts that ended communism.

2. *An illegal, or "black," market often arises to supply the commodity.* Usually some individuals are willing to take the risks involved in meeting unsatisfied demands illegally. Example: Although most states ban the practice, ticket "scalping" (the sale of tickets at higher than regular prices) occurs at most popular sporting events and rock concerts.

3. *The prices charged on illegal markets are almost certainly higher than those that would prevail in free markets.* After all, lawbreakers expect some compensation for the risk of being caught and punished. Example: Illegal drugs are normally quite expensive. (See the accompanying Policy Debate box, "Economic Aspects of the War on Drugs" on page 77.)

4. A substantial portion of the price falls into the hands of the illicit supplier instead of going to those who produce the good or perform the service. Example: With the introduction of official ticket resellers such as TicketExchange, hockey fans can buy secondhand tickets to watch the Toronto Maple Leafs. The NHL team gets a share of the resale, and it is believed that prices will be cheaper than if scalping laws prohibited such resale.

5. *Investment in the industry generally dries up.* Because price ceilings reduce the monetary returns that investors can legally earn, less capital will be invested in industries that are subject to price controls. Even fear of impending price controls can have this effect. Example: Price controls on farm products in Zambia have prompted peasant farmers and large agricultural conglomerates alike to cut back production rather than grow crops at a loss. The result has been thousands of lost jobs and widespread food shortages.

Case Study: Rent Controls in New York City

These points and others are best illustrated by considering a concrete example involving price ceilings. New York is the only major city in North America that has continuously legislated rent controls in much of its rental housing since World War II. Rent controls, of course, are intended to protect the consumer from high rents. But most economists believe that rent control does not help the cities or their residents and that, in the long run, it leaves almost everyone worse off. As we saw in Chapter 1, 80 percent of economists agreed without restriction that a ceiling on rents reduces the quantity and quality of housing available. Elementary supply–demand analysis shows us why.

Figure 11 is a supply–demand diagram for rental units in New York. Curve *DD* is the demand curve and curve *SS* is the supply curve. Without controls, equilibrium would be at point *E*, where rents average $2,000 per month and 3 million housing units are occupied. If rent controls are effective, the ceiling price must be below the equilibrium price of $2,000. But

FIGURE 11

Supply–Demand Diagram for Rental Housing

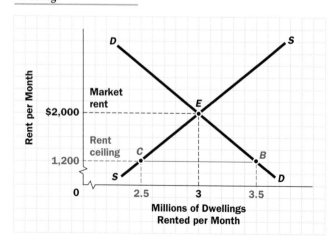

with a low rent ceiling, such as $1,200, the quantity of housing demanded will be 3.5 million units (point *B*) whereas the quantity supplied will be only 2.5 million units (point *C*).

The diagram shows a shortage of 1 million apartments. This theoretical concept of a "shortage" manifests itself in New York City as an abnormally low vacancy rate—typically about half the national urban average. Naturally, rent controls have spawned a lively black market in New York. The black market raises the effective price of rent-controlled apartments in many ways, including bribes, so-called key money paid to move up on a waiting list, or the requirement that prospective tenants purchase worthless furniture at inflated prices.

According to Figure 11, rent controls reduce the quantity supplied from 3 million to 2.5 million apartments. How does this reduction show up in New York and in other cities that have rent control? First, some property owners, discouraged by the low rents, have converted apartment buildings into office space or other uses. Second, some apartments have been inadequately maintained. After all, rent controls create a shortage, which makes even dilapidated apartments easy to rent. Third, some landlords have actually abandoned their buildings rather than pay rising tax and fuel bills. These abandoned buildings rapidly become eyesores and eventually pose threats to public health and safety.

With all of these problems, why does rent control persist in New York City? And why do other cities, in Canada and elsewhere, sometimes move in the same direction?

Part of the explanation is that most people simply do not understand the problems that rent controls create. Another part is that landlords are unpopular politically. But a third, and very important, part of the explanation is that not everyone is hurt by rent controls—and those who benefit from controls fight hard to preserve them. In New York and in other cities such as Paris, many tenants still pay rents that are only a fraction of what their apartments would fetch on the open market. They are, naturally enough, quite happy with this situation. This last point illustrates another very general phenomenon:

Virtually every price ceiling or floor creates a class of people that benefits from the regulations. These people use their political influence to protect their gains by preserving the status quo, which is one reason why it is so difficult to eliminate price ceilings or floors.

■ Case Study: Rent Controls in Canada

While most economists agree that rent freezes or strict rent controls, as exist in New York and in some European cities such as Paris, have devastating effects on the quality and quantity of rental housing, some economists argue that second-generation rent controls, like those that have been put into place in many Canadian cities since the mid-1970s (although some were discontinued in the 1990s), have achieved their purposes without generating disastrous effects. These second-generation rent regulations provide annual rent guideline increases, allowing, for instance, 2.1 and 2.6 percent increases in Ontario in 2006 and 2007, respectively. Rental unit owners can apply for further increases when they undertake major repairs and upgrading of their properties and when they face above-normal increases in property taxes and heating or electricity costs. This allows owners to earn a *fair* or *reasonable* rate of return on their residential investment (much as regulated monopolies are allowed to earn a fair rate of return).

Research done for the Canada Mortgage and Housing Corporation seems to demonstrate that there is "no convincing evidence that rent regulations, as they existed in various provinces in Canada . . . had significant effects on rents, on the construction of rental units, or on vacancy rates." In addition, rent controls had no reported effect on the proportion of occupied rental units that were in need of major repairs.

In addition to protecting tenants from unreasonable rent increases and ensuring rental unit owners a fair or reasonable rate of return on their investment, proponents of second-generation rent controls claim that these controls take away some of the monopolistic power of rental unit owners, thus somewhat reducing the overall average rental cost. In addition, they claim, rent controls tend to stabilize rent prices, preventing major rent increases when the market is tight (when vacancy rates are low) and also preventing rents from falling when the market is slack (when vacancy rates are high and owners of rental units would normally take a beating). Whether or not these claims are correct, rent control still remains an issue in several Canadian provinces, in particular in cities where few downtown rental apartments are affordable.

■ Restraining the Market Mechanism: Price Floors

Interferences with the market mechanism are not always designed to keep prices low. Agricultural price supports and minimum wage laws are two notable examples in which the law keeps prices *above* free-market levels. Such **price floors** are typically accompanied by a standard series of symptoms:

A **price floor** is a legal minimum below which the price charged for a commodity is not permitted to fall.

1. *A surplus develops as sellers cannot find enough buyers.* Example: Surpluses of various agricultural products have been a persistent—and costly—problem for the U.S. government. The problem is even worse in the European Union (EU), where the common agricultural policy holds prices even higher. This policy accounts for about half of all EU spending.
2. *Where goods, rather than services, are involved, the surplus creates a problem of disposal.* Something must be done about the excess of quantity supplied over quantity demanded. For instance, both the U.S. government and the European Union have often been forced to purchase, store, and then dispose of large amounts of surplus agricultural commodities.
3. *To get around the regulations, sellers may offer discounts in disguised—and often unwanted—forms.* Back when airline fares were regulated by the government, airlines offered more and better food and more stylishly uniformed flight attendants instead of lowering fares. Today, the food is worse, but tickets cost much less.
4. *Regulations that keep prices artificially high encourage overinvestment in the industry.* Even inefficient businesses whose high operating costs would doom them in an unrestricted market can survive beneath the shelter of a generous price floor. This is why airline industries throughout the world went through painful "shakeouts" of the weaker companies since the 1980s, after they were deregulated and allowed to charge market-determined prices.

Once again, a specific example is useful for understanding how price floors work.

■ Case Study: Farm Price Supports

One of the ironies of world capitalism is that those countries that most strongly argue in favour of free competitive markets and trade liberalization are precisely those countries that have the most extensive agricultural price support programs. Both the United States and the European Union heavily subsidize their agricultural sectors, including sugar beet, cotton, and wheat growers and dairy farmers. Indeed, these agricultural subsidies were an important component of the Doha round of trade negotiations, set up by the World Trade Organization, and the negotiations faltered in 2006 precisely on this issue.

American farm price supports began during the Great Depression when unemployed people could not afford to buy food and farmers were going broke in droves in the midst of excess supplies of agricultural products. Farm price supports in Europe got started a few years after World War II, as the founding members of the European Union were slowly emerging from more than a decade of food shortages.

One of the consequences of these price supports has been the creation of unsellable surpluses—more output of crops such as grains than consumers were willing to buy at the inflated prices yielded by the supports. Warehouses were filled to overflowing. New storage facilities had to be built, and the government was forced to set up programs in which grain from the unmanageable surpluses was shipped to poor foreign countries to combat malnutrition and starvation in those nations. Realistically, if price supports are to be effective in keeping prices above the equilibrium level, then *someone* must be prepared to purchase the surpluses that invariably result. Otherwise, those surpluses will somehow find their way into the market and drive down prices, undermining the price support program. The buyer of the surpluses has usually turned out to be the government, which makes its purchases at the expense of taxpayers who are forced to pay twice—once through taxes to finance the government purchases, and a second time in the form of higher prices for the farm products bought by the public.

Figure 12 illustrates the likely consequences of price support programs. Curve DD is the demand curve for a farm product, say wheat, and S_0S_0 is the supply curve. If there was no subsidization program, market forces would bring the price of wheat to $140 per tonne and 150 million tonnes would be produced and sold. If the government was to impose by decree a price of $220 per tonne, only 100 million tonnes would be demanded and 190 million tonnes would be produced. There would thus be a surplus of 90 million tonnes, produced in excess of the quantities being demanded at the $220 price. The government would have to purchase the surplus and store it away, waiting for an increase in demand. This additional demand could come from Third World markets, where the overproduction is now being dumped (at any price), potentially putting Third World farmers out of business.

An alternative is for government to pay a subsidy to wheat producers, thus shifting the supply curve to S_1S_1 (in perfect symmetry to the shift in the supply curve that was induced by an increase in the gasoline tax, as shown in Figure 10). This downward shift in the supply curve occurs because the net cost of production for the wheat grower will be reduced by the amount of the subsidy per tonne. In the case illustrated in Figure 12, to sustain a support price of $220 per tonne of wheat, which would induce a production of 190 millions of tonnes, the price being demanded on the market would have to fall to $108 and the government would be forced to grant a subsidy of $112 per tonne. It is estimated by the Organisation for Economic Co-operation and Development (OECD) that the government subsidy per tonne of wheat has been $150 per tonne in the European Union, $112 in the United States, $28 in Canada, and $7 in Australia over the 1999–2003 period.

Another possibility is to impose **quotas**. Farmers would be allowed to produce only a certain amount of wheat or to farm only a given amount of land. In the former case, the supply curve would become vertical at the production level of 100 tonnes of wheat. In the latter case, the supply curve would shift backward until it became S_2S_2. Through these restricting mechanisms, the quantities being supplied would be exactly equal to the quantities being demanded at the $220 price. In this case, there would no

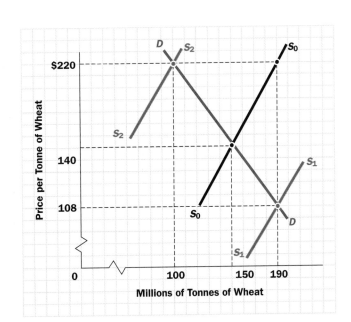

FIGURE 12

Price Support Programs

A **producer's quota** is the maximum amount that a producer is allowed to produce or the maximum area that a farmer is allowed to farm.

longer be a government subsidy, but output (and consumption) would be reduced relative to the free competitive market solution, and prices paid by consumers would be higher: $220 dollars.

■ Case Study: Farm Products Supply Management in Canada

In Canada, several farm products are produced under a form of quota system, where supply is managed by a central agency and products are marketed at set prices. There are many such agencies, such as the Canadian Dairy Commission, which covers milk, cream, cheese, and butter; the Canadian Egg Marketing Agency; the Canadian Turkey Marketing Agency, and the Chicken Farmers of Canada, which obviously cover eggs and poultry.

Although the details are different, all of these organizations operate under similar principles. The national agency first makes an estimate of future demand by both domestic consumers and processors of farm products; an estimate of possible exports and imports is also made. These estimates indicate the required level of national production. Production quotas are then assigned to each provincial board, in proportion to shares previously agreed upon. The provincial boards in turn allot quotas to registered local producers. The farmers then sell their products at prices that have been set by the national or the provincial agencies, taking into consideration a cost-of-production formula designed to provide a fair rate of return on the operations of an efficient farmer. Revenues are often pooled, as they are in the case of the Canadian Wheat Board, which markets the wheat, durum, and barley produced by western Canada farmers, although no quotas are imposed in this case.

Supply management of Canadian farm products as it now exists was mainly put in place in the 1970s. Before that, farm products faced unstable markets and highly variable producer revenues, with unpredictable production cycles and situations in which producers undercut each other when demand relative to supply was weak. Since consumers cannot drastically change their eating habits, a small excess supply of farm products can lead to a large decrease in farm product prices, thus leading to substantial decreases in farm revenues, as it did at the time of the Great Depression. Price support and supply management have been introduced to avoid this drawback of free competitive markets. There were some hitches in the initial stages of supply management, when quotas were not properly enforced or when overly high quotas, in particular in the dairy industry in 1975, were mistakenly granted, thus leading to huge surpluses. This is not the case today. Through quotas, national agencies attempt to strike the best balance between the supply of and the demand for agricultural products, thus ensuring stable prices for the consumers and stable revenues for the producers. A system with properly set quotas thus avoids the excess production associated with pure price support programs, with their storage and disposal costs.

The downside of the quota system is that milk and other dairy products, eggs, chickens, and bread are perhaps more expensive than they would otherwise be on average in a competitive market without quotas, as is obvious from Figure 12. Consumers are not alone in possibly paying higher prices: Milk quotas now sell for $30,000 per cow, which means that anybody who wants to start a dairy farm needs at least $1.2 million, since an efficient farm requires at least 40 head of cattle. But this may be the price that must be paid for a stable agricultural sector.

Another advantage of the farm product marketing boards is that these boards act as a countervailing force to the power of processors of farm products. These processors are often large firms that can take advantage of farmers, so it is argued that without the marketing boards, farm product producers would be at a disadvantage when negotiating prices. In other words, the forces of supply and demand were already distorted before the arrival of marketing boards. Indeed, the Canadian Wheat Board claims explicitly that by acting on behalf of all wheat and barley producers in western Canada, it exercises monopoly power that allows it to extract higher revenues for

POLICY DEBATE

Should the Canadian Wheat Board Be Dismantled?

Conservatives are popular in western Canada, but free-market policies are not welcomed by all Westerners. In the fall of 2006, the Harper federal government initiated steps to dismantle the Canadian Wheat Board. As of mid 2008, the government and the Wheat Board are still battling in court. The following newspaper story illustrates well the ideological conflict between those who believe in the laws of supply and demand and those who believe that markets are not as perfect as economists would like them to be.

Mr. Chorney, a 41-year-old grain farmer, believes the federal government is about to make an enormous mistake by dismantling the monopoly power of the Canadian Wheat Board. "They're really floundering on this issue," he says.

The debate over the future of the Wheat Board runs to the heart of Western Canadian history and politics, pitting traditional Prairie collectivism against the ideology of the free market. It's an issue that has waxed and waned over the years. Now, the federal government is on the brink of creating what it calls "marketing choice," a world in which farmers could choose either to sell their product on their own, or to whatever version of the Wheat Board survived the end of the monopoly. . . .

Ken Ritter is the elected chairman of the Canadian Wheat Board. Mr. Ritter was first elected as an opponent of the Wheat Board monopoly, but after nine months of handling the board's rail-transport negotiations, he had a change of mind. "I saw how the other players had . . . almost scorn for farmers. They felt they should run their railroad exactly the way they want, and farmers' economic interests were minimized," he says. "I'm a believer in a market economy. But in a market economy, the players all have to have reasonable weight to be effective. That's what

the Wheat Board helps farmers do. The main grain traders are huge corporations who hold some 83 per cent of the market. If you're not big, you're not in the game.". . .

Cherilyn Jolly-Nagel, the president of the Western Canadian Wheat Growers Association, is one of those who can't wait to see the market opened up to competition. She's a 27-year-old graduate of an agriculture college who runs a 6,500-acre operation with her husband in western Saskatchewan, and she sees herself as part of farming's new wave, a savvy group of young farmers able to find more money in international markets. "The current system doesn't allow me to capitalize on what I see as marketing opportunities," Ms. Jolly-Nagel says. . . .

Mr. Chorney, whose family has farmed an area 40 kilometres north of Winnipeg for the past 77 years, scoffs at the assertions of the Western Canadian Wheat Growers. He doesn't want to get into a debate about ideology; he's interested in the bottom line. The Canadian Wheat Board is the largest seller of wheat and barley in the world, with sales in the range of $3-billion to $4-billion a year. It was granted a monopoly over wheat exports by the government in 1943 and has been a constant target for U.S. trade challenges. One of the most well-known studies of the Wheat Board, hotly contested by economists on both sides of the debate, argued that over a 14-year period the board averaged sales of $265-million more per year than would have been realized by multiple sellers.

SOURCE: Joe Friesen, "Farmers fretting over Wheat Board's future." Posted October 10, 2006, on *GlobeandMail.com* at http://www.theglobeandmail.com. Reprinted with permission of *The Globe and Mail.*

western grain growers. This also explains why other farmers (for instance, potato growers in Prince Edward Island and in some northeastern U.S. states) organize themselves into cooperatives.

■ A Can of Worms

Our case studies—rent controls and farm price support programs—illustrate some of the possible side effects of price floors and ceilings, but barely hint at others. Problems that we have not yet mentioned may arise, such as favouritism and corruption. For instance, with price ceilings, there are shortages and someone must decide who gets the limited quantity that is available. In the former Soviet Union, queuing for certain goods was quite common. Even so, Communist Party officials and other favoured groups were somehow able to purchase the scarce commodities that others could not buy. Misallocation of resources is also likely to occur. For example, Russian farmers used to feed their farm animals bread instead of unprocessed grains because price ceilings kept the price of bread ludicrously low. Praiseworthy intentions—here the government's desire to provide all Russian citizens with low-cost food—may cause serious damage elsewhere in the economy.

A SIMPLE BUT POWERFUL LESSON

The law of supply and demand in unfettered markets looks simple enough. Tampering with the price mechanism by imposing ceilings or floors can generate all kinds of major negative side effects. Despite this, modern governments still interfere and impose regulations. Why is this so? There are essentially two reasons. The first explanation is that many people in authority still do not understand the law of supply and demand. But there is sometimes a deeper reason. The law of supply and demand assumes that market mechanisms are unhampered to start with, and that none of the market participants have any control over supply or demand. But this is clearly not the case in many, perhaps in most, markets. Even in agricultural markets, which are usually considered excellent illustrations of supply and demand laws, farmers are squeezed by input suppliers and large purchasers such as supermarket chains, which flex their market power muscles. As the quote at the beginning of the chapter reminds us, the free competitive market mechanisms of supply and demand are powerful indeed, but we must not forget that most markets are neither free nor fully competitive, but rather are dominated by a few large participants on either the supply or the demand side.

SUMMARY

1. The quantity of a product that is demanded is not a fixed number. Rather, **quantity demanded** depends on such factors as the price of the product, consumer incomes, and the prices of other products.

2. The relationship between quantity demanded and price, holding constant all other things, can be displayed graphically on a **demand curve.**

3. For most products, the higher the price, the lower the quantity demanded. As a result, the demand curve usually has a negative slope.

4. The quantity of a product that is supplied depends on its price and many other influences. A **supply curve** is a graphical representation of the relationship between **quantity supplied** and price, holding constant all other influences.

5. For most products, supply curves have positive slopes, meaning that higher prices lead to supply of greater quantities.

6. A change in quantity demanded that is caused by a change in the price of the good is represented by a movement *along* a fixed demand curve. A change in quantity demanded that is caused by a change in any other determinant of quantity demanded is represented by a **shift of the demand curve.**

7. This same distinction applies to the supply curve: Changes in price lead to movements along a fixed supply curve; changes in other determinants of quantity supplied lead to shifts of the entire supply curve.

8. A market is said to be in **equilibrium** when quantity supplied is equal to quantity demanded. The equilibrium price and quantity are shown by the point on the supply–demand graph where the supply and demand curves intersect. The **law of supply and demand** states that price and quantity tend to gravitate to this point in a free market.

9. Changes in consumer incomes, tastes, technology, prices of competing products, and many other influences lead to shifts in either the demand curve or the supply curve and produce changes in price and quantity that can be determined from **supply-demand diagrams.**

10. A tax on a good generally leads to a rise in the price at which the taxed product is sold. The rise in price is generally less than the tax, so consumers usually pay less than the entire tax.

11. Consumers generally pay only part of a tax because the resulting rise in price leads them to buy less and the cut in the quantity they demand helps to force price down.

12. An attempt to use government regulations to force prices above or below their equilibrium levels is likely to lead to **shortages** or **surpluses,** to black markets in which goods are sold at illegal prices, and to a variety of other problems. The market always strikes back at attempts to repeal the law of supply and demand.

13. A **ceiling** imposed on the price of a good will generally lead to a **shortage** of this good. A **floor** imposed on prices will generally lead to a **surplus.** The only way to avoid these surpluses is to impose **quotas** on the amounts that can be produced.

KEY TERMS

Invisible hand   62

Quantity demanded   63

Demand schedule   63

Demand curve   63

Shift in a demand curve   64

Quantity supplied   67

Supply schedule   68

Supply curve   68

Supply–demand diagram   71

Shortage   71

Surplus   71

Equilibrium   71

Law of supply and demand   72

Price ceiling   78

Price floor   80

Producer's Quota   81

TEST YOURSELF

1. What shapes would you expect for demand curves for the following:

   a. A medicine that means life or death for a patient

   b. French fries in a food court with kiosks offering many types of food

2. The following are the assumed supply and demand schedules for hamburgers in Unitown:

Demand Schedule		Supply Schedule	
Price	Quantity Demanded per Year (thousands)	Price	Quantity Supplied per Year (thousands)
$2.25	12	$2.25	30
2.00	16	2.00	28
1.75	20	1.75	26
1.50	24	1.50	24
1.25	28	1.25	22
1.00	32	1.00	20

   a. Plot the supply and demand curves and indicate the equilibrium price and quantity.

   b. What effect would a decrease in the price of beef (a hamburger input) have on the equilibrium price and quantity of hamburgers, assuming all other things remained constant? Explain your answer with the help of a diagram.

   c. What effect would an increase in the price of pizza (a substitute commodity) have on the equilibrium price and quantity of hamburgers, assuming again that all other things remain constant? Use a diagram in your answer.

3. Suppose the supply and demand schedules for bicycles are as they appear below.

   a. Graph these curves and show the equilibrium price and quantity.

Price	Quantity Demanded per Year (millions)	Quantity Supplied per Year (millions)
$160	40	24
200	36	28
240	32	32
280	28	36
320	24	40
360	20	44

   b. Now suppose that it becomes unfashionable to ride a bicycle, so that the quantity demanded at each price falls by 8 million bikes per year. What is the new equilibrium price and quantity? Show this solution graphically. Explain why the quantity falls by less than 8 million bikes per year.

   c. Suppose instead that several major bicycle producers go out of business, thereby reducing the quantity supplied by 8 million bikes at every price. Find the new equilibrium price and quantity, and show it graphically. Explain again why quantity falls by less than 8 million.

   d. What are the equilibrium price and quantity if the shifts described in Test Yourself Questions 3(b) and 3(c) happen at the same time?

4. The following table summarizes information about the market for principles of economics textbooks:

Price	Quantity Demanded per Year	Quantity Supplied per Year
$40	4,200	200
50	2,200	600
60	1,200	1,200
70	700	2,000
80	550	3,000

   a. What is the market equilibrium price and quantity of textbooks?

   b. To quell outrage over tuition increases, the president of the university places a $50 limit on the price of textbooks. How many textbooks will be sold now?

   c. While the price limit is still in effect, automated publishing increases the efficiency of textbook production. Show graphically the likely effect of this innovation on the market price and quantity.

5. How are the following demand curves likely to shift in response to the indicated changes?

   a. The effect of a drought on the demand curve for umbrellas

   b. The effect of higher popcorn prices on the demand curve for movie tickets

   c. The effect on the demand curve for coffee of a decline in the price of Coca-Cola

6. The two accompanying diagrams show supply and demand curves for two substitute commodities: tapes and compact discs (CDs).

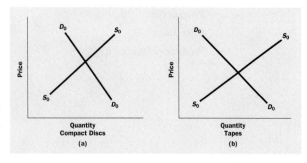

a. On the right-hand diagram, show what happens when rising raw material prices make it costlier to produce tapes.

b. On the left-hand diagram, show what happens to the market for CDs.

7. Consider the market for milk discussed in this chapter (Tables 1, 3, and 5 and Figures 1, 4, and 7). Suppose that the government decides to fight kidney stones by levying a tax of 40 cents per litre on sales of milk. Follow these steps to analyze the effects of the tax:

a. Construct the new supply schedule (to replace Table 3) that relates quantity supplied to the price that consumers pay.

b. Graph the new supply curve constructed in Test Yourself Question 7(a) on the supply–demand diagram depicted in Figure 7. What are the new equilibrium price and quantity?

c. Does the tax succeed in its goal of reducing the consumption of milk?

d. How much does the equilibrium price increase? Is the price rise greater than, equal to, or less than the 40-cent tax?

e. Who actually pays the tax, consumers or producers? (This may be a good question to discuss in class.)

8. (More difficult) The demand and supply curves for T-shirts in Touristtown are given by the following equations:

$$Q = 24,000 - 500P \qquad Q = 6,000 + 1,000P$$

where P is measured in dollars and Q is the number of T-shirts sold per year.

a. Find the equilibrium price and quantity algebraically.

b. If tourists decide they do not really like T-shirts that much, which of the following might be the new demand curve?

$$Q = 21,000 - 500P \qquad Q = 27,000 - 500P$$

Find the equilibrium price and quantity after the shift of the demand curve.

c. If, instead, two new stores that sell T-shirts open up in town, which of the following might be the new supply curve?

$$Q = 4,000 + 1,000P \qquad Q = 9,000 + 1,000P$$

Find the equilibrium price and quantity after the shift of the supply curve.

(Hint: See the appendix to this chapter.)

DISCUSSION QUESTIONS

1. How often do you rent videos? Would you do so more often if a rental cost half as much? Distinguish between your demand curve for home videos and your "quantity demanded" at the current price.

2. Discuss the likely effects of the following:

a. Rent ceilings on the market for apartments

b. Floors under wheat prices on the market for wheat

Use supply–demand diagrams to show what may happen in each case.

3. Suppose that Canadian quotas on milk have been miscalculated, not taking sufficient account of the reduction in births in Canada in the twenty-first century, and that huge milk and butter surpluses have accumulated. In an effort to reduce surpluses, the government offers to pay dairy farmers to slaughter cows. Use two diagrams, one for the milk market and one for the meat market, to illustrate how this policy should affect the price of meat. (Assume that meat is sold in an unregulated market.)

4. It is claimed in this chapter that either price floors or price ceilings reduce the actual quantity exchanged in a market. Use a diagram or diagrams to test this conclusion, and explain the common sense behind it.

5. The same rightward shift of the demand curve may produce a very small or a very large increase in quantity, depending on the slope of the supply curve. Explain this conclusion with diagrams.

6. Suppose that you expect the price of gasoline to go up in the very near future, say, in a few days. How would that change your demand for gasoline today? If everyone had the same expectations, what would happen to the demand curve for gasoline? Assuming that the supply curve will remain unchanged, what is the likely effect on the current price of gasoline?

7. From 1997 to 2005 in Canada, the number of working men over 25 years old grew by 12 percent; the number of working women in the same age group grew by 20 percent. During this time, average wages for men grew by 17.5 percent, while the average wages for women grew by 25 percent. Which of the following two explanations seems more consistent with the data?

a. Women decided to work more, raising their relative supply (relative to men).

b. Discrimination against women declined, raising the relative (to men) demand for female workers.

APPENDIX: *The Simple Algebra of Market Equilibrium*

Economists often resort to systems of two equations to deal with simple problems of supply and demand. Question 8 in the Test Yourself section provides an example of such a two-equation system. Knowing how to solve such systems will allow you to compute the equilibrium price and the equilibrium output when you are given supply and demand equations. In economics, the two key variables, price and quantity, are often called P and Q. Thus, the demand and supply curves could be given by:

$$Q = a - bP \qquad \text{(the demand equation)}$$

$$Q = c + dP \qquad \text{(the supply equation)}$$

where a, b, c, and d are the parameters being involved, b and d both being positive numbers.

The first equation represents demand because there is a negative relationship between quantities and prices, as there should be with a demand curve, whereas in the second equation, there is a positive relationship between quantities and prices, as is normally the case for a supply curve. For every \$1 increase in price, quantities demanded decrease by b units; similarly, for every \$1 increase in price, quantities supplied increase by d units.

What is the graphical representation of these two equations? Usually, in algebra, the variable on the left-hand side of an equation, such as $y = a + bx$, is to be found on the vertical axis (the y-axis). But economists do the opposite: As you must have noted, prices P are found on the vertical axis, and quantities Q are on the horizontal axis, so that our two equations can be reinterpreted as being:

$$P = a/b - (1/b)Q$$
$$\text{(the demand curve)}$$

$$P = -c/d + (1/d)Q$$
$$\text{(the supply curve)}$$

Thus, the slope of the demand curve as it appears on a demand and supply diagram is equal to $-1/b$ while the slope of the supply curve is $+1/d$, as shown in Figure 13. The vertical intercept of the demand curve (when $Q = 0$) is thus a/b. The horizontal intercepts of the demand and supply curves (when $P = 0$), as can be seen by looking at the two equations with which we started, are obviously a and c, respectively.

What are the equilibrium price and quantity, located at the intersection of the demand and supply curves? To find out, we must solve our system of two equations with two unknown variables (P and Q). One way to do so is to get rid of the Q variable by multiplying the second equation by -1 and subtracting it from the first equation:

$$Q = a - bP$$

$$-Q = -c - dP$$

thus getting:

$$0 = (a - c) - (b + d)P$$

Solving for P, we immediately obtain the equilibrium price:

$$P^* = \frac{a - c}{b + d}$$

Having found the value of P we then need only to introduce this value in either of the two equations of the system to find the equilibrium quantity. If there is no mistake, the value of Q should turn out to be the same, regardless of the chosen equation. Let us introduce the value of P^* in the demand equation. We get the equilibrium quantity:

$$Q^* = a - bP^* = a - b\frac{(a - c)}{(b + d)}$$

$$Q^* = \frac{ad + cb}{b + d}$$

You now know how to find the market equilibrium price and quantity when you are given the demand and supply equations. Obviously, any change in the intercepts of the curves or in the slopes of the curves will modify the equilibrium values.

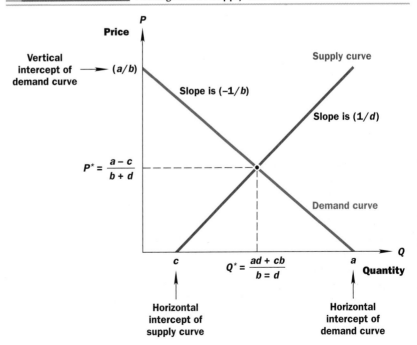

FIGURE 13   The Algebra of Supply and Demand

THE MACROECONOMY: AGGREGATE SUPPLY AND DEMAND

Macroeconomics is the headline-grabbing part of economics. When economic news appears on the front page of your daily newspaper or is reported on the nightly television news, you are most likely reading or hearing about some macroeconomic development in the national or world economy. The Bank of Canada has just raised interest rates. Inflation remains low. Jobs are scarce—or plentiful. The federal government's budget is in deficit. The euro is rising in value. These developments are all macroeconomic news stories. But what do they mean?

Part II begins your study of macroeconomics. It will first acquaint you with some of the major concepts of macroeconomics—things that you hear about every day, such as gross domestic product (GDP), inflation, unemployment, and economic growth (Chapters 5 and 6). Then it will introduce the basic theory that we use to interpret and understand macroeconomic events (Chapters 7 through 10). By the time you finish Chapter 10—which is only six chapters away—those newspaper articles should make a lot more sense.

5

AN INTRODUCTION TO MACROECONOMICS

Where the telescope ends, the microscope begins. Which of the two has the grander view?

VICTOR HUGO

By time-honoured tradition, economics is divided into two fields: *microeconomics* and *macroeconomics*. These inelegant words are derived from the Greek, where *micro* means something small and *macro* means something large. Chapters 3 and 4 introduced you to microeconomics. This chapter does the same for macroeconomics.

How do the two branches of the discipline differ? It is *not* a matter of using different tools. As we will see in this chapter, supply and demand provide the basic organizing framework for constructing macroeconomic models, just as they do for microeconomic models. Rather, the distinction is based on the issues addressed. For an example of a macroeconomic question, turn to the next page.

CONTENTS

ISSUE: *Was It the Conservatives' Fault?*

The worst pounding ever taken by a major Canadian federal party occurred in 1993, when the Conservatives, who had been in power for nine years by winning two elections in a row under the leadership of Brian Mulroney, decided to call an election. This occurred six months after the appointment of Kim Campbell as the new Conservative prime minister. The election resulted in the Conservatives, with Campbell at their helm, being trounced in the polls by Jean Chrétien and the Liberals, losing no fewer than 167 MPs and managing to salvage only 2 out of 303 seats in the entire country.

Mulroney and his government were highly unpopular at the time for several reasons. For example, Mulroney implemented a free trade agreement with the United States after his 1988 election and in 1991, he introduced the Goods and Services Tax (the GST), both of which the Liberals were promising to do away with. In addition, federal public finances were saddled with a large budget deficit; and Canada's rate of unemployment had risen to as high as 12 percent just a few months before the election, showing no sign of early improvement. The cherry topping, however, was Kim Campbell's statement, while on the election campaign trail, that the unemployment problem was too complex to be discussed during an election campaign.

Obviously the voters thought that Campbell was wrong: The economic policies pursued by the federal government can influence the number of jobs created or destroyed by the economy, so they are obviously relevant to an election campaign even though they are by no means the only influence.

DRAWING A LINE BETWEEN MACROECONOMICS AND MICROECONOMICS

In microeconomics, the spotlight is on *how individual decision-making units behave.* For example, the dairy farmers of Chapter 4 are individual decision makers; so are the consumers who purchase the milk. How do they decide which actions are in their own best interests? How are these millions of decisions coordinated by the market mechanism, and with what consequences? Questions such as these lie at the heart of microeconomics.

Although Plato and Aristotle might wince at the abuse of their language, microeconomics applies to the decisions of some astonishingly large units. The annual sales of such transnational enterprises of General Electric and General Motors, for example, exceed the total production of many nations. Yet someone who studies GE's pricing policies is a microeconomist, whereas someone who studies inflation in a small country like Monaco is a macroeconomist. The micro–macro distinction in economics is certainly not based solely on size.

What, then, is the basis for this long-standing distinction? The answer is that, whereas microeconomics focuses on the *decisions of individual units*, no matter how large, macroeconomics concentrates on *the behaviour of entire economies*, no matter how small. Microeconomists might look at a single company's pricing and output decisions. Macroeconomists study the overall price level, unemployment rate, and other things that we call *economic aggregates*.

Aggregation and Macroeconomics

An "economic aggregate" is simply an *abstraction* that people use to describe some salient feature of economic life. For example, although we observe the prices of gasoline, telephone calls, and movie tickets every day, we never actually see "the price level." Yet many people—not just economists—find it meaningful to speak of "the cost of living." In fact, the government's attempts to measure it are widely publicized by the news media each month.

Among the most important of these abstract notions is the concept of *domestic product*, which represents the total production of a nation's economy. The process by which real objects such as software, baseballs, and theatre tickets are combined into an abstraction called *total domestic product* is **aggregation**, and it is one of the foundations of macroeconomics. We can illustrate it by a simple example.

An imaginary nation called Agraria produces nothing but foodstuffs to sell to consumers. Rather than deal separately with the many markets for pizzas, candy bars, hamburgers, and so on, macroeconomists group them all into a single abstract "market for output." Thus, when macroeconomists announce that output in Agraria grew 10 percent last year, are they referring to more potatoes or hot dogs, more soybeans or green peppers? The answer is: They do not care. In the aggregate measures of macroeconomics, output is output, no matter what form it takes.

Aggregation means combining many individual markets into one overall market.

The Foundations of Aggregation

Amalgamating many markets into one means ignoring distinctions among different products. Can we really believe that no one cares whether the national output of Agraria consists of $800,000 worth of pickles and $200,000 worth of ravioli rather than $500,000 each of lettuce and tomatoes? Surely this is too much to swallow. Macroeconomists certainly do not believe that no one cares; instead, they rest the case for aggregation on two foundations:

1. Although the *composition* of demand and supply in the various markets may be terribly important for *some* purposes (such as how relative prices are determined and the diets people enjoy), it may be of little consequence for the economy-wide issues of growth, inflation, and unemployment—the issues that concern macroeconomists.

2. During economic fluctuations, markets tend to move up or down together. When demand in the economy rises, there is more demand for potatoes *and* tomatoes, more demand for artichokes *and* pickles, more demand for ravioli *and* hot dogs.

Although there are exceptions to these two principles, both seem serviceable enough as approximations. In fact, if they were not, there would be no discipline called macroeconomics, and a full-year course in economics could be reduced to a half-year. Lest this cause you a twinge of regret, bear in mind that many people believe that unemployment and inflation would be far more difficult to control without macroeconomics—which would be a lot worse.

The Line of Demarcation Revisited

These two principles—that the composition of demand and supply may not matter for some purposes, and that markets normally move together—enable us to draw a different kind of dividing line between microeconomics and macroeconomics.

In macroeconomics, we typically assume that most details of resource allocation are relatively unimportant to the study of the overall rates of inflation and unemployment. In microeconomics, we generally ignore inflation, unemployment, and growth, focusing instead on how individual markets allocate resources and distribute income.

To use a well-worn metaphor, a macroeconomist analyzes the size of the proverbial economic "pie," paying scant attention to what is inside it or to how it gets divided among the dinner guests. A microeconomist, by contrast, assumes that the pie is of the right size and shape, and frets over its ingredients and who gets to eat it. If you have ever baked or eaten a pie, you will realize that either approach alone is a trifle myopic.

Economics is divided into macroeconomics and microeconomics largely for the sake of pedagogical clarity: we can't teach you everything at once. But in reality, the crucial interconnection between macroeconomics and microeconomics is with us all the time. There is, after all, only one economy.

SUPPLY AND DEMAND IN MACROECONOMICS

Whether you are taking a course that concentrates on macroeconomics or one that focuses on microeconomics, the discussion of supply and demand in Chapter 4 served as an invaluable introduction. Supply and demand analysis is just as fundamental to macroeconomics as it is to microeconomics.

A Quick Review

Figure 1 shows two diagrams that should look familiar from Chapter 4. In Figure 1(a), we find a downward-sloping demand curve, labelled DD, and an upward-sloping supply curve, labelled SS. Because the figure is a multipurpose diagram, the "Price" and "Quantity" axes do not specify any particular commodity. To start on familiar terrain, first imagine that this graph depicts the market for milk, so the vertical axis measures the price of milk and the horizontal axis measures the quantity of milk demanded and supplied. As we know, if nothing interferes with the operation of the market, equilibrium will be at point E with a price P_0 and a quantity of output Q_0.

Next, suppose something happens to shift the demand curve outward. For example, we learned in Chapter 4 that an increase in consumer incomes might do that. Figure 1(b) shows this shift as a rightward movement of the demand curve from D_0D_0 to D_1D_1. Equilibrium shifts from point E to point A, so both price and output rise.

Moving to Macroeconomic Aggregates

Now let's switch from microeconomics to macroeconomics. To do so, we reinterpret Figure 1 as representing the market for an abstract object called *domestic product*—one of those economic aggregates that we described earlier. No one has ever seen, touched, or eaten a unit of domestic product, but these are the kinds of abstractions we use in macroeconomic analysis. The actual outputs that are seen, touched, or eaten

FIGURE 1

Two Interpretations of a Shift in the Demand Curve

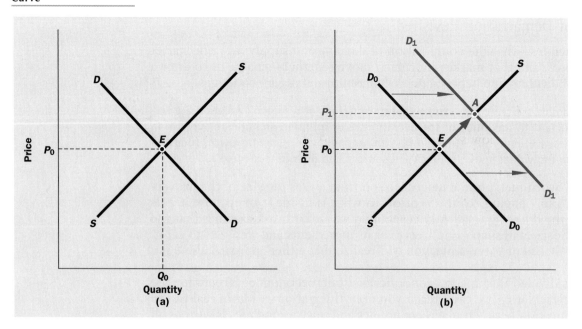

are merely heterogeneous commodities, such as apples and automobiles, that are produced and purchased by consumers in actual individual markets. However, we will abstract from the specific characteristics of these various commodities and treat them as individual components of domestic product. The way economists actually measure this aggregate output in an economy will be discussed later in this chapter and in Chapter 8.

Consistent with this reinterpretation, think of the price measured on the vertical axis as being another abstraction—the overall price index, or "cost of living."[1] Then the curve *DD* in Figure 1(a) is called an **aggregate demand curve**, and the curve *SS* is called an **aggregate supply curve**. We will develop an economic theory to derive these curves explicitly in Chapters 7 through 10. As we will see there, the curves have rather different origins from the microeconomic counterparts we encountered in Chapter 4.

> The **aggregate demand curve** shows the relationship between the quantity of domestic product that is being demanded and the overall price level.

> The **aggregate supply curve** shows the relationship between the quantity of domestic product that is being supplied and the overall price level.

Inflation

With this macroeconomic reinterpretation, Figure 1(b) depicts the problem of **inflation**. We see from the figure that the outward shift of the aggregate demand curve, whatever its cause, pushes the price level up. If aggregate demand keeps shifting out month after month, the economy is likely to suffer from inflation—meaning a sustained increase in the general price level.

Recession and Unemployment

The second principal issue of macroeconomics, recession and unemployment, also can be illustrated on a supply–demand diagram, this time by shifting the demand curve in the opposite direction. Figure 2 repeats the supply and demand curves of Figure 1(a) and in addition depicts a leftward shift of the aggregate demand curve from D_0D_0 to D_2D_2. Equilibrium now moves from point E to point B so that domestic product (total output) declines. This is what we normally mean by a **recession**—a period of time during which production falls and people lose jobs.

Economic Growth

Figure 3 illustrates macroeconomists' third area of concern: the process of economic growth. Here the original aggregate demand and supply curves are, once again, D_0D_0 and S_0S_0, which intersect at point E. But now we consider the possibility that *both* curves shift to the right over time, moving to D_1D_1 and S_1S_1, respectively. The new intersection point is C, and the blue arrow running from point E to point C shows the economy's growth path. Over this period of time, domestic product grows from Q_0 to Q_1.

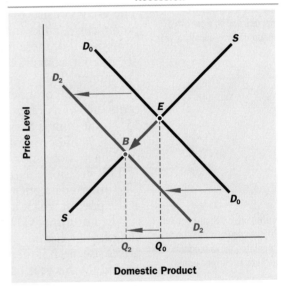

FIGURE 2   An Economy Slipping into a Recession

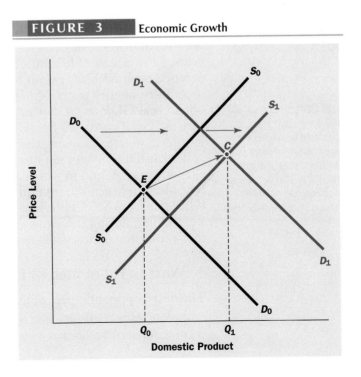

FIGURE 3   Economic Growth

---

[1] The appendix to Chapter 6 explains how such price indexes are calculated.

GROSS DOMESTIC PRODUCT

Inflation refers to a sustained increase in the general price level.

A **recession** is a period of time during which the total output of the economy declines.

Gross domestic product (GDP) is the sum of the money values of all final goods and services produced in the domestic economy and sold on organized markets during a specified period of time, usually a year.

Up to now, we have been somewhat cavalier in using the phrase *domestic product*. Let's now get more specific. Of the various ways to measure an economy's total output, the most popular choice by far is the **gross domestic product**, or **GDP** for short—a term you have probably encountered in the news media. GDP is the most comprehensive measure of the output of all the factories, offices, and shops in Canada. Specifically, it is the sum of the *money values* of all *final* goods and services *produced* in the *domestic* economy within the year.

Several features of this definition need to be underscored.[2] First, you will notice that:

We add up the money values of things.

Money as the Measuring Rod: Real versus Nominal GDP

The GDP consists of a bewildering variety of goods and services: computer chips and potato chips, tanks and textbooks, ballet performances and rock concerts. How can we combine all of these into a single number? To an economist, there is a natural way to do so: First, convert every good an d service into *money* terms, and then add up all of the money. Thus, contrary to the cliché, we *can* add apples and oranges. To add 10 apples and 20 oranges, first ask: How much *money* does each cost? If apples cost 20 cents each and oranges cost 25 cents, then the apples count for $2 and the oranges for $5, so the sum is $7 worth of "output." The market *price* of each good or service is used as an indicator of its *value* to society for a simple reason: *Someone* is willing to pay that much money for it.

This decision raises the question of what prices to use in valuing different outputs. The official data offer two choices. Most obviously, we can value each good and service at the price at which it was actually sold. If we take this approach, the resulting measure is called **nominal GDP**, or *GDP in current dollars*. This seems like a perfectly sensible choice, but it has one serious drawback as a measure of output: Nominal GDP rises when prices rise, even if there is no increase in actual production. For example, if hamburgers cost $2.00 this year but cost only $1.50 last year, then 100 hamburgers will contribute $200 to this year's nominal GDP whereas they contributed only $150 to last year's nominal GDP. But 100 hamburgers are still 100 hamburgers—output has not grown.

Nominal GDP, also called GDP at current prices, is calculated by valuing all outputs at current prices.

For this reason, government statisticians have devised alternative measures that correct for inflation by valuing goods and services produced in *different* years at the *same* set of prices. For example, if the hamburgers were valued at $1.50 each in both years, $150 worth of hamburger output would be included in GDP *in each year*. In practice, such calculations can be quite complicated, but the details need not worry us in an introductory course. Suffice it to say that, when the calculations are done, we obtain **real GDP** or *GDP in constant dollars*. The news media often refer to this measure as "GDP corrected for inflation." Throughout most of this book, and certainly whenever we are discussing the nation's output, we will be concerned with *real* GDP.

Real GDP, also called GDP at constant prices, is calculated by valuing outputs of different years at constant prices. Therefore, real GDP is a far better measure than nominal GDP of changes in total production.

The distinction between nominal and real GDP leads us to a working definition of a *recession* as a period in which *real* GDP declines. For example, during Canada's last recession (between the first quarter of 1990 and the first quarter of 1992), nominal GDP *rose* from $677 billion to $693 billion, but real GDP *fell* from $770 billion to $751 billion during the same time period. In fact, it has become conventional to say that a recession occurs when real GDP declines for two or more consecutive quarters.

What Gets Counted in GDP?

The next important aspect of the definition of GDP is that:

The GDP for a particular year includes only goods and services produced within the year. Sales of items produced in previous years are explicitly excluded.

---

[2] Certain exceptions to the definition are dealt with in the appendix to Chapter 8. Some instructors may prefer to take up that material here.

For example, suppose you buy a perfectly beautiful 1985 Thunderbird from a friend next week and are overjoyed by your purchase. The national income statistician will not share your glee. She counted that car in the GDP of 1985, when it was first produced and sold, and will never count it again. The same is true of houses. The resale values of houses do not count in GDP because they were counted in the years that the houses were built.

Next, you will note from the definition of gross domestic product that:

Only **final goods and services** count in the GDP.

The adjective *final* is the key word here. For example, when GM Canada in Oshawa, Ontario, buys auto parts from Magna International based in Aurora, Ontario, the transaction is not included in the GDP because GM Canada does not want the auto parts for itself. It buys them only to manufacture automobiles, which it sells to consumers. Only the automobiles are considered a final product. When GM Canada buys parts from Magna International, economists consider the auto parts to be **intermediate goods**. The GDP excludes sales of intermediate goods and services because, if they were included, we would wind up counting the same outputs several times.[3] For example, if the auto parts sold to automobile manufacturers were included in GDP, we would count the same auto part when it was sold to the carmaker and then again as a component of the automobile when it was sold to a consumer.

Final goods and services are those that are purchased by their ultimate users.

An intermediate good is a good purchased for resale or for use in producing another good.

Next, note that:

The adjective *domestic* in the definition of GDP denotes production within the geographic boundaries of Canada.

Some Canadians work abroad, and many Canadian companies have offices or factories in foreign countries. All of these people and businesses produce valuable outputs, but none of it counts in the GDP of Canada. (It counts, instead, in the GDPs of the other countries.) On the other hand, a number of foreigners and foreign companies produce goods and services in Canada. All that activity does count in our GDP.[4]

Finally, the definition of GDP notes that:

For the most part, only goods and services that pass through organized markets count in the GDP.

This restriction, of course, excludes many economic activities. For example, illegal activities are not included in the GDP. Thus, cigarette sales in convenience stores are part of GDP, but cigarette sales from smuggled merchandise are not. Garage sales, although sometimes lucrative, are not included either. The definition reflects the statisticians' inability to measure the value of many of the economy's most important activities, such as housework, do-it-yourself repairs, and leisure time. These activities certainly result in currently produced goods or services, but they all lack that important measuring rod—a market price.

This omission results in certain oddities. For example, suppose that each of two neighboring families hires the other to clean their house, generously paying $1,000 per week for the services. Each family can easily afford such generosity because it collects an identical salary from its neighbour. Nothing real has changed, but GDP goes up by $104,000 per year. If this example seems trivial, you may be interested to know that, according to one estimate made several years ago, Canada's GDP might be a stunning 42 percent higher if unpaid housework were valued at market prices and counted in GDP.[5]

---

[3] Actually, there is another way to add up the GDP by counting a portion of each intermediate transaction. This is explained in the appendix to Chapter 8.

[4] There is another concept, called gross *national* product, which counts the goods and services produced by all Canadians, regardless of where they work. For consistency, the outputs produced by foreigners working in Canada are not included in GNP. In practice, the two measures—GDP and GNP—are very close.

[5] William Chandler, "The Value of Household Work in Canada, 1992." National Income and Expenditure Accounts, Statistics Canada, Catalogue No. 13-001, April 1994, pp. xxxv-xlviii.

■ Limitations of the GDP: What GDP Is Not

Now that we have seen in some detail what the GDP *is*, let's examine what it *is not*. In particular:

> Gross domestic product is not a measure of the nation's economic well-being.

The GDP is not intended to measure economic well-being and does not do so for several reasons:

Only Market Activity Is Included in GDP   As we have just seen, a great deal of work done in the home contributes to the nation's well-being but is not counted in GDP because it has no price tag. One important implication of this exclusion arises when we try to compare the GDPs of developed and less developed countries. Canadians are always amazed to hear that the per-capita GDPs of the poorest African countries are less than $250 per year. Surely, no one could survive in Canada on $5 per week. How can Africans do it? Part of the answer, of course, is that these people are terribly poor. But another part of the answer is that:

> International GDP comparisons are vastly misleading when the two countries differ greatly in the fraction of economic activity that each conducts in organized markets.

This fraction is relatively large in Canada and relatively small in the poorest countries. So when we compare their respective measured GDPs, we are not comparing the same economic activities. Many things that get counted in the Canadian GDP are not counted in the GDPs of very poor nations because they do not pass through markets. It is ludicrous to think that these people, impoverished as they are, survive on what a Canadian thinks of as $5 per week.

A second implication is that GDP statistics take no account of the so-called underground economy—a term that includes not just criminal activities, but also a great deal of legitimate business that is conducted in cash or by barter to escape the tax collector. Naturally, we have no good data on the size of the underground economy. Observers at Statistics Canada believe that the market-based production of legal goods and services not covered by GDP represents, at most, 3 percent of GDP, and probably less than that. It could reach 4 percent of GDP if illegal activities are taken into account.[6] These estimates seem to be higher in the United States and in some other foreign countries.

GDP Places No Value on Leisure   As a country becomes richer and more productive, its citizens historically tend to take more and more leisure time. That was certainly the case in Canada during the first half of the twentieth century, when a standard workweek fell sharply from about 64 hours per week in Canadian manufacturing in 1901 to approximately 44 hours per week by 1950. However, over the last half century, that decline slowed down and has shown only a moderate fall since then, with standard workweeks in the Canadian manufacturing sector being roughly 37.5 hours nowadays. Since the length of the average workweek has fallen over the last 100 years, this has meant that growth in GDP over this period systematically *underestimated* the growth in national well-being. However, there is some evidence to suggest that this downward trend in hours of work has stopped and may even have reversed. (See the boxed feature "Are North Americans Working More?")

"Bads" as Well as "Goods" Get Counted in GDP   There are also reasons why the GDP *overstates* how well-off we are. Here are a few examples. Several major natural disasters struck Canada in a little over a decade, including the Red River Flood of April–May 1997 in Manitoba; the devastating ice storm of January 1998, which hit parts of Quebec, Ontario, and New Brunswick; Hurricane Juan, which reached the coasts of Nova Scotia in November of 2003; and the terrible wind storms that battered Vancouver Island in December of 2006. No one would doubt that these natural disasters made many Canadians worse off by destroying trees, as in Halifax's Point Pleasant Park and

---

[6] Philip Smith, "Assessing the Size of the Underground Economy: The Statistics Canada Perspective." Research paper, *Income and Expenditure Accounts* technical series, Statistics Canada, Catalogue no. 13-604-MIB, No. 28, May 1994.

Are North Americans Working More?

According to conventional wisdom, the workweek is steadily shrinking, leaving us with more and more leisure time to enjoy. But a 1991 book by economist Juliet Schor pointed out that this view was wrong: Americans were really working longer and longer hours. Her findings were both provocative and controversial at the time. But since then, the gap between the typical American and European workweeks has widened.

SOURCE: © Comstock Images/Getty Images

> In the last twenty years the amount of time Americans have spent at their jobs has risen steadily. . . . Americans report that they have only sixteen and a half hours of leisure a week, after the obligations of job and household are taken care of. . . . If present trends continue, by the end of the century Americans will be spending as much time at their jobs as they did back in the nineteen twenties.
>
> The rise in worktime was unexpected. For nearly a hundred years, hours had been declining. . . . Equally surprising, but also hardly recognized, has been the deviation from Western Europe. After progressing in tandem for nearly a century, the United States veered off into a trajectory of declining leisure, while in Europe work has been disappearing. . . . U.S. manufacturing employees currently work 320 more hours [per year]—the equivalent of over two months—than their counterparts in West Germany or France. . . . We have paid a price for prosperity. . . . We are eating more, but we are burning up those calories at work. We have color televisions and compact disc players, but we need them to unwind after a stressful day at the office. We take vacations, but we work so hard throughout the year that they become indispensable to our sanity.

Juliet Schor's provocative research on working hours in the United States was followed over a decade later by an important study published in 2003 by Statistics Canada researchers Andrew Heisz and Sébastien LaRochelle-Côté. These researchers analyzed the evolution of average annual working hours in both Canada and the United States and measured hours of work in a similar way in the two countries, using comparable survey data—that is, total annual working hours of the 16–69 age group divided by the working-age population, whether working or not, of that same age group. Heisz and LaRochelle-Côté found that, throughout the 1990s, Americans aged 16 to 69 worked increasingly more hours (when measured on a per working-age-person basis) than Canadians did. In 1979, average hours worked per working-age-person per year were 1,260 in Canada and 1,279 in the United States—approximately the same number of hours.

Two decades later in 2000, as can be seen from the accompanying chart, working hours had risen somewhat to 1,332 in Canada (a 5.7 percent increase) while, in the United States, the overall average had jumped to 1,455 hours (a 13.6 percent increase), with most of this gap emerging during the 1990s. Both countries had seen an increase in working hours, but the increase was much higher in the United States. In contrast, on the European continent, countries such as France and Germany saw average working hours drop significantly over those two decades.

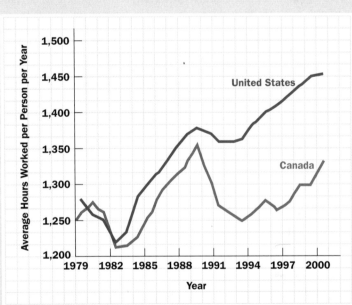

SOURCE: Statistics Canada, "Working Hours in Canada and the United States," *The Daily*, September 11, 2003. Retrieved from www.statcan.ca/Daily/English/030911/d030911b.htm

Average Hours Worked Per Person Per Year, Canada and the United States

SOURCES: Juliet B. Schor, *The Overworked American* (New York: Basic Books; 1991), pp. 1–2, 10–11; Andrew Heisz and Sébastien La Rochelle-Côté, *Working Hours in Canada and the United States*, Statistics Canada, Analytical Studies Branch Research Paper No. 209, September 2003.

Vancouver's Stanley Park, and damaging physical infrastructure, such as hydro lines and transmission towers during the ice storm. Yet these disasters almost certainly raised the GDP. Federal, provincial, and local governments spent more for cleanup and disaster relief, as well as for replanting trees and repairing infrastructure. Businesses and households also spent more to clean up and repair buildings. No one can imagine that Canadians were better off after any of these disasters, despite the additional GDP.

Wars represent an extreme example. Mobilization for a war fought on some other nation's soil normally causes a country's GDP to rise rapidly. But men and women serving in the military could be producing civilian output instead. Factories assigned to produce armaments could instead be making cars, washing machines, and televisions. A country at war is surely worse off than a country at peace, but this fact will not be reflected in its GDP.

Ecological Costs Are Not Netted Out of the GDP   Many productive activities of a modern industrial economy have undesirable side effects on the environment. Automobiles provide an essential means of transportation, but they also despoil the atmosphere. Factories pollute rivers and lakes while manufacturing valuable commodities. Almost everything seems to produce garbage, which creates serious disposal problems. None of these ecological costs are deducted from the GDP in an effort to give us a truer measure of the

Indexes of Well-Being

We pointed out earlier in this chapter that gross domestic product is *not* a measure of well-being. But social scientists are also concerned about welfare and social indicators, not just the amount of market-based economic activity. Over the past decades, many researchers, both at the community and the international levels, motivated by their conviction that GDP is inadequate to assess overall welfare, have designed indicators reflecting a combined measure of economic, health, and social well-being. Since these indicators reflect heterogeneous concerns, they are to some extent arbitrary. How can we add up, for instance, consumption per capita with life expectancy, or even something as subjective as happiness? Understandably, each researcher can come up with his or her own answer. Still, the quest to assess well-being continues. In Canada, there have been at least five such indicators, some of them even computed at Statistics Canada, but it is difficult to obtain up-to-date series.

Some indicators start from GDP and add or deduct various things such as the long-term costs of environmental damage (the greenhouse effect and ozone depletion) and of ecological damage (the harvesting of old-growth forests or the loss of wetlands). Also deducted are some consumer expenditures, such as the cost of commuting (the transport cost of going to work), lawyers' costs, spending on crime prevention (alarm systems), and the cost of family breakdown (two residences instead of a single one). The value of leisure, along with the value of unpaid housework and of volunteer work, is then added to this revised GDP estimate.

Other researchers may keep GDP as just one component of a series of indicators used to measure well-being. For instance, Lars Osberg of Dalhousie University and Andrew Sharpe of the Centre for the Study of Living Standards have developed an index of economic well-being for Canada where well-being depends on per-capita

SOURCE: Andrew Sharpe, *A Survey of Indicators of Economic and Social Well-Being* (Ottawa: Centre for the Study of Living Standards). Retrieved from www.csls.ca

consumption, income distribution, economic security, and a measure of additions to physical and human capital.

Community organizations sometimes set up quality-of-life indexes that take into account things as diverse as the number of new cancer cases, the ratio of low birth weight babies, the size of waiting lists (public housing, elderly long-term care), the number of hours with poor air quality, the number of social assistance beneficiaries, and the number of bankruptcies reported.

Perhaps the best-known cross-country social indicator in Canada is that of the United Nations Development Programme—the Human Development Index. The reason for its popularity is that, for more than six years in a row, the index ranked Canada as the best country in the world to live in, inducing much bragging by politicians and the media. The Human Development Index is composed of three indicators: a standard of living index, as measured by real GDP per capita; a longevity index, based on life expectancy at birth; and an education index, combining adult literacy and the overall enrollment ratio for primary, secondary, and postsecondary educational institutions. More recently this index has not been as kind to Canada: Canada's ranking has fallen to fourth place, as shown in the accompanying table.

2007/2008 United Nations Human Development Index	
1. Iceland	6. Sweden
2. Norway	7. Switzerland
3. Australia	8. Japan
4. Canada	9. Netherlands
5. Ireland	10. France

SOURCE: United Nations Human Development, Human Development Programme Report 2007. Human Development Index rankings. Retrieved from http://hdr.undp.org/en/media/lp1-hdr07-hdipr-e_final.pdf

net increase in economic welfare that our economy produces. Is this omission foolish? Not if we remember that national income statisticians are trying to measure economic activity conducted through organized markets, not national welfare.

Now that we have defined several of the basic concepts of macroeconomics, let us breathe some life into them by perusing Canadian economic history.

■ THE ECONOMY ON A ROLLER COASTER

▨ Growth, but with Fluctuations

The most salient fact about the Canadian economy has been its seemingly limitless *growth*; it gets bigger almost every year. Nominal gross domestic product in 2007 was $1,531 billion, more than 37 times as much as in 1961. In Figure 4, the black curve shows that extraordinary upward march. But, as the discussion of nominal versus real GDP suggests, a large part of this apparent growth was simply inflation. Because of higher prices, the *purchasing power* of each 2007 dollar was less than one-seventh of each 1961 dollar. Corrected for inflation, we see that *real* GDP (the red curve in the figure) was only five times greater in 2007 than in 1961.

Another reason for the growth of GDP is population growth. A nation becomes richer only if its GDP grows *faster* than its population. To see how much richer Canada has actually become since 1961, we must divide real GDP by the size of the population to obtain **real GDP per capita**—which is the blue line in Figure 4. It turns out that real output per person in 2005 was roughly 2.7 times as much as in 1961. That is still not a bad performance.

If aggregate supply and demand grew smoothly from one year to the next, as was depicted in Figure 3, the economy would expand at some steady rate. But Canadian economic history displays a far less regular pattern—one of alternating periods of rapid and slow growth that are called *macroeconomic fluctuations*, or sometimes just *business cycles*. In some time periods—seven since 1961, to be exact—real GDP actually declined. Such *recessions*, and their attendant problem of rising unemployment, have been a persistent feature of Candian economic performance—one to which we will pay much attention in the coming chapters.

Real GDP per capita is the ratio of real GDP divided by population.

| FIGURE 4 | Nominal GDP, Real GDP, and Real GDP per Capita, Since 1961 |

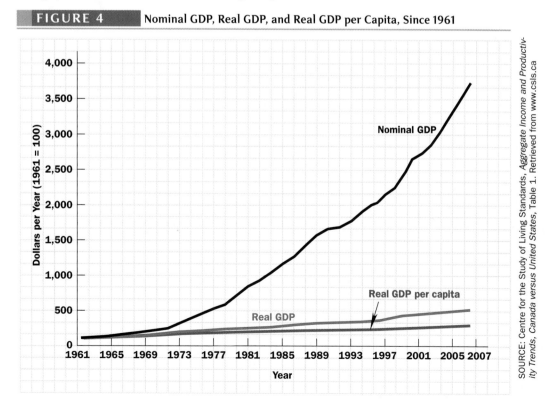

SOURCE: Centre for the Study of Living Standards, *Aggregate Income and Productivity Trends, Canada versus United States*, Table 1. Retrieved from www.csls.ca

FIGURE 5	The Growth Rate of Canadian Real Gross Domestic Product Since 1871

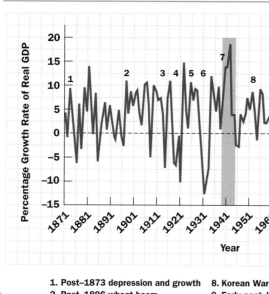

SOURCES: Created by the authors based on: Centre for the Study of Living Standards, *Aggregate Income and Productivity Trends Canada versus United States*, Table 1; F. H. Leacy (Ed.), *Historical Statistics of Canada*, 2nd ed. (Ottawa: Statistics Canada, 1983, Series F33-55); M. C. Urquhart, *Gross National Product, Canada, 1870–1926: The Derivation of the Estimates*, Table 1.6 (Kingston and Montreal: McGill–Queen's University Press, 1993).

1. Post–1873 depression and growth
2. Post–1896 wheat boom
3. World War I
4. Post–World War I recession
5. Roaring 1920s expansion
6. Great Depression
7. World War II
8. Korean War
9. Early post–World War II growth era
10. First oil crisis
11. Second oil crisis and 1981–1982 recession
12. 1990–1992 recession
13. Low inflation and steady growth decade

The bumps encountered along the Canadian economy's historic growth path stand out more clearly in Figure 5, which displays the same data in a different way and extends the time period back to 1871. Here we plot not the *level* of real GDP each year but, rather, its *growth rate*—the percentage change from one year to the next. Now the booms and busts that delight and distress people—and swing elections—stand out more clearly. For example, the fact that GDP growth was relatively high during the first term of Brian Mulroney's Conservatives (between 1984 and 1988) probably helped him to win a second term. Similarly, Jean Chrétien, the Liberal prime minister, easily won a third term in 2000, following a string of

Canadian Recessions Often Induced by U.S. Recessions

Canadian economic activity is heavily dependent on the economic health of the United States. This is not surprising, since the United States is by far our main trading partner, with Canada's GDP being approximately one-tenth of the U.S. GDP. The accompanying table shows the durations (and the dates) of each of the economic recessions, as assessed by Statistics Canada, that have occurred in this country since 1926 (you can check whether you were born during a recession!). It also shows the recessions that took place in the United States during that time period, according to the National Bureau of Economic Research.

We can see that several Canadian and American recessions occurred almost simultaneously, with the American recession usually preceding the Canadian one, but not always, as in 1990. Also, in some cases, our recessions were home-grown, while in other cases the Canadian economy avoided a recession while our neighbour did not, as in 2001. These recessions, which should correspond to periods of negative real growth, are somewhat difficult to decipher in Figure 5. This is either because the data used for the figure are annual statistics that hide the wide monthly variations within a year, or because Statistics Canada's revisions of some past data might have actually erased some of these recessions because of changes to the estimates of real GDP growth.

Dates of Economic Recessions in Canada and in the United States

Duration in Canada	PERIOD	
	Canada	United States
		October 1926 to November 1927
33 months	June 1929 to February 1933	August 1929 to March 1933
7 months	December 1937 to June 1938	May 1937 to June 1938
		February 1945 to October 1945
7 months	September 1947 to March 1948	
6 months	February 1949 to July 1949	November 1948 to October 1949
7 months	June 1951 to December 1951	
13 months	April 1953 to April 1954	April 1953 to April 1954
10 months	April 1957 to January 1958	August 1957 to April 1958
14 months	February 1960 to March 1961	April 1960 to February 1961
4 months	March 1970 to June 1970	December 1969 to November 1970
3 months	January 1975 to March 1975	November 1973 to March 1975
5 months	February 1980 to June 1980	January 1980 to July 1980
16 months	July 1981 to October 1982	July 1981 to November 1982
25 months	April 1990 to April 1992	July 1990 to March 1991
		March 2001 to November 2001
3 months	January 2008 to March 2008	

SOURCE: Philip Cross, "Tracking the Business Cycle: Monthly Analysis of the Economy at Statistics Canada, 1926–2001," *Canadian Economic Observer*, December 2001, Catalogue No. 11-010-PXB

years with strong economic growth. By contrast, as we pointed out in the introduction to this chapter, Kim Campbell and her Progressive Conservative government were wiped out during the 1993 election, following several years of slow or negative GDP growth, along with high rates of unemployment. Apart from this, it is also clear that the Canadian economy faced a much bumpier ride before World War II (1939–1945) than it did afterward.

Inflation and Deflation

The history of the inflation rate depicted in Figure 6 also shows more positive numbers than negative ones—more inflation than **deflation**. Although the price level has risen more than 18-fold since 1914, the upward trend is of rather recent vintage. Prior to World War II, Figure 6 shows periods of inflation and deflation, with little or no tendency for one to be more common than the other. Indeed, prices 30 years after Confederation were no higher than they were in 1867, and prices in 1940 were no higher than what they were in 1917, near the end of World War I. However, the figure does show some large gyrations in the inflation rate, including sharp bursts of price inflation during and immediately after the two world wars and dramatic deflations in the early 1920s and 1930s. Important deflations also occurred in the late 1870s, mid-1880s, and mid-1890s. By contrast, after another burst of inflation during the 1970s, inflation recently has been both low and stable, as you can see on the far right-hand side of the figure.

In sum, although both real GDP, which measures the economy's output, and the price level have grown a great deal over the past 140 years, neither has grown smoothly. The ups and downs of both real growth and inflation are important economic events that need to be explained. We need to build a macroeconomic theory designed to do precisely that. The remainder of Part II explains aggregate supply and develops a model of aggregate demand. Part III will explain the tools that the government uses to try to manage aggregate demand, and will detail the trade-offs encountered when dealing with inflation and output growth.

Deflation refers to a sustained decrease in the general price level.

| FIGURE 6 | The Inflation Rate in Canada since 1868 |

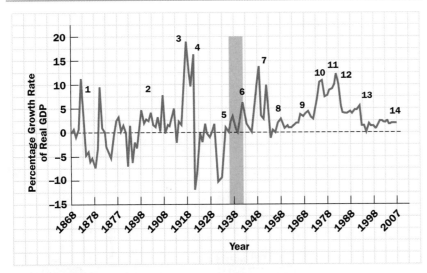

SOURCES: Calculated from the Statistics Canada Consumer Price Index for the years 1914–2006, CANSIM, series V737344; from the implicit price index for the years 1870–1914, M. C. Urquhart, *Gross National Product, Canada, 1870–1926: The Derivation of the Estimates*, Table 1.6 (Kingston and Montreal: McGill–Queen's University Press, 1993); and from a wholesale price index for the years 1867–1870, F. H. Leacy (Ed.), *Historical Statistics of Canada*, 2nd ed. (Ottawa: Statistics Canada, 1983, Series K33-43). Key time periods as shown in *Your Guide to the Consumer Price Index*, Statistics Canada, Catalogue No. 62-557-XPB, December 1996.

1. 1873–1896 stagnation
2. 1896–1914 wheat boom era
3. World War I inflation
4. Post–World War I recession
5. Great Depression
6. World War II and price controls
7. Explosion of pent-up demand
8. Korean War
9. Early post–World War II period of sustained growth
10. First oil crisis
11. Anti-Inflation Board
12. Second oil crisis and 1980s disinflation
13. 1990–1992 recession
14. Sustained low-inflation era

The Great Depression

As you look at Figures 5 and 6, the Great Depression of the 1930s is bound to catch your eye. The decline in economic activity from 1929 to 1933 indicated in Figure 5 was the most severe in Canada's history, and the rapid deflation in Figure 6 was almost as severe as the post-1873 and the post-World War I deflations. The Depression is but a dim memory now, but those who lived through it—including some of your grandparents and great-grandparents—will never forget it.

Human Consequences   Statistics often conceal the human consequences and drama of economic events, but in the case of the Great Depression, they stand as bitter testimony to its severity. The production of goods and services dropped an astonishing 30 percent, business investment dried up almost entirely by falling by a whopping 80 percent, household consumption spending fell by almost 20 percent, exports fell by about 30 percent, and the unemployment rate rose ominously from less than 3 percent in 1929 to about 20 percent in 1933—one person in five was jobless! From the data alone, you can conjure up pictures of soup lines, homeless beggars on street corners, closed factories, and relief camps where the unemployed could painfully eke out a meagre living (see the boxed feature "Federal Relief Camps and the 'On-to-Ottawa Trek'").

The Great Depression was centred in the United States but, given its international linkages, no country was spared its ravages. It literally changed the histories of many nations. In Germany, it facilitated the ascendancy of Nazism. In the United States, it

Federal Relief Camps and the "On-to-Ottawa Trek"

The October 1929 Great Crash of stock markets in Toronto, Montreal, New York, and other financial centres of the world caused tremendous hardship for both central Canadian industrial workers, many of whom lost their jobs, and western farmers, who faced a severe collapse of international grain prices. The official unemployment rate hovered around 20 percent of the labour force, and national income had fallen by over 30 percent by 1933 in relation to its 1929 peak level.

In the depth of the Great Depression, the newly elected Bennett Conservative government was under tremendous pressure to deal with the growing social unrest caused by mass unemployment. By 1933, the Bennett government took direct action and authorized, through the Department of National Defence, the creation of a Canada-wide system of work camps for many of the hundreds of thousands of unemployed transients who were threatening public order in Canadian cities. Through the Employment Service of Canada, unemployed men would be provided with bunkhouse facilities, three meals daily, medical care, and 20 cents per day for their labour. These men would work 44 hours per week in rural relief camps to clear brush and build basic infrastructure such as roads, bridges, and public buildings. Until their abolishment in 1936, 170,248 men had worked in these voluntary relief camps.

The harsh working conditions at these outposts made them fertile ground for trade union activity, especially since 20 cents a day was about one-tenth of the average industrial wage at the time. The most famous of these trade union actions was a strike of some 1,600 relief workers in British Columbia. In 1935, these strikers boarded railway freight cars and travelled eastward from the Pacific coast in an attempt to take their grievances to the government in Ottawa in what became known as the famous "On-to-Ottawa Trek." Prime Minister Bennett's excessively negative reaction to the "trekkers,"

which led to riots in Regina, may ultimately have caused the Conservative defeat, as public opinion swung away from Bennett. With the Liberal slogan "King or Chaos," Mackenzie King's Liberals came back to power in 1935, set up a federally run unemployment insurance program in 1940, and eventually laid the foundation for the post-World War II Canadian welfare state.

For more information, see R. B. Bryce, "The Canadian Economy in the 1930s: Unemployment Relief under Bennett and Mackenzie King," *Explorations in Canadian Economic History, Essays in Honour of Irene M. Spry,* D. Cameron (Ed.) (Ottawa: University of Ottawa Press, 1985).

SOURCE: Library and Archives Canada/J.G. Cote collection/C-029399. Retrieved from www.collectionscanada.ca/obj/026020/f1/c029399-v5.jpg

The "On-to-Ottawa Trek" getting under way in Kamloops, British Columbia, June 1935.

led and enabled Franklin D. Roosevelt to engineer and push through a host of political and economic reforms based on increased government intervention, commonly referred to as the "New Deal." It was largely those changes south of our border that pressured Canadian authorities to adopt a number of similar measures, many of which came to fruition during the early post-World War II period.

A Revolution in Economic Thought The worldwide depression also caused a much-needed revolution in economic thinking. Until the 1930s, the prevailing economic theory held that a capitalist economy occasionally misbehaved but had a natural tendency to cure recessions or inflations by itself. The roller coaster bounced around but did not run off the tracks.

John Maynard Keynes

But the stubbornness of the Great Depression shook almost everyone's faith in the ability of the economy to correct itself. In England, this questioning attitude led John Maynard Keynes, one of the world's most renowned economists, to write *The General Theory of Employment, Interest, and Money* (1936). Probably the most important economics book of the twentieth century, it carried a rather revolutionary message. Keynes rejected the idea that the economy naturally gravitated toward smooth growth and high levels of employment, asserting instead that if pessimism led businesses and consumers to curtail their spending, the economy might be condemned to years of stagnation.

In terms of our simple demand–supply framework, Keynes was suggesting that a shock, such as the Great Crash of the stock markets, could affect the overall behaviour of investors and firms and lead to an inward shift in demand across many sectors. As employment and incomes fall, household demand for goods and services will continue to decline. As Figure 2 (on page 95) shows, when generalized across all sectors of the economy, the consequence will be declining domestic product and deflation.

This doleful prognosis sounded all too realistic at the time. But Keynes closed his book on a hopeful note by showing how certain government actions—the things we now call monetary and fiscal policy—might prod the economy out of a depressed state. The lessons he taught the world then are among the lessons we will be learning in the rest of Part II and in Part III—along with many qualifications that economists have learned since 1936. These lessons show how governments can manage their economies so that recessions will not turn into depressions and depressions will not last as long as the Great Depression.

While Keynes was working on *The General Theory*, he wrote to his friend George Bernard Shaw that "I believe myself to be writing a book on economic theory which will largely revolutionize . . . the way the world thinks about economic problems." In many ways, he was right.

From World War II to 1973

The Great Depression finally ended when Canada entered World War II in 1939. Unlike during the Great Depression, when both Bennett and Mackenzie King feared increases in public spending, government spending almost immediately rose to extraordinarily high levels and gave a big boost to overall demand in the economy. Thus, **fiscal policy** was suddenly being used in a big way, thanks to such important ministers as C.D. Howe, who by the end of the war was nicknamed the "Minister of Everything" and who mobilized the Canadian economy for the war effort. The economy boomed, and the unemployment rate fell to as low as 1.4 percent by 1944.

The government's **fiscal policy** is its plan for spending and taxation. It can be used to steer aggregate demand in the desired direction.

Figure 1(b) on page 94 suggested that spending spurts such as this one should lead to inflation. But much of the *potential* inflation during World War II was contained by price controls; between 1941 and 1945, the Wartime Prices and Trade Board imposed a general ceiling on prices, wages, and rents. With prices held below the levels at which quantity supplied equalled quantity demanded (as suggested by Figure 3), shortages of consumer goods were common. Sugar and gasoline were strictly rationed. When controls were slowly lifted after the war, prices shot up as a result of the pent-up demand.

With the federal government's commitment to high employment in 1946, a period of strong growth marred by a few recessions after the war then gave way to the fabulous 1960s, a period of unprecedented—and noninflationary—growth that was credited to the success of the economic policies that Keynes had prescribed in the 1930s. For a while, it looked as if Canada could avoid both unemployment and inflation, as overall demand and supply expanded in approximate balance. But the optimistic verdicts proved somewhat premature.

As the economy reached high employment levels (with unemployment rates at 3.6 percent in 1966) and without the wartime price controls, Canada witnessed a creeping inflation that many analysts attributed to the Vietnam War. The high employment of the period, accompanied by increasing war expenditures, was putting upward pressure on wages and prices in the United States, with strong spillover effects on all of its trading partners internationally. Despite a short and mild recession in 1970, inflation continued during the early Trudeau years at levels higher than had been seen since the Korean War. Indeed, inflation worsened dramatically in 1973, mainly because of an explosion in food prices caused by poor harvests around the world.

The Great Stagflation, 1973–1984

In 1973, things started to become much worse for all oil-importing countries internationally, including Canada, which was both an oil importing and exporting country. A war between Israeli and Arab nations precipitated a quadrupling of oil prices by the Organization of the Petroleum Exporting Countries (OPEC). At the same time, continuing poor harvests in many parts of the globe pushed world food prices higher. Prices of other raw materials also skyrocketed.

Stagflation is inflation that occurs while the economy is growing slowly ("stagnating") or in a recession.

Monetary policy refers to actions taken by the Bank of Canada to influence aggregate demand by changing interest rates.

Much as suggested by Figure 7, an inward shift in supply arising from higher energy costs that affected virtually all sectors of the domestic economy pushed up the inflation rate to double-digit levels. At the same time, the Canadian economy slipped into a short recession at the beginning of 1975, and unemployment rose. With both inflation and unemployment unusually virulent in 1974 and 1975, the press coined a new term—**stagflation**—to refer to the simultaneous occurrence of economic *stag*nation and rapid in*flation*.

Policy makers in Canada became ever more concerned with fighting inflation, even at the cost of significantly lower growth and higher unemployment. The federal government implemented two policy measures in 1975 to bring down the inflation rate. The first of these was a restrictive **monetary policy** of what the Bank of Canada termed "monetary gradualism"—a policy of high interest rates—the effect of which was a slowdown in overall spending in the economy, thereby restraining demand. The second was a policy of wage and price controls administered by the Anti-Inflation Board between 1975 and 1978 that would further restrain the growth of costs, thus impacting on inflation via the supply side.

Thanks to a combination of these two factors and the lower overall growth rate of the economy, the inflation rate did slow down—but policy makers were frustrated yet again in 1979 by a second OPEC oil price shock. Hence, stagflation came roaring back with a vengeance in 1979, as inflation reached ever higher double-digit levels. In the belief that monetary policy was the only effective policy tool to combat inflation and following the lead of the Federal Reserve in the United States, the Bank of Canada brought interest rates to such excruciatingly high levels (in 1981, for instance, the 91-day treasury bill rate reached as high as 21 percent) that it essentially provoked the 1981–1982 "Great Recession." Inflation did come down, but only at the cost of double-digit mass unemployment not seen since the Great Depression.

FIGURE 7

The Effects of an Adverse Supply Shift

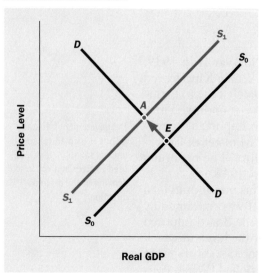

The Mulroney Years, 1984–1993

The 1981–1982 recession coincided with the end of the Trudeau era. Hence, at the time when John Turner replaced Pierre Trudeau at the helm of the Liberal Party and became prime minister in 1984, the economy was still hurting from the mass unemployment caused by restrictive monetary policy. At the same time, the low growth in the economy (which meant that government expenditures rose while government revenues fell) and the high interest rate policy of the Bank of Canada (which raised the servicing cost of government debt) destabilized the public finances to such an extent that all levels of government were confronted with ever-increasing budget deficits. It is no wonder that Canadian voters abandoned the Liberals and brought to power the Progressive Conservatives under the leadership of Brian Mulroney.

During Mulroney's first term in office, the Canadian economy followed a moderate growth path with a period of significant disinflation. However, by the time of the adoption of the Canada–U.S. Free Trade Agreement in 1989, the economy was showing signs of accelerating inflation that coincided with another spike in oil prices before the Persian Gulf War. With a strong commitment to price stability, John Crow, as newly appointed governor of the Bank of Canada, sought to rein in inflation with strong doses of high interest rates, much as his predecessor, Gerald Bouey, had done in 1981. Predictably, the outcome was the same: A deep recession between 1990 and 1992, which was then followed by what was termed at the time a "jobless recovery." Moreover, despite the attempts of the Conservatives to cut public spending and introduce new taxes, such as the Goods and Services Tax in 1991, government budget deficits and debt exploded. The Conservatives' record in relation to the economy was therefore such that, by the time Kim Campbell became leader of the Progressive Conservative Party and called an election in 1993, the Conservatives practically disappeared from the federal political scene for over a decade, until their merger with the former Canadian Alliance and the creation of the new Conservative Party of Canada in December 2003.

The Chrétien and Martin Era, 1993–2006: Deficit Reduction and the "New Economy"

Although Jean Chrétien had run on a platform to eliminate the Goods and Services Tax and do away with the Canada–U.S. Free Trade Agreement, the yawning budget deficit gave the new Liberal government an opportunity to refocus its agenda on slaughtering the so-called deficit dragon. With Paul Martin as federal minister of Finance, the anti-deficit strategy rested on two major pillars: restrictive fiscal policy (that is, major cuts in federal spending, particularly the significant cutting and reengineering of federal transfers to the provinces to support programs such as health care and social assistance) and expansionary monetary policy—a low interest rate policy made possible by the sharp decline in the inflation rate that resulted from the deep and prolonged 1990–1992 recession. The outcome of these changes was that, by the mid-1990s, federal finances went from the chronic deficits of the previous era to ever-increasing budget surpluses.

The Chrétien government did get a lot of assistance from the booming American economy during the Clinton administration. As the stock market soared (notably in the high-tech sectors), business investment perked up in the United States, and with the help of the North American Free Trade Agreement (NAFTA), Canadian exports grew to record levels as a share of GDP, with their prime destination being the United States. The upshot was high overall growth accompanied by a steady decline in Canada's unemployment rate throughout the latter half of the 1990s, both of which occurred in the context of a low inflation environment. Some optimists heralded the arrival of an exciting "New Economy"—a product of globalization and computerization—that somehow performed better than the economy of the past.

The new economy was certainly an alluring vision. But was it real? Most economists would answer: yes and no. On the one hand, advances in computer and information

The Effects of a Favourable Supply Shift

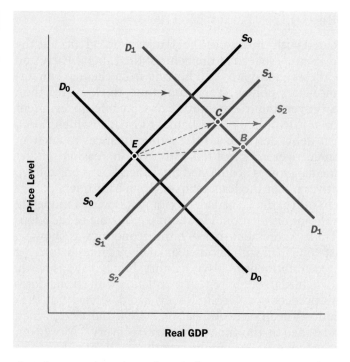

technology did seem to lead to faster growth in the second half of the 1990s. In that respect, Canada did get a "New Economy," largely shaped by the emerging technologies. But something perhaps more mundane also happened, associated with a particular alignment of factors—a major spurt in productivity arising from the high-tech sectors pushed overall supply significantly outward (as is shown in Figure 8) but without any concomitant growth in labour costs that would have otherwise offset it by shifting the supply curve upward. Hence, as demand grew, supply was growing almost as rapidly, thereby guaranteeing a low inflation environment brought about by favourable shifts in supply, not just to point C in Figure 3 on page 95, but also to point B in Figure 8.

By the latter half of 2000, this rapid growth had petered out in the United States with the collapse of the "dot-com" bubble, and the American economy went through a short recession in 2001. Despite the difficulties faced by our high-tech sector, the Canadian economy was less severely hit. Indeed, it has shown great resilience, despite the difficulties faced by our export sector after September 11, 2001. Much of this sustained growth has rested on the importance of consumer spending in the housing sector.

The Harper Years, 2006–: Domestic Tax Cuts and Global Finance

When the Conservatives came to power in January 2006 as a minority government, they inherited an economy that was experiencing solid growth. Consumer spending in the housing sector continued to expand rapidly and, during three consecutive federal budgets between 2006 and 2008, the Conservatives cut taxes significantly—the federal Goods and Services Tax, as well as corporate and personal income taxes. The effect was further stimulation of consumer spending and a lowering of Canada's unemployment rate to levels not seen in over three decades.

Mirroring somewhat the experience in the United States, this growth in household spending was accompanied by a phenomenal expansion in mortgage debt, which finally peaked when the U.S. mortgage market collapsed during 2007–2008; this collapse took its toll on the world economy. American mortgage companies for some time had been making a large number of subprime (risky) loans. When the growth in American housing prices started to slow down, soon followed by falling property prices, many borrowers were forced to default on their mortgage payments. This created a worldwide financial crisis in August 2007, as several banks and financial institutions suddenly discovered that some of their financial assets were based on these risky mortgages and that their value was now being questioned. Many banks and financial institutions around the world declared some heavy losses. As a result, bank lending became much more restrictive, as these lending institutions sought to remain liquid in times of financial crisis.

For a while during the latter half of 2007, it looked as if the financial crisis was under control. But by January 2008, it became clear that the United States was plunging deeper into recession, with its financial system facing serious meltdown. It was

ISSUE REVISITED: *Was It the Conservatives' Fault?*

As we noted at the start of this chapter, the weak economy proved to be one of the major issues of the 1993 federal election. The Canadian economy had been in a recession for no less than 25 months, from April 1990 to April 1992—the longest recession since the Great Depression of the 1930s. Despite a short recovery later in 1992, growth slowed down again in 1993. Before the election, rates of unemployment hovered around or above 11 percent, high rates that had not been experienced since the 1982–1984 period, when they led to the overturn of the Liberal government.

The Liberals did not do much better for several years after they took power in 1993, as unemployment rates remained at or near double-digit numbers, while growth rates remained low. There is little evidence that they could have done any better than the Conservatives under the circumstances. At the time, federal governments were less concerned about unemployment and more concerned about high inflation rates and government deficits. When the Liberals and Jean Chrétien took power, they put policies in place to reduce government deficits, partly by increasing taxes but mostly by reducing federal government expenditures. This, as we will see, normally has the effect of slowing down the economy, *all else being equal*. But the miraculous "New Economy," accompanied by low interest rates and a cheap Canadian dollar, negated that.

only by systematic intervention of the U.S. government, coupled with similar government actions internationally, that a collapse of the world financial system was averted in 2008. Interestingly, some of the Conservative tax cuts kicked in just around the time when the Canadian economy faced a slump in export demand, thereby somewhat stabilizing domestic spending. At the time of writing, Canada was experiencing a significant slowdown and facing gyrations in its exchange rate, but the Conservative Party was voted in, once more, as minority government.

THE PROBLEM OF MACROECONOMIC STABILIZATION: A SNEAK PREVIEW

This brief look at the historical record shows that our economy has not generally produced steady growth without inflation. Rather, it has been buffeted by periodic bouts of unemployment or inflation, and sometimes it has been plagued by both. We have also hinted that government policies may have had something to do with this performance. Let us now expand on and systematize this hint.

To provide a preliminary analysis of **stabilization policy**, the name given to government programs designed to shorten recessions and to counteract inflation, we can once again use the basic tools of aggregate supply and demand analysis. To facilitate this discussion, we have reproduced as Figures 9 and 10 two diagrams found earlier in this chapter, but we now give them slightly different interpretations.

Stabilization policy is the name given to government programs designed to prevent or shorten recessions and to counteract inflation (that is, to *stabilize* prices).

Combating Unemployment

Figure 9 offers a simplified view of government policy to fight unemployment. Suppose that, in the absence of government intervention, the economy would reach an equilibrium at point E, where the aggregate demand curve D_0D_0 crosses the aggregate supply curve SS. Now if the output corresponding to point E is too low, leaving many workers unemployed, *the government can reduce unemployment by increasing aggregate demand*. Subsequent chapters will consider in detail how this is done. But our brief historical review has already mentioned three methods: governments can spend more or reduce taxes ("fiscal policy"), and the Bank of Canada can lower interest rates ("monetary policy"). In the diagram, any of these actions would shift the demand curve outward to D_1D_1, causing equilibrium to move to point A.

FIGURE 9

Stabilization Policy to Fight Unemployment

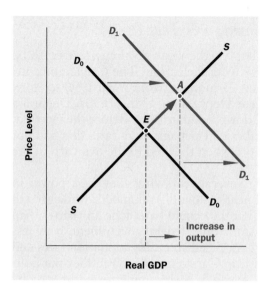

In general:

Recessions and unemployment are often caused by insufficient aggregate demand. When such situations occur, fiscal or monetary policies that successfully augment demand can be effective ways to increase output and reduce unemployment. But they could also raise prices.

Combating Inflation

The opposite type of demand management is called for when inflation is the main macroeconomic problem. Figure 10 illustrates this case. Here again, point E, the intersection of aggregate demand curve D_0D_0 and aggregate supply curve SS, is the equilibrium the economy would reach in the absence of government policy. But now suppose the price level corresponding to point E is considered "too high," meaning that the price level would be rising too rapidly if the economy were to move to point E. A government program that reduces demand from D_0D_0 to D_2D_2 (for example, a reduction in government spending) can keep prices down and thereby reduce inflation. Thus:

FIGURE 10

Stabilization Policy to Fight Inflation

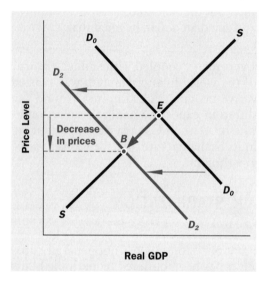

Inflation is frequently caused by aggregate demand racing ahead too fast. When this is the case, fiscal or monetary policies that reduce aggregate demand can be effective anti-inflationary devices. But such policies also decrease real GDP and raise unemployment.

This, in brief, summarizes the *intent* of stabilization policy. When aggregate demand fluctuations are the source of economic instability, the government can limit both recessions and inflations by pushing aggregate demand ahead when it would otherwise lag, and restraining it when it would otherwise grow too quickly.

Does It Really Work?

Can the government actually stabilize the economy, as these simple diagrams suggest? That is a matter of some debate.

We will deal with the pros and cons in Part III. But a look back at Figures 5 and 6 (pages 102 and 103) may be instructive right now. First, cover the portions of the two figures that deal with the period after 1939, the portions from the shaded area rightward in each figure. The picture that emerges for the 1871–1939 period is that of an economy with frequent and sometimes quite pronounced fluctuations. Now do the reverse. Cover the data before 1946 and look only at the post-war period. There is indeed a difference. The fluctuations of real GDP growth between 1871 and 1939 are clearly much wider than they have been since 1946 in Canada. Instances of negative real GDP growth are less common and business fluctuations look less severe. Although government policies have not achieved perfection, things do look much better.

When we turn to inflation, however, matters look rather different. While the fluctuations in the inflation rate appear less severe, gone are the periods of deflation and price stability that occurred before World War II. Prices seem only to rise. Some may say that this has been better for growth than an economy plagued by serious episodes of deflation. This may be true, but this quick tour through the data suggests that something has changed. The Canadian economy behaved differently from 1946 to 2006 than it did from 1871 to 1939.

Although controversy over this point continues, many economists attribute this shift in the economy's behaviour to lessons the government has learned about managing the economy—lessons you will be learning in Part III. When you look at the pre-war data, you see the fluctuations of an unmanaged economy that went through booms and recessions for "natural" economic reasons. The government did little about either. When you examine the post-war data, on the other hand, you see an economy that has been increasingly managed by government policy—sometimes successfully and sometimes unsuccessfully. Although the recessions are less severe, this improvement has come at a cost: The economy appears to be more inflation-prone than it was in the more distant past. These two changes in our economy may be connected. But to understand why, we will have to provide some relevant economic theory.

We have, in a sense, spent much of this chapter running before we have learned to walk—that is, we have been using aggregate demand and aggregate supply curves extensively before developing the theory that underlies them. That is the task before us in the rest of Part II.

SUMMARY

1. Microeconomics studies the decisions of individuals and firms, the ways in which these decisions interact, and their influence on the allocation of a nation's resources and the distribution of income. Macroeconomics looks at how entire economies behave and studies the pressing social problems of economic growth, inflation, and unemployment.

2. Although they focus on different subjects, microeconomics and macroeconomics rely on virtually identical tools. Both use the supply and demand analysis introduced in Chapter 4.

3. Macroeconomic models use abstract concepts like "the price level" and "gross domestic product" that are derived by combining many different markets into one. This process is known as **aggregation;** it should not be taken literally but rather viewed as a useful approximation.

4. The best specific measure of the nation's economic output is **gross domestic product (GDP)**, which is obtained by adding up the money values of all **final goods and services** produced in a given year. These outputs can be evaluated at current market prices (to get **nominal GDP**) or at some fixed set of prices (to get **real GDP**). Neither **intermediate goods** nor transactions that take place outside organized markets are included in GDP.

5. GDP measures an economy's production, not the increase in its well-being. For example, the GDP places no value on housework, other do-it-yourself activities, or leisure time.

On the other hand, even commodities that might be considered as "bads" rather than "goods" are counted in the GDP (for example, activities that harm the environment).

6. Canada's economic history shows steady growth punctuated by periodic **recessions**—that is, periods in which real GDP declined. Although the distant past included some periods of falling prices (**deflation**), more recent history shows only rising prices (**inflation**).

7. The Great Depression of the 1930s was the worst in Canadian history. It profoundly affected both our nation and countries throughout the world. It also led to a revolution in economic thinking, thanks largely to the work of John Maynard Keynes.

8. From World War II to the early 1970s, the Canadian economy exhibited steadier growth than in the past. Many observers attributed this more stable performance to the implementation of the **monetary** and **fiscal policies** (collectively called **stabilization policy**) that Keynes had suggested. At the same time, however, the price level seems only to rise—never to fall—in the modern economy. The economy seems to have become more "inflation-prone."

9. Between 1973 and 1992, the Canadian economy suffered through several serious recessions. In the first part of that period, inflation was also unusually virulent. This unhappy combination of economic stagnation with rapid inflation was nicknamed "**stagflation**." Since 1982, however, inflation has been low.

10. Canada enjoyed high growth in the late 1990s, and unemployment fell to its lowest level in 30 years by the early 2000s. Yet inflation also fell. One explanation for this happy combination of rapid growth and low inflation is that the **aggregate supply curve** shifted out unusually rapidly.

11. One major cause of inflation is that aggregate demand may grow more quickly than does aggregate supply. In such a case, a government policy that reduces aggregate demand may be able to stem the inflation.

12. Recessions often occur because aggregate demand grows too slowly. In this case, a government policy that stimulates demand may be an effective way to fight the recession.

KEY TERMS

Aggregation   93

Aggregate demand curve   95

Aggregate supply curve   95

Inflation   96

Recession   96

Gross domestic product (GDP)   96

Nominal GDP   96

Real GDP   96

Final goods and services   97

Intermediate good   97

Real GDP per capita   101

Deflation   103

Fiscal policy   105

Stagflation   106

Monetary policy   106

Stabilization policy   109

TEST YOURSELF

1. Which of the following problems are likely to be studied by a microeconomist and which by a macroeconomist?

   a. The rapid growth of Microsoft

   b. Why unemployment in the Canada rose from 1990 to 1991

   c. Why Japan's economy grew faster than the U.S. economy in the 1980s, but slower in the 1990s

   d. Why university tuition costs have risen so rapidly in recent years

2. Use an aggregate supply and demand diagram to study what would happen to an economy in which the aggregate supply curve never moved while the aggregate demand curve shifted outward year after year.

3. Which of the following transactions are included in gross domestic product, and by how much does each raise GDP?

   a. Smith pays a carpenter $25,000 to build a garage.

   b. Smith purchases $5,000 worth of materials and builds himself a garage, which is worth $25,000.

   c. Smith goes to the woods, cuts down a tree, and uses the wood to build himself a garage that is worth $25,000.

   d. The Jones family sells its old house to the Reynolds family for $200,000. The Joneses then buy a newly constructed house from a builder for $250,000.

   e. You purchase a used computer from a friend for $100.

   f. Your university purchases a new mainframe computer from IBM, paying $50,000.

   g. You win $300 at the Montreal casino.

   h. You make $300 in the stock market.

   i. You sell a used economics textbook to your university bookstore for $30.

   j. You buy a new economics textbook from your university bookstore for $60.

DISCUSSION QUESTIONS

1. You probably use "aggregates" frequently in everyday discussions. Try to think of some examples. (Here is one: Have you ever said, "The students at this university generally think . . ."? What, precisely, did you mean?)

2. Try asking a friend who has not studied economics in which year he or she thinks prices were higher: 1870 or 1900? 1920 or 1940? (In both cases, prices were higher in the earlier year.) Most young people think that prices have always risen. Why do you think they have this opinion?

3. Give some reasons why gross domestic product is not a suitable measure of the well-being of the nation. (Have you noticed newspaper accounts in which journalists seem to use GDP for this purpose?)

6

THE GOALS OF MACROECONOMIC POLICY

Unemployment is like a headache or a high temperature—unpleasant and exhausting but not carrying in itself any explanation of its cause.

WILLIAM HENRY BEVERIDGE (1879–1963), *CAUSES AND CURES OF UNEMPLOYMENT,* 1931

Lenin is said to have declared that the best way to destroy the Capitalist System was to debauch its currency. By a continuing process of inflation, governments can confiscate, secretly and unobserved, an important part of the wealth of their citizens.

JOHN MAYNARD KEYNES (1883–1946), *THE ECONOMIC CONSEQUENCES OF THE PEACE,* 1920

Inputs are the labour, machinery, buildings, and other resources used to produce outputs.

Outputs are the goods and services that the economy produces.

Someone once quipped that you could turn a parrot into an economist by teaching him just two words: supply and demand. Sure enough, economists think of the process of *economic growth* as having two essential ingredients:

- The first ingredient is the *supply side*. Given the available supplies of **inputs** like labour and capital, and the technology at its disposal, an economy is able to produce a certain volume of **outputs**, measured by GDP. This *capacity to produce* normally increases from one year to the next as the supplies of inputs grow and the technology improves. The supply side will be our focus in Chapters 7 and 10.
- The second ingredient is the *demand side*. How much of the capacity to produce is actually *utilized* depends on how many of these goods and services people and businesses want to *buy*. We begin building a theory of aggregate demand in Chapters 8 and 9.

CONTENTS

Corresponding to these two ingredients, and going beyond the obvious fact that the main goal of politicians is to get reelected, economists visualize a dual task for those who make macroeconomic policy. First, *policy should create an environment in which the economy can expand its productive capacity rapidly*, because that is the ultimate source of higher living standards. This first task is the realm of **growth policy**, and it is taken up in the next chapter. Second, *policy makers should manage aggregate demand so that it grows in line with the economy's capacity to produce*, avoiding as much as possible the cycles of boom and bust that we saw in the last chapter. This is the realm of *stabilization policy*. As we noted in the last chapter, inadequate growth of aggregate demand can lead to high *unemployment*, while excessive growth of aggregate demand can lead to high *inflation*. Both are to be avoided.

Thus, the goals of macroeconomic policy can be summarized succinctly as *achieving rapid but relatively smooth growth with low unemployment and low inflation*. Unfortunately, that turns out to be a tall order. In chapters to come, we will explain why these goals cannot be attained with machine-like precision, and why improvement on one front often spells deterioration on another. Along the way, we will pay a great deal of attention to both the *causes* of and *cures* for sluggish growth, high unemployment, and high inflation.

But before getting involved in such weighty issues of theory and policy, we pause in this chapter to take a close look at the three goals themselves. How fast can—or should—the economy grow? Why does a rise in unemployment cause such social distress? Why is inflation so loudly deplored? The answers to some of these questions may seem obvious at first. But, as you will see, there is more to them than meets the eye.

The chapter is divided into three main parts, corresponding to the three goals. An appendix explains how inflation is measured.

> **Growth policy** refers to government policies intended to make the economy grow faster in the long run.

▦ PART 1: THE GOAL OF ECONOMIC GROWTH

To residents of a prosperous society like ours, economic growth—the notion that standards of living rise from one year to the next—seems like part of the natural order of things. But it is not. Historians tell us that living standards barely changed from the Roman Empire to the dawn of the Industrial Revolution—a period of some 16 centuries! Closer in time, per-capita incomes have tragically declined in most of the former Soviet Union and some of the poorest countries of Africa in recent decades. Economic growth is *not* automatic.

Growth is also a very slow, and therefore barely noticeable, process. The typical Canadian will consume about 2.2 percent more goods and services in 2008 than he or she did in 2007. Can you perceive a difference that small? Perhaps not, but such tiny changes, when compounded for decades or even centuries, transform societies. During the second half of the twentieth century, for example, living standards in Canada increased by a factor of more than three—which means that your grandparents in the year 1951 consumed roughly 33 percent as much food, clothing, shelter, and other amenities as you do today. Try to imagine how your family would fare on one-third of its current income.

▪ PRODUCTIVITY GROWTH: FROM LITTLE ACORNS . . .

Small differences in growth rates make an enormous difference—*eventually*. To illustrate this point, think about the relative positions of five nations—Canada, the United States, the United Kingdom, Japan, and Uruguay—at two points in history: 1870 and 2001. In 1870, the United Kingdom was the preeminent economic and military power of the world. The Victorian era was at its height, and the sun never set on the British Empire, of which Canada was part. The United States was in no sense a major power, but was among the most prosperous countries in the world, as was Uruguay, which was much richer than Canada. Meanwhile, somewhere across the Pacific was an inconsequential and economically backward island nation called Japan.

The Wonders of Compound Interest

Growth rates, like interest rates, *compound* so that, for example, 10 years of growth at 3 percent per year leaves the economy *more than* 30 percent larger. How much more? The answer is 34.4 percent. To see how we get this figure, start with the fact that $100 left in a bank account for one year at 3 percent interest grows to $103, which is 1.03 × $100. If left for a second year, that $103 will grow another 3 percent—to 1.03 × $103 = $106.09, which is already more than $106. Compounding has begun.

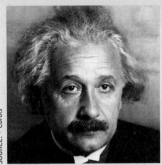

SOURCE: © Corbis

Notice that 1.03 × $103 is $(1.03)^2$ × $100. Similarly, after three years the original $100 will grow to $(1.03)^3$ × $100 = $109.27. As you can see, each additional year adds another 1.03 growth factor to the multiplication. Now to answer our original question, after 10 years of compounding, the depositor will have $(1.03)^{10}$ × $100 = $134.39 in the bank. Thus, her balance will have grown by 34.4 percent. By identical logic, an economy growing at 3 percent per year for ten years will expand 34.4 percent in total.

You may not be impressed by the difference between 30 percent and 34.4 percent. If so, follow the logic for longer periods. After 20 years of 3 percent growth, the economy will be 80.6 percent bigger (because $(1.03)^{20}$ = 1.806) , not just 60 percent bigger. After 50 years, cumulative growth will be 338 percent, not 150 percent. And after a century, it will be 1,822 percent, not just 300 percent. Now we are talking about large discrepancies! No wonder Einstein once said, presumably in jest, that compounding was the most powerful force in the universe.

The arithmetic of growth leads to a convenient "doubling rule" that you can do in your head. If something (the money in a bank account, the GDP of a country, and so on) grows at an annual rate of *g* percent, how long will it take to double? The approximate answer is 70/*g*, so the rule is often called "the Rule of 70." For example, at a 2 percent growth rate, something doubles in about 70/2 = 35 years. At a 3 percent growth rate, doubling takes roughly 70/3 = 23.33 years. Yes, small differences in growth rates can make a large difference.

Now fast forward 130 years. As can be seen in Figure 1, the rankings based on GDP per capita had changed substantially. By 2001, the United States had become the world's preeminent power, Canada and Japan had caught up with the United Kingdom, and Uruguay had fallen far behind. Obviously, some countries grew faster than others or else this stunning transformation of positions would not have occurred. But the magnitudes of the differences in growth rates may astound you.

Over the 130-year period, GDP per capita in the United States grew at a 1.9 percent compound annual rate, while the United Kingdom's growth rate was 1.5 percent—a difference of merely 0.4 percent per annum. During that time period, a growth rate of 2.5 percent propelled Japan from obscurity into the front rank of nations, while Uruguay moved from the front rank to obscurity, with an average growth rate of 1.0 percent. These numbers show vividly what a huge difference a one percentage point change in the growth rate can make, *if sustained for a long time*. This gives us some insight as to the future relative position of China if that country continues to grow at its current incredibly fast pace.

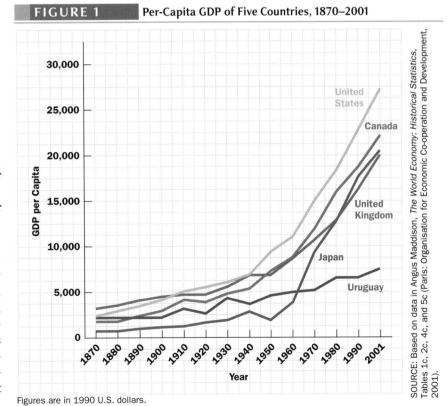

FIGURE 1   **Per-Capita GDP of Five Countries, 1870–2001**

Figures are in 1990 U.S. dollars.

SOURCE: Based on data in Angus Maddison, *The World Economy: Historical Statistics*, Tables 1c, 2c, 4c, and 5c (Paris: Organisation for Economic Co-operation and Development, 2001).

ISSUE: *Is Faster Growth Always Better?*

How fast should the Canadian economy, or any economy, grow? At first, the question may seem silly. Isn't it obvious that we should grow as fast as possible? After all, that will make us all richer. For the most part, economists agree; faster growth is generally preferred to slower growth. But as we will see in a few pages, further thought suggests that the apparently naive question is not quite as silly as it sounds. Growth comes at a cost. So more may not always be better.

Labour productivity is the amount of output a worker turns out in an hour (or a week, or a year) of labour. If output is measured by GDP, it is GDP per hour of work.

Economists define the *productivity* of a country's labour force (or **"labour productivity"**) as the amount of output a typical worker turns out in an hour of work. For example, if output is measured by GDP, productivity would be measured by GDP divided by the total number of hours of work. It is the growth rate of productivity that determines whether living standards will rise rapidly or slowly.

Only rising productivity can raise standards of living in the long run. Over long periods of time, small differences in rates of productivity growth compound like interest in a bank account and can make an enormous difference to a society's prosperity. Nothing contributes more to material well-being, to the reduction of poverty, to increases in leisure time, and to a country's ability to finance education, public health, environmental improvement, and the arts than its productivity growth rate.

■ THE CAPACITY TO PRODUCE: POTENTIAL GDP AND THE PRODUCTION FUNCTION

Potential GDP is the real GDP that the economy would produce if its labour and other resources were fully employed.

The **labour force** is the number of people holding or seeking jobs.

Questions like how fast our economy can or should grow require quantitative answers. Economists have invented the concept of **potential GDP** to measure the economy's normal capacity to produce goods and services. Specifically, potential GDP is the real gross domestic product (GDP) an economy *could* produce if its **labour force** were fully employed.

Note the use of the word *normal* in describing capacity. Just as it is possible to push a factory beyond its normal operating rate (by, for example, adding a night shift), it is possible to push an economy beyond its normal full-employment level by working it very hard. For example, we observed in the last chapter that the unemployment rate dropped as low as 1.2 percent under abnormal conditions during World War II. So when we talk about employing the labour force fully, we do not mean a measured unemployment rate of zero.

Conceptually, we estimate potential GDP in two steps. First, we count up the available supplies of labour, capital, and other productive resources. Then we estimate how much *output* these *inputs* could produce if they were all fully utilized. This second step—the transformation of inputs into outputs—involves an assessment of the economy's *technology*. The more technologically advanced an economy, the more out-

---

FIGURE 2

The Economy's Production Function

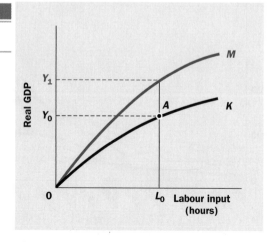

(a) Effect of Better Technology

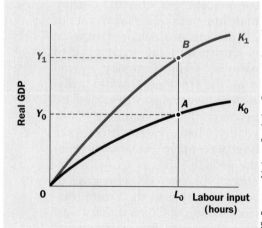

(b) Effect of More Capital

SOURCE: Bureau of Labour Statistics. Data pertain to the non-farm business sector.

put it will be able to produce from any given bundle of inputs—as we emphasized in Chapter 3's discussion of the production possibilities frontier.

To help us understand how technology affects the relationship between inputs and outputs, it is useful to introduce a tool called the **production function**—which is simply a mathematical or graphical depiction of the relationship between inputs and outputs. We will use a graph in our discussion.

For a given level of technology, Figure 2 shows how output (measured by real GDP on the vertical axis) depends on labour input (measured by hours of work on the horizontal axis). To read these graphs, and to relate them to the concept of potential GDP, begin with the black curve $0K$ in Panel (a), which shows how GDP depends on labour input, *holding both capital and technology constant*. Naturally, output rises as labour inputs increase as we move outward along the curve $0K$, just as you would expect. If the country's labour force can supply L_0 hours of work when it is fully employed, then *potential GDP* is Y_0 (see point A). If the technology improves, the production function will shift upward—say, to the blue curve labelled $0M$—meaning that the *same* amount of labour input will now produce *more* output. The graph shows that potential GDP increases to Y_1.

Now what about capital? Panel (b) shows two production functions. The black curve $0K_0$ applies when the economy has some lower capital stock, K_0. The higher, blue curve $0K_1$ applies when the capital stock is some higher number, K_1. Thus, the production function tells us that potential GDP will be Y_0 if the capital stock is K_0 (see point A) but Y_1 if the capital stock is K_1 instead (see point B). Once again, this relationship is just what you expect: The economy can produce *more* output with the *same* amount of labour if workers have more capital to work with.

You can hardly avoid noticing the similarities between the two panels of Figure 2: Better technology, as in Panel (a), or more capital, as in Panel (b), affects the production function in more or less the same way. In general:

> Either more capital or better technology will shift the production function upward and therefore raise potential GDP.

The economy's **production function** *shows the volume of output that can be produced from given inputs (such as labour and capital), given the available technology.*

THE GROWTH RATE OF POTENTIAL GDP

With this new tool, it is but a short jump to potential growth rates. If the *size* of potential GDP depends on the size of the economy's labour force, the amount of capital and other resources it has, and its technology, it follows that the *growth rate* of potential GDP must depend on:

- The growth rate of the labour force
- The growth rate of the nation's capital stock
- The rate of technical progress

To sharpen the point, observe that real GDP is, by definition, the product of the total hours of work in the economy times the amount of output produced per hour— what we have just called *labour productivity*:

GDP = Hours of work × Output per hour = Hours of work × Labour productivity.

For example, in Canada in 2007, using very rough numbers, GDP was about $1,500 billion and total hours of work per year were about 30 billion. Thus labour productivity was roughly $1,500 billion/30 billion hours = $50 per hour.

How fast can the economy increase its productive capacity? By transforming the preceding equation into growth rates, we have our answer: The growth rate of potential GDP is the *sum* of the growth rates of labour input (hours of work) and labour productivity:[1]

---

[1] You may be wondering about what happened to capital. The answer, as we have just seen in our discussion of the production function, is that one of the main determinants of potential GDP, and thus of labour productivity, is the amount of capital that each worker has to work with. Accordingly, the role of capital is incorporated into the productivity number. The numbers in this paragraph and the following one are drawn from *Aggregate Income and Productivity Trends Canada versus United States*, Table 4, Centre for the Study of Living Standards. Retrieved from www.csls.ca

TABLE 1

Annual Growth Rates of Real GDP in Canada

Year	Real GDP Growth
1961–1973	5.34 %
1973–1981	3.45
1981–1989	3.06
1989–1996	1.49
1996–2000	4.77
2000–2007	2.60

SOURCE: Centre for the Study of Living Standards, *Aggregate Income and Productivity Trends, Canada versus United States,* Table 4. Retrieved from www.csls.ca

Growth rate of potential GDP = Growth rate of labour input + Growth rate of labour productivity

In Canada in the 1960s, 1970s, and 1980s, total hours worked (labour input) increased at a rate of about 2 percent per year. Until 1973, the annual growth rate of labour productivity per hour worked was 3 percent, but it then fell to about 1.25 percent, implying an estimated growth rate of potential GDP in the 3.25 to 5.0 percent range. Since 1989, labour productivity per hour has grown at about 1.5 percent per year, while labour input grew at 1.2 percent per year on average. However, during this time period, these two growth rates were highly erratic, so it is not easy to estimate the growth rate of potential GDP in Canada. Given past experience, however, many economists would put it at around 3.0 or 3.5 percent.

Do the growth rates of potential GDP and actual GDP match up? The answer is an important one to which we will return often in this book:

> Over long periods of time, the growth rates of actual and potential GDP are normally quite similar. But the two often diverge sharply over short periods owing to cyclical fluctuations.

Table 1 illustrates this point with some Canadian data. Actual growth rates in real GDP were as high as 5.34 percent in the 1961–1973 period and 4.77 percent in the more recent 1996–2000 period, and they were as low as 1.49 percent between 1989 and 1996. Over the entire 45-year period, the average annual growth rate has been 3.6 percent, which corresponds to the 3.5 percent growth rate of potential output that we were talking about earlier. However, if we look only at the 1973–2007 period, this average annual growth rate falls to 2.95 percent. Thus, it is not clear whether 3.5 or 3.0 percent is the correct estimate of the growth rate of potential GDP. What is clear however is that the actual growth rates of GDP, even over periods as long as five or ten years, are often quite different from these averages, and that growth rates in the early 1990s were below potential, while growth rates in the late 1990s were above potential.

The next chapter is devoted to studying the *determinants* of economic growth and some *policies* that might speed it up. But we already know from the production function that there are two basic ways to boost a nation's growth rate—other than faster population growth and simply working harder. One is accumulating more capital. Other things being equal, a nation that builds more capital for its future will grow faster. The other way is by improving technology. When technological breakthroughs are coming at a fast and furious pace, an economy will grow more rapidly. We will discuss both of these factors in detail in the next chapter. First, however, we need to address the more basic question posed earlier in this chapter (see "Issue Revisited").

ISSUE REVISITED: *Is Faster Growth Always Better?*

It might seem that the answer to this question is obviously yes. After all, faster growth of either labour productivity or GDP per person is the route to higher living standards. But exceptions have been noted.

For openers, some social critics have questioned the desirability of faster economic growth as an end in itself, at least in the rich countries. Faster growth brings more wealth, and to most people the desirability of wealth is beyond question. "I've been rich and I've been poor. Believe me, honey, rich is better," singer Sophie Tucker once told an interviewer. And most people seem to share her sentiment. To those who hold this belief, a healthy economy is one that produces vast quantities of jeans, pizzas, cars, and computers.

Yet the desirability of further economic growth for a society that is already quite wealthy has been questioned on several grounds. Environmentalists worry that the sheer increase in the volume of goods imposes enormous costs on society in the form of pollution, crowding, and proliferation of wastes that need disposal. It has, they argue, dotted our roadsides with junkyards, filled our air with pollution, and poisoned our food with dangerous chemicals.

Some psychologists and social critics argue that the never-ending drive for more and better goods has failed to make people happier. Instead, industrial progress has transformed the satisfying and creative tasks of the artisan into the mechanical and dehumanizing routine of the assembly-line worker. Who are better off, the Americans who are working longer and longer hours, the Europeans who have much longer vacations and much shorter work hours, or the Canadians who are somewhere in between? The question is whether the vast outpouring of material goods is worth all the stress and environmental damage. In fact, surveys of self-reported happiness show that residents of richer countries are no happier, on average, than residents of poorer countries.

But despite this, most economists continue to believe that more growth is better than less. For one thing, slower growth would make it extremely difficult to finance programs that improve the quality of life—including efforts to protect the environment. Such programs are costly, and economic growth makes the additional resources available. Second, it would be difficult to prevent further economic growth even if we were so inclined; we cannot order people to stop being inventive and hard-working. Third, slower economic growth would seriously hamper efforts to eliminate poverty—perhaps within our own country and certainly throughout the world. Much of the earth's population still lives in a state of extreme want. These unfortunate people are far less interested in clean air and fulfillment in the workplace than they are in more food, better clothing, and sturdier shelters.

All that said, economists concede that faster growth is not *always* better. One important reason will occupy our attention later in Chapter 10 and Part III: an economy that grows too fast may generate inflation. Why? An economy will become inflationary when people's demands for goods and services expand faster than its capacity to produce them. So we probably do not want to grow faster than the growth rate of potential GDP, at least not for long.

Should society then seek the maximum possible growth rate of *potential* GDP? Well, maybe not. After all, more rapid growth does not come for free. We have noted that building more capital is one good way to speed the growth of potential GDP. But the resources used to manufacture jet engines and computer servers could be used to make home air conditioners and video games instead. Building more capital imposes an obvious cost on a society: the citizens must consume less today. This point does not constitute a brief against investing for the future. Indeed, most economists believe we need to do more of that. But we must realize that faster growth through capital formation comes at a cost—an *opportunity cost*. Here, as elsewhere, you don't get something for nothing.

▦ PART 2: THE GOAL OF LOW UNEMPLOYMENT

We noted earlier that actual GDP growth can differ sharply from potential GDP growth over periods as long as several years. These *macroeconomic fluctuations* have major implications for employment and unemployment. In particular:

> When the economy grows more *slowly* than its potential, it fails to generate enough new jobs for its ever-growing labour force. Hence, the **unemployment rate** *rises*. Conversely, GDP growth *faster* than the economy's potential leads to a *falling unemployment rate*.

The unemployment rate is the number of unemployed people, expressed as a percentage of the labour force.

High unemployment is socially wasteful. When the economy does not create enough jobs to employ everyone who is willing to work, a valuable resource is lost. Potential goods and services that might have been produced and enjoyed by consumers are lost forever. This lost output is the central economic cost of high unemployment, and we can measure it by comparing actual and potential GDP.

That cost is considerable. Table 2 summarizes the idleness of workers and machines, and the resulting loss of national output, for some of the years of low economic activity over the last 20 years. The second column lists the unemployment rate, and thus measures unused labour resources. The third lists the percentage of industrial capacity that

TABLE 2

The Economic Costs of High Unemployment

Year	Unemployment Rate	Capacity Utilization Rate	Real GDP Lost Due to Idle Resources
1991	10.3%	78.2%	3.4%
1992	11.2	78.8	3.7
1993	11.4	80.6	2.9
1996	9.7	82.0	1.9
1997	9.1	83.6	2.5
1998	8.3	84.6	1.3
2001	7.2	84.3	0.2
2003	7.6	84.2	0.5

SOURCES: Bank of Canada, Output Gap Measure, *Indicators of Capacity and Inflation Pressures for Canada* (retrieved from www.bankofcanada.ca), CANSIM Series V2062815, V4331081, copyright © 1995–2007, Bank of Canada. Permission is granted to reproduce or cite portions herein, if attribution is given to the Bank of Canada.

Canadian industrial producers were actually using, which indicates the extent to which plants and equipment went unused. The fourth column estimates the shortfall between potential and actual real GDP. We see that unemployment has cost the people of Canada as much as 3.7 percent reduction in their real incomes in 1992.

Of course, Table 2 presents only *estimates* of real GDP losses by the Bank of Canada, since potential output cannot be computed with much confidence. Also, many economists believe that the central bank tends to underestimate the size of lost output.

It should be noted that these losses cannot be recovered at a later stage. The labour wasted in 1991 or 1992 cannot be utilized in 2008.

THE HUMAN COSTS OF HIGH UNEMPLOYMENT

If these numbers seem a bit dry and abstract, think about the human costs of being unemployed. Years ago, job loss meant not only enforced idleness and a catastrophic drop in income, it often led to hunger, cold, ill health, even death. Here is how one unemployed worker during the Great Depression described his family's plight in a mournful letter to regional authorities:

> I have been out of work for over a year and a half. Am back almost thirteen months and the landlord says if I don't pay up before the 1 of 1932 out I must go, and where am I to go in the cold winter with my children? If you can help me please for God's sake and the children's sakes and like please do what you can and send me some help, will you, I cannot find any work. . . . Thanksgiving dinner was black coffee and bread and was very glad to get it. My wife is in the hospital now. We have no shoes to were [sic]; no clothes hardly. Oh what will I do I sure will thank you.[2]

Nowadays, unemployment does not hold quite such terrors for most families, although its consequences remain dire enough. Our system of Employment Insurance (discussed later in this chapter) has taken part of the sting out of unemployment, as have other social welfare programs that support the incomes of the poor. Yet most families still suffer painful losses of income and, often, severe noneconomic consequences when a breadwinner becomes unemployed.

Even families that are well protected by Employment Insurance suffer when joblessness strikes. Ours is a work-oriented society. A man's place has always been in the office or shop, and lately this has become true for women as well. A worker forced into idleness by a recession endures a psychological cost that is no less real for our inability to measure it. Martin Luther King Jr., the famous leader of the American civil rights movement, put it graphically: "In our society, it is murder, psychologically, to deprive a man of a job. . . . You are in substance saying to that man that he has no right to exist."[3] High unemployment has been linked to psychological and physical disorders, divorces, suicides, and crime.

It is important to realize that these costs, whether large or small in total, are distributed most unevenly across the population. In 2007, for example, the unemployment rate among all workers averaged 6.0 percent. But, as Figure 3 shows, workers between the ages of 25 and 44 who had eight years of schooling or less faced an unemployment rate of 14.1 percent. The situation for individuals between the ages of

---

[2] From *Brother, Can You Spare a Dime? The Great Depression 1929–1933*, by Milton Meltzer, p. 103. Copyright 1969 by Milton Meltzer. Reprinted by permission of Alfred A. Knopf, Inc.

[3] Quoted in Coretta Scott King (Ed.), *The Words of Martin Luther King* (New York: Newmarket Press, 1983), p. 45.

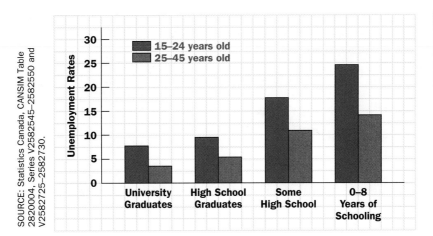

SOURCE: Statistics Canada, CANSIM Table 2820004. Series V2582545–2582550 and V2582725–2582730.

FIGURE 3

Unemployment Rates, Both Sexes, by Educational Attainment and Age Group, Canada, 2007

15 and 24 who had eight years of schooling or less was even worse: their unemployment rate reached 24.4 percent. By contrast, only 7.7 percent of workers between 15 and 24 who had a university degree faced unemployment, and workers between 25 and 44, also with a university degree, had unemployment rates as low as 3.7 percent.

> In good times and bad, workers with a high level of education experience the least unemployment, and those with a lower level of education suffer the most.

It is worth noting that unemployment in Canada has been about average among industrialized countries in recent years. For example, during 2007, when the Canadian rate of unemployment averaged 6.0 percent, the comparable figure for all OECD countries was 5.3 percent. Some European countries had high rates of unemployment, with 8.3 percent in France and Spain, 8.4 percent in Germany, and 9.6 percent in Poland. By contrast, the rates of unemployment in Australia and the United States were only 4.4 and 4.6 percent, respectively.[4]

■ COUNTING THE UNEMPLOYED: THE OFFICIAL STATISTICS

We have been using unemployment figures without considering where they come from or how accurate they are. The basic data come from Statistics Canada's monthly *Labour Force Survey*—of about 54,000 households throughout Canada. The census taker asks several questions about the employment status of each member of the household and, on the basis of the answers, classifies each person as *employed, unemployed,* or *out of the labour force.*

The Employed   The first category is the simplest to define. It includes everyone currently at work, including part-time workers. Although some part-timers work less than a full week by choice, others do so only because they cannot find suitable full-time jobs. Nevertheless, these workers are counted as employed, even though many would consider them "underemployed."

The Unemployed   The second category is a bit trickier. For persons not currently working, the survey first determines whether they are temporarily laid off from a job to which they expect to return. If so, they are counted as unemployed. The remaining workers are asked whether they actively sought work during the previous four weeks. If they did, they are also counted as unemployed.

Out of the Labour Force   But if they failed to look for a job, they are classified as *out of the labour force* rather than unemployed. This seems a reasonable way to draw the distinction—after all, not *everyone* wants to work. Yet there is a problem: research

---

[4] See *OECD Main Economic Indicators, Standardised Unemployment Rates.* Retrieved from www.stats.oecd.org

FIGURE 4

Canadian Labour
Market Participation,
Males and Females, 25
to 54, 1976–2007

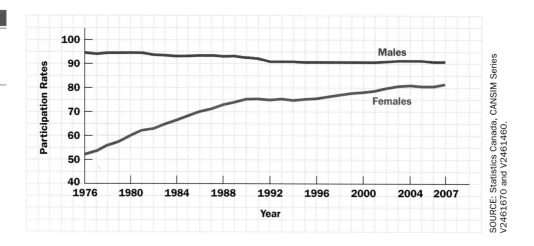

SOURCE: Statistics Canada, CANSIM Series V2461670 and V2461460.

A **discouraged worker** is
an unemployed person who
gives up looking for work
and is therefore no longer
counted as part of the
labour force.

shows that many unemployed workers give up looking for jobs after a while. These so-called **discouraged workers** are victims of poor job prospects, just like the officially unemployed. But when they give up hope, the measured unemployment rate—which is the ratio of the number of unemployed people to the total labour force—actually declines.

Involuntary part-time work, loss of overtime or shortened work hours, and discouraged workers are all examples of "hidden" or "disguised" unemployment. People concerned about such phenomena argue that we should include them in the official unemployment rate because, if we do not, the magnitude of the problem will be underestimated. Others, however, argue that measured unemployment overestimates the problem because, to count as unemployed, potential workers need only *claim* to be looking for jobs, even if they are not really interested in finding them.

Sticking with the official data, Figure 4 displays the participation rate of Canadians, that is, the percentage of the Canadian population in the labour force. This measure usually takes into account all Canadians aged 15 and older, but here we look at the evolution of the core working-age population—the participation rate of males and females between the ages of 25 and 54. It is interesting to note that the participation rate of women in the labour market keeps rising strongly—a truly important social phenomenon. By contrast, the participation rate of men shows a slight downward trend. This downward trend has been partially reversed lately, however, since the rate of unemployment in Canada has fallen recently to its lowest level in three decades.

■ TYPES OF UNEMPLOYMENT

Frictional unemployment is unemployment that
is due to normal turnover in
the labour market. It includes
people who are temporarily
between jobs because they
are moving or changing
occupations, or are unem-
ployed for similar reasons.

**Structural unemploy-
ment** refers to workers who
have lost their jobs because
they have been displaced by
automation, because their
skills are no longer in
demand, or because of similar reasons.

Providing jobs for those willing to work is one principal goal of macroeconomic policy. How are we to define this goal?

We have already noted that a zero-measured unemployment rate would clearly be an *incorrect* answer. Ours is a dynamic, highly mobile economy. Households move from one province to another. Individuals quit jobs to seek better positions or retool for more attractive occupations. These and other decisions produce some minimal amount of unemployment—people who are literally between jobs. Economists call this **frictional unemployment**, and it is unavoidable in our market economy. The critical distinguishing feature of frictional unemployment is that it is short-lived. A frictionally unemployed person has every reason to expect to find a new job soon.

A second type of unemployment can be difficult to distinguish from frictional unemployment but has very different implications. **Structural unemployment** arises when jobs are eliminated by changes in the economy, such as automation or permanent changes in demand. The crucial difference between frictional and structural unemployment is that, unlike frictionally unemployed workers, structurally unemployed workers cannot realistically be considered "between jobs." Instead, their skills

POLICY DEBATE

Does the Minimum Wage Cause Unemployment?

Elementary economic reasoning—summarized in the simple supply-demand diagram to the right—suggests that setting a minimum wage (*W* in the graph) above the free-market wage (*w* in the graph) must cause unemployment. In the graph, unemployment is the horizontal gap between the quantity of labour supplied (point *B*) and the quantity demanded (point *A*) at the minimum wage. Indeed, the conclusion seems so elementary that generations of economists took it for granted. The argument seems compelling. Indeed, earlier American editions of this book, for example, confidently told students that a higher minimum wage must lead to higher unemployment.

A recent empirical study, done in 2007 by Morley Gunderson of the University of Toronto, supports this example of elementary economics, claiming that a 25 percent raise of the Ontario minimum wage, from $8 to $10, would reduce the 1.2 million Ontario jobs that paid less than $10 by 7.5 to 15 percent, thus leading to a loss of 90,000 to 180,000 jobs. In addition, says Morley, a high minimum wage encourages youngsters to forgo schooling.

But some surprising economic research published in the 1990s cast serious doubt on this conventional wisdom. For example, economists David Card (a Canadian) and Alan Krueger compared employment changes at fast-food restaurants in New Jersey and nearby Pennsylvania after New Jersey, but not Pennsylvania, raised its minimum wage in 1992. To their surprise, the New Jersey stores did *more* net hiring than their Pennsylvania counterparts. Similar results were found for fast-food stores in Texas after the federal minimum wage was raised in 1991, and in California after the statewide minimum wage was increased in 1988. In none of these cases did a higher minimum wage seem to reduce employment—in contrast to the implications of simple economic theory. David Green, of the University of British Columbia, also found that minimum wage increases had hardly any negative effect on youth employment in four Canadian provinces between 1968 and 1997.

Why is this so? First, most minimum wage workers are in the service or retail industry, where businesses compete with other local businesses. Since they are all affected by a wage increase, the consequences on employment are negligible. Secondly, the supply and

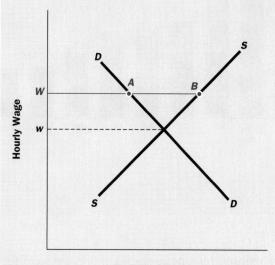

Number of Workers

demand apparatus does not fully reflect reality: Workers at the minimum wage level are not really in a position to bargain freely with their employers, so their wages are probably lower than they ought to be. In addition, there is some evidence that if there is a somewhat lower minimum wage for entry-level workers, say teenagers, then the consequences of higher minimum wages on the employment of young workers are truly negligible.

The research of Card and Krueger, and of others who reached similar conclusions in the 2000s, was controversial from the start, and remains so. Thus, a policy question that had been deemed closed now seems to be open: Does the minimum wage really cause unemployment?

Indeed, a 2003 survey of American economists showed that 25 percent of them answered this question in the negative, while only 45 percent gave a definite positive reply (compare this with the results of the survey of Canadian economists, which occurred before the new minimum wage studies, as outlined in Chapter 1, page 13). More recently, five Nobel Prize winners and six past presidents of the American Economics Association signed a statement stating that minimum wage increases "can significantly improve the lives of low-income workers and their families, without the adverse effects that critics have claimed."

Resolution of this debate is of more than academic interest. Increases in the minimum wage are now justified in part on the basis of new research suggesting that unemployment will not rise as a result of these increases. It is now much more difficult to deny demands for higher minimum wages on the grounds that those that the government wants to help would be most hurt by a new higher minimum wage. Take the case of Ontario, where a provincial NDP MP put forth a private bill asking that the minimum wage be set immediately at $10. Despite the Gunderson study mentioned above, the Liberal government decided to raise the minimum wage from $7.25 to $8 in 2007, with promises to raise it gradually up to $10.25 in 2010. Research can have consequences.

SOURCES: David Card and Alan Krueger, *Myth and Measurement: The New Economics of the Minimum Wage* (Princeton, NJ: Princeton University Press, 1995); Michael Goldberg and David Green, *Raising the Floor: The Social and Economic Benefits of Minimum Wages in Canada* (Ottawa: Canadian Centre for Policy Alternatives, 1999).

and experience may be unmarketable in the changing economy in which they live. They are thus faced with either prolonged periods of unemployment or the necessity of making major changes in their skills or occupations.

An instance of structural unemployment can be found in the widely different rates of unemployment in the various provinces and territories of Canada. As shown in Figure 5, unemployment rates in western Canada are systematically lower than they are in the Maritime provinces.

SOURCE: Statistics Canada, CANSIM Tables 282-0002 and 282-0055.

FIGURE 5

Annual Unemployment Rates by Province and Territory, Persons Aged 15 and Older, 2007

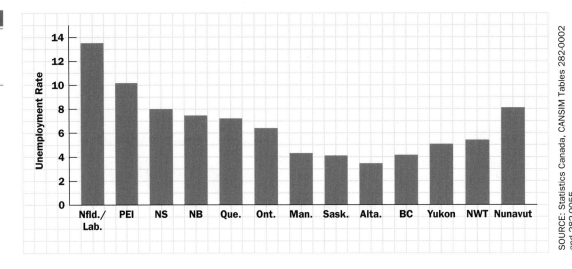

Cyclical unemployment is the portion of unemployment that is attributable to a decline in the economy's total production. Cyclical unemployment rises during recessions and falls as prosperity is restored.

The remaining type of unemployment, **cyclical unemployment**, will occupy most of our attention. Cyclical unemployment rises when the level of economic activity declines, as it does in a recession. Thus, when macroeconomists speak of maintaining "full employment," they mean limiting unemployment to its frictional and structural components—which means, roughly, producing at potential GDP. A key question, therefore, is: How much measured unemployment constitutes full employment?

■ HOW MUCH EMPLOYMENT IS "FULL EMPLOYMENT"?

Full employment is a situation in which everyone who is willing and able to work can find a job. At full employment, the measured unemployment rate is still positive.

How much employment is **full employment**? That is the question! After World War II, it seemed that the federal government could commit itself to pursue a policy of full employment with very low rates of unemployment. As late as 1970, the Economic Council of Canada (an agency that was created in 1963 by the federal government and then dissolved in 1993) estimated that full employment, or the full use of potential output, meant a rate of unemployment in the 3 to 4 percent range. But as the actual unemployment rate kept creeping up, and as achievement of this full employment target never even came close to being realized, estimates of what full employment meant kept changing. By the late 1970s, many economists claimed that full employment came at measured unemployment rates as high as 6 or 6.5 percent. These estimates were further revised upward when actual unemployment rates reached double digits in both the early 1980s and the early 1990s. In the late 1980s, researchers at the Bank of Canada thought that an 8 percent unemployment rate was good enough for full employment. While some economists thought that even such a high rate was unduly optimistic, others thought that the central bank was far too conservative.

This 8 percent estimate looked reasonable during most of the 1990s, with actual unemployment rates in Canada hovering at 8 percent or much higher. As it happened, real-world events decisively negated the notion that the full employment unemployment rate was that high. Since the spring of 1999, the actual rate of unemployment has been below 8 percent every month. The boom of the late 1990s pushed the unemployment rate down to 6.7 percent in the spring of 2000, and it fell below 6 percent in 2007. A similar phenomenon, on an even larger scale, was occurring in the United States, with the rate of unemployment falling as low as 3.9 percent in 2000. All of this has left economists guessing at what full employment might be. There is now much less confidence among economists in assessing a meaningful full employment unemployment rate.

■ EMPLOYMENT INSURANCE: THE INVALUABLE CUSHION

■ Features of the Program

One major reason why Canada's unemployed workers no longer experience the complete loss of income that devastated so many during the 1930s is our **Employment Insurance plan**—one of the most valuable institutional innovations to emerge from the trauma of the Great Depression.

The Unemployment Insurance Act was passed by Parliament in 1940. Because social welfare, and hence unemployment insurance, was one of the responsibilities assigned exclusively to the provinces in 1867, the 1940 Act required an amendment to the British North America Act and, therefore, the approval of all provinces. Unemployment insurance then became a federal responsibility. After periodic changes to the Act, the law became the Employment Insurance Act in 1996. Several provisions of the program were then modified, and further amendments have been made since (more than 20 bills over a period of 10 years!). Since 2008, the program has been run by a Crown corporation.

Employment Insurance has gradually been used as a means to provide other social programs. The Employment Insurance Act covers situations that go beyond unemployment, such as maternity and parental leaves. But the main target of the program remains laid-off workers. The generosity of the regular program depends essentially on five parameters that change through time according to political winds and ideological fads. These changes can have a substantial impact on the living standards of unemployed persons.

Maximum Annual Insurable Earnings   If you lose your $80,000 job, your unemployment benefits will be based on earnings of $40,000—the 2007 maximum annual insurable earnings (about $770 per week). The good news is that any labour income that you make beyond $40,000 is not liable to the 1.8 percent payroll tax that employees must pay to finance the Employment Insurance plan.

Amount of Weekly Benefits   Unemployed workers can get at most 55 percent of weekly insurable earnings, that is, in 2007, 55 percent of $770 or $423.50 per week, obviously not a large sum of money (indeed barely above the poverty line for a single individual in an urban dwelling). But most Employment Insurance recipients do not receive this amount, either because they did not earn the maximum weekly insurable amount while they were working, or because they had already claimed benefits in the past.

Qualification Requirements   The program is designed for people who are truly laid-off or who have reached the end of their fixed-term employment without having found another job. Individuals who quit without just cause or who are fired for misconduct, as well as recipients who refuse a job offer, are penalized by losing their benefits for a number of weeks.

Number of Work Hours Required to Qualify for Benefits   Not all workers have access to Employment Insurance, even though they have been laid-off or their contracts have expired, because applicants must have worked a certain number of hours during a 52-week qualifying period. Broadly speaking, applicants who come from regions where the rate of unemployment is low need many more hours of work (about 20 weeks of work at 35 hours per week) than applicants who come from regions where the rate of unemployment is high (about 12 weeks of 35 hours per week).

Number of Weeks for Payment Receipt   This depends both on the region's rate of unemployment and on the number of hours of insurable earnings accumulated by the applicant during the 52-week qualifying period. For instance, workers living in Alberta, where unemployment rates are below 6 percent, are eligible for only 14 weeks of benefits once they qualify; this is extended to 36 weeks of benefits if work hours exceed 1,820. At the other extreme, in areas where unemployment rates are above 16 percent, a qualified applicant would receive 32 weeks of Employment Insurance payments, and as much as 45 weeks of benefits could be granted in some cases.

> **Employment Insurance** is a government program that replaces some of the wages lost by eligible workers who lose their jobs.

▨ Implications of the Program

The importance of Employment Insurance to the unemployed is obvious. But significant benefits also accrue to citizens who never become unemployed. During recessions, billions of dollars are paid out in unemployment benefits. And because recipients probably spend most of their benefits, Employment Insurance limits the severity of recessions by providing additional purchasing power when and where it is most needed.

> The Employment Insurance system is one of several cushions built into our economy since 1935 to prevent another Great Depression. By giving money to those who become unemployed, the system helps prop up aggregate demand during recessions.

Although some say the Canadian economy is now "depression-proof," this should not be a cause for too much rejoicing, because the many recessions we have had since the 1950s—with the longest one in 1990–1992—amply demonstrate that we are far from "recession-proof."

The fact that Employment Insurance and other social welfare programs replace a significant fraction of lost income has led some skeptics to claim that unemployment is no longer a serious problem. But the fact is that Employment Insurance is just what the name says—an *insurance* program. And insurance can never prevent a catastrophe from occurring; it simply spreads the costs among many people instead of letting all of the costs fall on the shoulders of a few unfortunate souls. As we noted earlier, unemployment robs the economy of output it could have produced, and no insurance policy can insure society against such losses.

> Our system of payroll taxes and unemployment benefits spreads the costs of unemployment over the entire population. But it does not eliminate the basic economic cost.

In that case, you might ask, why not cushion the blow even more by making Employment Insurance much more generous, as many European countries have done and as it used to be in Canada? The answer is that there is also a downside to Employment Insurance. When unemployment benefits are very generous, people who lose their jobs may be less than eager to look for new jobs. The right level of Employment Insurance strikes an appropriate balance between the benefit of supporting the incomes of unemployed people and the cost of raising the unemployment rate a bit.

This issue has given rise to serious debate in Canada over the last two decades. From the 1970s until 1990, when coverage started to shrink, about 80 percent of the unemployed obtained Employment Insurance benefits. Now, because of the more stringent requirements of the program, only about 40 percent of the unemployed have access to regular Employment Insurance benefits. The numbers are even lower for unemployed women. The other unemployed persons must rely on provincial social welfare programs if they are self-employed, do not meet the plan qualification requirements, or have exhausted their benefits.

While some economists insist that the rules should be even tougher to induce people to work, others are in favour of a low, uniform entrance requirement throughout the country, arguing that in the current globalized world, plant closings and hence structural unemployment can occur in any part of Canada, even where unemployment rates are low (for instance in southern Ontario, when autoworkers are laid off). A 2000 study conducted by Stephen Jones of the University of McMaster, on behalf of Human Resources and Social Development Canada, showed that a less generous insurance program did reduce the duration of people's unemployment spells, but it did so by only a small amount.[5] In other words, a generous unemployment insurance program does induce some individuals to remain unemployed, but this effect remains relatively unimportant overall.

---

[5] See Stephen Jones, *EI Impacts on Unemployment Duration and Benefit Receipt*, Final Report (Ottawa: Human Resources Development Canada, October 2000). Retrieved from www.hrsdc.gc.ca/en/cs/sp/hrsdc/edd/reports/2000–000426/eiiudbre.pdf

PART 3: THE GOAL OF LOW INFLATION

Both the human and economic costs of inflation are less obvious than the costs of unemployment. But this does not make them any less real, for if one thing is crystal clear about inflation, it is that people do not like it.

With inflation very low for years now, inflation barely registers as a problem in national public opinion polls. But when inflation was high, it often headed the list—generally even ahead of unemployment. Surveys also show that inflation, like unemployment, makes people unhappy. Finally, studies of elections suggest that voters penalize the party that runs the government when inflation is high. The fact is beyond dispute: People dislike inflation. The question is, why?

INFLATION: THE MYTH AND THE REALITY

At first, the question may seem ridiculous. During inflationary times, people pay higher prices for the same quantities of goods and services they had before. So more and more income is needed just to maintain the same standard of living. Is it not obvious that this erosion of **purchasing power**—that is, the decline in what money will buy—makes everyone worse off?

> The **purchasing power** of a given sum of money is the volume of goods and services that it will buy.

Inflation and Real Wages

This would indeed be the case were it not for one very significant fact. The wages that people earn are also prices—prices for labour services. During a period of inflation, wages also rise. In fact, the average wage typically rises more or less in step with prices. Thus, contrary to popular myth, workers as a group are not usually victimized by inflation.

> The purchasing power of wages—what is called the **real wage rate**—is not systematically eroded by inflation. Sometimes wages rise faster than prices, and sometimes prices rise faster than wages. In the long run, wages tend to outstrip prices as new capital equipment and innovation increase output per worker.

> The **real wage rate** is the wage rate adjusted for inflation. Specifically, it is the nominal wage divided by the price index. The real wage thus indicates the volume of goods and services that the nominal wages will buy.

Figure 6 illustrates this simple fact. The blue line shows the rate of increase of prices in Canada for each year since 1946, and the red line shows the rate of increase of wages. The difference between the two, shaded in yellow in the diagram, indicates the rate of growth of *real* wages. Generally, wages rise faster than prices, reflecting

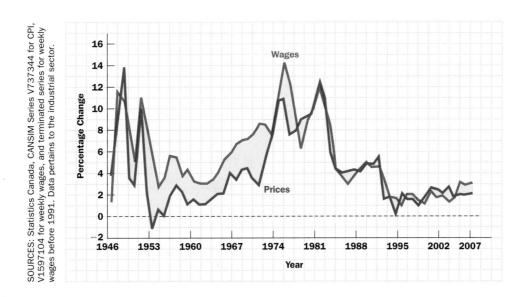

SOURCES: Statistics Canada, CANSIM Series V737344 for CPI, V1597104 for weekly wages, and terminated series for weekly wages before 1991. Data pertains to the industrial sector.

FIGURE 6

Rates of Change of Wages and Prices in Canada since 1946

Calculating the Real Wage: A Real Example

The *real* wage shows not how many dollars a worker is paid for an hour of work (that is called the *nominal* wage), but rather the *purchasing power* of that money. It indicates what an hour's worth of work can buy. As noted in the definition of the real wage in the margin, we calculate the real wage by *dividing* the nominal wage by the price level. The rule is:

$$\text{Real wage} = \frac{\text{Nominal wage}}{\text{Price level}}$$

Here's a concrete example. Between 2001 and 2007, the average hourly wage in Canada rose from $23 to $27, an increase of about 17 percent over six years. Sounds pretty good for Canadian workers.

But over those same five years, the Consumer Price Index, the most commonly used index of the price level, rose from 97.8 to 111.5 (with the index at 100 in 2002). This means that the real wages in the two years were:

$$\text{Real wage in 2001} = \$23 \times \frac{100}{97.8} = \$23.50$$

$$\text{Real wage in 2007} = \$27 \times \frac{100}{111.5} = \$24.20$$

for a 3 percent real increase over the six-year period, which is much less than the apparent nominal increase of 17 percent!

the steady advance of labour productivity; therefore, real wages rise. But this is not always the case; the graph shows several instances in which inflation outstripped wage increases.

The feature of Figure 6 that virtually jumps off the page is the way the two lines dance together. With two exceptions (first in 1946–1947 and more recently in 1978, at the end of the 1975–1978 Canadian experiment with wage and price controls designed to slow down inflation), wages normally rise rapidly when prices rise rapidly, and they rise slowly when prices rise slowly. But you should not draw any hasty conclusions from this association. It does not, for example, imply that rising prices *cause* rising wages or that rising wages *cause* rising prices. Remember the warnings given in Chapter 1 about trying to infer causation just by looking at data. But analyzing cause and effect is not our purpose right now. We merely want to dispel the myth that inflation inevitably erodes real wages.

Why is this myth so widespread? Imagine a world without inflation in which wages are rising 2 percent per year because of the increasing productivity of labour. Now imagine that, all of a sudden, inflation sets in and prices start rising 3 percent per year but nothing else changes. Figure 6 suggests that, with perhaps a small delay, wage increases will accelerate to 2 + 3 = 5 percent per year.

Will workers view this change with equanimity? Probably not. To each worker, the 5 percent wage increase will be seen as something he earned by the sweat of his brow. In his view, he *deserves* every penny of his 5 percent raise. In a sense, he is right because "the sweat of his brow" earned him a 2 percent increment in real wages that, when the inflation rate is 3 percent, can be achieved only by increasing his money wages by 5 percent. An economist would divide the wage increase in the following way:

Reason for Wages to Increase	Amount
Higher productivity	2%
Compensation for higher prices	3%
Total	5%

But the worker will probably keep score differently. Feeling that he earned the entire 5 percent raise by his own merits, he will view inflation as having "robbed" him of three-fifths of his just desserts. The higher the rate of inflation, the more of his raise the worker will feel has been stolen from him.

Of course, nothing could be farther from the truth. Basically, the economic system rewards the worker with *the same 2 percent real wage increment for higher productivity, regardless of the rate of inflation.* The "evils of inflation" are often exaggerated because people fail to understand this point. Indeed, examination of Figure 6 shows that ever since inflation rates have been brought down to around 2 percent, since 1991, wage gains have barely surpassed price inflation rates. In fact, since 1978, the rate of growth of Canadian average weekly wages has just kept pace with the rate of growth of the Consumer Price Index—a rather dismal situation for Canadian wage earners.

■ The Importance of Relative Prices

A related misperception results from failure to distinguish between a *rise in the general price level* and a change in **relative prices**, which is a rise in one price relative to another. To see the distinction most clearly, imagine first a *pure inflation* in which *every* price rises by 10 percent during the year, so that relative prices do not change. Table 3 gives an example in which the price of movie tickets increases from $6.00 to $6.60, the price of candy bars from 50 cents to 55 cents, and the price of automobiles from $9,000 to $9,900. After the inflation, just as before, it will still take 12 candy bars to buy a movie ticket, 1,500 movie tickets to buy a car, and so on. A person who manufactures candy bars in order to purchase movie tickets is neither helped nor harmed by the inflation. Neither is a car dealer with a sweet tooth.

> An item's **relative price** is its price in terms of some other item rather than in terms of dollars.

But real inflations are not like this. When there is 10 percent general inflation—meaning that the "average price" rises by 10 percent—some prices may jump 20 percent or more while others actually fall.[6] Suppose that, instead of the price increases shown in Table 3, prices rise as shown in Table 4. Movie prices go up by 25 percent, but candy prices do not change. Surely, candy manufacturers who love movies will be disgruntled because it now costs 15 candy bars instead of 12 to get into the theatre. They will blame inflation for raising the price of movie tickets, even though their real problem stems from the *increase in the price of movies relative to candy.* (They would have been hurt as much if movie tickets had remained at $6 while the price of candy fell to 40 cents.)

Because car prices have risen by only 5 percent, theatre owners in need of new cars will be delighted by the fact that an auto now costs only 1,260 movie admissions—just as they would have cheered if car prices had fallen to $7,560 while movie tickets remained at $6. However, they are unlikely to attribute their good fortune to inflation. Indeed, they should not. What has actually happened is that *cars became cheaper relative to movies.*

Because real-world inflations proceed at uneven rates, relative prices are always changing. There are gainers and losers, just as some would gain and others lose if relative prices were to change without any general inflation. Inflation, however, gets a bad name because losers often blame inflation for their misfortune, whereas gainers rarely credit inflation for their good luck.

TABLE 3			
Pure Inflation			
Item	Last Year's Price	This Year's Price	Increase
Candy bar	$0.50	$0.55	10%
Movie ticket	6.00	6.60	10
Automobile	9,000	9,900	10

TABLE 4			
Real-World Inflation			
Item	Last Year's Price	This Year's Price	Increase
Candy bar	$0.50	$0.50	0%
Movie ticket	6.00	7.50	25
Automobile	9,000	9,450	5

Inflation is not usually to blame when some goods become more expensive relative to others.

These two kinds of misconceptions help explain why respondents to public opinion polls often cite inflation as a major national issue, why higher inflation rates depress consumers, and why voters express their ire at the polls when inflation is high. But not all of the costs of inflation are mythical. Let us now turn to some of the real costs.

---

[6] How statisticians figure out "average" price increases is discussed in the appendix to this chapter.

INFLATION AS A REDISTRIBUTOR OF INCOME AND WEALTH

We have just seen that the *average* person is neither helped nor harmed by inflation. But almost no one is exactly average! Some people gain from inflation and others lose. For example, senior citizens trying to scrape by on pensions or other fixed incomes suffer badly from inflation. Because they earn no wages, it is little solace to them that wages keep pace with prices. Their pension incomes do not.[7]

This example illustrates a general problem. Think of pensioners as people who "lend" money to an organization (the pension fund) when they are young, expecting to be paid back with interest when they are old. Because of the rise in the price level during the intervening years, the unfortunate pensioners get back dollars that are worth less in purchasing power than those they originally loaned. In general:

Those who lend money are often victimized by inflation.

Although lenders may lose heavily, borrowers may do quite well. For example, homeowners who borrowed money from banks in the form of mortgages back in the 1960s, when interest rates were 5 or 6 percent, gained enormously from the surprisingly virulent inflation of the 1970s. They paid back dollars of much lower purchasing power than those that they borrowed. The same is true of other borrowers.

Borrowers often gain from inflation.

Because the redistribution caused by inflation generally benefits borrowers at the expense of lenders,[8] and because both lenders and borrowers can be found at every income level, we conclude that:

Inflation does not systematically steal from the rich to aid the poor, nor does it always do the reverse.

Why, then, is the redistribution caused by inflation so widely condemned? Because its victims are selected capriciously. No one legislates the redistribution. No one enters into it voluntarily. The gainers do not earn their spoils, and the losers do not deserve their fate. Moreover, inflation robs particular classes of people of purchasing power year after year—people living on private pensions, families who save money and "lend" it to banks, and workers whose wages and salaries do not adjust to higher prices. Even if the average person suffers no damage from inflation, that fact offers little consolation to those who are its victims. This is one fundamental indictment of inflation.

Inflation redistributes income in an arbitrary way. Society's income distribution should reflect the interplay of the operation of competitive markets and the purposeful efforts of government to alter that distribution. Inflation interferes with and distorts this process.

REAL VERSUS NOMINAL INTEREST RATES

But wait. Must inflation always rob lenders to bestow gifts upon borrowers? If both parties see inflation coming, won't lenders demand that borrowers pay a higher interest rate as compensation for the coming inflation? Indeed they will. For this reason, economists draw a sharp distinction between *expected* inflation and *unexpected* inflation.

What happens when inflation is fully expected by both parties? Suppose Diamond Jim wants to borrow $1,000 from Scrooge for one year, and both agree that, in the absence of inflation, a fair rate of interest would be 3 percent. This means that Diamond Jim would pay back $1,030 at the end of the year for the privilege of having $1,000 now.

If both men expect prices to increase by 6 percent, Scrooge may reason as follows: "If Diamond Jim pays me back $1,030 one year from today, that money will buy less

---

[7] The same is not true of Canada Pension Plan benefits, which are automatically increased to compensate recipients for changes in the price level.

[8] By the same token, *deflation* generally benefits lenders at the expense of borrowers, because the borrowers must pay back money of greater purchasing power.

than $1,000 buys today. Thus, I'll really be *paying him* to borrow from me! I'm no philanthropist. Why don't I charge him 9 percent instead? Then he'll pay back $1,090 at the end of the year. With prices 6 percent higher, this will buy roughly what $1,030 is worth today. So I'll get the same 3 percent increase in purchasing power that we would have agreed on in the absence of inflation and won't be any worse off. That's the least I'll accept."

Diamond Jim may follow a similar chain of logic. "With no inflation, I was willing to pay $1,030 one year from now for the privilege of having $1,000 today, and Scrooge was willing to lend it. He'd be crazy to do the same with 6 percent inflation. He'll want to charge me more. How much should I pay? If I offer him $1,090 one year from now, that will have roughly the same purchasing power as $1,030 today, so I won't be any worse off. That's the most I'll pay."

This kind of thinking may lead Scrooge and Diamond Jim to write a contract with a 9 percent interest rate—3 percent as the increase in purchasing power that Diamond Jim pays to Scrooge and 6 percent as compensation for expected inflation. Then, if the expected 6 percent inflation actually materializes, neither party will be made better or worse off by inflation.

This example illustrates a general principle. The 3 percent increase in purchasing power that Diamond Jim agrees to turn over to Scrooge is called the **real rate of interest**. The 9 percent contractual interest charge that Diamond Jim and Scrooge write into the loan agreement is called the **nominal rate of interest**. The nominal rate of interest is calculated by adding the *expected rate of inflation* to the real rate of interest. The general relationship is roughly:

Nominal interest rate = **Real interest rate** + **Expected inflation rate**

Expected inflation is added to compensate the lender for the loss of purchasing power that the lender expects to suffer as a result of inflation. Because of this:

> Inflation that is accurately predicted need not redistribute income between borrowers and lenders. If the *expected* rate of inflation that is embodied in the nominal interest rate matches the *actual* rate of inflation, no one gains and no one loses. However, to the extent that expectations prove incorrect, inflation will still redistribute income.[9]

It need hardly be pointed out that errors in predicting the rate of inflation are the norm, not the exception. Published forecasts bear witness to the fact that economists have great difficulty in predicting the rate of inflation. The task is no easier for businesses, consumers, and banks. This is another reason why inflation is so widely condemned as unfair and undesirable: it sets up a guessing game that no one likes.

> The **real rate of interest** is the percentage increase in purchasing power that the borrower pays to the lender for the privilege of borrowing. It indicates the increased ability to purchase goods and services that the lender earns.

> The **nominal rate of interest** is the percentage by which the money the borrower pays back exceeds the money that she borrowed, making no adjustment for any decline in the purchasing power of this money that results from inflation.

■ INFLATION DISTORTS MEASUREMENTS

So inflation imposes costs on society because it is difficult to predict. But other costs arise even when inflation is predicted accurately. Many such costs stem from the fact that people are simply unaccustomed to thinking in inflation-adjusted terms and so make errors in thinking and calculation. Many laws and regulations that were designed for an inflation-free economy malfunction when inflation is high. Here are some important examples.

■ Confusing Real and Nominal Interest Rates

People frequently confuse *real* and *nominal* interest rates. For example, most Canadians viewed the 14 percent one-year mortgage interest rates that banks charged in 1980 as scandalously high (until they reached 21 percent a year later!) but saw the 8 percent mortgage rates in 1992 as great bargains. In truth, with inflation around 2 percent in 1992 and 10 percent in 1980, the real interest rate in 1992 (about 6 percent) was

---

[9] *Exercise:* Who gains and who loses if the inflation turns out to be only 4 percent instead of the 6 percent that Scrooge and Diamond Jim expected? What if the inflation rate is 8 percent?

above real rates in 1980 (about 4 percent). Indeed, mortgage rates became really low both in nominal and real terms only in 2004, when they reached 4.3 percent in nominal terms while the inflation rate was 1.8 percent, thus yielding an approximate 2.5 percent in real terms.

The Malfunctioning Tax System

The tax system is probably the most important example of inflation illusion at work. The law does not recognize the distinction between nominal and real interest rates; it simply taxes *nominal* interest regardless of how much real interest it represents. Similarly, **capital gains**—the difference between the price at which an investor sells an asset and the price that she paid for it—are taxed in nominal, not real, terms. As a result, our tax system can do strange things when inflation is high. An example will show why.

Between 1982 and 2007, the price level roughly doubled. Consider some stock that was purchased for $20,000 in 1982 and sold for $35,000 in 2007. The investor actually *lost* purchasing power while holding the stock because $20,000 of 1982 money could buy roughly what $40,000 could buy in 2007. Yet because the law levies taxes on nominal capital gains, with no correction for inflation, the investor would have been taxed on the $15,000 *nominal* capital gain—even though she suffered a *real* capital loss of $5,000.

Many economists have proposed that this (presumably unintended) feature of the law be changed by taxing only real capital gains, that is, capital gains in excess of inflation. This has not been done. Instead, as some kind of approximation, Canadian governments include in taxable income only 50 percent of the capital gains that are realized when the asset is actually sold. This little example illustrates a pervasive and serious problem:

> Because it fails to recognize the distinction between nominal and real capital gains, or between nominal and real interest rates, our tax system levies high, and presumably unintended, tax rates on capital income when there is high inflation. Thus the laws that govern our financial system can become counterproductive in an inflationary environment, causing problems that were never intended by legislators. Some economists feel that the high tax rates caused by inflation discourage saving, lending, and investing—and therefore retard economic growth.

Thus, failure to understand that high *nominal* interest rates can still be low *real* interest rates has been known to make the tax code misfire, to impoverish savers, and to inhibit borrowing and lending. And it is important to note that *these costs of inflation are not purely redistributive.* Society as a whole loses when mutually beneficial transactions are prohibited by dysfunctional legislation.

Why, then, do such harmful laws stay on the books? The main reason appears to be a lack of understanding of the difference between real and nominal interest rates. People fail to understand that it is normally the *real* rate of interest that matters in an economic transaction because only that rate reveals how much borrowers pay and lenders receive *in terms of the goods and services that money can buy.* They focus on the high *nominal* interest rates caused by inflation, even when these rates correspond to low real interest rates.

> The difference between real and nominal interest rates, and the fact that the real rate matters economically whereas the nominal rate is often politically significant, are matters that are of the utmost importance and yet are understood by very few people—including many who make public policy decisions.

OTHER COSTS OF INFLATION

Another cost of inflation is that rapidly changing prices make it risky to enter into long-term contracts. In an extremely severe inflation, the "long term" may be only a few days from now. But even moderate inflations can have remarkable effects on long-term loans. Suppose a corporation wants to borrow $1 million to finance the purchase

A **capital gain** is the difference between the price at which an asset is sold and the price at which it was bought.

of some new equipment and needs the loan for 20 years. If inflation averages 2 percent over this period, the $1 million it repays at the end of 20 years will be worth $672,971 in today's purchasing power. But if inflation averages 5 percent instead, it will be worth only $376,889.

Lending or borrowing for this long a period is obviously a big gamble. With the stakes so high, the outcome may be that neither lenders nor borrowers want to get involved in long-term contracts. But without long-term loans, business investment may become impossible. The economy may stagnate.

Inflation also makes life difficult for the shopper. You probably have a group of stores that you habitually patronize because they carry the items you want to buy at (roughly) the prices you want to pay. This knowledge saves you a great deal of time and energy. But when prices are changing rapidly, your list quickly becomes obsolete. You return to your favourite clothing store to find that the price of jeans has risen drastically. Should you buy? Should you shop around at other stores? Will they have also raised their prices? Business firms have precisely the same problem with their suppliers. Rising prices force them to shop around more, which imposes costs on the firms and, more generally, reduces the efficiency of the entire economy.

■ THE COSTS OF LOW VERSUS HIGH INFLATION

The preceding litany of the costs of inflation alerts us to one very important fact: *Predictable inflation is far less burdensome than unpredictable inflation*. When is inflation most predictable? When it proceeds year after year at a modest and more or less steady rate. Thus, the *variability of the inflation rate* is a crucial factor. Inflation of 3 percent per year for three consecutive years will exact lower social costs than inflation that is 2 percent in the first year, zero in the second year, and 7 percent in the third year. In general:

Steady inflation is more predictable than variable inflation and therefore has smaller social and economic costs.

But the *average level of inflation* also matters. Partly because of the inflation illusions mentioned earlier and partly because of the more rapid breakdown in normal customer relationships that we have just mentioned, steady inflation at 6 percent per year is more damaging than steady inflation at 3 percent per year.

High inflation is more damaging than low inflation because it creates more uncertainty in the economy, thus leading people to confuse absolute price changes with relative price changes. Since resource allocation and decisions in market economies ought to be guided by relative prices, which measure relative scarcities, being confused about these relative prices induces agents to take mistaken and inefficient decisions. Higher inflation rates, along with their associated increased variability, generate more errors in the assessment of relative price changes, and thus may lead to slower productivity growth.

What is at issue among economists of various persuasions is the importance of the economic costs of these mistaken decisions. Economists distinguish between *low inflation*, which is a modest economic problem, and *high inflation*, which can be a devastating one, partly on the basis of the average level of inflation and partly on its variability. If inflation remains steady and low, prices may rise for a long time, but at a moderate and fairly constant pace, allowing people to adapt. For example, annual inflation in Canada has been remarkably steady since 1992, never dropping below 0.2 percent nor rising above 3 percent until the summer of 2008.

Very high inflations typically last for short periods of time and are often marked by highly variable inflation rates from month to month or year to year. In recent decades, for example, countries ranging from Argentina to Israel to Russia have experienced bouts of inflation exceeding 100 percent or even 1,000 percent per year. (See "Hyperinflation in Zimbabwe" on the next page.) Each of these episodes severely disrupted the affected country's economy.

Hyperinflation in Zimbabwe

Whereas mild inflation is barely noticeable in everyday life, hyperinflation makes all sorts of normal activities more difficult and transforms a society in strange and unexpected ways. The inflation rate in Zimbabwe is expected to reach between 1 million and 500 million percent per year in October 2008. In May 2008, ATMs were being emptied after only four or five customers had used them, so the monetary authorities were obliged to introduce ever-larger bank note denominations. Customers had to carry 1 billion Zimbabwe dollars to purchase even a small amount of coffee. The following is a BBC report that summarizes the situation.

SOURCE: AFP/Getty Images

"Prices are now doubling every week instead of every month and it is hard to see how we can survive to the end of June or how an election will be feasible at all if things continue to deteriorate at this pace," said Harare economist John Robertson.

This is the fourth set of new banknotes to be introduced this year. At independence in 1980, one Zimbabwe dollar was nearly at par with the U.S. dollar. Just one in five of the adult population is believed to have a formal job and some three million people have left the country for a new life in South Africa. The economy has been in trouble for several years, with supplies of basic foodstuffs, cooking oil and petrol all running low. The government has also suspended import duty on some basic goods, such as cooking oil, rice and soap in a bid to counter inflation.

The central bank of Zimbabwe has issued a 500 million Zimbabwe dollar banknote, worth US$2, to try to ease cash shortages amid the world's highest rate of inflation. The previous highest denomination note was for Z$250 million, issued 10 days ago. One economist said prices now double every week.

SOURCE: Adapted from BBC News online report, May 15, 2008. Retrieved from http://news.bbc.co.uk/1/hi/world/africa/7402943.stm. Reprinted by permission.

The German hyperinflation after World War I is perhaps the most famous episode of runaway inflation. Between December 1922 and November 1923, when a hard-nosed reform program finally broke the spiral, wholesale prices in Germany increased by almost 100 million percent! But even this experience was dwarfed by the great Hungarian inflation of 1945–1946, the greatest inflation of them all. For a period of one year, the *monthly* rate of inflation averaged about 20,000 percent. In the final month, the price level skyrocketed 42 quadrillion percent!

If you review the costs of inflation that have been discussed in this chapter, you will see why the distinction between low and high inflation is so fundamental. Many economists think we can live rather nicely in an environment of steady, low inflation. No one believes we can survive very well under extremely high inflation.

When inflation is steady and low, the rate at which prices rise is relatively easy to predict. It can therefore be taken into account in setting interest rates. Under high inflation, especially if prices are rising at ever-increasing or highly variable rates, this is extremely difficult, and perhaps impossible, to do. The potential redistributions become monumental, and lending and borrowing may cease entirely.

Any inflation makes it difficult to write long-term contracts. Under low, creeping inflation, the "long term" may be twenty years, or ten years, or five years. By contrast, under high, galloping inflation, the "long term" may be measured in days or weeks. Restaurant prices may change daily. Airfares may go up while you are in flight. When it is impossible to enter into contracts of any duration longer than a few days, economic activity becomes paralyzed. We conclude that:

The horrors of hyperinflation are very real. But they are either absent in low, steady inflations or present in such muted forms that they can scarcely be considered horrors.

LOW INFLATION DOES NOT NECESSARILY LEAD TO HIGH INFLATION

We noted earlier that inflation is surrounded by a mythology that bears precious little relation to reality. It seems appropriate to conclude this chapter by disposing of one particularly persistent myth: that low inflation is a slippery slope that invariably leads to high inflation.

There is neither statistical evidence nor theoretical support for the belief that low inflation inevitably leads to high inflation. To be sure, inflations sometimes speed up. At other times, however, they slow down.

Although creeping inflations have many causes, runaway inflations have occurred only when the government has printed incredible amounts of money, usually to finance wartime expenditures. In the German inflation of 1923, the government finally found that its printing presses could not produce enough paper money to keep pace with the exploding prices. Not that it did not try— by the end of the inflation, the *daily* output of currency exceeded 400 quadrillion marks! The Hungarian authorities in 1945–1946 tried even harder: the average growth rate of the money supply was more than 12,000 percent *per month*. Needless to say, these are not the kind of inflation problems that are likely to face industrialized countries in the foreseeable future.

But that does not mean there is nothing wrong with low inflation. We have spent several pages analyzing the very real costs of even modest inflation. A case against moderate inflation can indeed be built, but it does not help this case to shout slogans like "Creeping inflation always leads to galloping inflation." Fortunately, it is simply not true.

These children in Germany during the hyperinflation of the 1920s are building a pyramid with cash, worth no more than the sand or sticks used by children elsewhere.

SOURCE: © Camera Press/Globe Photos, Inc.

SUMMARY

1. Macroeconomic policy strives to achieve rapid and reasonably stable growth while keeping both unemployment and inflation low.

2. Only rising productivity can raise standards of living in the long run. And seemingly small differences in productivity growth rates can compound to enormous differences in living standards.

3. The **production function** tells us how much output the economy can produce from the available supplies of labour and capital, given the state of technology.

4. The growth rate of **potential GDP** is the sum of the growth rate of the **labour force** plus the growth rate of **labour productivity**. The latter depends on, among other things, technological change and investment in new capital.

5. Over long periods of time, the growth rates of actual and potential GDP match up quite well. But, owing to macroeconomic fluctuations, the two can diverge sharply over short periods.

6. Although some psychologists, environmentalists, and social critics question the merits of faster economic growth, economists generally assume that faster growth of potential GDP is socially beneficial.

7. When GDP is below its potential, unemployment is above its "**full employment**" level. High unemployment exacts heavy financial and psychological costs from those who are its victims, costs that are borne quite unevenly by different groups in the population.

8. **Frictional unemployment** arises when people are between jobs for normal reasons. Thus, most frictional unemployment is desirable.

9. **Structural unemployment** is due to shifts in the pattern of demand or to technological change that makes certain skills obsolete.

10. **Cyclical unemployment** is the portion of unemployment that rises when real GDP grows more slowly than potential GDP and falls when the opposite is true.

11. Today, after years of extremely low unemployment, economists are unsure where full employment lies. Some think it may be at a measured unemployment rate near 5 percent.

12. **Employment Insurance** replaces up to about one-half of the lost income of unemployed persons who are insured. But fewer than half of the unemployed actually collect benefits, and no insurance program can bring back the lost output that could have been produced had these people been working.

13. People have many misconceptions about inflation. For example, many believe that inflation systematically erodes **real wages** and blame inflation for any unfavorable changes in relative prices. Both of these ideas are myths.

14. Other costs of inflation are real, however. For example, inflation often redistributes income from lenders to borrowers.

15. This redistribution is ameliorated by adding the expected rate of inflation to the interest rate. But such expectations often prove to be inaccurate.

16. The **real rate of interest** is the **nominal rate of interest** minus the **expected rate of inflation**.

17. Because the real rate of interest indicates the command over real resources that the borrower surrenders to the lender, it is of primary economic importance. But public attention often is riveted on nominal rates of interest, and this confusion can lead to costly policy mistakes.

18. Because nominal—not real—**capital gains** and interest are taxed, our tax system levies overly high taxes on income from capital when inflation is high. This, however, is compensated for by the fact that only half of the realized capital gains are included in taxable income.

19. Low inflation that proceeds at moderate and fairly predictable rates year after year carries far lower social costs than does high or variable inflation. Many of these costs arise because inflation sends confused messages about relative price changes, which induce people to make inefficient decisions, thus reducing productivity.

20. The notion that low inflation inevitably accelerates into high inflation is a myth with no foundation in economic theory and no basis in historical fact.

KEY TERMS

TEST YOURSELF

1. Two countries start with equal GDPs. The economy of Country A grows at an annual rate of 2 percent while the economy of Country B grows at an annual rate of 3 percent. After 25 years, how much larger is Country B's economy than Country A's economy? Why is the answer *not* 25 percent?

2. If output rises by 35 percent while hours of work increase by 40 percent, has productivity increased or decreased? By how much?

3. Most economists would argue that actual GDP in Canada grew more slowly than potential output in the first half of the 1990s. What then should have happened to the unemployment rate from, say, 1990 to 1994? Then, in the second half of the 1990s, actual GDP grew faster than potential GDP. What should have happened to the unemployment rate during the 1995–2000 time period? (Check the data table on the inside back cover of this book to see what actually happened.)

4. Country A and Country B have identical population growth rates of 1.1 percent per annum, and everyone in each country always works 40 hours per week. Labour productivity grows at a rate of 2 percent in Country A and a rate of 2.5 percent in Country B. What are the growth rates of potential GDP in the two countries?

5. What is the *real interest rate* paid on a credit-card loan bearing 14 percent nominal interest per year, if the rate of inflation is
   a. zero?
   b. 3 percent?
   c. 6 percent?
   d. 12 percent?
   e. 16 percent?

6. Suppose you agree to lend money to your friend on the day you both enter university at what you both expect to be a zero *real* rate of interest. Payment is to be made at graduation, with interest at a fixed *nominal* rate. If inflation proves to be *lower* during your university years than you both had expected, who will gain and who will lose?

DISCUSSION QUESTIONS

1. If an earthquake destroys some of the factories in Poorland, what happens to Poorland's potential GDP? What happens to Poorland's potential GDP if it acquires some new advanced technology from Richland, and starts using it?

2. Why is it not as terrible to become unemployed nowadays as it was during the Great Depression?

3. "Unemployment is no longer a social problem because unemployed workers receive unemployment benefits and other benefits that make up for most of their lost wages." Comment.

4. Why is it so difficult to define *full employment*? What unemployment rate should the government be shooting for today?

5. Show why each of the following complaints is based on a misunderstanding about inflation:
   a. "Inflation must be stopped because it robs workers of their purchasing power."
   b. "Inflation makes it impossible for working people to afford many of the things they were hoping to buy."
   c. "Inflation must be stopped today, for if we do not stop it, it will surely accelerate to ruinously high rates and lead to disaster."

6. China has been growing at a rate of about 10 percent over the last decade. How many years will it take for its GDP to double? Can this go on forever?

APPENDIX *How Statisticians Measure Inflation*

■ INDEX NUMBERS FOR INFLATION

Inflation is generally measured by the change in some index of the general price level. For example, between 1977 and 2007, the all-items Consumer Price Index (CPI), the most widely used measure of the price level, rose from 33.6 to 111.5—an increase of over 230 percent. The meaning of the *change* is clear enough. But what are the meanings of the 33.6 figure for the price level of 1977 and the 111.5 figure for 2007? Both are **index numbers**.

> An **index number** expresses the cost of a market basket of goods relative to its cost in some "base" period, which is simply the year used as a basis of comparison.

Because the CPI currently uses 2002 as its base period, the CPI of 111.5 for 2007 means that it cost $111.50 in 2007 to purchase the same basket of several hundred goods and services that cost $100 in 2002.

Now, in fact, the particular list of consumer goods and services under scrutiny did not actually cost $100 in 2002. When constructing index numbers, by convention the index is set at 100 in the base period. This conventional figure is then used to obtain index numbers for other years in a very simple way. Suppose that the budget needed to buy the roughly 600 goods and services included in the CPI was $2,000 per month in 2002 and $2,230 per month in 2007. Then the index is defined by the following rule:

$$\frac{\text{CPI in 2007}}{\text{CPI in 2002}}$$
$$= \frac{\text{Cost of market basket in 2007}}{\text{Cost of the market basket in 2002}}$$

Because the CPI in 2002 is set at 100:

$$\frac{\text{CPI in 2007}}{100} = \frac{\$2,230}{\$2,000} = 1.115$$

or

$$\text{CPI in 2007} = 111.5$$

Exactly the same sort of equation enables us to calculate the CPI in any other year. We have the following rule:

$$\text{CPI in given year} = \frac{\text{Cost of market basket in given year}}{\text{Cost of market basket in base year}} \times 100$$

Of course, not every combination of consumer goods that cost $2,000 in 2002 rose to $2,230 in 2007. For example, a colour TV that cost $600 in 2002 might have cost only $500 in 2007, but a $600 dental bill in 2002 might have ballooned to $750. The index number problem refers to the fact that there is no perfect cost-of-living index because no two families buy precisely the same bundle of goods and services, and hence no two families suffer precisely the same increase in prices. Economists call this **the index number problem**:

> When relative prices are changing, there is no such thing as a "perfect price index" that is correct for every consumer. Any statistical index will understate the increase in the cost of living for some families and overstate it for others. At best, the index can represent the situation of an "average" family.

■ THE CONSUMER PRICE INDEX

The **Consumer Price Index (CPI)**, which is calculated and announced each month by Statistics Canada, is surely the most closely watched price index. One major reason is that many collective agreements contain a clause indexing wage increases to increases in the CPI. When you read in the newspaper or see on television that the "cost of living rose by 0.2 percent last month," chances are the reporter is referring to the CPI.

> The **Consumer Price Index (CPI)** is measured by pricing the items on a list representative of a typical household budget.

To know which items to include and in what amounts, Statistics Canada conducts an extensive survey of spending habits every year—the *Survey of Household Spending*. However, the *same* bundle of goods and services is used as a standard for four years or more, whether or not spending habits change. Economists call this the *base-period weight index* because the relative importance it attaches to the price change of each item depends on how much money consumers actually chose to spend on the item during the base period. The base-period weight index was changed in May 2007. The weights for the various components of the basket of goods and services, which were previously based on the 1996 basket and then on the 2001 basket, have been updated on the basis of the 2005 Statistics Canada *Survey of Household Spending*.

Canadian consumers were asked at the beginning of 2006 about the amounts they spent on various items during 2005. The share of each class of expenditures is then established on this basis. For instance, in 2005, fresh fruit carried a weight share of 0.73 percent, with electricity, gasoline, tuition fees, and textbooks at 2.46, 4.49, 1.93, and 0.38 percent, respectively. These weights can change considerably from one province to another, but the switch to the new weights had only a small effect on the all-items inflation rate, which moved from 2.1 to 2.2 percent in May 2007 as a result of the switch. Statistics Canada also takes this opportunity to introduce new goods into the basket. For instance, in the new 2005 base-period weight index, rentals of video games have been added.

A simple example will help us understand how the CPI is constructed. Imagine that university students purchase only three items—hamburgers, jeans, and movie tickets—and that we want to devise a cost-of-living index (call it SPI, or "Student Price Index") for them. First, we would conduct a survey of spending habits in the base year. (Suppose it is 2002.) Table 5 represents the hypothetical results. You will note that the frugal students of that day spent only $100 per month: $56 on hamburgers, $24 on jeans, and $20 on movies.

Table 6 presents hypothetical prices of these same three items in 2008. Each price has risen by a different amount, ranging from 25 percent for jeans up to 50 percent for hamburgers. By how much has the SPI risen?

TABLE 5

Results of Student Expenditure Survey, 2002

Item	Average Price	Average Quantity Purchased per Month	Average Expenditure per Month
Hamburger	$ 0.80	70	$56
Jeans	24.00	1	24
Movie ticket	5.00	4	20
Total			$100

TABLE 6

Prices in 2008

Item	Price	Increase over 2002
Hamburger	$1.20	50%
Jeans	30.00	25
Movie ticket	7.00	40

Pricing the 2002 student budget at 2008 prices, we find that what once cost $100 now costs $142, as the calculation in Table 7 shows. Thus, the SPI, based on 2002 = 100, is:

$$\text{SPI} = \frac{\text{Cost of budget in 2008}}{\text{Cost of budget in 2002}} \times 100 = \frac{\$142}{\$100} \times 100 = 142$$

So, the SPI in 2008 stands at 142, meaning that students' cost of living has increased 42 percent over the 6 years.

TABLE 7

Cost of 2002 Student Budget in 2008 Prices

70 Hamburgers at $1.20	$84
1 pair of jeans at $30	30
4 movie tickets at $7	28
Total	$142

USING A PRICE INDEX TO "DEFLATE" MONETARY FIGURES

One of the most common uses of price indexes is in the comparison of monetary figures relating to two different points in time. The problem is that, if there has been inflation, the dollar is not a good measuring rod because it can buy less now than it did in the past.

Here is a simple example. Suppose the average student spent $100 per month in 2002 but $140 per month in 2008. If there was an outcry that students had become spendthrifts, how would you answer the charge?

The obvious answer is that a dollar in 2008 does not buy what it did in 2002. Specifically, our SPI shows us that it takes $1.42 in 2008 to purchase what $1 would purchase in 2002. To compare the spending habits of students in the two years, we must divide the 2008 spending figure by 1.42. Specifically, *real* spending per student in 2008 (where "real" is defined by 2002 dollars) is:

$$\text{Real spending in 2008} = \frac{\text{Nominal spending in 2008}}{\text{Price index of 2004}} \times 100$$

Thus:

$$\text{Real spending in 2008} = \frac{\$140}{142} \times 100 = \$98.59$$

This calculation shows that, despite appearances to the contrary, the change in nominal spending from $100 to $140 actually represented a small *decrease* in real spending.

This procedure of dividing by the price index is called **deflating**, and it serves to translate noncomparable monetary figures into more directly comparable real figures.

> **Deflating** is the process of finding the real value of some monetary magnitude by dividing by some appropriate price index.

A good practical illustration is the real wage, a concept we have discussed in this chapter. As we saw in the boxed insert on page 128, we obtain the real wage by dividing the nominal wage by the price level.

USING A PRICE INDEX TO MEASURE INFLATION

Three measures of inflation are commonly found in news reports. They all start from the monthly measures of the CPI. Inflation can be measured between:

1. A given month and the preceding month
2. A given month and the same month of the preceding year
3. The annual average index of a given year and that of the previous year

Each of these measures will give a different answer, so we have to know which one is being discussed. Suppose you are given the data in Table 8, which reflects the all-items CPI basket for Canada (with the 2002 index set at 100).

TABLE 8	
Consumer Price Indexes	
December 2007	112.0
November 2007	111.9
December 2006	109.4
Average 2007	111.5
Average 2006	109.1

For all measures, we want to compute the *change* in the price index divided by the *initial* value of the price index. The first measure, the percentage change between December and November 2007, is given by the following formula:

$$\frac{(112.0 - 111.9)}{111.9} \times 100\% = +0.089\%$$

The initial value is 111.9, the CPI for the month of November 2007, and so it appears in the denominator. Thus, the *month-to-month price change* tells us that prices rose by 0.089 percent. Statistics Canada would round this up and say that prices rose by 0.1 percent in December 2007.

If we want to ascertain this measure on an annual basis, we would need to multiply this number by 12. In this case, on an annual basis, the month-to-month change would be equivalent to 1.1 percent (0.089% × 12 = 1.068% ≈ 1.1%).

The second measure, the percentage change between December 2007 and December 2006 is calculated by a similar formula:

$$\frac{(112.0 - 109.4)}{109.4} \times 100\% = +2.4\%$$

Thus, the *price change over 12 months*, or the rate of inflation between December 2006 and December 2007, is 2.4 percent.

Finally, we can also compute the *annual rate of inflation* for 2007 by comparing the average index for 2007 with the average index for 2006. The average index for 2007 is obtained simply by adding all 12 monthly indexes of 2007 and dividing the total by 12. Make use of the data in Table 8 and rely on the same formula as before to obtain:

$$\frac{(111.5 - 109.1)}{109.1} \times 100\% = +2.2\%$$

Thus, prices rose by 2.2 percent on average between 2006 and 2007.

In this case, the second and third measures give close results, but it could turn out otherwise. Which measure is best depends on your purpose. If you are interested in the latest change, then the month-to-month price change (the first measure) is the best. If you want to know what happened over the last 12 months, then the second measure is the most appropriate. If you want to compare annual rates or use historical series, you should use the third measure.

■ What the CPI Is Not

The CPI is useful for calculating *changes* in consumer prices. There are provincial measures of the CPI, and Statistics Canada also provides CPI measures for a series of metropolitan areas. All of these indexes allow you to measure price changes in a given province or in a given city. But you cannot use these CPI data to find out whether the price level in Vancouver is any higher than that in other Canadian cities. To do this, you must rely on another, lesser known index: the Inter-City Index of Consumer Price Levels.

Table 9 illustrates the difference between these two concepts. The second column gives measures of the well-known CPI. We see that, since 2002, prices in Edmonton rose by over 17 percent, while those in Montreal, Ottawa, Toronto, Winnipeg, and Vancouver rose by about 10 percent. Does this mean that prices in Toronto are lower than those in Edmonton, and that prices in Vancouver are the same as those in Winnipeg? Not at all. The CPI indicator cannot answer such a question. Only the Inter-City Index can. As the figures in the third column show, it is still much more expensive to live in Toronto (inter-city index at 109) than it is to live in Edmonton (97), and it is more expensive to live in Vancouver (104) than it is in Winnipeg (92).

TABLE 9		
Consumer Price Index vs. Inter-City Index of Consumer Price Levels		
City	Consumer Price Index, 2007 (2002 = 100)	Inter-City Index of Consumer Price Levels, October 2006 (all cities = 100)
Saint John (NB)	111.2	92
Montreal	110.3	93
Ottawa	110.7	102
Toronto	110.5	109
Winnipeg	110.8	92
Edmonton	117.4	97
Vancouver	110.2	104

SOURCE: Adapted from Statistics Canada, *The Consumer Price Index*, Tables 8-2 and 15, January 2008, Catalogue No. 62-001-XIB.

■ THE GDP DEFLATOR

In macroeconomics, one of the most important of the monetary magnitudes that we have to deflate is the nominal gross domestic product (GDP).

The price index used to deflate nominal GDP is called the **GDP deflator**. It is a broad measure of economy-wide inflation; it includes the prices of all goods and services in the economy.

Our general principle for deflating a nominal magnitude tells us how to go from nominal GDP to real GDP:

$$\text{Real GDP} = \frac{\text{Nominal GDP}}{\text{GDP deflator}} \times 100$$

As with the CPI, the 100 simply serves to establish the base of the index as 100, rather than 1.00.

Some economists consider the GDP deflator to be a better measure of overall inflation than the Consumer Price Index. The main reason is that the GDP deflator is based on a broader market basket. As mentioned earlier, the CPI is based on the budget of a typical family. By contrast, the GDP deflator is constructed from a market basket that includes *every* item in the GDP—that is, every final good and service produced by the economy. Thus, in addition to prices of consumer goods, the GDP deflator includes the prices of airplanes, lathes, and other goods purchased by businesses—especially computers, which fall in price every year. It also includes government services.

For this reason, the two indexes rarely give the same measure of inflation. Usually the discrepancy is minor, but sometimes it can be noticeable. For instance, in 2004 and 2005, the CPI rose by 1.9 and 2.2 percent, respectively, while the GDP deflator recorded an inflation rate of 2.9 and 3.1 percent during the same two years. The opposite occurred in 2002, when the CPI inflation rate was 2.2 percent, while the GDP deflator rose by only 1.0 percent.

The way the GDP deflator is calculated was changed by Statistics Canada in 2001. Quick changes arising from the technology and information sector forced this modification, which had actually been recommended by the United Nations 1993 System of National Accounts. Under the old measure, the so-called Laspeyres Index, the prices of the base period were used as weights to compute changes in GDP arising from changes in the volumes of production. This tended to overestimate growth when there were substantial increases in the sales of products whose prices were briskly falling, such as high-tech products. This occurred in particular in 1999–2000. Using a possible alternative measure, the Paasche Index, the weights are given by prices of the current period, but this index tends to underestimate growth when the prices of more popular products are falling. The new measure is the Fisher Index, which is simply an average of the two alternative indexes, thus giving a more reliable measure.

SUMMARY

1. Inflation is measured by the percentage increase in an **index number** of prices, which shows how the cost of some basket of goods has changed over a period of time.

2. Because relative prices are always changing, and because different families purchase different items, no price index can represent precisely the experience of every family.

3. The **Consumer Price Index (CPI)** tries to measure the cost of living for an average household by pricing a typical fixed basket every month.

4. Price indexes such as the CPI can be used to **deflate** nominal figures to make them more comparable. Deflation amounts to dividing the nominal magnitude by the appropriate price index.

5. The inflation rate between two adjacent years is computed as the percentage change in the price index between the first year and the second year.

6. The **GDP deflator** is a broader measure of economy-wide inflation than the CPI because it includes the prices of all goods and services in the economy.

KEY TERMS

Index number   137

Index number problem   137

Consumer Price Index   137

Deflating   138

GDP deflator   139

TEST YOURSELF

1. To the right you will find the values of the Standard and Poor's/Toronto Stock Exchange (S&P/TSX) composite index, for six different years, all assessed in the month of December. The Canadian all-items Consumer Price Index for each of these months (on a base of 1992 = 100) is also provided. Use these numbers to deflate all six stock market values. Do real stock prices always rise every decade? What happened more recently?

Year	S&P/TSX	CPI
December 1960	544	18.7
December 1970	947	24.2
December 1980	2,268	55
December 1990	3,256	95.1
December 2000	8,933	115.1
December 2006	12,908	130.2

2. Below you will find nominal GDP and the GDP deflator (based on 1997 = 100) for the years 1985, 1995, and 2005.

   a. Compute real GDP for each year.

   b. Compute the percentage change in nominal and real GDP from 1985 to 1995, and from 1995 to 2005.

   c. Compute the percentage change in the GDP deflator over these two periods. Verify that the percentage change in real GDP is *not* equal to the percentage change in nominal GDP minus the percentage change in the GDP deflator.

GDP Statistics	1985	1995	2005
Nominal GDP (billions of dollars)	485	810	1,371
GDP deflator	73.1	97.2	118.5

3. Fill in the blanks in the following table of GDP statistics.

	2003	2004	2005
Nominal GDP	1,213		1,371
Real GDP	1,088	1,124	
GDP deflator		114.8	118.4

4. Use the following data to compute the University Price Index for 2008 using the base 1982 = 100.

Item	Price in 1982	Quantity per Month in 1982	Price in 2008
Button-down shirts	$10	1	$25
Loafers	25	1	55
Sneakers	10	3	35
Textbooks	12	12	40
Jeans	12	3	30
Restaurant meals	5	11	14

5. Average weekly earnings in the Canadian economy during the several past years were as follows, with the CPI numbers being provided on the basis of the 2002 year (2002 = 100).

	1961	1971	1981	1991	2001
Weekly earnings	74	130	337	553	667
CPI	15.7	20.9	49.5	82.8	97.8

   a. On this basis, calculate the real wage (in 2002 dollars) for each of these years.

   b. Knowing that the 2006 CPI index is 109.1, calculate the real wage in 2006 dollars for each of these years.

   c. Which decade had the fastest growth of money wages; the slowest?

   d. Which decade had the fastest growth of real wages; the slowest?

6. The example in the appendix showed that the Student Price Index (SPI) rose by 42 percent from 2002 to 2008. You can understand the meaning of this better if you do the following:

   a. Use Table 5 to compute the fraction of total spending accounted for by each of the three items in 2002. Call these values the "expenditure weights."

   b. Compute the weighted average of the percentage increases of the three prices shown in Table 6, using the expenditure weights you just computed.

   You should get 42 percent as your answer. This shows that "inflation," as measured by the SPI, is a weighted average of the percentage price increases of all the items that are included in the index.

7

ECONOMIC GROWTH: THEORY AND POLICY

Once one starts to think about . . . [differences in growth rates among countries], it is hard to think about anything else.

ROBERT E. LUCAS (1937–), 1995 RECIPIENT OF THE BANK OF SWEDEN PRIZE IN ECONOMIC SCIENCES IN MEMORY OF ALFRED NOBEL, 1988

Why do some economies grow rapidly while others grow slowly—or not at all? As the opening quotation suggests, there is probably no more important question in all of economics. From 1990 to 2006, according to the International Monetary Fund, the Canadian economy grew at a 2.65 percent annual rate, while China's grew 9.7 percent per year and Russia's *declined* by .05 percent per year. Those are very large differences. What factors account for the disparities?

The discussion in Chapter 6 of the goal of economic growth focused our attention on two crucial but distinct tasks for macroeconomic policy makers, both of which are quite difficult to achieve:

1. *Growth policy:* Ensuring that the economy sustains a high long-run growth rate of potential GDP (although not necessarily the *highest possible* growth rate).
2. *Stabilization policy:* Keeping actual GDP reasonably close to potential GDP in the short run, so that society is plagued by neither high unemployment nor high inflation.

This chapter is devoted to the theory of economic growth and to the policies that this theory suggests.

Corresponding to the two tasks listed above, there are two ways to think about what is to come in this and subsequent chapters. In discussing *growth policy* in this chapter, we will study the factors that determine an economy's *long-run* growth rate of *potential GDP*, and we will consider how policy makers can try to speed it up. When we turn to *stabilization policy*, starting in the next chapters, we will investigate how and why *actual GDP* deviates from potential GDP in the *short run* and how policy makers can try to minimize these deviations. Thus the two views of the macroeconomy complement one another.

CONTENTS

PUZZLE: *Why Does University Education Keep Getting More Expensive?*

Have you ever wondered why the cost of a university education rises more rapidly than most other prices year after year? If you have not, your parents surely have! And it's not a myth. Between 1992 and 2006, the component of the Consumer Price Index (CPI) that measures university tuition costs rose by a cumulative 150 percent—compared to just 30 percent for the overall CPI. That is, the *relative* price of university tuition increased massively.

Economists understand at least part of the reason, and it has little, if anything, to do with the efficiency (or lack thereof) with which universities are run. Rather, it is a natural companion to the economy's long-run growth rate. Furthermore, there is good reason to expect the relative price of university tuition to keep rising, and to rise more rapidly in faster-growing societies. Economists believe that the same explanation for the unusually rapid growth in the cost of attending university applies to services as diverse as visits to the doctor, theatrical performances, and restaurant meals—all of which also have become relatively more expensive over time. Later in this chapter, we will see precisely what this explanation is.

SOURCE: Peter Spiro/iStock Photo

THE THREE PILLARS OF PRODUCTIVITY GROWTH

As we learned in the previous chapter, the growth rate of potential GDP is the *sum* of the growth rates of *hours of work* and *labour productivity*. It is hardly mysterious that an economy will grow if its people keep working harder and harder, year after year. And a few societies have followed that recipe successfully for relatively brief periods of time. But there is a limit to how much people can work or, more important, to how much they want to work. In fact, people typically want more leisure time, not longer hours of work, as they get richer. In consequence, the natural focus of growth policy is on enhancing productivity—on working *smarter* rather than working *harder*.

The last chapter introduced a tool called the *production function*, which tells us how much *output* the economy can produce from specified *inputs* of labour and capital, given the state of *technology*. The discussion there focused on two of the three main determinants of productivity growth:[1]

1. The rate at which the economy builds up its stock of *capital*
2. The rate at which *technology* improves

Before introducing the third determinant, let us review how these first two pillars work.

Capital

Figure 1 resembles Figure 1 of the last chapter (see page 116). The lower curve $0K_1$ is the production function when the capital stock is some low number, K_1. Its upward

---

[1] If you need review, see pages 116-117 of Chapter 6.

slope indicates, naturally enough, that larger quantities of labour input produce more output. (Remember, technology is held constant in this graph.) The middle curve $0K_2$ is the production function corresponding to some larger capital stock, K_2, and the upper curve $0K_3$ pertains to an even larger capital stock, K_3.

To keep things simple at first, suppose hours of work do not grow over time, but rather remain fixed at L_1. However, the nation's businesses invest in new plant and equipment, so the capital stock grows from K_1 in the first year to K_2 in the second year and K_3 in the third year. Then the economy's capacity to produce will move up from point a in year 1 to point b in year 2 and point c in year 3. Potential GDP will therefore rise from Y_a to Y_b to Y_c. Because hours of work do not change in this example (by assumption), every bit of this growth comes from rising *productivity*, which is in turn due to the accumulation of more capital.[2] In general:

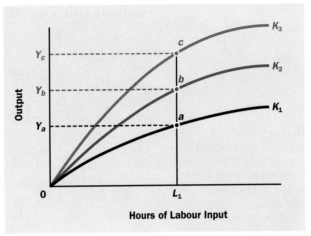

FIGURE 1

Production Functions Corresponding to Three Different Capital Stocks

> For a given technology and a given labour force, labour productivity will be higher when the capital stock is larger.

This conclusion is hardly surprising. Employees who work with more capital can obviously produce more goods and services. Just imagine manufacturing a desk, first, with only hand tools, then with power tools, and finally with all the equipment available in a modern furniture factory. Or think about selling books from a sidewalk stand, in a bookstore, or over the Internet. Your productivity would rise in each case. Furthermore, workers with *more* capital are almost certainly blessed with *newer*—and, hence, *better*—capital as well. This advantage, too, makes them more productive. Again, compare one of Henry Ford's assembly-line workers of a century ago to an autoworker in a Ford plant today.

It is important to note that while labour productivity depends on the amount of effort being exerted by the workers, it also depends, more fundamentally, on the quality and efficiency of the equipment that is provided for the workforce.

■ Technology

In Chapter 6, we saw that a graph like Figure 1 can also be used to depict the effects of *improvements in technology*. So now imagine that curves $0K_1$, $0K_2$, and $0K_3$ all correspond to the *same* capital stock, but to *different* levels of technology. Specifically, the economy's technology improves as we move up from $0K_1$ to $0K_2$ to $0K_3$. The graphical (and commonsense) conclusion is exactly the same: Labour becomes more productive from year 1 to year 2 to year 3, so improving technology leads directly to growth. In general:

> For given inputs of labour and capital, labour productivity will be higher when the technology is better.

Once again, this conclusion hardly comes as a surprise—indeed, it is barely more than the definition of technical progress. When we say that a nation's technology improves, we mean, more or less, that firms in the country can produce more output from the same inputs. And of course, superior technology is a major factor behind the vastly higher productivity of workers in rich countries versus poor ones. Textile plants in Quebec, for example, use technologies that are far superior to those employed in Africa.

---

[2] Because productivity is the ratio Y/L, it is shown on the graph by the *slope* of the straight line connecting the origin to point a, or point b, or point c. Clearly, that slope is rising over time and hence labour productivity rises over time.

Labour Quality: Education and Training

It is now time to introduce the third pillar of productivity growth, the one not mentioned in Chapter 6: *workforce quality*. It is generally assumed—and supported by reams of evidence—that more highly educated workers can produce more goods and services in an hour than can less well-educated workers. And the same lesson applies to training that takes place outside the schools, such as on the job: Better-trained workers are more productive. The amount of education and training embodied in a nation's labour force is often referred to as its stock of **human capital**.

Conceptually, an increase in human capital has the same effect on productivity as does an increase in physical capital or an improvement in technology, that is, the same *quantity* of labour input becomes capable of producing more output. So we can use the ever-adaptable Figure 1 for yet a third purpose—to represent increasing *workforce quality* as we move up from $0K_1$ to $0K_2$ to $0K_3$. Once again, the general conclusion is obvious:

> For a given capital stock, labour force, and technology, labour productivity will be higher when the workforce has more education and training.

This third pillar is another obvious source of large disparities between rich nations, which tend to have well-educated populations, and poor nations, which do not. So we can add a third item to our list of the principal determinants of a nation's productivity growth rate:

3. The rate at which *workforce quality* (or "human capital") is improving

In contemporary Canada, average educational attainment is high and workforce quality changes little from year to year. But in some rapidly developing countries improvements in education can be an important engine of growth. For example, average years of schooling in South Korea soared from less than five in 1970 to more than nine in 1990 and to as much as twelve in 2004. This contributed mightily to South Korea's remarkably rapid economic development.

Although there is no unique formula for growth, the most successful growth strategies of the post–World War II era, beginning with the Japanese "economic miracle," made ample use of all three pillars. Starting from a base of extreme deprivation after World War II, Japan showed the world how a combination of high rates of investment, a well-educated workforce, and the adoption of state-of-the-art technology could catapult a poor nation into the leading ranks within a few decades. The lessons were not lost on the so-called Asian Tigers—including Taiwan, South Korea, Singapore, and Hong Kong—which developed rapidly using their own versions of the Japanese model. Today, a number of other countries in Asia, Eastern Europe, and Latin America are trying to apply variants of this growth formula.

> **Human capital** is the amount of skill embodied in the workforce. It is most commonly measured by the amount of education and training.

LEVELS, GROWTH RATES, AND THE CONVERGENCE HYPOTHESIS

Notice that, where productivity *growth rates* are concerned, it is the *rates of increase* of capital, technology, and workforce quality that matter, rather than their current *levels*. The distinction is important.

Productivity *levels* are vastly higher in the rich countries—that is why they are called rich. The wealthy nations have more bountiful supplies of capital, more highly skilled workers, and superior technologies. Naturally, they can produce more output per hour of work. Table 1 shows that labour productivity in the United States used to be much higher than anywhere else in the world. Labour productivity in Canada used to follow closely behind, with an hour of labour in Canada in 1960 and 1975 producing nearly 90 percent as much output as an hour of labour in the United States. At the other extreme, labour productivity in Turkey was only 13 percent of that of the United States in 1960, and in 2007, this figure stood at 29 percent.

But the *growth rates* of capital, workforce skills, and technology are not necessarily higher in the rich countries. For example, Country A might have abundant capital, but the amount may be increasing at a snail's pace, whereas in Country B capital may be scarce but growing rapidly. When it comes to determining the long-run growth rate, it is the *growth rate* rather than the current *levels* of these underpinnings of the country's well-being that matter.

In fact, GDP per hour of work actually grew faster in several countries that had lower average incomes than Canada and the United States. Indeed, all of the countries listed in Table 1, with the exception of Mexico, experienced labour productivity growth in the 1960–2007 period that surpassed that of Canada and the United States. In some cases, such as Norway and Ireland, the productivity levels in 2007 were even higher than they were in North America. Why has productivity growth in the European and Asian countries in Table 1 been so much faster? While a typical Irish worker in 1960 or even in 1980 had less physical and human capital than a typical Canadian worker and used less advanced technology, the capital stock, average educational attainment, and the level of technology probably all increased faster in Ireland than in Canada or in the United States.

> The level of productivity in a nation depends on its supplies of human and physical capital and the state of its technology. But the growth rate of productivity depends on the rates of increase of these three factors.

The distinction between productivity levels and productivity growth rates may strike you as a piece of boring arithmetic, but it has many important practical applications. Here is a particularly striking one:

If the productivity growth rate is higher in poorer countries than in richer ones, then poor countries will close the gap on rich ones. The so-called **convergence hypothesis** suggests that this is what normally happens.

> The convergence hypothesis: The productivity growth rates of poorer countries tend to be higher than those of richer countries.

The idea behind the convergence hypothesis, as illustrated in Figure 2, is that productivity growth will typically be faster where the initial level of productivity is lower. In this hypothetical example, the poorer country starts out with a per-capita GDP of $2,000, just one-fifth that of the richer country. But the poor country's real GDP per capita grows faster, so it gradually narrows the relative income gap.

Why might we expect convergence to be the norm? In some poor countries, the supply of capital may be growing very rapidly. In others, educational attainment may be rising quickly, albeit from a low base. But the main reason to expect convergence in the long run is that *low-productivity*

TABLE 1

Productivity Levels and Productivity Growth Rates in Selected Countries, 1960–2007

Country	GDP per Hour of Work 1960 (as % of U.S. GDP)				Compounded Growth Rate
	1960	1975	1990	2007	1960–2007
United States	100	100	100	100	1.8%
Canada	89	92	85	81	1.65
Norway	70	95	121	140	3.2
United Kingdom	58	67	79	89	2.7
France	54	76	100	99	3.0
Mexico	41	44	33	27	1.0
Ireland	35	52	76	92	3.9
Spain	30	57	87	71	3.7
Japan	25	54	69	71	4.1
South Korea	12	16	27	45	4.9
Turkey	12	19	25	29	3.6

Note: South Korea data start in 1963.

SOURCES: Authors' calculations and The Conference Board and Groningen Growth and Development Centre, *Total Economy Database,* "Labour productivity per hour worked in 2007 U.S. dollars, with purchasing power parity adjustment." Retrieved from www.ggdc.net/dseries/totecon.html

> The **convergence hypothesis** holds that nations with low levels of productivity tend to have high productivity growth rates, so that international productivity differences shrink over time.

FIGURE 2

The Convergence Hypothesis

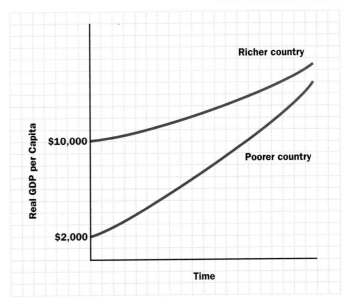

TABLE 2		
GDP per Capita and GDP Growth Rates in Selected Poor Countries		
Country	GDP per Capita 2007*	GDP Average Growth Rate, 1990–2007
Burundi	$704	0%
Democratic Republic of Congo	893	−2.0
Haiti	1,913	+0.1
Sierra Leone	958	0
Zimbabwe	2,395	−0.5

* In U.S. dollars, based on purchasing power parity measures.

Note: For reference, in 2007, the Canadian GDP per capita was US$36,983.

SOURCE: International Monetary Fund, *World Economic Outlook Database*. Retrieved from www.imf.org

countries should be able to learn from high-productivity countries as scientific and managerial know-how spreads around the world.

A country that is operating at the technological frontier can improve its technology only by *innovating*. It must constantly figure out ways to do things better than it was doing them before. By comparison, a less advanced country can boost its productivity simply by *imitating*, by adopting technologies that are already in common use in the advanced countries. Not surprisingly, it is much easier to "look it up" than to "think it up."

Modern communications assist the convergence process by speeding the flow of information around the globe. The Internet was invented mainly in the United States, but it quickly spread to almost every corner of the world. Likewise, advances in human genomics and stem-cell research are now originating in some of the most advanced countries, but they are communicated rapidly to scientists all over the world. A poor country that is skilled at importing scientific and engineering advances from the rich countries can achieve very rapid productivity growth. Indeed, when Japan was a poor nation, successful imitation was one of its secrets to getting rich. India and China appear to be trying that now.

Unfortunately, not all poor countries seem able to participate in the convergence process. For a variety of reasons (some of which will be mentioned later in this chapter), a number of developing countries seem incapable of adopting and adapting advanced technologies. When discussing Table 1, we pointed out that labour productivity in Mexico grew more slowly than that in Canada and the United States and hence much more slowly than that of many European countries. Sadly, this kind of dismal performance on the part of poor countries relative to rich countries is not at all unusual. South American countries such as Peru, Uruguay, and Argentina have also experienced overly slow labour productivity growth. Real incomes have stagnated or even fallen in some of the poorest countries of the world, especially in Africa, as can be seen in Table 2. Convergence certainly cannot be taken for granted.

> Technological laggards can, and sometimes do, close the gap with technological leaders by imitating and adapting existing technologies. Within this "convergence club," productivity *growth rates* are higher where productivity *levels* are lower. Unfortunately, some of the world's poorest nations have been unable to join the club.

A nation's capital is its available supply of plant, equipment, and software. It is the result of past decisions to make *investments* in these items.

■ GROWTH POLICY: ENCOURAGING CAPITAL FORMATION

Let us now see how the government might spur growth by working on these three pillars, beginning with capital.

First, we need to clarify some terminology. We have spoken of the supply of **capital**, by which we mean the volume of plant (factories, office buildings, and so on), equipment (drill presses, computers, and so on), and software currently available. Businesses *add* to the existing supply of capital whenever they make **investment** expenditures—purchases of new plant, equipment, and software. In this way, the *growth* of the capital stock depends on how much businesses spend on investment. That is the process called **capital formation**—literally, forming new capital.

But you don't get something for nothing. Devoting more of society's resources to producing investment goods generally means devoting fewer resources to producing consumer goods. A *production possibilities frontier* like those introduced in Chapter 3 can be used to depict the nature of this trade-off—and the choices open to a nation. Given its technology and existing resources of labour, capital, and so on, the country can in principle select one of the points on the production possibilities frontier shown

Investment is the *flow* of resources into the production of new capital. It is the labour, steel, and other inputs devoted to the *construction* of factories, warehouses, railroads, and other pieces of capital during some period of time.

Capital formation is synonymous with investment. It refers to the process of building up the capital stock.

as curve *AICD* in Figure 3. If it picks a point like *C*, its citizens will enjoy many consumer goods, but it will not be investing much for the future. *So it will grow slowly.* If, on the other hand, it selects a point like *I*, its citizens will consume less today, but its higher level of investment means *it will grow more quickly.* Thus, at least within limits, the amount of capital formation and growth can be chosen.

Now suppose the government wants the capital stock to grow faster, that is, it wants to move from a point like *C* toward a point like *I* in Figure 3. In a capitalist, market economy such as ours, private businesses make almost all investment decisions—how many factories and office buildings to build, how many drill presses and computers to purchase, and so on. To speed up the process of capital formation, the government must somehow persuade private businesses to invest more. But how?

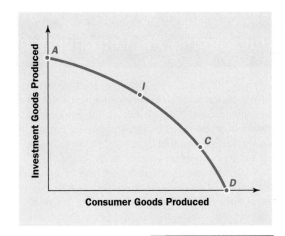

FIGURE 3

Choosing between Investment and Consumption

Interest Rates   The most obvious way to increase investment by private businesses is to lower real interest rates. When real interest rates fall, investment normally rises. Why? Because businesses often borrow to finance their investments, and the real interest rate indicates how much firms must pay for that privilege. An investment project that looks unattractive at an interest rate of 10 percent may look highly profitable if the firm has to pay only 6 percent.

> The amount that businesses invest depends on the real interest rate they pay to borrow funds. The lower the real rate of interest, the more investment there will be.

In subsequent chapters, we will learn how government policy, especially monetary policy, influences interest rates—which gives policy makers some leverage over private investment decisions. That relationship, in fact, is why monetary policy will play such a crucial role in subsequent chapters. But we might as well come clean right away: For reasons to be examined later, the government's ability to control interest rates is imperfect. Furthermore, the rate of interest is only one of several determinants of investment spending. So policy makers have only a limited ability to affect the level of investment by manipulating interest rates.

Tax Provisions   The government also can influence investment spending by altering various provisions of the tax code. For example, some economists argue that a reduced tax rate on capital gains would encourage risky investment and the development of small businesses. Following up on this idea, the 1984 Liberal government's budget fully exempted the first $100,000 of capital gains, but this tax shelter was terminated in 1994—again by the Liberals. The Conservatives, also acting on the belief that low tax rates on capital gains encourage investment, increased the share of realized capital gains exempted from taxable income from 50 percent to 75 percent in 1990, but this was also overturned in 2000 by the Liberals. Obviously the issue of capital gains taxation is highly controversial.

A number of economists argue that the best fiscal means to encourage business investment is to provide firms with generous amortization allowances. For instance, when a firm purchases a capital good, depending on the class of the good, it can deduct a certain percentage of the purchasing cost of this good from its taxable income. For instance, if it is believed that the machine should last 10 years, then one-tenth of the cost could be deducted each year. It is sometimes argued that accelerated amortization tax provisions, where in this instance perhaps 25 percent of the cost could be deducted for four years, would induce businesses to spend more on investment.

> The tax law gives the government several ways to influence business spending on investment goods. But influence is far from total control.

Questioning the Consumption–Investment Production Possibilities Frontier

On page 148, we pointed out that societies, just like individuals, have a choice to make between more consumption now or more consumption later (through more investment now and hence faster growth of productive capacity). This was illustrated with the help of the production possibilities frontier shown in Figure 3; this trade-off will be discussed on other occasions in this chapter.

Some economists question the relevance of a production possibilities frontier in this case, however. They provide two kinds of arguments. First, they say that the economy is seldom on the frontier, that most often it is *inside* the frontier, meaning that, even over the long run, there are usually unutilized labour and capital resources, so that the economy can increase both consumption and investment production. This will be the topic of the next two chapters. Second, they argue that faster sales growth arising from high consumption expenditures can generate faster technical progress and thus faster growth rates of potential output. In other words, more consumption expenditures may displace the entire production possibilities frontier outward. This relationship, which has been observed in the case of several countries, is called Verdoorn's Law, in honour of the Dutch economist Petrus Johannes Verdoorn (1911–1982), who first identified this relationship in 1948. The following excerpt from a book by Edward J. Nell illustrates

well the thinking of those economists who question the unavoidable trade-off between consumption and investment.

The system and the individual face different conditions. For the individual, high consumption must come at the expense of high consumption later. . . . Savings is the key to growth, for individuals. But not for the system as a whole. . . . Consumption is demand, and demand is the key to production; investment occurs only when there is the expectation of further pressures on the facilities of production; or when there is pressure to innovate to keep up with the competition. . . . Hence the current demand is required to provide business with a stimulus to invest, and it is chiefly through such investment that technical progress takes place. Thus high consumption and high public spending not only mean investment in human beings, making for a more productive, healthier, better educated labour force; they also stimulate investment in physical plant and equipment, bringing improvements and better organization.

SOURCE: Excerpted from Edward J. Nell, *Making Sense of a Changing Economy* (London: Routledge, 1996), p. 112.

Technical Change   Technology, which we have listed as a separate pillar of growth, also drives investment. New business opportunities suddenly appear when a new product such as the mobile telephone is invented, or when a technological breakthrough makes an existing product much cheaper or better, as happened with Internet services in the 1990s. In a capitalist system, entrepreneurs pounce on such opportunities—building new factories, stores, and offices, and buying new equipment. Thus, if the government can figure out how to spur technological progress (a subject discussed later in this chapter), those same policies will probably boost investment.

The Growth of Demand   High growth itself can induce businesses to invest more. When demand presses against capacity, executives are likely to believe that new factories and machinery can be employed profitably—and that creates strong incentives to build new capital. Thus it was no coincidence that investment soared in Canada during the boom years of the 1990s and collapsed during the early 1980s and early 1990s. By contrast, if machinery and factories stand idle, businesses may find new investments unattractive. In summary:

> High levels of sales and expectations of rapid economic growth create an atmosphere conducive to investment.

This situation creates a kind of virtuous cycle in which high rates of investment boost economic growth, and rapid growth boosts investment. Of course, the same process can also operate in reverse—as a vicious cycle: When the economy stagnates, firms do not want to invest much, which damages prospects for further growth. (See "Questioning the Consumption–Investment Production Possibilities Frontier.")

Political Stability and Property Rights   There is one other absolutely critical determinant of investment spending that North Americans simply take for granted.

A business thinking about committing funds to, say, build a factory faces any number of risks. Construction costs might run higher than estimates. Interest rates might rise. Demand for the product might prove weaker than expected. The list goes on and on. These are the normal hazards of entrepreneurship, an activity that is not for the faint-hearted. But, at a minimum, business executives contemplating a long-term investment want assurances that their property will not be taken from them for capricious or political reasons. Businesspeople in Canada who have tight links with Conservative politicians do not worry that their property will be seized if the Liberals win the next election. Nor do they worry that court rulings will deprive them of their **property rights** without due process.

By contrast, in many less well-organized societies, the rule of law is regularly threatened by combinations of arbitrary government actions, political instability, anticapitalist ideology, rampant corruption, or runaway crime. Such problems have posed serious impediments to long-term investment in many poor countries throughout history. They are among the chief reasons these countries have remained poor. And the litany of problems that threaten property rights is not just a matter of history—these issues remain relevant in countries as different as Russia, much of Africa, and parts of Latin America today. Where businesses fear that their property may be expropriated, a drop in interest rates of, say, two percentage points will not encourage much investment.

Needless to say, the strength of property rights, adherence to the rule of law, the level of corruption, and the like are not easy to measure. Anyone who attempts to rank countries on such criteria must make many subjective judgments. Nevertheless, some results from one heroic attempt to do so are displayed in Table 3. The relative rankings of the various countries is roughly what you might expect.

TABLE 3

Selected Countries Ranked by Legal Structure and Security of Property Rights, 2005

Country	Ranking	Rating
Denmark	1	9.4
Norway	2	9.3
New Zealand	3	9.3
United Kingdom	12	8.7
Canada	14	8.6
Japan	17	8.3
United States	21	7.7
South Korea	34	7.2
India	46	6.7
Italy	52	6.4
China	63	5.8
Mexico	72	5.7

SOURCE: James D. Gwartney and Robert A. Lawson, *Economic Freedom of the World: 2007 Annual Report,* Exhibit 1.3 (Fraser Institute, 2007). Retrieved from www.fraserinstitute.org/commerce.web/publication_details.aspx?pubID=4872

Property rights are laws and/or conventions that assign owners the rights to use their property as they see fit (within the law)—for example, to sell the property and to reap the benefits (such as rents or dividends) while they own it.

GROWTH POLICY: IMPROVING EDUCATION AND TRAINING

Numerous studies in many countries support the view that more-educated and better-trained workers earn higher wages. Economists naturally assume that people who earn more are more productive. Thus, more education and training presumably contribute to higher productivity. Although private institutions play a role in the educational process, in most societies the state bears the primary responsibility for educating the population. So *educational policy* is an obvious and critical component of growth policy.

A modern industrial society is built more on brains than on brawn. Even ordinary blue-collar jobs often require a high school education. For this reason, policies that raise

To Grow Fast, Get the Institutions Right

The World Bank surveyed the ways the governments of around 100 countries either encourage or discourage market activity. Its conclusion, as summarized in *The Economist*, was that "when poor people are allowed access to the institutions richer people enjoy, they can thrive and help themselves. A great deal of poverty, in other words, may be easily avoidable."

The World Bank study highlighted the importance of making simple institutions accessible to the poor—such as protection of property rights (especially over land), access to the judicial system, and a free and open flow of information—as key ingredients in successful economic development. *The Economist* put it graphically:

If it is too expensive and time-consuming, for example, to open a bank account, the poor will stuff their savings under the mattress. When it takes 19 steps, five months and more than an average person's annual income to register a new business in Mozambique, it is no wonder that aspiring, cash-strapped entrepreneurs do not bother.

The Bank's conclusion reminded many people of the central message of a best-selling 2000 book by Peruvian economist and businessman Hernando de Soto—who found to his dismay that, in his own country, it took 700 bureaucratic steps to obtain legal title to a house!

SOURCES: "Now, think small," *The Economist*, September 15, 2001, pp. 40–42. Hernando de Soto, *The Mystery of Capital: Why Capitalism Triumphs in the West and Fails Everywhere Else* (New York: Basic Books), 2000.

rates of high school attendance and completion and, perhaps more importantly, improve the *quality* of secondary education can make genuine contributions to growth. Unfortunately, such policies have proven difficult to devise and implement. As evidence of this, according to international surveys conducted in 1994 and 2003, there was no increase whatsoever over that decade in the literacy skills of Canadians aged between 16 and 25.[3]

Finally, if knowledge is power in the Information Age, then sending more young people to colleges and universities may be crucial to economic success. The Statistics Canada 2001 census showed that, when taking into account the whole population aged 15 years and over, individuals with university diplomas or degrees earned nearly twice as much on average as those with high school graduation certificates. It is also well documented that the earnings gap between high school and university graduates in Canada has risen dramatically since 1980. In Canada, however, this has occurred mainly because high school graduates have seen their real earnings drop, and not because university graduates earn more in real dollars.

All of this is shown in Figure 4, which records the change in real weekly earnings of men and women in two age groups and with various levels of education from 1980 to 2000, and then from 2000 to 2005. The 1980 to 2000 data shows that for men and for young women working full-time, the job market rewarded more generously than ever the skills acquired in university *relative* to those acquired in high school (strangely, this was not the case for women between 35 and 54). Indeed, as the numbers in Figure 4 show, those individuals (especially men) who did not invest in an education actually saw their real earnings fall by as much as 20 percent compared to the earnings of their predecessors 20 years earlier. This trend was partially reversed in the 2000s, however, with workers with less education, especially men, making some gains relative to university degree holders.

FIGURE 4   Changes in Real Weekly Earnings, Men and Women, by Level of Education and Age Group, Canada, 1980–2000 and 2000–2005

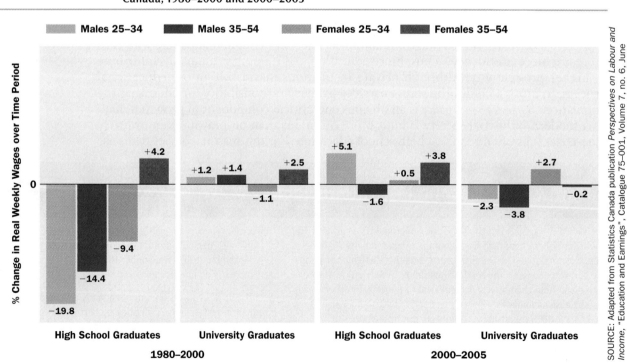

SOURCE: Adapted from Statistics Canada publication *Perspectives on Labour and Income*, "Education and Earnings", Catalogue 75–001, Volume 7, no. 6, June 2006, Table 4.

---

[3] See Statistics Canada, *Building Our Competencies: Canadian Results of the International Adult Literacy and Skills Survey 2003*, November 2005, Catalogue No. 89-617-XIE. This can be seen by comparing Annex A Tables 2.1 and 2.4.

The Yule Paradox

A statistical puzzle appears when comparing the data in Figure 4 on page 152 with those in Figure 6 on page 127. There, we saw that, overall, real wages of workers went up slightly between 1980 and 2000 (wages grew faster than prices), whereas the numbers in the accompanying table seem to indicate that most workers lost out during this 20-year period. How can we reconcile these two apparently contradictory sets of facts? The answer is that the *composition* of the workforce has changed, as the accompanying table shows.

Percentage of the Canadian Workforce with a University Degree, 1980–2005			
Age Group	1980	2000	2005
25 to 34	14%	24%	27%
35 to 54	10	19	22

SOURCE: Adapted from Statistics Canada publication *Perspectives on Labour and Income,* "Education and Earnings", Catalogue 75–001, Volume 7, no. 6, June 2006, Table 1.

In 1980, in the case of workers between 25 and 34, for instance, only 14 percent held a university degree, whereas this proportion increased to 24 percent and 27 percent in 2000 and 2005, respectively. Similar increases have been observed for older workers. So, more workers have a university degree and hence earn high wages, thus pushing up the overall real wage despite the fact that, *for a given level of education*, real wages have gone down or remained almost the same. This is a famous statistical paradox, called the *Yule Paradox*, named after the statistician (George Udny Yule) who first encountered this enigma in 1903.

Baseball provides another example of this statistical paradox: How can a Toronto Blue Jays baseball player have a lower overall batting average than a New York Yankees player despite the Blue Jays player having a higher batting average in each half of the season?

The data in Figure 4 combined with the table shown here yields a second puzzle. Why is it that the real wages of university degree holders have gone up relative to high school graduates, at least in the case of men and young women, when the relative supply of university graduates has gone up? By the law of demand and supply, one would have thought that their relative remuneration would have gone down. A very simple answer, which does not take us very far, is to reply that the demand for university graduates must have risen even faster than its supply. A slightly more sophisticated, but also more controversial argument is that globalization, with the resulting competition presented by low-skill workers from all over the world, has reduced the bargaining power of Canadian high school graduates and hence led to a reduction of their real wages.

To the extent that high wages reflect high productivity, low-cost tuition (such as that in Quebec), student loans to low-income families, and other policies to encourage university attendance may yield rich dividends for society.

Devoting more resources to education should, therefore, raise an economy's growth rate. By suitable reinterpretation, Figure 3 (on page 149) can again be used to illustrate the trade-off between present and future. Because expenditures on education are naturally thought of as *investments* in *human* capital, just think of the vertical axis now as representing educational investments. If a society spends more on them and less on consumer goods (thus moving from point *C* toward point *I*), it should grow faster.

But education is not a panacea for all an economy's ills. Education in the former Soviet Union was, at least in some respects, probably outstanding. Ultimately, however, it proved insufficient to prevent the Soviet economy from falling ever further behind the capitalist economies in terms of economic growth.

On-the-job training may be just as important as formal education in raising productivity, but it is less amenable to influence by the government. For the most part, private businesses decide how much, and in what ways, to train their workers. Various public policy initiatives—ranging from government-run training programs, to subsidies for private sector training, to mandated minimum training expenditures by firms—have been tried in various countries with mixed results. In Canada, constitutional issues complicate the design and delivery of training programs, as those ought to be under provincial jurisdiction. Evaluations of existing and past training programs usually conclude that their impact is positive but small, with their economic benefits outweighing their costs. Ironically, there is some evidence that training programs led to a percentage improvement of the earnings of older trainees, which is higher than that of younger trainees.

On-the-job training refers to skills that workers acquire while at work, rather than in school or in formal vocational training programs.

■ GROWTH POLICY: SPURRING TECHNOLOGICAL CHANGE

Our third pillar of growth is *technology*, or getting more output from given supplies of inputs. Some of the most promising policies for speeding up the pace of technical progress have already been mentioned:

More Education   Although some inventions and innovations are the product of dumb luck, most result from the sustained application of knowledge, resources, and brainpower to scientific, engineering, and managerial problems. We have just noted that more-educated workers appear to be more productive per se. In addition, a society is likely to be more innovative if it has a greater supply of scientists, engineers, and skilled business managers who are constantly on the prowl for new opportunities. Modern growth theory emphasizes the pivotal role in the growth process of committing more human, physical, and financial resources to the acquisition of knowledge.

> High levels of education, especially scientific, engineering, and managerial education, contribute to the advancement of technology.

There is little doubt that Canadian universities run high-quality graduate programs in business and in many of the scientific and engineering disciplines. As evidence of this, one need only look at the thousands of foreign students who flock to Canada to attend graduate school. Many economists endorse policies designed to induce more bright people to pursue scientific and engineering careers. Some well-known examples of such incentives include scholarships, fellowships, and research grants.

More Capital Formation   We are all familiar with the fact that the latest versions of cell phones, PCs, personal digital assistants (PDAs), and even televisions embody new features that were unavailable a year or even six months ago. The same is true of industrial capital. Indeed, new investment is the principal way in which the latest technological breakthroughs are hard-wired into the nation's capital stock. As we mentioned in our earlier discussion of capital formation, newer capital is normally better capital. In this way:

> High rates of investment contribute to rapid technical progress.

So all of the policies we discussed earlier as ways to bolster capital formation can also be thought of as ways to speed up technical progress.

Invention is the act of discovering new products or new ways of making products.

Innovation is the act of putting new ideas into effect by, for example, bringing new products to market, changing product designs, and improving the way in which things are done.

Research and development (R&D) refers to activities aimed at inventing new products or processes, or improving existing ones.

Research and Development   But there is a more direct way to spur **invention** and **innovation**: devote more of society's resources to **research and development (R&D)**.

Driven by the profit motive, businesses have long invested heavily in industrial R&D. According to the old saying, "Build a better mousetrap, and the world will beat a path to your door." And innovative companies have been engaged in research on "better mousetraps" for decades. Polaroid invented instant photography, Xerox developed photocopying, and Apple pioneered the desktop computer. Boeing and Airbus improved jet aircraft several times. Pharmaceutical companies have discovered many new, life-enhancing drugs. Intel has developed generation after generation of ever-faster microprocessors. In Canada, a high-tech company—Research in Motion, in Waterloo, Ontario—invented the BlackBerry, an all-in-one electronic communication device, which is now being widely imitated. Ballard Power Systems (located in Burnaby, British Columbia) has been developing fuel-cell technology as an environmentally friendly alternative to the standard combustion motor for automobiles and buses. The list goes on and on.

All of these companies and others have spent untold billions of dollars on R&D to discover new products, to improve old ones, and to make their industrial processes more efficient. While many research dollars are inevitably "wasted" on false starts and experiments that don't pan out, numerous studies have shown that the average dollar invested in R&D has yielded high returns to society. Heavy spending on R&D is, indeed, one of the keys to high productivity growth.

Unfortunately, when it comes to private expenditures on R&D, Canada is not really a world leader, as Canadian private expenditures on R&D, as a percentage of GDP, are much smaller than those of other large industrialized countries in the world. This can probably be attributed to our geographic location next to the United States, where a substantial amount of R&D is being performed by American-owned parent companies of Canadian subsidiaries (for instance, Ford Motor Company of the United States and Ford Canada). There are nevertheless sectors where Canada holds its ground, making large R&D expenditures relative to their sales. These sectors are most notably utilities (such as hydro companies); radio, television, and communication equipment; office, accounting, and computing equipment; textiles, textile products, leather goods, and footwear; pharmaceuticals manufacturing; real estate sales and rental activities; aircraft and spacecraft; refined petroleum products; and nuclear fuel.

The Canadian government supports and encourages R&D in several ways. First, it subsidizes private R&D spending through specific tax provisions. Tax credits of 20 to 35 percent, which reduce business taxable income, can be claimed on expenditures for scientific research and experimental development carried out in Canada.

Second, Canadian governments themselves participate in R&D. Today, in Canada, 10 percent of R&D expenditures—more than $2.5 billion per year—are performed by government agencies, mainly federal departments and agencies. Research is conducted and patents and licences are being acquired by various federal institutions, such as the Canadian Space Agency, the Department of National Defence, Agriculture Canada, Environment Canada, Health Canada, Transport Canada, Natural Resources Canada, the Department of Fisheries and Oceans, and the Communications Research Centre of Industry Canada.

Last but not least, federal and provincial governments have over the years funded about 25 percent of the R&D activity in Canada—over $6.5 billion in 2005—either directly as detailed above or indirectly through universities and through the National Sciences and Engineering Research Council and the Canadian Institutes of Health Research.

Our multipurpose Figure 3 again illustrates the choice facing society. Now interpret the vertical axis as measuring investments in R&D. Devoting more resources to R&D—that is, choosing point *I* rather than point *C*—leads to less current consumption but more growth.

THE PRODUCTIVITY SLOWDOWN AND SPEED-UP IN CANADA

Around 1973, productivity growth in Canada suddenly and mysteriously slowed down—from the rate of about 3.75 percent per year that had characterized the 1947–1973 period to about 1.2 percent thereafter (see Figure 5). Hardly anyone anticipated this productivity slowdown. Then, starting around 1996, productivity growth suddenly speeded up again—from about 1.0 percent per year during the

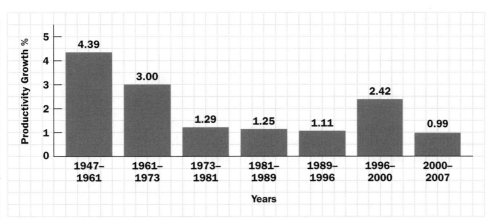

FIGURE 5

Annual Growth Rates of Labour Productivity Growth (GDP per hour worked), Canada, 1961–2007

1989–1996 period to about 2.5 percent (see Figure 5 again). Once again, the abrupt change in the growth rate caught most people by surprise. Unfortunately, this productivity growth spurt was short-lived. The rate of labour productivity growth came back down to 1.0 percent between 2000–2007, following the meltdown of the technology and information sector.

Recall from the discussion of compounding and the Rule of 70 in Chapter 6 that a change in the growth rate of just 1 percentage point, if sustained for decades, makes an enormous difference in living standards. So understanding these two major events is of critical importance. Yet even now, more than 30 years later, economists remain puzzled about the 1973 productivity slowdown, and the reasons behind the 1996 productivity speed-up are only partly understood. Let us see what economists know about these two episodes.

■ The Productivity Slowdown, 1973–1995

The productivity slowdown after 1973 was certainly a disconcerting development, and economists have been struggling to explain it ever since. But before we provide possible explanations of this phenomenon, it should be pointed out that the productivity slowdown of 1973 was a universal feature among advanced economies, as Table 4 shows.

Among the leading explanations of the 1973 slowdown are:

Lagging Investment   During the 1980s and early 1990s, many people suggested that inadequate investment was behind Canada's productivity problem. Countries such as Germany and Japan, these critics observed, saved and invested far more than Canadians did, thereby equipping their workers with more modern equipment that boosted labour productivity. Canadian tax policy, they argued, should create stronger incentives for business to invest and for households to save.

Although the argument was logical, the facts do not support it. While it is true that right after World War II business investment was quite high, the share of Canadian GDP accounted for by business investment did not actually decrease during the period of slow productivity growth.

TABLE 4		
Annual Growth Rates of Labour Productivity (GDP per hour worked), Various Countries, 1950–1973 and 1973–1984		
Country	1950–1973	1973–1984
France	5.1	3.4
Germany	6.0	3.0
Japan	7.7	3.2
Netherlands	4.4	1.9
United Kingdom	3.2	2.4
United States	2.5	1.0

SOURCE: Angus Maddison, "Growth and Slowdown in Advanced Capitalist Economies: Techniques of Qualitative Assessment," Table 2, *Journal of Economic Literature*, June 1987. Reprinted with permission.

High Energy Prices   A second explanation begins with a tantalizing fact: The productivity slowdown started around 1973, just when the Organization of the Petroleum Exporting Countries (OPEC) jacked up the price of oil. As a matter of logic, higher oil prices should reduce business use of energy, which should make labour less productive. Furthermore, productivity growth fell just at the time that energy prices rose, not just in Canada but all over the world—which is quite a striking coincidence.

Once again, the argument sounds persuasive—until you remember another important fact: Energy prices dropped sharply in the mid-1980s, but productivity growth did not revive. So the energy explanation of the productivity slowdown has many skeptics.

Inadequate Workforce Skills   Could it be that the skills of the Canadian labour force failed to keep pace with the demands of new technology after 1973? Although workforce skills are notoriously difficult to measure, there was and is a widespread feeling that the quality of education in Canada has declined. Yet standard measures such as school attendance rates, graduation rates, and average levels of educational attainment have all continued to register gains. Clearly, the proposition that the quality of the Canadian workforce declined is at least debatable.

The Shift toward Service Industries   Another possible explanation is that all industrialized economies have experienced a shift of their activities toward service industries. As we have already pointed out, labour productivity growth mainly occurs in the manufacturing sector; little productivity growth is possible in the service sector, such as elementary school teaching or medical services. As employment in the service industries takes a larger share of GDP, labour productivity growth is bound to fall. Statistics show that the greater part of the Canadian labour force—75 percent in 2005—works in the service industries. But while this can explain a gradual slowdown, it can explain neither the rapid 1973 slowdown nor the 1996 upturn in labour productivity growth.

The Breakdown of Industrial Labour Relations   Some economists believe that deteriorating industrial relations between workers and their employers could have caused the productivity slowdown. At the end of the 1960s and in the early 1970s, labour union leaders became more radical, with workers becoming more resistant to change. All of this happened in economies where labour was apparently getting the upper hand over management, with low unemployment rates, low layoffs, and high quit rates. Economies were also rocked by many workers' strikes, many of which were wildcat strikes—spontaneous strikes not mandated by union leaders. There were twice as many person-days lost in work stoppages in the decade starting in 1973 than there were in the decade before 1973. This increased willingness to quit and strike could have led to slower productivity growth. Following the recession of 1980–1982, and certainly that of 1990–1992, labour unrest was less of a factor, however, so it could explain the productivity slowdown of the 1970s, but seems less relevant to events in the years that followed.

Austerity Policies Pursued by Government   As just pointed out, Canada faced two very bad recessions in the early 1980s and early 1990s. As we will see in later chapters, these recessions were generated by the keen anti-inflation policies pursued by the Bank of Canada. Some economists believe that there is a tight causal link that goes from fast growth in aggregate demand and productivity growth (refer back to "Questioning the Consumption–Investment Production Possibilities Frontier" feature). While this may explain what happened after 1982, it can hardly provide an explanation for the slowdown in productivity growth that occurred before, starting in 1973. In addition, Canada also experienced many recessions before 1973, including a long one in 1960–1961, as shown on page 102 in Chapter 5, achieving high rates of productivity growth nonetheless.

A Technological Slowdown?   Could the pace of innovation have slowed in the 1973–1995 period? Most people instinctively answer "no." After all, the microchip and the personal computer were invented in the 1970s, opening the door to what can only be called a revolution in computing and information technology (IT). Workplaces were transformed beyond recognition. Entirely new industries (such as those related to PCs and Internet services) were spawned. Didn't these technological marvels raise productivity by enormous amounts?

The paradox of seemingly rapid technological advance coupled with sluggish productivity performance puzzled economists for years. How could the contribution of technology to growth have *fallen*? A satisfactory answer was never given. And then, all of a sudden, the facts changed.

▨ The Productivity Speed-Up, 1996–2000

Figure 5 shows that productivity growth speeded up remarkably after 1996, rising from about 1.0 percent per annum before that year to about 2.5 percent until 2000. This time, the causes are better understood—and most of them relate to the IT revolution.

Surging Investment   Bountiful new business opportunities in the IT sector and elsewhere, coupled with a strong national economy, led to a small surge in business investment spending in the 1990s. Business investment as a percentage of real GDP rose from 10.5 percent in 1995 to 12.9 percent in 1999, and most of that increase was concentrated in computers, software, and telecommunications equipment. Indeed, between 1997 and 1999, the information and communication technology sector grew at an amazing rate of 19 percent per year. Real investment in information and technology as

Where Have the Productivity Gains Gone?

The statistical facts of the last decade have created yet another puzzle. Normally, one would expect the increases in labour productivity—GDP per hour worked—to be reflected in increases in real hourly wages. However, this has not really been the case since 1981. Figure 5 showed that productivity gains, although relatively weak, have stayed above 1 percent per year since 1981. By contrast, real hourly compensation during the same time period increased at a much lower pace and even decreased between 2000 and 2005, as can be seen in the accompanying table and deduced from a close examination of Figure 6 in Chapter 6.

Time Period	Annual Growth Rate of Hourly Compensation
1981–1989	0.27%
1989–2000	0.76
2000–2005	− 0.11

SOURCE: Andrew Sharpe and Jean-François Arsenault, "The Living Standard Domain of the Canadian Index of Wellbeing," unpublished report prepared for the Atkinson Charitable Foundation (Ottawa: Centre for the Study of Living Standards, n.d.).

Why is it that the growth rate of labour productivity and the growth rate of real labour compensation can be so different over a long time period? In the present case, there are basically three explanations. The first is a technical reason: GDP and wages are deflated by two different indexes. As explained in Chapter 6, GDP is deflated by the GDP deflator, while wages are deflated by the Consumer Price Index. The GDP deflator index has grown much more slowly than the CPI over this 25-year period, because of low growth rates in the price index of investment goods due to the falling absolute price of information and communication technologies. As a result, real wages could not grow as fast as labour productivity. This explains about half of the discrepancy.

The second and third explanations, which explain the other half of the discrepancy, are linked to issues of income distribution. As in many other countries, there has been a shift in income distribution in Canada over the last two decades. The profit share is now much larger than it used to be, implying that the labour share is now smaller than it was at the beginning of the first productivity slowdown. This implies that an excessive portion of the productivity gains of the last two decades have been captured by profit recipients in the form of higher dividends or higher corporate retained earnings.

Finally, there has been a distributional change *within* the labour share of national income, with a large increase in inequality. The labour share includes the very high employment income of CEOs, top athletes, performers, etc. But weekly earnings are not a comprehensive measure of labour compensation, since they exclude nonwage components of labour compensation and benefits such as stock options and bonuses. Growth in the nonwage components of labour compensation has outstripped wage growth. This explains further the weak rate of increase in real hourly wages.

Why has this been so? Some economists say that, along with the anti-inflation policies that were initiated in the early 1980s, economies have been slowly moving from managerial capitalism, where all employees share the productivity gains, toward finance capitalism, where corporate executives and shareholders receive a greater proportion of these productivity gains.

a share of GDP doubled during the second half of the 1990s. We have observed several times in this chapter that the productivity growth rate should rise when the capital stock grows faster—and it did.

Falling Energy Prices?   For part of this period, especially the years 1996–1998, energy prices were falling. By the same logic used earlier, falling energy prices should have enhanced productivity growth. But, as we noted earlier, this argument did not seem to work so well when energy prices fell in the 1980s. Why, then, should we believe it for the 1990s?

Advances in Information Technology   We seem to be on safer ground when we look to technological progress, especially in computers and semiconductors, to explain the speed-up in productivity growth. First, innovation seemed to explode in the 1990s. Computers became faster and much, much cheaper—as did telecommunications equipment and services. Corporate intranets became commonplace. The Internet grew from a scientific curiosity into a commercial reality, and so on. We truly entered the Information Age.

Second, it probably took Canadian businesses some time to learn how to use the computer and telecommunications technologies that were invented and adopted between, say, 1980 and the early 1990s. It was only in the late 1990s, some observers argue, that Canadian industry was positioned to reap the benefits of these advances in the form of higher productivity. Such long delays are not unprecedented. Research has shown, for example, that it took a long time for the availability of electric power at the end of the nineteenth century to contribute much to productivity growth. Like electric power, computers were a novel input to production, and it may have taken years for prospective users to find the most productive ways to employ them.

In summary:

Two of the three main pillars of productivity growth—capital formation and technological change—seem to do a credible job of explaining why productivity accelerated in Canada at the end of the 1990s.

The Second Productivity Slowdown, 2000–2007

The productivity speed-up in Canada was short-lived, however, which presents another puzzle for productivity specialists. Whereas labour productivity growth has continued unabated in the United States, the rate of productivity growth in Canada

PUZZLE RESOLVED:
Why the Relative Price of University Tuition Keeps Rising

Earlier in this chapter, we observed that the relative prices of services such as university tuition, dental care, and theatre tickets seem to rise year after year. And we suggested that one main reason for this perpetual increase is tied to the economy's long-run growth rate. We are now in a position to understand precisely how that mechanism works. Rising productivity is the key. The argument is based on three simple ideas.

Idea 1 It stands to reason, and is amply demonstrated by historical experience, that *real wages tend to rise in proportion to labour productivity.* This relationship makes sense: Labour normally gets paid more when and where it produces more. Thus, real wages will rise most rapidly in those economies with the fastest productivity growth.

Idea 2 Although average labour productivity in the economy increases from year to year, *there are a number of personally provided services for which productivity (output per hour) cannot or does not grow.* We have already mentioned several of them. Your university can increase the "productivity" of its faculty by increasing class size, but most students and parents would view that as a decrease in educational quality. Similarly, a dentist takes roughly as long to repair a cavity as his counterparts did 25 or 50 years ago. It also takes *exactly* the same time for an orchestra to play one of Beethoven's symphonies today as it did in Beethoven's time.

There is a common ingredient in each of these diverse examples: The major sources of higher labour productivity that we have studied in this chapter—more capital and better technology—are completely or nearly irrelevant. It still takes one lecturer to teach a class, one doctor to examine a patient, and four musicians to play a string quartet—just as it did a hundred years ago. Saving on labour by using more and better equipment is more or less out of the question.[4] These so-called *personal services* stand in stark contrast to, say, working on an automobile assembly line or in a semiconductor plant, or even to working in service industries such as telecommunications—all instances in which both capital formation and technical progress regularly raise labour productivity.

Idea 3 *Real wages in different occupations must rise at similar rates in the long run.* This point may sound wrong at first: Haven't the wages of computer programmers risen faster than those of schoolteachers in recent years? Yes they have, and that is the market's way of attracting more young people into computer programming. But in

---

[4] However, some people foresee a world in which education and medical care are delivered long distance over the Internet. We'll see!

the long run, these growth rates must (more or less) equilibrate, or else virtually no one would want to be a schoolteacher any more.

Now let's bring the three ideas together. University professors are no more productive than they used to be, but autoworkers are (Idea 2). But in the long run, the real wages of university teachers and autoworkers must grow at roughly the same rate (Idea 3), which is the economy-wide productivity growth rate (Idea 1). As a result, wages of university teachers and doctors will rise *faster* than their productivity does, and so their services must grow ever more expensive compared to, say, computers and phone calls.

That is, indeed, the way things seem to have worked out. Compared to the world in which your parents grew up, computers and telephone calls are now very cheap while university tuition and plumbers' and electricians' bills are very expensive. The same logic applies to the services of police officers (two per squad car), soccer players (11 per team), chefs, and many other occupations where productivity improvements are either impossible or undesirable. All of these services have grown much more expensive over the years. This phenomenon has been called the **cost disease of the personal services**.

Ironically, the villain of the piece is actually the economy's strong productivity growth. If manufacturing and telecommunications workers did *not* become more productive over time, their real wages would not rise. In that case, the real wages of teachers, plumbers, and doctors would not have to keep pace, so their services would not have to grow ever more expensive. Paradoxically, the enormous productivity gains that have blessed our economy and raised our standard of living also account for the problem of rising tuition costs. In the most literal sense, we are the victims of our own success.

> According to the **cost disease of the personal services**, service activities that require direct personal contact tend to rise in price relative to other goods and services.

has gone back down to about 1 percent per year in 2000–2007, as can be seen in Figure 5. Two main explanations have been advanced so far. First, the meltdown of the high-tech sector, where productivity growth is very high, has led to an overall lower measure of labour productivity growth. Also, Canadian firms have reduced their investments in information and technology, so productivity-enhancing techniques have not been introduced at the same fast pace that characterized the second half of the 1990s. Second, Canada has experienced a *decrease* in the productivity of the mining and oil and gas extraction industries, which also has an impact on overall productivity. Higher energy prices have induced Canadian companies to exploit natural resources that are more costly and that take more time to extract. Hopefully, these investments in less traditional resources (the Alberta tar sands, for instance) will pay off one day.

▪ GROWTH IN THE DEVELOPING COUNTRIES[5]

Ernest Hemingway once answered a query of F. Scott Fitzgerald's by agreeing that, yes, the rich *are* different—they have more money! Similarly, whereas the main determinants of economic growth—increases in capital, improving technology, and rising workforce skills—are the same in both rich and poor countries, they look quite different in what is often called the Third World. This chapter has focused on growth in the industrialized countries so far. So let us now review the three pillars of productivity growth from the standpoint of the developing nations.

▪ The Three Pillars Revisited

Capital   We noted earlier that many poor countries are poorly endowed with capital. Given their low incomes, they simply have been unable to accumulate the volumes of business capital (factories, equipment, and the like) and public capital (roads, bridges, airports, and so on) that we take for granted in the industrialized world. In a rich coun-

---

[5] This section can be skipped in shorter courses.

try like Canada, $100,000 or more worth of capital stands behind a typical worker, while in a poor African country, the corresponding figure may be less than $500. No wonder the Canadian worker is vastly more productive than his African counterpart.

But accumulating more capital can be exceptionally difficult in the developing world. We noted earlier that rich countries have a *choice* about how much of their resources to devote to current consumption versus investment for the future. (See Figure 3 on page 149.) But building capital for the future is a far more difficult task in poor countries, where much of the population may be living on the edge and have little if anything to save for the future. For this reason, it has long been believed that **development assistance**, sometimes called *foreign aid*, is a crucial ingredient for growth in the developing world. Indeed, the World Bank was established in 1944 precisely to make low-interest development loans to poor countries.

Development assistance has always been controversial. Critics of foreign aid argue that the money is often not well spent. Without honest and well-functioning governments, well-defined property rights, and so on, they argue, the developing countries cannot and will not make good use of the assistance they receive. Supporters of foreign aid counter that the donor countries have been far too stingy. Canada, for example, donates only about 0.25 percent of its GDP each year. The Canadian International Development Agency (CIDA) is in charge of administering Canada's official assistance programs. But can grants that amount to $60 per person—which is a fairly typical figure for the recipient countries—really be expected to make much difference? This is why the Canadian government has decided to focus its help on a few countries, most of which are in Africa, instead of spreading its funds all over the globe. In 2000, as part of an agreed set of ambitious new development goals, the wealthy members of the United Nations pledged to increase their assistance to the developing nations. (See the box "The Millennium Development Goals.")

> **Development assistance** ("foreign aid") refers to outright grants and low-interest loans to poor countries from both rich countries and multinational institutions like the World Bank. The purpose is to spur economic development.

Technology   You need only visit a poor country to see that the level of technology is generally far below what we in the West are accustomed to. In principle, this handicap should be easy to overcome. As we noted in our discussion of the convergence hypothesis, people in poor countries don't have to invent anything; they can just adopt technologies that have already been invented in the rich countries. And indeed, a number of formerly poor countries have followed this strategy with great success. South Korea, which was destitute in the mid-1950s, is a prime example.

But as we observed earlier, many of the developing nations, especially the poorest ones, have been unable to join this "convergence club." They may lack the necessary

The Millennium Development Goals

To celebrate the arrival of the new millennium in 2000, the member states of the United Nations established an ambitious set of *Millennium Development Goals* to be achieved by the year 2015. Where the goals are numerical, they refer to conditions in the year 1990 as the starting point for measurement. The twelve goals fall under eight categories:

1. **Poverty and hunger**
   Halve the proportion of people living on less than $1 a day.
   Halve the proportion of people who suffer from hunger.

2. **Education**
   Ensure that both boys and girls achieve universal primary education.

3. **Gender equality**
   Eliminate gender disparities at all levels of education.

4. **Child mortality**
   Reduce the under-five mortality rate by two-thirds.

5. **Maternal health**
   Reduce maternal mortality by three-quarters.

6. **Disease**
   Reverse the spread of HIV/AIDS.

7. **Environment**
   Halve the proportion of people without access to potable water.
   Significantly improve the lives of at least 100 million slum dwellers.
   Reverse the loss of environmental resources.

8. **Global partnership for development**
   Raise official development assistance.
   Expand market access for poor countries' exports.

scientific and engineering know-how. They may be short on educated workers. They may be woefully undersupplied with the necessary infrastructure, such as transportation and communications systems. Or they may simply be plagued by incompetent or corrupt governments. Whatever the reasons, they have been unable to emulate the technological advances of the West.

There are no easy solutions to this problem. One common suggestion is to encourage **foreign direct investment** by **multinational corporations**. Industrial giants like Toyota (Japan), IBM (United States), Siemens (Germany), and others bring their advanced technologies with them when they open a factory in a developing nation. They can train local workers and improve local transportation and communications networks. But, of course, these companies are *foreign*, and they come to make a *profit*—both of which may cause resentment in the local population.

For this and other reasons, many developing countries have not always welcomed foreign investment. In addition, multinationals are rarely tempted to open factories in the poorest developing countries, such as those in sub-Saharan Africa, where skilled labour is in short supply, transportation systems may be inadequate, and governments are often unstable and unreliable.

Education and Training   Huge discrepancies exist between the average levels of educational attainment in the rich and poor countries. Table 5, on next page, shows some data on average years of schooling in selected OECD and non-OECD countries, including some of the countries listed in Table 1. The differences are dramatic—ranging from a high of 13.9 years in Norway (with Canada not far behind at 13.2 years) to less than 3 years in Haiti and Burundi. Countries with high average educational attainment by and large have high productivity levels, but some countries, such as Romania, are poorer than one would expect from their average years of schooling. In most industrialized countries, universal primary education and high rates of high school completion are already realities. But in many poor countries, even completing grade school may be the exception, leaving rudimentary skills such as reading, writing, and basic arithmetic in short supply. In such cases, expanding and improving primary education—including keeping children in school until they reach the age of 12—may be among the most cost-effective growth policies available. (See boxed feature "The Importance of Literacy for Productivity.")

> **Foreign direct investment** is the purchase or construction of real business assets—such as factories, offices, and machinery—in a foreign country.
>
> **Multinational corporations** are corporations, generally large ones, which do business in many countries. Most, but not all, of these corporations have their headquarters in developed countries.

The Importance of Literacy for Productivity

Table 1, page 147, showed that Canada has been losing ground in the labour productivity race, as its ranking has deteriorated in relation to both the United States and several European countries. A possible explanation of this phenomenon is that the literacy skills of Canadians have gone downward *relative* to those of the citizens of other countries since 1975. These literacy skills (proficiency in finding information and understanding documents, and in numeracy) are associated with high national productivity. The implication for Canada and poor countries is that more effort should be put into teaching basic reading and arithmetic skills to all citizens, as the following newspaper article points out.

ECONOMIST PREFERS ABC TO PHD

As a university professor, Jean-Francois Tremblay is pleased to see Ottawa and the provinces investing in post-secondary education after a 10-year hiatus. But as an economist, he is not convinced that pouring more public money into universities and colleges is the best way to boost Canada's economic growth.

Tremblay and his colleague Serge Coulombe, who teach economics at the University of Ottawa, have just completed a study for the C.D. Howe Institute, which shows that improving literacy among lower-income citizens would have a greater impact on Canada's standard of living than producing more highly educated graduates.

By most international measures, Canada has a high-quality education system. Yet Canadians do not perform particularly well in standardized tests of literacy and numeracy. In a 14-nation survey conducted by the Organisation for Economic Co-operation and Development, Canada ranked a less-than-impressive eighth, behind the Scandinavian countries, Belgium, the Netherlands and Germany. What's more, Canada's score peaked in 1975, then began a long decline.

A mediocre literacy rating drags down a country's productivity more than a mid-place ranking in university enrolment, Tremblay explained. He and Coulombe demonstrate in their paper that a 1 percent jump in Canada's literacy score, relative to the international average, would boost national productivity by 2.5 percent and raise per capita gross domestic product by 1.5 percent.

SOURCE: Adapted from Carol Goar, "Economist prefers ABC to PhD," *Toronto Star,* October 17, 2005, p. A22.

The problem is particularly acute in many traditional societies, where women are second-class citizens—or worse. In such countries, the education of girls may be considered unimportant or even inappropriate.

Some Special Problems of the Developing Countries

Accumulating capital, improving technology, and enhancing workforce skills are common ingredients of growth in rich and poor countries alike. But Third World countries also must contend with some special handicaps to growth that are mostly absent in the West.

Geography   Canadians often forget how blessed we are geographically. We live in a temperate (but at times very cold!) climate zone, on a land mass that has literally millions of hectares of flat, fertile land that is ideal for agriculture. The fact that our nation literally stretches "from sea to sea to sea" also means we have many fine seaports. Contrast this splendid set of geographical conditions with the situation of the world's poorest region: sub-Saharan Africa. Many African nations are landlocked and/or terribly short of arable land.

Health   People in rich countries rarely think about such debilitating tropical diseases as malaria. But they are rampant in many developing nations, especially in Africa. The AIDS epidemic, of course, is ravaging the continent. Although improvements in public health are important in all countries, they are literally matters of life and death in the poorest nations. And there is a truly vicious cycle here: Poor health is a serious impediment to economic growth, and poverty makes it hard to improve health standards.

Governance   Complaining about the low quality of government is a popular pastime in many Western democracies. Canadians do it every day. But most governments in industrialized nations are paragons of virtue and efficiency compared to the governments of some (but not all) developing nations. As we have noted in this chapter, political stability, the rule of law, and respect for property rights are all crucial requirements for economic growth. By the same token, corruption and over-regulation of business are obvious deterrents to investment. Lawlessness, tyrannical rule, and war are even more serious impediments. Unfortunately, too many poor nations have been victimized by a succession of corrupt dictators and tragic wars. It need hardly be said that those conditions are not exactly conducive to economic growth.

TABLE 5	
Average Educational Attainment in Selected Countries, 2004	
OECD countries	
Norway	13.9
United States	13.3
Canada	13.2
Ireland	13.0
United Kingdom	12.6
Japan	12.4
South Korea	12.0
France	11.6
Mexico	8.8
Non-OECD countries	
Romania	9.5
India	4.8
Brazil	4.6
Haiti	2.7
Burundi	1.2

Note: Data for OECD countries are for 2004 for people aged between 25 and 64; non-OECD data are for 2000 for people older than 25.

SOURCES: For OECD countries: OECD, *OECD Education at a Glance, 2006*, Table A1.5; retrieved from www.oecd.org. For non-OECD countries: Robert J. Barro and Jong-Wha Lee, *International Data on Educational Attainment: Updates and Implications*, National Bureau of Economic Research Working Paper No. 42, April 2000; appendix data tables retrieved from www.cid.harvard.edu/ciddata/ciddata.html

FROM THE LONG RUN TO THE SHORT RUN

Most of this chapter has been devoted to explaining and evaluating the factors underpinning the growth rate of *potential* GDP. Over long periods of time, the growth rates of actual and potential GDP match somewhat. But, just like people, economies do not always live up to their potential. As we observed in the previous chapter, GDP in Canada often diverges from potential GDP as a result of macroeconomic fluctuations. Sometimes it is higher; often it is lower. Indeed, whereas this chapter has studied the factors that determine the rate at which the GDP of a particular country *grows* from one year to the next, we know that GDP occasionally *shrinks*—during periods we call *recessions*. To study these fluctuations, we must supplement the long-run theory of *aggregate supply*, which we have just described, with a short-run theory of *aggregate demand*—a task that begins in the next chapter.

SUMMARY

1. More **capital**, improved workforce quality (which is normally measured by the amount of education and training), and better technology all raise labour productivity and therefore shift the production function upward. They constitute the three main pillars of growth.

2. The growth rate of labour productivity depends on the rate of capital formation, the rate of improvement of workforce quality, and the rate of technical progress. So growth policy concentrates on speeding up these processes.

3. **Capital formation** can be encouraged by low real interest rates, favourable tax treatment, rapid technical change, rapid growth of demand, and a climate of political stability that respects **property rights**. Each of these factors is at least influenced by policy.

4. Policies that increase education and training—the second pillar of growth—can be expected to make a country's workforce more productive. They range from universal primary education to post-graduate fellowships in science and engineering.

5. Technological advances can be encouraged by more education, by higher rates of **investment**, and also by direct expenditures—both public and private—on **research and development (R&D)**.

6. The **convergence hypothesis** holds that countries with lower productivity levels tend to have higher productivity growth rates, so that poor countries gradually close the gap on rich ones.

7. One major reason to expect convergence is that technological know-how can be transferred quickly from the leading nations to the laggards. Unfortunately, not all countries seem able to benefit from this information transfer.

8. Productivity growth slowed precipitously in Canada and elsewhere around 1973, and economists are still not sure why.

9. Productivity growth in Canada has speeded up again between 1996-2000, probably mainly as a result of the information technology revolution and the large investments that accompanied it.

10. Because many personal services—such as education, dental and medical care, and police protection—are essentially handicraft activities that are not amenable to labour-saving innovations, they suffer from a **cost disease** that makes them grow ever more expensive over time.

11. The same three pillars of economic growth—capital, technology, and education—apply in the developing countries. But on all three fronts, conditions are much more difficult there—and improvements are harder to obtain.

12. The rich countries try to help with all three pillars by providing **development assistance**, and **multinational corporations** sometimes provide capital and better technology via **foreign direct investment**. But both of these mechanisms are surrounded by controversy.

13. Growth in many of the poor countries is also held back by adverse geographical conditions and/or corrupt governments.

KEY TERMS

Human capital   146

Convergence hypothesis   147

Capital   148

Investment   148

Capital formation   148

Property rights   151

On-the-job training   153

Invention   154

Innovation   154

Research and development (R&D)   154

Cost disease of the personal services   160

Development assistance   161

Foreign direct investment   162

Multinational corporations   162

TEST YOURSELF

1. The table below shows real GDP per hour of work in four imaginary countries in the years 1995 and 2005. By what percentage did labour productivity grow in each country? Is it true that productivity *growth* was highest where the initial *level* of productivity was the lowest? For which countries?

	Output per Hour	
	1995	2005
Country A	$40	$48
Country B	$25	$35
Country C	$ 2	$ 3
Country D	$ 0.50	$ 0.60

2. Imagine that new inventions in the computer industry affect the growth rate of productivity as follows:

Year of Invention	Following Year	5 Years Later	10 Years Later	20 Years Later
0%	−1%	0%	+2%	+3%

Would such a pattern help explain Canadian productivity performance since the mid-1970s? Why?

3. Which of the following prices would you expect to rise rapidly? Why?

   a. cable television rates

   b. hockey tickets

   c. Internet access

   d. household cleaning services

   e. driving lessons

4. Two countries have the production possibilities frontier (PPF) shown in Figure 3 on page 149. But Consumia chooses point *C*, whereas Investia chooses point *I*. Which country will have the higher PPF the following year? Why?

5. Show on a graph how capital formation shifts the production function. Use this graph to show that capital formation increases labour productivity. Explain in words why labour is more productive when the capital stock is larger.

6. This exercise should help you to understand the Yule Paradox, discussed on page 153. The following table gives the batting averages of two baseball players during the first and the second halves of the season. Knowing that the overall batting average depends on the number of at-bats during the entire season, which player has the highest overall batting average? How is this related to the Yule Paradox?

Player	First Half of Season		Second Half of Season		Overall Season	
	At-Bats	Batting Average	At-Bats	Batting Average	At-Bats	Batting Average
Blue Jays player	300	0.300	100	0.400	400	_____
Yankees player	100	0.260	300	0.380	400	_____

DISCUSSION QUESTIONS

1. Explain the different objectives of (long-run) growth policy versus (short-run) stabilization policy.

2. Explain why economic growth might be higher in a country with well-established property rights and a stable political system compared with a country where property rights are uncertain and the government is unstable.

3. Chapter 6 pointed out that, because faster capital formation comes at a cost (reduced current consumption), it is possible for a country to invest too much. Suppose the government of some country decides that its businesses are investing too much. What steps might it take to slow the pace of capital formation?

4. Explain why, under some circumstances, it might be possible to simultaneously increase both investment expenditures and current consumption.

5. Explain why the best educational policies to promote faster growth might be different in the following countries.

   a. Mozambique

   b. Brazil

   c. France

6. Comment on the following: "Sharp changes in the volume of investment in Canada help explain both the productivity slowdown in 1973 and the productivity speed-up in 1996."

7. Discuss some of the pros and cons of increasing development assistance, both from the point of view of the donor country and the point of view of the recipient country.

8

THE CIRCULAR FLOW OF SPENDING AND THE POWERFUL CONSUMER

Men are disposed, as a rule and on the average, to increase their consumption as their income increases, but not by as much as the increase in their income.

JOHN MAYNARD KEYNES (1883–1946), 1936

The last chapter focused on the determinants of *potential GDP*—the economy's capacity to produce. We turn our attention now to the factors determining *actual GDP*—how much of that potential is actually utilized. Will the economy be pressing against its capacity, and therefore perhaps also having trouble with inflation? Or will there be a great deal of unused capacity, and therefore high unemployment?

In this chapter and the next, we tackle the demand side of macroeconomics, in contrast to the supply side that we examined in the previous chapter. While the supply side may rule the roost in the long run, Chapter 5's whirlwind tour of Canadian economic history suggested that the strength of aggregate demand holds the key to the economy's condition in the short run. When aggregate demand grows briskly, the economy booms. When aggregate demand is weak, the economy stagnates.

The model we develop to understand aggregate demand in this chapter and the next will teach us much about this process. But it is too simple to deal with policy issues effectively, because the government and the financial system are largely ignored. We remedy these omissions in Part III, where we give government spending, taxation, and interest rates appropriately prominent roles. The influence of the exchange rate between the Canadian dollar and foreign currencies will also be considered in Part III, but its full implications will be examined in Part IV.

CONTENTS

ISSUE: *Demand Management and the Ornery Consumer*

In Chapter 5, we suggested that the government sometimes wants to shift the aggregate demand curve. It can do so a number of ways. One direct approach is to alter its own spending, becoming extravagant when private demand is weak or miserly when private demand is strong. Alternatively, the government can take a more indirect route, by using taxes and other policy tools to influence *private* spending decisions. Because consumer expenditures constitute close to 60 percent of gross domestic product, the consumer presents the most tempting target.

A case in point arose when the long boom of the 1990s ended abruptly and economic growth in the United States slowed to a crawl, threatening the health of the Canadian economy. The Canadian government had already decided to grant long-awaited reductions in individual tax rates in its budget of February 2000, but, with the poor outlook of the economy in the fall, Paul Martin—the Liberal finance minister—decided to speed up the tax reductions, enacting them all in January 2001. Marginal tax rates of 29, 24, and 17 percent were moved down to 26, 22, and 16 percent, respectively, and a surtax was abolished. Finance Canada assessed that the enacted changes meant a 20 percent reduction in personal taxation on average, representing about 2 percent of household disposable income.

In the United States, newly elected President George W. Bush and his economic advisers also decided that consumer spending needed a boost, and Congress passed a multiyear tax cut in 2001. One provision of the tax cut gave taxpayers an advance rebate on their 2001 taxes. Cheques ranging as high as $600 went out starting in July 2001. There should be no mystery about how changes in personal taxes are expected to affect consumer spending. Any reduction in personal taxes leaves consumers with more after-tax income to spend; any tax increase leaves them with less. The linkage from taxes to spendable income to consumer spending seems direct and unmistakable, and, in a certain sense, it is.

Yet, while growth slowed down in Canada in 2001, there was no recession despite the fears of many forecasters. Growth became negative in the United States for about three-quarters of 2001, however, and the United States was hit with its first recession in a decade. So, while in Canada the tax cuts were successful in avoiding a recession, this was not the case for our southern neighbour. Why is this? It seems that Canadian consumers understood very well that the tax cuts were there to stay, and spent their extra income. In contrast, Americans understood the tax cut to be temporary, and as a consequence they saved a substantial share of their tax cuts, rather than spending them. As a result, the economy did not receive the expected boost.

◼ COMPONENTS OF AGGREGATE SPENDING

Aggregate demand is the total amount that all consumers, business firms, and government agencies wish to spend on final goods and services.

First, some vocabulary. We have already introduced the concept of *gross domestic product* as the standard measure of the economy's total output.[1]

For the most part, firms in a market economy produce goods only if they think they can sell them. **Aggregate demand** is the total amount that all consumers, business firms, government agencies, and foreigners wish to spend on Canadian final goods and services. Aggregate demand is a schedule, not a fixed number. It depends on a variety of factors—such as consumer incomes, various government policies, and events in foreign countries. To understand the nature of aggregate demand, it is best to break it up into its four major components, as we do in this chapter.

Each component of aggregate demand is associated with a component of gross domestic product, seen from the expenditure side. Each element of this expenditure-based gross domestic product is a fixed number, and can be related to the national accounts, as these are described in the appendix to this chapter. Thus, by examining the four components of aggregate demand, we also examine the components of gross domestic product, seen from the expenditure side.

[1] See Chapter 5, pages 96–101.

Consumer expenditure (*consumption* for short) is simply the total value of all consumer goods and services demanded. Because consumer spending constitutes between 55 and 60 percent of total spending, it is the main focus of this chapter. We represent it by the letter *C*.

Investment spending, represented by the letter *I*, was discussed extensively in the last chapter. It is the amount that firms spend on factories, machinery, software, and the like, plus the amount that families spend on new houses. Notice that this usage of the word *investment* differs from common parlance. Most people speak of *investing* in the stock market or in a bank account. But that kind of investment merely swaps one form of financial asset (such as money) for another form (such as a share of stock). These financial investments are called *placements* by French-speaking economists, and this is a word that Anglophones would be well-advised to adopt, so as to avoid confusion with the real thing! When economists speak of *investment*, they mean instead the purchase of some *new, physical asset*, such as a drill press, a computer, or a house. The distinction is important here because it is only the economists' kinds of investments that constitute direct additions to the demand for newly produced goods.

Government purchases of goods and services are the third major component of aggregate demand. In Canada, they represent about 20 percent of overall expenditures. Government purchases include items such as paper, computers, airplanes, ships, and labour bought by all levels of government. We use the symbol *G* for this variable.

Net exports constitute the fourth and last component of aggregate demand. Net exports are simply defined as Canadian exports *minus* Canadian imports. The reasoning here is simple. Part of the demand for Canadian goods and services originates beyond our borders—as when foreigners buy our wheat, software, and banking services. So to obtain total demand for Canadian products, these goods and services must be added to Canadian domestic demand. Similarly, some items included in *C* and *I* are made abroad. Think, for example, of beer from Germany, cars from Japan, and shirts from Malaysia. These must be subtracted from the total amount demanded by Canadian consumers if we want to measure total spending *on Canadian products*. The addition of exports, *X*, and the subtraction of imports, *IM*, leads to the following shorthand definition of aggregate demand:

Aggregate demand is the sum $C + I + G + (X - IM)$.

These are also the four main components of the gross domestic product, seen from the expenditure side. We need two further concepts for our vocabulary to be complete. We will need to assess the gross domestic product, but this time as seen from the income side. We will also need to define a more restrictive concept of income, called **disposable income**.[2] The term *disposable income*, which we will abbreviate *DI*, is meant to be descriptive—it tells us how much consumers actually have available to spend or to save. For that reason, it will play a prominent role in this chapter and in subsequent discussions.

Consumer expenditure (*C*) is the total amount spent by consumers on newly produced goods and services (excluding purchases of new homes, which are considered investment goods).

Investment spending (*I*) is the sum of the expenditures of business firms on new plant and equipment and households on new homes. Financial "investments" are not included, nor are resales of existing physical assets.

Government purchases (*G*) refer to the goods (such as airplanes and paper clips) and services (such as school teaching and police protection) purchased by all levels of government.

Net exports, or *X − IM*, is the difference between exports (*X*) and imports (*IM*). It indicates the difference between what we sell to foreigners and what we buy from them.

Disposable income (*DI*) is the sum of the incomes of all individuals in the economy after all taxes have been deducted and all transfer payments have been added.

■ THE CIRCULAR FLOW OF SPENDING, PRODUCTION, AND INCOME

Enough definitions. How do these three concepts—domestic product, domestic expenditure, and domestic income—interact in a market economy? We can answer this best with a rather elaborate diagram (Figure 1). For obvious reasons, Figure 1 is called a *circular flow diagram*. It depicts a large tube in which an imaginary fluid circulates in a clockwise direction. At several points along the way, some of the fluid leaks out or additional fluid is injected into the tube.

Let's examine this system, beginning on the far left. At point 1 on the circle, we find consumers. Disposable income (*DI*) flows into their pockets, and two things flow out: consumption (*C*), which stays in the circular flow, and saving (*S*), which "leaks out." This outflow depicts the fact that consumers normally spend less than they earn and

---

[2] More detailed information on these and other concepts is provided in the appendix to this chapter.

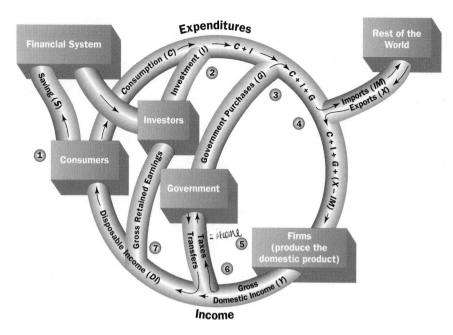

The Circular Flow of Expenditures and Income

save the balance. The "leakage" to saving, of course, does not disappear; it flows into the financial system via banks, mutual funds, and so on. We defer consideration of what happens inside the financial system to Chapters 12 and 13.

The upper loop of the circular flow represents expenditures, and as we move clockwise to point 2, we encounter the first "injection" into the flow: investment spending (I). The diagram shows this injection as coming from "investors"—a group that includes both business firms and home buyers.[3] As the circular flow moves past point 2, it is bigger than it was before: Total spending has increased from C to $C + I$.

At point 3, there is yet another injection. The government adds its demand for goods and services (G) to those of consumers and investors ($C + I$). Now aggregate demand has grown to $C + I + G$.

The next leakage and injection come at point 4. Here we see export spending entering the circular flow from abroad and import spending leaking out. The net effect of these two forces may increase or decrease the circular flow, depending on whether net exports are positive or negative. (In Canada, they are usually positive.) In either case, by the time we pass point 4, we have accumulated the full amount of aggregate demand, $C + I + G + (X - IM)$.

The circular flow diagram shows this aggregate demand for goods and services arriving at the business firms, which are located at point 5. Responding to this demand, firms produce the domestic product. As we will discuss in Chapter 9, the domestic product may wind up being equal to aggregate demand, but it may also turn out to be somewhat smaller or larger than aggregate demand.[4] As the circular flow emerges from the firms, we rename it *gross domestic product, income-based,* or more simply, **gross domestic income**. Why? The reason is that:

Domestic income and domestic product must be equal.

Why is this so? When a firm produces and sells $100 worth of output, it pays most of the proceeds to its workers, to people who have lent it money, and to the landlord who owns the property on which the plant is located. All of these payments represent *income* to some individuals. But what about the rest? Suppose, for example, that the firm pays wages, interest, payroll taxes, and indirect sales taxes totalling $90 million and sells its output for $100 million. What happens to the remaining $10 million? The firm's owners receive it as *profits*. Thus, when we add up all of the wages, interest, payroll taxes, indirect taxes, and profits in the economy to obtain the *domestic income*, we must arrive at the *value of output*, that is, the domestic product.

Gross domestic income is GDP seen from the income side; valued at market prices, it incorporates all wages, interest, and profits, and all taxes on factors of production and sales taxes; it excludes transfer payments from the government.

---

[3] Remember that expenditure on housing is part of I, not part of C.

[4] However, we will see in the appendix to this chapter and in Appendix A of Chapter 9 that national accountants redefine aggregate expenditures in such a way that any discrepancy between aggregate demand and domestic product is made good by an additional entry in the investment expenditure category, so that the flow of domestic product is identically equal to the flow of expenditures.

The lower loop of the circular flow diagram shows domestic income leaving firms and heading for consumers. But some of the flow takes a detour along the way. At point 6, the government does two things. First, it siphons off a portion of the domestic income in the form of *taxes*. Second, it adds back government **transfer payments**, such as Employment Insurance and social welfare benefits, which government agencies give to certain individuals as outright *grants* rather than as payments for goods or services rendered.

At point 7, there is a further flow away from consumers. This flow is made up of two components: amortization funds and undistributed corporate profits. The sum of these two components is the share of the gross profits of corporations that are not distributed to households. These are the gross **retained earnings** of corporations, in other words, the gross saving of corporations that go straight to the "investors." The firms will use these funds to invest in new physical capital and to replace worn-out machines and structures, without going through the financial system. Until we deal with it in the appendix, from now on, for simplification purposes, we will omit from our discussion this saving "leakage" arising from firms.

$$DI = \text{GDP} - \text{Taxes} + \text{Transfer payments}$$
$$= \text{GDP} - (\text{Taxes} - \text{Transfers})$$
$$= Y - T$$

where Y represents GDP and T represents taxes *net of transfers* or simply *net taxes*. Disposable income flows unimpeded to consumers at point 1, and the cycle repeats.

Figure 1 raises several complicated questions, which we pose now but will not try to answer until subsequent chapters:

- Does the flow of spending and income grow larger or smaller as we move clockwise around the circle? Why?
- Is the output that firms produce at point 5 (the GDP) equal to aggregate demand? If so, what makes these two quantities equal? If not, what happens?

The next chapter provides the answers to these two questions.

- Do the government's accounts balance, so that what flows in at point 6 (net taxes) is equal to what flows out at point 3 (government purchases)? What happens if they do not balance?

This important question is first addressed in Chapter 11 and then recurs many times, especially in Chapter 15, which discusses budget deficits and surpluses in detail.

- Is our international trade balanced, so that exports equal imports at point 4? More generally, what factors determine net exports, and what consequences arise from trade deficits or surpluses?

We take up these questions in the next two chapters and then deal with them more fully in Part IV.

However, we cannot dig very deeply into any of these issues until we first understand what goes on at point 1, where consumers make decisions. So we turn next to the determinants of consumer spending.

Transfer payments are sums of money that the government gives to certain individuals as outright grants rather than as payments for services rendered to employers. Some common examples are social welfare and Employment Insurance benefits.

Retained earnings (or plowback) are the portion of a corporation's profits that management decides to keep and reinvest in the firm's operations rather than paying out as dividends to shareholders.

CONSUMER SPENDING AND INCOME: THE IMPORTANT RELATIONSHIP

Recall that we started the chapter with a puzzle: Why did consumers respond so weakly to the 2001 tax rebate in the United States, whereas the response was much more favourable in Canada? An economist interested in predicting how consumer spending will respond to a change in income taxes must first ask how consumption (C) relates to disposable income (DI), for a tax increase obviously decreases after-tax income, and a tax reduction increases it. This section, therefore, examines what we know about how consumer spending is influenced by changes in disposable income.

FIGURE 2

Consumer Spending and Disposable Income

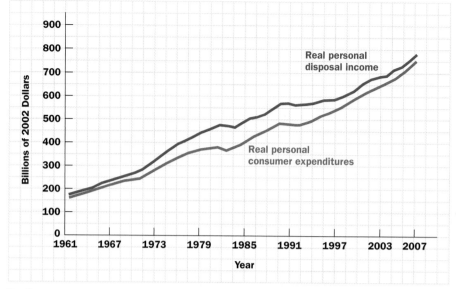

SOURCES: Centre for the Study of Living Standards, *Aggregate income and productivity trends: Canada vs. the United States*, Table 1 (real disposable income), retrieved from www.csls.ca/data/ipt1.asp CAN-SIM, Series v499334 (Personal expenditure on consumer goods and services at current prices) and v737344 (CPI).

Note: Figures are all in billions of 2002 dollars.

Figure 2 depicts the historical paths of *C* and *DI* for Canada since 1961. The association is extremely close, suggesting that consumption will rise whenever disposable income rises and fall whenever income falls. The vertical distance between the two lines represents personal saving: disposable income minus consumption. Notice how much apparent household saving there was in the late 1970s and in the 1980s, and how little saving consumers did in the early 1960s and over the most recent years.

Of course, knowing that *C* will move in the same direction as *DI* is not enough for policy planners. They need to know *how much* one variable will go up when the other rises by a given amount. Figure 3 presents the same data as in Figure 2, but in a way designed to help answer the "how much" question.

A **scatter diagram** is a graph showing the relationship between two variables (such as consumer spending and disposable income). Each year is represented by a point in the diagram, and the coordinates of each year's point show the values of the two variables in that year.

Economists call such pictures **scatter diagrams**, and they are very useful in predicting how one variable (in this case, consumer spending) will change in response to a change in another variable (in this case, disposable income). Each dot in the diagram represents the data on *C* and *DI* corresponding to a particular year. For example, the point labelled "2000" shows that real consumer expenditures in 2000 were $625 billion (which we read off the vertical axis), while real disposable incomes amounted to $670 billion (which we read off the horizontal axis). Similarly, each year from 1961 to 2007 is represented by its own dot in Figure 3.

To see how such a diagram can assist fiscal policy planners, imagine that it is 2000 and that Paul Martin, then the minister of Finance, is contemplating a tax cut. Martin and his advisers want to know how much consumer spending might be stimulated by tax cuts of various sizes. To assist your imagination, the scatter diagram in Figure 4 removes the points from 2000 onward that appear in Figure 3; after all, these data were unknown in 2000. Years prior to 1969 have also been removed, on the grounds that Finance officials may feel that going back 30 years ought to be enough. With no more training in economics than you have right now, what would you suggest?

One rough-and-ready approach is to get a ruler, set it down on Figure 4, and sketch a straight line that comes as close as possible to hitting all the points. That has been done for you in the figure, and you can see that the resulting line is reasonably close to touching all the points. The line summarizes, in a very rough way, the normal relationship between income and consumption. The two variables certainly appear to be closely related.

The *slope* of the straight line in Figure 4 is very important.[5] Specifically, we note that it is:

$$\text{Slope} = \frac{\text{Vertical change}}{\text{Horizontal change}} = \frac{\$90 \text{ billion}}{\$100 \text{ billion}} = 0.90$$

---

[5] To review the concept of *slope*, see the appendix to Chapter 1, pages 20–22.

SOURCES: Centre for the Study of Living Standards, *Aggregate income and productivity trends: Canada vs. the United States*, Table 1 (real disposable income), retrieved from www.csls.ca/data/ipt1.asp CAN-SIM, Series v499334 (Personal expenditure on consumer goods and services at current prices) and v737344 (CPI).

FIGURE 3

Scatter Diagram of Consumer Spending and Disposable Income

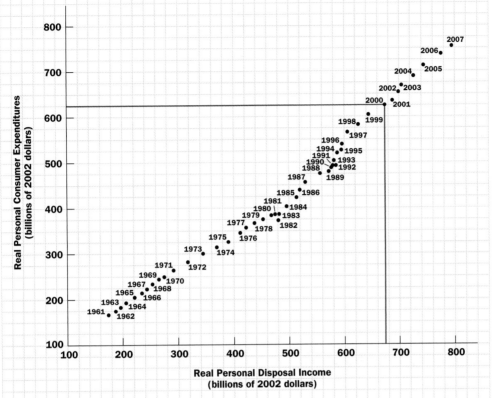

Note: Figures are in billions of 2002 dollars.

SOURCES: Centre for the Study of Living Standards, *Aggregate income and productivity trends: Canada vs. the United States*, Table 1 (real disposable income), retrieved from www.csls.ca/data/ipt1.asp CAN-SIM, Series v499334 (Personal expenditure on consumer goods and services at current prices) and v737344 (CPI).

FIGURE 4

Scatter Diagram of Consumer Spending and Disposable Income, 1969–1999

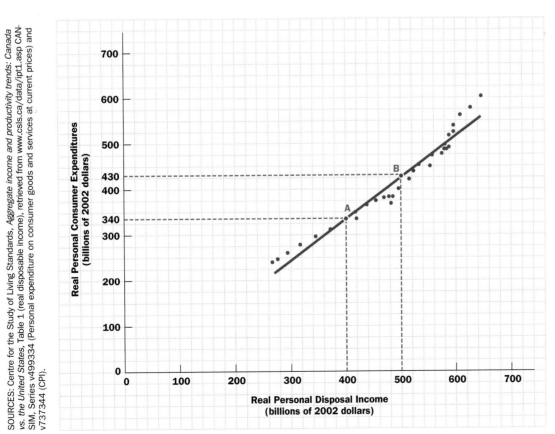

Note: Figures are in billions of 2002 dollars.

Because the horizontal change involved in the move from A to B represents a rise in disposable income of $100 billion (from $400 billion to $500 billion), and the corresponding vertical change represents the associated $90 billion rise in consumer spending (from $340 billion to $430 billion), the slope of the line indicates how consumer spending responds to changes in disposable income. In this case, we see that each additional $1 of income leads to 90 cents of additional spending.

Now let us return to tax policy. First, recall that each dollar of tax cut increases disposable income by exactly $1. Next, apply the finding from Figure 4 that each additional dollar of disposable income increases consumer spending by about 90 cents. The conclusion is that a tax cut of, say, $20 billion—which is what happened in 2001—would be expected to increase consumer spending by about $20 \times 0.9 = \$18$ billion.

■ THE CONSUMPTION FUNCTION AND THE MARGINAL PROPENSITY TO CONSUME

The **consumption function** shows the relationship between total consumer expenditures and total disposable income in the economy, holding all other determinants of consumer spending constant.

The **marginal propensity to consume (MPC)** is the ratio of changes in consumption relative to changes in disposable income that produce the change in consumption. On a graph, it appears as the slope of the consumption function.

It has been said that economics is just systematized common sense. So let us now organize and generalize what has been a completely intuitive discussion up to now. One thing we have discovered is the apparently close relationship between consumer spending, C, and disposable income, DI. Economists call this relationship the **consumption function**.

A second fact we have gleaned from these figures is that the *slope* of the consumption function is relatively constant. We infer this constancy from the fact that the straight line drawn in Figure 4 comes so close to touching every point. If the slope of the consumption function had varied widely, we could not have done so well with a single straight line. Because of its importance in applications such as the tax cut, economists have given this slope a special name—the **marginal propensity to consume**, or **MPC** for short. The MPC tells us how much more consumers will spend if disposable income rises by $1.

$$\text{MPC} = \frac{\text{Change in } C}{\text{Change in } DI \text{ that produces the change in } C}$$

The MPC is best illustrated by an example, and for this purpose we turn away from Canadian data for a moment and look at consumption and income in a hypothetical country, Niceland, whose data come in nice round numbers—which facilitates computation.

Columns (1) and (2) of Table 1 show annual consumer expenditure and disposable income, respectively, from 2003 to 2008. These two columns constitute the consumption function, and they are plotted in Figure 5. Column (3) in the table shows the marginal propensity to consume (MPC), which is the slope of the line in Figure 5; it is derived from the first two columns. We can see that between 2005 and 2006, DI rose by $400 billion (from $4,000 billion to $4,400 billion) while C rose by $300 billion (from $3,300 billion to $3,600 billion). Thus, the MPC was:

$$\text{MPC} = \frac{\text{Change in } C}{\text{Change in } DI} = \frac{\$300}{\$400} = 0.75$$

As you can easily verify, the MPC between any other pair of years in Table 1 is also 0.75. This relationship explains why the slope of the line in Figure 4 was so crucial in estimating the effect of a tax cut. This slope, which we found there to be 0.90, is simply the MPC for Niceland. The MPC tells us how much *additional* spending will be induced by each dollar *change* in disposable income. For each $1 of tax cut, economists expect consumption to rise by $1 times the marginal propensity to consume.

To estimate the *initial* effect of a tax cut on consumer spending, economists must first estimate the MPC and then multiply the amount of the tax cut by the estimated MPC.[6] Because they never know the true MPC with certainty, their prediction is always subject to some margin of error.

---

[6] The word *initial* in this sentence is an important one. The next chapter will explain why the effects discussed in this chapter are only the beginning of the story.

TABLE 1			
Consumption and Income in a Hypothetical Economy, Niceland			
Year	(1) Consumption, C	(2) Disposable Income, DI	(3) Marginal Propensity to Consume, MPC
2003	$2,700	$3,200	
2004	3,000	3,600	0.75
2005	3,300	4,000	0.75
2006	3,600	4,400	0.75
2007	3,900	4,800	0.75
2008	4,200	5,200	0.75

Note: Amounts are in billions of dollars.

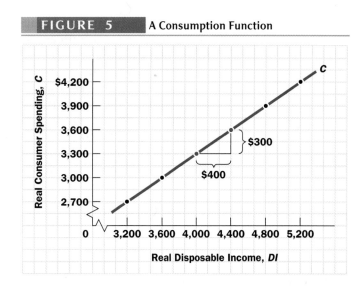

FIGURE 5   A Consumption Function

FACTORS THAT SHIFT THE CONSUMPTION FUNCTION

Unfortunately for policy planners, the consumption function does not always stand still. Recall from Chapter 4 the important distinction between a *movement along* a demand curve and a *shift* of the curve. A demand curve depicts the relationship between quantity demanded and *one* of its many determinants—price. Thus a change in price causes a *movement along the demand curve.* But a change in any other factor that influences quantity demanded causes a *shift of the entire demand curve.*

Because factors other than disposable income influence consumer spending, a similar distinction is vital to understanding real-world consumption functions. Look back at the definition of the consumption function in the margin of page 174. A change in disposable income leads to a *movement along the consumption function* precisely because the consumption function depicts the relationship between C and DI. Such movements, which are what we have been considering so far, are indicated by the blue arrows in Figure 6.

But consumption also has other determinants, and a change in any of them will *shift the entire consumption function*—as indicated by the red arrows in Figure 6. Such shifts account for many of the errors in forecasting consumption. To summarize:

> Any change in disposable income moves us *along a given consumption function.* A change in any of the other determinants of consumption *shifts the entire consumption schedule* (see Figure 6).

Because disposable income is far and away the main determinant of consumer spending, the real-world data in Figure 3 come *close* to lying along a straight line. But if you use a ruler to draw such a line, you will find that it misses a number of points badly. These deviations reflect the influence of the "other determinants" just mentioned. Let us see what some of them are.

Wealth   One factor affecting spending is consumers' *wealth*, which is a source of purchasing power in addition to income. Wealth and income are different things. For example, a wealthy retiree with a huge bank balance may earn little current *income* when interest rates are low. But a high-flying investment banker who spends every penny of the high income she earns will not accumulate much *wealth*.

FIGURE 6

Shifts of the Consumption Function

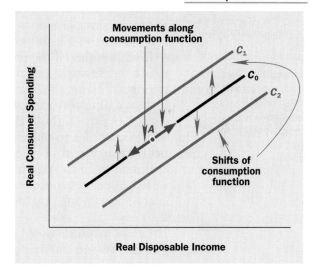

To appreciate the importance of the distinction, think about two recent university graduates, each of whom earns $40,000 per year. If one of them has $100,000 in the bank, and the other has no assets at all, who do you think will spend more? Presumably the one with the big bank account. The general point is that current income is not the only source of spendable funds; households can also finance spending by cashing in some of the wealth they have previously accumulated.

One important implication of this analysis is that the stock market can exert a major influence on consumer spending. A stock market boom adds to wealth and thus raises the consumption function, as depicted by the shift from C_0 to C_1 in Figure 6. That is what happened in the late 1990s, when the stock market soared and Canadian consumers went on a spending spree. Correspondingly, a collapse of stock prices, like the one that occurred in 2000–2002, should shift the consumption function down (see the shift from C_0 to C_2).

The Price Level   Stock market shares are hardly the only form of wealth. People hold a great deal of wealth in forms that are fixed in money terms. Bank accounts are the most obvious example. The purchasing power of such **money-fixed assets** obviously declines whenever the price level rises, and hence whenever we observe inflation in product prices. Canadian consumers hold about $1,000 billion worth of deposits and currency, so that each 1 percent rise in the price level reduces the purchasing power of consumer wealth by $10 billion, a tidy sum worth a bit more than 0.6 percent of GDP.

Of course, such a process also operates in reverse. Canadian consumers (individuals and unincorporated businesses) also have **money-fixed liabilities**—essentially consumer credit and mortgage debts—that also amount to about $1,000 billion. Any time the price level rises by 1 percent, their real liabilities fall by 1 percent. Thus, a 1 percent rise in the price level increases the purchasing power of Canadian consumers by about $10 billion (the consumption function would shift from C_0 to C_1).

It follows that, if the price level rises without anything else changing, it is not clear which effect—the negative **wealth effect** or the positive debt effect—will be strongest. All we can say is that, referring back to Figure 2, saving rates were rather high at a time when inflation rates were high as well, starting in the mid-1970s and continuing throughout the 1980s. High inflation rates seem to have induced Canadian households to reduce consumer spending. Thus, the wealth effect seems to have been strongest, as people attempted to save more to recover their previous stock of real wealth. In the rest of the book, we will make the standard assumption that the wealth effect is stronger than the debt effect, and hence that higher prices reduce the overall purchasing power of consumers.

The Real Interest Rate   A higher real rate of interest raises the rewards for saving. For this reason, many people believe it is "obvious" that higher real interest rates must encourage saving and therefore discourage spending. Surprisingly, however, statistical studies of this relationship suggest otherwise. With very few exceptions, they show that interest rates have little effect on aggregate consumption in most countries. Hence, in developing our initial model of the economy, we will assume that changes in real interest rates do not shift the consumption function. (See "Using Tax Provisions to Spur Saving.")

Future Income Expectations   It is hardly earth-shattering to suggest that consumers' expectations about their *future* incomes should affect how much they spend today. Indeed, to make predictions about the strength of the Canadian economy, the Conference Board of Canada—a major forecasting agency—uses a consumer confidence index, based on the likelihood of respondents to make major purchases in the near future. Other forecasters also try to measure changes in consumers' optimism or pessimism, based on questions relating to the respondents' assessment of their personal financial situation and that of the entire economy.

A **money-fixed asset** is an asset whose value is a fixed number of dollars.

An example of a **money-fixed liability** is a mortgage taken to purchase a house, the value of which is a fixed number of dollars.

The **wealth effect** is the negative effect that higher output prices have on real consumer spending, as the real value of the money-fixed assets of households fall when prices are higher.

Using Tax Provisions to Spur Saving

Compared to the citizens of virtually every other industrial nation, Canadians save rather little—only about 2 percent of disposable income in recent years. Many policy makers consider this lack of saving to be a serious problem, so they have proposed numerous tax incentives to induce people to save. Among these is the well-known Registered Retirement Saving Plan (RRSP), the contributions to which reduce taxable income. Whereas contributions could be no bigger than $13,500 per year in the early 2000s, this amount has been increased gradually, reaching $19,000 in 2007 and being projected to reach $22,000 in 2010. Also, under new legislation proposed by the Harper Conservative government, starting in 2009, Canadians will be able to contribute $5,000 annually to a Tax-Free Savings Account, any income from which will be tax-free.

All of these tax changes are designed to increase the after-tax return on saving. For example, if you put away money in a bank at a 5 percent rate of interest and your income is taxed at a 30 percent rate, your after-tax rate of return on saving is just 3.5 percent (70 percent of 5 percent). But if the interest is earned tax-free, you get to keep the full 5 percent. Over long periods of time, this seemingly small interest differential compounds to make an enormous difference in returns. For example, $100 invested for 20 years at 3.5 percent interest grows to $199. But at 5 percent, it grows to $265. Advocates of tax incentives for saving argue that lower tax rates will induce Canadians to save more.

This idea seems reasonable and has many supporters. Unfortunately, the evidence runs squarely against it. Economists have conducted many studies of the effect of higher rates of return on saving. With very few exceptions, they detect little or no impact. Although the evidence fails to support the "commonsense" solution to the undersaving problem, the debate goes on. Many people, it seems, refuse to believe the evidence.

ISSUE REVISITED: *Why the 2001 Tax Rebates Failed in the United States but Not in Canada*

To understand how expectations of future incomes affect current consumer expenditures, consider the abbreviated life histories of three consumers given in Table 2. (The reason for giving our three imaginary individuals such odd names will be apparent shortly.) The consumer named "Constant" earned $100 in each of the years considered in the table. The consumer named "Temporary" earned $100 in three of the four years, but had a good year in 2001. The consumer named "Permanent" enjoyed a permanent increase in income in 2001 and was therefore clearly the richest.

Now let us use our commonsense to figure out how much each of these consumers might have spent in 2001. Temporary and Permanent had the same income that year. Do you think they spent the same amount? Not if they had some ability to foresee their future incomes, because Permanent was richer in the long run.

Now compare Constant and Temporary. Temporary had a 20 percent higher income in 2001 ($120 versus $100), but only 5 percent more over the entire four-year period ($420 versus $400). Do you think his spending in 2001 was closer to

20 percent above Constant's, or closer to 5 percent above it? Most people guess the latter.

The point of this example is that consumers very reasonably decide on their current consumption spending by looking at their long-run income prospects. This should come as no surprise to a university student. You are probably spending more than you earn this year, but that does not make you a foolish spendthrift. On the contrary, you know that your university education gives you a strong expectation of much higher incomes in the future, and you are spending with that idea in mind.

To relate this example to the failure of the U.S. 2001 income tax cut, imagine that the three rows in Table 2 represent the entire economy under three different government policies. The first row (Constant) shows the unchanged path of disposable income in the absence of any tax cut. The second (Temporary) shows an increase in disposable income attributable to a tax cut for one year only. The bottom row (Permanent) shows a policy that increases *DI* in every future year by cutting taxes permanently in 2001. Which of the two lower rows do you imagine would have generated more consumer spending in 2001? The bottom row (Permanent), of course. What we have concluded, then, is this:

TABLE 2					
Incomes of Three Consumers					
	Incomes in Each Year				
Consumer	2000	2001	2002	2003	Total Income
Constant	$100	$100	$100	$100	**$400**
Temporary	100	120	100	100	420
Permanent	100	120	120	120	460

Permanent cuts in income taxes cause greater increases in consumer spending than do temporary cuts of equal magnitude.

The application of this analysis to the 2001 tax rebates that occurred in Canada and in the United States is immediate. In Canada, taxpayers were sufficiently convinced that the tax rebate was there to stay, as the tax cut was widely advertised as a five-year plan involving $100 billion in tax reductions. They acted as would consumer Permanent in Table 2. On the other hand, although the tax cuts provided by the Bush administration were also of the permanent kind, American taxpayers understood these tax reductions to be a one-shot deal. The tax rebate cheques that were sent through the mail as the first installment of tax reduction were perceived by American consumers to be of a temporary nature, probably because these cheques were so widely advertised as a one-time event. As a result, in 2001, American taxpayers acted like consumer Temporary in Table 2.

We have, then, what appears to be a general principle, backed up by both historical evidence and common sense. Permanent changes in income taxes have more significant effects on consumer spending than do temporary ones. This conclusion may seem obvious, but it is not a lesson you would have learned from an introductory textbook 30 years ago. In addition, this anecdote shows the powerful impact that perceptions and expectations can have on the economy.

THE EXTREME VARIABILITY OF INVESTMENT

Next, we turn to the most *volatile* component of aggregate demand: investment spending.[7] While consumer spending follows movements in disposable income quite closely, investment spending swings from high to low levels with astonishing speed. For example, when real GDP in Canada slowed abruptly from a 2.6 percent growth

---

[7] We repeat the warning given earlier about the meaning of the word *investment*. It *includes* spending by businesses and individuals on newly produced factories, machinery, and houses. But it *excludes* sales of used industrial plants, equipment, and homes as well as purely financial transactions, such as the purchases of stocks and bonds.

rate in 1989 to a sluggish 0.3 percent in 1990, a drop of over 2 percentage points, the growth rate of real investment spending went from 5.0 percent to *minus* 5.9 percent, a swing of nearly 11 percentage points. What accounts for such dramatic changes in investment spending?

Several factors that influence how much businesses want to invest were discussed in the previous chapter, including interest rates, tax provisions, technical change, and the strength of the economy. Sometimes these determinants change abruptly, leading to dramatic variations in investment. But perhaps the most important factor accounting for the volatility of investment spending was not discussed much in Chapter 7: the *state of business confidence*, which in turn depends on *expectations about the future*.

Although confidence is tricky to measure, it does seem obvious that businesses will build more factories and purchase more new machines when they are optimistic. Correspondingly, their investment plans will be very cautious if the economic outlook appears bleak. Keynes pointed out that psychological perceptions such as these are subject to abrupt shifts, so that fluctuations in investment can be a major cause of instability in aggregate demand (see "Investment and the State of Business Confidence").

Unfortunately, neither economists nor, for that matter, psychologists have many good ideas about how to *measure*—much less *control*—business confidence. So economists usually focus on several more objective determinants of investment that are easier to quantify, such as rates of capacity utilization or profit rates, and even influence—factors such as interest rates and tax rates. Nevertheless, in their efforts to predict turning points in economic activity, some forecasting agencies such as the Conference Board of Canada conduct regular surveys purporting to assess business confidence, surveys that are similar to those assessing consumer sentiments.

THE DETERMINANTS OF NET EXPORTS

Another highly variable source of demand for Canadian products is foreign purchases of Canadian goods—our *exports*. As we observed earlier in this chapter, we obtain the *net* contribution of foreigners to Canadian aggregate demand by subtracting *imports*, which is the portion of domestic demand that is satisfied by foreign producers, from our exports to get *net exports*. What determines net exports?

National Incomes

Although both exports and imports depend on many factors, the predominant one is *income levels in different countries*. When Canadian consumers and firms spend more

Investment and the State of Business Confidence

John Maynard Keynes had some very noteworthy thoughts about the concept of uncertainty and economic matters:

> It would be foolish, in forming our expectations, to attach great weight to matters which are uncertain. (By very "uncertain" I do not mean the same thing as "very improbable.") It is reasonable, therefore, to be guided to a considerable degree by the facts about which we feel somewhat confident, even though they may be less decisively relevant to the issue than other facts about which our knowledge is vague and scanty. . . .
>
> The state of long-term expectations, upon which our decisions are based, does not solely depend, therefore, on the most

probable forecast we can make. It also depends on the *confidence* with which we make this forecast—on how highly we rate the likelihood of our best forecast turning out quite wrong. If we expect large changes but are uncertain as to what precise form these changes will take, then our confidence will be weak.

The *state of confidence*, as they term it, is a matter to which practical men always pay the closest and most anxious attention. But economists have not analysed it carefully and have been content, as a rule, to discuss it in general terms.

SOURCE: Excerpted from John Maynard Keynes, *The General Theory of Employment, Interest and Money* (London: Macmillan, 1936), p. 148.

on consumption and investment, some of this new spending goes toward the purchase of foreign goods. Therefore:

> Our imports rise when our GDP rises and fall when our GDP falls.

Similarly, because our *exports* are the *imports* of other countries, our exports depend on *their* GDPs, not on our own. Thus:

> Our exports are relatively insensitive to our own GDP, but are quite sensitive to the GDPs of other countries.

Putting these two ideas together leads to a clear implication: When our economy grows faster than the economies of our trading partners, our net exports tend to shrink. Conversely, when foreign economies grow faster than ours, our net exports tend to rise. For instance, in early 2008, because of the impending American recession, Merrill Lynch—the financial management and banking institution—predicted a swing of about $40 billion in our trade balance, with Canadian net exports moving from a highly positive number to something close to zero by 2009.

Relative Prices and Exchange Rates

Although GDP levels here and abroad are important influences on a country's net exports, they are not the only relevant factors. International prices matter, too.

To make things concrete, let's focus on trade between the Canada and Japan. Suppose Canadian prices rise while Japanese prices fall, making Canadian goods more expensive *relative to Japanese goods*. If Canadian consumers react to these new relative prices by buying more Japanese goods, Canadian *imports rise*. If Japanese consumers react to the same relative price changes by buying fewer Canadian products, Canadian *exports fall*. Both reactions reduce Canada's *net* exports.

Naturally, a decline in Canadian prices (or a rise in Japanese prices) does precisely the opposite. Thus:

> A rise in the prices of a country's goods will lead to a reduction in that country's net exports. Analogously, a decline in the prices of a country's goods will raise that country's net exports. Similarly, price increases abroad raise the home country's net exports, whereas price decreases abroad have the opposite effect.

This simple idea holds the key to understanding how exchange rates among the world's currencies influence exports and imports—an important topic that we will consider in depth in Chapters 18 and 19. The reason is that exchange rates translate foreign prices into terms that are familiar to home-country customers—their own currencies.

Consider, for example, Canadians interested in buying Japanese cars that cost ¥3,000,000. If it takes ¥100 to buy a dollar, these cars cost Canadian buyers $30,000. But if the dollar is worth ¥150, those same cars cost Canadians just $20,000, and consumers in Canada are likely to buy more of them. These sorts of responses help explain why American automakers lost their market share to Japanese imports when the American dollar rose against the yen in the late 1990s.

HOW PREDICTABLE IS AGGREGATE DEMAND?

We have now learned enough to see why economists often have difficulty predicting aggregate demand. Consider the four main components, starting with consumer spending.

Because wealth affects consumption, forecasts of spending can be thrown off by unexpected movements of the stock market or by poor forecasts of future inflation rates. It may also be difficult to anticipate how taxpayers will view changes in the income tax law. Will they be perceived as temporary changes or permanent ones? Consumer decisions may also be swayed by sudden changes in consumer sentiment. For example, speculation about impending financial and banking crises may precipitate a slowdown in consumer spending.

Swings in investment spending are even more difficult to predict, partly because they are tied so closely to business confidence and expectations. Developments abroad also often lead to surprises in the net export account. Even the final component of aggregate demand, government purchases (G), is subject to the vagaries of politics and to sudden national security events such as 9/11 in the United States.

We could say much more about the determinants of aggregate demand, but it is best to leave the rest to more advanced courses. For we are now ready to apply our knowledge of aggregate demand to the construction of the first model of the economy. Although it is true that income determines consumption, the consumption function in turn helps to determine the level of income. If that sounds like circular reasoning, read the next chapter!

SUMMARY

1. **Aggregate demand** is the total volume of goods and services purchased by consumers, businesses, government units, and foreigners. It can be expressed as the sum $C + I + G + (X - IM)$, where C is consumer spending, I is investment spending, G is **government purchases**, and $X - IM$ is **net exports**. These components are similar to those of the expenditure-based gross domestic product.

2. Aggregate demand is a schedule that depends on a variety of factors, including consumer incomes, events in foreign countries, and government policies.

3. Economists reserve the term **investment spending** to refer to purchases of newly produced factories, machinery, software, and houses.

4. Gross domestic product is the total volume of final goods and services produced in the country.

5. **Gross domestic income** is GDP seen from the income side. Because it is valued at market prices, it incorporates all wages, interest, and profits, as well as all taxes on factors of production and sales taxes. By necessity, it is identically equal to gross domestic product.

6. **Disposable income** is the sum of the incomes of all individuals in the economy after taxes and transfers. It is the chief determinant of **consumer expenditures**.

7. All of these concepts, and others, can be depicted in a circular flow diagram that shows expenditures on all four sources flowing into business firms and national income flowing out.

8. The close relationship between consumer spending (C) and disposable income (DI) is called the **consumption function**.

Its slope, which is used to predict the change in consumption that will be caused by a change in income taxes, is called the **marginal propensity to consume (MPC)**.

9. Changes in disposable income move us along a given consumption function. Changes in any of the other variables that affect C shift the entire consumption function. Among the most important of these other variables are total consumer wealth, the inflation rates, and expected future incomes.

10. Because consumers hold so many **money-fixed assets**, they lose purchasing power when prices rise, which leads them to reduce their spending. This effect is however partially compensated for by the presence of **money-fixed liabilities**, the real value of which diminishes when prices rise.

11. The government often tries to manipulate aggregate demand by influencing private consumption decisions, usually through changes in the personal income tax.

12. Consumer spending is also strongly affected by consumer sentiment. This explains why identical changes in tax policy may produce different results at different times.

13. Investment is the most volatile component of aggregate demand, largely because it is closely tied to confidence and expectations.

14. Policy makers cannot influence confidence in any reliable way, so policies designed to spur investment focus on more objective, although possibly less important, determinants of investment—such as interest rates and taxes.

15. Net exports depend on GDPs and relative prices both domestically and abroad.

KEY TERMS

Aggregate demand   168

Consumer expenditure (*C*)   169

Investment spending (*I*)   169

Government purchases (*G*)   169

Net exports (*X − IM*)   169

$C + I + G + (X - IM)$ 169

Disposable income (*DI*)   169

Gross domestic income   169

Transfer payments   171

Retained earnings   171

Scatter diagram   172

Consumption function   174

Marginal propensity to consume (MPC)   174

Movements along versus shifts of the consumption function   175

Money-fixed assets   176

Money-fixed liabilities   176

Wealth effect   176

TEST YOURSELF

1. What are the four components of aggregate demand? Which is the largest? Which is the smallest?

2. Which of the following acts constitute *investment* according to the economist's definition of that term ?

   a. Intel builds a new factory to manufacture semi-conductors.

   b. You buy 100 shares of Intel stock.

   c. A small chipmaker goes bankrupt, and Intel purchases its factory and equipment.

   d. Your family buys a newly constructed home from a developer.

   e. Your family buys an older home from another family. (*Hint:* Are any *new* products demanded by this action?)

3. On a piece of graph paper, construct a consumption function from the data given below and determine the MPC.

Year	Consumer Spending	Disposable Income
2003	$1,200	$1,500
2004	1,440	1,800
2005	1,680	2,100
2006	1,920	2,400
2007	2,160	2,700

4. In which direction will the consumption function shift if the price level rises? Show this on your graph from the previous question.

DISCUSSION QUESTIONS

1. Explain the difference between *investment* as the term is used by most people and *investment* as defined by an economist?

2. What would the circular flow diagram (Figure 1) look like in an economy with no government? Draw one for yourself.

3. The marginal propensity to consume (MPC) for Canada as a whole was estimated to be roughly 0.90. Explain in words what this means. What is your personal MPC at this stage in your life? How might that change by the time you are your parents' age?

4. Look at the scatter diagram in Figure 3. What does it tell you about what was going on in this country in the years around 1982–1983?

5. What is a consumption function, and why is it a useful device for government economists planning a tax cut?

6. Explain why permanent tax cuts are likely to lead to bigger increases in consumer spending than are temporary tax cuts.

7. There has been a large increase in the values of houses throughout most of Canada since 2001. What impact should this have on the consumption function? Distinguish between house owners and soon-to-be house owners.

8. Household saving in Canada and in the United States is at nearly 0 percent. If households do not save, who does?

APPENDIX *National Income Accounting*

The type of macroeconomic analysis presented in this book dates from the publication of John Maynard Keynes's *The General Theory of Employment, Interest, and Money* in 1936. But at that time, there was really no way to test Keynes's theories because the necessary data did not exist. It took some years for the theoretical notions used by Keynes to find concrete expression in real-world data.

The system of measurement devised for collecting and expressing macroeconomic data is called **national income accounting**.

The development of this system of accounts ranks as a great achievement in applied economics, perhaps as important in its own right as was Keynes's theoretical work. Indeed, the British economist Richard Stone (1913–1991), who worked with colleagues of Keynes during World War II, received the Bank of Sweden Prize in Economic Sciences in Memory of Alfred Nobel in 1984, for his efforts in setting up the United Nations System of National Accounts, the latest edition of which was produced in 1993, and the standards of which are now followed in all countries.

Without this system of accounts, the practical value of Keynesian analysis would be severely limited. Economists spent long hours wrestling with the many difficult conceptual questions that arose as they translated the theory into numbers. Along the way, some more-or-less arbitrary decisions and conventions had to be made. You may not agree with all of them, but the accounting framework that was devised, though imperfect, is eminently serviceable.

In the remainder of this appendix, we deal with what Statistics Canada calls the *national income and expenditure accounts*. There are, however, three other components to the Canadian national accounts. First are the *input–output accounts* that measure productive activity according to both the commodities produced and the industries that produce them, as well as the use of such commodities in the production process of an industry. The accounts are useful to estimate the so-called "multipliers," about which more will be said in the next chapter. These multipliers are used in economic models for simulating the impact of a specific event on the economy—for example, the Vancouver Olympic Games in 2010—or higher spending by government on roads.

Second are the *financial and wealth accounts*, which measure the financial flows from and into each sector of the economy, along with the balance sheet (the stocks of financial and tangible assets, as well as their liabilities) of each sector. This is particularly useful to monitor what we prefer to call the *placements* of economic agents, by contrast with their physical *investments*. Finally, there are the *balance of payments accounts*, which track the commercial and financial transactions of Canadians in relation to the rest of the world. The data of the latter two of these national accounts will be used in some of the following chapters. But for now, we will discuss the national income and expenditure accounts and their key measure, the gross domestic product.

■ DEFINING GDP: EXCEPTIONS TO THE RULES

We first encountered the concept of **gross domestic product (GDP)** in Chapter 5.

Gross domestic product (GDP) is the sum of the money values of all final goods and services produced during a specified period of time, usually one year. More specifically, this is GDP *at market prices*.

However, the definition of GDP has certain exceptions that we have not yet noted.

First, the treatment of government output involves a minor departure from the principle of using market prices. Unlike private products, the "outputs" of government offices are not sold; indeed, it is sometimes even difficult to define what those outputs are. Lacking prices for outputs, national income accountants fall back on the only prices they have: prices for the inputs from which the outputs are produced. Thus:

Government outputs are valued at the cost of the inputs needed to produce them.

This means, for example, that if a clerk at the Department of Motor Vehicles who earns $16 per hour spends one-half hour torturing you with explanations of why you cannot get a driver's licence, that particular government "service" increases GDP by $8.

Second, some goods that are produced during the year but not yet sold are nonetheless counted in that year's GDP. Specifically, goods that firms add to their *inventories* count in the GDP even though they do not pass through markets.

National income statisticians treat inventories as if they were "bought" at their current production cost by the firms that produced them, even though these "purchases" do not actually take place.

Finally, the treatment of investment goods runs slightly counter to the rule that GDP includes only final goods. In a broad sense, factories, generators, machine tools, and the like might be considered to be intermediate goods. After all, their owners want them only for use in producing other goods, not for any innate value that they possess. But this classification would present a real problem. Because factories and machines normally are never sold to consumers, when would we count them in GDP? National income statisticians avoid this problem by defining investment goods as final products demanded by the *firms* that buy them.

Now that we have a more complete definition of what the GDP is, let us turn to the problem of actually measuring it. National income accountants have devised three ways to perform this task, and we consider each in turn.

GDP AS THE SUM OF FINAL GOODS AND SERVICES

The first way to measure GDP seems to be the most natural, because it follows so directly from the circular flow diagram (Figure 1). It also turns out to be the most useful definition for macroeconomic analysis. We simply add up the final demands of all consumers, business firms, government, and foreigners. Using the same symbols that we introduced in the chapter, with one exception, we have gross domestic product, expenditure-based, or in short, gross domestic expenditure:

$$\text{GDP} = C + I_{\text{na}} + G + (X - IM)$$

The exception is the new symbol I_{na} that replaces I. The symbol I_{na} stands for **gross private domestic investment** as it appears in the actual Statistics Canada national accounts. We will explain the word *gross* later. *Private* indicates that government investment is not included in I_{na} and is instead part of G. *Domestic* means that machinery sold by Canadian firms to foreign companies are included in exports X rather than in investment.

Gross private domestic investment is made up of two major components, which will be discussed in detail in the next chapter. Investment is the sum of *fixed business investment* and *business investment in inventories*. The latter is the value of the change in business inventories—the goods that have been produced but not yet sold and that firms are presumed to have bought themselves. It is this component that ensures that domestic product and domestic expenditure are identically equal to each other in the national accounts, barring any statistical error. We will say more about this in the next chapter. Fixed business investment is subdivided into investment in residential structures (the construction of houses and apartment buildings) and nonresidential investment, that is, investment in commercial and industrial structures (plants and buildings) and investment in machinery and equipment (including computers and software). In 2007, residential investment represented 36 percent of all fixed business investment.

> **Gross private domestic investment** includes business investment in plant, equipment, and software; residential construction; and inventory investment.

We repeat again that *only* these three things are *investment* in national income accounting terminology.

As defined in the national income accounts, *investment* includes only newly produced capital goods, such as machinery, factories, and new homes. It does not include exchanges of existing assets.

The symbol G, for government purchases, represents the volume of *current goods and services purchased by all levels of government*. Thus, all government payments to its employees are counted in G, as are all of its purchases of goods. Few citizens realize, however, that *the federal government spends most of its money, not for purchases of goods and services, but rather on transfer payments*—literally, giving away money—either to individuals or to other levels of government.

The importance of this conceptual distinction lies in the fact that G represents the part of the national product that government uses up for its own purposes—to pay for the armed forces, bureaucrats, paper, and ink—whereas transfer payments merely shuffle purchasing power from one group of citizens to another. Except for the administrators needed to run these programs, real economic resources are not used up in this process.

In adding up the nation's total output as the sum of $C + I + G + (X - IM)$, we sum the shares of GDP that are used up by consumers, investors, government, and foreigners, respectively. Because transfer payments merely give someone the capability to spend on C, it is logical to exclude transfers from our definition of G, including in C only the portion of these transfer payments that consumers spend. If we included transfers in G, the same spending would get counted twice: once in G and then again in C.

The final component of GDP is net exports, which are simply exports of goods and services minus imports of goods and services. Table 3 shows GDP for 2007,

TABLE 3		
Gross Domestic Product in 2007 from the Expenditure Side		
Item	Nominal Amount*	Share of GDP
Personal consumption expenditures (*C*)	$ 854	55.7%
Fixed business investment	298	19.5
Business investment in inventories	+7	0.5
Government current expenditures and investment (*G*)	342	22.3
Net exports (*X* − *IM*)	+31	2.0
Exports (*X*)	535	
Imports (*IM*)	504	
Gross domestic product (Y)	**1,532**	**100.0**

* In billions of current dollars.

SOURCE: Statistics Canada, *National Income and Expenditure Accounts*, Catalogue No. 13-001-XIE, Table 2.

from the expenditure side, in nominal terms, with the share of GDP for each of the major components. Note that gross private domestic investment I_{na} is equal to $305 billion, being the sum of fixed business investment and business investment in inventories. Normally, Table 3 should include an entry for a statistical discrepancy, as national accountants cannot avoid small errors in the measurement of the value of production, expenditures, and income. Usually, in Canada, these errors amount to less than 0.1 percent of GDP, so such statistical discrepancies are omitted here.

■ GDP AS THE SUM OF ALL FACTOR PAYMENTS

We can count up the GDP another way: by *adding up all incomes in the economy*. Let's see how this method handles some typical transactions. Suppose Goodyear Canada produces tires and sells them to General Motors of Canada for $1 million. The first method of calculating GDP simply counts the $1 million as part of *I*. The second method asks: What incomes resulted from producing these tires? The answer might be something like this:

Wages of Goodyear employees	$400,000
Interest to bondholders	50,000
Indirect taxes paid	50,000
Profits of Goodyear stockholders	100,000

The total is $600,000. The remaining $400,000 is accounted for by inputs that Goodyear Canada purchased from other companies: rubber, steel, processing equipment, and so on. But if we traced this $400,000 back even further, we would find that it is accounted for by the wages, interest, and indirect taxes paid by these other companies, *plus* their profits, *plus* their purchases from other firms. In fact, for *every* firm in the economy, there is an accounting identity that says:

$$\text{Revenue from sales} = \begin{cases} \text{Wages paid +} \\ \text{Interest paid +} \\ \text{Indirect taxes paid +} \\ \text{Profits earned +} \\ \text{Purchases from other firms} \end{cases}$$

Why must this always be true? Because profits are the balancing item; they are what is *left over* after the firm has made all other payments. In fact, this accounting identity really reflects the definition of profits: sales revenue less all costs.

Now apply this accounting identity to *all firms in the economy*. Total purchases from other firms are precisely what we call *intermediate goods*. What, then, do we get if we subtract these intermediate transactions from both sides of the equation?

$$\begin{matrix} \text{Revenue from sales minus} \\ \text{Purchases from other firms} \end{matrix} = \begin{cases} \text{Wages paid +} \\ \text{Interest paid +} \\ \text{Indirect taxes paid +} \\ \text{Profits earned} \end{cases}$$

On the right-hand side, we have the sum of all factor incomes: payments to labour, land, and capital. On the left-hand side, we have total sales minus sales of intermediate goods. This means that we have sales of *final goods*, which is precisely our definition of GDP. Thus, the accounting identity for the entire economy can be rewritten as follows:

GDP = Wages + Interest + Indirect taxes + Profits

This definition gives national income accountants another way to measure the GDP.

Table 4 shows how to obtain GDP from the sum of all incomes. Things are slightly more complicated than indicated in our previous discussion. By adding up labour income (which includes wages, salaries, and supplementary labour income—that is, both employees' and employers' contributions to Employment Insurance and the Canada or Quebec Pension Plans, as well as other

TABLE 4	
Gross Domestic Product in 2007 from the Income Side	
Item	Nominal Amount*
Labour income	$ 782
plus	
Interest and profit income	385
Interest and investment income	69
Corporate profits	210
Government enterprise profits	16
Unincorporated business income (including rents)	90
equals	1,167
Inventory valuation adjustment	+3
plus	
Taxes less subsidies on factors of production	67
equals	
Net domestic product at basic prices	1,237
plus	
Taxes less subsidies on sales	101
equals	
Net domestic product at market prices (NDP)	1,338
plus	
Capital consumption allowance	194
equals	
Gross domestic product at market prices (GDP)	1,532

* In billions of current dollars.

SOURCE: Statistics Canada, *National Income and Expenditure Accounts*, Table 1, Catalogue No. 13-001-XIE.

pension plans, Workers' Compensation, Medicare, dental plans, disability insurance, etc.; interest and investment income; profit income (corporate profits, government enterprise profits); and the net income (including rents) of unincorporated businesses—independent business operators (including farmers) and self-employed professionals whose income is partly labour income and partly profit income—we obtain only $1,167 billion, whereas GDP in 2007 was $1,532 billion.

By adding taxes on factors of production (such as additional taxes on employment, and taxes on the ownership or use of land, business structures, and equipment), we arrive at *net domestic product at basic prices*, here $1,237 billion.[8] Thus, this aggregate takes into account all of the factor payments, plus the taxes, including payroll taxes, that are associated with labour, land, and capital. By also adding sales taxes, such as the Goods and Services Tax (GST), the provincial sales taxes, and various excise taxes on fuel, tobacco, and alcohol, we obtain what is called *net domestic product at market prices*. This we abbreviate as "NDP," since this is the net equivalent of our broad measure of economic activity—the GDP. NDP in 2007 reached $1,338 billion.

From a conceptual point of view, most economists feel that NDP is a more meaningful indicator of the economy's output than is GDP. After all, the depreciation component of GDP represents the output that is needed just to repair and replace worn-out factories and machines; it is not available for anybody to consume.[9] Therefore, NDP seems to be a better measure of production than GDP.

Alas, GDP is much easier to measure because depreciation is a particularly tricky item. What fraction of his tractor did Farmer Jones "use up" last year? How much did the CN Tower depreciate during 2007? If you ask yourself these difficult questions, you will understand why most economists believe that we can measure GDP more accurately than NDP. For this reason, most economic models are based on GDP.

> The *net domestic product at market prices (NDP)* is simply GDP less amortization.

> The *net domestic product at basic prices* is simply NDP less all of the various sales taxes.

The only difference between net domestic product and gross domestic product is *amortization* of the nation's capital stock, or what the statisticians at Statistics Canada call *capital consumption allowance*, here $194 billion. So, the adjective "net" in this case means that amortization is excluded, and "gross" means that it is included. GDP is thus a measure of *all* final production, making no adjust-

ment for the fact that some capital is used up each year and thus depreciates. It should be clearly understood that GDP is calculated first, without any adjustment, from the figures that are provided by businesses, while NDP is calculated later, on the basis of an *estimate* of the capital consumption allowance, to arrive at a net production figure.

> Amortization, or *capital consumption allowance*, is the value of the portion of the nation's capital equipment that is used up within the year. It tells us how much output is needed just to maintain the economy's capital stock.

■ GDP AS THE SUM OF VALUES ADDED

It may strike you as strange that national income accountants include only *final* goods and services in GDP. Aren't *intermediate* goods part of the nation's product? Of course they are. The problem is that, if all intermediate goods were included in GDP, we would wind up double- and triple-counting certain goods and services and therefore get an exaggerated impression of the actual level of economic activity.

To explain why, and to show how national income accountants cope with this difficulty, we must introduce a new concept, called **value added**.

> The **value added** by a firm is its revenue from selling a product minus the amount paid for goods and services purchased from other firms.

The intuitive sense of this concept is clear: If a firm buys some inputs from other firms, does something to them, and sells the resulting product for a price higher than it paid for the inputs, we say that the firm has "added value" to the product. If we sum up the values added by all firms in the economy, we must get the total value of all final products. Thus:

> GDP can be measured as the sum of the values added by all firms.

To verify this fact, look back at the accounting identity at the top of page 185. The left-hand side of this equation, sales revenue minus purchases from other firms, is precisely the firm's value added. Thus:

$$\text{Value added} = \text{Wages} + \text{Interest} + \text{Indirect taxes} + \text{Profits}$$

Because the second method we gave for measuring GDP is to add up wages, interest, indirect taxes, and profits, the value-added approach must yield the same answer.

The value-added concept is useful in avoiding double-counting. Often, however, intermediate goods are difficult to distinguish from final goods. Paint bought by a painter, for example, is an intermediate good. But paint bought by a do-it-yourselfer is a final good. What happens, then, if the professional painter buys some paint to refurbish his own garage? The intermediate good becomes a final good.

---

[8] An inventory valuation adjustment must also be made; this can be a large number, either because firms hold a lot of inventory or inflation rates are high.

[9] If the capital stock is used for consumption, it will decline, and the nation will wind up poorer than it was before.

You can see that the line between intermediate goods and final goods is a fuzzy one in practice.

If we measure GDP by the sum of values added, however, we need not make such subtle distinctions. In this method, every purchase of a new good or service counts, but we do not count the entire selling price, only the portion that represents value added.

To illustrate this idea, consider the data in Table 5 and how they would affect GDP as the sum of final products. Our example begins when a farmer who grows soybeans sells them to a mill for $3 per bushel. This transaction does *not* count in the GDP, because the miller does not purchase the soybeans for her own use. The miller then grinds up the soybeans and sells the resulting bag of soy meal to a factory that produces soy sauce. The miller receives $4, but GDP still has not increased because the ground beans are also an intermediate product. Next, the factory turns the beans into soy sauce, which it sells to your favourite Chinese restaurant for $8. Still no effect on GDP.

But then the big moment arrives: The restaurant sells the sauce to you and other customers as a part of your meals, and you eat it. At this point, the $10 worth of soy sauce becomes part of a final product and *does* count in the GDP. Notice that if we had also counted the three intermediate transactions (farmer to miller, miller to factory, factory to restaurant), we would have come up with $25—2½ times too much.

TABLE 5
An Illustration of Final and Intermediate Goods

Item	Seller	Buyer	Price
Bushel of soybeans	Farmer	Miller	$3
Bag of soy meal	Miller	Factory	4
Litre of soy sauce	Factory	Restaurant	8
Litre of soy sauce used as seasoning	Restaurant	Consumers	10
		Total: $25	
Addendum: Contribution to GDP $10			

Why is it too much? The reason is straightforward. Neither the miller, the factory owner, nor the restaurateur values the product we have been considering *for its own sake*. Only the customers who eat the final product (the soy sauce) have increased their material well-being, so only this last transaction counts in the GDP. However, as we will now see, value-added calculations enable us to come up with the right answer ($10) by counting only *part* of each transaction. The basic idea is to count at each step only the contribution to the value of the ultimate final product that is made at that step, excluding the values of items produced at other steps (the same point was made in Chapter 18 of *Microeconomics: Principles and Policy*).

Ignoring the minor items (such as fertilizer) that the farmer purchases from others, the entire $3 selling price

of the bushel of soybeans is new output produced by the farmer; that is, the whole $3 is value added. The miller then grinds the beans and sells them for $4. She has added $4 minus $3, or $1 to the value of the beans. When the factory turns this soy meal into soy sauce and sells it for $8, it has added $8 minus $4, or $4 more in value. Finally, when the restaurant sells it to hungry customers for $10, a further $2 of value is added.

The last column of Table 6 shows this chain of creation of value added. We see that the total value added by all four firms is $10, exactly the same as the restaurant's selling price. This is as it must be, for only the restaurant sells the soybeans as a final product.

TABLE 6
An Illustration of Value Added

Item	Seller	Buyer	Price	Value Added
Bushel of soybeans	Farmer	Miller	$3	$3
Bag of soy meal	Miller	Factory	4	1
Litre of soy sauce	Factory	Restaurant	8	4
Litre of soy sauce used as seasoning	Restaurant	Consumers	10	2
		Total:	$25	$10

Addendum: Contribution to GDP

Final products	$10
Sum of values added	$10

ADDITIONAL MEASURES OF THE INCOME OF THE NATION

GDP versus GNP

So far we have evaded a complication that may have some importance in open economies such as Canada. Domestic production, in particular GDP, measures the economic activity that occurs within the borders of Canada. Looking at it from the income side, GDP measures the income that is generated by businesses located inside Canada's borders, regardless of who is the recipient of this income. This we have called the *gross domestic income*. But income recipients could be foreigners, either foreigners working for companies located in Canada or foreign owners of companies operating in Canada. Similarly, there are Canadians who work abroad and contribute to the GDP of foreign countries (although Canadian diplomats working at Canadian embassies abroad are considered as part of the Canadian *domestic* activity), and there are Canadians who hold securities issued by companies or governments located abroad. To take all of this into account, national accountants have created another concept: the *gross national product (GNP)*, or looking at it from the income side, *gross national income*, which reflects the income received by Canadians. Thus, if Quebec were to secede from the rest of Canada, the salaries of Quebec residents still working in Ottawa would be part of Canadian GDP but would not be part of Canadian GNP.

> Gross national product (GNP) is the sum of the money values of all final goods and services produced by the factors of production owned by the *nationals* of a country, during a specified period of time, usually a year.

In symmetry to the *net domestic product* (NDP), there is also a *net national product* (NNP). It is a rather simple matter to translate GDP into GNP, as can be seen from Table 7. Starting with GDP, one adds the income received from abroad and subtracts the income paid to other countries (essentially investment income). In the case of Canada, more income was paid than received; hence, net foreign income (NFY) is negative. As a result, Canadian GNP is currently about 1 percent smaller than Canadian GDP, so Canadian national income is smaller than its domestic production. This difference occurs because of Canada's large buildup of foreign debt in the 1970s and 1980s, which led to a discrepancy between GDP and GNP that was as large as 4 percent. But the trend has now reversed. In 1970, GNP and GDP were approximately equal, and it is estimated that we may be back to this situation in the near future.

TABLE 7

GDP versus GNP in 2007 (in billions of current dollars)

Gross domestic product	GDP	$1,532
+ Net foreign income	+ NFY	−20
= Gross national product	= GNP	1,512

SOURCE: Statistics Canada, *National Income and Expenditure Accounts,* Table 1, Catalogue No. 13-001-XIE.

Which measure is the best? Until the 1968 revision of the United Nations System of National Accounts, which is constructed around the GDP concept, GNP was the most popular measure. National accountants then slowly migrated toward national accounting systems based on GDP measures. The European Community did so in 1970, and Statistics Canada made its move in July 1986, followed by the United States in 1991. National accountants now prefer to focus the accounts around a measure of the economic activity that occurs within the borders of a nation (GDP), rather than around the income collected by the citizens or the residents of a country. But because some economists believe that the strength of gross national income relative to gross domestic product is of some significance, most national accounts still keep track of GNP.

■ Disposable Income

On page 169, we defined a rough-and-ready measure of disposable income, a variable that is crucial when dealing with concepts such as the marginal propensity to consume, since this propensity is measured on the basis of changes in consumption expenditures and disposable income. We then claimed on page 171 that disposable income was approximately equal to GDP minus taxes net of transfers ($DI = Y - T$). It is now time to give a more precise definition of disposable income, and we will do this with the help of Table 8.

TABLE 8

Personal Income and Disposable Income, 2007

	Item	Nominal Amount*
1	Labour income	$ 782
2	+ Unincorporated business income	90
3	+ Interest and investments income	133
4	+ Current transfers from government	151
5	+ Other incoming transfers	5
6	= Total personal income	1,161
7	− Transfers to government	272
8	= Disposable income	889
9	− Current transfers to corporations	17
10	− Current transfers to nonresidents	4
11	− Personal consumption expenditures	854
12	= Personal saving	14

* In billions of current dollars.

SOURCE: Statistics Canada, *Canadian Economic Observer,* Table 2, Catalogue No. 10-010-XIB.

In Canada, individuals and the unincorporated businesses of individuals are amalgamated in a single sector, which represents households, as we can see from rows 1 and 2 in Table 8. To get total personal income, we need to add income interest and all investment income (row 3)—which now includes the profits of corporations paid out as dividends as well as interest payments on government debt, both from Canada and abroad—as well as government transfers to individuals (row 4). These include the Child Tax Benefit, Employment Insurance, welfare, the Canada Pension Plan, Old Age Security benefits, scholarships, and research grants. Other incoming transfers (row 5), such as received charitable donations and pensions paid by foreign governments to Canadians, also need to be added.

To determine disposable income, subtract from total personal income all transfers to government (row 7), which include individual income taxes and all taxes that were included in supplementary labour income and hence in labour income, such as payroll taxes tied to contributions to Employment Insurance, Workers' Compensation, and the Canada and Quebec Pension Plans.

Disposable income (row 8) can then be split among payments on consumer debt (row 9), remittances to foreign countries (mainly religious and charitable organizations, row 10), and personal consumption expenditures (row 11, the same item that appeared at the top of Table 3 as *C*). Personal saving, or household saving, is what is left over, a meagre $14 billion, or 1.5 percent of disposable income!

If we compare disposable income ($889 billion) to GDP ($1,532 billion) in 2007, we see that there is a large discrepancy, a portion of which can be explained by the subtraction of all taxes that were included in GDP. Other large adjustment items include capital consumption allowances, the undistributed profits of corporate firms (their retained earnings), and income taxes (both personal and corporate). In Canada in 2007, corporate retained earnings amounted to no less than $107 billion, or 7.0 percent of GDP, and the capital consumption allowance was $122 billion, so that corporate gross retained earnings—the gross profits that firms keep for themselves to invest in new machinery and replace used-up capital—were $229 billion, or 15.0 percent of GDP.

SUMMARY

1. **Gross domestic product** (**GDP**) is the sum of the money values of all final goods and services produced within the borders of a nation during a year and sold on organized markets. There are, however, certain exceptions to this definition.

2. One way to measure the GDP is to add up the final demands of consumers, investors, government, and foreigners: GDP = $C + I + G + (X - IM)$, taking into account business investment in inventories.

3. A second way to measure GDP is to start with all factor payments—wages, interest, and profits—and then add all indirect taxes on factors of production and sales, thus obtaining the **net domestic product**. By also adding **capital consumption allowances** (**amortization**), you obtain GDP.

4. A third way to measure the GDP is to sum up the **value added** by every firm in the economy (and then once again add indirect business taxes and depreciation).

5. Except for possible bookkeeping and statistical errors, all three methods must give the same answer.

6. An alternative to GDP is the concept of **gross national product** (**GNP**). It is the sum of the money values of all final goods and services produced by the factors of production owned by the *nationals* of a country, instead of the final goods and services produced *inside the borders of a nation*. Since 1986, Statistics Canada has based its national accounts on GDP rather than GNP.

KEY TERMS

National income accounting   183

Gross domestic product (GDP)   183

Gross private domestic investment (I_{na})   184

Net domestic product at basic prices   186

Net domestic product at market prices (NDP)   186

Amortization   186

Capital consumption allowances   186

Value added   186

Gross national product (GNP)   188

TEST YOURSELF

1. Which of the following transactions are included in the gross domestic product, and by how much does each raise GDP?

   a. You buy a new Toyota, made in Canada, paying $18,000.

   b. You buy a new Honda, imported from Japan, paying $18,000.

   c. You buy a used Cadillac, paying $3,000.

   d. Rogers spends $100 million to increase its Internet capacity.

   e. Your grandmother receives a Old Age Security cheque for $1,200.

   f. Chrysler manufactures 1,000 automobiles at a cost of $12,000 each. Unable to sell them, the company holds the cars as inventory.

   g. Mr. Black and Mr. Blue, each out for a Sunday drive, have a collision in which their cars are destroyed. Black and Blue each hire a lawyer to sue the other, paying the lawyers $3,000 each for services rendered. The judge throws the case out of court.

   h. You sell a used computer to your friend for $100.

2. The following outline provides a complete description of all economic activity in Trivialand for 2004. Draw up versions of Tables 3 and 4 for Trivialand showing GDP computed in two different ways.

   i. There are thousands of farmers but only two big business firms in Trivialand: Specific Motors (an auto company) and Super Duper (a chain of food markets). There is no government and no amortization.

   ii. Specific Motors produced 1,000 small cars, which it sold at $6,000 each, and 100 trucks, which it sold at $8,000 each. Consumers bought 800 of the cars, and the remaining 200 cars were exported to the United States. Super Duper bought all the trucks.

   iii. Sales at Super Duper markets amounted to $14 million, all of it sold to consumers.

   iv. All farmers in Trivialand are self-employed and sell all of their wares to Super Duper.

   v. The costs incurred by all of Trivialand's businesses were as shown in the accompanying table:

	Specific Motors	Super Duper	Farmers
Wages	$3,800,000	$4,500,000	$ 0
Interest	300,000	1,200,000	2,700,000
Purchases of food	0	7,000,000	0

DISCUSSION QUESTIONS

1. Explain the difference between final goods and intermediate goods. Why is it sometimes difficult to apply this distinction in practice? In this regard, why is the concept of value added useful?

2. Explain the difference between government spending and government purchases of goods and services (G). Which is larger?

9

DEMAND-SIDE EQUILIBRIUM: THE INCOME MULTIPLIER

A definite ratio, to be called the Multiplier, can be established between income and investment.

JOHN MAYNARD KEYNES (1883–1946), 1936

Let's briefly review where we have just been. In Chapter 8, we learned that aggregate demand has four components: consumer expenditure (C), investment (I), government purchases (G), and net exports ($X - IM$). We also saw that consumer expenditures depend on gross domestic product (GDP); more specifically, they are a function of disposable income. But then, how is gross domestic product itself determined? It is now time to start building a theory that puts all of the pieces together.

Our approach is sequential. Because it is best to walk before you try to run, we begin in this chapter by assuming that the price level, the rate of interest, and the international value of the Canadian dollar are all constant. None of these assumptions is true, of course, and we will dispense with them all in subsequent chapters. But we reap two important benefits from making these unrealistic assumptions now. First, they enable us to construct a simple but useful model of how the strength of aggregate demand influences the level of gross domestic product—a model we will use to derive specific numerical solutions. Second, this model gives us an initial answer to a question of great importance to policy makers: can we expect the economy to achieve full employment if the government does not intervene?

CONTENTS

ISSUE: *Why Does the Market Permit Unemployment?*

Economists are fond of pointing out, with some awe, the achievements of competitive markets. Without central direction, they somehow get businesses to produce just the goods and services that consumers want—and to do so cheaply and efficiently. If consumers want less meat and more fish, markets respond. If people subsequently change their minds, markets respond again. Markets seem able to coordinate literally millions of decisions effortlessly and seamlessly.

Yet for hundreds of years and all over the globe, market economies have stumbled over one particular coordination problem: the periodic bouts of mass unemployment that we call *recessions* and *depressions*. Widespread unemployment represents a failure to coordinate economic activity in the following sense. If the unemployed were hired, they would be able to buy the goods and services that businesses cannot sell. The revenues from those sales would, in turn, allow firms to pay the workers. So a seemingly straightforward "deal" offers jobs for the unemployed and sales for the firms. But somehow this deal is not made. Workers remain unemployed and firms get stuck with unsold output.

Thus, free markets, which somehow manage to get rough diamonds dug out of the ground in South Africa and turned into beautiful rings that grooms buy for brides in Montreal or Vancouver, cannot seem to solve the coordination problem posed by unemployment. Why not? For centuries, economists puzzled over this question. By the end of the chapter, we will be well on the way toward providing an answer.

THE MEANING OF EQUILIBRIUM GDP

We begin by putting the four components of aggregate demand together to see how they interact, using as our organizing framework the circular flow diagram from the last chapter. In doing so, we initially ignore the possibility, raised in earlier chapters, that the government might use monetary and fiscal policy to steer the economy in some desired direction. Aside from pedagogical simplicity, there is an important reason for doing so. One of the crucial questions surrounding stabilization policy is whether the economy would *automatically* gravitate toward full employment if the government simply left it alone. Contradicting the teachings of generations of economists before him, Keynes claimed it would not. But Keynes's views remain controversial to this day. We can study the issue best by imagining an economy in which the government never tried to manipulate aggregate demand, which is just what we do in this chapter.

To begin to construct a simple model of the size of the economy, we must first understand what we mean by *equilibrium GDP*. Figure 1, which repeats Figure 1 from the last chapter, is a circular flow diagram that will help us do this. As explained in the last chapter, total *production* and total *income* must be equal. But the same need not be true of total spending. Imagine that, for some reason, the total expenditures made after point 4 in the figure, $C + I + G + (X - IM)$, exceed the output produced by the business firms at point 5. What happens then?

Because consumers, businesses, government, and foreigners together are buying more than firms are producing, businesses will start taking goods out of their warehouses to meet customer demand. Thus, inventory stocks will fall—which signals retailers that they need to increase their orders and manufacturers that they need to step up production. Consequently, output is likely to rise.

At some later date, if evidence indicates that the high level of spending is not just a temporary aberration, either manufacturers or retailers (or both) may also respond to buoyant sales performances by raising their prices. Economists therefore say that neither output nor the price level is in **equilibrium** when total spending exceeds current production.

The definition of *equilibrium* in the margin tells us that the economy cannot be in equilibrium when total spending exceeds production, because falling inventories

Equilibrium refers to a situation in which neither consumers nor firms have any incentive to change their behaviour. They are content to continue with things as they are.

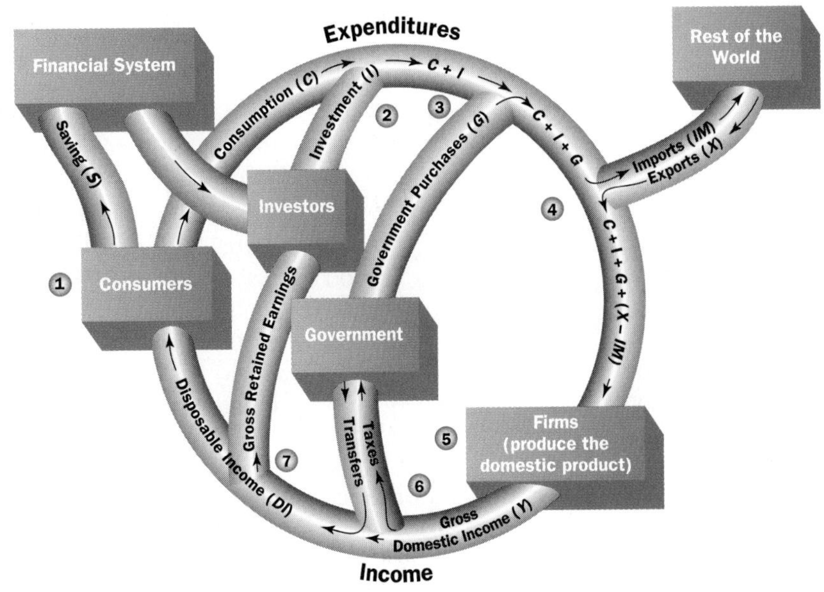

demonstrate to firms that their production and pricing decisions were not quite appropriate.[1] Thus, because we normally use GDP to measure output:

> The equilibrium level of GDP on the demand side cannot be one at which total spending exceeds output because firms will notice that they are depleting their inventory stocks. Firms may first decide to increase production sufficiently to meet the higher demand. Later they may decide to raise prices.

Now imagine the other case, in which the flow of spending reaching firms falls short of current production. Unsold output winds up as additional inventories. The inventory pile-up signals firms that either their pricing or output decision was wrong. Once again, they will probably react first by cutting back on production, causing GDP to fall (at point 5 in Figure 1). If the imbalance persists, they may also lower prices in the hope of stimulating sales. But they certainly will not be happy with things as they are. Thus:

> The equilibrium level of GDP on the demand side cannot be one at which total spending is less than output, because firms will not allow inventories to pile up. They may decide to decrease production, or they may decide to cut prices in order to stimulate demand.

We have now determined, by process of elimination, the only level of output that is consistent with people's desires to spend. We have reasoned that GDP will *rise* whenever it is less than total spending, $C + I + G + (X - IM)$, and that GDP will fall whenever it exceeds $C + I + G + (X - IM)$. Equilibrium can occur, then, only when there is just enough spending to absorb the current level of production. Under such circumstances, producers conclude that their price and output decisions are correct and have no incentive to change. We conclude that:

> The **equilibrium level of GDP on the demand side** is the level at which total spending equals production. In such a situation, firms find their inventories remaining at desired levels, so they have no incentive to change output or prices.

Thus, the circular flow diagram has helped us to understand the concept of equilibrium GDP and has shown us how the economy is driven toward this equilibrium. It leaves unanswered, however, three important questions:

- How large is the equilibrium level of GDP?
- Will the economy suffer from unemployment, inflation, or both?
- Is the equilibrium level of GDP on the demand side also consistent with firms' desires to produce? That is, is it also an equilibrium on the *supply* side?

The first two questions will occupy our attention in this chapter; the third is reserved for later chapters.

FIGURE 1

The Circular Flow Diagram

THE MECHANICS OF INCOME DETERMINATION

Our first objective is to determine precisely the equilibrium level of GDP on the demand side. To make the analysis more concrete, we turn to a numerical example.

---

[1] All the models in this book assume, strictly for simplicity, that firms seek constant inventories. Deliberate inventory changes are treated in more advanced courses.

TABLE 1

The Total Expenditure Schedule

(1) GDP (Y)	(2) Consumption (C)	(3) Investment (I)	(4) Government Purchases (G)	(5) Net Exports ($X - IM$)	(6) Total Expenditure
4,800	3,000	900	1,300	−100	5,100
5,200	3,300	900	1,300	−100	5,400
5,600	3,600	900	1,300	−100	5,700
6,000	3,900	900	1,300	−100	6,000
6,400	4,200	900	1,300	−100	6,300
6,800	4,500	900	1,300	−100	6,600
7,200	4,800	900	1,300	−100	6,900

An **expenditure schedule** shows the relationship between national income (GDP) and total spending.

FIGURE 2

Construction of the Expenditure Schedule

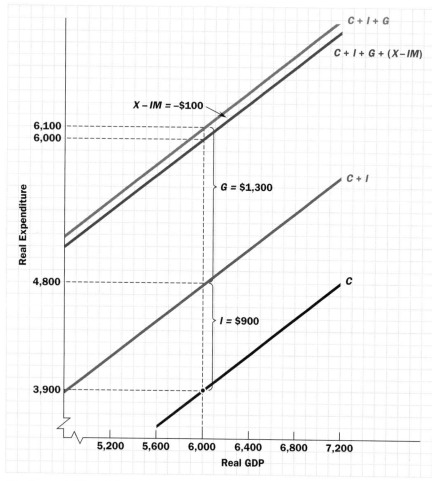

Note: Figures are in billions of dollars per year.

Specifically, we examine the relationship between total spending and GDP in the hypothetical economy we introduced in the last chapter.

Columns (1) and (2) of Table 1 repeat the consumption function that we first encountered in Table 1 of Chapter 8 (see page 175). They show how consumer spending, C, depends on GDP, which we symbolize by the letter Y. Columns (3) through (5) provide the other three components of total spending, I, G, and $X - IM$, through the simplifying assumptions that each is just a fixed number regardless of the level of GDP. Specifically, we assume that investment spending is $900 billion, government purchases are $1,300 billion, and net exports are −$100 billion—meaning that in this hypothetical economy (it could be our neighbour, the United States), imports exceed exports.

By adding Columns (2) through (5), we calculate $C + I + G + (X - IM)$, or total expenditure, which appears in Column (6) of Table 1. Columns (1) and (6) are shown in blue to indicate how total expenditure depends on income. We call this relationship the **expenditure schedule**.

Figure 2 shows the construction of the expenditure schedule graphically. The black line labelled C is the consumption function; it plots on a graph the numbers given in Columns (1) and (2) of Table 1.

The red line, labelled $C + I$, displays our assumption that investment is fixed at $900 billion. It lies a fixed distance (corresponding to $900 billion) above the C line. If investment were not always $900 billion, the two lines would either move closer together or grow farther apart. For example, our analysis of the determinants of investment spending suggested that I might be larger when GDP is higher. Such added investment as GDP rises—which is called **induced investment**—would give the resulting $C + I$ line a steeper slope than the C line. But we ignore that possibility here for simplicity.

The green line, which is labelled $C + I + G$, adds government purchases. Because they are assumed to be $1,300 billion regardless of the size of GDP, the green line is parallel to the red line and $1,300 billion higher.

Finally, the blue line labelled $C + I + G + (X - IM)$ adds in net exports. It is parallel to the green line and $100 billion lower, reflecting our assumption that net exports are always −$100 billion.

Once again, if imports depended on GDP, as the previous chapter suggested, the $C + I + G$ and $C + I + G + (X - IM)$ lines would not be parallel. We deal with this more complicated case in Appendix D to this chapter.

Induced investment is the part of investment spending that rises when GDP rises and falls when GDP falls.

We are now ready to determine demand-side equilibrium in our hypothetical economy. Table 2 presents the logic of the circular flow argument in tabular form. The first two columns reproduce the expenditure schedule that we have just constructed. The other columns explain the process by which the economy approaches equilibrium. Let us see why a GDP of $6,000 billion must be the equilibrium level.

Consider first any output level below $6,000 billion. For example, at output level $Y = \$5,200$ billion, total expenditure is $5,400 billion, as shown in Column (2). This is $200 billion more than production. With spending greater than output, as noted in Column (3), inventories will fall (see Column (4)). As the table suggests in Column (5), this will signal producers to raise their output. Clearly, then, no output level below $Y = \$6,000$ billion can be an equilibrium, because output is too low.

A similar line of reasoning eliminates any output level above $6,000 billion. Consider, for example, $Y = \$6,800$ billion. The table shows that total spending would be $6,600 billion if output were $6,800 billion, so $200 billion would go unsold. This would raise producers' inventory stocks and signal them that their rate of production was too high.

Just as we concluded from our circular flow diagram, equilibrium will be achieved only when total spending, $C + I + G + (X - IM)$, exactly equals GDP, Y. In symbols, our condition for equilibrium GDP is:

$$Y = C + I + G + (X - IM)$$

Table 2 shows that this equation holds only at a GDP of $6,000 billion, which must be the equilibrium level of GDP.

Figure 3 on the next page depicts the same conclusion graphically, by adding a 45° line to Figure 2. Why a 45° line? Recall from the appendix to Chapter 1 that a 45° line marks all points on a graph at which the value of the variable measured on the horizontal axis (in this case, GDP) equals the value of the variable measured on the vertical axis (in this case, total expenditure).[2] Thus, the 45° line in Figure 3 shows all the

TABLE 2				
The Determination of Equilibrium Output				
(1) Output (Y)	(2) Total Spending [C + I + G + (X − IM)]	(3) Balance of Spending and Output	(4) Inventory Status	(5) Producer Response
4,800	5,100	Spending exceeds output	Falling	Produce more
5,200	5,400	Spending exceeds output	Falling	Produce more
5,600	5,700	Spending exceeds output	Falling	Produce more
6,000	**6,000**	**Spending = output**	**Constant**	**No change**
6,400	6,300	Output exceeds spending	Rising	Produce less
6,800	6,600	Output exceeds spending	Rising	Produce less
7,200	6,900	Output exceeds spending	Rising	Produce less

Note: Amounts are in billions of dollars.

points at which output and spending are equal—that is, where $Y = C + I + G + (X - IM)$. *The 45° line therefore displays all the points at which the economy can possibly be in demand-side equilibrium,* for firms will be content with current output levels only if total spending equals production.

Now we must compare these *potential* equilibrium points with the *actual* combinations of spending and output that are consistent with the current behaviour of consumers and investors. That behaviour is described by the $C + I + G + (X - IM)$ line in Figure 3, which shows how total expenditure varies as income changes. *The economy will always be on the expenditure line* because only points on the $C + I + G + (X - IM)$ line describe the spending plans of consumers and investors. Similarly, *if the economy is in equilibrium, it must be on the 45° line.* As Figure 3 shows, these two requirements imply that the only viable equilibrium is at point E, where the $C + I + G + (X - IM)$ line intersects the 45° line. Only this point is consistent with

---

[2] If you need review, see the appendix to Chapter 1, especially page 22.

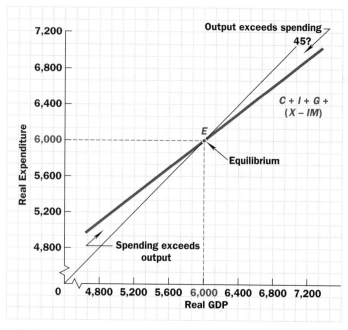

FIGURE 3

Income–Expenditure
Diagram

Note: Figures are in billions of dollars per year.

both equilibrium and people's actual desires to consume and invest.

Notice that to the left of the equilibrium point, E, the expenditure line lies *above* the 45° line. This means that total spending exceeds total output, as we have already noted. Hence, inventories will be falling and firms will conclude that they should increase production. Thus, production will rise toward the equilibrium point, E. The opposite is true to the right of point E. Here spending falls short of output, inventories rise, and firms will cut back production—thereby moving closer to E.

In other words, whenever production is *above* the equilibrium level, market forces will drive output *down*. And whenever production is *below* equilibrium, market forces will drive output *up*. In either case, deviations from demand-side equilibrium will gradually be eliminated.

Diagrams such as Figure 3 will recur so frequently in this and the next several chapters that it will be convenient to have a name for them. We call them **income–expenditure diagrams**, because they show how expenditures vary with income, or simply **45° line diagrams**.

THE AGGREGATE DEMAND CURVE

An **income–expenditure diagram**, or **45° line diagram**, plots total real expenditure (on the vertical axis) against real income (on the horizontal axis). The 45° line marks off points where income and expenditure are equal.

Chapter 5 introduced aggregate demand and aggregate supply curves relating aggregate quantities demanded and supplied to the price level. The expenditure schedule graphed in Figure 3 is certainly *not* the aggregate demand curve, for we have yet to bring the price level into our discussion. It is now time to remedy this omission and derive the aggregate demand curve.

To do so, we need only recall something we learned in the last chapter. As we noted on page 176, households own a great deal of *money-fixed assets* whose real value declines when the price level rises. The money in your bank account is a prime example. If prices rise, it will buy less. Because of that fact, consumers' *real* wealth declines whenever the price level rises—and that affects their spending. As discussed in Chapter 8, this is often called the *wealth effect*. We also know from the previous chapter that a higher price level reduces the burden of household debt, but we will assume that the latter effect is weaker, and that the overall effect of higher prices is an erosion of the purchasing power of households. Specifically:

Higher prices decrease the demand for goods and services because they erode the purchasing power of consumer wealth. Conversely, lower prices increase the demand for goods and services by enhancing the purchasing power of consumer wealth.

For these reasons, a change in the price level will shift the entire consumption function. To represent this shift graphically, Figure 4 repeats Figure 6 from the previous chapter. It shows that:

A higher price level leads to lower real wealth and therefore to less spending *at any given level of real income*. Thus, a higher price level leads to a lower consumption function (such as C_1 in Figure 4), and a lower price level leads to a higher consumption function (such as C_2 in Figure 4).

Because students are sometimes confused by this point, it is worth repeating that the depressing effect of the price level on consumer spending works through real *wealth*, not through real *income*. The consumption function is a relationship between *real consumer income* and *real consumer spending*. Thus, any decline in real income, regardless of its cause, moves the economy leftward *along a fixed consumption function;* it does not shift the consumption function.[3] By contrast, a decline in *real wealth* will *shift the entire consumption function downward,* meaning that people spend less at any given level of real income.

In terms of the 45° line diagram, a rise in the price level will therefore pull down the consumption function depicted in Figure 2, and hence will pull down the total expenditure schedule as well. Conversely, a fall in the price level will raise both the C and $C + I + G + (X - IM)$ schedules in the diagram. The two panels of Figure 5 illustrate both of these shifts.

How, then, do changes in the price level affect the equilibrium level of real GDP on the demand side? Common sense says that, with lower spending, equilibrium GDP should fall, and Figure 5 shows that this conclusion is correct. Panel (a) shows that a rise in the price level, by shifting the expenditure schedule downward, leads to a reduction in the equilibrium quantity of real GDP demanded from Y_0 to Y_1. Conversely, Panel (b) shows that a fall in the price level, by shifting the expenditure schedule upward, leads to a rise in the equilibrium quantity of real GDP demanded from Y_0 to Y_2. In summary:

A rise in the price level leads to a lower equilibrium level of real aggregate quantity demanded. This relationship between the price level and real GDP (depicted in Figure 6) is precisely what we called the aggregate demand curve in earlier chapters. It comes directly from the 45° line diagrams in Figure 5. Thus, points E_0, E_1, and E_2 in Figure 6 correspond precisely to the points bearing the same labels in Figure 5.

The effect of higher prices on consumer wealth is just one of several reasons why the aggregate demand curve slopes downward. A second reason comes from international trade. In Chapter 8's discussion of the determinants of net exports (see pages 179–180), we pointed out that higher Canadian prices (holding foreign prices constant) will depress exports (X) and stimulate imports (IM). That means that, other

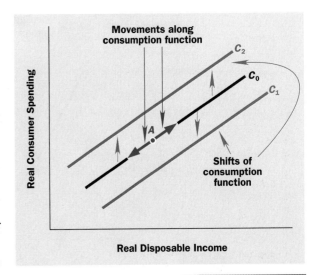

FIGURE 4

Shifts of the Consumption Function

FIGURE 5

The Effect of the Price Level on Equilibrium Aggregate Quantity Demanded

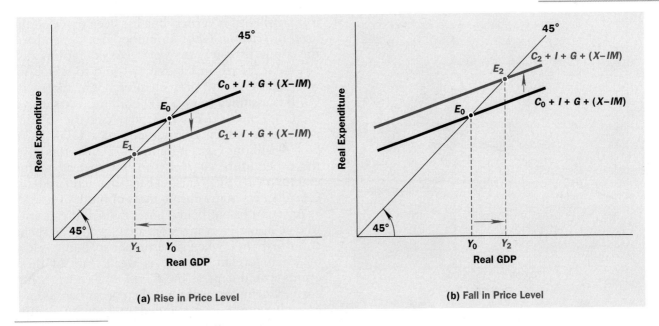

(a) Rise in Price Level

(b) Fall in Price Level

---

[3] This is true even if a rise in the price level lies behind the decline in real income.

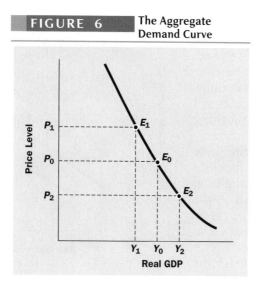

FIGURE 6   The Aggregate Demand Curve

things equal, a higher Canadian price level will reduce the $(X - IM)$ component of total expenditure, thereby shifting the $C + I + G + (X - IM)$ line downward and lowering real GDP, as depicted in Figure 5(a). Thus:

An income–expenditure diagram like Figure 3 can be drawn only for a *specific* price level. At different price levels, the $C + I + G + (X - IM)$ schedule will be different and, hence, the equilibrium quantity of GDP demanded will also differ.

As we will now see, this seemingly technical point about graphs is critical to understanding the genesis of unemployment and inflation.

DEMAND-SIDE EQUILIBRIUM AND FULL EMPLOYMENT

We now turn to the second major question posed on page 193: Will the economy achieve an equilibrium at full employment without inflation, or will we see unemployment, inflation, or both? This question is a crucial one for stabilization policy, for if the economy always gravitates toward full employment *automatically*, then the government should simply leave it alone.

In the income–expenditure diagrams used so far, the equilibrium level of GDP demanded appears as the intersection of the expenditure schedule and the 45° line, regardless of the GDP level that corresponds to full employment. However, as we will see now, when equilibrium GDP falls above potential GDP, the economy probably will be plagued by inflation, and when equilibrium falls below potential GDP, unemployment and recession will result.

This remarkable fact was one of the principal messages of Keynes's *General Theory of Employment, Interest, and Money*. Writing during the Great Depression, it was natural for Keynes to focus on the case in which equilibrium falls short of full employment, leaving some resources unemployed. Figure 7 illustrates this possibility. A vertical line has been drawn at the level of *potential GDP*, a number that depends on the kinds of *aggregate supply* considerations discussed at length in Chapter 7—and to which we will return in the next chapter. Here, potential GDP is assumed to be $7,000 billion. We see that the $C + I + G + (X - IM)$ curve cuts the 45° line at point E, which corresponds to a GDP ($Y = $6,000 billion) *below* potential GDP. In this case, the expenditure curve is too low to lead to full employment. Such a situation characterized the Canadian economy during most of the 1990s.

An equilibrium below potential GDP can arise when consumers or investors are unwilling to spend at normal rates, when government spending is low, or when foreign demand is weak. Any of these events would depress the $C + I + G + (X - IM)$ curve. Unemployment must then occur because not enough output is demanded to keep the entire labour force at work.

FIGURE 7

A Recessionary Gap

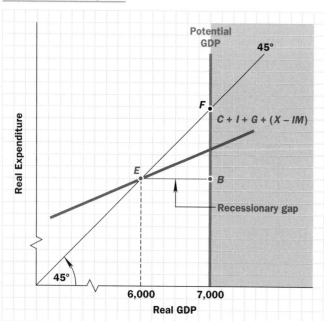

Note: Figures are in billions of dollars per year.

The distance between the *equilibrium* level of output demanded and the *full-employment* level of output (that is, potential GDP) is called the **recessionary gap**; it is shown by the horizontal distance from point E to point B in Figure 7. Although the figure is entirely hypothetical, real-world gaps of precisely this sort have been a pervasive feature of Canadian economic history.

Figure 7 clearly shows that full employment can be reached only by raising the total expenditure schedule to eliminate the recessionary gap. Specifically, the C + I + G + (X − IM) line must move upward until it cuts the 45° line at point F. Can this happen without government intervention? This is a highly contentious issue among economists, and indeed their answers to this question help to define the various schools of thought in macroeconomics. We will return to this question in the following chapters, after we bring the supply side into the picture. First, however, let us briefly consider the other case—when equilibrium GDP exceeds full employment.

Figure 8 illustrates this possibility, which economists at the Bank of Canada believe characterized the Canadian economy in 2000 and between 2004 and 2007. Now the expenditure schedule intersects the 45° line at point E, where GDP is $8,000 billion. But this exceeds the full-employment level, Y = $7,000 billion. A case such as this can arise when consumer or investment spending is unusually buoyant, when foreign demand is particularly strong, or when the government spends too much.

To reach an equilibrium at full employment, something has to give to drive the expenditure schedule *down* until it passes through point F. The horizontal distance BE—which indicates the amount by which the quantity of GDP demanded exceeds potential GDP—is now called the **inflationary gap**. If there is an inflationary gap, a reduction in one of the components of total expenditure is necessary to reach an equilibrium at full employment. In sum:

> Only if spending plans are "just right" will the expenditure curve intersect the 45° line precisely at full employment, so that neither a recessionary gap nor an inflationary gap occurs.

Are there reasons to expect this outcome? Does the economy have a self-correcting mechanism that automatically eliminates recessionary or inflationary gaps and propels it toward full employment? And why do inflation and unemployment sometimes rise or fall together? We are not ready to answer these questions yet because we have not yet brought *the supply side* into the picture. However, it is not too early to get an idea about why things can go wrong during a recession.

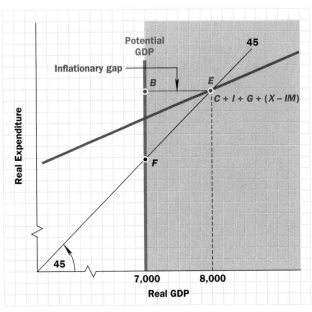

Note: Figures are in billions of dollars per year.

FIGURE 8

An Inflationary Gap

The **recessionary gap** is the amount by which the equilibrium level of real GDP falls short of potential GDP.

The **inflationary gap** is the amount by which equilibrium real GDP exceeds the full-employment level of GDP.

THE COORDINATION OF SAVING AND INVESTMENT

To do so, it is useful to pose the following question: Must the full-employment level of GDP be a demand-side equilibrium? Decades ago, economists thought the answer was yes. Since Keynes, most economists believe the answer is "not necessarily."

To help us see why, Figure 9 offers a simplified circular flow diagram that ignores exports, imports, and the government. In this version, income can "leak out" of the circular flow only at point 1, where consumers save some of their income. Similarly, lost spending can be replaced only at point 2, where investment enters the circular flow.

What happens if firms produce exactly the full-employment level of GDP at point 3 in the diagram? Will this income level be maintained as we move around the circle, or will it shrink or grow? The answer is that full-employment income will be maintained

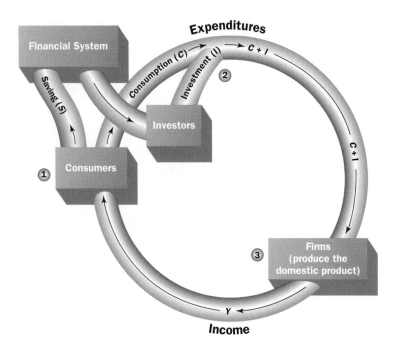

FIGURE 9

A Simplified Circular Flow

only if the spending by investors at point 2 exactly balances the saving done by consumers at point 1. In other words:

> The economy will reach an equilibrium at full employment on the demand side only if the amount that consumers wish to save out of their full-employment incomes happens to equal the amount that investors want to invest. If these two magnitudes are unequal, full employment will not be an equilibrium.

Thus, the basic answer to the puzzle we posed at the start of this chapter is:

> The market will permit unemployment when total spending is too low to employ the entire labour force.

Now, how can that occur? The circular flow diagram shows that, if saving exceeds investment at full employment, the total demand received by firms at point 3 will fall short of total output because the added investment spending will not be enough to replace the leakage to saving. With demand inadequate to support production at full employment, GDP must fall below potential. There will be a recessionary gap. Conversely, if investment exceeds saving when the economy is at full employment, then total demand will exceed potential GDP and production will rise above the full-employment level. There will be an inflationary gap.

A **coordination failure** occurs when party A would like to change his behaviour if party B would change hers, and vice versa, and yet the two changes do not take place because the decisions of A and B are not coordinated.

Now, this discussion does nothing but restate what we already know in different words. But these words provide the key to understanding why the economy sometimes finds itself stuck above or below full employment, for *the people who invest are not the same as the people who save.* In a modern capitalist economy, investing is done by one group of individuals (primarily corporate executives and home buyers), whereas saving is done by another group.[4] It is easy to imagine that their plans may not be well coordinated. If they are not, we have just seen how either unemployment or inflation can occur.

Neither of these problems would arise if the acts of saving and investing were perfectly coordinated. While perfection is never attainable, the analysis in the boxed feature, "Unemployment and Inflation as Coordination Failures," raises a tantalizing possibility. If both high unemployment and high inflation arise from **coordination failures**, might the government be able to do something about this problem? Keynes suggested that it could, by using its powers over monetary and fiscal policy. His idea will be examined in detail in later chapters. But even the simple football analogy described in the box reminds us that a central authority may not find it easy to solve a coordination problem.

■ CHANGES ON THE DEMAND SIDE: MULTIPLIER ANALYSIS

The **multiplier** is the ratio of the change in equilibrium GDP (Y) divided by the original change in spending that causes the change in GDP.

We have just learned how demand-side equilibrium depends on the consumption function and the amounts spent on investment, government purchases, and net exports. But none of these is a constant of nature; they all change from time to time. How does equilibrium GDP change when the consumption function shifts or when I, G, or $(X - IM)$ changes? As we will see now, the answer is simple: *by more!* A remarkable result called the **multiplier** says that a change in spending will bring about an *even larger* change in equilibrium GDP on the demand side. Let us see why.

---

[4] In a modern economy, not only do households save, but businesses also save in the form of retained earnings, as was explained on page 171 of Chapter 8. The firms that gather the retained earnings may not be those that decide or want to invest.

Unemployment and Inflation as Coordination Failures

The idea that unemployment stems from a *lack of coordination* between the decisions of savers and investors may seem abstract. But we encounter coordination failures in the real world quite frequently. The following familiar example may bring the idea down to earth.

Picture a crowd watching a football game. Now something exciting happens and the fans rise from their seats. People in the front rows begin standing first, and those seated behind them are forced to stand if they want to see the game. Soon everyone in the stadium is on their feet.

But with everyone standing, no one can see any better than when everyone was sitting. And the fans are enduring the further discomfort of being on their feet. (Never mind that stadium seats are uncomfortable!) Everyone in the stadium would be better off if everyone sat down. Sometimes this happens. But the crowd rises to its feet again on every exciting play. There is simply no way to coordinate the individual decisions of tens of thousands of football fans.

Unemployment poses a similar coordination problem. During a deep recession, workers are unemployed and businesses cannot sell their wares. Figuratively speaking, everyone is "standing" and unhappy about it. If only the firms could agree to hire more workers, those newly employed people could afford to buy more of the goods and services the firms want to produce. But, as at the football stadium, there is no central authority to coordinate these millions of decisions.

SOURCE: © Jonathan Nourok/PhotoEdit

The coordination failure idea also helps to explain why it is so difficult to stop inflation. Virtually everyone prefers stable prices to rising prices. But now think of yourself as the seller of a product. If all other participants in the economy would hold their prices steady, you would happily hold yours steady, too. But, if you believe that others will continue to raise their prices at a rate of, say, 5 percent per year, you may find it dangerous not to increase your prices apace. Hence, society may get stuck with 5 percent inflation even though everyone agrees that zero inflation is better.

■ The Magic of the Multiplier

Because it is subject to abrupt swings, investment spending often causes business fluctuations in Canada and elsewhere. So let us ask what would happen if firms suddenly decided to spend more on investment goods. As we will see next, such a decision would have a *multiplied* effect on GDP, that is, each $1 of additional investment spending would add *more* than $1 to GDP.

To see why, refer first to Table 3, which looks very much like Table 1. The only difference is that we assume here that firms now want to invest $200 billion more than previously—for a total of $1,100 billion. As indicated by the blue numbers, only income level $Y = \$6,800$ billion is an equilibrium on the demand side of the economy now, because only at this level is total spending, $C + I + G + (X - IM)$, equal to production (Y).

The *multiplier* principle says that GDP will rise by *more than* the $200 billion increase in investment. Specifically, the multiplier is defined as the ratio of the change in equilibrium GDP (Y) to the original change in spending that caused GDP to change. In shorthand, when we deal with the multiplier for investment (I), the formula is:

TABLE 3					
Total Expenditure after a $200 Billion Increase in Investment Spending					
(1)	(2)	(3)	(4)	(5)	(6)
Income (Y)	Consumption (C)	Investment (I)	Government Purchases (G)	Net Exports ($X - IM$)	Total Expenditure
4,800	3,000	1,100	1,300	−100	5,300
5,200	3,300	1,100	1,300	−100	5,600
5,600	3,600	1,100	1,300	−00	5,900
6,000	3,900	1,100	1,300	−100	6,200
6,400	4,200	1,100	1,300	−100	6,500
6,800	**4,500**	**1,100**	**1,300**	**−100**	**6,800**
7,200	4,800	1,100	1,300	−100	7,100

Note: Figures are in billions of dollars per year.

$$\text{Multiplier} = \frac{\text{Change in } Y}{\text{Change in } I}$$

Let us verify that the multiplier is, indeed, greater than 1. Table 3 shows how the new expenditure schedule is constructed by adding up C, I, G, and $(X - IM)$ at each level of Y, just as we did earlier—only now $I = \$1,100$ billion rather than $900 billion.

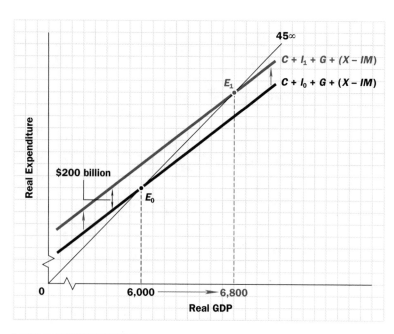

FIGURE 10

Illustration of the Multiplier

Note: Figures are in billions of dollars per year.

If you compare the last columns of Table 1 (page 194) and Table 3, you will see that the new expenditure schedule lies uniformly above the old one by $200 billion.

Figure 10 depicts this change graphically. The curve marked $C + I_0 + G + (X - IM)$ is derived from the last column of Table 1, while the higher curve marked $C + I_1 + G + (X - IM)$ is derived from the last column of Table 3. The two expenditure lines are parallel and $200 billion apart.

So far things look just as you might expect. But one more step will bring the multiplier rabbit out of the hat. Let us see what the upward shift of the expenditure line does to equilibrium income. In Figure 10, equilibrium moves outward from point E_0 to point E_1, or from $6,000 billion to $6,800 billion. The difference is an increase of $800 billion in GDP. All this from a $200 billion stimulus to investment? That is the magic of the multiplier.

Because the change in I is $200 billion and the change in equilibrium Y is $800 billion, by applying our definition, the multiplier is:

$$\text{Multiplier} = \frac{\text{Change in } Y}{\text{Change in } I} = \frac{\$800}{\$200} = 4$$

This tells us that, in our example, each additional $1 of investment demand will add $4 to equilibrium GDP!

This result does, indeed, seem mysterious. Can something be created from nothing? Let's first check that the graph has not deceived us. The first and last columns of Table 3 show in numbers what Figure 10 shows graphically. Notice that equilibrium now comes at $Y = $6,800 billion, because only at that point is total expenditure equal to production (Y). This equilibrium level of GDP is $800 billion higher than the $6,000 billion level found when investment was only $900 billion. Thus, a $200 billion rise in investment does indeed lead to an $800 billion rise in equilibrium GDP; the multiplier really is 4.

Demystifying the Multiplier: How It Works

The multiplier result seems strange at first, but it loses its mystery once we recall the circular flow of income and expenditure and the simple fact that one person's spending is another person's income. To illustrate the logic of the multiplier and see why it is exactly 4 in our example, think about what happens when businesses decide to spend $1 million on investment goods.

Suppose that Microhard—a major corporation in our hypothetical country—decides to spend $1 million on a new office building. Its $1 million expenditure goes to construction workers and owners of construction companies as wages and profits. That is, the $1 million becomes their *income*.

But the construction firm's owners and workers will not keep all of their $1 million in the bank; instead, they will spend most of it. If they are "typical" consumers, their spending will be $1 million times the marginal propensity to consume (MPC). In our example, the MPC is 0.75, so assume they spend $750,000 and save the rest. *This $750,000 expenditure is a net addition to the nation's demand for goods and services, just as Microhard's original $1 million expenditure was.* So, at this stage, the $1 million investment has already pushed GDP up by some $1.75 million. But the process is by no means over.

Shopkeepers receive the $750,000 spent by construction workers, and they in turn also spend 75 percent of their new income. This activity accounts for $562,500 (75 percent of $750,000) in additional consumer spending in the "third round." Next follows a fourth round in which the recipients of the $562,500 spend 75 percent of this amount, or $421,875, and so on. At each stage in the spending chain, people spend 75 percent of the additional income they receive, and the process continues—with consumption growing in every round.

Where does it all end? Does it all end? The answer is that, yes, it does eventually end—with GDP a total of $4 million higher than it was before Microhard built the original $1 million office building. The multiplier is, indeed, 4.

Table 4 displays the basis for this conclusion. In the table, "Round 1" represents Microhard's initial investment, which creates $1 million in income for construction workers. "Round 2" represents the construction workers' spending, which creates $750,000 in income for shopkeepers. The rest of the table proceeds accordingly; each entry in Column (2) is 75 percent of the previous entry. Column (3) tabulates the running sum of Column (2).

We see that after 10 rounds of spending, the initial $1 million investment has mushroomed to $3.77 million—and the sum is still growing. After 20 rounds, the total increase in GDP is over $3.98 million—near its eventual value of $4 million. Although it takes quite a few rounds of spending before the multiplier chain nears 4, we see from the table that it hits 3 rather quickly. If each income recipient in the chain waits, say, two months before spending his new income, the multiplier will reach 3 in only about 10 months.

Figure 11 provides a graphical presentation of the numbers in the last column of Table 4. Notice how the multiplier builds up rapidly at first and then tapers off to approach its ultimate value (4 in this example) gradually.

Although this is only a hypothetical example, the same thing occurs every day in the real world. For instance, a burst of new housing creates a multiplier effect on everything from appliances and furniture to carpeting and insulation. Similarly, when a large company such as the SNC-Lavalin Group makes an investment in a developing country, the multiplier effect boosts business activity in many sectors.

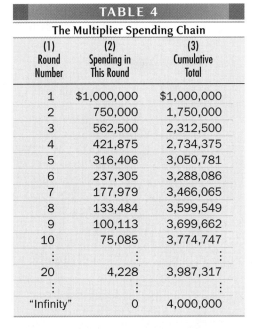

	TABLE 4	
The Multiplier Spending Chain		
(1) Round Number	(2) Spending in This Round	(3) Cumulative Total
1	$1,000,000	$1,000,000
2	750,000	1,750,000
3	562,500	2,312,500
4	421,875	2,734,375
5	316,406	3,050,781
6	237,305	3,288,086
7	177,979	3,466,065
8	133,484	3,599,549
9	100,113	3,699,662
10	75,085	3,774,747
⋮	⋮	⋮
20	4,228	3,987,317
⋮	⋮	⋮
"Infinity"	0	4,000,000

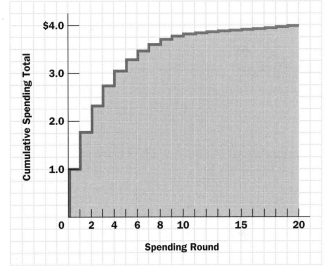

Note: Amounts are in millions of dollars.

FIGURE 11

How the Multiplier Builds

Algebraic Statement of the Multiplier

Figure 11 and Table 4 probably make a persuasive case that the multiplier eventually reaches 4. But for the remaining skeptics, we offer a simple algebraic proof.[5] Most of you learned about something called an *infinite geometric progression* in high school. This term refers to an infinite series of numbers, each one of which is a fixed fraction of the previous one. The fraction is called the *common ratio*. A geometric progression beginning with 1 and having a common ratio of 0.75 looks like this:

$$1 + 0.75 + (0.75)^2 + (0.75)^3 + \ldots$$

---

[5] Students who blanch at the sight of algebra should not be put off. Anyone who can balance a chequebook (even many who cannot!) will be able to follow the argument.

More generally, a geometric progression beginning with 1 and having a common ratio R would be:

$$1 + R + R^2 + R^3 + \ldots$$

A simple formula enables us to sum such a progression as long as R is less than 1.[6] The formula is:[7]

Sum of infinite geometric progression $= \dfrac{1}{1 - R}$

We now recognize that the multiplier chain in Table 4 is just an infinite geometric progression with 0.75 as its common ratio. That is, each \$1 that Microhard spends leads to a $(0.75) \times \$1$ expenditure by construction workers, which in turn leads to a $(0.75) \times (0.75 \times \$1) = (0.75)^2 \times \$1$ expenditure by the shopkeepers, and so on. Thus, for each initial dollar of investment spending, the progression is:

$$1 + 0.75 + (0.75)^2 + (0.75)^3 + (0.75)^4 + \ldots$$

Applying the formula for the sum of such a series, we find that:

$$\text{Multiplier} = \frac{1}{1 - 0.75} = \frac{1}{0.25} = 4$$

Notice how this result can be generalized. If we did not have a specific number for the marginal propensity to consume, but simply called it MPC, the geometric progression in Table 4 would have been:

$$1 + \text{MPC} + (\text{MPC})^2 + (\text{MPC})^3 + \ldots$$

This progression uses the MPC as its common ratio. Applying the same formula for summing a geometric progression to this more general case gives us the following general result:

Oversimplified Multiplier Formula

$\text{Multiplier} = \dfrac{1}{1 - \text{MPC}}$

We call this formula "oversimplified" because it ignores many factors that are important in the real world. You can begin to appreciate just how unrealistic the oversimplified formula is by considering some real numbers for the Canadian economy. The current MPC is probably about 0.95. From our oversimplified formula, then, it would seem that the multiplier should be:

$$\text{Multiplier} = \frac{1}{1 - 0.95} = \frac{1}{0.05} = 20$$

In fact, the actual multiplier for the Canadian economy is less than 2. That is quite a discrepancy!

This disagreement does not mean that anything we have said about the multiplier so far is incorrect. Our story is simply incomplete. As we progress through this and subsequent chapters, you will learn why the multiplier in Canada is less than 2 even though the country's MPC is close to 0.95. One such reason relates to *international trade*—in particular, the fact that a country's imports depend on its GDP. We deal

---

[6] If R exceeds 1, no one can possibly sum it—not even with the aid of a modern computer—because the sum is not a finite number.

[7] The proof of the formula is simple. Let the symbol S stand for the (unknown) sum of the series:

$S = 1 + R + R^2 + R^3 + \ldots$

Then, multiplying by R,

$RS = R + R^2 + R^3 + R^4 + \ldots$

By subtracting RS from S, we obtain:

$S - RS = 1$ or $S = \dfrac{1}{1 - R}$

with this complication in Appendix D to this chapter. A second factor is *inflation*, a complication we will address in the next chapter. The final factor is *income taxation*, a point we will elaborate in Chapter 11. As you will see, each of these factors *reduces* the size of the multiplier. So:

> Although the multiplier is larger than 1 in the real world, it cannot be calculated with any degree of accuracy from the oversimplified formula. The actual multiplier is much lower than the formula suggests.

■ THE MULTIPLIER IS A GENERAL CONCEPT

Although we have used business investment to illustrate the workings of the multiplier, it should be clear from the logic that *any* increase in spending can kick off a multiplier chain. To see how the multiplier works when the process is initiated by an upsurge in consumer spending, we must distinguish between two types of change in consumer spending.

To do so, look back at Figure 4 on page 197. When *C* rises because income rises— that is, when consumers move outward *along a fixed consumption function*—we call the increase in *C* an **induced increase in consumption**. (See the blue arrows in the figure.) When *C* rises because the entire consumption function *shifts upward* (such as from C_0 to C_2 in the figure), we call it an **autonomous increase in consumption**. The name indicates that consumption changes *independently* of income. The discussion of the consumption function in Chapter 8 pointed out that a number of events, such as a change in the value of the stock market, can initiate such a shift.

If consumer spending were to rise autonomously by $200 billion, we would revise our table of aggregate demand to look like Table 5. Comparing this new table to Table 3, we note that each entry in Column (2) is $200 billion *higher* than the corresponding entry in Table 3 (because consumption is higher), and each entry in Column (3) is $200 billion *lower* (because in this case investment is only $900 billion).

Column (6), the expenditure schedule, is identical in both tables, so the equilibrium level of income is clearly *Y* = $6,800 billion once again. The initial rise of $200 billion in consumer spending leads to an eventual rise of $800 billion in GDP, just as it did in the case of higher investment spending. In fact, Figure 10 (page 202) applies directly to this case once we note that the upward shift is now caused by an autonomous change in *C* rather than in *I*. The multiplier for autonomous changes in consumer spending, then, is also 4 (= $800/$200).

The reason is straightforward. It does not matter who injects an additional dollar of spending into the economy—business investors or consumers. Whatever the source of the extra dollar, 75 percent of it will be respent if the MPC is 0.75, and the recipients of this second round of spending will, in turn, spend 75 percent of their additional income, and so on. That continued spending constitutes the multiplier process. Thus a $200 billion increase in government purchases (*G*) or in net exports (*X − IM*) would have the same multiplier effect as depicted in Figure 10. The multipliers are identical because the logic behind them is identical.

The idea that changes in *G* have multiplier effects on GDP will play a central role in the discussion of government stabilization policy that begins in Part III. So it is worth noting here that:

> Changes in the volume of government purchases of goods and services will change the equilibrium level of GDP on the demand side in the same direction, but by a multiplied amount.

An **induced increase in consumption** is an increase in consumer spending that stems from an increase in consumer incomes. It is represented on a graph as a movement along a fixed consumption function.

An **autonomous increase in consumption** is an increase in consumer spending without any increase in consumer incomes. It is represented on a graph as a shift of the entire consumption function.

	TABLE 5				
	Total Expenditure after Consumers **Decide to Spend $200 Billion More**				
(1)	(2)	(3)	(4)	(5)	(6)
			Government	Net	
Income	Consumption	Investment	Purchases	Exports	Total
(*Y*)	(*C*)	(*I*)	(*G*)	(*X − IM*)	Expenditure
4,800	3,200	900	1,300	−100	5,300
5,200	3,500	900	1,300	−100	5,600
5,600	3,800	900	1,300	−100	5,900
6,000	4,100	900	1,300	−100	6,200
6,400	4,400	900	1,300	−100	6,500
6,800	**4,700**	**900**	**1,300**	**−100**	**6,800**
7,200	5,000	900	1,300	−100	7,100

Note: Figures are in billions of dollars per year.

To cite a recent example, the federal government has announced that it will spend billions of dollars on public infrastructures, such as roads and airports. The G component of $C + I + G + (X-IM)$ increases, which has a multiplier effect on GDP.

Applying the same multiplier idea to exports and imports teaches us another important lesson: Booms and recessions tend to be transmitted across national borders. Why is that? Suppose a boom abroad raises GDPs in foreign countries. With rising incomes, foreigners, mostly Americans, will buy more Canadian goods—which means that Canadian exports will increase. But an increase in our exports will, via the multiplier, raise GDP in Canada. By this mechanism, rapid economic growth abroad contributes to rapid economic growth here. And, of course, the same mechanism also operates in reverse. Thus:

> The GDPs of the major economies are linked by trade. A boom in one country tends to raise its imports and hence push up exports and GDP in other countries. Similarly, a recession in one country tends to pull down GDP in other countries.

THE PARADOX OF THRIFT

A Reduction in Autonomous Consumer Spending

So far, we have emphasized the effects that an increase in any of the four major components of aggregate expenditures has on the equilibrium level of GDP, through the action of the income multiplier. We have emphasized the effects of an increase in autonomous demand, in particular the increase in investment demand. But, naturally, all these effects operate in reverse if there is a *decrease* in any autonomous component of spending. A good way to check your understanding of the multiplier process is to run it precisely in reverse. What happens if, for example, consumers autonomously decide to spend $200 billion less than in the previous year? The answer is that, given that the multiplier is equal to 4, the equilibrium level of income should fall by $800 billion. And indeed, this is what we observe by comparing the data in Table 5 with that in Table 1, where all expenditures are identical except for a $200 billion decrease in autonomous consumption; the equilibrium level of GDP is $6,000 billion in Table 1, whereas it is $6,800 in Table 5—a decrease of $800 billion.

But this result is somewhat surprising. Households initially decided to *reduce* their consumption spending by $200 billion. Seen from the opposite angle, they decided to *increase* their saving by $200 billion. But at the end of the adjustment process, when income reaches its new equilibrium, GDP has gone down by $800 billion, which means, under the assumption that taxes are constant, that disposable income has also gone down by $800 billion. Because all of the tables in our examples are built on the assumption that the MPC is equal to 0.75, this implies that consumer expenditures must have fallen by $600 billion, while saving has *decreased* by $200 billion. Thus, in the end, saving is no larger than what it was before households decided to increase their saving. Households took the discretionary decision to increase their saving, but ultimately their saving has not increased! What is going on?

The Saving and Investment Approach

To understand what is going on, let us simplify our little model of income determination to the utmost. Suppose that there is no government (and hence no taxes in this Eden!) and no foreign trade, as was assumed in Figure 9 on page 200. Under those conditions, with $G = T = X = IM = 0$, the condition for equilibrium GDP that we outlined on page 193, is simplified to:

$$Y = C + I$$

Because there is no taxation, gross domestic income and disposable income are one and the same, so that gross domestic income is also the sum of consumption and saving.

Calling S the saving of our households, it follows that:

$$Y = C + S$$

and hence that:

$$C + S = C + I$$

or

$$S = I$$

It will always turn out that, once equilibrium output has been reached, investment and saving will be equal.[8]

Thus, as long as there is no change in the level of investment I decided by firms, the level of saving at the new equilibrium level of output can be no different than it was at the initial equilibrium of output. Thus, households can try to save until they are all blue in the face—this will not change the fact that, in the aggregate, the saving of the community *in equilibrium* can be no different than the given level of investment. Thus, if households attempt to consume less or save more on their current income than the given level of investment, spending will exceed output and income, so that the inventories of firms will be rising, inducing the firms to reduce production. This will happen until output, and hence income, is so much reduced that household saving is once more equal to the given level of investment. In this case, in a very strong sense, investment is *causing* the equilibrium level of saving.

■ A Reduction in the Marginal Propensity to Consume

So far we have simply made changes to the autonomous components of spending. In all of our experiments, we have assumed that the multiplier remained constant or, in other words, that the marginal propensity to consume, the MPC, remained the same. Since the MPC is the slope of the expenditure schedule in our income-multiplier diagram, this implied that the slope of our expenditure schedule—the $C + I + G + (X - IM)$ line in Figure 10, say—did not change when we changed a component of autonomous spending.

But let us now pursue a new kind of experiment. Let us suppose that some economists insist that the entire economy behaves no differently than the finances of an individual, and that they launch an immense thrift campaign on the basis that individuals become wealthier when they save than when they are spendthrifts. Let us suppose that this advertising campaign in favour of household saving—not much different from the one we observe every year in February, when financial institutions run last-minute advertisements to promote the purchase of RRSPs—is so successful that it reduces the marginal propensity to consume. Consumers now decide that they will spend a smaller fraction of each dollar they earn.

Table 6 illustrates what will happen. The table starts from an equilibrium position, at the top of the table, with output at \$6,000 billion, where the MPC is 0.75, and hence the **marginal propensity to save** is 0.25, since the marginal propensity to consume and the marginal propensity to save must sum to unity. As a result of the thrift campaign, the economy switches to a lower MPC, which we assume to be 5/8 or 0.625 (and hence households switch to a higher marginal propensity to save, MPS, at 0.375). The economy moves out of its equilibrium position into a disequilibrium position, caused by the thrift campaign, where output is still at \$6,000 billion but where spending is now only \$5,250 billion. Eventually, the new equilibrium, at \$4,000 billion, is reached.

The **marginal propensity to save** is the ratio of changes in saving relative to changes in disposable income that produce the change in saving.

---

[8] This is true in all cases, but when we assume away the government and the foreign sectors, as we do here, then investment and *household* saving have to be equal, as we claim. See Appendix B.

TABLE 6
The Effects of the Paradox of Thrift

	(1)	(2)	(3) = (1) − (2)	(4)	(5) = (2) + (4)	
	Income or GDP (Y)	Consumption (C)	Saving (S = Y − C)	Investment (I)	Total Spending (C + I)	Inventory Status
MPC = 0.75	6,000	5,000	1,000	1,000	6,000	No change
MPC = 0.625	6,000	4,250	1,750	1,000	5, 250	Rising
	5,250	3,781	1,469	1,000	4,781	Rising
	4,781	3,488	1,293	1,000	4,488	Rising
	4,488	3,300	1,188	1,000	4,300	Rising
	...	...	...	...	...	...
	4,000	3,000	1,000	1,000	4,000	No change

Note: Figures are in billions of dollars per year.

Table 6 is based on the assumption that autonomous consumption is $500 billion. With investment spending at $1,000 billion, this implies that overall autonomous expenditures are equal to $1,500 billion. With an MPC of 0.75 and income at $6,000 billion, induced consumption is $4,500 billion, so that overall consumption is indeed $5,000 billion. Total spending is thus $5,000 billion (consumption) plus $1,000 billion (investment), so that total spending is also $6,000 billion, as is income. Equilibrium income is simply the amount of autonomous expenditures times the multiplier (here, $1,500 billion times 4). With the new MPC of 5/8 = 0.625, you can compute that the multiplier ought to be 8/3 = 2.666, implying an equilibrium level of income equal to $4,000 billion. For those who enjoy more formal demonstrations, an algebraic derivation of this result in the general case can be found in Appendix C.

All of this can be illustrated with the help of Figure 12. With a lower MPC, the multiplier is now smaller, and the slope of the expenditure schedule is now flatter. The original expenditure schedule, with an MPC equal to 0.75, crosses the 45° line at the initial GDP equilibrium of $6,000 billion; the new schedule, with an MPC of 0.625, crosses the 45° line at $4,000 billion, which is the new output equilibrium. As producers adapt to the lower expenditures by reducing production, say by producing the amounts that correspond to the total expenditures of the previous round, income falls gradually, until it reaches its new equilibrium position at $4,000 billion.

Saving, which had initially risen to $1,750 billion at the peak of the thrift campaign, is now back to $1,000 billion in the new equilibrium—the value of investment spending, no more and no less. The thrift campaign has led to a recession. Real output and real income have fallen by $2,000 billion.

The equilibrium condition for output is shown in the bottom part of Figure 12. Since investment is taken to be a fixed number irrespective of income, the investment schedule is just a horizontal line. As for the saving schedule, it rises with the level of income. Its slope is given by the marginal propensity to save. Point E_0 is the initial equilibrium, at the old MPC of 0.75. Point E_1 represents the new equilibrium level of GDP, with the new MPC of 0.625, where the investment horizontal line and the new saving schedule intersect, and hence where the amount of investment is exactly equal to the amount of saving. Notice that, with this new lower MPC, at all income levels above $4,000 billion, saving exceeds investment.

The fact that the efforts of all individuals to increase overall saving proves to be unsuccessful, leading only to a fall in GDP and a lower level of equilibrium income, is called the **paradox of thrift**. It is one of the great achievements of Keynes to have uncovered and explained this macroeconomic paradox. As we pointed out in Chapter 1, economists and noneconomists alike are subjected to the possibility of fallacies of composition. To believe that what is true for an individual is necessarily true for society as a whole is a fallacy of composition.

The **paradox of thrift** is the surprising fact that individual efforts to save more will ultimately be unsuccessful at the aggregate level, leading instead to lower equilibrium income and output levels and failing to raise aggregate saving.

The paradox of thrift uncovers one of the most famous fallacies of composition—the belief that higher household saving leads to greater community wealth. Rather, it is higher levels of investment that will induce greater community saving and hence lead to the accumulation of greater wealth for the entire community.

Thus, we see that any attempt to reduce consumption, either through a reduction in autonomous consumption demand or through a reduction in the propensity to consume, will lead to a reduction in the equilibrium level of income. Some economists are worried about the low saving rates of Canadian and American households in the 2000s. However, these low saving rates have sustained the growth of demand in the Canadian and the American economies recently, thus helping business firms to operate at high rates of capacity utilization and to make record profits.

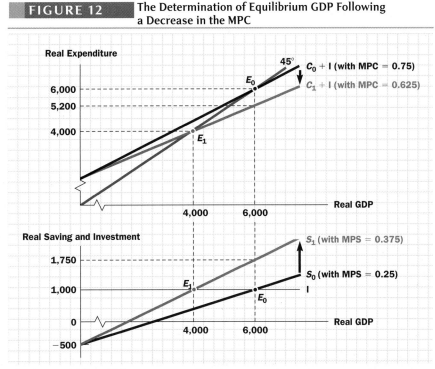

FIGURE 12   The Determination of Equilibrium GDP Following a Decrease in the MPC

NOTE: Figures are in billions of dollars per year.

The Paradox of Thrift and the Banana Parable

The discovery of the paradox of thrift is a great accomplishment. As we pointed out earlier, on page 200, it is tied to a coordination failure. If the thrift campaign could be accompanied by a simultaneous increase in investment expenditures, none of this would happen. But why would investment increase? In Chapter 8 on page 179, we argued that investment would increase if business confidence solidified. But if sales are falling and stocks of inventories are rising, unplanned, this will in no way convince entrepreneurs to increase the pace of investment in fixed capital and capacity.

Some students may however see a flaw in our presentation of the paradox of thrift. All along, we have assumed that prices were constant or that they did not play any role. What if prices fell as real sales declined? Would this make any difference to the paradox of thrift? The issue is whether we take into account the debt effect—the fact that wealth is often the counterpart of the debt of someone else. Keynes first conceived the paradox of thrift in the context of an economy where prices were free to decrease. Based on the banana parable provided by Keynes in 1930, the following is how Robert Skidelsky (1939–)—Keynes' famous biographer—imagined Keynes might summarize his views to an audience with limited economic understanding. Basically, Keynes's banana parable calls for the saving of all households to be accumulated as deposits in bank accounts, with all of these deposits to be lent out to the firms to make up their losses.

Well, let me give you a parable which I have found helpful, with some people who have not had the benefits of attending my lectures at Cambridge, in getting my theory down to its simplest terms. Imagine a community, initially in a state of equilibrium, which produces only bananas. A thrift campaign is started, as a result of which people start saving more and consuming less, the rate of investment in plantations staying the same. The price of

bananas then falls by the amount of the increased saving. Virtue is rewarded: people get the same amount of bananas as before for less money, and they have "saved" as well. But the producers of bananas have now made an unexpected loss, since they have been forced to sell their bananas at below cost price. They cannot, of course, "hoard" them, because they will rot. The increased saving has not increased the aggregate wealth of the community at all: it has simply transferred part of it from producers to the consumers of bananas. So nothing has happened to reduce their excess saving. . . .

In the next phase, the loss-making businessmen try to protect themselves by reducing their wage bills, which means in practice, throwing workers out of jobs. But this will not help, since the income of the community will be reduced by just as much as the aggregate costs of production. Thus the entrepreneurs continue to make losses as long as the community continues to save more than it invests and the output of bananas continues to decline until either all production stops and the population starves to death, or the thrift campaign is called off or peters out as a result of growing poverty. . . .

The fact that you do not spend . . . means that some businessman has to accept a lower price for what he sells you and is, therefore, poorer by the exact amount that you are richer. And very likely, without knowing it, you as a shareholder in a banana plantation are that much poorer as well. Why on earth, with producers of consumption goods making a loss, should anyone think it worthwhile investing in new facilities for making these goods?

SOURCE: Excerpted from Robert Skidelsky, *John Maynard Keynes, Volume Two: The Economist as Saviour, 1920–1937* (London: Macmillan, 1986), pp. 323–325.

■ THE MULTIPLIER AND THE AGGREGATE DEMAND CURVE

One last mechanical point about the multiplier: Recall that income–expenditure diagrams such as Figure 3 (page 196) can be drawn only for a given price level. Different price levels lead to different total expenditure curves. This means that our oversimplified multiplier formula indicates *the increase in real GDP demanded that would occur if the price level were fixed.* Graphically, this means that it measures the *horizontal shift* of the economy's aggregate demand curve.

Figure 13 illustrates this conclusion by supposing that the price level that underlies Figure 3 is $P = 100$. The top panel simply repeats Figure 10 (page 202) and shows how an increase in investment spending from $900 to $1,100 billion leads to an increase in GDP from $6,000 to $6,800 billion.

The bottom panel shows two downward-sloping aggregate demand curves. The first, labelled $D_0 D_0$, depicts the situation when investment is $900 billion. Point E_0 on this curve indicates that, at the given price level ($P = 100$), the equilibrium quantity of GDP demanded is $6,000 billion. It corresponds exactly to point E_0 in the top panel. The second aggregate demand curve, $D_1 D_1$, depicts the situation after investment has risen to $1,100 billion. Point E_1 on this curve indicates that the equilibrium quantity of GDP demanded when $P = 100$ has risen to $6,800 billion, which corresponds exactly to point E_1 in the top panel.

As Figure 13 shows, the horizontal distance between the two aggregate demand curves is exactly equal to the increase in real GDP shown in the income–expenditure diagram—in this case, $800 billion. Thus:

An autonomous increase in spending leads to a horizontal shift of the aggregate demand curve by an amount given by the oversimplified multiplier formula.

So everything we have just learned about the multiplier applies to *shifts of the economy's aggregate demand curve.* If businesses decide to increase their investment spending, if the consumption function shifts upward, or if the government or foreigners decide to buy more goods, then the aggregate demand curve moves horizontally to the right—as indicated in Figure 13. If any of these variables move downward instead, the aggregate demand curve moves horizontally to the left.

Thus, the economy's aggregate demand curve cannot be expected to stand still for long. Autonomous changes in one or another of the four components of total spending will cause it to move around. But to understand the *consequences* of such shifts of aggregate demand, we must bring the *aggregate supply* curve back into the picture. That is the task for the next chapter.

FIGURE 13

Two Views of the Multiplier

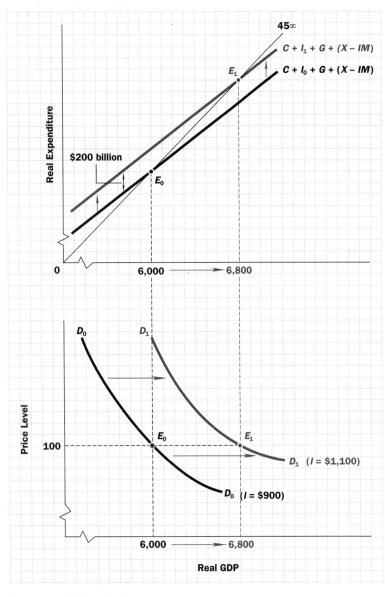

Note: Figures are in billions of dollars per year.

SUMMARY

1. The *equilibrium level of GDP on the demand side* is the level at which total spending just equals production. Because total spending is the sum of consumption, investment, government purchases, and net exports, the condition for equilibrium is $Y = C + I + G + (X - IM)$.

2. Income levels below **equilibrium** are bound to rise because, when spending exceeds output, firms will see their inventory stocks being depleted and will react by stepping up production.

3. Income levels above equilibrium are bound to fall because, when total spending is insufficient to absorb total output, inventories will pile up and firms will react by curtailing production.

4. The determination of the equilibrium level of GDP on the demand side can be portrayed on a convenient **income–expenditure diagram** as the point at which the **expenditure schedule**—defined as the sum of $C + I + G + (X - IM)$—crosses the 45° line. The 45° line is significant because it marks off points at which spending and output are equal—that is, at which $Y = C + I + G + (X - IM)$, which is the basic condition for equilibrium.

5. An income–expenditure diagram can be drawn only for a specific price level. Thus, the equilibrium GDP so determined depends on the price level.

6. Higher prices reduce the real debt of consumers, but they also reduce their real wealth. Economists presume that this second effect is stronger, and hence that higher prices reduce the purchasing power of consumers. Higher prices thus reduce total expenditures on the 45° line diagram. Equilibrium real GDP demanded is therefore lower when prices are higher. This downward-sloping relationship is known as the **aggregate demand curve**.

7. Equilibrium GDP can be above or below **potential GDP**, which is defined as the GDP that would be produced if the labour force were fully employed.

8. If equilibrium GDP exceeds potential GDP, the difference is called an **inflationary gap**. If equilibrium GDP falls short of potential GDP, the resulting difference is called a **recessionary gap**.

9. Such gaps can occur because of the problem of **coordination failure**: the saving that consumers want to do at full-employment income levels may differ from the investing that investors want to do.

10. Any **autonomous increase in consumption** has a multiplier effect on GDP; that is, it increases GDP by more than the original increase in spending.

11. The **multiplier** effect occurs because one person's additional expenditure constitutes a new source of income for another person, and this additional income leads to still more spending, and so on.

12. The multiplier is the same for an autonomous increase in consumption, investment, government purchases, or net exports.

13. A simple formula for the multiplier says that its numerical value is $1/(1 - MPC)$. This formula is too simple to give accurate results, however.

14. Rapid (or sluggish) economic growth in one country contributes to rapid (or sluggish) growth in other countries because one country's imports are other countries' exports.

15. A cut in autonomous consumer expenditures leads to a reduction in the equilibrium level of income. But then, this means that an increase in household saving eventually leads to a fall in income and disposable income, bringing back household saving to the level it had reached before the attempt to boost it—a paradoxical result.

16. A reduction in the marginal propensity to consume, and hence an increase in the **marginal propensity to save**, as a result of a thrift campaign, leads to a fall in the equilibrium level of income. In the simplified case with no government and foreign sectors, despite the efforts of all individuals to boost their saving, aggregate household saving at the new (lower) income equilibrium will be no different from what it was before the thrift campaign, at the level set by investment spending. This is the **paradox of thrift**.

KEY TERMS

TEST YOURSELF

1. From the following data, construct an expenditure schedule on a piece of graph paper. Then use the income–expenditure (45° line) diagram to determine the equilibrium level of GDP.

Income	Consumption	Investment	Government Purchases	Net Exports
$3,600	$3,220	$240	$120	$40
3,700	3,310	240	120	40
3,800	3,400	240	120	40
3,900	3,490	240	120	40
4,000	3,580	240	120	40

Now suppose investment spending rises to $260, and the price level is fixed. By how much will equilibrium GDP increase? Derive the answer both numerically and graphically.

2. From the following data, construct an expenditure schedule on a piece of graph paper. Then use the income–expenditure (45° line) diagram to determine the equilibrium level of GDP. Compare your answer with your answer to the previous question.

Income	Consumption	Investment	Government Purchases	Net Exports
$3,600	$3,280	$180	$120	$40
3,700	3,340	210	120	40
3,800	3,400	240	120	40
3,900	3,460	270	120	40
4,000	3,520	300	120	40

3. Suppose that investment spending is always $250, government purchases are $100, net exports are always $50, and consumer spending depends on the price level in the following way:

Price Level	Consumer Spending
$ 90	$740
95	720
100	700
105	680
110	660

On a piece of graph paper, use these data to construct an aggregate demand curve. Why do you think this example supposes that consumption declines as the price level rises?

4. **(More difficult)**[9] Consider an economy in which the consumption function takes the following simple algebraic form:

$$C = 300 + 0.75DI$$

and in which investment (I) is always $900 and net exports are always −$100. Government purchases are fixed at $1,300 and taxes are fixed at $1,200. Find the equilibrium level of GDP, and then compare your answer to Table 1 and Figure 2. (*Hint:* Remember that disposable income is GDP minus taxes: $DI = Y − T = Y − 1,200$.)

5. **(More difficult)** Keep everything the same as in Test Yourself Question 4 *except* change investment to $I = $1,100. Use the equilibrium condition $Y = C + I + G + (X − IM)$ to find the equilibrium level of GDP on the demand side. (In working out the answer, assume the price level is fixed.) Compare your answer to Table 3 and Figure 10. Now compare your answer to the answer to Test Yourself Question 4. What do you learn about the multiplier?

6. **(More difficult)** An economy has the following consumption function:

$$C = 200 + 0.8DI$$

The government budget is balanced, with government purchases and taxes both fixed at $1,000. Net exports are $100. Investment is $600. Find equilibrium GDP.
  What is the multiplier for this economy? If G rises by $100, what happens to Y? What happens to Y if both G and T rise by $100 at the same time?

7. Use both numerical and graphical methods to find the multiplier effect of the following shift in the consumption function in an economy in which investment is always $220, government purchases are always $100, and net exports are always −$40. (*Hint:* What is the marginal propensity to consume?)

Income	Consumption before Shift	Consumption after Shift
$1,080	$ 880	$ 920
1,140	920	960
1,200	960	1,000
1,260	1,000	1,040
1,320	1,040	1,080
1,380	1,080	1,120
1,440	1,120	1,160
1,500	1,160	1,200
1,560	1,200	1,240

8. Higher prices reduce the purchasing power of consumers by reducing their real wealth, but higher prices increase the purchasing power of consumers by also reducing their net debt, when all of these are money-fixed assets or money-fixed liabilities. Make a sketch of what the aggregate demand curve would look like if the debt effects were larger than the wealth effects. (Check your result by referring to Figure 6 in Chapter 10.)

---

[9] The answer to this question is provided in Appendix C to this chapter.

DISCUSSION QUESTIONS

1. For over 20 years now, imports have consistently exceeded exports in the U.S. economy. Many people consider this imbalance to be a major problem. Does this chapter give you any hints about why? (You may want to discuss this issue with your instructor. You will learn more about it in later chapters.)

2. Look back at the income–expenditure diagram in Figure 3 (page 196) and explain why some level of real GDP other than $6,000 (say, $5,000 or $7,000) is *not* an equilibrium on the demand side of the economy. Do not give a mechanical answer to this question. Explain the economic mechanism involved.

3. Does the economy this year seem to have an inflationary gap or a recessionary gap? (If you do not know the answer from reading the newspaper, ask your instructor.)

4. Try to remember where you last spent a dollar. Explain how this dollar will lead to a multiplier chain of increased income and spending. (Who received the dollar? What will he or she do with it?)

APPENDIX A *National Accounting and Inventories*

The discussion surrounding the determination of equilibrium output has underlined the important role played by changes in inventories. In particular, in Table 2, we saw that inventories (a stock) fall when spending exceeds output, and that inventories rise when output exceeds spending.

However, in the appendix to Chapter 8, we also emphasized the fact that, from a national accounting point of view, gross domestic output is *always* the same, however it is measured, from a value-added point of view, or from the expenditure side, or from the income side (it is an identity). So how can spending exceed output, while at the same time, domestic output is equal to domestic expenditures? For those brought up in the Christian faith, this looks a bit like the mystery of the Holy Trinity, where three are only one.

In this case, the mystery is resolved by noting that national accountants use a definition of investment, and hence of total expenditures, that is just slightly different from the one that we use in macroeconomics.

In the model in this chapter, investment expenditures include only *fixed business investment*, that is, investment in fixed capital. This is what we call I in our model of output equilibrium. By contrast, national accountants include in investment expenditures both *fixed business investment* and *business investment in inventories*, the sum of which we call I_{na}.

Business investment in inventories represents the value of the change in business inventories. It represents the difference between the volume of goods that have been produced and the volume of goods that have been sold (times the current production cost of each good). Thus, if output exceeds spending, the unsold goods will be added to the stock of inventories, so these unsold goods will constitute an investment in inventories (a flow). Similarly, if spending exceeds output, inventory stocks will diminish, thus implying a negative investment in inventories. Any discrepancy between output and spending, from the macroeconomic point of view, will lead to the creation of an investment in inventories (either positive or negative), which will equate domestic production with domestic expenditures, as verified by the national accounts. Investment in inventories thus constitutes the entry that adjusts domestic expenditures to domestic output.

This adjustment is shown in Table 7, starting with out-of-equilibrium values taken from Table 1. For instance, suppose (as in the second column) that fixed capital investment was $900 billion, and that spending ($5,100 billion) exceeds output ($4,800). This means that firms will have to deplete their inventories to respond to demand, up to a value of $300 billion. Thus, there is a disinvestment in inventories, or a negative investment in inventories, of $300 billion. From the point of view of the national accounts, business investment, which is the sum of fixed

TABLE 7
Investment in Inventories a Means to Make National Accounts Sing in Tune

	Spending Exceeds Output	Output Exceeds Spending
GDP	$4,800	$7,200
Fixed business investment (I)	900	900
Spending: $C + I + G + (X - IM)$	5,100	6,900
+ Investment in inventories	−300	+300
= GDP, expenditure-based	4,800	7,200
Investment, national accounts (I_{na})	600 (= 900 − 300)	1,200 (= 900 + 300)

Note: Figures are in billions of dollars per year; values taken from Table 1.

investment and investment in inventories, is now equal to only $600 billion. But this will make gross national product, expenditure-based, exactly equal to the value added of what has been produced during the year.

Changes in inventories also allow us to explain how saving and investment are always equal to each other (it is another identity) from the point of view of the national accounts, while the equality of investment and saving is an equilibrium condition in macroeconomics.

This can easily be seen in the case of our most simplified model, with no government and no international trade. In this case, saving as defined in the national accounts is identical to household saving. If saving is any different from fixed capital investment, as defined in macroeconomics, investment in inventories will make up the difference. As a result, saving and investment, as defined by the national accounts (that is, including both fixed capital investment and investment in inventories), are always equal. Table 8, based on the figures of Table 6, makes this point.

In its initial stages, the thrift campaign described on page 206 looks highly successful. As the third row of

TABLE 8

Investment in Inventories as a Means of Equalizing Saving and Investment in the National Accounts

(1)	(2)	(3) = (1) − (2)	(4)	(5) = (2) + (4)	(6) = (1) − (5)	(7) = (4) + (6)
Income or GDP (Y)	Consumption (C)	Saving (S = Y − C)	Investment in Fixed Capital (I)	Total Spending	Investment in Inventories	Investment, National Accounts (I$_{na}$)
$6,000	$5,000	$1,000	$1,000	$6,000	$0	$1,000
6,000	4,250	1,750	1,000	5, 250	750	1,750
5,250	3,781	1,469	1,000	4,781	469	1,469
4,781	3,488	1,293	1,000	4,488	293	1,293
4,488	3,300	1,188	1,000	4,300	188	1,188
…	…	…	…	…	…	…
4,000	3,000	1,000	1,000	4,000	0	1,000

Note: Figures are in billions of dollars per year; values taken from Table 6.

Table 8 shows, saving, which stood at only $1,000 billion before the change in MPC, moved up to $1,750 billion. From the national accounting viewpoint, investment also moved up to $1,750 billion, but $750 billion came from increases in inventories, that is, from $750 billion worth of goods that have been produced but not sold. Eventually, through changes in the level of output, overall saving diminished gradually, until it became equal to the given level of fixed capital investment by firms, $1,000 billion, as shown in the last row.

SUMMARY

1. In the model in this chapter, investment expenditures include only *fixed business investment*, that is, investment in fixed capital. This is what we call *I* in our model of output equilibrium. By contrast, national accountants include in investment expenditures both *fixed business investment* and *business investment in inventories*.

2. A discrepancy between total spending and GDP is made up for by changes in inventories, so that, in the national accounts, total expenditures are exactly equal to GDP since total expenditures include total spending as defined by macroeconomists plus business investment in inventories.

3. A discrepancy between saving and investment spending in macroeconomics is made up for in the national accounts by the adjustment provided by business investment in inventories. However, as the economy moves gradually to its new equilibrium position, it is saving that adjusts to the level of investment spending, as a result of the changing level of income.

DISCUSSION QUESTION

Explain how an increase in the marginal propensity to consume could lead to the appearance of a *negative* entry for investment in business inventories in the national accounts.

APPENDIX B *The General Saving and Investment Identity*

In the general case with government and foreign sectors, investment must still be equal to saving, but saving will now need to be defined as something more than household saving.

We begin by recalling a few equations. First, we pointed out on page 171 of Chapter 8 that disposable income (*DI*) is equal to GDP minus taxes net of transfers:

$$DI = Y - T$$

In an open economy, where residents may receive investment income from abroad, this is not quite exact, however. Disposable income will really depend on gross national income (GNP), which, as we pointed out in the appendix to Chapter 8, on page 188, includes both gross domestic income (GDP) and net foreign income (*NFY*), so that:

$$DI = (Y + NFY) - T$$

Disposable income can either be spent or saved. Hence:

$$DI = C + S$$

These two definitions jointly imply that:

$$Y + NFY = C + S + T$$

Combining this with our standard condition defining equilibrium GDP:

$$Y = C + I + G + (X - IM)$$

we obtain:

$$C + I + G + (X - IM) + NFY = C + S + T$$

Subtracting *C* from both sides, and keeping only *I* on the left-hand side, we get:

$$I = S + (T - G) + (IM - X - NFY)$$

The sum of the three terms on the right-hand side is overall saving in the general case. The sum must be equal to investment. The three components of overall saving are private saving (*S*), government saving (*T − G*), and saving from abroad (*IM − X − NFY*). The sum of the first two terms is often called *national saving*. The last term, also called *nonresident saving*, is the current account deficit of the balance of payments, as we will find out in Chapter 18. Naturally, with no government and foreign trade, we are back to the simpler equality, *I = S*. This simpler equality is also verified in the special case where both the government budget (*G = T*) and the current account (*X + NFY = IM*) are balanced. The more complex equality will be discussed again in Chapter 18 and more explanation will be provided there in the course of our discussion of trade balance and international capital flows.

SUMMARY

1. In an open economy with a government sector, investment must still be equal to saving. But saving will now be made up of three components: private saving, government saving, and nonresident saving.

2. The sum of private and government saving is called *national saving*.

APPENDIX C *The Simple Algebra of Income Determination and the Multiplier*

The model of demand-side equilibrium that the chapter presented graphically and in tabular form can also be handled with some simple algebra. Written as an equation, the consumption function in our example is

$$C = 300 + 0.75DI$$

$$= 300 + 0.75(Y - T)$$

because, by definition, $DI = Y - T$. This is simply the equation of a straight line with a slope of 0.75 and an intercept of $300 - 0.75T$. Because $T = 1,200$ in our example, the intercept is -600 and the equation can be written more simply as follows:

$$C = -600 + 0.75Y$$

Investment in the example was assumed to be 900, regardless of the level of income, government purchases were 1,300, and net exports were -100. So the sum $C + I + G + (X - IM)$ is

$$C + I + G + (X - IM) = -600 + 0.75Y + 900 + 1,300 - 100$$

$$= 1,500 + 0.75Y$$

This equation describes the expenditure curve in Figure 3. Because the equilibrium quantity of GDP demanded is defined by

$$Y = C + I + G + (X - IM)$$

we can solve for the equilibrium value of Y by substituting $1,500 + 0.75Y$ for $C + I + G + (X - IM)$ to get:

$$Y = 1,500 + 0.75Y$$

To solve this equation for Y, first subtract $0.75Y$ from both sides to get:

$$0.25Y = 1,500$$

Then divide both sides by 0.25 to obtain the answer:

$$Y = 6,000$$

This, of course, is precisely the solution we found by graphical and tabular methods in the chapter.

We can easily generalize this algebraic approach to deal with any set of numbers in our equations. Suppose that the consumption function is as follows:

$$C = a + bDI = a + b(Y - T)$$

(In the example, $a = 300$, $T = 1,200$, and $b = 0.75$.) Then the equilibrium condition that $Y = C + I + G + (X - IM)$ implies that:

$$Y = a + bDI + I + G + (X - IM)$$

$$= a - bT + bY + I + G + (X - IM)$$

Subtracting bY from both sides leads to:

$$(1 - b)Y = a - bT + I + G + (X - IM)$$

and dividing through by $1 - b$ gives:

$$Y = \frac{a - bT + I + G + (X - IM)}{1 - b}$$

This formula is valid for any numerical values of a, b, T, G, I, and $(X - IM)$ (so long as b is between zero and 1).

From this formula, it is easy to derive the oversimplified multiplier formula algebraically and to show that it applies equally well to a change in investment, autonomous consumer spending, government purchases, or net exports. To do so, suppose that *any* of these autonomous components of spending, found in the numerator of the multiplier formula, increases by one unit. Then GDP would rise from the previous formula to:

$$Y = \frac{a - bT + I + G + (X - IM) + 1}{1 - b}$$

By comparing this expression with the previous expression for Y, we see that a one-unit change in any component of spending changes equilibrium GDP by

$$\text{Change in } Y = \frac{a - bT + I + G + (X - IM) + 1}{1 - b}$$
$$- \frac{a - bT + I + G + (X - IM)}{1 - b}$$

or

$$\text{Change in } Y = \frac{1}{1 - b}$$

Recalling that b is the marginal propensity to consume, we see that this is precisely the oversimplified multiplier formula.

TEST YOURSELF

1. Find the equilibrium level of GDP demanded in an economy in which investment is always $300, net exports are always −$50, the government budget is balanced with purchases and taxes both equal to $400, and the consumption function is described by the following algebraic equation:

$$C = 150 + 0.75DI$$

(*Hint:* Do not forget that $DI = Y - T$.)

2. Referring to Test Yourself Question 1, do the same for an economy in which investment is $250, net exports are zero, government purchases and taxes are both $400, and the consumption function is as follows:

$$C = 250 + 0.5DI$$

3. In each of these cases, how much saving is there in equilibrium? (*Hint:* Disposable income not consumed must be saved by households.) Is household saving equal to investment?

4. Imagine an economy in which consumer expenditure is represented by the following equation:

$$C = 50 + 0.75DI$$

Imagine also that investors want to spend $500 at every level of income ($I = 500), net exports are zero ($X - IM = 0$), government purchases are $300, and taxes are $200.

a. What is the equilibrium level of GDP?

b. If potential GDP is $3,000, is there a recessionary or inflationary gap? If so, how much?

c. What will happen to the equilibrium level of GDP if investors become optimistic about the country's future and raise their investment to $600?

d. After investment has increased to $600, is there a recessionary or inflationary gap? How much?

5. Fredonia has the following consumption function:

$$C = 100 + 0.8DI$$

Firms in Fredonia always invest $700 and net exports are zero, initially. The government budget is balanced with spending and taxes both equal to $500.

a. Find the equilibrium level of GDP.

b. How much is saved? Is saving equal to investment?

c. Now suppose that an export-promotion drive succeeds

in raising net exports to $100. Answer (a) and (b) under these new circumstances.

6. **(More difficult)**[10] So far we have assumed that taxes T were an autonomous component of the consumption function. This would be the case if taxes were all head taxes. This is a useful simplifying assumption, but is not very realistic. What if taxes were an induced component, where taxes were proportional to income, as are income taxes. So far, and in all the tables in the chapter, we assumed that the consumption function was of the form $C = a + b(Y - T)$. Assume now that taxes are induced and equal to $T = tY$, where t is the tax rate. Show that, in this case, the multiplier would be smaller than when taxes were an autonomous element.

DISCUSSION QUESTIONS

1. Explain the basic logic behind the multiplier in words. Why does it require b, the marginal propensity to consume, to be between zero and one?

2. **(More difficult)** What would happen to the multiplier analysis if $b = 0$? If $b = 1$?

APPENDIX D *The Multiplier with Variable Imports*

In the chapter, we assumed that net exports were a fixed number, -100 in the example. In fact, a nation's imports vary along with its GDP for a simple reason: Higher GDP leads to higher incomes, some of which is spent on foreign goods. Thus:

Our imports rise as our GDP rises and fall as our GDP falls.

Similarly, our *exports* are the *imports* of other countries, so it is to be expected that our exports depend on *their* GDPs, not on our own. Thus:

Our exports are relatively insensitive to our own GDP, but are quite sensitive to the GDPs of other countries.

This appendix derives the implications of these rather elementary observations. In particular, it shows that once we recognize the dependence of a nation's imports on its GDP:

International trade lowers the value of the multiplier.

To see why, we begin with Table 9, which adapts the example of our hypothetical economy to allow imports to depend on GDP. Columns (2) through (4) are the same as in Table 1; they show C, I, and G at alternative levels of GDP. Columns (5) and (6) record revised assumptions about the behaviour of exports and imports. Exports are fixed at $650 billion regardless of GDP. But imports are assumed to rise by $60 billion for every $400 billion rise in GDP, which is a simple numerical example of the idea that imports depend on GDP. Column (7) subtracts imports from exports to get net exports, $(X - IM)$, and Column (8) adds up the four components of total expenditure, $C + I + G + (X - IM)$. The equilibrium, you can see, occurs at $Y = $6,000$ billion, just as it did in the chapter.

Figures 14 and 15 display the same conclusion graphically. The upper panel of Figure 14 shows that exports are fixed at $650 billion regardless of GDP, whereas imports increase as GDP rises, just as in Table 9. The difference between exports and imports, or net exports,

TABLE 9							
Equilibrium Income with Variable Imports							
(1) Gross Domestic Product (Y)	(2) Consumer Expenditures (C)	(3) Investment (I)	(4) Government Purchases (G)	(5) Exports (X)	(6) Imports (IM)	(7) Net Exports (X − IM)	(8) Total Expenditure [C + I + G + (X − IM)]
4,800	3,000	900	1,300	650	570	+80	5,280
5,200	3,300	900	1,300	650	630	+20	5,520
5,600	3,600	900	1,300	650	690	−40	5,760
6,000	**3,900**	**900**	**1,300**	**650**	**750**	**−100**	**6,000**
6,400	4,200	900	1,300	650	810	−160	6,240
6,800	4,500	900	1,300	650	870	−220	6,480
7,200	4,800	900	1,300	650	930	−280	6,720

Note: Figures are in billions of dollars per year.

---

[10] The answer to this question can be found in Appendix B to Chapter 11.

FIGURE 14   The Dependence of Net Exports on GDP

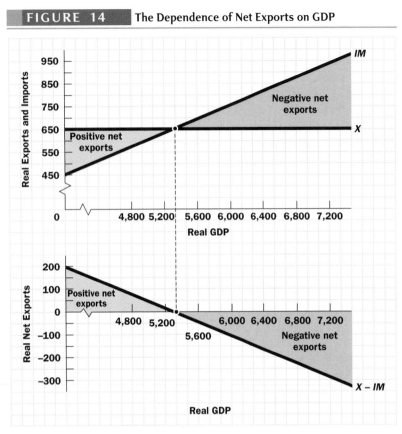

Note: Figures are in billions of dollars per year.

line in black. Previously, we simply assumed that net exports were fixed at −$100 billion regardless of GDP. Now that we have amended our model to note that net exports decline as GDP rises, the sum $C + I + G + (X − IM)$ rises more slowly than we previously assumed. This change is shown by the blue line. Note that it is less steep than the black line.

Let us now consider what happens if exports rise by $160 billion while imports remain as in Table 9. Table 10 shows that equilibrium now occurs at a GDP of $Y = $6,400$ billion. Naturally, higher exports have raised domestic GDP. But consider the magnitude. A $160 billion increase in exports (from $650 billion to $810 billion) leads to an increase of $400 billion in GDP (from $6,000 billion to $6,400 billion). So the multiplier is 2.5 (= $400/$160).[11]

This same conclusion is shown graphically in Figure 16, where the line $C + I + G + (X_0 − IM)$ represents the original expenditure schedule and the line $C + I + G + (X_1 − IM)$ represents the expenditure schedule after the $160 billion increase in exports. Equilibrium shifts from point E to point A, and GDP rises by $400 billion.

Notice that the multiplier in this example is 2.5, whereas in the chapter, with net exports taken to be a fixed number, it was 4. This simple example illustrates a general result: *International trade lowers the numerical value of the multiplier.* Why is this so? Because, in an open economy, any autonomous increase in spending is partly dissipated in purchases of foreign goods, which creates additional income for *foreigners* rather than for domestic citizens.

Thus, international trade gives us the first of what will eventually be several reasons why the oversimplified multiplier formula overstates the true value of the multiplier.

If we want to express this more formally, we can go back to the equations in Appendix B, now assuming that imports IM depend on GDP, that is, assuming that imports are an *induced* element of aggregate demand instead of an *autonomous* component, so that:

$$IM = mY$$

The parameter m may be described as the *propensity to import.* Aggregate demand and the equilibrium condition can now be rewritten as:

$$Y = A − bT + bY + I + G + X − mY$$

is positive until GDP approaches $5,300 billion and negative once GDP surpasses that amount. The bottom panel of Figure 14 shows the subtraction explicitly by displaying *net exports*. It shows clearly that:

Net exports decline as GDP rises.

Figure 15 carries this analysis over to the 45° line diagram. We begin with the familiar $C + I + G + (X − IM)$

FIGURE 15   Equilibrium GDP with Variable Imports

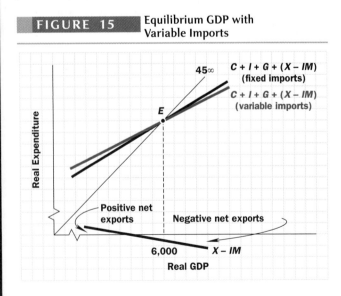

---

[11] *Exercise:* Construct a version of Table 9 to show what would happen if imports rose by $160 billion at every level of GDP while exports remained at $650 billion. You should be able to show that the new equilibrium would be $Y = $5,600$.

TABLE 10

Equilibrium Income after a $160 Billion Increase in Exports

(1) Gross Domestic Product (Y)	(2) Consumer Expenditures (C)	(3) Investment (I)	(4) Government Purchases (G)	(5) Exports (X)	(6) Imports (IM)	(7) Net Exports (X − IM)	(8) Total Expenditure [C + I + G + (X − IM)]
4,800	3,000	900	1,300	810	570	+240	5,440
5,200	3,300	900	1,300	810	630	+180	5,680
5,600	3,600	900	1,300	810	690	+120	5,920
6,000	3,900	900	1,300	810	750	+60	6,160
6,400	4,200	900	1,300	810	810	0	6,400
6,800	4,500	900	1,300	810	870	−60	6,640
7,200	4,800	900	1,300	810	930	−120	6,800

Note: Figures are in billions of dollars per year.

FIGURE 16 | The Multiplier with Variable Imports

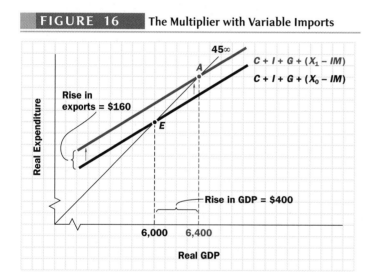

Moving all of the terms containing Y to the left-hand side, we obtain:

$$(1 - b + m)Y = A - bT + I + G + X$$

Dividing through by $(1 - b + m)$, we get the new formula that determines the equilibrium level of income:

$$Y = \frac{A - bT + I + G + X}{1 - b + m}$$

The multiplier, with induced imports, is now $\frac{1}{1 - b + m}$ instead of $\frac{1}{1 - b}$. If, for instance, $b = 0.9$ while $m = 0.3$, the multiplier will fall to a value of 2.5, instead of a value of 10 when there are no induced imports (the denominator goes from 0.1 to 0.4). If, as in the chapter, $b = 0.75$, the multiplier is equal to 4, and it will fall to 2.5 if we assume the existence of a propensity to import, $m = 0.15$. Obviously, economies that are widely open have smaller multipliers. Thus, autonomous expenditures will have a much smaller multiplier impact inside a small community that must import most of its products than in the country taken as a whole, which is a relatively less open entity.

SUMMARY

1. Because imports rise as GDP rises, while exports are insensitive to (domestic) GDP, net exports decline as GDP rises.

2. If imports depend on GDP, international trade reduces the value of the multiplier.

TEST YOURSELF

1. Suppose exports and imports of a country are given by the following:

GDP	Exports	Imports
$2,500	$400	$250
3,000	400	300
3,500	400	350
4,000	400	400
4,500	400	450
5,000	400	500

Calculate net exports at each level of GDP.

2. If domestic expenditure (the sum of $C + I + G$ in the economy described in Test Yourself Question 1) is as shown in the following table, construct a 45° line diagram and locate the equilibrium level of GDP.

GDP	Domestic Expenditures
$2,500	$3,100
3,000	3,400
3,500	3,700
4,000	4,000
4,500	4,300
5,000	4,600

3. Now raise exports to $650 and find the equilibrium level of GDP again. How large is the multiplier?

DISCUSSION QUESTION

1. Explain the logic behind the finding that variable imports reduce the numerical value of the multiplier.

10

SUPPLY-SIDE INTERACTING WITH DEMAND: UNEMPLOYMENT *AND* INFLATION?

When a further increase in the quantity of effective demand produces no further increase in output and entirely spends itself on an increase in the cost-unit fully proportionate to the increase in effective demand, we have reached a condition which might be appropriately designated as one of true inflation.

JOHN MAYNARD KEYNES (1883–1946), *THE GENERAL THEORY OF EMPLOYMENT, INTEREST AND MONEY*, (LONDON: MACMILLIAN), 1936

C hapter 9 has taught us that the position of the economy's total expenditure $(C + I + G + (X - IM))$ schedule governs whether the economy will experience a recessionary or an inflationary gap. Too little spending leads to a *recessionary gap*. Too much leads to an *inflationary gap*. Which sort of gap actually occurs is of considerable practical importance, because a recessionary gap translates into *unemployment* while an inflationary gap leads to *inflation*.

But the tools provided in Chapter 9 cannot tell us which sort of gap will arise because, as we learned, the position of the expenditure schedule depends on the price level—and the price level is determined by *both* aggregate demand *and* aggregate supply. So this chapter has a clear task: to bring the supply side of the economy back into the picture.

Doing so will put us in a position to deal with the crucial question raised in earlier chapters: Does the economy have an efficient self-correcting mechanism? We will see that the answer is "perhaps," but only under very special circumstances. This chapter will also enable us to explain the vexing problem of *stagflation*—the simultaneous occurrence of stagnating output *and* high inflation—that plagued the economy in the 1980s and that reappeared in 2008.

CONTENTS

PUZZLE: *Why Did Inflation Fall While the Economy Boomed?*

For years, economists have talked about the agonizing trade-off between inflation and unemployment—a notion that we will develop in more detail in Chapter 16. Very low unemployment is supposed to make the inflation rate rise. Yet the high growth in both Canada and the United States during the latter half of the 1990s and early in the 2000s seemed to belie this idea. The unemployment rate fell below 4 percent in the United States and to about 6 percent in Canada, the lowest rates in 30 years. But inflation did not rise; in fact, it *fell* for part of this period. How can we explain this exceptional conjunction of events—relatively low unemployment coupled with falling inflation? Does it mean—as many pundits said at the time—that standard economic theory does not apply to the "New Economy"? Before this chapter is over, we will have some answers.

THE AGGREGATE SUPPLY CURVE

In earlier chapters, we noted that aggregate demand is a schedule, not a fixed number. The same point applies to *aggregate supply*: The concept of aggregate supply does not refer to a fixed number, but rather to a schedule (an *aggregate supply curve*).

The exact relationship between the overall price level and the domestic product that is being supplied depends on wages and other production costs, on the capital stock, on the state of technology, among other things. Figure 1 shows a typical aggregate supply curve. It slopes upward, meaning that there usually is a positive relationship between the price level and aggregate output, *other things held constant*. Let's see why.

Why the Aggregate Supply Curve Slopes Upward

There are several reasons why one could argue that the aggregate supply curve usually slopes upward. The main reason is the *principle of increasing costs* that we encountered on page 50 of Chapter 3. As production expands, the opportunity cost of producing additional units increases. Simply put, the pricing decision of firms can be summarized by the following equation:

Price = Cost per unit + Profit per unit

This is nearly an identity since the profit per unit is, by definition, the difference between the price of the sold good minus the cost of producing it. However, we give a behavioural twist to the equation by supposing that prices are set by firms, on the basis of their unit cost and a certain *costing margin*, that is, the *profit margin* that will be such that producers will realize a target profit per unit.

The aggregate supply curve will be upward-sloping if prices rise when aggregate output rises. This, as can be seen from the above equation, will arise when profit per unit or cost per unit, or both, rise as more output is being produced. As long as the principle of increasing costs holds, the cost per unit is likely to increase as production rises, and hence there will be a positive relationship between the price level and the quantity of real GDP supplied.[1] In other words the aggregate supply curve is upward-sloping.

Note that, on a given aggregate supply curve as constructed here, costs per unit rise because it becomes harder and harder to produce more, not because wage rates or the prices of other inputs rise. Many of the costs that firms

FIGURE 1

An Aggregate Supply Curve

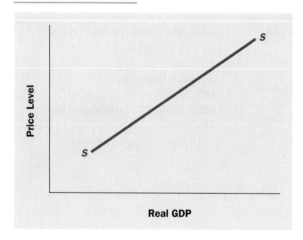

---

[1] Provided profit per unit does not drop as more output is being produced.

A Flat Aggregate Supply Curve

Some economists argue that the aggregate supply curve is likely to be flat, instead of upward-sloping, for a large range of output levels, as depicted in the accompanying graph. These economists, usually of a Keynesian pedigree, argue that the principle of increasing costs applies only at very high output levels, when production is being pushed to its capacity limit (called *full capacity output*). Evidence shows, so they say, that firms operate most of the time with large reserves of capacity, and are thus capable of increasing production without facing rising unit costs. Unit costs are thus approximately constant as long as firms are below full-capacity output. These economists also argue that firms will keep constant their target profit per unit, at least in the short run. Combining these two hypotheses, a constant cost per unit and a constant target profit per unit, it follows that firms will keep prices constant as long as they are producing not too far from their normal rate of capacity utilization.* It follows that the aggregate supply curve is flat, up to full-capacity output, or up to a level near potential output.

Perceptive students will note that this flat aggregate supply curve is consistent with the analysis that was pursued in the previous two chapters, where changes in prices were mostly ignored.

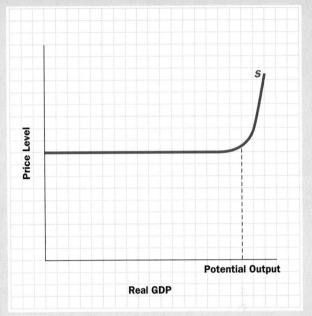

*The case for a flat aggregate supply curve corresponds to the alternative models of the oligopolistic firm that can be found in Chapter 12 of our textbook *Microeconomics: Principles and Policy*.

incur for labour and other inputs remain fixed for periods of time—although certainly not forever. For example, workers and firms often enter into long-term labour contracts that set nominal wages for one to three years in advance. Even when no explicit contracts exist, wage rates typically adjust only annually. Similarly, a variety of material inputs are delivered to firms, for some period of time, at prearranged prices.

The phrase "for some period of time" alerts us to an important fact: the aggregate supply curve may not stand still for long. If wages or prices of other inputs change, as they surely will during inflationary times, then the aggregate supply curve will shift.

Shifts of the Aggregate Supply Curve

We have concluded so far that, holding constant the levels of wages and other input prices, there is an upward-sloping aggregate supply curve relating the price level to aggregate quantity supplied. Now let's consider what happens when input prices change.

The Nominal Wage Rate   The most obvious determinant of the aggregate supply curve's position is the *nominal wage rate*. Wages are the major element of cost in the economy, accounting for more than 60 percent of all inputs. Because higher wage rates mean higher unit costs, they imply higher prices for each level of aggregate output.

Graphically, the aggregate supply curve *shifts to the left* (or inward), as shown in Figure 2 on the next page. In this diagram, firms are willing to supply $6,000 billion in real goods and services at a price level of 100 when wages are low (point *A*). But after wages increase, firms are willing to supply the same amount only if the price level rises to 110 (point *B*). By similar reasoning, the aggregate supply curve will shift to the right (or outward) if wages fall. In this case, firms will be willing to provide the same output at a lower price.

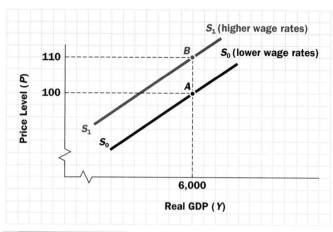

FIGURE 2

A Shift of the Aggregate Supply Curve

An increase in the money wage rate shifts the aggregate supply curve *inward*, meaning that the quantity supplied at any price level *declines*. A decrease in the money wage rate shifts the aggregate supply curve *outward*, meaning that the quantity supplied at any price level *increases*.

Prices of Other Inputs   In this regard, wages are not unique. An increase in the price of *any* input that firms buy will shift the aggregate supply curve in the same way. That is:

The aggregate supply curve is shifted inward (to the left) by an increase in the price of any input to the production process, and it is shifted outward (to the right) by any decrease.

The logic is exactly the same.

Although producers use many inputs other than labour, the one that has attracted the most attention in recent decades is energy. Increases in the prices of imported energy, such as those have taken place in recent years since 2003, push the aggregate supply curve inward—as shown in Figure 2. By the same token, decreases in the price of imported oil, such as the ones we enjoyed in 2001, shift the aggregate supply curve in the opposite direction—outward.

Technology and Productivity   Another factor that can shift the aggregate supply curve is the state of technology. The idea that technological progress increases the **productivity** of labour is familiar from earlier chapters. Holding wages constant, any increase of productivity will *decrease* business unit costs, thus allowing firms to reduce prices when producing the same output level.

Productivity is the amount of output produced by a unit of input.

For instance, suppose that the hourly wage rate of workers producing a gadget is $10 per hour, but that the labour input required to manufacture the gadget decreases from eight hours to seven hours, while the target profit per unit is $30. Then the price of this gadget is likely to diminish from $110 to $100. In brief, we can conclude that:

Improvements in productivity shift the aggregate supply curve outward.

We can therefore interpret Figure 2 as illustrating the effect of a *decline* in productivity. As we mentioned in Chapter 7, a slowdown in productivity growth was a persistent problem for Canada for more than two decades.

Available Supplies of Labour and Capital   The last determinants of the position of the aggregate supply curve are the ones we studied in Chapter 7: The bigger the economy—as measured by its available supplies of labour and capital—the more it is capable of producing. Thus:

As the labour force grows or improves in quality, and as investment increases the capital stock, the aggregate supply curve shifts *outward* to the right, meaning that more output can be produced at any given price level.

So, for example, the relatively high growth of investment during the latter half of the 1990s, by boosting the supply of capital, left the Canadian economy with a greater capacity to produce goods and services—that is, it shifted the aggregate supply curve outward.

These factors, then, are the major "other things" that we hold constant when drawing an aggregate supply curve: nominal wage rates, prices of other inputs (such as energy), technology, labour force, and capital stock. A change in the price level moves the economy *along a given supply curve*, but a change in any of these determinants of aggregate quantity supplied *shifts the entire supply schedule*.

■ EQUILIBRIUM OF AGGREGATE DEMAND AND SUPPLY

In Chapter 9, we constructed an aggregate demand curve, showing that this curve, for each different price level, was the set of real gross domestic product levels such that what was produced was actually what was being demanded. In other words, the aggregate demand curve gives us, for each price level, the real GDP level that ensures that spending is equal to output. But among all of the possible prices, what was the actual price level? Our analysis in terms of aggregate demand and aggregate supply can now provide us with an answer. The actual price level is given by the intersection of the aggregate demand and aggregate supply curves. That will be our short-term macroeconomic equilibrium, which takes jointly into account the price level and real GDP. In Figure 3, this macroeconomic equilibrium is given, under the initial conditions, by point E_0.

To illustrate the importance of the *slope* of the aggregate supply curve, we return to a question we posed in the last chapter: What happens to equilibrium GDP if the aggregate demand curve shifts outward? We saw there that such changes have a *multiplier* effect, and we noted that the actual numerical value of the multiplier is considerably smaller than suggested by the oversimplified multiplier formula. One of the reasons, variable imports, emerged in an appendix to that chapter. We are now in a position to understand a second reason:

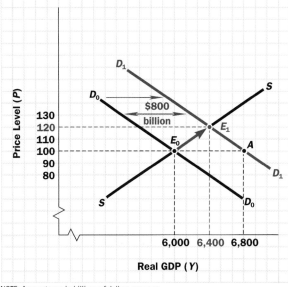

NOTE: Amounts are in billions of dollars per year.

FIGURE 3

Macroeconomic Equilibrium, Inflation, and the Multiplier

Inflation reduces the size of the multiplier.

The basic idea is simple. In Chapter 9, we described a multiplier process in which one person's spending becomes another person's income, which leads to further spending by the second person, and so on. But this story was confined to the *demand* side of the economy; it ignored what is likely to be happening on the *supply* side. The question is: As the multiplier process unfolds, will the additional demand be taken care of by firms without raising prices?

If the aggregate supply curve slopes upward, the answer is no. More goods will be provided only at *higher* prices. Thus, as the multiplier chain progresses, pulling income and employment up, prices will rise in tandem. This development, as we know from earlier chapters, will reduce net exports and dampen consumer spending because rising prices erode the purchasing power of consumers' wealth. As a consequence, the multiplier chain will not proceed as far as it would have in the absence of inflation.

How much inflation results from the rise in demand? How much is the multiplier chain muted by inflation? The answers to these questions depend on the slope of the economy's aggregate supply curve.

For a concrete example, let us return to the $200 billion increase in investment spending used in Chapter 9. There we found (see especially Figure 10 on page 202) that $200 billion in additional investment spending would eventually lead to $800 billion in additional spending *if the price level does not rise*—that is, *it tacitly assumed that the aggregate supply curve was horizontal*. But that may not be so. The slope of the aggregate supply curve tells us how any expansion of aggregate demand gets apportioned between higher output and higher prices.

In our example, Figure 3 shows the $800 billion rightward shift of the aggregate demand curve, from D_0D_0 to D_1D_1, that we derived from the oversimplified multiplier formula in Chapter 9. We see that, as the economy's equilibrium moves from point E_0 to point E_1, real GDP does not rise by $800 billion. Instead, prices rise, which cancels out part of the increase in quantity demanded. As a result, output rises from $6,000 billion to $6,400 billion—an increase of only $400 billion. Thus, in the example, inflation reduces the multiplier from $800/$200 = 4 to $400/$200 = 2. In general:

> As long as the aggregate supply curve slopes upward, any increase in aggregate demand will push up the price level. Higher prices, in turn, will drain off some of the higher real demand by eroding the purchasing power of consumer wealth and by reducing net exports. Thus, inflation reduces the value of the multiplier below that suggested by the oversimplified formula.

Notice also that the price level in this example has been pushed up (from 100 to 120, or 20 percent) by the rise in investment demand. This, too, is a general result:

> As long as the aggregate supply curve slopes upward, any outward shift of the aggregate demand curve will cause some rise in prices.

The economic behaviour behind these results is certainly not surprising. Firms faced with large increases in quantity demanded at their original prices respond to these changed circumstances in two natural ways: They raise production (so that real GDP rises), and they also raise prices (so the price level rises), because of increases in unit costs. But this rise in the price level, in turn, reduces the purchasing power of the bank accounts and bonds held by consumers, and they, too, react in the natural way: They cut down on their spending. Such a reaction amounts to a movement *along* aggregate demand curve D_1D_1 in Figure 3 from point A to point E_1.

Figure 3 also shows us exactly where the oversimplified multiplier formula goes wrong. By ignoring the effects of the higher price level, the oversimplified formula erroneously supposes that the economy moves horizontally from point E_0 to point A—which it would do only if the aggregate supply curve were horizontal. As the diagram clearly shows, output does not actually rise this much, which is one reason why the oversimplified formula exaggerates the size of the multiplier.

■ RECESSIONARY AND INFLATIONARY GAPS REVISITED

With this understood, let us now reconsider the question we have been deferring: Will equilibrium occur at, below, or beyond potential GDP?

We could not answer this question in Chapter 9 because we had no way to determine the equilibrium price level, and therefore no way to tell which type of gap, if any, would arise. But we find that our answer is still the same: Anything can happen.

The reason is that Figure 3 tells us nothing about where *potential* GDP falls. The factors determining the economy's capacity to produce were discussed extensively in Chapter 7. But that analysis might leave potential GDP above the $6,000 billion equilibrium level or below it. Depending on the locations of the aggregate demand and aggregate supply curves, then, we can reach equilibrium *beyond* potential GDP (an inflationary gap), *at* potential GDP, or *below* potential GDP (a recessionary gap). All three possibilities are illustrated in Figure 4.

The three upper panels duplicate diagrams that we encountered in Chapter 9. (Recall that each income–expenditure diagram considers *only* the demand side of the economy by holding the price level fixed.) Start with the upper-middle panel, in which the expenditure schedule $C + I_1 + G + (X − IM)$ crosses the 45° line exactly at potential GDP—which we take to be $7,000 billion in the example. Equilibrium is at point E, with neither a recessionary nor an inflationary gap. Now suppose that total expenditures either *fall* to $C + I_0 + G + (X − IM)$ (producing the upper-left diagram) or *rise* to $C + I_2 + G + (X − IM)$ (producing the upper-right diagram). As we read across the page from left to right, we see equilibrium occurring with a recessionary gap, at full employment, or with an inflationary gap—depending on the position of the $C + I + G + (X − IM)$ line.[2] In Chapter 9, we learned of several variables that

---

[2] These three diagrams hold potential GDP at $7,000 billion and vary the expenditure schedule. You can draw equivalent diagrams by holding the $C + I + G + (X − IM)$ line constant and changing the presumed level of potential GDP. Try it as an exercise.

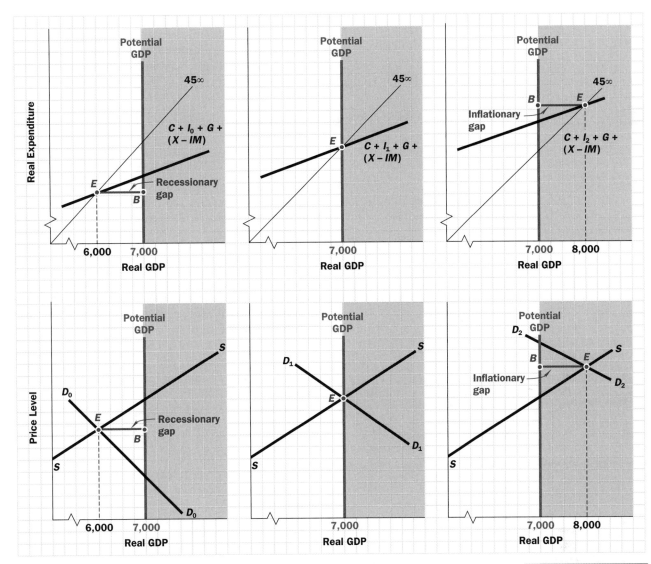

Note: Real GDP is in billions of dollars per year.

FIGURE 4

Recessionary and
Inflationary Gaps
Revisited

might shift the expenditure schedule up and down in this way. One of them was the price level.

The three lower panels portray the same three cases differently—in a way that can tell us what the price level will be. These diagrams consider *both* aggregate demand *and* aggregate supply, and therefore determine *both* the equilibrium price level *and* the equilibrium GDP at point *E*—the intersection of the aggregate supply curve *SS* and the aggregate demand curve *DD*. But the same three possibilities emerge nonetheless.

In the lower-left panel, aggregate demand is too low to provide jobs for the entire labour force, so we have a recessionary gap equal to distance *EB*, or $1,000 billion. This situation corresponds precisely to the one depicted on the income–expenditure diagram immediately above it.

In the lower-right panel, aggregate demand is so high that the economy reaches an equilibrium well beyond potential GDP. An inflationary gap equal to *BE*, or $1,000 billion, arises, just as in the diagram immediately above it.

In the lower-middle panel, the aggregate demand curve D_1D_1 is at just the right level to produce an equilibrium at potential GDP. Neither an inflationary gap nor a recessionary gap occurs, as in the diagram just above it.

It may seem, therefore, that we have simply restated our previous conclusions. But, in fact, we have done much more. For now that we have studied the determination of the equilibrium price level, we are able to examine how the economy adjusts to either a recessionary gap or an inflationary gap. Specifically, because wages are fixed in the short run, any one of the three cases depicted in Figure 4 can occur. But, in the long run, wages will adjust to labour market conditions, which will shift the aggregate supply curve. It is to that adjustment that we now turn.

■ ADJUSTING TO A RECESSIONARY GAP: DEFLATION OR UNEMPLOYMENT?

Suppose the economy starts with a recessionary gap—that is, an equilibrium *below* potential GDP—as depicted in the lower-left panel of Figure 4. Such a situation might be caused, for example, by inadequate consumer spending or by anemic investment spending. From 1990 to 1992, most observers believe that the Canadian economy was in just such straits—for the second time in a decade. And in Japan, recessionary gaps have been the norm since the early 1990s. What happens when an economy experiences a recessionary gap?

With equilibrium GDP below potential, jobs will be difficult to find. The ranks of the unemployed will exceed the number of people who are jobless because of moving, changing occupations, and so on. In the terminology of Chapter 6, the economy will experience a considerable amount of *cyclical unemployment*. Businesses, by contrast, will have little trouble finding workers, and their current employees will be eager to hang on to their jobs.

Such an environment makes it difficult for workers to win wage increases. Indeed, in extreme situations, wages may even fall—thereby shifting the aggregate supply curve *outward*. (Recall that an aggregate supply curve is drawn for a *given* money wage.) But as the aggregate supply curve shifts outward—eventually moving from S_0S_0 to S_1S_1 in Figure 5—prices decline and the recessionary gap could shrink. As long as net exports rise sufficiently and consumer spending increases because of strong wealth effects, by this process, deflation could gradually erode the recessionary gap—leading the economy to equilibrium at potential GDP (point *F* in Figure 5).

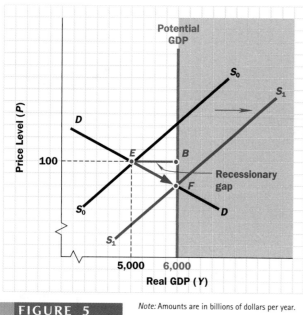

FIGURE 5

The Elimination of a Recessionary Gap

Note: Amounts are in billions of dollars per year.

But there is an important catch. In our modern economy, this adjustment process proceeds slowly—painfully slowly. Our brief review of the historical record in Chapter 5 showed that the economic history of Canada includes several examples of *deflation* before World War II but none since then. Not even severe recessions have forced average prices and wages down—although they have certainly slowed their rates of increase to a crawl. The only protracted episode of deflation in an advanced economy since the 1930s is the recent experience of Japan.

Exactly why wages and prices rarely fall in our modern economy is a subject of intense debate among economists. Some economists emphasize institutional factors such as minimum wage laws, union contracts, Employment Insurance, and a variety of government regulations that place legal floors under particular wages and prices. Because most of these factors are of recent vintage, this theory may successfully explain why wages and prices fall less frequently now than they did before World War II. But rigid wages and prices were a factor also (although less so) prior to World War II. Also, given the trend toward deregulation since the 1970s, it seems doubtful that legal restrictions can take us very far in explaining sluggish wage–price adjustments in Canada.

Other observers, going as far back as John Maynard Keynes in the 1930s, suggest that workers have a profound psychological resistance to accepting a wage reduction, especially if one group suffers *relative* to others. This theory certainly has the ring of truth. Think how you would react if your boss announced he was cutting your hourly wage rate. You might quit, or you might devote less care to your job. If the boss suspects you will react this way, he may be reluctant to cut your wage. Nowadays, genuine wage reductions are rare enough to be newsworthy. But although no one doubts that wage cuts can damage morale, this psychological theory has one major drawback: It fails to explain why the psychological resistance to wage cuts apparently started only after World War II. Until a satisfactory answer to this question is provided, many economists will remain skeptical of this hypothesis.

A third explanation is based on a fact we emphasized in Chapter 5—that business cycles have been less severe in the post-war period than they were in the pre-war period. As workers and firms came to realize that recessions would not turn into depressions, the argument goes, they decided to wait out the bad times rather than accept wage or price reductions that they would later regret.

Yet another theory is based on the old adage, "You get what you pay for." The idea is that workers differ in productivity, but that the productivities of individual employees are difficult to identify. Firms therefore worry that they will lose their best employees if they reduce wages—because these workers have the best opportunities elsewhere in the economy. Rather than take this chance, the argument goes, firms prefer to maintain high wages even in recessions.

Other theories also have been proposed, none of which commands a clear majority of professional opinion. But regardless of the cause, we may as well accept it as a well-established fact that wages fall only sluggishly, if at all, when demand is weak.

For a number of economists, the implications of this rigidity are quite serious. If a recessionary gap cannot cure itself without some deflation, and if wages and prices do not fall, recessionary gaps like *EB* in Figure 5 could linger for a long time. That is:

> When aggregate demand is low, the economy may get stuck with a recessionary gap for a long time. If wages and prices fall very slowly, the economy could endure a prolonged period of production below potential GDP.

Does the Economy Have a Self-Correcting Mechanism?

Now a situation like that described earlier would, presumably, not last forever. As the recession lengthened and perhaps deepened, more and more workers would be unable to find jobs at the prevailing "high" wages. Eventually, their need to be employed would overwhelm their resistance to wage cuts.

Firms, too, would become increasingly willing to cut prices as the period of weak demand persisted and managers became convinced that the slump was not merely a temporary aberration. Prices and wages did, in fact, fall in many countries during the Great Depression of the 1930s, and they have even fallen in Japan in recent times, albeit very slowly.

However, as observed by John Maynard Keynes during the 1930s, the strength of the factors pushing for greater net exports and higher consumer spending may not be sufficiently potent. For instance, while it is true that a fall in prices makes a country's products more competitive in the international economy and, therefore, could stimulate net exports, this is only true if competitors in other countries do not suffer the same deflation by also cutting their prices. Moreover, while falling prices can stimulate consumption because one's stock of wealth is rising in real terms, you must not abstract from the fact that the counterpart of this rising real wealth is the concomitant growth of private real debt held by firms and households. As mentioned on page 176 of Chapter 8, the negative effect on consumer (and investment) spending of falling incomes and rising real debt can possibly more than outweigh the positive contribution to consumption expenditures of the rising purchasing power of household wealth that results from the falling prices. In such a case, the aggregate demand curve would be upward-sloping, rather than downward-sloping.

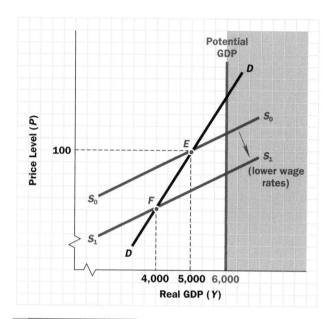

FIGURE 6

The Perverse Effects of Declining Wages and Prices with an Upward-Sloping Aggregate Demand Curve

The **Fisher debt effect** is the negative effect that lower commodity prices have on real spending, as the real value of the money-fixed liabilities of households and firms rise when prices are lower.

The economy's **self-correcting mechanism** refers to the way changes in wages brought about by competitive forces drive the economy back to potential output, thus eliminating the inflationary gap or the recessionary gap.

Figure 6 illustrates this unusual but possible case—the aggregate demand curve *DD* is upward-sloping—which James Tobin (1918–2002) called the *Fisher effect* in honour of his predecessor at Yale University, Irving Fisher (1867–1947), who had noted the negative consequences of the rising burden of debt during the deflation times of the Great Depression. Fisher was struck by the devastation—loan defaults, bankruptcies, property seizures—that the rising real debt had brought to debtors, whether corporations, homeowners or farmers. In the case of what we will call the **Fisher debt effect**, as wages and prices fall, as illustrated by the shift in the aggregate supply curve from S_0S_0 to S_1S_1, aggregate spending would actually decline, thereby intensifying the recession. In Figure 6, starting from a macroeconomic equilibrium *E*, at $5,000 billion, below potential output, declining wages and prices would drive the economy to an even lower real GDP level, $4,000 billion, at *F.*

Nowadays, policy makers believe that it is folly to wait for falling wages and prices to eliminate a recessionary gap. They agree that government action is both necessary and appropriate under recessionary conditions. Nevertheless, vocal—and highly partisan—debate continues over how much and what kind of intervention is warranted. One reason for the disagreement is that, at the macroeconomic level, the **self-correcting mechanism** may not operate at all and, if it does, it may do so only weakly to cure recessionary gaps.

An Example from Recent History: Deflation in Japan

Fortunately for us, recent Canadian economic history offers no examples of long-lasting recessionary gaps of the type experienced during the 1930s. But the world's second-largest economy does. The Japanese economy has been consistently weak since the early 1990s—including several recessions. As a result of low domestic demand, Japan has experienced persistent recessionary gaps for over a decade. During the 1980s, growth in real GDP averaged at about 4 percent annually; during the 1990s, this rate declined sharply to just slightly over 1 percent annually. Unsurprisingly, Japan's modest inflation rate in the early 1990s evaporated and turned into a small *deflation* rate from the mid-1990s to the mid-2000s. Of course, you can always argue that eventually the Japanese economy did start to show signs of some improvement, but still nowhere near the pre-1990s spectacular growth rates. Hence, if the self-correcting mechanism is at work in modern economies, at best it is an extremely slow one.

ADJUSTING TO AN INFLATIONARY GAP: INFLATION

Let us now turn to what happens when the economy finds itself *beyond* full employment—that is, with an *inflationary* gap like that shown in Figure 7. When the aggregate supply curve is S_0S_0 and the aggregate demand curve is *DD*, the economy will initially reach equilibrium (point *E*) with an inflationary gap, shown by the segment *BE*.

According to some economists, this situation has prevailed in Canada in recent years, as the unemployment rate fell to below the 6 percent threshold during certain months. What should happen under such circumstances? As we will now see, the relatively tight labour market should produce inflation that eventually eliminates the inflationary gap, although perhaps in a slow and painful way. Let us see how.

When equilibrium GDP exceeds potential GDP, jobs are plentiful and labour is in great demand. Firms are likely to have trouble recruiting new workers or even holding onto their old ones as other firms try to lure workers away with higher wages.

Rising wages add to business costs, which shift the aggregate supply curve *inward*. As the aggregate supply curve moves from S_0S_0 to S_1S_1 in Figure 7, the inflationary gap shrinks. In other words, inflation eventually erodes the inflationary gap and brings the economy to an equilibrium at potential GDP (point F).

There is a straightforward way of looking at the economics underlying this process. Inflation arises because buyers are demanding more output than the economy can produce at normal operating rates. To paraphrase an old cliché, there is too much demand chasing too little supply. Such an environment encourages price hikes.

Ultimately, rising prices eat away at the purchasing power of consumers' wealth, forcing them to cut back on consumption, as explained in Chapter 8. In addition, exports fall and imports rise, as we learned in Chapter 9. Eventually, aggregate quantity demanded is scaled back to the economy's capacity to produce—graphically, the economy moves back along curve DD from point E to point F. At this point, the self-correcting process stops. In brief:

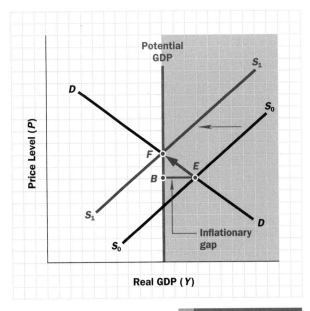

FIGURE 7

The Elimination of an Inflationary Gap

> If aggregate demand is exceptionally high, the economy may reach a temporary state above full employment (an *inflationary gap*). When this occurs, the tight situation soon forces wages and prices to rise, which could feed on each other to create an inflationary spiral. However, as higher prices cut into consumer purchasing power and net exports, the inflationary gap begins to close, with output falling and prices continuing to rise. The gap is finally eliminated at a higher price level and with GDP equal to potential GDP.

Some economists would argue that this was indeed the case during the early post-World War II years with Canadian unemployment rates at historically low levels of just over 3 percent (as during the mid-1960s) and it may have also been the case since 2001 with unemployment rates in recent times at less than 6 percent. Yet the inflation rate has not accelerated. Why not? We will have an answer in just a few more pages.

But first we repeat an important caveat: *The self-correcting mechanism takes time* because wages and prices do not adjust quickly or, under certain conditions, the mechanism may not materialize at all. Thus, while an inflationary gap sows the seeds of its own destruction, the seeds germinate slowly. So, once again, policy makers may want to speed up the process.

▨ Demand Inflation and Stagflation

Simple as it is, this model of how the economy adjusts to an inflationary gap teaches us a number of important lessons about inflation in the real world. First, Figure 7 reminds us that the real culprit is an *excess of aggregate demand* relative to potential GDP. The aggregate demand curve is initially so high that it intersects the aggregate supply curve well beyond full employment. The resulting intense demand for goods and labour pushes prices and wages higher. Although aggregate demand in excess of potential GDP is not the only possible cause of inflation, it certainly is the cause in our example.

Nonetheless, business managers and journalists may blame inflation on rising wages. In a superficial sense, of course, they are right, because higher wages do indeed lead firms to raise product prices. But in a deeper sense they are wrong. Both rising wages and rising prices are symptoms of the same underlying malady: too much

Stagflation is inflation that occurs while the economy is growing slowly or having a recession.

aggregate demand. Blaming labour for inflation in such a case is a bit like blaming high drug prices for making you ill.

Second, notice that output *falls* while prices *rise* as the economy adjusts from point *E* to point *F* in Figure 7. This is our first (but not our last) explanation of the phenomenon of **stagflation**—the conjunction of in*flation* and economic *stag*nation. Specifically:

A period of stagflation is part of the normal aftermath of a period of excessive aggregate demand.

It is easy to understand why. When aggregate demand is excessive, the economy will temporarily produce beyond its normal capacity. Labour markets tighten and wages rise. Machinery and raw materials may also become scarce and so start rising in price. Faced with higher costs, business firms quite naturally react by charging higher prices. That is stagflation.

A careful look at recent periods of recession over the last few decades in Canada, as shown in Figures 5 and 6 in Chapter 5 (on pages 102 and 103, respectively), would indicate that such is generally the case. Even after real GDP starts to decline, the inflation rate continues to rise for a while, until it eventually falls.

From this we can conclude the following about the economy's ability to right itself:

If the wealth effects on consumption spending are strong and the forces of international competition are potent, the self-correcting mechanism may eliminate either unemployment or inflation. But this mechanism works slowly and unevenly, as the forces involved are weak. In addition, its beneficial effects on either inflation or unemployment are sometimes swamped by strong forces pushing in the opposite direction (such as rapid increases or decreases in aggregate demand). Finally, the economy may be subjected to overwhelming perverse debt-deflation effects, so that the self-correcting mechanism may not work at all. Thus, the self-correcting mechanism is not particularly reliable.

A Tale of Two Graduating Classes: 1983 versus 2007

SOURCE: © Felicia Martinez/PhotoEdit

Timing matters in life. The university graduates of 2007 were pretty lucky. The unemployment rate in Canada was gravitating around 6 percent—at the time the lowest in over 30 years—with many employers scrambling for new hires. Starting salaries continued to rise, many graduates had numerous job offers, and some firms even offered bonuses to students who signed on the dotted line!

Nearly 25 years earlier, in 1983, when some of their parents were just graduating, the state of the labour market was dramatically different. The Canadian economy was in a deep slump, with an unemployment rate of approximately 12 percent—the highest level since the Great Depression a half-century earlier. Companies that had stocked up on recent university graduates during the tight labour market of the 1970s found themselves with more employees than they knew what to do with in 1982 and 1983. They were not eager to hire more. Bonuses and other "perks" were practically nonexistent; job offers were scarce. With unemployment rates of 12 percent in May and June of 1983, the job market was in its most saturated state in 50 years, just as the new graduates were hitting the streets. In sharp contrast, we have the glory days of 2007 when the unemployment rate had bottomed out at 5.3 percent in October of that year—a rate that had not been seen in Canada since the early 1970s.

◼ STAGFLATION FROM A SUPPLY SHOCK

We have just discussed the type of stagflation that follows in the wake of an inflationary boom. However, that is not what happened when unemployment and inflation both soared in the 1970s and early 1980s. What caused this more virulent strain of stagflation? Several things, although the principal culprit was rising energy prices.

In 1973, the Organization of the Petroleum Exporting Countries (OPEC) quadrupled the international price of crude oil. Even though Canada was itself an oil exporting country with oil-producing regions benefiting from the oil price hike, Canadian consumers were soon faced with the prices of gasoline and home heating fuels increasing sharply, and Canadian businesses saw an important cost of doing business—energy prices—rising drastically. OPEC struck a second time in the period 1979–1980, this time doubling the price of oil. Then the same thing happened again, albeit on a smaller scale, when Iraq invaded Kuwait in 1990. Oil prices surged upward again because of the protracted war in Iraq and the continued hostilities in the Persian Gulf area since 2003, as well as other more random factors such as the impact of Hurricane Katrina of 2005. More recently, the growing speculation in world commodity markets has pushed up the prices of raw materials and, more specifically, oil.

Higher energy prices, we observed earlier, shift the economy's aggregate supply curve *inward* in the manner shown in Figure 8. If the aggregate supply curve shifts inward, as it surely did following each of these "oil shocks," production must decline as the higher prices bring about reductions in aggregate demand. The result is the worst of both worlds: falling production and rising prices.

This conclusion is shown graphically in Figure 8, which shows an aggregate demand curve, *DD*, and two aggregate supply curves. When the supply curve shifts inward, the economy's equilibrium shifts from point *E* to point *A*. Thus, output falls while prices rise—exactly our definition of stagflation. In sum:

> Stagflation is the typical result of adverse shifts of the aggregate supply curve.

Figure 8 represents well what happened as a result of both the first and second oil price shocks in 1973–1975 and 1979–1981, respectively. For instance, between 1979 (represented by the supply curve S_0S_0 and point *E*) and 1981 (represented by supply curve S_1S_1 and point *A*), the figure shows real GDP falling, while the price level rises over the two years. The general lesson to be learned from the Canadian experience with supply shocks is both clear and important:

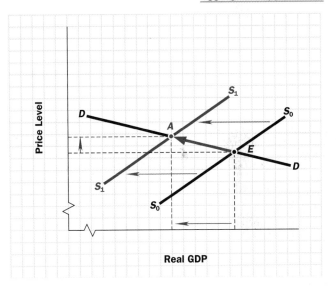

FIGURE 8

Stagflation from an Adverse Shift in Aggregate Supply

> The typical results of an adverse supply shock are lower output and higher inflation. This is one reason why the world economy was plagued by stagflation in the mid-1970s and early 1980s. And it can happen again if another series of major supply-reducing events takes place.

Indeed, there was mounting evidence by mid-2008 that Canada was likely to be plagued by another episode of stagflation inflicted by a large adverse supply shock—mainly the result of the world price of oil having doubled within a year.

◼ APPLYING THE MODEL TO A GROWING ECONOMY

You may have noticed that ever since Chapter 5 we have been using the simple aggregate supply and aggregate demand model to determine the equilibrium *price level* and the equilibrium *level of real GDP*, as depicted in several graphs in this chapter. But in

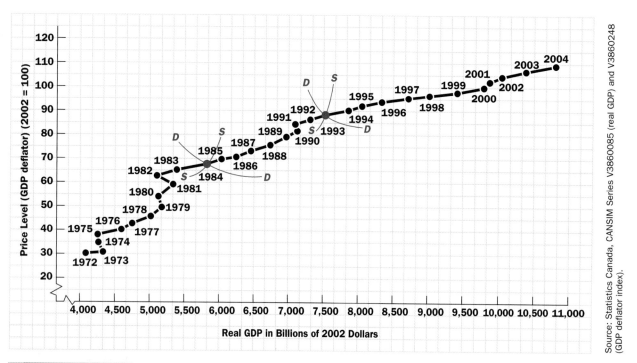

Source: Statistics Canada, CANSIM Series V3860085 (real GDP) and V3860248 (GDP deflator index).

the real world, neither the price level nor real GDP remains constant for long. Instead, both normally rise from one year to the next.

The growth process is illustrated in Figure 9, which is a scatter diagram of the Canadian price level and the level of real GDP for every year from 1970 to 2007. The labelled points show the clear upward march of the economy through time—toward higher prices and higher levels of output.

This upward trend is hardly mysterious, for both the aggregate demand curve and the aggregate supply curve normally shift to the right each year. Aggregate supply grows because more workers join the workforce each year and because investment and technology improve productivity (Chapter 7). Aggregate demand grows because a growing population generates more demand for both consumer and investment goods and because the government increases its purchases (Chapters 8 and 9). We can think of each point in Figure 9 as the intersection of an aggregate supply curve and an aggregate demand curve for that particular year. To help you visualize this idea, the

curves for 1984 and 1993 are sketched in the diagram.

Figure 10 is a more realistic version of the aggregate supply and demand diagram that illustrates how our theoretical model applies to a growing economy. We have chosen the numbers so that the black curves D_0D_0 and S_0S_0 roughly represent the year 2004, and the blue curves D_1D_1 and S_1S_1 roughly represent 2005—except that we use nice round numbers to facilitate computations. Thus, the equilibrium in 2004 was at point A, with a real GDP of $1,200 billion (in 2002 dollars) and a price level of 107. A year later, the equilibrium was at point B, with real GDP at $1,250 billion and the price level at 110. The red arrow in

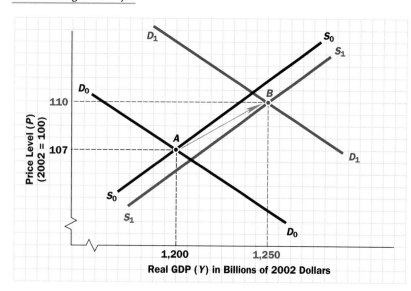

the diagram shows how equilibrium moved from 2004 to 2005. It points upward and to the right, meaning that both prices and output increased. In this case, the economy grew by 4.2 percent and prices rose about 2.8 percent, which is close to what actually happened in Canada over that year.

Demand-Side Fluctuations

Let us now use our theoretical model to rewrite history. Suppose that aggregate demand grew *faster* than it actually did between 2004 and 2005. What difference would this have made to the performance of the Canadian economy? Figure 11 provides answers. Here the black demand curve D_0D_0 is exactly the same as in the previous diagram, as

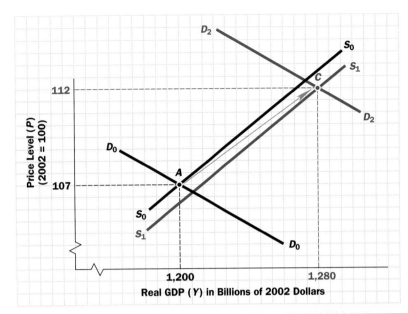

FIGURE 11

The Effects of Faster Growth of Aggregate Demand

are the two supply curves, indicating a given rate of aggregate supply growth. But the blue demand curve D_2D_2 lies farther to the right than the demand curve D_1D_1 in Figure 10. Equilibrium is at point A in 2004 and point C in 2005. Comparing point C in Figure 11 with point B in Figure 10, we see that *both* output *and* prices would have increased more over the year—that is, the economy would have experienced faster *growth* and more *inflation*. This is generally what happens when the growth rate of aggregate demand speeds up.

> For any given growth rate of aggregate supply, a faster growth rate of aggregate demand will lead to more inflation and faster growth of real output.

Figure 12 illustrates the opposite case. Here we imagine that the aggregate demand curve shifted out *less* than in Figure 10. That is, the blue demand curve D_3D_3 in Figure 12 lies to the left of the demand curve D_1D_1 in Figure 10. The consequence, we see, is that the shift of the economy's equilibrium from 2004 to 2005 (from point A to point E) would have entailed *less inflation* and *slower growth* of real output than actually took place. Again, that is generally the case when aggregate demand grows more slowly.

FIGURE 12

The Effects of Slower Growth of Aggregate Demand

> For any given growth rate of aggregate supply, a slower growth rate of aggregate demand will lead to less inflation and slower growth of real output.

Putting these two findings together gives us a clear prediction:

> If fluctuations in the economy's real growth rate from year to year arise primarily from variations in the rate at which *aggregate demand* increases, then the data should show the most rapid inflation occurring when output grows most rapidly and the slowest inflation occurring when output grows most slowly.

Is it true? For the most part, yes. Our brief review of Canadian economic history back in Chapter 5 found that

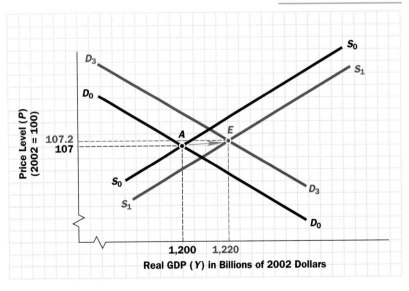

most episodes of high inflation came with rapid growth. But not all. Some surges of inflation resulted from the kinds of supply shocks we have considered in this chapter.

Supply-Side Fluctuations

As a historical example, let's return to the events of 1973 to 1975 and 1979 to 1981 that were considered in Figure 8 (page 233), but now add in something we ignored there: While the aggregate supply curve was shifting *inward* because of the oil shock, the aggregate demand was shifting *outward*. In Figure 13, the black aggregate demand curve D_0D_0 and aggregate supply curve S_0S_0 represent the economic situations in 1973 and 1979, respectively before the major oil price shocks, with equilibrium at point E. By 1975 and 1981, respectively, the aggregate demand curve had shifted out to the position indicated by the blue curve D_1D_1, but, because of the higher oil prices, the aggregate supply curve had shifted *inward* to the blue curve S_1S_1. After the short-lived slumps of 1975 and 1980 (see the boxed information in Chapter 5 on page 102), the new equilibrium point B therefore wound up to the left of the original equilibrium point E. Real output fell slightly (indeed, because these mild declines in output were merely three and five months in duration, the annual real GDP averages did not even register a decline for 1975 and 1980 in Canada), while prices—led by energy costs—rose rapidly.

What about the opposite case? Suppose the economy experiences a *favourable* supply shock, as it did in the late 1990s (albeit primarily in the United States), so that the aggregate supply curve shifts *outward* at an unusually rapid rate.

Figure 14 depicts the consequences. The aggregate demand curve shifts out from D_0D_0 to D_1D_1 as usual, but the aggregate supply curve shifts all the way out to S_1S_1. (The dotted line indicates what would happen in a "normal" year.) So the economy's equilibrium winds up at point B rather than at point C. Compared to C, point B represents *faster economic growth* (B is to the right of C) and *lower inflation* (B is lower than C). In brief, the economy wins on both fronts: Inflation falls while GDP grows rapidly, as happened in the late 1990s.

Combining these two cases, we conclude that:

If fluctuations in economic activity emanate mainly from the supply side, higher rates of inflation will be associated with *lower* rates of economic growth.

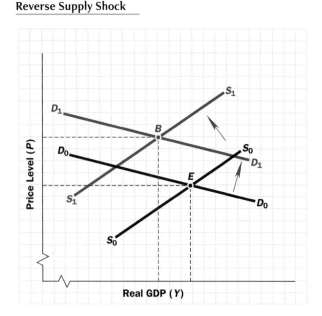

FIGURE 13

Stagflation from a
Reverse Supply Shock

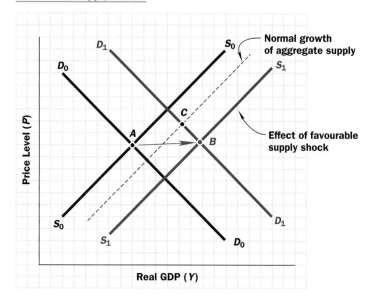

FIGURE 14

The Effects of a
Favourable Supply Shock

PUZZLE RESOLVED: *Explaining the Roaring Late 1990s*

The situation depicted in Figure 14 holds the key to understanding why the North American economy performed so well in the late 1990s. As we observed at the beginning of this chapter, inflation *fell* while unemployment was relatively low, leading many observers to proclaim that some of the most basic precepts of macroeconomics no longer applied in the "New Economy."

What really happened? Several things, but one of them was a favourable oil shock. The world oil market weakened in 1997 and 1998, and oil prices plummeted from about US$26 per barrel to just US$11 per barrel. This sharp drop in the price of oil constituted a favourable supply shock that shifted the aggregate supply curve outward—just as shown in Figure 14. So Canadian and U.S. economic growth speeded up while inflation declined. In addition, productivity accelerated in the late 1990s—as we discussed in Chapter 7—and this constituted another favourable supply shock. Thus, North America enjoyed the happy combination of falling unemployment and declining inflation at the same time.

Lucky? Yes. But mysterious? No. What was happening was that the economy's aggregate supply curve was shifting outward much faster than it normally does. As we know from turning our previous analysis of adverse supply shocks in the opposite direction:

Favourable supply shocks tend to push output up and reduce inflation. It was mainly favourable supply shocks, including a speed-up in productivity growth, that accounted for the stunningly good news in the late 1990s.

A ROLE FOR STABILIZATION POLICY

We have pointed out that, while the growth path of the economy is not a violently unstable one, it does display sharp fluctuations. Chapter 8 emphasized the volatility of investment spending, and Chapter 9 noted that changes in investment have multiplier effects on aggregate demand. This chapter took the next step by showing how shifts in the aggregate demand curve cause fluctuations in *both* real GDP *and* prices—fluctuations that are widely decried as undesirable. It also suggested that the economy's self-correcting mechanism may not necessarily work and, if it does work, it acts rather slowly. This leaves room for government stabilization policy to improve the workings of an advanced market economy. Can the government really accomplish this goal of stabilizing the economy's performance? If so, how? These are some of the important questions for Part III.

SUMMARY

1. The economy's **aggregate supply curve** relates the quantity of goods and services that will be supplied to the price level. It normally slopes upward to the right because of the principle of increasing costs. As it becomes harder to produce more, unit costs rise, inducing firms to raise prices.

2. The position of the aggregate supply curve can be shifted by changes in money wage rates, prices of other inputs, technology, or quantities or qualities of labour and capital.

3. The **equilibrium price level** and the **equilibrium level of real GDP** are jointly determined by the intersection of the economy's aggregate supply and aggregate demand schedules.

4. Among the reasons why the oversimplified multiplier formula is wrong is the fact that it ignores the inflation that is caused by an increase in aggregate demand. Such **inflation decreases the multiplier** by reducing both consumer spending and net exports.

5. The equilibrium of aggregate supply and demand can come at full employment, below full employment (a **recessionary gap**), or above full employment (an **inflationary gap**).

6. The economy has a **self-correcting mechanism** that erodes a recessionary gap, but it is both slow and weak, or even nonexistent. Specifically, a depressed labour market reduces wage increases and, in extreme cases, may drive wages down. Lower wages shift the aggregate supply curve outward and lead to higher growth only if the positive effect on net exports is strong and private wealth effects stimulate consumption adequately. Otherwise, as occurs

with the **Fisher debt effect**, lower wages and prices may drive down real GDP instead, as borrowers must cut spending because of their rising real debt burden.

7. If an inflationary gap occurs, the economy has a similar self-correcting mechanism that erodes the gap through a process of inflation. Unusually strong job prospects push wages up, which shifts the aggregate supply curve to the left and reduces the inflationary gap.

8. One consequence of this self-correcting mechanism is that, if a surge in aggregate demand opens up an inflationary gap, the economy's subsequent natural adjustment will lead to a period of **stagflation**—that is, a period in which prices are rising while output is falling.

9. An inward shift of the aggregate supply curve will cause output to fall while prices rise—that is, it will produce stagflation. Among the events that have caused such a shift are abrupt increases in the price of foreign oil.

10. Adverse supply shifts like this plagued the Canadian economy during the mid- and late 1970s, leading to stagflation each time.

11. But things reversed in 1997–1998, when falling oil prices and rising **productivity** shifted the aggregate supply curve out more rapidly than usual, thereby boosting real growth and reducing inflation simultaneously.

12. Inflation can be caused either by rapid growth of aggregate demand or by sluggish growth of aggregate supply. When fluctuations in economic activity emanate from the demand side, prices will rise rapidly when real output grows rapidly. But when fluctuations in economic activity emanate from the supply side, output will grow slowly when prices rise rapidly.

KEY TERMS

Productivity   224

Equilibrium of real GDP and the price level   225

Inflation and the multiplier   225

Recessionary gap   226

Inflationary gap   226

Fisher debt effect   230

Self-correcting mechanism   230

Stagflation   232

TEST YOURSELF

1. In an economy with the following aggregate demand and aggregate supply schedules, find the equilibrium levels of real output and the price level. Graph your solution. If full employment comes at $2,800 billion, is there an inflationary or a recessionary gap?

Aggregate Quantity Demanded	Price Level	Aggregate Quantity Supplied
$3,200	90	$2,750
3,100	95	2,900
3,000	100	3,000
2,900	105	3,050
2,800	110	3,075

Note: Amounts are in billions of dollars.

2. Suppose a worker receives a wage of $20 per hour. Compute the real wage (money wage deflated by the price index) corresponding to each of the following possible price levels: 85, 95, 100, 110, 120. What do you notice about the relationship between the real wage and the price level? Relate your finding to the slope of the aggregate supply curve.

3. Add the following aggregate supply and demand schedules to the example in Test Yourself Question 2 in Chapter 9 (page 212) to see how inflation affects the multiplier.

(1) Price Level	(2) Aggregate Demand When Investment Is $240	(3) Aggregate Demand When Investment Is $260	(4) Aggregate Supply
90	$3,860	$4,060	$3,660
95	3,830	4,030	3,730
100	3,800	4,000	3,800
105	3,770	3,970	3,870
110	3,740	3,940	3,940
115	3,710	3,910	4,010

Draw these schedules on a piece of graph paper.

a. Notice that the difference between Columns (2) and (3), which show the aggregate demand schedule at two different levels of investment, is always $200. Discuss how this constant gap of $200 relates to your answer in the previous chapter.

b. Find the equilibrium GDP and the equilibrium price level both before and after the increase in investment. What is the value of the multiplier? Compare that to the multiplier you found in Test Yourself Question 2 in Chapter 9.

4. Use an aggregate supply and demand diagram to show that multiplier effects are smaller when the aggregate supply curve is steeper. Which case gives rise to more inflation—the steep aggregate supply curve or the flat one? What happens to the multiplier if the aggregate supply curve is vertical?

5. Derive an upward-sloping aggregate demand curve (as shown in Figure 6), based on the assumption that when prices decrease, the positive effects of holding fixed-denominated assets are overtaken by the negative effects of holding fixed-denominated liabilities (real debt effects overcome real wealth effects). To draw the curve, make use of the analysis found in Figures 5 and 6 of Chapter 9.

DISCUSSION QUESTIONS

1. Explain why a decrease in the price of foreign oil shifts the aggregate supply curve outward to the right. What are the consequences of such a shift?

2. Comment on the following statement: "Inflationary and recessionary gaps are nothing to worry about because the economy has a built-in mechanism that cures either type of gap automatically."

3. Give two different explanations of how the economy can suffer from stagflation.

4. Why do you think wages tend to be rigid in the downward direction?

5. Explain in words why rising prices reduce the multiplier effect of an autonomous increase in aggregate demand.

6. Wage and price deflation can have perverse effects on the economy. In addition to the argument that can be drawn from Figure 6 in Chapter 10, what other reasons could lead economists to be fearful of deflation? As an entrepreneur, what would you do if you thought that wage costs would fall for a few more months or a couple of additional quarters? As a consumer, what would you do if you believed that the prices of various durable goods were bound to decrease for a few more quarters? What impact would these expectations have on real spending or output?

FISCAL AND MONETARY POLICY

Part II constructed a framework for understanding the macroeconomy. The basic theory came in three parts. We started with the determinants of the long-run growth rate of potential GDP in Chapter 7, added some analysis of short-run fluctuations in aggregate demand in Chapters 8 and 9, and finally considered short-run fluctuations in aggregate supply in Chapter 10. Part III *uses* that framework to consider a variety of public policy issues—the sorts of things that make headlines in the newspapers and on television.

At several points in earlier chapters, we suggested that the government may be able to manage aggregate demand by using its *fiscal and monetary policies*. Chapters 11–13 pick up and build on that suggestion. You will learn how the government tries to promote rapid growth and low unemployment while simultaneously limiting inflation—and why its efforts do not always succeed. Then, in Chapters 14–16, we turn explicitly to a number of important controversies related to the government's *stabilization policy*. How should the Bank of Canada do its job? Why is it considered so important to balance public budgets? Is there a trade-off between inflation and unemployment?

By the end of Part III, you will be in an excellent position to understand some of the most important debates over national economic policy—not only today but also in the years to come.

11

MANAGING AGGREGATE DEMAND: FISCAL POLICY

Cicero said that man plants trees for future generations. Had he rather remarked that man levies taxes for future generations, he would have founded fiscal theory (instead of capital theory).

EDMUND S. PHELPS (1933–), 2006 RECIPIENT OF THE BANK OF SWEDEN PRIZE IN ECONOMIC SCIENCES IN MEMORY OF ALFRED NOBEL, 1979

I n the model of the economy we constructed in Part II, the government played a rather passive role. It did some spending and collected taxes, but that was about it. We hinted that well-designed government policies might improve the economy's performance. It is now time to expand on that hint—and to learn about some of the difficulties that must be overcome if stabilization policy is to succeed.

We begin in this chapter with **fiscal policy**. The next three chapters take up the government's other main tool for managing aggregate demand, *monetary policy*. In a later chapter, Chapter 15, we will discuss the long-term implications of fiscal policy for public deficits and public debt.

The government's **fiscal policy** is its plan for spending and taxation. It is designed to steer aggregate demand in some desired direction.

CONTENTS

ISSUE: *An Increase in Government Spending or a Tax Cut?*

During the 2006 federal election that produced a minority Conservative government, two views of fiscal policy emerged. On the one hand, the New Democratic Party and the Bloc Québécois were essentially proposing to increase both government expenditures and taxes. On the other hand, the Liberals and the Conservatives seemed to share the view that both government expenditures and taxes ought to be reduced. All federal parties felt that it was best for the federal government budget to be roughly in balance. All parties also argued, as one would expect, that their proposed fiscal policy would be best for the Canadian economy.

From what we saw in Chapter 9, there are two ways in which governments can raise aggregate demand: one is to increase government expenditures and the other is to cut taxes. Which way is best? And what happens to aggregate demand if both taxes and government expenditures are raised (or cut) together?

All taxes were not created equal. Some taxes have a greater impact on the poor, and others on the rich. What are the consequences for aggregate demand? Also, different taxes are likely to have different incentive effects (on working hours, for instance) and hence affect aggregate supply differently.

The debates over fiscal policy that occur around election time often revolve around three concepts that we study in this chapter:

1. The multiplier effect of tax cuts versus higher government spending
2. The multiplier effects of different types of tax cuts (e.g., those for the poor versus those for the rich)
3. The incentive effects of tax cuts

By the end of the chapter, you will be in a much better position to form your own opinion on this important public policy issue.

INCOME TAXES AND THE CONSUMPTION SCHEDULE

To understand how taxes affect equilibrium gross domestic product (GDP), we begin by recalling that taxes (T) are *subtracted* from gross domestic product (Y) to obtain disposable income (DI):

$$DI = Y - T$$

and that disposable income, not GDP, is the amount actually available to consumers, and is therefore the principal determinant of consumer spending (C). Thus, *at any given level of GDP*, if taxes rise, disposable income falls—and hence so does consumption. What we have just described in words is summarized graphically in Figure 1:

Any increase in taxes shifts the consumption schedule *downward*, and any tax reduction shifts the consumption schedule *upward*.

Of course, if the C schedule moves up or down, so does the $C + I + G + (X - IM)$ schedule. And we know from Chapter 9 that such a shift will have a multiplier effect on aggregate demand. So it follows that:

An increase or decrease in taxes will have a mutiplier effect on equilibrium GDP on the demand side. Tax reductions increase equilibrium GDP, and tax increases reduce it.

So far, this analysis just echoes our previous analysis of the multiplier effects of government spending. But there is one important difference. Government purchases of goods and services add to total spending *directly*—through the G

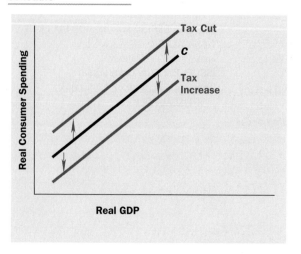

FIGURE 1

How Tax Policy Shifts the Consumption Schedule

component of $C + I + G + (X - IM)$. But taxes reduce total spending only *indirectly*—by lowering disposable income and thus reducing the C component of $C + I + G + (X - IM)$. As we will now see, that little detail turns out to be quite important.

◼ THE MULTIPLIER REVISITED

To understand why, let us return to the example used in Chapter 9, in which we learned that the multiplier works through a chain of spending and respending, as one person's expenditure becomes another's income. In the example, the spending chain was initiated by Microhard's decision to spend an additional $1 million on investment. With a marginal propensity to consume (MPC) of 0.75, the complete multiplier chain was:

$$\$1,000,000 + \$750,000 + \$562,500 + \$421,875 + \ldots$$
$$= \$1,000,000 (1 + 0.75 + (0.75)^2 + (0.75)^3 + \ldots)$$
$$= \$1,000,000 \times 4 = \$4,000,000$$

Thus, each dollar originally spent by Microhard eventually produced $4 in additional spending.

◼ The Tax Multiplier

Now suppose the initiating event was a $1 million *tax cut* instead. As we just noted, a tax cut affects spending only *indirectly*. By adding $1 million to disposable income, it increases consumer spending by $750,000 (assuming again that the MPC is 0.75). Thereafter, the chain of spending and respending proceeds exactly as before, to yield:

$$\$750,000 + \$562,500 + \$421,875 + \ldots$$
$$= \$750,000 (1 + 0.75 + (0.75)^2 + \ldots)$$
$$= \$750,000 \times 4 = \$3,000,000$$

Notice that the mutiplier effect of each dollar of tax cut is 3, not 4. The reason is straightforward. Each new dollar of additional autonomous spending—regardless of whether it is C or I or G—has a multiplier of 4. But each dollar of tax cut creates only 75 cents of new consumer spending. Applying the basic expenditure multiplier of 4 to the 75 cents of first-round spending leads to a multiplier of 3 for each dollar of tax cut. This numerical example illustrates a general result:[1]

> The multiplier for changes in taxes is smaller than the multiplier for changes in government purchases because not every dollar of tax cut is spent.

◼ Income Taxes and the Multiplier

But this is not the only way in which taxes force us to modify the multiplier analysis of Chapter 9. If the volume of taxes collected depends on GDP—which, of course, it does in reality—there is another.

To understand this new wrinkle, return again to our Microhard example, but now assume that the government levies a 20 percent *income tax*—meaning that individuals pay 20 cents in taxes for each $1 of income they receive. Now when Microhard spends $1 million on salaries, its workers receive only $800,000 in *after-tax* (that is, disposable) income. The rest goes to the government in taxes. If workers spend 75 percent of the $800,000 (because the MPC is 0.75), spending in the next round will be only $600,000. Notice that this is only *60 percent* of the original expenditure, not *75 percent*—as was the case before.

---

[1] You may notice that the tax multiplier of 3 is the spending multiplier of 4 times the marginal propensity to consume, which is 0.75. See the appendix to this chapter for an algebraic explanation.

Thus, the multiplier chain for each original dollar of spending *shrinks* from

$$1 + 0.75 + (0.75)^2 + (0.75)^3 + \ldots = \frac{1}{1 - 0.75} = \frac{1}{0.25} = 4$$

in Chapter 9's example to

$$1 + 0.6 + (0.6)^2 + (0.6)^3 + \ldots = \frac{1}{(1 - 0.6)} = \frac{1}{0.4} = 2.5$$

This is clearly a large reduction in the multiplier. Although this is just a numerical example, the appendix to this chapter shows that the basic finding is quite general:

> The multiplier is reduced by an income tax because an income tax reduces the fraction of each dollar of GDP that consumers actually receive and spend.

We thus have a third reason why the oversimplified multiplier formula of Chapter 9 exaggerates the size of the multiplier: It ignores income taxes.

REASONS WHY THE OVERSIMPLIFIED FORMULA OVERSTATES THE MULTIPLIER

1. It ignores variable imports, which reduce the size of the multiplier.
2. It ignores price-level changes, which reduce the multiplier.
3. It ignores income taxes, which also reduce the size of the multiplier.

FIGURE 2

The Multiplier in the Presence of an Income Tax

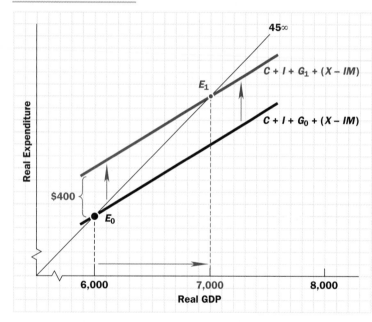

Note: Figures are in billions of dollars per year.

The last of these three reasons is the most important in practice.

This conclusion about the multiplier is shown graphically in Figure 2, which can usefully be compared to Figure 10 of Chapter 9 (page 202). Here we draw our $C + I + G + (X - IM)$ schedules with a slope of 0.6, reflecting an MPC of 0.75 and a tax rate of 20 percent, rather than the 0.75 slope we used in Chapter 9. Figure 2 then illustrates the effect of a $400 billion increase in government purchases of goods and services, which shifts the total expenditure schedule from $C + I + G_0 + (X - IM)$ to $C + I + G_1 + (X - IM)$. Equilibrium moves from point E_0 to point E_1—a GDP increase from $Y = \$6,000$ billion to $Y = \$7,000$ billion. Thus, if we ignore for the moment any increases in the price level (which would further reduce the multiplier), a $400 billion increment in government spending leads to a $1,000 billion increment in GDP. So, when a 20 percent income tax is included in our model, the multiplier is only $\$1,000/\$400 = 2.5$, as we concluded above.

Thus, we now have noted two different ways in which taxes modify the multiplier analysis:

1. Tax changes have a smaller multiplier effect than spending changes by government or others.
2. An income tax reduces the multipliers for both tax changes and changes in spending.

■ Automatic Stabilizers

The size of the multiplier may seem to be a rather abstract notion with little practical importance. But that is not so. Fluctuations in one or another of the components of total spending—*C*, *I*, *G*, or *X* − *IM*—occur all the time. Some come unexpectedly; some are even difficult to explain after the fact. We know from Chapter 9 that any such fluctuation will move GDP up or down by a multiplied amount. If the multiplier is smaller, GDP will be less sensitive to such shocks—that is, the economy will be less volatile.

Features of the economy that reduce its sensitivity to shocks are called **automatic stabilizers**. The most obvious example is the one we have just been discussing: the personal income tax. The income tax acts as a shock absorber because it makes disposable income, and thus consumer spending, less sensitive to fluctuations in GDP. As we have just seen, when GDP rises, disposable income (*DI*) rises *less* because part of the increase in GDP is siphoned off by the federal and provincial governments. This leakage helps limit any increase in consumption spending. When GDP falls, *DI* falls less sharply because part of the loss is absorbed by governments rather than by consumers. So consumption does not drop as much as it otherwise might. Thus, the much-maligned personal income tax is one of the main features of our modern economy that helps ensure against a repeat performance of the Great Depression.

But our economy has other automatic stabilizers. For example, Chapter 6 discussed the Canadian system of Employment Insurance. This program serves as an automatic stabilizer as well: When GDP drops and people lose their jobs, unemployment benefits prevent disposable incomes from falling as dramatically as earnings do. As a result, unemployed workers can maintain their spending better, and consumption fluctuates less than employment does.

The list could continue, take for instance the agricultural supply management programs that we discussed in Chapter 4, but the basic principle remains the same: Each automatic stabilizer serves, in one way or another, as a shock absorber, thereby lowering the multiplier. And each does so quickly, without the need for any decision maker to take action. In a word, they work *automatically*.

A case in point arose when the economy of our neighbour, the United States, sagged in the early part of this decade. The budget deficit naturally rose as tax receipts came in lower than had been expected. While there was much hand-wringing over the rising U.S. deficit, most economists viewed it as a good thing in the short run: The automatic stabilizers were propping up spending, as they should.

> An **automatic stabilizer** is a feature of the economy that reduces its sensitivity to shocks, such as sharp increases or decreases in spending.

▨ Government Transfer Payments

To complete our discussion of multipliers for fiscal policy, let us now turn to the last major fiscal tool: *government transfer payments*. Transfers, as you will remember, are payments to individuals that are not compensation for any direct contribution to production. How are transfers treated in our models of income determination—like purchases of goods and services (*G*) or like taxes (*T*)?

The answer to this question follows readily from the circular flow diagram on page 170 of Chapter 8 or the accounting identity on page 171. The important thing to understand about transfer payments is that they intervene between gross domestic product (*Y*) and disposable income (*DI*) in precisely the *opposite* way from income taxes. They add to earned income rather than subtract from it.

Specifically, starting with the wages, interest, rents, and profits that households earn, we *subtract* income taxes to calculate disposable income. We do so because these taxes represent the portion of incomes that consumers *earn* but never *receive*. But then we must *add* transfer payments because they represent sources of income that are *received* although they were not *earned* in the process of production. Thus:

Transfer payments function basically as negative taxes.

As you may recall from Chapter 8, we use the symbol *T* to denote taxes *minus* transfers. Thus giving consumers $1 in the form of transfer payments is treated in the 45° line diagram as a $1 decrease in taxes.

ISSUE REVISITED: *The Political Debate over Taxes and Spending*

What we have learned already has some bearing on the debate between the New Democratic Party and the Bloc Québécois on the one hand and the Liberal Party of Canada and the Conservative Party of Canada on the other. Remember that the first two parties would rather increase both taxes and government expenditures. We have learned that the multiplier for *T* is smaller than the multiplier for *G*. That means that an increase in government spending balanced by an equal increase in taxes should *raise* total spending.

Next, consider the claim, often made by members of the New Democratic Party, that tax cuts are mostly for wealthy taxpayers and do not stimulate much spending. This assertion assumes that the rich have lower marginal propensities to consume than the poor, as many people naturally assume. Remember, a low MPC leads to a lower multiplier. Canadian data drawn from 2002 actually supports this belief. Figure 3 shows the relationship between saving rates and current income. Households that have low income—in the lowest quintile—have saving rates below zero. They spend more than they earn! High-income couples have high saving rates, nearly 10 percent. Therefore, poor people do have a high MPC, while rich people have a low MPC. The situation is the same in other countries. In Japan, for instance, the propensity to consume in 2006 is 80 percent for the lowest income group and only 67 percent for the highest one.

SOURCE: Based on Mario Seccareccia, "Rising Household Indebtedness and the Plummeting Saving Rate in Canada: An Explanatory Note," Table 1, *Economic and Labour Relations Review*, 16(1), July 2005, pp. 133–151.

FIGURE 3

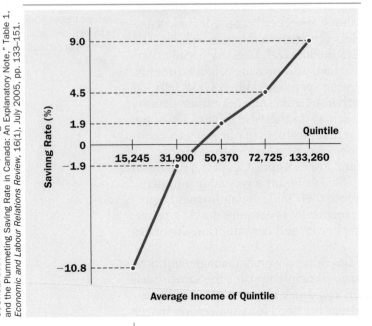

Saving Rates per Household Current Income Quintiles, Canada, 2002

PLANNING EXPANSIONARY FISCAL POLICY

We will have more to say about this debate. But first imagine you are the federal minister of Finance trying to decide whether to use fiscal policy to stimulate the Canadian economy in 2008—when it is expected to be hit by the economic recession of our major trading partner, the United States—and, if so, by how much. Suppose the economy would have a GDP of $1,400 billion if the government simply reenacted last year's budget. Suppose further that your goal is to achieve a fully employed labour force, and that staff economists tell you that reaching this target requires a GDP of approximately $1,500 billion. Finally, just to keep the calculations simple, imagine that there is no inflation. What sort of budget should you present?

This chapter has taught us that the government has three ways to raise GDP by $100 billion. The federal government can close the recessionary gap between actual and potential GDP by:

1. Raising government purchases
2. Reducing taxes
3. Increasing transfer payments

Figure 4 illustrates the problem, and its cure through higher government spending, on our 45° line diagram. Figure 4(a) shows the equilibrium of the economy if no changes are made in the budget. With an expenditure multiplier of 2.5, you can figure out that an additional $40 billion of government spending will be needed to push GDP up by $100 billion and eliminate the gap ($40 × 2.5 = $100).

FIGURE 4

Fiscal Policy to
Eliminate a
Recessionary Gap

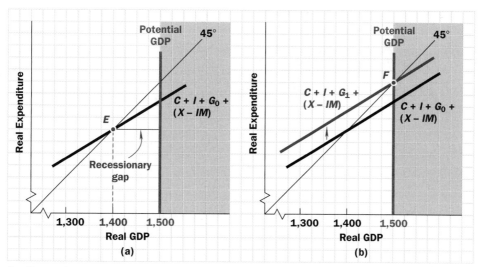

Note: Figures are in billions of dollars per year.

So you might vote to raise G by \$40 billion, hoping to move the $C + I + G + (X - IM)$ line in Figure 4(a) up to the position indicated in Figure 4(b), thereby achieving full employment. Or you might prefer to achieve this fiscal stimulus by lowering taxes. Or you might opt for more generous transfer payments. The point is that a variety of budgets are capable of increasing GDP by \$100 billion. Figure 4 applies equally well to any of them.

PLANNING CONTRACTIONARY FISCAL POLICY

The preceding example assumed that the basic problem of fiscal policy is to close a recessionary gap, as was probably the case in 2008 in the United States and in Canada. But only a year before, in 2007, many economists believed that the major macroeconomic problem in Canada was just the opposite. Economists at the Bank of Canada thought that real GDP exceeded potential GDP by about \$12 billion, leading to an inflationary gap. In such a case, the government would wish to adopt more restrictive fiscal policies to reduce aggregate demand.

It does not take much imagination to run our previous analysis in reverse. If an inflationary gap would arise from a continuation of current budget policies, contractionary fiscal policy tools can eliminate it. By cutting spending, raising taxes, or by some combination of the two, the government can pull the $C + G + I + (X - IM)$ schedule down to a noninflationary position and achieve an equilibrium at full employment. A restrictive fiscal policy can avoid inflation by limiting aggregate demand to the level that the economy can produce at full employment.

THE CHOICE BETWEEN SPENDING POLICY AND TAX POLICY

In principle, fiscal policy can nudge the economy in the desired direction equally well by changing government spending or by changing taxes. For example, if the government wants to expand the economy, it can raise G or lower T. Either policy would shift the total expenditure schedule upward, as depicted in Figure 4(b), thereby raising equilibrium GDP on the demand side.

In terms of our aggregate demand and supply diagram, either policy shifts the aggregate demand curve outward, as illustrated in the shift from D_0D_0 to D_1D_1 in Figure 5. As a result, the economy's equilibrium moves from point E to point A. Both real GDP and the price level rise. As this diagram points out:

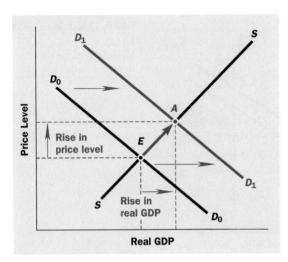

FIGURE 5

Expansionary Fiscal
Policy

Any combination of higher spending and lower taxes that produces the same aggregate demand curve leads to the same increases in real GDP and prices.

How, then, do policy makers decide whether to raise spending or to cut taxes? The answer depends mainly on how large a public sector they want to create—a major issue in the long-running debate in Canada over the proper size of government.

The small-government point of view is typically found among advocates of free markets; for instance, among the economists working for think-tanks such as the Fraser Institute. Over recent years, both the federal Conservative and Liberal parties, the latter with Paul Martin as its long-standing Finance minister, have endorsed such a view. At the provincial level, this small-government platform was most popular under the Ontario Conservatives led by Mike Harris and the Alberta Conservatives under Ralph Klein. Conservatives generally say that we are foolish to rely on the public sector to do what private individuals and businesses can do better on their own. Conservatives believe that the growth of government interferes too much in our everyday lives, thereby curtailing our freedom. Those who hold this view can argue for *tax cuts* when macroeconomic considerations call for expansionary fiscal policy, and for *lower public spending* when contractionary policy is required.

An opposing opinion is expressed most often by left-wing or centre-left-wing economists and politicians, in particular by members of the New Democratic Party and by the authors of the annual *Alternative Federal Budget* published by the Canadian Centre for Policy Alternatives. These individuals hold that something is amiss when a country as wealthy as Canada has such an impoverished public sector and such large inequalities in income distribution. According to them, Canada's most pressing needs are not for more fast food and video games but, rather, for better schools, a truly universal health system, more efficient public transport, affordable housing, better water and sewer systems, more food inspection, cleaner cities, more environment-friendly measures, and a better welfare system. People on this side of the debate believe that we should *increase* spending when the economy needs stimulus and pay for these improved public services by *increasing taxes* when it is necessary to rein in the economy.

The use of fiscal policy for economic stabilization is sometimes erroneously associated with a large and growing public sector—that is, with "big government." This need not be so.

Individuals favouring a smaller public sector can advocate an active fiscal policy just as well as those who favour a larger public sector. Advocates of bigger government should seek to expand demand (when appropriate) through higher government spending and contract demand (when appropriate) through tax increases. By contrast, advocates of smaller government should seek to expand demand by cutting taxes and reduce demand by cutting expenditures.

? ISSUE REDUX: *Increase Spending or Cut Taxes—or Something Else?*

In the United States, there has been no hesitation in eliminating the recessionary gap through expansionary fiscal policy, but this has not been the case in Canada. One reason, as we will see in Chapter 15, is that most Canadian politicians fear that tax cuts and increases in government spending will fuel public deficits. As a result, at least since the mid-1990s, both Liberal and Conservative federal governments have been essentially concerned with "balancing the books" and reducing the public debt, rather than closing the recessionary or the inflationary gap, leaving this duty to monetary policy.

■ SOME HARSH REALITIES

The mechanics outlined so far in this chapter make the fiscal policy planner's job look pretty simple. The elementary diagrams suggest, rather misleadingly, that policy makers can drive GDP to any level they please simply by manipulating spending and tax programs. It seems they should be able to hit the full employment bull's-eye every time. In fact, a better analogy is to a poor rifleman shooting through dense fog at an erratically moving target with an inaccurate gun and slow-moving bullets.

The target is moving because, in the real world, the investment, net exports, and consumption schedules constantly shift about as expectations, technology, events abroad, and other factors change. For all of these reasons and others, the policies decided on today, which will take effect at some future date, may no longer be appropriate by the time that future date rolls around.

The second misleading feature of our diagrams (the "inaccurate gun") is that we do not know multipliers with the precision of our examples. Although our best guess may be that a $20 billion increase in government purchases will raise GDP by $35 billion (a multiplier of 1.75), the actual outcome may be as little as $20 billion or as much as $50 billion. It is therefore impossible to "fine-tune" every wobble out of the economy's growth path. Economic science is simply not that precise.

A third complication is that our target—full employment GDP—may be only dimly visible, as if through a fog. For example, as we noted in Chapter 6, a lively debate has raged for years over what the unemployment rate that corresponds to full employment truly is.

A fourth complication is that the fiscal policy "bullets" travel slowly: Tax and spending policies affect aggregate demand only after some time elapses. Consumer spending, for example, may take months to react to an income tax cut. Because of these time lags, fiscal policy decisions must be based on *forecasts* of the future state of the economy. And no one has yet discovered a foolproof method of economic forecasting. The combination of long lags and poor forecasts may occasionally leave the government fighting the last inflation just as the new recession gets under way.

And, finally, the people aiming the fiscal "rifle" are politicians, not economic technicians. Sometimes political considerations lead to policies that deviate markedly from what textbook economics would suggest. And even when they do not, it may take a long time for bureaucrats to design a new program or assess the implications of a tax change.

In addition to all of these operational problems, legislators trying to decide whether to push the unemployment rate lower would like to know the answers to two further questions. First, since either higher spending or lower taxes will increase the government's budget deficit, what are the long-run costs of running large budget deficits? This is a question we will take up in depth in Chapter 15. Second, how large is the inflationary cost likely to be? As we know, an expansionary fiscal policy that reduces a recessionary gap by increasing aggregate demand will lower unemployment. But, as Figure 5 reminds us, it also tends to be inflationary. This undesirable side effect may make the government hesitant to use fiscal policy to combat recessions.

Is there a way out of this dilemma? Can we carry on the battle against unemployment without aggravating inflation? For almost 30 years, a small but influential minority of economists, journalists, and politicians have argued that we can. They call their approach "supply-side economics." These ideas have had immense influence in the United States, helping the Republicans, through Ronald Reagan and George Bush, to achieve three successive electoral victories in the 1980s, and they have been revived under President George W. Bush in 2001 and 2005. In Canada, supply-side economics were received with less enthusiasm, with, for instance, only some of its arguments being part of the "commonsense revolution" of Ontario Prime Minister Mike Harris between 1995 and 2002. A similar "commonsense revolution" occurred in the United Kingdom, under the leadership of the "Iron Lady," Margaret Thatcher, from 1979 to 1990. Just what is supply-side economics?

THE IDEA BEHIND SUPPLY-SIDE TAX CUTS

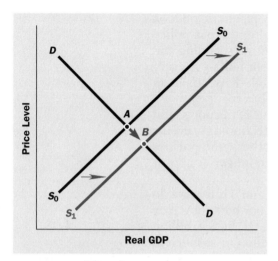

The central idea of supply-side economics is that certain types of tax cuts will increase aggregate supply. For example, taxes can be cut in ways that raise the rewards for working, saving, and investing. *If people actually respond to these incentives,* such tax cuts will increase the total supplies of labour and capital in the economy, thereby increasing aggregate supply.

Figure 6 illustrates the idea on an aggregate supply and demand diagram. If policy measures can shift the economy's aggregate supply to position $S_1 S_1$, then prices will be lower and output higher than if the aggregate supply curve remained at $S_0 S_0$. Policy makers will have reduced inflation and raised real output at the same time—as shown by point B in the figure. The trade-off between inflation and unemployment will therefore have been defeated. That is the goal of supply-side economics.

Policies Advocated by Supply-Siders

What sorts of policies do supply-siders advocate? Economists at the Fraser Institute located in Vancouver believe that some taxes are worse than others: They are more costly to administer and they reduce the incentives to work, save, and invest.[2] These are the taxes that ought to be eliminated or reduced. Here are the suggestions of supply-siders.

Lower Business Taxes   Corporate income taxes ought to be reduced, thus raising the profitability of investment. In addition, the capital tax on businesses should be eliminated. Indeed in their 2007 budget, the federal Conservatives provided financial incentives to encourage provincial governments to suppress the capital tax on business, which should soon be completely eliminated.[3]

Lower Personal Income Taxes   A reduction in personal income tax rates will reduce taxes not only on labour income, but also on capital income and capital gains. It is particularly important to reduce rates in the upper tax brackets. The argument of the supply-siders is that if tax rates on rich people—presumably the individuals who are the entrepreneurs responsible for the dynamism of the economy—can be lowered enough, these individuals will augment their supplies of both labour and capital, and provide employment for the rest of the workforce. This influence was felt in Canada, as in the rest of the world, as the highest combined provincial and federal tax bracket rate fell from 61 percent in 1973 to 51 percent in 1987, and then to 43 percent by 2005.

Encourage Saving   Supply-siders propose that income arising from saving be tax-free (as in the federal government's 2008 budget Tax-Free Savings Account) or that income that is being saved be exempted from taxation. This is already the case for money put into registered retirement saving plans (RRSP) or registered pension plans (RPP). But there are limits to the amounts that can be put into these plans. The limits have been substantially relaxed over the last few years. Supply-siders suggest that the limits be entirely removed, so that all saved income would be tax-free.

Some Flies in the Ointment

Critics of supply-side economics rarely question the basic idea that lower taxes improve incentives. They argue, instead, that supply-siders exaggerate the beneficial

---

[2] See "Tax efficiency: Not all taxes were created equal," *Studies in Economic Prosperity*, January 2007 (Vancouver: The Fraser Institute).

[3] Ironically, 1988 Nobel Prize laureate French economist Maurice Allais used to argue that this was the best tax since it could not be avoided and would pressure firms to be more efficient in order to overcome the burden of the tax.

effects of tax cuts and ignore some undesirable side effects. Here is a brief rundown of some of their main objections.

Small Magnitude of Supply-Side Effects   The first objection is that supply-siders are simply too optimistic: No one really knows how to do what Figure 6 shows. Although it is easy, for example, to design tax incentives that make working more *attractive* financially, people may not actually respond to these incentives. In fact, most of the statistical evidence suggests that we should not expect much from such tax incentives. As the economist Charles Schultze once quipped: "There's nothing wrong with supply-side economics that division by 10 couldn't cure."

Demand-Side Effects   The second objection is that supply-siders ignore the effects of tax cuts on aggregate demand. If you cut personal taxes, for example, individuals *may possibly* work more. But they *will certainly* spend more.

   The joint implications of these two objections appear in Figure 7. This figure depicts a *small* outward shift of the aggregate supply curve (which reflects the first objection) and a *large* outward shift of the aggregate demand curve (which reflects the second objection). The result is that the economy's equilibrium moves from point E (the intersection of S_0S_0 and D_0D_0) to point C (the intersection of S_1S_1 and D_1D_1). Prices rise as output expands. The outcome differs only a little from the straight "demand-side" fiscal stimulus depicted in Figure 5.

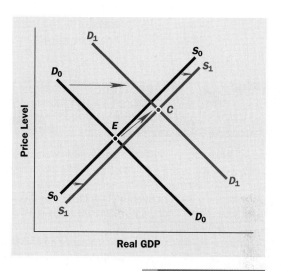

FIGURE 7

A More Pessimistic View of Supply-Side Tax Cuts

Confusing Means and Ends   Some supply-side proposals are intended to reduce taxation on saving and increase the rate of saving. But as we observed in Chapter 9 when studying the paradox of thrift, what ought to be increased is the amount of investment—real, tangible investment. If the rate of saving increases without a simultaneous rise in investment, aggregate demand will fall and the economy will be worse off. Any incentives that are created should be targeted toward investment and research and development.

Effects on Income Distribution   There is an ironic twist to supply-side economics. On the one hand, there is a call to reduce the generosity of social programs, as if more money given to the poor would destroy their character and their desire to work. On the other hand, it is claimed that more money to the rich will induce them to work harder. Still, despite reductions in the tax rates of high-income brackets and increases in their hourly earnings, the data show that the 10 percent richest Canadians do not work more than before, whereas all other Canadians work longer hours.

Losses of Tax Revenue   Supply-siders initially intimated that tax rate cuts would not generate reduced tax revenues. The large-scale experiments conducted in the United States have proven this claim to be false: Budget deficits have skyrocketed when personal income tax rates were drastically cut in the early 1980s and 2000s. As a result, supply-siders now recommend increases in tax rates on consumption, such as the GST, to compensate for the decrease in other taxes.

? ISSUE: *Tax Cuts Once Again*

   Some critics of supply-side economics question the motives of supply-siders. Since it is very likely that cuts in tax rates will lead to reduced government revenues, the obvious response to such a situation is to reduce government expenditures, thus ensuring that the public books get balanced and that the public debt does not rise. The call for tax cuts, as occurred during the "commonsense revolution" of Ontario Prime Minister Mike Harris, is enticing to most taxpayers. But many social activists and political analysts see it as a ploy, led by business think-tanks and other right-wing organizations, to convey a hidden agenda: reduce the share of government expenditure in national income. Because of reduced revenues, governments are being forced to cut back on social programs, public education, public health care, and other government programs, or they are being induced to sell Crown corporations. This then gives additional investment opportunities to the private sector and more room to expand their activities.

In Canada, as in Western Europe, politicians were put under tremendous pressure to balance public budgets. As a result, when tax cuts were voted in, the cuts were usually accompanied by reductions in public spending programs, even by provincial governments that had left-wing leanings, so as to avoid the creation of large budget deficits. Indeed, perhaps with the exception of oil-rich Alberta, provincial governments in the 1990s felt squeezed by the high cost of servicing the provincial debt, the reduction in federal transfer payments, and the pressure for tax cuts brought about by interprovincial tax competition.

Some Surprising Anti-Keynesian Episodes

In the 1990s and early 2000s, a new view of the impact of fiscal policy emerged, a view held mostly by some European economists. This new *anti-Keynesian* view of public finance asserts that *reductions* in government expenditure will lead to an *increase* in GDP—exactly the opposite of what we have been claiming since Chapter 9! How can that be?

The anti-Keynesian view of public finance is based on a theoretical argument and some empirical and historical evidence. European economists have observed several instances of contractions in government expenditures that have been followed by episodes of economic expansion, notably in Denmark, Sweden, and Italy, but also in Japan during the first half of the 1980s and in Canada in 1979–1981 and 1986–1987. A further episode was observed in Canada between 1996 and 2000, when the Canadian economy grew at a real rate of 4.75 percent—quite a high rate—just after a series of major cutbacks in government expenditures; this was particularly true following the 1995 federal budget prepared by Liberal Finance Minister Paul Martin. Doesn't this episode contradict the Keynesian theory of aggregate demand that we have been discussing in this book?

The answer to this conundrum is that every one of these anti-Keynesian episodes can be explained by a change in some other factor that influences the economy. This reminds us how difficult it is to do forecasting in macroeconomics, but also that any of our assertions with respect to the impact of a given factor, such as government expenditure, depends on the assumption that other factors do not simultaneously change, creating an opposite effect.

The 1996–2000 episode in Canada, for instance, can be explained by several factors that mitigated the negative impact of the reduction in government expenditure. First, and most obviously, the Canadian economy was very much influenced by the strong economic expansion that was occurring in the United States. With the help of the North American Free Trade Agreement (signed in 1994), which expanded the Canada–U.S. Free Trade Agreement of 1989, Canadian firms were able to export more freely to the United States, thus benefitting from the booming American economy.

In addition, during the 1996–2000 episode, the Canadian dollar, which was already weak at about US$0.75, became even weaker, moving to about US$0.66 during this time period, which also helped Canadian producers with their exports to the United States. Finally, in 1996 and 1997, interest rates in Canada were particularly low, both in nominal and in real terms, thus boosting private expenditures such as investment and the consumption of durable goods. Thus, overall, the fall in public expenditures was more than compensated for by large increases in net exports and in private expenditures.

Partisans of the new anti-Keynesian view would argue that private expenditures rose because the fall in government expenditures benefitted the private sector, with the initial reduction in government expenditures, as announced in the 1995 Liberal budget, signalling a reduction in public deficits and hence in future taxes and future interest rates. This encouraged consumers to spend and businesses to invest. All of these arguments will be discussed in the following chapters. Suffice it to say at this stage that many economists believe that the historical evidence supports the Keynesian view: The United States managed to quickly overcome the 2001 recession through a hugely expansionary fiscal policy, whereas Europe, which essentially followed the precepts of the anti-Keynesian view by refusing to let government expenditures overcome government revenues, is still suffering from slow growth and high rates of unemployment.

SOURCE: Rosaria Rita Canale, Pasquale Foresti, Ugo Marani, and Oreste Napolitano, *On Keynesian Effects of (Apparent) Non-Keynesian Fiscal Policies* (Naples, Italy: Facoltà di Economia, University "Federico II," 2007, unpublished). Retrieved from http://mpra.ub.uni-muenchen.de/3742

SUMMARY

1. The government's **fiscal policy** is its plan for managing aggregate demand through its spending and taxing programs. This policy is made jointly by the Minister of Finance, subject to approval in the House of Commons.

2. Because consumer spending (*C*) depends on disposable income (*DI*), and *DI* is GDP minus taxes, any change in taxes will shift the consumption schedule on a 45° line diagram. Such shifts in the consumption schedule have multiplier effects on GDP.

3. The multiplier for changes in taxes is smaller than the multiplier for changes in government purchases because each $1 of tax cuts leads to less than $1 of increased consumer spending.

4. An income tax reduces the size of the multiplier.

5. Because an income tax reduces the multiplier, it reduces the economy's sensitivity to shocks. It is therefore considered an **automatic stabilizer**.

6. Government transfer payments are like negative taxes, rather than like government purchases of goods and services, because they influence total spending only indirectly through their effect on consumption.

7. If the multipliers were known precisely, it would be possible to plan a variety of fiscal policies to eliminate either a recessionary gap or an inflationary gap. Recessionary gaps can be cured by raising *G* or cutting *T*. Inflationary gaps can be cured by cutting *G* or raising *T*.

8. Active stabilization policy can be carried out either by means that tend to expand the size of government (by raising either *G* or *T* when appropriate) or by means that reduce the size of government (by reducing either *G* or *T* when appropriate).

9. Expansionary fiscal policy can mitigate recessions, but it also raises the budget deficit.

10. Expansionary fiscal policy also normally exacts a cost in terms of higher inflation. This last dilemma has led to a great deal of interest in "supply-side" tax cuts designed to stimulate aggregate supply.

11. **Supply-side tax cuts** aim to push the economy's potential output outward to the right. When successful, they can expand the economy and reduce inflation at the same time—a highly desirable outcome.

12. But critics point out at least four serious problems with supply-side tax cuts: They also stimulate aggregate demand; the beneficial effects on aggregate supply may be small; they make the income distribution more unequal; and large tax cuts lead to large budget deficits.

KEY TERMS

Fiscal policy   243

Effect of income taxes on
the multiplier   245

Automatic stabilizer   247

Supply-side tax cuts   252

TEST YOURSELF

1. Consider an economy in which tax collections are always $400 and in which the four components of aggregate demand are as follows:

GDP	Taxes	DI	C	I	G	(X − IM)
$1,360	$400	$960	$720	$200	$500	$30
1,480	400	1,080	810	200	500	30
1,600	400	1,200	900	200	500	30
1,720	400	1,320	990	200	500	30
1,840	400	1,440	1,080	200	500	30

Find the equilibrium of this economy graphically. What is the marginal propensity to consume? What is the multiplier? What would happen to equilibrium GDP if government purchases were reduced by $60 and the price level remained unchanged?

2. Consider an economy similar to that in the preceding question in which investment is also $200, government purchases are also $500, net exports are also $30, and the price level is also fixed. But taxes now vary with income and, as a result, the consumption schedule looks like the following:

GDP	Taxes	DI	C
$1,360	$320	$1,040	$810
1,480	360	1,120	870
1,600	400	1,200	930
1,720	440	1,280	990
1,840	480	1,360	1,050

Find the equilibrium graphically. What is the marginal propensity to consume? What is the tax rate? Use your diagram to show the effect of a decrease of $60 in government purchases. What is the multiplier? Compare this answer to your answer to Question 1 above. What do you conclude?

3. Return to the hypothetical economy in Question 1, and now suppose that *both* taxes and government purchases are increased by $120. Find the new equilibrium under the

assumption that consumer spending continues to be exactly three-quarters of disposable income (as it is in Question 1).

4. Suppose you are put in charge of fiscal policy for the economy described in Question 1 above. There is an inflationary gap, and you want to reduce income by $120. What specific actions can you take to achieve this goal?

5. Now put yourself in charge of the economy in Question 2 and suppose that full employment comes at a GDP of $1,840. How can you push income up to that level?

DISCUSSION QUESTIONS

1. The U.S. federal budgets for national defence and homeland security both rose rapidly after the September 11 attacks. How would GDP in the United States have been affected if this higher spending on national security led to:

   a. Larger budget deficits?

   b. Less spending elsewhere in the budget, so that total government purchases remained the same?

2. Explain why G has the same multiplier as I, but taxes have a different multiplier.

3. If the government decides that aggregate demand is excessive and is causing inflation, what options are open to it? What if the government decides that aggregate demand is too weak instead?

4. Which of the proposed supply-side tax cuts appeals to you most? Draw up a list of arguments for and against enacting such a cut right now.

5. **(More difficult)** Advocates of lower taxes on capital gains argue that this type of tax cut will raise aggregate supply by spurring business investment. But, of course, any increase in investment spending will also raise aggregate demand. Compare the effects on aggregate supply, aggregate demand, and tax revenues of three different ways to cut the capital gains tax:

   a. Reduce capital gains taxes on *all* investments, including those that were made before tax rates were cut.

   b. Reduce capital gains taxes only on investments made after tax rates are cut.

   c. Reduce capital gains taxes only on certain types of placements, such as corporate stocks and bonds.

   Which of the three options seems most desirable to you? Why?

APPENDIX *Algebraic Treatment of Fiscal Policy*

In this appendix, we explain the simple algebra behind the fiscal policy multipliers discussed in the chapter. In so doing, we deal only with a simplified case in which prices do not change. Although it is possible to work out the corresponding algebra for the more realistic aggregate demand and supply analysis with variable prices, the analysis is rather complicated and is best left to more advanced courses.

Most of the taxes collected by the Canadian government—indeed, by all national governments—rise and fall with GDP. In some cases, the reason is obvious: *Personal* and *corporate income tax* collections, for example, depend on how much income there is to be taxed. *Sales tax* receipts depend on GDP because consumer spending is higher when GDP is higher. However, other types of tax receipts—such as property taxes—do not vary with GDP. We call the first kind of tax **variable taxes** and the second kind **fixed taxes**. We first deal with variable taxes.

We start with the example used in Appendix C of Chapter 9. The government spends $1,300 billion on goods and services (G = 1,300) and levies an income tax equal to 20 percent of GDP. So, if the symbol T denotes tax receipts,

$$T = 0.20Y$$

Because the consumption function we have been working with is

$$C = 300 + 0.75DI$$

where *DI* is disposable income, and because disposable income and GDP are related by the accounting identity

$$DI = Y - T$$

it follows that the C schedule used in the 45° line diagram is described by the following algebraic equation:

$$C = 300 + 0.75(Y - T)$$
$$= 300 + 0.75(Y - 0.20Y)$$
$$= 300 + 0.75(0.80Y)$$
$$= 300 + 0.60Y$$

We can now apply the equilibrium condition:

$$Y = C + I + G + (X - IM)$$

Because investment in this example is I = 900 and net exports are −100, substituting for C, I, G, and (X − IM) into this equation gives:

$$Y = 300 + 0.60Y + 900 + 1,300 - 100$$
$$0.40Y = 2,400$$
$$Y = 6,000$$

This is all there is to finding equilibrium GDP in an economy with a government.

To find the multiplier for government spending, increase G by 1 and solve the problem again:

$$Y = C + I + G + (X - IM)$$

$$Y = 300 + 0.60Y + 900 + 1,301 - 100$$

$$0.40Y = 2,401$$

$$Y = 6,002.5$$

Thus, the multiplier is $6,002.5 - 6,000 = 2.5$, as stated in the text.

To find the multiplier for an increase in fixed taxes, change the tax schedule as follows:

$$T = 0.20Y + 1$$

Disposable income is then

$$DI = Y - T = Y - (0.20Y + 1) = 0.80Y - 1$$

so the consumption function is

$$C = 300 + 0.75DI$$

$$= 300 + 0.75(0.80Y - 1)$$

$$= 299.25 + 0.60Y$$

Solving for equilibrium GDP as usual gives:

$$Y = C + I + G + (X - IM)$$

$$Y = 299.25 + 0.60Y + 900 + 1,300 - 100$$

$$0.40Y = 2,399.25$$

$$Y = 5,998.125$$

So a \$1 increase in fixed taxes lowers Y by \$1.875. The tax multiplier is -1.875, which is 75 percent of -2.5.

Now let us proceed to a more general solution, using symbols rather than specific numbers. The equations of the model are as follows:

$$Y = C + I + G + (X - IM) \qquad (1)$$

is the usual equilibrium condition.

$$C = a + bDI \qquad (2)$$

is the same consumption function we used in Appendix C of Chapter 9.

$$DI = Y - T \qquad (3)$$

is the accounting identity relating disposable income to GDP.

$$T = T_0 + tY \qquad (4)$$

is the tax function, where T_0 represents fixed taxes (which are zero in our numerical example) and t represents the tax rate (which is 0.20 in the example). Finally, I, G, and $(X - IM)$ are just fixed numbers.

We find the solution by first substituting Equations (3) and (4) into Equation (2) to derive the consumption schedule relating C to Y:

$$C = a + bDI$$

$$C = a + b(Y - T)$$

$$C = a + b(Y - T_0 - tY)$$

$$C = a - bT_0 + b(1 - t)Y \qquad (5)$$

Notice that a change in fixed taxes (T_0) shifts the *intercept* of the C schedule, whereas a change in the tax rate (t) changes its *slope*.

Next, substitute Equation (5) into Equation (1) to find equilibrium GDP:

$$Y = C + I + G + (X - IM)$$

$$Y = a - bT_0 + b(1 - t)Y + I + G + (X - IM)$$

$$[1 - b(1 - t)]\, Y = a - bT_0 + I + G + (X - IM)$$

or

$$Y = \frac{a - bT_0 + I + G + (X - IM)}{1 - b(1 - t)} \qquad (6)$$

Equation (6) shows us that the multiplier for G, I, a, or $(X - IM)$ is

$$\text{Multiplier} = \frac{1}{1 - b(1 - t)}$$

To see that this is in fact the multiplier, raise any of G, I, a, or $(X - IM)$ by one unit. In each case, Equation (6) would be changed to read:

$$Y = \frac{a - bT_0 + I + G + (X - IM) + 1}{1 - b(1 - t)}$$

Subtracting Equation (6) from this expression gives the change in Y stemming from a one-unit change in G, I, or a:

$$\text{Change in } Y = \frac{1}{1 - b(1 - t)}$$

In Chapter 9 (page 204), we noted that if there were no income tax ($t = 0$), a realistic value for b (the marginal propensity to consume) would yield a multiplier of 20, which is much bigger than the true multiplier. Now that we have added taxes to the model, our multiplier formula produces much more realistic numbers. Approximate values for these parameters for the Canadian economy are $b = 0.95$ and $t = \frac{1}{3}$. The multiplier formula then gives

$$\text{Multiplier} = \frac{1}{1 - 0.95(1 - \frac{1}{3})}$$

$$= \frac{1}{1 - 0.633} = \frac{1}{0.367} = 2.72$$

which is much closer to its actual estimated value—between 1.5 and 2 (to find an actual value of 1.5, combine the above analysis with that of induced imports on page 219).

Finally, we can see from Equation (6) that the multiplier for a change in fixed taxes (T_0) is:

$$\text{Tax Multiplier} = \frac{-b}{1 - b(1 - t)}$$

For the example considered in the text and earlier in this appendix, $b = 0.75$ and $t = 0.20$; so the formula gives:

$$\frac{-0.75}{1 - 0.75(1 - 0.20)} = \frac{-0.75}{1 - 0.75(0.80)}$$

$$= \frac{-0.75}{1 - 0.60} = \frac{-0.75}{0.40} = -1.875$$

According to these figures, each \$1 *increase* in T_0 *reduces* Y by \$1.875.

SUMMARY

1. Precisely *how* a tax change affects the consumption schedule depends on whether **fixed taxes** or **variable taxes** are changed.

2. Shifts of the consumption function caused by tax policy are subject to the same multiplier as autonomous shifts in G, I, or $X - IM$.

3. Because tax changes affect C only indirectly, the multiplier for a change in T is smaller than the multiplier for a change in G.

4. The government's net effect on aggregate demand—and hence on equilibrium output and prices—depends on whether the expansionary effects of its spending are greater or smaller than the contractionary effects of its taxes.

KEY TERMS

Variable taxes   256

Fixed taxes   256

TEST YOURSELF

1. Consider an economy described by the following set of equations:

$$C = 120 + 0.80DI$$
$$I = 320$$
$$G = 480$$
$$(X - IM) = -80$$
$$T = 200 + 0.25Y$$

Find the equilibrium level of GDP. Next, find the multipliers for government purchases and for fixed taxes. If full employment comes at $Y = 1,800$, what are some policies that would move GDP to that level?

2. This question is a variant of the previous problem that approaches things in the way that a fiscal policy planner might. In an economy whose consumption function and tax function are as given in Question 1, with investment fixed at 320 and net exports fixed at -80, find the value of G that would make GDP equal to 1,800.

3. You are given the following information about an economy:

$$C = 0.90DI$$
$$I = 100$$
$$G = 540$$
$$(X - IM) = -40$$
$$T = \tfrac{1}{3}Y$$

a. Find equilibrium GDP and the budget deficit.

b. Suppose the government, unhappy with the budget deficit, decides to cut government spending by precisely the amount of the deficit you just found. What actually happens to GDP and the budget deficit, and why?

4. **(More difficult)** In the economy considered in Question 3, suppose the government, seeing that it has not wiped out the deficit, keeps cutting G until it succeeds in balancing the budget. What level of GDP will then prevail?

DISCUSSION QUESTIONS

1. When the income tax rate declines, as it has in Canada recently, does the multiplier go up or down? Explain why.

2. Discuss the pros and cons of having a higher or lower multiplier.

12

MONEY AND THE BANKING SYSTEM

[Money] is a machine for doing quickly and commodiously what would be done, though less quickly and commodiously, without it.

JOHN STUART MILL (1806–1873), 1848

The circular flow diagrams of earlier chapters had a "financial system" in the upper-left corner. (Look back, for example, at Figure 1 of Chapter 9 on page 193.) Saving flowed into this system and investment flowed out. Something obviously goes on *inside* the financial system where savings are deposited and funds are borrowed to finance spending, and it is time we learned just what this something is.

There is another, equally important, reason for studying the financial system. The government exercises significant control over aggregate demand by manipulating *monetary policy* as well as fiscal policy. Indeed, nowadays monetary policy is the most widely accepted tool for macroeconomic stabilization. To understand how monetary policy works (the subject of Chapters 13 and 14), we must first acquire some understanding of the banking and financial system. By the end of this chapter, you will have that understanding.

CONTENTS

ISSUE: *Why Are Banks So Heavily Regulated?*

In all countries, banking has long been one of the most heavily regulated industries. Governments have determined who could participate in the industry, what could be sold, to whom it could be sold, and at what price it could be sold (that is, how high the interest rate could be). With the exception of the regulation of certain strategic sectors such as parts of the communication and energy sectors, there are few examples of such strict regulation.

Much of what is supplied by the banking sector today would not have been available to us over a century ago. For instance, in the nineteenth century, banks could make only short-term loans to businesses. Personal consumer loans were not available in Canada before 1936. The residential mortgage market (loans to purchase homes) was opened up to banks only in 1954. Following the trend in the United States, most restrictions on interest rates were lifted in Canada during the 1960s. Before 1980, foreign banks were not authorized to operate in the same way as domestic banks. The ownership of insurance and trust subsidiaries became possible for banks only in 1992. The slow but steady deregulation of the banking sector over the last century has gradually blurred the distinction between banks and other financial institutions. Despite these major changes, a quick trip to the website of the Canadian Bankers Association would reveal that banks are still heavily regulated.

How much bank regulation is enough—or too much? To answer this question, we must first address a more basic one: why are banks so heavily regulated in the first place? The main answer is that banking is a very special industry. But why? Reading this chapter will provide you with the answer to this question.

BANKING AS A SPECIAL INDUSTRY

Banking is special because the major "output" of the banking industry is the *nation's money supply*. As purveyors of liquidity, banks play a strategic role in the financing of aggregate spending and, therefore, in the determination of aggregate demand. The macroeconomic performance of an economy depends critically on its financial sector. While banks advance credit to households and firms based on purely private profit considerations, the government must set the framework for banking activity on the basis of more than what may be good for bank managers and bank shareholders. Above all, the monetary authorities must set the parameters for banking operation by considering what is best for the economy as a whole.

A second reason for the extensive web of bank regulation is concern for the *financial viability* of the entire system and, particularly, the safety of depositors. In a market economy, new businesses are born and die every day, and no one other than the people directly involved take much notice. When a firm goes bankrupt, employees lose their jobs and shareholders lose the funds they had invested. But, except for the case of very large firms where more than the local employer and workers are affected, that is about all that happens.

If banks were treated like other firms, depositors would lose money whenever one went bankrupt. That outcome would be bad enough by itself, but the real danger when a bank appears to be in trouble is the possibility of a **bank run**. When depositors become nervous about the security of their money, they may all rush to close out their accounts. For reasons we will learn about in this chapter, most banks cannot survive such a "run" and would be forced to shut their doors.

Worst yet, this disease is highly contagious. If one family hears that their neighbours just lost their life savings because their bank went broke, they are likely to rush to their own bank to withdraw their funds. In fact, that is precisely what happened in Argentina when people lost confidence in the local banks in 2002.[1]

A **bank run** (also called a run on a bank) occurs when many depositors withdraw cash from their accounts all at once.

---

[1] As will be explained in Chapter 18, the Argentine crisis had much to do with worries about the exchange rate between the Argentine peso and the U.S. dollar.

Without modern forms of bank regulation, therefore, one bank failure might lead to another. For reasons having to do with the concentrated system of banking in Canada and because of regulatory measures put in place by successive federal governments going back to the nineteenth century, bank failures have not been as common an occurrence as they were during the nineteenth century prior to the tightening of banking regulations and in the early twentieth century. Indeed, the last major bank default in Canada was the Home Bank in 1923. Since then, only three small regional banks and one foreign subsidiary have failed: The Canadian Commercial Bank and the Northland Bank went under in 1985, the Bank of British Columbia in 1986, and the Bank of Credit and Commerce Canada in 1991. Ideally, there should not be any bank defaults, but five bank failures in a little less than a century does not look so bad when compared to the literally thousands of banks that failed in the United States during the same period. On the other hand, almost 40 non-bank financial institutions—mainly trust and mortgage companies—have gone bankrupt in Canada since 1967, suggesting that we are not that far from the kind of financial instabilities that were still plaguing the American financial system as this book was being written.

THE NATURE OF MONEY

Competing Views on the Origin of Money

Money is so much a part of our daily life that we take it for granted and fail to understand its role and how it came to be. But money is in no sense "natural." Like the wheel, it had to be invented.

Where does money come from? Why did it have to be invented? Although ancient writings do provide valuable insights on how this came about, economists have been and still remain somewhat divided on the origin of money. Broadly speaking, economists have offered at least two different accounts on why money was invented.

The first of these is the tale of the emergence of **barter**—a system in which people exchange one good directly for another so as to reap the rewards of the division of labour—and how then money had to be invented to minimize the transaction costs associated with barter exchange. Once humans discovered the benefits arising from the division of labour, the historical sequence is simple: First, markets characterized by barter exchange that predate money appeared, and then money, usually in the form of precious metals, emerged for efficiency reasons to facilitate exchange.

> **Barter** is a system of exchange in which people directly trade one good for another, without using money as an intermediate step.

Barter is extremely cumbersome. If you grow corn and crave peanuts, you must find someone who is a peanut farmer and craves corn (a situation called the *double coincidence of wants*). In addition, unlike money, commodities are not easily portable, divisible, fungible, nor storable. Because money has these unique features, it facilitates the task of exchanging goods. Hence, the invention of money was the natural outcome of the cost-minimizing behaviour of private participants in the context of market exchange. Government played no role in this process, other than to officially recognize a particular commodity as its legal tender. This approach is sometimes referred to as the **metallist** or **commodity view of money**, a view that was strongly supported by Austrian economist Carl Menger (1840–1921).

> The **metallist** or **commodity concept of money** identifies money primarily as a commodity possessing an intrinsic value that emerged spontaneously to facilitate exchange of goods or services and to overcome the problem of double coincidence of wants related to barter exchange.

The second tale deemphasizes the market exchange aspect of money. It points, instead, to the strategic role of government (the state) in explaining the origin and evolution of money. According to this alternative view, money is a creation of the state that allowed individuals to discharge their obligation (or debt) to the state.

Regardless of the nature of the economic system, the citizens of all organized communities must ultimately pay for the proper functioning of the state sector. In ancient command economies, this obligation was paid in kind. This could be in the form of a *corvée*, where an individual had to work directly for the state for a certain part of the year to build a road, for instance, or it could be a tax levied in proportion to the physical quantities of goods produced by households during the year—for example, as a percentage of the wheat harvested by a farmer.

To facilitate the task of discharging one's tax obligation, money was invented that could relieve the government of ordering individuals to directly pay taxes in kind. Instead of requiring each citizen to work, say, one day per week to build a road, the state could hire a contractor to build the road, pay the contractor with state-issued money, and then require that all individuals pay their taxes with state-issued money. This token money would thus be demanded by whoever (1) needed to discharge their own tax liability levied by the state in money form or (2) wished to claim part of existing private sector output exchanged in the marketplace by others also in need of this state-issued money, so that they could free themselves of their own tax obligations to the government. This latter approach is often described as the **state** or **chartalist theory of money**, and is mainly associated with German monetary theorist Georg Friedrich Knapp (1842–1926) and well-known British economist John Maynard Keynes (1883–1946).

Notwithstanding the fact that the first approach traces the origin of money to a market phenomenon while the second sees it as a creature of the state, both approaches recognize the superiority of a monetary to a barter economy. Each approach presents interesting and relatively plausible explanations of the origin of money, even though there is probably greater historical evidence supporting the latter view.[2] Because of its greater simplicity and logical plausibility, the concept of money emerging from barter remains the dominant approach in economics. However, regardless of the exact origin of money, almost all economists see a monetary economy as a tremendous improvement when compared to a nonmonetary economy. Indeed, the best way to appreciate what monetary exchange accomplishes is to imagine a world without it.

The **state** or **chartalist concept of money** identifies money primarily as a unit of account created by the state to permit individuals to discharge their obligations to the state, which evolved also as a medium of exchange in market transactions.

The Conceptual Definition of Money

Under monetary exchange, people trade **money** for goods when they purchase something, and they trade goods for money when they sell something, but they do not trade goods directly for other goods. This practice defines money's principal role as the **medium of exchange**. But once it has become accepted as the medium of exchange, whatever serves as money is bound to serve other functions as well. For one, it will inevitably become the **unit of account**—that is, the standard unit for quoting prices. Thus, if inhabitants of an idyllic tropical island use coconuts as money, they would be foolish to quote prices in terms of seashells.

Money also may come to be used as a **store of value**. If the corn sales of farmers bring in more value than they want to spend right away, they may find it convenient to store the difference temporarily in the form of money. They know that money can be "sold" easily for goods and services at a later date, whereas land, gold, and other stores of value might not be. Of course, if inflation is substantial, they may decide to forgo the convenience of money and store their wealth in some other form rather than see its purchasing power eroded. So money's role as a store of value is far from inevitable.

Because money may not always serve as a store of value, and because other commodities may act as stores of value, we will not include the store-of-value function as part of our conceptual definition of money. Instead, we simply label as "money" whatever serves as the medium of exchange.

Money is the standard object used in exchanging goods and services. In short, money is the **medium of exchange**.

The **medium of exchange** is the object or objects used to buy and sell other items such as goods and services.

The **unit of account** is the standard unit for quoting prices.

A **store of value** is an item used to store wealth from one point in time to another.

What Serves as Money?

Although questions are sometimes raised as to whether some ancient societies can be correctly described as "monetary" economies, anthropologists and historians can testify that a bewildering variety of objects have served as money in different times and

---

[2] See Charles Goodhart, "The Two Concepts of Money: Implications for the Analysis of Optimal Currency Areas," *European Journal of Political Economy, 14*(3), 1998, pp. 407–432.

The Changing Face of Canadian Bank Notes

Until 1934, when the Bank of Canada—the Canadian central bank—was founded, the supply of paper money had been a shared responsibility between private banks and the government, beginning with the establishment of Canada's first chartered bank (the Bank of Montreal) in 1817. Between 1817 and Confederation, notes in circulation were predominantly privately issued chartered bank notes. However, between Confederation and 1934, the composition changed in favour of government notes—the "Dominion notes." In 1935, with the central bank having been awarded a monopoly over the issue of bank notes, the first series of Bank of Canada notes appeared.

In addition to satisfying public desire for a certain quantity of paper money, the Bank of Canada must also ensure high-quality bank notes that are not easily counterfeited, with special security features such as holographic stripe, security thread, ghost image, see-through number, and fluorescence. Canada's bank notes are made of 100 percent cotton paper—a material that is more resistant to wear and tear than wood-pulp paper. Given the relative use that the Canadian public makes of these bank notes in circulation, $5 and $10 bills last only about one to two years, while at the other extreme, a $100 bill lasts between seven and nine years before replacement is required.

Since the original series of 1935, Bank of Canada notes have gone through periodic redesigning. The images of British monarchs and famous Canadian prime ministers decorate the front of the bank notes and various themes are represented on the back, depicting Canadian physical and industrial landscapes, Canadian wildlife, and Canadian culture. Since 1935, the Bank of Canada has designed six such distinct series, as shown in the accompanying illustrations.

SOURCE: Bank of Canada. Retrieved from www.bank-banque-canada.ca/en/banknotes/general/character/index.html

SOURCE: Jonathan Noden-Wilkinson/Shutterstock

2001–2004 Series: *Canadian Journey* These notes (presently in circulation) are distinguished by new and enhanced security features, world-class designs, and a tactile feature to help the blind and visually impaired identify the different denominations.

SOURCE: Kenneth V. Pilon/Shutterstock

1954 Series *Significant changes to the design of Canada's paper currency gave it a whole new look that set the standard for the future.*

SOURCE: Alphonse Tran/Shutterstock

1986 Series: *Birds of Canada* The 1986 series of bank notes was designed with enhanced security features to counter developments in colour-copier technology.

SOURCE: Kenneth V. Pilon/Shutterstock

1937 Series *The 1937 series of bank notes saw the portrait of King George VI replace those of other members of the royal family.*

SOURCE: Alphonse Tran/Shutterstock

1969–1979 Series *The main characteristic of this series was the use of multicoloured tints beneath the dominant colour.*

SOURCE: National Currency Collection, Currency Museum, Bank of Canada

1935 Series *On March 11, 1935, the Bank of Canada issued its first series of bank notes.*

Commodity money is an object in use as a medium of exchange, but which also has a substantial value in alternative (nonmonetary) uses.

places. Cattle, stones, candy bars, cigarettes, woodpecker scalps, porpoise teeth, and giraffe tails provide a few of the more colourful examples.

In primitive or less organized societies, the commodities that served as money generally held value in themselves. If not used as money, cattle could be slaughtered for food, cigarettes could be smoked, and so on. But such **commodity money** generally runs into several severe difficulties. To be useful as a medium of exchange, a commodity must be easily divisible—which makes cattle a poor choice. It must also be of uniform, or at least readily identifiable, quality so that inferior substitutes are easy to recognize. This shortcoming may be why woodpecker scalps never achieved great popularity. The medium of exchange must also be storable and durable, which presents a serious problem for candy-bar money. Finally, because people will carry and store commodity money, it is helpful if the item is compact—that is, if it has high value per unit of volume and weight.

All of these traits make it natural that gold and silver have circulated as money since the first coins were struck about 2,500 years ago. Because they have high value in nonmonetary uses, a lot of purchasing power can be carried without too much weight. Pieces of gold are also storable, divisible (with a little trouble), and of identifiable quality (with a little more trouble).

The same characteristics suggest that paper would make an even better money. The Chinese invented paper money in the eleventh century, and Marco Polo brought the idea to Europe. Because we can print any number on it that we please, we can make paper money as divisible as we like. People can also carry a large value of paper money in a lightweight and compact form. Paper is easy to store and, with a little cleverness, we can make counterfeiting challenging, although never impossible. (See the box on Canada's bank notes.)

Paper cannot, however, serve as commodity money because its value per square centimetre in alternative uses is so low. A paper currency that is repudiated by its issuer can, perhaps, be used as wallpaper or to wrap fish, but these uses will surely represent only a small fraction of the paper's value as money. Contrary to the popular expression, such a currency literally *is* worth the paper it is printed on—which is to say that it is not worth much. Thus, paper money is always **fiat money**.

Fiat money is money that is decreed as such by the government. It is of little value as a commodity, but it maintains its value as a medium of exchange because people have faith that the issuer will stand behind the pieces of printed paper and limit their production.

Money in contemporary Canada is almost entirely fiat money. Look at, for example, a five-dollar bill. Just to the left of the image of Sir Wilfrid Laurier is the statement: "This note is legal tender," and the bill is signed in the bottom right-hand corner by the Governor and Deputy Governor of the Bank of Canada. Nowhere on the bank note is there a promise, stated or implied, that the Canadian government will exchange it for anything else. A five-dollar bill is convertible into, say, five "loonies" or 20 quarters—but not into milligrams of gold, kilograms of chocolate, or any other commodity.

Why do people hold these pieces of paper? It is because they know that the government will ultimately accept them in payment of taxes, while other participants in the economy are willing to accept them for things of intrinsic value—food, rent, shoes, and so on. If this confidence ever evaporated, your various Bank of Canada notes would cease serving as a medium of exchange and, given that they would probably make ugly wallpaper, would become virtually worthless.

But don't panic. Unless the government collapsed because of a war or a revolution and the new regime repudiated the previous bank notes and issued a new currency, as has happened at times in certain countries, there is no cause for concern. It is of interest to note that our monetary system has evolved over hundreds of years, during which *commodity money* was replaced by *full-bodied paper money*—paper certificates that were backed by gold and silver of equal value, supposedly held in the issuer's vaults. Then the full-bodied paper money was replaced by certificates that were only partially backed by gold and silver. Finally, we arrived at our present system, in which paper money has no "backing" whatsoever. Yet we continue to engage in monetary exchange, regardless of what "backs" our money. This proves, therefore, that what matters in determining the degree of confidence in a currency is whether others will accept it, particularly the government, and not whether it is backed by precious metals.

HOW THE QUANTITY OF MONEY IS MEASURED

Our conceptual definition of money as the medium of exchange raises difficult questions about just which items to include and which items to exclude when we count up the money supply. Such questions have long made the statistical definition of money a subject of dispute. In fact, the Bank of Canada has several official definitions of the money supply, two of which we will meet shortly.

Some components are obvious. All of our coins and paper money—the small change of our economic system—clearly should count as money. The sum of coins and paper money is called **currency**. But we cannot stop there if we want to include the main vehicle for making payments in our society, for the lion's share of our nation's payments are made neither in metal nor in paper money, but by cheque.

> **Currency** is the sum of coins and bank notes.

Chequable deposits are actually no more than bookkeeping entries in bank ledgers. Many people think of cheques as a convenient way to pass coins or dollar bills to someone else. But that is not so. For example, when you pay your sports club membership with a cheque for $500, dollar bills rarely change hands. Instead, that cheque normally travels back to your bank, where $500 is deducted from the bookkeeping entry that records your account and $500 is added to the bookkeeping entry for your club's account. (If you and the sports club hold accounts at different banks, more books get involved, but still no coins or bills will likely move.) The volume of money held in the form of chequable deposits far exceeds the volume of currency.

M1 and M1+

So it seems imperative to include chequable deposits in any useful definition of the money supply. Unfortunately, this is not an easy task nowadays, because of the wide variety of ways to transfer money by cheque. Traditional chequable accounts in commercial banks are the most familiar vehicle. But many people can also write cheques on their savings accounts, on their deposits at credit unions, on their mutual funds, on their accounts with stockbrokers, and so on.

One popular definition of the money supply, often referred to as the narrow definition of money, draws the line early and includes only currency held by the public and all chequable deposits at banks, credit unions, caisses populaires, and trust and mortgage loan companies. In the official Bank of Canada statistics, this narrowly defined concept of money is called **M1+**. Why is there a plus sign? It is because, up until very recently, the Bank of Canada kept track of an even narrower measure of money, called M1, which included only currency and conventional chequable accounts at banks. The upper part of Figure 1 shows the composition of the M1+ stock in December 2007. Currency represents only about 12 percent of the narrow definition of money.

> The narrowly defined money supply (M1+) is the sum of currency held by the public and all chequable deposits at banks, credit unions, caisses populaires, and trust and mortgage loan companies.

SOURCES: Bank of Canada, Weekly Financial Statistics, and computations by the authors.

M2+ and Other Definitions of the Money Supply

But the fact that an account is non-chequable does not mean that it should not be included in the money supply. Although you cannot write a cheque on a savings account, modern banking procedures have blurred the distinction

Two Definitions of the Money Supply, December 2007

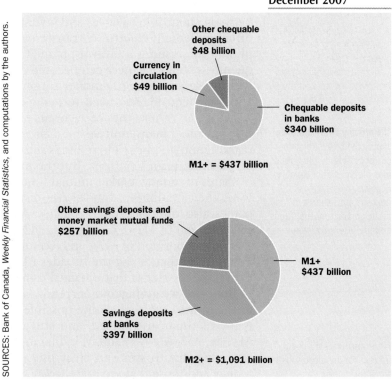

Other chequable deposits $48 billion

Currency in circulation $49 billion

Chequable deposits in banks $340 billion

M1+ = $437 billion

Other savings deposits and money market mutual funds $257 billion

M1+ $437 billion

Savings deposits at banks $397 billion

M2+ = $1,091 billion

Debit Cards, Credit Cards, and Electronic Money

Our discussion of the stock of money has emphasized the role of chequable deposit accounts. While cheques are still used to make payments, a lot of Canadians now use debit cards or credit cards when they purchase goods. What is the relationship between money and debit or credit cards? Take first the case of debit cards. These cards are a convenient means of payments that play the role of cheques. When you use your debit card to purchase goods from a merchant, the operation takes funds from your deposit account at your bank or financial institution and transfers these funds to the deposit account of the merchant, just like a cheque would, except that the operation is nearly instantaneous. Thus, debit cards are not "plastic money" as some people say; rather they are "plastic cheques" that transfer money from one deposit account to another.

Now what about credit cards? These are not money, either. Credit cards, as their name indicate, allow you to draw on a line of credit granted by the financial institution issuing the card, up to a maximum amount. When you use your credit card to pay a merchant, a loan is being automatically granted to you, while the financial institution transfers funds to the deposit account of the merchant. Whenever you use your credit card, money is being created, but that money is the addition to the deposit balance of the merchant. Similarly, when you wish to settle your credit card account, you do so by using the chequable deposit balance (the money) that you have at your financial institution.

SOURCE: Johnny Lye/Shutterstock

Since the 1990s, various forms of electronic money have been tested. Among these is the "smart card" or "electronic purse," which has an embedded memory chip that records the amount of money stored in the card, perhaps at an ATM, taken from your own deposit account. This is why these cards are also called *prepaid cards*. You can use the cash stored on the card to make purchases simply by inserting your card into specially designed slots in vending machines and store cash register equipment. Smart cards are another form of currency, designed to replace coins and bank notes.

Students who make transactions on eBay and other auction sites, or who purchase goods from online vendors, certainly know about PayPal. For a small percentage fee, this company allows individuals to make and receive payments on the Internet without knowing each other's bank account number or credit card number. Only PayPal has this information. Using their PayPal accounts to pay for purchases, participants transfer money from their bank into PayPal (or make use of a credit card). Those who receive payments can leave their balances in the PayPal account, and possibly earn interest, or they can transfer their funds to a bank account. The balances held in PayPal or other similar Internet payment accounts can be considered as electronic money, although these balances are not yet considered to be part of the money supply.

---

between chequable balances and savings balances. For example, most banks these days offer convenient electronic transfers of funds from one account to another by telephone, by pushing a button on an ATM, or by punching a computer key. Consequently, savings balances can become chequable almost instantly. For this reason, in a broader definition of the money supply, not only chequable deposits are included, but also nonchequable and fixed-term deposits.

However, other types of accounts also allow limited withdrawal rights by cheque. For instance, many mutual fund organizations and brokerage houses offer money market mutual funds. These funds sell shares and use the proceeds to purchase a variety of short-term securities. But the important point for our purposes is that owners of shares in money market mutual funds can withdraw their funds by writing cheques, using their holdings of fund shares just like chequable accounts. Life insurance companies also offer similar products. When all of these funds are added to savings accounts and to M1+, one obtains **M2+**.

The composition of M2+ in December 2007 is shown on the lower part of Figure 1. You can see that, using the broader M2+ definition of money results in a sum more than twice the size of that obtained using the narrow M1+ definition.

But once we go beyond currency and chequable deposits, many other definitions of the money supply become possible. The Bank of Canada has experimented with many of them in the past, and still uses measures of monetary aggregates called M1++, M2, M2++, and M3. The inescapable problem, however, is that there is no obvious place to stop, no clear line of demarcation between those assets that *are* money and those that are merely *close substitutes* for money—so-called **near moneys**.

The broadly defined money supply (**M2+**) is the sum of currency held by the public, plus all types of chequable deposits, plus savings deposits, plus shares in money market mutual funds and life insurance annuities.

Near moneys are liquid assets that are close substitutes for money.

If we define an asset's liquidity as the ease with which its holder can convert it into cash, there is a spectrum of assets of varying degrees of **liquidity**. Everything in M1+ is completely liquid, but money market fund shares are a bit less so, and so on, until we encounter items such as short-term government bonds, Canada Savings Bonds, and even standard mutual funds, which, while still liquid, would not normally be included in the money supply. Any number of different money supply variations can be defined—and have been—by drawing the line in different places. But an introductory course in economics is not the place to get bogged down in complex definitional issues. So we will simply adhere to the convention that:

> "Money" consists only of coins, bank notes, and chequable deposits.

An asset's **liquidity** refers to the ease with which it can be converted into cash.

■ THE BANKING SYSTEM

Now that we have defined money and seen how to measure it, we turn our attention to the principal creators of money—the banks. Banking is a complicated business—and getting more so. If you go further in your study of economics, you will probably learn more about the operations of banks. But for our present purposes, a few simple principles will suffice.

▨ Principles of Bank Management: Profits versus Safety

Bankers have a reputation for conservatism in politics, dress, and business affairs. From what has been said so far, the economic rationale for this conservatism should be clear. Chequable deposits are pure fiat money. Years ago, these deposits were partially backed by gold or silver, with the guarantee of banks to convert their clients' deposits into these precious metals. Then deposits became backed by nothing more than a particular bank's promise to convert them into currency on demand. If depositors lost trust in a bank, they would run to the bank to claim their gold or to obtain currency. The bank was then doomed, as the deposit balances of their depositors far exceeded the amounts of gold or currency that the bank held as reserves in its vaults.[3]

Thus, bankers have always relied on a reputation for prudence, which they have achieved in two principal ways. First, they have applied time-tested rules in providing loans, because any large losses on their loans would undermine their depositors' confidence. Second, they have been cautious in making financial investments and have maintained a sufficiently high level of liquid assets, such as government treasury bills, to minimize risk. Banks also used to hold a generous level of cash reserves to minimize their vulnerability to runs, as much as one-quarter of their liabilities, either of their own volition or as a result of compulsory reserve requirements. But, because of institutional changes, banks' holdings of liquid assets have gradually diminished, and cash reserves have practically disappeared nowadays (at about $5 billion, they represent only 1 percent of M1+).

It is important to realize that banking is an inherently risky business that is rendered safe only by cautious and prudent management and, as we will discuss below, by a body of regulations that minimize the risk to the public from unscrupulous banking practices. The history of banking does suggest that, unlike during the nineteenth century when bank failures were common, bank insolvencies are now a rare phenomenon. When complemented with an improved regulatory system in place, the Canadian banking industry seems to have learned from its past. But the risk is ever-present. Why?

Banks, like other enterprises, are in business to earn profits. The forerunners of bankers, goldsmiths, made profits from the direct services that they provided by storing the public's wealth for safekeeping. As goldsmiths became bankers, they also made profits by getting deposits at zero interest and lending some of the money out at positive interest rates. The history of banking as a profit-making industry has continued to this day, with about half of the banks' revenues being earned directly from the services they render to

---

[3] From this arose the idea, found in most textbooks, that the amount of bank deposits is some multiple of the banks' reserves. But this mechanism does not fit current institutions, and so will not be discussed here.

the public (including storage fees for keeping secure some of our most valuable items in safety deposit boxes) and the other half on the interest spread, that is, on the difference between the interest that they charge on bank loans and the interest they pay on bank deposits. But risky loans are normally associated with higher expected returns. Profits are high when a bank minimizes its portfolio of low-return liquid assets and maximizes the number of loans to some borrowers with questionable credit standing, who are charged higher interest rates. There is thus always an incentive to take on greater risk.

This was certainly demonstrated in the course of the so-called *subprime crisis*, which started in August 2007 and culminated in early 2008, when several banks and other financial institutions throughout the world ran into great financial difficulties. These banks had either made risky mortgage loans (so-called *subprime loans*) or had purchased financial assets backed by these risky loans. When housing prices in the United States stopped going up, an unusually high percentage of borrowers defaulted on their loans.

The art of bank management is to strike the appropriate balance between the lure of profits and the need for safety. If a banker errs by being too stodgy, his bank will earn inadequate profits. If he errs by taking unwarranted risks, his bank may not survive at all.

■ Bank Regulation

Banking is the cornerstone of the Canadian financial industry and accounts for more than 50 percent of the overall domestic assets of the financial sector. As of 2008, the Canadian financial sector included not only the 20 domestic banks, 24 foreign bank subsidiaries, and 22 foreign branch banks operating here, but also many trust companies, insurance companies, credit unions, and caisses populaires. About 90 percent of all of the assets of the banking sector are accounted for by Canada's six major banks, which have both domestic and international branches. These are all highly profitable enterprises that have played a crucial role in Canada's economic development.

Governments in virtually every society have decided that profit-minded bankers will not necessarily strike the right balance between profits and safety. So they have thrown up a web of regulations designed to ensure depositors' safety and the stability of the financial system. In Canada, there are five federal agencies with either a regulatory or a quasi-regulatory role, as well as a number of provincial agencies, whose overall purpose is to constitute Canada's "financial safety net." The five federal agencies are the Bank of Canada (because, as the Canadian central bank, it oversees the payment system), the Canadian Deposit Insurance Corporation (which insures deposits and sets the terms under which insurance is made available to its members), the federal Department of Finance (which develops rules and regulations applicable to financial institutions), the Financial Consumer Agency of Canada (which enforces the consumer-related provisions of the federal financial institution statutes), and the Office of the Superintendent of Financial Institutions (which is responsible for direct supervision of Canada's financial institutions). Let us look at a couple of these activities.

Deposit insurance is a system that guarantees that depositors will not lose money even if their bank goes bankrupt.

Deposit Insurance   The principal innovation that guarantees the safety of bank deposits is **deposit insurance**. Today, all deposits at chartered banks and most deposits in other financial institutions are insured against loss by the Canadian Deposit Insurance Corporation (CDIC), a federal Crown corporation established by Parliament in 1967, together with 10 provincial deposit insurers, including a special arrangement with Quebec's Autorité des Marchés Financiers (AMF). If your bank or other financial institution belongs to the CDIC, as almost all do, your account is insured for up to $100,000, regardless of what happens to the bank. Thus, while bank failures may spell disaster for the bank's shareholders, they are of little concern to many depositors, unless your deposits exceed $100,000 or unless you have chosen to hold more risky, uninsured bank liabilities. Deposit insurance eliminates the motive for customers to rush to their bank just because they hear some bad news about the bank's finances, thus greatly reducing the risk of a bank run.

While the purpose of the CDIC is to contribute to the stability of Canada's financial system, there has been some controversy as to how well it has done so since its creation in 1967. Some critics of deposit insurance worry that depositors who are freed from any risk of loss from a failing bank will not bother to shop around for safer banks. This problem is an example of what is called **moral hazard**—the general idea that, when people are well insured against a particular risk, they will put little effort into making sure that the risk does not occur. (Example: A business with good fire insurance may not install an expensive sprinkler system.) Hence, unlike most supporters who would agree that we have a safer system today than before 1967 (especially since each member institution is rated annually and is charged a premium on the basis of its score based on such factors as capital adequacy and asset quality), some of the critics argue that high levels of deposit insurance actually make the banking system less safe.

Moral hazard is the idea that people insured against the consequences of risk will engage in riskier behaviors.

Bank Supervision   Partly for this reason, the government takes several steps to see that banks do not get into financial trouble. The principal regulatory body that supervises financial institutions is the Office of the Superintendent of Financial Institutions (OSFI), which conducts periodic risk assessments of Canadian financial institutions (as well as pension plans) to determine whether they are on a sound financial footing and are complying with the OSFI's supervisory requirements. The OSFI's role of supervising chartered banks goes back to 1925, when it was established in response to the Home Bank failure of 1923. However, its present structure goes back to 1987, with further revisions in 1996, following the report of the Estey Commission of Inquiry on two bank failures that occurred in 1985. In particular, the OSFI must verify that a bank's capital is large enough relative to the size of its assets—a rule known as *capital adequacy requirements*. These minimum requirements, and their generalization to banks of many countries, have been spearheaded by the Bank for International Settlements, an international organization located in Basel, Switzerland. The OSFI can order external audits and ensure that the requirements are met, in extreme cases by taking direct control of the recalcitrant financial institution. Such supervision is clearly aimed at keeping banks safe.

■ HOW BANKERS KEEP BOOKS

Our objective is to understand how the money supply is determined. But before we can fully understand the process by which money is "created," we must acquire at least a nodding acquaintance with the mechanics of modern banking.

The first thing to know is how to distinguish assets from liabilities. An **asset** of a bank is something of value that the bank *owns*. This "thing" may be a physical object, such as the bank building or a computer, or it may be a piece of paper, such as an IOU from a customer to whom the bank has made a loan. A **liability** of a bank is something of value that the bank *owes*. Most bank liabilities take the form of bookkeeping entries. For example, if you have an account in the Main Street Bank, your bank balance is a liability of the bank. (It is, of course, an asset to you.)

There is an easy test for whether some piece of paper or bookkeeping entry is a bank's *asset* or *liability*. Ask yourself a simple question: If this paper were converted into cash, would the bank receive the cash (if so, it is an asset) or pay it out (if so, it is a liability)? This test makes it clear that loans to customers are assets of the bank (when a loan is repaid, the bank collects), whereas customers' deposits are bank liabilities (when a deposit is cashed in, the bank pays). Of course, things are just the opposite to the bank's customers: The loans are liabilities and the deposits are assets.

When accountants draw up a complete list of all the bank's assets and liabilities, the resulting document is called the bank's **balance sheet**. Typically, the value of all the bank's assets exceeds the value of all its liabilities. (On the rare occasions when this is not so, the bank is in serious trouble.) In what sense, then, do balance sheets "balance"?

They balance because accountants have invented the concept of **net worth** to balance the books. Specifically, they define the net worth of a bank to be the *difference* between the value of all its assets and the value of all its liabilities. Thus, by definition, when accountants add net worth to liabilities, the sum they get must be

An **asset** of an individual or business firm is an item of value that the individual or firm owns.

A **liability** of an individual or business firm is an item of value that the individual or firm owes. Many liabilities are known as *debts*.

A **balance sheet** is an accounting statement listing the values of all assets on the left side and the values of all liabilities and *net worth* on the right side.

Net worth is the value of all assets minus the value of all liabilities.

TABLE 1			
Balance Sheet of Bank-a-Mythica, as of December 31, 2008			
Assets		Liabilities and Net Worth	
Assets		**Liabilities**	
Currency (bank notes, and coin)	$100,000	Chequable deposits	$5,000,000
Securities	$1,000,000	**Net Worth**	
Loans outstanding	$4,400,000	Bank's capital	$500,000
Total	**$5,500,000**	Total	**$5,500,000**

equal to the value of the bank's assets:

Assets = Liabilities + Net worth

Table 1 illustrates this point with the balance sheet of a fictitious bank, Bank-a-Mythica, whose finances are extremely simple. On December 31, 2008, the bank had only three kinds of assets (listed on the left side of the balance sheet): $100,000 in bank notes and coin (cash), held in its vault or in ATMs; $1 million in securities, that is bills or bonds issued by the Canadian government or by private corporations and purchased by the bank; and $4.4 million in outstanding loans to its customers, that is, in customers' IOUs. And it had only one type of liability (listed on the right side)—$5 million in chequing deposits. The difference between total assets ($5.5 million) and total liabilities ($5.0 million) was the bank's net worth ($500,000), also shown on the right side of the balance sheet. The net worth is often called the bank's *capital* or *shareholders' equity*. It is this bank's capital that must remain large enough relative to total assets, in agreement with existing **capital adequacy requirements**, as pointed out on page 269.

To meet **capital adequacy requirements**, a bank's capital must be large enough relative to the size of its assets, most notably the size of its loans.

MONEY CREATION IN A BANKING SYSTEM WITH A SINGLE BANK

The process of money creation is perhaps the most intriguing aspect of the economic system and has given rise to the most extraordinary and extravagant theories. Besides economists, it has attracted the attention of all sorts of people, from majors in the army to chemistry Nobel laureates. Still, the process of money creation is very simple and can be easily understood by all. Money creation, or rather bank deposit creation as we will analyze it here, is not alchemy. It relies mainly on three features of the banking system: the willingness of banks to grant loans, the creditworthiness of borrowers, and the willingness of borrowers to take on the burden of loans.

Loans Make Deposits

To understand how money deposits are created, start by imagining that the banking system is made up of a single bank that has a total monopoly on the provision of loans and deposits in the economy—a *monocentric system*. All financial transactions have to transit through this single bank. Every economic agent has an account at this bank. Some agents have a negative account, in which case they have outstanding loans at the bank; other agents have a positive account, in which case they have deposits at the bank. How are new bank deposits created? Here we will deal with only the major creation channel.

Suppose that an individual wants to purchase some goods or services, but does not have the funds to do so. It may be a student who wants to purchase a new car, or an entrepreneur who is anxious to hire new workers and increase production, having just received additional orders for her product. To make their objectives possible, both the student and the entrepreneur have to borrow from the bank. Will the loan be granted? The answer is yes, as long as the borrower is **creditworthy**, that is, has an acceptable credit rating or has an asset that can be used to secure the loan (**collateral**). The word *credit* comes from the Latin word *credere*, which means to believe or to trust. Trustworthy people or organizations with a history of repaying their debts or with collateral can get bank loans.

How can the borrowers demonstrate their creditworthiness? They can prove that their past credit record is impeccable, that they have repaid previous loans, with interest, in full. Or they can show that their current income is high compared to the pay-

Creditworthiness is demonstrated by providing collateral or by demonstrating the ability to fulfill loan obligations.

Collateral is property (e.g., car, house, business inventory, government securities) that is pledged by the borrower as security for a loan.

ments required for the loan they want (such ratios are now generated automatically by bank computer programs, which identify whether the customer is not creditworthy or tell the loan officer how much can be lent, and at what rate). Or they can show proof that the goods that they are about to produce have already been ordered by some other firm that is capable of paying for the goods. Or they can provide collateral that the bank can seize in case they are unable to repay the loan. In the case of a loan to purchase a house—a mortgage loan—the collateral is the house being purchased. In the case of a car loan, the collateral is likely to be the car itself. Sometimes collateral is financial assets, such as stocks, corporate bonds, and government securities. In some cases, expected future income is accepted as the basis for a loan, as seems to be the case for some medical and dentistry students. If a person has none of the above qualification requirements for a loan, someone else may back the loan (e.g., a student's mother), in which case, that person must be approved by the bank as being creditworthy and must meet one or more of the criteria listed above.

So let us suppose that indeed the borrower is creditworthy. What happens next? The answer is simple: A bank loan is created *ex nihilo*—Latin for *out of nothing*—with the stroke of a pen, or rather, in our modern world, by pressing a key on a computer. Simultaneously, as the bank loan is created, a new bank deposit is also created.

Suppose that on January 2, 2009, a creditworthy borrower is granted a new loan of $40,000 (for quite a nice car!). The effects on Bank-a-Mythica, which holds a monopoly on banking services, are shown in Table 2. The bank now has $40,000 more in loans on the asset side of its balance sheet, but simultaneously, on the liability side, there is an increase of $40,000 in bank deposits. The minute the loan is granted, the car purchaser is credited with a money deposit of $40,000. This is money that the bank now owes to the car purchaser. This is why it is on the liability side of the bank's balance sheet. Tables such as this one, which shows *changes* in balance sheets rather than the balance sheets themselves, will help us follow the process of money creation and destruction.

There is nothing more to money creation. Since chequable bank deposits are part of M1+, the current narrowest money aggregate, Table 2 shows how most money is created in the modern world.

> For money creation to occur, all we need is a bank willing to lend and a creditworthy person willing to borrow.

What then happens next? Suppose that the car is purchased the next day, on January 3. The purchaser goes to the car dealer, most likely with a certified cheque in hand, and after having paid and signed all the papers, she drives off with the car. The car dealer deposits the cheque, still at Bank-a-Mythica, since this is the only bank in the country. The balance sheet of Bank-a-Mythica will show the changes indicated in Table 3.

By combining Tables 2 and 3, we arrive at Table 4, which summarizes the bank's overall transactions for those two days. The car purchaser still owes $40,000 to the bank, but all of the money is now in the car dealer's account.

As we pointed out on page 269, all of our balance sheet tables, such as Table 1 or Table 4, must *balance*. In all such tables, which are called *T-accounts*, the two sides of the ledger must carry equal

TABLE 2	
Changes in the Balance Sheet of Bank-a-Mythica, January 2, 2009	
Assets	Liabilities and Net Worth
Loan to car purchaser +$40,000	Deposit into car purchaser's account +$40,000

TABLE 3	
Changes in the Balance Sheet of Bank-a-Mythica, January 3, 2009	
Assets	Liabilities and Net Worth
	Deposit of car purchaser −$40,000
	Deposit of car dealer +$40,000

TABLE 4	
Changes in the Balance Sheet of Bank-a-Mythica, January 2–3, 2009	
Assets	Liabilities and Net Worth
Loan to car purchaser +$40,000	Deposit of car dealer +$40,000

total amounts. This balance is required because changes in assets and liabilities must be equal if the balance sheet is to balance both before and after the transactions.

▇ The Limits to Money Creation

One of the most striking features of the money creation process is that there seems to be no limit to how much money can be created. In a sense, this is true. The creation of money in the modern world is not limited by some scarce resource, such as the amount of gold that banks have accumulated in their vaults. Still, there are economic incentives that restrict the creation of money, even in a monocentric banking system.

The amount that the monopoly bank can lend is limited only by the three crucial features of the banking system that we identified earlier: the willingness of the bank to grant loans, the creditworthiness of borrowers, and the willingness of borrowers to take on loans. As in all economic transactions, both partners in the transaction need to be willing to engage in the transaction, both the bank and the borrower. But why would anyone but a lunatic turn down loan or credit card offers? The reason is that the borrower may be unwilling to get into debt and pay interest on this debt. Potential borrowers may also have no reason to spend more, or they may be afraid of going bankrupt and losing all of their wealth if they borrow too much, which is sometimes called the *borrower's risk*. Thus, borrowers, on their own, may willingly put limits on the amounts they wish to borrow.

Now let us look at the other side of the coin. Why would a monopoly bank be unwilling to lend? The primary reason is that the bank fears that some of its clients may be unable to repay their loans or make the interest payments that are due. This is the *lender's risk*. What are the consequences of this risk? First, banks are in the business of making profits, of having their revenues exceed their costs. Besides service fees, their revenues are the interest payments that they receive on their assets (their loans and the securities that they hold). The costs are the interest payments that they have to make on their liabilities (essentially on the deposits that people hold at the bank), plus the costs of operating a bank (such as employees' salaries, equipment purchases and rentals, and the costs of running the ATMs). If borrowers do not fulfill their loan repayment obligations, banks will experience losses, instead of making profits.

Bad loans have a second, less obvious, implication. Suppose the bank, by mistake, makes a loan of $200,000 to a person who is not creditworthy, and that this person turns out to be a crook. Instead of building a prosperous business with the borrowed money, the crook spends it all in bars, cars, and casinos. At the end of the year, the borrower has defaulted on the loan and has vanished, and the collateral that was offered to get the loan is worthless. There is no way that the loan can be recovered; it has to be considered as a bad loan, and thus must be entirely written off. While this is an extreme case, small businesses regularly go bankrupt (as do large corporations sometimes), because of poor planning, bad luck, or changing economic conditions. Their banks can recover only a portion of the loans that they granted. The rest has to be written off.

How will the bank accountants write off the debt? Since the $200,000 loan is now worth nothing, $200,000 must be removed from the bank assets on its balance sheet. But a T-account must always balance by definition. What other change must be made for the balance sheet to balance? Since the bank has suffered a $200,000 capital loss, it must be subtracted from the bank's capital, as shown in Table 5. Thus, the owners of the bank have lost $200,000, in addition to the forgone interest. Compared to the original situation described by Table 1, the bank has only $300,000 of its own funds left.

TABLE 5			
Balance Sheet of Bank-a-Mythica, December 31, 2009, After Accounting for Bad Loan			
Assets		Liabilities and Net Worth	
Assets		**Liabilities**	
Currency	$100,000	Chequable deposits	$5,000,000
Securities	$1,000,000	**Net Worth**	
Loans outstanding		Bank's capital	
($4,400,000 − $200,000)	$4,200,000	($500,000 − $200,000)	$300,000
Total	**$5,300,000**	Total	**$5,300,000**

Although Bank-a-Mythica is not in as good a shape as it was in Table 1, it is still **solvent**. In other words, despite the bad loan, the bank's capital is still positive, as its assets are still greater than its liabilities. However, if $900,000 worth of loans had turned out to be bad loans that year, $900,000 worth of loans would have been subtracted from the asset side of the balance sheet of Bank-a-Mythica, and $900,000 would have been subtracted from the bank's capital. But wait! The bank's capital was shown as being only $500,000 in Table 1. What happens now? The net worth of the bank becomes negative, standing at −$400,000. The bank is **insolvent**. Its liabilities—the deposits of its customers—are not covered by enough assets (the sum of securities and loans). The bank must declare bankruptcy, or its assets and liabilities will have to be taken over by some other bank. This is why the Office of the Superintendent of Financial Institutions, as noted earlier, verifies that Canadian banks fulfill capital adequacy requirements, and hence have enough capital to withstand a string of bad loans.

> A **solvent bank** has a positive net worth—its assets are greater than its liabilities.

> An **insolvent bank** has a negative net worth—its liabilities are greater than its assets.

The lesson to be drawn from this is that Bank-a-Mythica faces no limit as to the amount of loans it can make, and therefore to the amount of money it can create, except for its own fear of making losses and of possibly becoming insolvent. What limits the creation of money is the number of creditworthy borrowers and the willingness of these potential borrowers to borrow. If no one is willing to go into debt, no new loan will be granted and bank deposits will not grow. As the saying goes, you can lead a horse to water, but you can't make it drink!

It should also be clear that monetary relations are based on conventions, or on customs. The definition of a creditworthy borrower will not be the same everywhere at the same time. Someone classified as a creditworthy person today in Canada may not have been in the past, or in some other country. For instance, criteria to obtain mortgage loans are now much less stringent than they were in the past. Also, different banks may have different opinions about the creditworthiness of the same person. Since we are talking about different banks, this is a good time to move on to a banking system with several banks.

The Subprime Crisis

Canada's GDP fell in the first quarter of 2008 for the first time since 2001. Besides the high value of the Canadian dollar, this was widely attributed to the subprime financial crisis that hit our main trading partner—the United States. Why was it called a *subprime crisis*? Because loans at a rate above the prime interest rate made to not-so-creditworthy borrowers are called *subprime loans*. Many of these loans had been granted to American mortgage borrowers over the previous few years by banks and mortgage-specialized financial institutions.

But why would banks and other financial institutions make such risky loans? As discussed earlier in this chapter, financial institutions are driven by profit motives. Subprime loans carry higher interest rates and hence yield higher profits if everything goes well. If borrowers cannot afford to honour their monthly mortgage obligations, they have the option of selling their property. However, housing prices kept rising in the United States until mid-2006, meaning that a financially strapped borrower could sell the property, pay back the loan, and even make a profit. The financial institutions came out as the winners, whatever.

In addition, mortgage-specialized institutions started a new *originate and distribute* policy that lulled them into paying less attention to the creditworthiness of their borrowers. Under this policy, financial institutions package together a number of loans they have granted and then sell the packages as high-return securities to other financial institutions, including Japanese, European, and Canadian banks—a process known as *securitization*.

Everything started to collapse in 2007, however, when U.S. housing prices fell rapidly. Defaulting borrowers were unable to sell their properties at fair prices, so the value of individual loans and of securitized loans fell just as rapidly, precipitating a financial crisis. Banks and other financial institutions experienced huge capital losses, so large that a number of them, including the prominent U.S. investment bank Bear Stearns, became insolvent. Moreover, Freddie Mac and Fannie Mae, the two largest American mortgage refinancing companies—the pillars of the housing credit market in the United States—suffered such large liquidity losses in the summer of 2008, after the failure of IndyMac (a similar but smaller financial institution), that they had to be rescued by the American government. In Canada, banks remained solvent, thanks to their adequate capital reserves and the granting of fewer securitized subprime loans, but the Canadian Imperial Bank of Commerce had to issue a substantial amount of new shares to continue fulfilling its capital adequacy requirements.

Various amusing but very informative accounts of the subprime crisis can be found at http://www.youtube.com, by searching for the following keywords: "Bird and Fortune, subprime crisis."

MONEY CREATION IN A BANKING SYSTEM WITH SEVERAL BANKS

We have seen that loans made to individuals or corporations, and hence money creation, are based on trust. The same is true of relationships between banks. Whenever they engage in transactions with each other, banks must trust each other; otherwise, the banking system would grind to a halt, or the banks that are not trusted by the other banks would soon be unable to operate and their clients would suffer great inconvenience. Well-functioning banking systems have regulations that allow banks to make their transactions with each other with great confidence. In Canada, transactions between banks are regulated through the federal Payment Clearing and Settlement Act, which was proclaimed in 1996, and through the bylaws of the Canadian Payments Association. The Bank of Canada is a key player in this, since it oversees the payment system, and its role will be discussed further in the next chapter.

The Canadian Clearing and Settlement System

To understand the functioning of a banking system with multiple banks—a *polycentric* banking system—let us use the example of a Chevrolet car dealer who must pay for an allotment of cars that was sent to him by GM Canada. Suppose that in order to do so, the car dealer must get a loan for $400,000, thus increasing the amount borrowed from his bank, say, the Bank of Montreal, by $400,000, and ordering his bank to pay this amount to GM Canada. Let us suppose that GM Canada does business with another bank, say, the Toronto-Dominion Bank.

The **large-value transfer system (LVTS)** is the main Canadian clearing and settlement system, where banks exchange and deposit payment items for their clients, determine the net amounts owed to each, and settle their accounts at the end of the day.

Because the amount involved is large, the payment will go through an electronic-only payment system (instead of a paper payment system, such as is the case with ordinary cheques). In Canada, this electronic-only wire system is called the **large-value transfer system (LVTS)**, which has been operating since 1999. This is a clearing and settlement system in which banks and a few other participants in the LVTS, such as the Fédération des caisses Desjardins and, more importantly, the Bank of Canada, clear their payments and settle their accounts. About 90 percent of the value of bank payments go through the LVTS. From now on, the participants in the LVTS, with the exception of the Bank of Canada, will be referred to simply as "banks."

In our car dealer example, as soon as the $400,000 payment from the Bank of Montreal to the Toronto-Dominion bank is cleared, a $400,000 amount is deposited in the bank account of the car producer, GM Canada. Thus, a loan is initially granted by the Bank of Montreal, with deposit money created therein, but the deposit eventually ends up in an account at the Toronto-Dominion Bank. How will all this be entered in the balance sheets of the two banks at the moment that the transfer to the account of GM Canada occurs? Let us look at Table 6.

The Chevrolet car dealer has ordered his bank to transfer $400,000 of his newly acquired money to the deposit account of GM Canada at the Toronto-Dominion Bank. Now, as shown in the bottom part of Table 6, once the transfer is recorded through the LVTS, the Bank of Montreal owes this $400,000 amount to the clearing system—it is said to have a *negative* **LVTS balance** or to have a *debit LVTS position*—while the Toronto-Dominion Bank is said to hold a *positive* LVTS balance or to have a *credit LVTS position*. The system owes the Toronto-Dominion Bank $400,000.

The **LVTS balance** (either negative or positive) of a bank is the multilateral clearing position that the bank has attained in the large-value transfer system in the course of a day.

Things may change quite rapidly however. During the same day, GM Canada might have to pay its suppliers, producers of metals or plastics, several of whom may have accounts at the Bank of Montreal. In that event, payments will have to flow from the Toronto-Dominion Bank to the Bank of Montreal, and the positive LVTS balance of the Toronto-Dominion Bank may be reduced to close to zero, or may even become negative. And as further payment orders come in during the day, there will be further changes to the net position of each bank.

The net amount that each participating financial institution is permitted to owe is subject to bilateral and multilateral limits. As with individuals, transactions between banks are closely monitored with the help of credit ratios. These ratios depend on the

TABLE 6

The Money Creation Channel with Two Different Banks: Intraday Changes in Balance Sheets

Bank of Montreal (BMO)		Toronto-Dominion Bank (TD)	
Assets	Liabilities	Assets	Liabilities
Loan to Chevrolet car dealer +$400,000 LVTS balance −$400,000		LVTS balance +$400,000	Deposit to GM Canada account +$400,000

LVTS	
Assets	Liabilities and Net Worth
	Balance of Toronto-Dominion Bank +$400,000
	Balance of Bank of Montreal −$400,000

amount of collateral that each bank is willing to provide to the LVTS and on the amount of bilateral credit limits that participants grant to each other. Various whistles go off when one bank goes too deeply into a negative position. In that case, the bank with the excessive negative position will have to wait till it receives transfers from the other banks before it can go ahead with the payments ordered by its depositors. The purpose of these controls is to ensure that the troubles of one bank will not snowball and cause other banks to run into trouble—the issue of **systemic risk**. Collateral and trust, or creditworthiness, are thus the kingpin of a monetary system.

A **systemic risk** is the possibility that the failure of one bank to meet its obligations could lead to the failure of other banks to meet their obligations, jeopardizing the functioning of the entire payment system.

Gross Flows of Payments and Net Balances in the LVTS

The following numerical example may help you to understand how the main Canadian clearing and settlement system—the LVTS—works in a multilateral setting. Suppose the following transactions occur among three banks that participate in the LVTS during the day. The numbers in the example are not unreasonable, given that, on average in 2007, no less than $183 billion worth of payments transited through the LVTS *every day*—about one ninth of Canada's *annual* GDP!

- The Bank of Montreal (BMO) makes payments of $30 billion to depositors at the Toronto-Dominion Bank (TD).
- The Bank of Montreal (BMO) makes payments of $30 billion to depositors at the Canadian Imperial Bank of Commerce (CIBC).
- TD makes payments of $22 billion to depositors at the BMO.
- TD makes payments of $20 billion to depositors at the CIBC.
- CIBC makes payments of $40 billion to depositors at the BMO.
- CIBC makes payments of $18 billion to depositors at the TD.

The following table sums up these transactions and their implications in relation to the settlement balances of the three banks.

Although there have been transactions totalling a gross amount of $160 billion, the net amounts involved are much smaller, with

the Bank of Montreal being left with a positive LVTS balance of $2 billion. In other words, the Bank of Montreal is in a net credit LVTS position. The Toronto-Dominion Bank has a LVTS positive balance of $6 billion, while the Canadian Imperial Bank of Commerce holds the difference, an $8 billion negative LVTS balance (a net debit LVTS position). It would be easy to build other examples where the total amount of positive balances is even smaller, despite actual daily transactions being large, but the size of positive LVTS balances is only very indirectly related to the amount of monetary transactions or the volume of economic activity. It is a random number that depends on the relative size of incoming and outgoing payments for each LVTS participant.

Owed to → Owed by ↓	BMO	TD	CIBC	Σ Amounts Owed by (debits)	Σ Amounts Owed to (credits)	LVTS Balances
BMO		30	30	60	62	+2
TD	22		20	42	48	+6
CIBC	40	18		58	50	−8
Σ amounts owed to	62	48	50	160	160	0

Σ stands for "the sum of."

■ The Overnight Market

Suppose now that we have reached the end of the day and, as shown in Table 6, the Bank of Montreal is still in a $400,000 debit LVTS position (a negative LVTS balance). Can such a situation last? As we will see in the next chapter, in a sense it could, but there are ways in which this situation could be reversed. For example, the financial institutions that have positive LVTS balances will usually lend them to those that have negative balances! This takes place on the **overnight market**, where banks and other financial institutions make loans to each other for one night. In the present case, at the end of the day, the Toronto-Dominion Bank can grant a one-night loan of $400,000 at the overnight rate of interest to the Bank of Montreal, allowing both banks to bring their LVTS balances to zero.

Once again, we can learn something from this example. It is clear that the banking system relies on trust and creditworthiness. Banks have to be sufficiently confident in other banks and in the clearing and settlement system to accept that other LVTS participants run temporary negative balance positions during the day, and to grant overnight loans to banks that end the day with a deficit LVTS position.[4] Indeed, as we noted earlier, regulations exist to ensure that transactions can be carried with very little risk. In addition, as long as all banking institutions are "moving in step," granting loans and collecting deposits at approximately the same pace, the situation of a polycentric banking system is not very different from a monocentric one, because on average, over a period of weeks, the positive and negative positions will compensate each other for each bank, although they will not on an hour-per-hour basis.

Things become slightly more complicated when some banks are growing faster than others, with their loans growing faster than those of other banks. Once again, however, this does not cause a problem as long as the fast-growing banks remain trustworthy in the eyes of other banks. When banks do not trust each other, a financial crisis arises, as happened in Europe in August 2007, when all financial institutions refused to lend to German banks on the overnight market, following the failure of two of the German banks. Similar fears arose at the time in our own Canadian payments system, when banks became reluctant to lend large amounts to each other.

The **overnight market** is the financial market where banks and other financial institutions lend and borrow surplus funds among themselves for one night.

■ THE NEED FOR MONETARY POLICY

At this stage, it should be clear that, in a modern monetary system such as the Canadian one, nothing limits the creation of credit and money other than the prudence of bankers and the self-restraint of borrowers. This feature of our monetary system—the fact that the creation of money is essentially endogenous—has advantages. It provides flexibility to the monetary system: Monetary units are easily created when the economy is expanding and there is a need for additional units of money for production and transaction purposes. However, as with most things, there is a downside to this flexibility.

In all likelihood, when economic perspectives are bad, bankers and their customers will tend to be extra prudent. However, when economic perspectives look good, both bankers and their clients may become overly enthusiastic. Demand for credit may quickly rise and bankers are likely to grant new loans at an accelerating pace, attributing creditworthy status to nearly all income earners. With loans increasing, so will the stock of money. With the rising demand for loans, you might think that this process would lead to rising interest rates—the cost of loans—and that this would then somewhat restrain the demand for loans and the growth of the money supply. But what happens is that *both* the demand for and the supply of loans increase in tandem, as bankers are very happy to finance the expenditures that their customers desire. Hence, with demand and supply growing together, there is no inherent market force pushing interest rates upward.

---

[4] This helps to explain why a bank cannot be started by just anybody. Partners need to use their own funds to start up a bank, and they need to be sufficiently creditworthy to be granted loans within the clearing and settlement system.

If such a process persists, at some stage the rising demand for credit and money will outpace the growth of potential output. An inflationary gap will appear, and the inflation rate will start rising. In addition, as has happened in the past, speculation might increase, leading to fast-rising prices in the stock market and in the real estate market, which could further disrupt the economy. Or, as has happened in the United States lately, overly enthusiastic banks will make large loans to people who are already overburdened. Some outside intervention is necessary.

> During an economic boom, profit-oriented banks will likely make the money supply expand, adding undesirable momentum to the booming economy and paving the way for inflation. The authorities must intervene to prevent this rapid money growth.

The flexibility of the monetary system may also create a problem when the economy is not performing well or when prospects are bleak. Bankers may then become overly prudent, and decrease the amount of loans and the supply of money. As Keynes once commented, "Banks and bankers are by nature blind. . . . A 'sound' banker, alas, is not one who foresees danger and avoids it, but one who, when he is ruined, is ruined in a conventional and orthodox way, along with his fellows, so that no one can really blame him."[5]

Some economists believe that this is what happened in Japan in the 1990s and the early 2000s. Because Japanese bankers had so many bad loans on their books as a result of the collapse in the prices of land and stocks, it is said that the bankers became super-cautious about lending money to any but their most creditworthy borrowers, thus further slowing down recovery from economic recession when some more optimistic borrowers requested new credit lines.

Regulation of the monetary system—monetary policy—is necessary, therefore, because profit-oriented bankers might otherwise provide the economy with lending and money creation that dance to and amplify the tune of the business cycle. There is a need for a monetary policy that will create the incentives that will be beneficial for the entire economy and that will steer the economy in the right direction. Precisely how the monetary authorities—more precisely the Bank of Canada—do that is the subject of the next chapter.

SUMMARY

1. There are two concepts of money: the **metallist** or **commodity** view of money, which sees money as evolving from **barter** exchange, and the **state** or **chartalist** theory, which sees money as a creation of the state.

2. It is more efficient to exchange goods and services by using **money** as a medium of exchange than by bartering them directly.

3. In addition to being the **medium of exchange**, whatever serves as money is likely to become the standard **unit of account** and a popular **store of value**.

4. Throughout history, all sorts of items have served as money. **Commodity money** gave way to full-bodied paper money (certificates backed 100 percent by some commodity, such as gold), which in turn gave way to partially backed paper money. Nowadays, our paper money has no commodity backing whatsoever; it is pure **fiat money**.

5. A narrow definition of the Canadian money supply is **M1+**, which includes coins, paper money, and chequable deposits in all financial institutions. There are broader definitions, such as **M2+**, which adds savings deposits as well as shares in money market mutual funds and life insurance annuities.

6. Money is mainly being created when new loans are being granted.

7. Money creation relies primarily on three features of the banking system: the willingness of banks to grant loans, the creditworthiness of borrowers, and the willingness of borrowers to take on loans.

8. **Creditworthiness** is at the core of the bank lending system. It is based on trust and conventions. It can be demonstrated by providing **collateral** or by demonstrating the ability to face the loan obligations.

9. There is no intrinsic limit to lending and money creation. The only limits are the lack of creditworthy economic agents willing to borrow, and the bankers' fear that they will make less profit and possibly incur large capital losses, thus becoming **insolvent**.

10. Bank transactions need to be cleared and settled. This is done through clearing houses. Large bank transactions transit via the **large-value transfer system (LVTS)**—the most important clearing house in the Canadian banking system.

---

[5] J. M. Keynes, "The Consequences to the Banks of the Collapse of Money Values," *Essays in Persuasion*, 1931 (New York: W. W. Norton, 1961).

11. The **LVTS balance** of a bank is its position at the LVTS clearing house. When the bank is in a net credit position, its balance is positive; when the bank is in a net debit position, its balance is negative.

12. Canadian banks usually target a zero level of LVTS balances. When they have negative balances at the end of the day, they can borrow from other banks on the **overnight market**.

13. The behaviour of profit-seeking bankers tends to amplify the business cycle. There is thus a need for monetary policy.

KEY TERMS

Bank run 260	Currency 265	Capital adequacy requirements 270
Barter 261	M1+ 265	Creditworthiness 270
Metallist or commodity concept of money 261	M2+ 266	Collateral 270
State or chartalist concept of money 262	Near moneys 266	Solvent bank 273
	Liquidity 267	Insolvent bank 273
Money 262	Deposit insurance 268	Large-value transfer system (LVTS) 274
Medium of exchange 262	Moral hazard 269	LVTS balance 274
Unit of account 262	Asset 269	Systemic risk 275
Store of value 262	Liability 269	Overnight market 276
Commodity money 264	Balance sheet 269	
Fiat money 264	Net worth 269	

TEST YOURSELF

1. With the help of Table 1, explain what happens to a bank balance sheet when each of the following transactions occur:

   a. You withdraw $100 from an ATM.

   b. Sam finds a $100 bill on the sidewalk and deposits it into his chequable account.

   c. Mary withdraws $1,000 in cash from her account at Hometown Bank, takes it to the city, and deposits it into her account at Big City Bank.

2. With the help of a balance sheet like the one shown in Table 6, explain what would happen if Mary was to close down her account at Hometown Bank and asked the manager to transfer her $80,000 deposit to her other account at Big City Bank.

3. With the help of a balance sheet like the ones in Tables 2 and 3, describe what would happen if Manufacturer Toy was to draw $500,000 on its line of credit (thereby taking a loan) to pay its employees, who also have their accounts at Bank-a-Mythica.

4. Using the type of balance sheet shown in Table 1, document the following transactions: Your mother decides to sell her Canada Savings Bonds for $10,000. The bonds are bought by Bank-a-Mythica and the funds are transferred to her deposit account at Bank-a-Mythica. Is there an increase or a decrease in the supply of money? (You have found a new way in which money can be created!)

5. How would your answer to Test Yourself Question 4 differ if your uncle bought the Canada Savings Bonds from your mother, instead of the bank? Your uncle's account is also at the Bank-a-Mythica.

6. **(More difficult)** Bank-Out-of-Luck is the victim of a holdup and $100,000 in cash has been stolen. How will that loss appear in the bank's balance sheet? Suppose that the bank initially had a balance sheet identical to that in Table 1. Would the situation be any different if a borrower of the bank had defaulted on a loan, with the bank being subjected to a $100,000 capital loss?

7. **(More difficult)** You are given the following transactions. With the help of a table similar to the table provided in the boxed feature "Gross Flows of Payments and Net Balances in the LVTS," on page 275, compute the LVTS balance of each bank. Which bank is likely to borrow on the overnight market?

   • The Bank of Montreal (BMO) makes payments of $45 billion to depositors at the Toronto-Dominion Bank (TD).

   • The Bank of Montreal (BMO) makes payments of $30 billion to depositors at the Canadian Imperial Bank of Commerce (CIBC).

   • TD makes payments of $35 billion to depositors at the BMO.

   • TD makes payments of $40 billion to depositors at the CIBC.

   • CIBC makes payments of $40 billion to depositors at the BMO.

   • CIBC makes payments of $20 billion to depositors at the TD.

DISCUSSION QUESTIONS

1. If ours were a barter economy, how would you pay your tuition bill? What if your college or university did not want the goods or services you offered in payment?

2. How is "money" defined, both conceptually and in practice? Does the Canadian money supply consist of commodity money, full-bodied paper money, or fiat money?

3. In the example in Table 1, currency (or cash—bank notes and coins) held by Bank-a-Mythica was a small percentage of its overall assets. Can you compute that percentage? In reality, banks hold about 0.2 percent of their assets in the form of currency. Why do banks hold such a relatively small amount of currency? What do you think banks could do if many depositors suddenly demanded a lot of cash?

4. Explain why capital adequacy requirements, such as those imposed by the Bank for International Settlements, help banking systems to be less susceptible to failure.

5. Each year during the December holiday shopping season, consumers and stores increase their holdings of cash (as was seen in Chapter 1 on page 11). Explain how this development may impact on banks' balance sheets.

6. Give two examples of creditworthy borrowers.

7. If the government takes over a failed bank with liabilities (mostly deposits) of $2 billion, pays off the depositors, and sells the assets for $1.5 billion, where does the missing $500 million come from? Why?

13

MANAGING AGGREGATE DEMAND: MONETARY POLICY

So long as prices remain unaltered the banks' rate of interest is to remain unaltered. If prices rise, the rate of interest is to be raised; and if prices fall, the rate of interest is to be lowered.

KNUT WICKSELL (1851–1926), 1898

Armed with our understanding of the rudiments of banking, we are now in a better position to understand how the levels of output and price inflation are affected by interest rate determination. Up to now, we have taken investment (*I*) to be a fixed number. But this is a poor assumption. Not only is investment highly variable, but it also depends on interest rates—which are, in turn, heavily influenced by *monetary policy*. The main task of this chapter is to explore how government pursues monetary policy through the actions of its central bank and explain how interest rate policy affects aggregate demand. You will see that the policies being pursued by modern central banks were already being advocated more than a century ago, as shown by the quote from Swedish economist Wicksell, above. By the end of this chapter, we will have constructed a complete macroeconomic model, which we will use in subsequent chapters to investigate a variety of important policy issues.

CONTENTS

? ISSUE: *Just Why Is the Governor of the Bank of Canada So Important?*

Mark Carney was chosen in October 2007 to act as the new governor of the Bank of Canada, starting in February 2008. The choice of the new governor generated some hype from the media. During the months that led to the selection of Carney, journalists and officials from various financial institutions evaluated the pros and cons of some likely candidates—and Carney was *not* one of them!

But why is the governor of the Bank of Canada so important? Why do the media pay so much attention to an economist who is usually rather low key? Because in the view of many economists, the decisions of the Bank of Canada on interest rates are the single most important influence on aggregate demand—and hence on economic growth, unemployment, and inflation.

The Bank of Canada, obviously, is a bank, but a very special kind of bank. Its customers are banks rather than individuals, and it performs some of the same services for them as your bank performs for you. Although this central bank makes large profits, profit is not its goal. Instead, the Bank of Canada tries to manage interest rates according to what it perceives to be the national interest. This chapter will teach you how the Bank of Canada does its job and why its decisions affect our economy so profoundly. In brief, it will teach you why people listen so carefully when the governor makes a speech or when the Bank of Canada makes an announcement.

■ MONEY AND INCOME: THE IMPORTANT DIFFERENCE

But first we must get some terminology straight. The words *money* and *income* are used almost interchangeably in common parlance. Here, however, we must be more precise.

Money is a snapshot concept. It answers questions such as "How much money do you have right now?" or "How much money did you have at 3:32 P.M. on Friday, November 5?" To answer these questions, you would add up the cash you are (or were) carrying and whatever checkable balances you have (or had), and answer something like: "I have $126.33," or "On Friday, November 5, at 3:32 P.M., I had $31.43."

Income, by contrast, is more like a motion picture; it comes to you over a period of time. If you are asked, "What is your income?", you must respond by saying "$1,000 *per week*," or "$4,000 *per month*," or "$50,000 *per year*," or something like that. Notice that a unit of time is attached to each of these responses. If you just answer, "My income is $45,000," without indicating whether it is per week, per month, or per year, no one will understand what you mean. To sum up, money is a *stock* while income is a *flow*.

That the two concepts are very different is easy to see. A typical Canadian family has an *income* of over $50,000 per year, but its *money* holdings at any point in time (using the M1+ definition) may be around $4,000. Similarly, at the national level, nominal GDP in 2007 was $1.5 trillion, while the money stock (M1+) at the end of 2007 was around $440 billion.

Monetary policy refers to actions that the Bank of Canada takes to affect the macroeconomic performance of the economy.

Although money and income are different, they are certainly related. In this chapter, we will see how these two variables are affected by **monetary policy**—including changes in interest rates under the control of the central bank.

■ CANADA'S CENTRAL BANK: THE BANK OF CANADA

A central bank is a bank for banks. The Bank of Canada is Canada's central bank and hence acts as Canada's monetary authority.

Both Canada and the United States were without **central banks** until early in the twentieth century, even though most European countries had established national central banks during the nineteenth century or even earlier. It took a major financial crisis in 1907 for the Americans to establish their central bank, the Federal Reserve System. In Canada, it was only after the Great Crash, in the midst of the Great Depression, that a central bank was created.

Origins and Structure

Acting on the advice of the Macmillan Commission studying the desirability of a central bank in Canada, the Conservative government of R. B. Bennett passed the Bank of Canada Act in July of 1934 and established Canada's central bank as a privately owned and politically independent institution. Soon however, the Bank of Canada Act was amended to ensure majority government ownership and then, through a subsequent amendment in 1938, the Bank of Canada became a fully publicly owned Crown corporation.

Much like other federal Crown corporations, the Bank of Canada is managed by a board of directors. The board comprises 12 directors from outside the Bank who are appointed for a three-year term by the minister of Finance on the basis of their expertise as well as on the basis of regional representation. There are also three additional directors: the governor, who chairs the board and is appointed by it; the senior deputy governor, who also holds voting rights and who, together with the governor, is appointed for a seven-year term; and the deputy minister of Finance, who sits as an *ex officio* nonvoting member. The board meets on a weekly basis, handling ongoing administrative and financial matters related to the running of the Bank, including matters pertaining to human resource management.

The Bank of Canada is responsible for conducting monetary policy that promotes the economic welfare of Canada. While no particular method of implementation is stipulated in the Bank of Canada Act, it is the powerful Governing Council, consisting of the governor, the senior deputy governor, and the four deputy governors, that determines the target overnight rate (which will be discussed further). This target rate is set via consensus within the Governing Council eight times per year at regular predetermined dates on the basis of what is deemed best by the council.

While its main function is the conduct of monetary policy, the Bank of Canada also holds other responsibilities: It functions as the fiscal agent of the federal government in collecting taxes and managing the public debt, and it oversees the clearing and settlement process of the Canadian payment system.

Central Bank Independence

For decades a debate has raged over the pros and cons of **central bank independence**.

Proponents of central bank independence argue that it enables the central bank to take the long view and to make monetary policy decisions on objective, technical criteria—thus keeping monetary policy out of the "political thicket." Without this independence, they argue, politicians with short time horizons might try to force the central bank to pursue overly expansionary monetary policy, especially before elections, thereby contributing to chronic inflation and undermining faith in the country's financial system. They point to historical evidence showing that countries with more independent central banks have, on average, experienced lower inflation.

Opponents of this view counter that there is something profoundly undemocratic about letting a group of unelected bankers and economists make decisions that affect every citizen's well-being. Monetary policy, they argue, should be formulated by the elected representatives of the people, just as fiscal policy is.

The high inflation of the 1970s and early 1980s helped resolve this issue by convincing many governments around the world that an independent central bank was essential to controlling inflation. Thus, one country after another has made its central bank independent over the past 20 to 25 years. For example, the Maastricht Treaty (1992), which committed members of the European Union to both low inflation and a single currency (the euro), required each member state to make its central bank independent. All did so, even though several have still not joined the monetary union. Japan also decided to make its central bank independent in 1998. In Latin America, several formerly high-inflation countries like Brazil and Mexico found that giving their central banks more independence helped them control inflation. And some of the formerly

Central bank independence refers to the central bank's ability to make decisions without political interference.

Is the Bank of Canada an Independent Central Bank?

Anybody visiting the website of the Bank of Canada will undoubtedly observe that the Bank makes a noticeable effort to point out that it is *not* a government department and that it holds considerable independence vis-à-vis the political authorities in Ottawa. For instance, the Bank of Canada affirms that:

- The governor and senior deputy governor are appointed by the Bank's board of directors (with the approval of Cabinet), not by the federal government.
- The deputy minister of Finance sits on the board of directors but has no vote.
- The Bank submits its expenditures to its board of directors. Federal government departments submit theirs to the Treasury Board.
- Bank employees are regulated by the Bank itself, not by federal public service agencies.
- The Bank's books are audited by external auditors appointed by Cabinet on the recommendation of the minister of Finance, not by the auditor general of Canada.*

While this does suggest a significant amount of institutional independence as a special Crown corporation, how far can the Bank of Canada assert its independence with regard to monetary policy? A famous example often referred to as the "Coyne Affair" will suggest that this political independence can reach its limit.

James Coyne became the governor of the Bank of Canada in 1955. He soon faced an economic slowdown accompanied by

SOURCE: Wayne Eardley/FirstLight

"creeping inflation." Supported by the Liberal government in power, Governor Coyne applied continuous doses of monetary restraint in an effort to reduce inflation. However, when the Conservatives led by John Diefenbaker replaced the Liberals in 1957, a disagreement arose between the objectives of the new minister of Finance, Donald Fleming, who demanded expansionary monetary policy to fight unemployment, and those of Governor Coyne, who defended restraint. The dispute reached its peak in July of 1961, with a government motion requiring the governor to vacate his post, leading to Coyne's resignation. As Minister Fleming was quoted as saying in *Time* magazine on June 23, 1961:

Mr. Coyne's continuation in office would stand in the way of a comprehensive, sound and responsible economic program. The government's policy is expansionist. The policies advocated by Mr. Coyne are restrictionist—restrictive of trade, of production, of jobs.

The Coyne affair crystallized the asymmetrical power relationship between the governor of the Bank of Canada and the federal government, with the latter ultimately overriding the former. When he was appointed, Louis Rasminsky, Coyne's successor, recognized officially that all formal issuance of directives from the minister of Finance requiring a change of policy would hold sway and would necessarily lead to the resignation of the governor if the latter's policy was in conflict.

The position articulated by Rasminsky regarding the ultimate supremacy of the authority of the minister of Finance has not yet been challenged and remains relevant to this day in setting the limits to central bank independence in Canada. On the other hand, other than Coyne, no governors have been forced to resign.

*SOURCE: Bank of Canada website. Retrieved from www.bank-banque-canada.ca /en/about/are.html

socialist countries of Europe, finding themselves saddled with high inflation and "unsound" currencies, made their central banks more independent for similar reasons.

Thus, for practical purposes, the debate over central bank independence is now all but over. The new debate is over how to hold such independent and powerful institutions *accountable* to the political authorities and to the broad public. For example, many central banks have now abandoned their former traditions of secrecy and have become far more open to public scrutiny.

■ MONETARY POLICY

Monetary policy implementation is the set of rules, instruments, and day-to-day actions that allow the central bank to achieve its operational target.

Monetary policy can be conceptually divided into two components: monetary policy implementation and monetary policy strategy. **Monetary policy implementation** deals with the day-to-day, or even the minute-to-minute, operations of the central bank. We can say that it corresponds to the nitty-gritty aspects of monetary policy. Monetary policy implementation is made up of two elements—the operational target and the operational instruments—both of which must be under the control of the central bank if monetary policy implementation is to be successful.

Today, there is wide consensus among central bankers that the operational target ought to be a short-term interest rate, which in Canada is the **overnight interest rate** on collateralized transactions. This is the rate of interest that arises from the overnight market, which we covered in Chapter 12 when discussing the Canadian banking clearing and settlement system. It is the rate of interest at which banks and other financial market participants lend and borrow among themselves for one night, using or searching for surplus funds fully secured by acceptable collateral. The operational target of the Bank of Canada is thus the **target overnight interest rate**.

Monetary policy strategy is closely tied to monetary macroeconomics. It deals with the macroeconomic goals of the central bank—for instance, a target inflation rate or a given growth rate of economic activity—and how best to achieve them. It also deals with the monetary stance of the Bank of Canada, that is, currently, its decision to keep constant or to change the target overnight interest rate. Monetary policy strategy is also linked with the transmission mechanism of monetary policy, that is, how any change in the target interest rate will impact the macroeconomic objectives of the Bank of Canada. In other words, monetary policy strategy depends on the macroeconomic model that lies behind the actions of the central bank.

In what follows, we first examine the big picture—the monetary policy strategy of the Bank of Canada. Monetary policy implementation will be studied afterward.

> The **overnight interest rate** is the interest rate that banks and other financial market participants pay and receive when they borrow and lend surplus funds among themselves for one night.
>
> The **target overnight interest rate** is the operational target of the Bank of Canada.
>
> **Monetary policy strategy** is the decision that the central bank makes about the level of the target overnight interest rate to try to influence or achieve, for example, a target inflation rate.

■ MONETARY POLICY STRATEGY

We now examine the macroeconomic goals that our monetary authorities are pursuing, and how changes in the target overnight interest rate allow the Bank of Canada to achieve these goals over time. The link between changes in interest rates under the control of the Bank of Canada and economic activity is called the *transmission mechanism*. We shall see how this mechanism relies on a negative relationship between interest rates and components of aggregate spending.

■ The Macroeconomic Goals of the Bank of Canada

When the Bank of Canada was created in the midst of the Great Depression, its goals were clearly set out in the preamble to the 1934 Bank of Canada Act:

> . . . to regulate credit and currency in the best interests of the economic life of the nation, to control and protect the external value of the national monetary unit, and to mitigate by its influence fluctuations in the general level of production, trade, prices, and employment so far as may be possible within the scope of monetary action, and generally to promote the economic and financial welfare of Canada.[1]

The goals, as defined by the Canadian Parliament, are thus multiple. According to the Act, the Bank of Canada must:

- Regulate credit.
- Provide currency in an adequate way.
- Protect the value of the Canadian dollar on foreign exchange markets.
- Take action to reduce fluctuations in prices, that is, to control inflation.
- Take action to reduce fluctuations in output and employment.
- Promote economic and financial welfare.

The preamble is both specific and vague. It says that the Bank of Canada should reduce the fluctuations in production, trade, and employment; but how does this fit with the fact that another of its goals is to promote the economic welfare of Canada? Does this mean that the Bank of Canada should pursue the full employment of

---

[1] Bank of Canada. Retrieved from http://bankofcanada.ca/en/about/act_loi_boc_bdc.pdf

Canada's human resources? Also, the Bank of Canada may be facing some trade-offs: What if its actions to reduce the inflation rate lead to reduced economic welfare? How far should the Bank of Canada go in reducing the rate of inflation?

Throughout the years, the Bank of Canada has given varying importance to these sometimes contradictory goals. Things started to change, however, in 1988. The then governor of the Bank of Canada, John Crow, in a famous speech (the Hanson Lecture at the University of Alberta) argued strongly in favour of a single goal, price stability, which most people interpreted as a goal of near-zero inflation, or low inflation.

In 1991, the Bank of Canada and the Department of Finance agreed to define a target inflation band, which was initially set between 3 and 5 percent but is now 1 to 3 percent. This 1 to 3 percent band has remained unchanged during subsequent agreements between the Bank and the government, the last of which occurred in 2006 (valid until 2011). Since 2001, the midpoint of the band, 2 percent, has become the official target rate of inflation. With the accord between the Bank of Canada and the Department of Finance, Canada became the second country after New Zealand to adopt **inflation targeting**.

> The goal of **inflation targeting** by the Bank of Canada is to keep the inflation rate at a particular level; currently, 2 percent is the target.

Inflation targeting—controlling inflation by maintaining a set level of inflation—has been the *main* macroeconomic goal of the Bank of Canada since 1991. The targeted inflation rate currently stands at 2 percent, the midpoint of the inflation target band of 1 and 3 percent.

The Bank of Canada uses the 12-month rate of increase in the total Consumer Price Index (CPI), prepared by Statistics Canada, as the country's inflation rate, because the CPI is the most commonly used indicator of inflation in the Canadian economy. For instance, many collective agreements base their escalator clauses on the precise estimate of past CPI growth rates, since the CPI is regarded as the most relevant estimate of the evolution of the cost of living for Canadians.

Why is there such a focus on the inflation rate, rather than on full employment or the exchange rate of the Canadian dollar? In the words of David Dodge, the governor of the Bank between February 2001 and January 2008, "Focusing on domestic price stability—however that term is defined—is the best contribution monetary policy can make to economic stabilization and sustainable long-term growth."[2] Thus, officials at the Bank of Canada, and indeed at many other central banks in the world, believe that keeping the rate of inflation steady at some low level is the best that central banks can do. By doing this, the Bank claims that overly large and unwarranted fluctuations in the Canadian exchange rate will be prevented, and that the economy will therefore not stray too far nor for too long from some optimal level of employment and output.

Central bankers believe, as was discussed on page 133 of Chapter 6, that high inflation is costly. As will be shown in more detail in Chapter 16, central bankers, along with a majority of macroeconomists, believe that "Monetary policy *cannot* have a systematic and *sustained* effect on macroeconomic variables other than the inflation rate."[3] Thus, it is best for the central bank to set its sights on the inflation rate rather than on any other macroeconomic variable. Indeed, officials at the Bank of Canada are convinced that in the long run the economy will be more productive if inflation is kept low and steady. These are the beliefs that have led the Bank of Canada to set inflation as its main macroeconomic goal, despite the preamble of the Bank of Canada Act.

The Transmission Mechanism of Monetary Policy

We discussed earlier that the monetary policy operational target is the overnight interest rate. We also know now that the monetary policy strategic target is the inflation rate. How are these two variables connected? What is the mechanism, or the chain of causation, that links the overnight interest rate to the inflation rate?

---

[2] David Dodge, "Inflation Targeting: A Canadian Perspective." Remarks to the National Association for Business Economics, Washington, DC, March 21, 2005. Retrieved from www.bank-banque-canada.ca/en/speeches/2005/sp05-2.html

[3] Christopher Ragan, "Why monetary policy matters—A Canadian perspective." Retrieved from the Bank of Canada website: www.bank-banque-canada.ca/en/ragan_paper/ragan_paper.pdf

TABLE 1

The Transmission Mechanism of Monetary Policy

With Overly High Inflation Rates	With Overly Low Inflation Rates
1. Actual or forecasted inflation rate is over the target inflation rate.	1. Actual or forecasted inflation rate is below the target inflation rate.
2. Bank of Canada raises the target overnight interest rate.	2. Bank of Canada lowers the target overnight interest rate.
3A. Other interest rates go up.	3A. Other interest rates go down.
3B. Canadian dollar rises relative to other currencies.	3B. Canadian dollar falls relative to other currencies.
Aggregate spending goes down:	Aggregate spending goes up:
4A. Investment and consumption expenditures on durable goods fall.	4A. Investment and consumption expenditures on durable goods rise.
4B. Net exports fall.	4B. Net exports rise.
5. Production (real GDP) goes down.	5. Production (real GDP) goes up.
6. The growth rate of costs and prices goes down (the inflation rate falls).	6. The growth rate of costs and prices goes up (the inflation rate rises).

Let us suppose that the rate of inflation is over its target, or that the Bank of Canada expects the rate of inflation soon to be over target. What action will the Bank of Canada take? And how will this action affect the economy? The chain of causation that links the inflation rate with the overnight rate can be seen in Table 1 and Figure 1. The numbers in the table relate to those in the diagram. In a nutshell, the central bank raises interest rates when inflation rates are too high, hoping to slow down the economy, and it decreases interest rates when inflation rates are too low, in an attempt to crank up the economy.

An implication of the transmission mechanism shown in Table 1 and Figure 1 is that the impact of monetary policy on inflation rates is only an indirect one. In the current view of central bankers, the best operational instrument is the short-term interest rate—the overnight rate. Interest rates have only an indirect effect on inflation rates, however. An increase in interest rates will slow down inflation rates by reducing economic activity, that is by reducing aggregate spending and hence production, thus

FIGURE 1

Diagrammatic Representation of the Transmission Mechanism

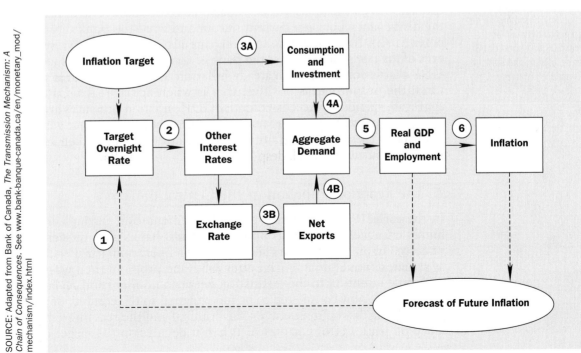

increasing unemployment. This reduction in real output and economic activity tends to slow down the growth rate of costs, including the costs of primary products and labour costs, as well as the rate of price inflation—the final objective of the Bank of Canada.

Guides to Future Inflation

Obviously, there is quite a way from the cup to the lip in the transmission mechanism. Any component in the long six-step chain that goes from the target overnight interest rate to the inflation rate can go wrong. It may also take a long time to go through the chain. Indeed, this explains why officials at the Bank of Canada claim that monetary policy takes from 12 to 18 months to have an effect on real GDP, and up to 18 or 24 months to have its full effect on the inflation rate. As a consequence, monetary policy has to be forward-looking. Not only must central bankers assess the implications of the most recent data on inflation rates provided by Statistics Canada, they must also make a forecast of future inflation rates over a period of about two years under the assumption that no change is made to monetary policy. What this implies is that monetary policy, like most of economics, is more an art than a science. Much depends on forecasts and modelling, but also on experience and hunches.

Starting with the first element of the transmission chain of monetary policy, officials at the Bank of Canada rely on a long list of indicators that help them to assess future inflation. We will discuss only two of them here. The first is **core inflation**, which is based on a modified CPI called the CPIX. This indicator excludes items with the most volatile prices (fruits and vegetables; gasoline; fuel oil; natural gas; intercity transportation; tobacco; the interest costs of mortgage; and the effects of changes in indirect taxes on the remaining CPI components). Bank of Canada officials consider that the inflation fluctuations of these eight components are mostly of a temporary nature and hence that core inflation provides a better indicator of underlying inflation and a good estimator of future inflation. Figure 2 shows the historical evolution of inflation and core inflation, along with the target inflation band, since February 1991, when the inflation targets were first announced. It can readily be seen that while CPI inflation sometimes moved outside the target band, core inflation tended to remain much closer to the target midpoint.

The second major indicator of future inflation rates is the **output gap**. This measure is an overall assessment of the degree of slack in the economy. It is an estimate of the strength of the pressures on capacity and inflation. The output gap is defined as the discrepancy between current output and what the Bank of Canada deems to be potential GDP, which was defined on page 116 of Chapter 6. More specifically, in the eyes of the decision makers at the Bank of Canada, potential output is the level of real GDP that is consistent with steady inflation. Inflation pressures are likely to mount when the output gap is positive, that is when actual real GDP, as determined by aggregate spending, exceeds potential GDP. Inflation pressures are likely to diminish when the output gap is negative. Assessing correctly the output gap is, however, a difficult task. Hence, rising (falling) core inflation is often taken as a sign of positive (negative) output gap.

The Reaction Function of the Central Bank

In the early 1970s, monetary policy implementation through interest setting was highly criticized by most economists. Central banks did not seem to have inflation under control, so it was argued that other operational targets, such as monetary aggregates, would do a much better job. One problem then was that central banks paid little attention to the distinction between nominal and real interest rates. This distinction is now considered to be fundamental to the conduct of monetary policy.

Recall the distinction between the nominal and the real interest rate that was provided on page 131 of Chapter 6. When it decides on the target overnight rate, the

Core inflation is the rate of change of a modified Consumer Price Index that excludes certain items whose prices are the most volatile, such as food and energy.

The **output gap** is a measure of the inflationary tensions that exist in the economy, based on the discrepancy between actual real GDP and potential GDP, as defined by the Bank of Canada.

SOURCE: Bank of Canada, Statistics Canada, Series V735319 and V41444252.

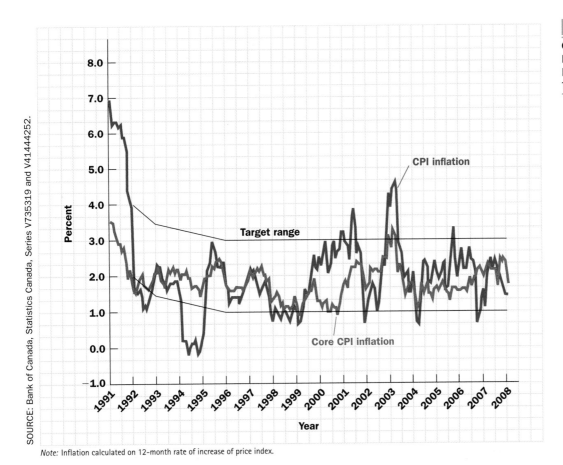

FIGURE 2

CPI Inflation, Core Inflation, and the Target Inflation Band, 1991–2008

Note: Inflation calculated on 12-month rate of increase of price index.

Bank of Canada sets the nominal short-term interest rate. However, as long as it is able to assess the inflation rate correctly, this means that it is also able to set the real short-term interest rate. Recalling the definition on page 131 in Chapter 6, and reorganizing the equation, we have (roughly):

Real interest rate = Nominal interest rate − Expected inflation rate

In the 1970s, with inflation rising, the Bank of Canada raised nominal interest rates, but not enough to raise real interest rates. Monetary policy strategy now requires central banks to raise nominal interest rates faster than inflation rises, thus raising *real* interest rates when inflation rises or is above target, and lowering *real* interest rates when inflation falls or is below target. This relationship is called the **reaction function** of the central bank.

The Taylor Rule is a well-known central bank reaction function that was proposed in 1993 by American economist John B. Taylor. This rule splits the forecasted inflation rate into two components: the current actual inflation rate and the forecasted increase in the inflation rate that can be attributed to the output gap. Based on U.S. data, Taylor argued that the overnight interest rate ought to be set in the following way:

Target overnight rate = 2 percent + Inflation rate
+ (0.5 × (Inflation rate − Target inflation rate)) + (0.5 × (% Output gap))

Thus, for a target inflation rate of 2 percent such as that in Canada, an inflation rate of 3 percent accompanied by a positive output gap of 2 percent would suggest a target overnight rate that would need to be set at 6.50 percent ($2 + 3 + (0.5 \times 1) + (0.5 \times 2)$). Under such a rule, the central bank will set higher real interest rates whenever inflation rates are higher.

The **reaction function** of the central bank is the relationship between the current inflation rate (or the expected future inflation rate) and the target overnight interest rate that the central bank sets in response to this inflation rate.

Links among Interest Rates

You might ask whether other interest rates will follow the upward or downward movement of the Bank of Canada's target overnight rate—element 2 in the causal chain of the transmission mechanism shown in Table 1 and Figure 1. The answer to this question generally depends on whether we are talking about short-term or long-term interest rates. In the case of short-term interest rates, both market rates (e.g., the treasury bill rate) and administered rates (e.g., the prime lending rate) follow closely the evolution of the target overnight rate. This is shown in Figure 3.[4] Indeed, since 1996, banks set the prime lending rate at exactly 175 basis points above the target overnight rate.

By contrast, as can be inferred from Figure 4, long-term rates, such as the yields on 10-year bonds, do not follow as closely the changes in the target overnight rate, although their evolution is not impervious to changes in short-term rates. However, as long as enough borrowers borrow on variable terms (for instance, mortgages that are amortized over a 20-year period, but at interest rates that are newly set every year), element 3A, to which we now turn, will not be compromised.

The Negative Relationship between Interest Rates and Spending

Let us now suppose that the Bank of Canada, facing rising inflation, has decided to raise real interest rates, and increases both the nominal and the real target overnight rate. How do we know that this will slow down the economy? While not all categories of aggregate spending are sensitive to interest rate movements, at least three important components of total expenditures are somewhat interest elastic: consumer expenditures on durable goods; investment spending by business enterprises and residential construction; and net exports (the latter via the associated exchange rate movement).

Although the evidence is weak (as was pointed out in Chapter 8, page 176), spending on consumer durables such as automobiles, furniture, and major household appliances may be responsive to interest rate changes. Since these tend to be big-ticket items that often require financing, the cost of borrowing funds could play a role in

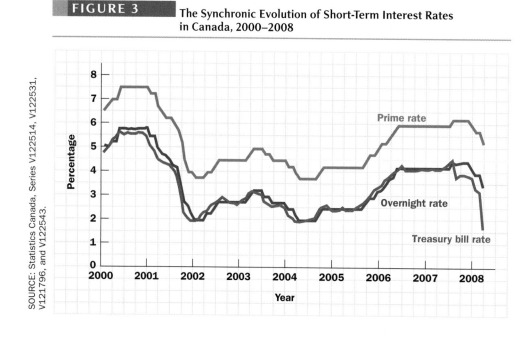

FIGURE 3   **The Synchronic Evolution of Short-Term Interest Rates in Canada, 2000–2008**

SOURCE: Statistics Canada, Series V122514, V122531, V121796, and V122543.

---

[4] It should be noted, however, that in early 2008, the treasury bill rate did not track the overnight rate anymore, being much lower. This peculiar situation arose as a consequence of the subprime financial crisis. When financial market participants lose confidence, they are reluctant to hold assets issued by the private sector and rush toward the safest assets—federal government securities—thus driving up the prices of these assets and consequently driving down their interest rates.

SOURCE: Statistics Canada, Series V122514 and V122543.

FIGURE 4	Long-Term Interest Rates versus the Overnight Interest Rate, 2000–2008

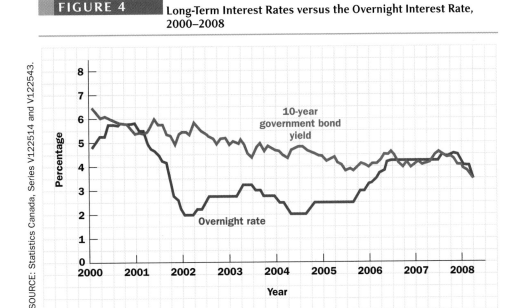

the household decision to purchase, say, a car. Hence, given household disposable income, the higher the level of interest rates is, the lower that consumption spending on durable goods might be.

The same reasoning applies to investment spending by private businesses for the building of plant and the purchase of capital equipment. Investment on fixed capital often occurs in spurts during periods of an investment boom. Because of the lumpiness of investment projects, as a rule, firms must borrow rather than rely exclusively on internal funds. While expectations about the future and investors' state of confidence play a critical role in the decision to invest, increases in interest costs impact negatively on the amount of borrowing and thus on the volume of investment. In addition, if businesses have to make higher interest payments on previously accumulated debt, then they have less cash flow left to finance investment and expansion.

The most immediate impact of increases in real interest rates is likely to be on residential investment. Housing construction is quite sensitive to changes in interest rates because purchasers must usually borrow large amounts in the form of housing mortgages. These mortgages are granted to borrowers on the basis of their capacity to make future mortgage payments, based in particular on the ratio of their housing expenditures relative to their income. When interest rates rise, fewer borrowers qualify, or they qualify for loans of a lesser amount. Investment in housing is thus likely to slow down when interest rates rise.

Finally, net exports are also negatively affected by the higher level of interest rates—this is element 3B in Table 1 and Figure 1. The reasoning here is somewhat more complex and will be discussed in more detail in Chapter 19, when foreign exchange markets will be analyzed. In the meantime, it will suffice to say that international financial capital movements are affected by the level of interest rates in one country. Hence, when interest rates rise in Canada vis-à-vis the rest of the world, financial capital is attracted to Canada and this pushes up the demand for Canadian dollars. The higher demand for our currency raises its exchange rate in terms of foreign currencies. This increases the prices of our exports in terms of foreign currencies and makes our goods less competitive internationally, while simultaneously reducing the price of foreign imports in Canadian dollars. The effect is a drop in exports and an increase in imports, resulting in a decline in our net exports to the rest of the world. The reverse mechanism would apply if interest rates were to fall in Canada, in which case, the Canadian dollar would depreciate and our net exports would rise.

There are therefore two channels through which monetary policy has an effect on all three private components of aggregate spending and real GDP: a direct channel

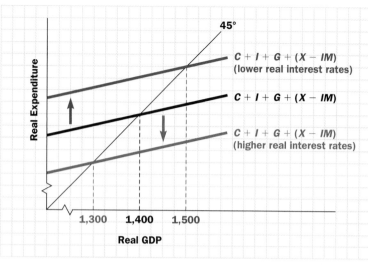

FIGURE 5

**The Effect of Real
Interest Rates on Real
Expenditures**

Note: Figures are in billions of dollars per year

through consumption and investment, as depicted by elements 3A and 4A in Table 1 and Figure 1, and an indirect channel through the exchange rate and net exports (elements 3B and 4B).

The negative relationship between real interest rates and real GDP is shown in Figure 5, which summarizes elements 3 through 5 of Table 1. Higher real interest rates, resulting from the reaction function of the central bank, induce decreases in the various components of aggregate spending, thus leading to a vertical downward shift of the expenditure schedule, from the black line to the red line. This kicks off a multiplier chain of decreases in output and employment, until the new equilibrium real GDP is attained, at $1,300 billion. Similarly, lower real interest rates would eventually propel the economy to a higher real GDP, at $1,500 billion.

Going back to Figure 1, only element 6 remains to be discussed. We already know that any restrictive policy will push the aggregate demand curve inward, while expansionary policies will push it outward. Thus, using the aggregate demand and aggregate supply framework that was developed in Chapter 10, it can easily be shown that higher real interest rates will have a negative effect on prices and output, while lower real interest rates will have the opposite effect.

■ MONETARY POLICY IMPLEMENTATION[5]

The **operating band** is the zone of overnight rates between the bank rate and the interest rate on bank deposits at the central bank.

The **interest rate on deposits at the central bank** is the rate of interest that banks receive on their deposits at the Bank of Canada as a result of the operation of the LVTS.

The **bank rate** is the interest rate charged to banks that still have negative LVTS balances at the end of the day and therefore must borrow funds for one night from the Bank of Canada in order to settle with the LVTS.

The **corridor system** is the Bank's operating framework that forces the overnight interest rate to remain close to the midpoint of the operating band, as defined by the target overnight rate.

While all central banks follow more or less a similar monetary policy strategy, the instruments used may differ from one country to another. Different monetary systems, with different institutions, provide different technical instruments that help the central bank achieve its operational target—the interest rate that it wants to control. We now study monetary policy implementation at the Bank of Canada. More precisely, we look at how the Bank of Canada succeeds on a day-to-day basis in achieving the target overnight interest rate. Three instruments will be considered: standing facilities, government deposit shifting, and open-market operations.

■ Standing Facilities and the Corridor System

How the operational target is implemented in the Canadian monetary system is a simple story. Unless there are special circumstances, the Bank of Canada makes an announcement eight times a year, in the early morning, on specific dates, as to what its target overnight interest rate will be until the next announcement. *Et voilà!* The actual overnight rate will immediately adjust to the new target.

The target overnight rate is accompanied by an **operating band**, which is made up of two additional interest rates that stand below and above the target overnight rate. These two rates are the **interest rate on deposits at the central bank** and the interest rate on advances (that is, loans) made by the Bank of Canada to the banks that participate in the large value transfer system . This latter rate is also called the **bank rate**. These two interest rates thus determine the operating band. This band looks like a corridor—a channel or a tunnel—which is why this operating framework is called the **corridor system**, as shown in Figure 6. Nearly identical corridor systems exist in New Zealand, Australia, England, and Sweden.

---

[5] Instructors may wish to cover only the "Standing Facilities and the Corridor System" section, as the other sections are more technical.

Figure 6 illustrates the case where the target overnight rate of interest is 4.00 percent (the rate may be quite different as you read this book). As a result, the bank rate is set at 4.25 percent, since the bank rate is always set at one-quarter of one percent (or 25 basis points, as financial market specialists say) above the target overnight rate. Symmetrically, the interest rate on deposits at the Bank of Canada is set at 25 basis points below the target overnight rate. The operating band is thus 50 basis points wide.

The Bank of Canada thus acts as a price fixer in relation to the short-term interest rate. It constrains the level of the overnight interest rate by setting both a floor and a ceiling to the values that can be taken by the overnight interest rate. The Bank of Canada promises to take as a deposit, paid at a 3.75 percent rate, any amount of a positive LVTS balance that happens to be held by an individual bank, and it promises to grant an advance, at a 4.25 percent cost, to any individual bank that turns out to have a negative LVTS balance (provided the borrowing bank has adequate collateral). These deposit and borrowing facilities are called **standing facilities**. They are a key element of all monetary systems that rely on a corridor framework, as is the case in Canada, as they greatly ease the task of the central bank in achieving the target overnight rate.

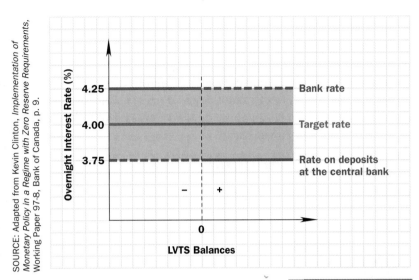

SOURCE: Adapted from Kevin Clinton, *Implementation of Monetary Policy in a Regime with Zero Reserve Requirements,* Working Paper 97-8, Bank of Canada, p. 9.

FIGURE 6

The Target Overnight Interest Rate with Its Operating Band

Standing facilities are routine monetary operations involving the central bank that banks can use *at their discretion at any moment;* they include both *borrowing* and *deposit* facilities.

The overnight rate can, in theory, take any value within the operating band, the range of which is given by the shaded area in Figure 6. But it cannot go outside this band because of the standing facilities. Why is this so? Why does the Bank of Canada have the power to so strongly influence the overnight rate? The essential reason for this is that in Canada, as in virtually all countries, all payments must eventually be settled on the books of the central bank, in this case, the Bank of Canada.

Payments go through two steps: First, they are cleared, then they are settled. *Clearing* is the daily process by which banks exchange and deposit payment items for their clients and determine the net amounts owed to each. Settlement is the procedure by which banks use claims on the Bank of Canada to fulfill their net obligations to all other banks at the end of the day.

The Bank of Canada is the settlement agent of the LVTS—the main payment system in Canada. Banks need to settle with the LVTS at the end of the day, and they must do so on the books of the Bank of Canada. The Bank of Canada provides settlement accounts to LVTS participants; it provides funds to those that need to cover their settlement obligations (those that have negative LVTS balances at the end of the day), and it transfers claims on itself for those banks ending the day with positive LVTS balances.

Suppose, as was the case in the example in Table 6 of Chapter 12, that the Bank of Montreal has a net debit LVTS position (a negative LVTS balance) at the end of the day. How much is it willing to pay other banks to borrow balances from them and bring its LVTS balance position back to zero? Clearly it is not willing to pay an interest rate higher than 4.25 percent, since this is the rate that the Bank of Canada will charge to banks with negative LVTS balances. If all other banks were offering to charge more than 4.25 percent to lend LVTS balances, the Bank of Montreal would turn down these offers and would simply take an advance from the Bank of Canada at the bank rate of 4.25 percent.

Now, what about the banks that have positive LVTS balances? What is their reasoning? Suppose, as was the case in Table 6 of Chapter 12, that the Toronto-Dominion Bank has a net credit LVTS position. What is the minimum interest rate that will induce the TD Bank to lend its balance to other banks (thus also bringing its LVTS balance position back to zero)? Clearly, it needs to be paid more than 3.75 percent, since this is the rate that it would get anyway if it were to leave its LVTS balances as a deposit at the Bank of Canada. If no deal can be struck between the Bank of Montreal and the Toronto-Dominion Bank, then the balance sheet of the Bank of Canada will be as shown in Table 2 below. The Toronto-Dominion Bank will be granted a claim on the Bank of Canada—its LVTS balance will be brought down to zero and transformed into an overnight deposit at the Bank of Canada. As for the Bank of Montreal, it will have to borrow $400,000 from the Bank of Canada to bring its LVTS balances back to zero.

TABLE 2

Balance Sheet of Bank of Canada with No Deal Struck between Banks

Bank of Canada	
Assets	Liabilities and Net Worth
Advance to the Bank of Montreal at 4.25 percent +$400,000	Deposits of Toronto-Dominion Bank at 3.75 percent +$400,000

The overnight interest rate that will arise from the negotiations between potential lenders and borrowers of overnight funds will thus have to be somewhere between 3.75 and 4.25 percent. Indeed, unless there are some unusual circumstances, the realized overnight rate will turn out to be very close to the middle of the operating band, at the target overnight rate—in the case described by Figure 6 it will stand at 4.00 percent or very close to it, perhaps at 4.02 or 3.98, or perhaps at 4.01 percent. There are essentially two reasons for this. First, the banks know that the Bank of Canada wishes the overnight rate to be around 4.00 and that it will intervene if the actual rate keeps drifting away from the target rate. Second, competition should bring the overnight interest rate to near the middle of the operating band because at that point, the opportunity gain of the lenders and that of the borrowers are precisely the same, being equal to 25 basis points for both groups of participants in the overnight market.

> The Canadian monetary policy implementation framework is such that the realized overnight interest rate is always, or nearly always, at the midpoint of the operational band, at the target overnight rate, or within just a few basis points of the target set by the Bank of Canada. The operational target of the Bank of Canada—the overnight interest rate—is strongly under its control.

■ Settlement Balances

As long as LVTS transactions involve only banks and not the public sector, whenever a bank is in a deficit position (whenever it has a negative LVTS balance), there is another bank, or a group of other banks, that has an identical surplus position (a posi-

The Role of Lender of Last Resort

In addition to its standing facilities, the Bank of Canada offers an additional access to borrowing, which is tied to its role of lender of last resort. One of the roles of the Bank of Canada is to prevent financial panics and to avoid the spread of bank defaults, where the failure of one bank would generate the failure of another bank, with a domino effect. Various rules and controls have been put in place in the clearing and settlement system, so that a defaulting or a failing bank should not jeopardize the health of the rest of the banking industry. In the unlikely event that several banks failed simultaneously, the Bank of Canada would be obliged to supply funds to the LVTS, thus acting as the lender of last resort.

The Bank of Canada may also act as a lender of last resort in another situation. An otherwise solvent bank may be subjected to a bank run, where depositors all want to turn their deposits into cash or to transfer their deposits to another institution. In such a case, the bank would be forced to sell some of its assets, many of which are likely to be nonmarketable and difficult to sell without incurring large losses. To prevent a liquidity problem from turning into a solvency problem, the Bank of Canada may decide to grant loans to this bank at the bank rate, for a maximum term to maturity of six months, and this would be called an Emergency Lending Assistance loan.

tive LVTS balance). In other words, *under the above condition*, the *net* overall amount of LVTS balances held by banks—the sum of the positive and negative LVTS balances of all of the banks—is zero at all times (this corresponds to the vertical dotted line at 0 in Figure 6).

Things are entirely different when payment transactions involve the federal government or the central bank, such as when the federal government pays its employees, when it collects taxes, when the Bank of Canada purchases or sells foreign currencies on foreign exchange markets on behalf of government, when it provides banks with currency, or when it undertakes transactions in government securities with banks or dealers. In all of these instances, one bank may be in a LVTS deficit position without any other bank being in a surplus position, or one bank may be in a LVTS surplus position, with none of the other banks being in a deficit position. In this case, the *net* overall amount of LVTS balances held by banks—the amount of **settlement balances** as they are called by the Bank of Canada—will not be zero.

Why do monetary transactions involving the federal government or the central bank disrupt the symmetrical behaviour of positive and negative individual LVTS balances? To examine the peculiarity of federal government transactions, let us suppose that it is the end of April, when taxpayers are sending in their tax returns with their tax payments. Take the example of a wealthy taxpayer—a customer of the Bank of Montreal—who has to send in an additional $60,000 in federal tax. Table 3 summarizes what happens in the payment system.

> **Settlement balances** are the *net* aggregate amount of LVTS balances held by banks, that is, the sum of positive and negative LVTS balances of all of the banks.

TABLE 3					
The Impact on Intraday Changes in Balance Sheets of the Federal Government Collecting Tax Revenues					
Bank of Montreal (BMO)		LVTS		Bank of Canada (B of C)	
Assets	Liabilities	Assets	Liabilities	Assets	Liabilities
LVTS balance −$60,000	Deposit of taxpayer −$60,000		Balance of BMO −$60,000		Deposit of Canadian government +$60,000
			Balance of B of C +$60,000	LVTS balance +$60,000	

First, note that the Bank of Canada is the fiscal agent of the Canadian government; in other words, the Bank of Canada handles the payments to the federal government. When the taxpayer orders the Bank of Montreal to make the $60,000 payment, the account of the federal government at the Bank of Canada is credited with $60,000 while the LVTS balance of the Bank of Montreal is diminished by $60,000. The *net* aggregate amount of LVTS balances held by banks thus diminishes by $60,000. Payments to the federal government constitute a drain on settlement balances. If nothing else occurs, the Bank of Montreal will be looking in vain for a counterparty in its efforts to borrow funds in the overnight market, since no bank has a compensatory positive LVTS balance. This will tend to push the overnight rate above the target overnight rate, toward the bank rate, since some banks, here the Bank of Montreal, will be forced to borrow from the Bank of Canada at the bank rate.

But the Bank of Canada wants the overnight rate to be at its target rate, not above it. What can it do to avoid such a situation? The Bank of Canada must pursue *neutralizing* operations that will compensate for the impact of government transactions on settlement balances. In other words, the Bank of Canada will take measures to bring back to zero the amount of settlement balances. The actions taken to modify settlement balances are described as **settlement-balance management**.

> **Settlement-balance management** is the action that the Bank of Canada takes to neutralize the impact of government transactions, thus bringing back the supply of settlement balances to their desired level, usually zero.

■ Government Deposit Shifting

Settlement-balance management in Canada is pursued by shifting government deposits. In the case described by Table 3, to neutralize the impact of tax collection, the Bank of Canada needs to shift Canadian government deposits back to the banks. Suppose that it does so, with $60,000 worth of government deposits being shifted to the government account at the Bank of Montreal, as shown in Table 3. In reality the deposits are auctioned off, with the banks that offer the highest deposit rate getting the government deposits. Suppose that in this case, the Bank of Montreal acquires $60,000 worth of LVTS balances when the auction is completed. Adding Tables 3 and 4, we obtain Table 5, which shows that the system is back to a zero amount of settlement balances. The payment flows involving the government sector have been entirely neutralized.

TABLE 4

The Impact on Intraday Changes in Balance Sheets of a Shift of Government Deposits into Banks

Bank of Montreal (BMO)			LVTS		Bank of Canada (B of C)	
Assets	Liabilities	Assets	Liabilities	Assets	Liabilities	
LVTS balance +$60,000	Deposit of government +$60,000		Balance of BMO $+60,000		Deposit of government −$60,000	
			Balance of B of C −$60,000	LVTS balance −$60,000		

When the federal government receives a payment (taxes), the banking system as a whole is put into a negative settlement-balance position; when the federal government makes a payment (expenditures), the banking system as a whole is put into a positive settlement-balance position.

To neutralize the effects of financial payments received by the federal government (or the central bank), the Bank of Canada shifts government deposits from its own accounts to banks; to neutralize the effects of financial payments made by the federal government (or those made by itself), the Bank of Canada shifts government deposits from banks to its own accounts.

The Bank of Canada transfers government deposits twice a day. It first does so in the early morning, when most of the bank payments go through the LVTS. It does so again late in the afternoon, after all bank payments involving the federal government have been made. When this second adjustment is being carried out, the Bank of

TABLE 5

The Neutralizing Impact of a Shift of Government Deposits into Banks, Following a Federal Government Revenue Inflow

Bank of Montreal (BMO)			LVTS		Bank of Canada (B of C)	
Assets	Liabilities	Assets	Liabilities	Assets	Liabilities	
LVTS balance $0	Deposit of taxpayer −$60,000		Balance of BMO $0		Deposit of government $0	
	Deposit of government +$60,000		Balance of B of C $0	LVTS balance $0		

Canada knows with certainty how many settlement balances are in the system. The Bank of Canada is thus able to calculate the exact amount of government deposits that need to be shifted to achieve a zero amount of settlement balances, as occurred in our example in Table 5. Unless there are some unusual circumstances, the amount of government deposits being auctioned will be such that the amount of settlement balances is indeed zero by the end of the day. In other words, the Bank of Canada normally targets a zero amount of settlement balances.

> Under normal circumstances, the net amount of settlement balances in the system is zero at the end of the day. The amounts of positive LVTS balances held by some banks are exactly equal to the amounts of negative LVTS balances held by the other banks.

Thus, despite the existence of government payment transactions, the situation by the end of the day is exactly the same as it would be if no such transactions had occurred. Any bank with a net debit LVTS position that needs to borrow funds to settle its position is aware that there is at least one other bank with an offsetting net credit LVTS position—a potential lender. These banks will meet on the overnight market and the rate of interest will tend to be the target overnight rate.

The Supply of Base Money

It follows that, whatever the size of GDP, the size of daily transactions, or the size of the money supply, *under normal circumstances*, bank deposits at the Bank of Canada are zero or very close to zero, while advances by the Bank of Canada are also zero or next to zero. The magnitude of these deposits and advances, a few dozen million dollars on average, with a few spikes into the hundreds of millions, is dwarfed by the size of daily transactions through the LVTS (more than $183 billion) and the size of monetary aggregates such as M2+ (over $1,000 billion). These few dozen millions are peanuts when measured by the scale of the Canadian monetary system, and hence can be considered as being virtually equal to zero. Actually, to grease the wheels of the payment system, the Bank of Canada purposefully targets a small amount of positive settlement balances—$25 million in 2007. A banking officer who lets this amount remain as an overnight deposit at the Bank of Canada, instead of lending it in the overnight market, would forgo about $2,775 in interest—a small amount of cash!

There are, however, abnormal or unusual circumstances, where the amount of settlement balances is not zero or close to zero. A well-known instance occurred when the World Trade Center in the financial centre of New York was subjected to two airplane attacks on September 11, 2001. The Bank of Canada, along with other central banks, made it clear that it would alleviate any fear of financial disruption by providing the monetary system with the additional liquidity that was being demanded by the banks and other financial institutions. For more than a week, the Bank of Canada set settlement balances at levels of several hundreds of millions of dollars.

More recently, in August 2007, the Bank of Canada felt compelled to supply more than $1,000 million in settlement balances during a couple of days because of a confidence crisis in the wake of the turmoil created by the meltdown of the subprime mortgage market in the United States. Large amounts of settlement balances were again provided later in 2007 and again in 2008, as the confidence crisis subsided. Technical factors also occasionally forced the Bank of Canada to set settlement balances at *negative* levels in 2006 and 2007.

What all this means is that the Bank of Canada sets the supply of settlement balances at the level demanded by banks: The supply is demand-led. In the case of the 9/11 and the 2007–2008 subprime crises, there was a temporary large demand for settlement balances because banks were highly reluctant to lend to each other. Banks preferred to hold secured deposits at the Bank of Canada rather than lend these funds to other banks at the slightly higher overnight interest rate and risk losing their funds. This induced the Bank of Canada to set the supply of settlement balances much above zero, to keep the overnight interest rate on target.

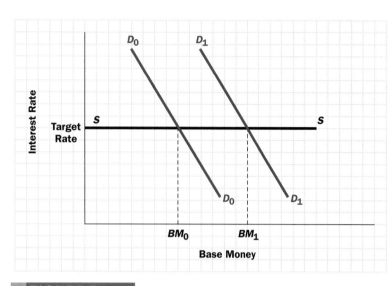

FIGURE 7

The Demand for and the Supply of Base Money

Base money is made up of two components of the liability side of the balance sheet of the central bank: currency and deposits received.

Open-market operations refer to the sale or purchase of government securities by the Bank of Canada through transactions in the open market.

Central banks also supply banks with currency on demand. Whenever banks need to fill their ATMs with more bank notes, the Bank of Canada sells these bank notes to the banks. Thus, if we call the sum of currency and bank deposits at the central bank **base money**, we can say that there is a horizontal supply of base money, SS, at the target overnight interest rate. Whenever the demand for base money increases, so does the supply of base money. This is illustrated in Figure 7, based on the standard assumption that the demand for base money is downward-sloping (the interest rate being a measure of the opportunity cost of holding coins or bank notes—the higher the interest rate, the less base money one wishes to hold). If there is a shift in the demand for base money from $D_0 D_0$ to $D_1 D_1$, the supply of base money will accommodate at the target overnight interest rate, moving from BM_0 to BM_1.

■ Open-Market Operations and Buyback Operations

The Bank of Canada can make use of another operational instrument when unusual circumstances arise. This instrument is called **open-market operations**, which traditionally involve the sale or the purchase of government securities by the central bank. The counterparty to this transaction could be a bank or a nonfinancial firm, or it involves a government securities distributor, called a *primary dealer*.

The bookkeeping related to purchases of securities by the central bank is shown in Table 6, where for simplicity it is assumed that a bank is the counterparty. The Bank of Montreal receives a payment inflow when it sells securities to the central bank, obtaining an LVTS balance in the process. The Bank of Canada thus adds $100,000 worth of settlement balances to the system.

The Balance Sheet of the Bank of Canada

As the fiscal agent of the Canadian government, the Bank of Canada is also in charge of the government's holdings of foreign currencies. These are held in the Exchange Fund Account. The balance sheet of the Canadian monetary authorities is thus the sum of the balance sheet of the Bank of Canada plus that of the Exchange Fund Account.

As can be seen from the accompanying table, foreign exchange reserves (assets held in foreign currencies such as U.S. dollars, euros, gold) comprise nearly half of the total assets of the Canadian monetary authorities, the other half being securities previously issued by the Canadian government. On the other side of the balance sheet, currency is the main liability of the monetary authorities. Deposits by banks into the Bank of Canada account represent only a minute proportion of these liabilities. The rest is made up of Canadian government deposits.

The Balance Sheet of the Canadian Monetary Authorities, December 2007

Assets		Liabilities	
Official foreign exchange reserves	$40	Currency	$52
Treasury bills issued by Canadian government	16	Deposits of banks	1
Long-term government bonds	29	Canadian government claims	41
Others	6	Net worth	−3
Total	**$91**	**Total**	**$91**

Note: All numbers are in billions of dollars.

SOURCE: Statistics Canada, *National Balance Sheet Accounts*, Catalogue No. 13-214-XIE, Table 12.

TABLE 6

**Effects on the Intraday Balance Sheets of a Bank
and the Bank of Canada of a Central Bank Open-Market Securities Purchase**

Bank of Montreal		Bank of Canada	
Assets	Liabilities	Assets	Liabilities
Canadian government securities −$100,000		Canadian government securities +$100,000	
LVTS balance +$100,000		LVTS balance −$100,000	

What is the impact of such operations on the overnight interest rate? When the central bank acquires securities on the open market (as in Table 6), it increases the net amount of settlement balances in the system. This will tend to push down the overnight interest rate since some banks will wind up with positive LVTS balances that they will be unable to lend on the overnight market. In symmetry, central bank sales on the open market decrease the net amount of settlement balances and hence push up the overnight interest rate.

Since 1995, the Bank of Canada no longer pursues *outright* open-market operations. Instead it pursues only **buyback operations**, whereby the Bank of Canada sells or purchases government securities, but with the promise to reverse the transaction the next day (or sometimes later) at a predetermined price. This instrument gives much more flexibility to central banks. When, for instance, the Bank of Canada makes a purchase and resale agreement, the settlement balances that are added to the system are removed automatically the next day, when the resale provision kicks in. It is thus equivalent to a collaterized one-day loan. The buyback operations, because they are *repurchase* operations, are called *repos*. This gives rise to the *repo* market, which is part of the overnight market.

Today, the Bank of Canada uses buyback operations occasionally, on average less than once a week, when it is unhappy with the evolution of the overnight interest rate relative to the target overnight rate. Banks transact with each other and with other financial entities on the overnight market all day long, on the basis of their current LVTS balance positions. When the overnight rate is trading above the target rate, for instance, the Bank of Canada might intervene on the repo market, typically a bit before noon, offering to purchase securities for one day at the target overnight rate, thus offering to lend funds for one day at the target rate. Banks that need to borrow funds will take the offer, borrowing, say, at 4.00 percent instead of the 4.10 or 4.15 percent market rate. The effects of these operations are usually quite fast: The actual overnight rate quickly comes back to its target.

> Central bank purchases of securities increase the amount of settlement balances and tend to decrease the overnight interest rate. Central bank sales of securities decrease the amount of settlement balances and tend to increase the overnight interest rate.

Under normal circumstances, open-market operations and buyback operations play only a supporting role in the determination and control of the Canadian overnight interest rate. The major operational instruments in Canada are the standing facilities of the corridor system and shifts in government deposits. But whatever the instrument, the main lesson is that the Bank of Canada supplies the amount of base money that is being demanded, so as to achieve the target overnight interest rate. The ability of the central bank to drive the overnight rate toward its target allows the Bank of Canada to pursue its monetary policy strategy. See Table 7 for a recap of the impact of various transactions on settlement balances and overnight interest rates.

Buyback operations, which occur on the repo market, are sales of securities accompanied by promises to repurchase the securities at a predetermined price on a specific day, usually the next day.

TABLE 7

Impact of Various Transactions on Settlement Balances and Overnight Interest Rates: A Recap

Action	Settlement Balances	Overnight Interest Rates
Citizens pay their federal taxes. Central bank sells securities. Central bank sells bank notes to banks. Central bank sells foreign currency on foreign exchange markets. Central bank transfers government deposits to its own accounts.	Fall (Banks make a payment outflow involving the Bank of Canada)	Tend to rise
Federal government pays its employees. Central bank buys securities. Central bank buys foreign currency on foreign exchange markets. Central bank transfers government deposits to other banks.	Rise (Banks receive a payment inflow involving the Bank of Canada)	Tend to fall

■ FROM MODELS TO POLICY DEBATES

You will no doubt be relieved to hear that we have now provided just about all the technical apparatus we need to analyze stabilization policy. To be sure, you will encounter many graphs in the next few chapters. Most of them, however, repeat diagrams with which you are already familiar. Our attention now turns from *building* a theory to *using* that theory to address several important policy issues.

The next three chapters take up a trio of controversial policy debates that surface regularly in the newspapers: the debate over the conduct of stabilization policy (Chapter 14), the continuing debate over budget deficits and the effects of fiscal and monetary policy on growth (Chapter 15), and the controversy over the trade-off between inflation and unemployment (Chapter 16).

SUMMARY

1. The Bank of Canada is the Canadian **central bank**. It is run by the governor and deputy governor. While the governor is appointed by the board of the Bank, subject to approval by the minister of Finance, the Bank of Canada enjoys a good amount of independence.

2. Over the past 20 or 25 years, many countries have decided that **central bank independence** is a good idea and have moved in that direction.

3. **Monetary policy** can be subdivided into two components: **monetary policy implementation**, which has to do with the operational targets and instruments used by a central bank, and **monetary policy strategy**, which has to do with the macroeconomic goals pursued by the central bank and the actions needed to achieve them.

4. The preamble to the Bank of Canada Act states that the Bank has several goals, but over the last 15 years the Bank of Canada has focused on low inflation as its main macroeconomic goal. Canada is under an **inflation targeting** regime, with a 2 percent inflation rate target and a target inflation band between 1 and 3 percent.

5. The Bank of Canada sets the **target overnight interest rate** with a view to keeping the inflation rate, as measured by the CPI, near the inflation target. This is the **reaction function** of the central bank. To assess future inflation, the Bank of Canada relies on measures of **core inflation**, which excludes certain CPI items whose prices are the most volatile, such as food and energy, and estimates of the **output gap**, which is an assessment of the pressures on capacity and inflation. A well-known reaction function is the Taylor Rule.

6. When the Bank of Canada fears that future inflation rates will exceed the target inflation rate, it raises the target overnight rate to achieve higher real interest rates. High real interest rates have a negative impact on all three major private components of aggregate expenditures. High interest rates discourage borrowers and reduce their cash flow. Also, high interest rates attract foreign investors, thus pushing up the value of the Canadian dollar and making it more difficult for domestic producers to compete with foreign producers. These effects help to explain the transmission mechanism of monetary policy.

7. The Bank of Canada uses a **corridor system**, with a target overnight interest rate that is at the midpoint of the **operating band**. The corridor system relies on **standing facilities**, whereby banks (with appropriate collateral) are free to borrow from the Bank of Canada at the **bank rate** to settle their LVTS obligations, as well as being able to deposit their surplus LVTS balances at the **interest rate on deposits at the central bank**, thus keeping the actual overnight rate within the operating band.

8. To achieve the target overnight interest rate, the Bank of Canada supplies bank notes on demand and it usually sets the supply of **settlement balances** to zero, unless there are some exceptional or technical factors. This is called **settlement-balance management**, which is done by shifting government deposits from the central bank to banks, or vice-versa.

9. When the government makes a payment, settlement balances are added to the monetary system; when the government receives a payment, settlement balances are withdrawn from the system.

10. When government deposits are shifted from the central bank to banks, settlement balances are added to the system; when government deposits are shifted from banks to the central bank, settlement balances are drained out of the system.

11. **Open-market operations** are conducted when the central bank purchases government securities on the open market, in which case, it adds settlement balances to the system, or when the central bank sells government securities, in which case it diminishes the amount of settlement balances in the monetary system.

12. In Canada, open-market operations are conducted solely through **buyback operations**, also called *repos*, where the central bank promises to reverse the operation, usually on the next day. On the days when they occur, buyback operations are usually conducted around noon, when the Bank of Canada is unhappy about the value taken by the overnight interest rate relative to its target.

KEY TERMS

Monetary policy 282

Central bank 282

Central bank independence 283

Monetary policy implementation 284

Monetary policy strategy 285

Overnight interest rate 285

Target overnight interest rate 285

Inflation targeting 286

Core inflation 288

Output gap 288

Reaction function 289

Operating band 292

Interest rate on deposits at the central bank 292

Bank rate 292

Corridor system 292

Standing facilities 293

Settlement balances 295

Settlement-balance management 295

Base money 298

Open-market operations 298

Buyback operations 299

TEST YOURSELF

1. Unlike in Europe, where central banks seemed to have naturally evolved over the centuries, neither Canada nor the United States had central banks before the twentieth century. What reasons could account for this obvious difference in the historical evolution of central banks?

2. Suppose that the Bank of Canada enlarges its building on Wellington Street in Ottawa at a cost of $100 million, and that the construction company has a bank account at the Bank of Montreal. Show how this will change the balance sheet of the Bank of Canada and that of the Bank of Montreal, as well as their LVTS balances. Compare this to the effect of an open-market purchase of securities by the Bank of Canada. What do you conclude?

3. Suppose that the Bank of Canada purchases $500 million worth of government bonds from a dealer that has a bank account at the Toronto-Dominion Bank. Show the effects on the balance sheets of the Bank of Canada, the Toronto-Dominion Bank, the dealer, and the LVTS. Does it make any difference if the Bank of Canada buys bonds from a bank or a dealer?

4. Treasury bills have a fixed face value (say, $1000) and pay interest by selling "at a discount." For example, if a one-year bill with a $1,000 face value sells today for $950, it will pay $1,000 − $950 = $50 in interest over its life. The interest rate on the bill is therefore $50/$950 = 0.0526, or 5.26 percent.

   a. Suppose the price of the treasury bill falls to $925. What happens to the interest rate?

   b. Suppose, instead, that the price rises to $975. What is the interest rate now?

   c. **(More difficult)** Now generalize this example. Let P be the price of the bill and r be the interest rate. Develop an algebraic formula expressing r in terms of P. (*Hint:* The interest earned is $1,000 − $P. What is the *percentage* interest rate?) Show that this formula demonstrates that higher bond prices mean lower interest rates.

5. When banks require bank notes, the bank notes are automatically supplied by the Bank of Canada. As a first step, show what will happen to the balance sheets of the Bank of Canada, the banks, and the LVTS, when $100 million worth of bank notes are being supplied to the banks. As a second step, show how the Bank of Canada will be using shifts of government deposits to neutralize the first operation.

6. In your answer to Test Yourself Question 5, you should have found that, at the end of the second step, government deposits at the Bank of Canada would be diminished by $100 million. As more and more bank notes are inserted into the Canadian economy, as the value of transactions grows, neutralization will require that more and more government deposits are shifted to banks. At some point, all of the government deposits at the Bank of Canada would vanish. Show that this process can be stopped and reversed when the Bank of Canada is purchasing securities newly issued by the Canadian government. Show the Bank of Canada balance sheet changes when $100 million worth of securities are purchased by the Bank of Canada when the issue is being auctioned.

7. **(More difficult)** Consider an economy in which government purchases, taxes, and net exports are all zero, the consumption function is

$$C = 300 + 0.75Y$$

and investment spending (I) depends on the rate of interest (r) in the following way:

$$I = 1,000 - 100r$$

Find the equilibrium GDP if the Bank of Canada makes the rate of interest (a) 2 percent ($r = 0.02$), (b) 5 percent, and (c) 10 percent.

8. According to the Taylor Rule, what target overnight interest rate would the Bank of Canada set, given the following conditions: the current inflation rate is 2.5 percent, the output gap is −1 percent, and the target inflation rate is 2 percent?

9. By drawing aggregate demand and supply curves, confirm the validity of elements 5 and 6 in Table 1 on page 287.

DISCUSSION QUESTIONS

1. Why does a modern industrial economy need a central bank?

2. What are some reasons behind the worldwide trend toward greater central bank independence? Are there arguments against such independence?

3. What advantages are there with inflation targeting? Do you see any disadvantages? What if inflation is high when a financial crisis hits the economy?

4. Between September 2005 and March 2006, the target overnight rate was hiked up by 25 basis points on no less than six occasions. What are the likely reasons for such interest rate increases?

5. Explain why both business investments and purchases of new homes rise when interest rates decline.

6. With the help of a graph, explain why interest rates need not rise when there is an increase in the demand for currency (bank notes)—an upward shift of the demand curve for currency.

7. By extrapolating the values of the table below, estimate what the target (nominal) overnight rate and the target real overnight rate would be if forecasted inflation stood at 10 percent? If inflation stood at −2 percent, in other words there is a 2 percent *deflation* (prices fall at a 2 percent rate)? And if *deflation* reaches 4 percent? What happens to the reaction function and the ability of the central bank to pursue monetary policy and set real interest rates if *deflation* rises above 2 percent?

A Possible Schedule of the Reaction Function of the Central Bank

Forecasted Inflation Rate	Target (Nominal) Overnight Rate	Target Real Overnight Rate
−1%	0.5%	1.5%
0	2	2
1	3.5	2.5
2	5	3
3	6.5	3.5
4	8	4
6	11	5

14

THE DEBATE OVER MONETARY AND FISCAL POLICY

Perhaps the single most important and most thoroughly documented yet obstinately rejected proposition is that "inflation is always and everywhere a monetary phenomenon."

MILTON FRIEDMAN (1912–2006), 1976 RECIPIENT OF THE BANK OF SWEDEN PRIZE IN ECONOMIC SCIENCES IN MEMORY OF ALFRED NOBEL, 1994

U p to now, our discussion of stabilization policy has been almost entirely objective and technical. In seeking to understand how the national economy works and how government policies affect it, we have mostly ignored the intense economic and political controversies that surround the actual conduct of monetary and fiscal policy. Chapters 14 through 16 cover precisely these issues.

We begin this chapter by introducing an alternative theory of how monetary policy affects the economy, known as *monetarism*. Although monetarist theories are not as dominant as they once were, some of the ideas are still highly influential or have paved the way for alternatives to Keynesian theories. We will see that important differences *do* arise among economists over the appropriate design and execution of monetary *policy*. These differences are the central concern of the chapter. We will learn about the continuing debates about the operational targets and goals of the Bank of Canada and about the relative virtues of monetary versus fiscal policy. As we will see, the resolution of these issues is crucial to the proper conduct of stabilization policy and, indeed, to the decision of whether the government should try to stabilize the economy at all.

CONTENTS

ISSUE: *Should We Forsake Stabilization Policy?*

We have suggested several times in this book that well-timed changes in fiscal or monetary policy can mitigate fluctuations in inflation and unemployment. For example, when the U.S. economy sagged after the terrorist attacks in September 2001, *both* fiscal policy *and* monetary policy in the United States turned more expansionary. These actions might be called "textbook responses," reflecting the lessons you have learned in Chapters 11 and 13.

But some economists argue that these lessons are best forgotten. In practice, they claim, attempts at macroeconomic stabilization are likely to do more harm than good. Policy makers are therefore best advised to follow fixed *rules* rather than use their best judgment on a case-by-case basis.

Nothing we have said so far leads to this conclusion. But we have not yet told the whole story. By the end of the chapter you will have encountered several arguments in favour of rules, so you will be in a better position to make up your own mind on this important issue.

MONETARISM

In the previous chapter, we studied how monetary policy influences real output and the inflation rate. The approach that we took relied on Keynesian macroeconomics, noting however that our focus on the interest rate as the key monetary policy operational tool and the central bank reaction function belong to the Wicksellian tradition—the tradition of Swedish economist Knut Wicksell (1851–1926) that was nearly forgotten until its recent rediscovery by central bankers.

The main advocate of monetarism as an alternative explanation of how money affects the economy, Milton Friedman (1912–2006), never liked the term *monetarism*, preferring to say that he restated a well-known and ancient theory, the *quantity theory of money*. Friedman and his colleagues and students at the University of Chicago developed a set of theories that contradicted Keynesianism. Their theories, in particular monetarism, are sometimes known as the Chicago School. These economic views have had, and still have, an enormous influence on economic policy throughout the world. An adversary of Keynesian economics and Keynesian policies, Friedman was a staunch advocate of free-market policies and reduced government intervention. One of his books (written with his wife Rose Friedman), *Capitalism and Freedom* (1962), the title of which says it all, was a worldwide bestseller. Friedman also hosted an award-winning television series in the 1980s called *Free to Choose*, which was also the title of another bestselling book written by him and his wife.

While some of Friedman's macroeconomic constructs are still highly influential in the economics profession and among central bankers today—we will discuss a very important one in Chapter 16—some of his other ideas, in particular, the revival of the quantity theory of money, while still popular among some academic economists, are not as highly regarded by central bankers and others in the economics profession.

Velocity and the Quantity Theory of Money

While Friedman had long been crusading for the dismissal of Keynesian economics and the return of another view of how monetary policy affects real output and inflation, it was only in the early 1970s that Friedman managed to resuscitate a model much older than the Keynesian model, a model known as the *quantity theory of money*. When central bankers got stuck with rising inflation despite rising nominal interest rates, they started paying attention to Friedman and his proposed theories and policies. Not knowing where to turn, for a number of years they embraced his proposals with some enthusiasm. This was the case in particular at the Bank of Canada, under the pressure of some devoted academic followers of Friedman, notably David Laidler and Michael Parkin of the University of Western Ontario, as well as Thomas Courchene of Queen's University.

The model of the quantity theory of money is easy to understand once we introduce a new concept: **velocity**.

In Chapter 12, we learned that because barter is so cumbersome, virtually all economic transactions in advanced economies use money. Thus, if there are $1,000 billion worth of transactions in an economy during a particular year, and there is an average money stock of $200 billion during that year, then each dollar of money must have been used an average of five times during the year.

The number 5 in this example is called the *velocity of circulation*, or *velocity* for short, because it indicates the *speed* at which money circulates. For example, a particular dollar bill might be used to buy a haircut in January; the barber might use it to purchase a sweater in March; the storekeeper might then use it to pay for gasoline in May; the gas station owner could pay it out to a house painter in October; and the painter might spend it on a Christmas present in December. In this way, the same dollar is used five times during the year. If it was used only four times during the year, its velocity would be 4, and so on.

No one has data on every transaction in the economy. To make velocity an operational concept, economists need a workable measure of the dollar volume of all transactions. As mentioned in the previous chapter, the most popular choice is nominal gross domestic product (GDP), even though it ignores many transactions that use money, such as the huge volume of activity in financial markets. If we accept nominal GDP as our measure of the money value of transactions, we are led to a concrete definition of velocity as the ratio of nominal GDP to the number of dollars in the money stock. Because nominal GDP is the product of real GDP (Y) times the price level (P), we can write this definition in symbols as follows:

$$\text{Velocity} = \frac{\text{Value of transactions}}{\text{Money stock}} = \frac{\text{Nominal GDP}}{M} = \frac{P \times Y}{M}$$

By multiplying both sides of the equation by M, we arrive at an identity called the **equation of exchange**, which relates the money supply and nominal GDP:

$$\text{Money supply} \times \text{Velocity} = \text{Nominal GDP}$$

Alternatively, stated in symbols, we have:

$$M \times V = P \times Y$$

Here we have an obvious link between the stock of money, M, and the nominal value of the nation's output. This connection is merely a matter of arithmetic, however—not of economics. For example, it does not imply that the Bank of Canada can raise nominal GDP by increasing M. Why not? Because V might simultaneously fall enough to prevent the product $M \times V$ from rising. In other words, if more dollar bills circulated than before, but each bill changed hands more slowly, total spending might not rise. Thus, we need an auxiliary assumption to change the arithmetic identity into an economic theory:

The **quantity theory of money** transforms the equation of exchange from an arithmetic identity into an economic model by assuming that changes in velocity are so minor that velocity can be taken to be virtually constant.

You can see that if V never changed, the equation of exchange would be a marvelously simple model of the determination of nominal GDP—far simpler than the Keynesian model that took us several chapters to develop. To see this, it is convenient to rewrite the equation of exchange in growth-rate form:

$$\%\Delta M + \%\Delta V = \%\Delta P + \%\Delta Y$$

If V was constant (making its percentage change zero), this equation could say, for example, that if the Bank of Canada wanted to make nominal GDP grow by 4.7 percent per year, it need merely raise the money supply by 4.7 percent per year. In such a simple world, economists could use the equation of exchange to *predict* nominal GDP

Velocity indicates the number of times per year that an "average dollar" is spent on goods and services. It is the ratio of nominal gross domestic product (GDP) to the number of dollars in the money stock. That is:

$$\text{Velocity} = \frac{\text{Nominal GDP}}{\text{Money stock}}$$

The **equation of exchange** states that the money value of GDP transactions must be equal to the product of the average stock of money times velocity. That is:

$$M \times V = P \times Y$$

The **quantity theory of money** assumes that velocity is (approximately) constant. In that case, nominal GDP is proportional to the money stock.

growth by predicting the growth rate of money. And policy makers could *control* nominal GDP growth by controlling the growth of the money supply.

In the real world, things are not so simple because velocity is not a fixed number. But variable velocity does not necessarily destroy the usefulness of the quantity theory. As we explained in Chapter 1, all economic models make assumptions that are at least mildly unrealistic. Without such assumptions, they would not be models at all, just tedious descriptions of reality. The question is really whether the assumption of constant velocity is a useful abstraction from annoying detail or a gross distortion of the facts.

Figure 1 sheds some light on this question by showing the behaviour of velocity since 1975. Note that the figure includes two different measures of velocity, labelled V_1 and V_2. Why? Recall from Chapter 12 that we can measure money in several ways, the most popular of which are M1+ and M2+. Because velocity (V) is simply nominal GDP divided by the money stock (M), we get a *different* measure of V for *each* measure of M. Figure 1 shows the velocities of both M1+ and M2+.

FIGURE 1

Velocity of Circulation of M1+ and M2+, 1968–2007

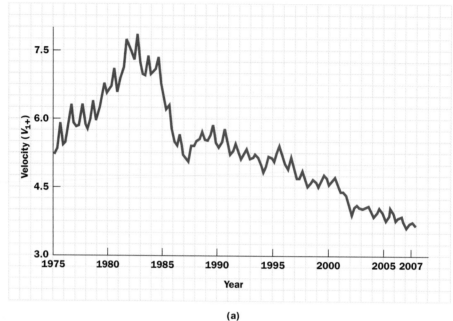

(a)

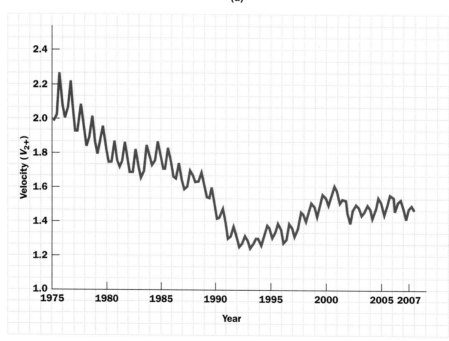

(b)

SOURCE: Created by the authors based on Statistics Canada, Series V37258 (M1+), V41552788 (M2+), and V498918 (GDP).

You will undoubtedly notice the stark difference in the behaviour of V_{1+} versus V_{2+}. The two velocities are far from moving in tandem. It is thus fundamental to know which measure of money is the most useful one. What is also remarkable is the quite erratic behaviour of both series, with substantial quarterly fluctuations. Clearly, neither measures of the velocity of money are constant. Because velocity is not stable in the short run, predictions of nominal GDP growth based on assuming constant velocity have not fared well, regardless of how M is measured. In a word, the strict quantity theory of money is not an adequate model of aggregate demand.

Some Determinants of Velocity

Because it is abundantly clear that velocity is a variable, not a constant, the equation of exchange is useful as a model of GDP determination only if we can explain movements in velocity. What factors decide whether a dollar will be used to buy goods and services four or five or six times per year? While numerous factors are relevant, two are important enough to merit discussion here.

Efficiency of the Payments System   Money is convenient for conducting transactions, which is why people hold it. But money has one important *dis*advantage: Cash pays no interest, and ordinary chequable accounts pay very little. Thus, if it were possible to convert interest-bearing assets into money on short notice and at low cost, a rational individual might prefer to use, say, credit cards for most purchases, making periodic transfers to her chequable account as necessary. That way, the same volume of transactions could be accomplished with lower money balances. By definition, velocity would rise.

The incentive to limit cash holdings thus depends on the ease and speed with which it is possible to exchange money for other assets—which is what we mean by the "efficiency of the payments system." As computerization has speeded up banks' bookkeeping procedures, as financial innovations have made it possible to transfer funds rapidly between chequable accounts and other assets, and as credit and debit cards have come to be used instead of cash, the need to hold money balances has declined and velocity has risen.

In practice, improvements in the payments system pose severe practical problems for analysts interested in predicting velocity. A host of financial innovations, beginning in the 1970s and continuing to the present day (some of which were mentioned in Chapter 12's discussion of the definitions of money), have transformed forecasting velocity into a hazardous occupation. In fact, many economists believe the task is impossible and should not even be attempted.

Interest Rates   A second key determinant of velocity is the rate of interest. The reason is implicit in what we have already said: The higher the rate of interest, the greater the *opportunity cost* of holding money. Therefore, as interest rates rise, people want to hold smaller cash balances (as illustrated in Figure 7 in Chapter 13). So the existing stock of money circulates faster, and velocity rises. Thus, we conclude that:

> Velocity is not a strict constant but depends on such things as the efficiency of the financial system and the rate of interest. Only by studying these determinants of velocity can we hope to predict the growth rate of nominal GDP from knowledge of the growth rate of the money supply.

The Quantity Theory Modernized

Adherents to the school of thought called **monetarism** try to do precisely that. Monetarists realize that velocity changes, but they claim that such changes are fairly *predictable*—certainly in the long run and perhaps even in the short run. As a result, they conclude that the best way to study economic activity is to start with the equation of exchange in growth-rate form:

$$\%\Delta M + \%\Delta V = \%\Delta P + \%\Delta Y$$

Monetarism is a mode of analysis that uses the equation of exchange to organize and analyze macroeconomic data.

From here, careful study of the determinants of money growth (which we provided in the previous two chapters) and of changes in velocity (which we just sketched) can be used to *predict* the growth rate of nominal GDP. Similarly, given an understanding of movements in V, controlling M can give the Bank of Canada excellent control over nominal GDP. These ideas are the central tenets of monetarism.

The monetarist and Keynesian approaches can be thought of as alternative theories of aggregate demand. Keynesians divide economic knowledge into four neat compartments marked C, I, G, and $(X - IM)$ and unite them all with the equilibrium condition that $Y = C + I + G + (X - IM)$. In Keynesian analysis, money affects the economy by first affecting interest rates. Monetarists, by contrast, organize their knowledge into two alternative boxes labelled M and V, and then use the identity $M \times V = P \times Y$ to predict aggregate demand. In the monetarist model, the role of money is not necessarily limited to working through interest rates.

The bit of arithmetic that multiplies M and V to get $P \times Y$ is neither more nor less profound than the one that adds up C, I, G and $(X - IM)$ to get Y, and certainly both are correct. The real question is which framework is more *useful* in practice. That is, which approach works better as a model of aggregate demand?

Although there is no generally correct answer for all economies in all periods of time, a glance back at Figure 1 will show you why most economists had abandoned monetarism by the early 1990s. Velocity behaved erratically even in the late 1970s, when it was first tried. In addition, as was detailed in Chapter 13, central bankers never felt comfortable with the idea that they could control the money supply, arguing instead that they could act on short-term interest rates. This, and the erratic velocity, explains why there are few true monetarists left.

Nonetheless, as we will see later in this chapter, some faint echoes of the debate between Keynesians and monetarists can still be heard. Furthermore, few economists doubt that there is a strong *long-run* relationship between M and P. This long-run relationship can be established by rewriting the growth-rate form of the equation of exchange in the following manner:

$$\%\Delta P = \%\Delta M + \%\Delta V - \%\Delta Y$$

assuming that the growth rates of V and Y are relatively stable in the long-run. Under these conditions, the growth rate of P (the inflation rate) is determined by the growth rate of the money supply M.

Most economists, however, would question whether this relationship between prices and the money supply is useful in the short run (see the boxed feature "Does Money Growth Always Cause Inflation?"). In addition, there is the crucial question of causality. As we pointed out in Chapter 1, while there may be a long-run relationship between money and prices, this does not necessarily imply that the causality runs from the money supply to prices. The relationship could exist because higher prices induce the banking system to increase the size of the money supply—a statement that is compatible with another theory, nearly as old as the *quantity theory of money*, called the **banking view**. Indeed, the reversed causality, from prices to the money supply, as argued by advocates of the banking view, is compatible with the Bank of Canada's position. As we saw in Chapter 13, the central bank automatically provides all of the currency that banks need for their customers' transactions, thus implying that the growth rate of the money supply is determined by the inflation rate (and the growth rate of real GDP).

The **banking view** holds that changes in nominal GDP cause changes in the stock of money, thus reversing the causality generally endorsed by adherents to the quantity theory of money.

■ DEBATE: SHOULD THE BANK OF CANADA CONTROL THE MONEY SUPPLY OR INTEREST RATES?

Another major controversy that raged for a couple of decades focused on how the Bank of Canada, along with central banks in the rest of the world, should implement monetary policy. Before the 1970s, most economists thought of monetary policy in terms of influencing short-term interest rates, such as the treasury bill rate. The

POLICY DEBATE

Does Money Growth Always Cause Inflation?

Monetarists have long claimed that, in the famous words of Milton Friedman, "inflation is always and everywhere a monetary phenomenon." By this statement, Friedman means that changes in the growth rate of the money supply ($\%\Delta M$) are far and away the principal cause of changes in the inflation rate ($\%\Delta P$)—in all places and at all times.

The accompanying chart uses recent Canadian economic history as an illustration. It helps to understand why so many economists rely on the dominant role of rapid money growth in accounting for high rates of inflation. In this scatter diagram, each point records both the growth rate of the M2+ money supply and the inflation rate (as measured by the Consumer Price Index) for a particular year between 1975 and 2007. Obviously, years of high inflation are associated with years of high money growth rates. There is thus an apparent positive relationship between the two variables.

However, years with similar inflation rates are sometimes associated with years of widely different growth rates of the money supply, as in 1992 and 1997; or years with similar money supply growth rates are associated with widely different

inflation rates, as in 1983 and 2002, so that the relationship between the two variables is not very clear-cut.

Such a graph, although it shows a positive link between money supply growth and inflation rates, cannot answer the more fundamental question of causality, which still remains an unsettled issue: Is inflation caused by money supply growth, or is money supply growth caused by inflation?

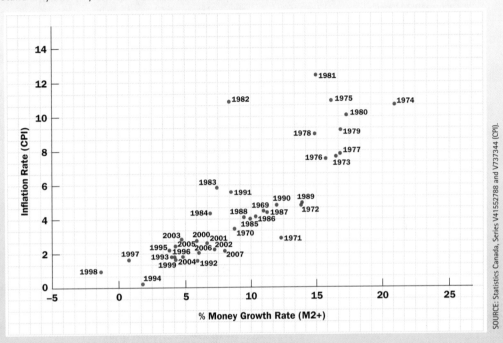

SOURCE: Statistics Canada, Series V41552788 and V737344 (CPI).

emphasis on interest rates again became the dominant view in the late 1980s and early 1990s, when the corridor system described in Chapter 13 was designed and then became the operating framework of the Bank of Canada.

But other economists, especially monetarists, insisted that the Bank of Canada should concentrate instead on controlling base money or some other measure of the money supply. Indeed, we saw in Chapter 1 that in 1986, Canadian economists were split nearly 50–50 as to whether the money supply was a more important target than interest rates for monetary policy. The Bank of Canada experimented with monetarist strictures for about seven years, between the fall of 1975 and November 1982. Other central banks pursued similar monetarist advice, but most of them gradually abandoned such policies. The debate still echoes today in Europe, where the European Central Bank, unlike the Bank of Canada and the Federal Reserve in the United States, still claims to pay attention to the growth of the money supply.

The monetarist advice looked pretty simple to understand and to implement. If one believes in the modernized quantity theory of money, then it follows that the growth rate of nominal GDP is approximately equal to the growth rate of the money stock. Thus, by controlling money supply growth, it is possible to influence the growth rate of nominal GDP, and if real GDP grows at a relatively stable rate, it follows that the monetary authorities can control the inflation rate by targeting and setting an appropriate money supply growth rate.

While the advice provided by monetarists looked straightforward enough, its implementation was not. During the period of monetarist experiment in Canada, several things went wrong and led to the abandonment of monetarism. First, most monetarists advised the Bank of Canada to target the growth rate of base money. As was pointed out in Chapter 13, base money is made up of two main components of the liability side of the central bank: currency and the deposits of banks at the Bank of Canada. These deposits at the central bank used to be called *reserves*. Monetarists were thus advising central bankers to use base money or reserves as their operating target. This recommendation relied on the belief that there was a stable ratio between broad money aggregates (for instance M1, M1+, or M2+) and the stock of base money. This ratio is determined by the **money multiplier** and is still found in most textbook explanations of the money supply process.

The **money multiplier** is the ratio of some broad money aggregate to base money (defined as the sum of currency and bank deposits at the central bank).

The officials at the Bank of Canada felt very uncomfortable with this money multiplier approach, even in the heyday of monetarism in the late 1970s. They argued that the money multiplier, just like the velocity of money, was bound to be highly unstable, as can be verified by examining Figure 2. Also, they argued that they could not target the supply of base money, claiming that they had to adjust the stock of base money to the forecasted changes in demand on a day-to-day basis. If the supply of base money were to be regulated in any other way, interest rates would be gyrating wildly every day, as shown in Figure 3. For instance, if the demand for base money moved from D_0D_0 to D_1D_1 within a day, interest rates would shoot up from 5 percent to 9 percent. To avoid this brisk hike in interest rates, the monetary authorities have to respond to the change in the demand for base money by increasing its supply from $8 billion to $9 billion. In other words, it was argued that the demand for base money was too unstable to allow the Bank of Canada to set the supply of money independently of the demand for it. As a result the Bank of Canada never pursued a full monetarist program, since it did not set or target base money.

The Bank of Canada, however, pursued the monetary policy strategy that was being recommended by monetarist economists, by setting and announcing targets of money supply growth based on measures of M1 (a money aggregate that is narrower than

---

FIGURE 2   The Evolution of the Money Multiplier (M1/Base Money) during the Heyday of Monetarism, 1970–1985

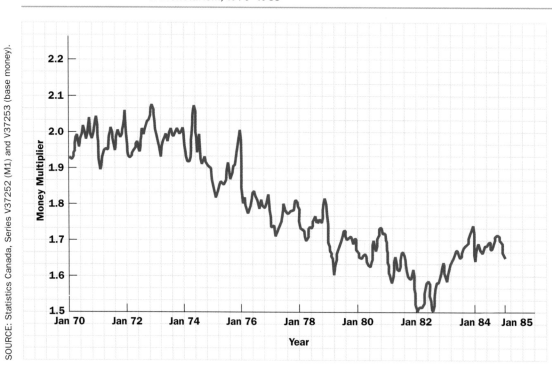

SOURCE: Statistics Canada, Series V37252 (M1) and V37253 (base money).

M1+, as defined in Chapter 12). These money growth targets were *intermediate* targets of the Bank of Canada, while interest rates remained operational targets because Bank of Canada officers tried to achieve these money growth targets by setting interest rates at levels that would steer the demand for money toward the targeted supply. However, two things happened that eventually led to the abandonment of these intermediate monetary targets. First, the Bank of Canada failed to achieve the targets on a number of occasions. Second, even when it did achieve the restrictive monetary targets, this was to no avail, since inflation rates remained high or continued to rise. For instance, between the end of 1980 and November 1982, M1 grew by almost 0 percent, while the inflation rate went above 10 percent. The quantity theory of money just did not hold up, as the velocity of money failed to remain stable.

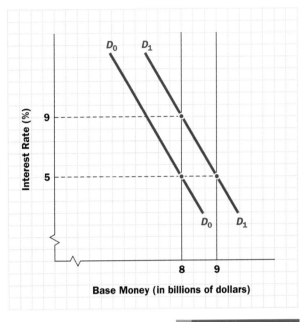

FIGURE 3

The Difficulties Associated with the Control of Base Money

Similar problems with the implementation of monetarism were plaguing other countries. For instance, many central banks that attempted to target wider monetary aggregates, such as M2, failed repeatedly to achieve their targets. In the United States in October 1982, the chairman of the Federal Reserve System announced that he was abandoning monetary targeting. This induced the Canadian central bank to do the same one month later. The then Bank of Canada governor, Gerald Bouey, made this memorable statement to the House of Commons Standing Committee on Finance, Trade, and Economics Affairs, after the monetary targets were withdrawn: "We did not abandon M1, M1 abandoned us."[1]

Despite all of the misgivings about money targeting that many Bank of Canada officials had, researchers there and in Canadian universities continued for some time to try to find stable monetary aggregates after 1982. A new monetary aggregate, broader than M1 and called M1A, was found at some point to be stable relative to GDP (in other words, it had a stable velocity), but it soon was discovered that this stability was the outcome of measurement errors! As late as 1988, Governor Crow was still expressing confidence in the ability of the Bank of Canada to use broader monetary aggregates, M2 and M2+, as useful intermediate targets.

The consensus view now, as pointed out in Chapter 13, is that central banks should give themselves a short-term interest rate—such as the overnight interest rate—as an operational target, moving the target rate so as to achieve a real interest rate that will have the appropriate effect on aggregate demand. Monetary aggregates, such as the growth rate of M1+ or M2+, should be used only as one element among many others that can help central bankers to estimate future values of the inflation rate. Indeed, on the website of the Bank of Canada, money supply growth does not appear among the indicators of capacity and inflation pressures. Instead, variables such as wage inflation, core inflation, commodity price indexes, rates of capacity utilization, office vacancy rates, and inflation expectations are to be found among the indicators of future inflation.

■ DEBATE: SHOULD WE RELY ON FISCAL OR MONETARY POLICY?

The Keynesian and monetarist approaches are like two different languages. But it is well known that language influences attitudes in many subtle ways. For example, the Keynesian language biases things toward thinking first about fiscal policy simply

---

[1] As reported by Charles Freedman, "Reflections on the Bank of Canada monetary policy framework," in P. Arestis, M. Baddeley, and J. McCombie (Eds.), *The New Monetary Policy: Implications and Relevance* (Cheltenham, UK: Edward Elgar, 2005), p.176.

because G is a part of $C + I + G + (X - IM)$. By contrast, the monetarist approach, working through the equation of exchange, $M \times V = P \times Y$, puts the spotlight on M. In fact, years ago economists engaged in a spirited debate in which extreme monetarists claimed that fiscal policy was futile, whereas extreme Keynesians argued that monetary policy was useless. Today, such arguments are rarely heard.

Instead of arguing over which type of policy is more *powerful*, economists nowadays debate which type of medicine—fiscal or monetary—cures the patient more *quickly*. Until now, we have ignored questions of timing and pretended that the authorities noticed the need for stabilization policy instantly, decided on a course of action right away, and administered the appropriate medicine at once. In reality, each of these steps takes time.

First, delays in data collection mean that the most recent data describe the state of the economy a few months ago. Second, one of the prices of democracy is that the government often takes a distressingly long time to decide what should be done, to muster the necessary political support, and to put its decisions into effect. Finally, our $1,500 billion economy is a bit like a sleeping elephant that reacts rather sluggishly to moderate fiscal and monetary prods. As it turns out, these *lags in stabilization policy*, as they are called, play a pivotal role in the choice between fiscal and monetary policy. Here's why.

The main policy tool for manipulating consumer spending (C) is the personal income tax, and Chapter 8 documented why the fiscal policy planner can feel fairly confident that each $1 of tax reduction will lead to about 90 to 95 cents of additional spending *eventually*. But not all of this extra spending happens at once.

First, consumers must learn about the tax change. Then they may need to be convinced that the change is permanent. Finally, there is simple force of habit: Households need time to adjust their spending habits when circumstances change. For all these reasons, consumers may increase their spending by only 30 to 50 cents for each $1 of additional income within the first few months after a tax cut. Only gradually will they raise their spending up to about 90 to 95 cents for each additional dollar of income.

Lags are much longer for investment (I), which provides the main vehicle by which monetary policy affects aggregate demand. Planning for capacity expansion in a large corporation is a long, drawn-out process. Ideas must be submitted and approved, plans must be drawn up, funding acquired, orders for machinery or contracts for new construction placed. And most of this activity occurs *before* any appreciable amount of money is spent. Economists have found that much of the response of investment to changes in either interest rates or tax provisions takes several *years* to develop. Similar but somewhat shorter lags are also observed in the case of housing investment, tied to the construction industry.

The fact that C responds more quickly than I has important implications for the choice among alternative stabilization policies. The reason is that the most common varieties of fiscal policy either affect aggregate demand directly—G is a component of $C + I + G + (X - IM)$—or work through consumption with a relatively short lag, whereas monetary policy primarily affects investment. Therefore:

> Conventional types of fiscal policy actions, such as changes in G or in personal taxes, probably affect aggregate demand much more promptly than do monetary policy actions.

So is fiscal policy a superior stabilization tool? Not quite. The lags we have just described, which are beyond policy makers' control, are not the only ones affecting the timing of stabilization policy. Additional lags stem from the behaviour of the policy makers themselves! We refer here to the delays that occur while policy makers study the state of the economy, contemplate which steps they should take, and put their decisions into effect.

Here monetary policy has a huge advantage. As pointed out in Chapter 13, page 283, the Governing Council of the Bank of Canada can change the target overnight interest rate eight times each year and more often if necessary. Thus, monetary policy decisions are made frequently. And once the Bank of Canada decides on a course of action, by tradition on Monday, it can execute its plan the following morning, on Tuesday at 9:00 A.M., when it announces the new interest rate target and the new operating band.

In contrast, federal budgeting procedures operate on an annual budget cycle. Except in unusual cases, major fiscal policy initiatives can occur only at the time of the annual budget. In principle, tax laws can be changed at any time, but the wheels of Parliament grind slowly and are often gummed up by partisan politics. For these reasons, it may take many months for Parliament to change fiscal policy. In sum, only in rare circumstances can the government take important fiscal policy actions on short notice. Thus:

Policy lags are normally much shorter for monetary policy than for fiscal policy.

So where does the combined effect of expenditure lags and policy lags leave us? With nothing very conclusive, we are afraid. In practice, most students of stabilization policy have come to believe that the unwieldy and often partisan nature of our political system make active use of fiscal policy for stabilization purposes difficult, if not impossible. Monetary policy, they claim, is the only realistic game in town, and therefore must bear the entire burden of stabilization policy.

■ DEBATE: THE SHAPE OF THE AGGREGATE SUPPLY CURVE

Another lively debate over stabilization policy revolves around the shape of the economy's aggregate supply curve. Many economists think of the aggregate supply curve as quite flat, as in Figure 4(a), so that large increases in output can be achieved with little inflation. But other economists envision the supply curve as steep, as shown in Figure 4(b), so that prices respond strongly to changes in output. The differences for public policy are substantial.

If the aggregate supply curve is flat, expansionary fiscal or monetary policy that raises the aggregate demand curve can buy large gains in real GDP at low cost in terms of inflation. In Figure 5(a) overleaf, stimulation of demand pushes the aggregate demand curve outward from D_0D_0 to D_1D_1, thereby moving the economy's equilibrium from point E to point A. The substantial rise in output ($40 billion) is accompanied by only a pinch of inflation (1 percent). So the antirecession policy is quite successful.

Conversely, when the supply curve is flat, a restrictive stabilization policy is not a very effective way to bring inflation down. Instead, it serves mainly to reduce real output, as Figure 5(b) shows. Here a leftward shift of the aggregate demand curve from D_0D_0 to D_2D_2 moves equilibrium from point E to point B, lowering real GDP by $40 billion but cutting the price level by merely 1 percent. Fighting inflation by contracting aggregate demand is obviously quite costly in this example.

FIGURE 4

Alternative Views of the Aggregate Supply Curve

Things are just the reverse if the aggregate supply curve is steep. In that case, expansionary fiscal or monetary policies will cause a good deal of inflation without boosting real GDP much. This situation is depicted in Figure 6(a), in which expansionary policies shift the aggregate demand curve outward from D_0D_0 to D_1D_1, thereby moving the economy's equilibrium from E to A. Output rises by only $10 billion but prices shoot up 10 percent.

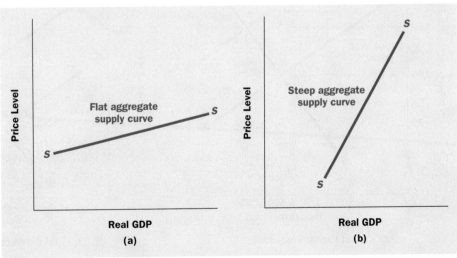

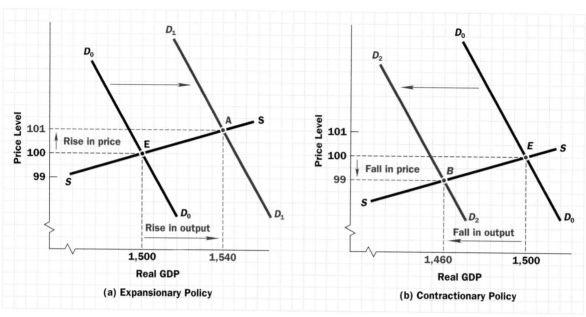

FIGURE 5

Stabilization Policy with a Flat Aggregate Supply Curve

Note: Real GDP in billions of dollars per year.

Similarly, contractionary policy is an effective way to bring down the price level without much sacrifice of output, as shown by the shift from E to B in Figure 6(b). Here it takes only a $10 billion loss of output (from $1,500 billion to $1,490 billion) to "buy" 10 percent less inflation.

As we can see, deciding whether the aggregate supply curve is steep or flat is clearly of fundamental importance to the proper conduct of stabilization policy. If the supply curve is flat, stabilization policy is much more effective at combating recession than inflation. If the supply curve is steep, precisely the reverse is true.

But why does the argument persist? Why can't economists just determine the shape of the aggregate supply curve and stop arguing? The answer is that supply conditions in the real world are far more complicated than our simple diagrams suggest. Some industries may have flat supply curves, whereas others have steep ones. For reasons explained in Chapter 10, supply curves shift over time. And, unlike laboratory scientists, economists cannot perform controlled experiments that would reveal the shape

FIGURE 6

Stabilization Policy with a Steep Aggregate Supply Curve

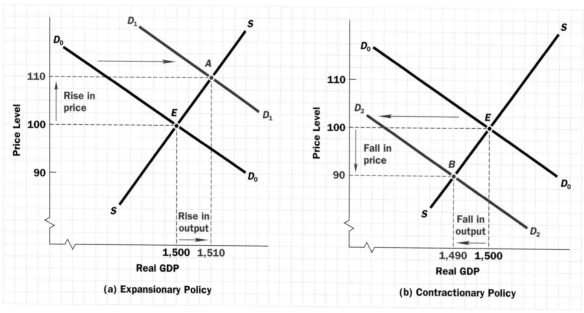

Note: Real GDP in billions of dollars per year.

of the aggregate supply curve directly. Instead, they must use statistical inference to make educated guesses.

Although empirical research continues, our understanding of aggregate supply remains less settled than our understanding of aggregate demand. Nevertheless, many economists believe that the outline of a consensus view has emerged. This view holds that *the steepness of the aggregate supply schedule depends on the time period under consideration.*

In the very short run, the aggregate supply curve is quite flat, making Figure 5 the more relevant picture of reality. Over short time periods, therefore, fluctuations in aggregate demand have large effects on output but only minor effects on prices. In the long run, however, the aggregate supply curve becomes quite steep, perhaps even vertical. In that case, Figure 6 is a better representation of reality, so that changes in demand affect mainly prices, not output.[2] The implication is that:

> Any change in aggregate demand will have most of its effect on *output* in the short run but on *prices* in the long run.

DEBATE: SHOULD THE GOVERNMENT INTERVENE?

We have yet to consider what may be the most fundamental and controversial debate of all—the issue posed at the beginning of the chapter. Is it likely that government policy can successfully stabilize the economy? Or are even well-intentioned efforts likely to do more harm than good?

This controversy has raged for decades, with no end in sight. The debate is partly political or philosophical. Left-of-centre economists tend to be more intervention-minded and hence more favourably disposed toward an activist stabilization policy. Conservative economists are more inclined to keep the government's hands off the economy and hence advise adhering to fixed rules. Such political differences are not surprising. But more than ideology propels the debate. We need to understand the economics.

Critics of stabilization policy point to the lags and uncertainties that surround the operation of both fiscal and monetary policies—lags and uncertainties that we have stressed repeatedly in this and earlier chapters. Will the central bank's decisions to change the target overnight interest rate have the desired effects on other interest rates and aggregate demand? Can fiscal policy actions be taken promptly? How large is the expenditure multiplier? The list could go on and on.

These skeptics look at this formidable catalog of difficulties, add a dash of skepticism about our ability to forecast the future state of the economy, and worry that stabilization policy may fail. They therefore advise both the fiscal and monetary authorities to pursue a passive policy rather than an active one—adhering to fixed rules that, although incapable of ironing out every bump in the economy's growth path, will at least keep it roughly on track in the long run.

Advocates of active stabilization policies admit that perfection is unattainable. But they are much more optimistic about the prospects for success, and they are much *less* optimistic about how smoothly the economy would function in the absence of demand management. They therefore advocate discretionary increases in government spending (or decreases in taxes) and lower interest rates when the economy has a recessionary gap—and the reverse when the economy has an inflationary gap. Such policies, they believe, will help keep the economy closer to its full-employment growth path.

The historical record of fiscal and monetary policy is far from glorious. Although the authorities have sometimes taken appropriate and timely actions to stabilize the economy, at other times they clearly either took inappropriate steps or did nothing at all. The question of whether the government should adopt passive rules or attempt an activist stabilization policy therefore merits a closer look. As we will see, the *lags* in the effects of policy discussed earlier in this chapter play a pivotal role in the debate.

---

[2] The reasoning behind the view that the aggregate supply curve is flat in the short run but steep in the long run will be developed in Chapter 16.

Central Banks Fighting Recessions and Financial Crises

In August 2007, the banking world was taken by surprise when many bankers suddenly realized that they had purchased financial assets that were not as safe as they had been told, and when they were forced to declare large losses (see the boxed feature "The Subprime Crisis" in Chapter 12). Many banks then decided to tighten their lending standards. By the beginning of 2008, signs of an impending major U.S. recession were accumulating, with the danger of a worldwide recession.

During the fall of 2007, fearing a major financial crisis that would bring about a huge recession, the Federal Reserve had already decided to drop its target interest rate—the federal funds rate, as the U.S. overnight rate is called—by 100 basis points, from 5.25 percent to 4.25 percent. But on January 22, 2008, the Federal Reserve Board made the extraordinary decision to announce a 75 basis points reduction in the target federal funds rate, *one week before the regular announcement date*. During the following week, there was a further 50 basis points reduction, with another 75 basis point reduction about a month later. Thus, the target interest rate in the United States dropped by 200 basis points in less than two months. A further reduction of 25 basis points took place on April 30. To sum up, the target interest rate in the United States moved down 325 basis points from 5.25 percent to 2.00 percent in the span of eight months.

During the same time period, the target overnight rate in Canada went down by only 150 basis points, from 4.50 percent to 3.00 percent. Economists working for banks mostly thought this was a good move, whereas university economists often favoured smaller reductions. As for the European central bank, its target interest rate did not bulge at all, remaining at 4 percent, despite the fact that many European banks were also being hit by the subprime mortgage crisis. Obviously, different central banks perceive the likelihood of a recession differently. But also some central banks may be keener than others to fight recessions, instead of inflation. In the United States, the Fed cut its target interest rate by 325 basis points despite rising inflation rates.

U.S. Federal Funds Rate Target and the Canadian Overnight Rate Target, 2007–2008

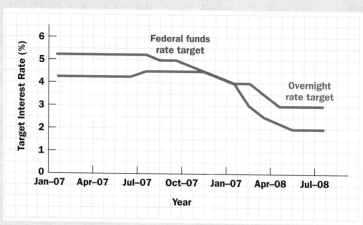

SOURCES: Statistics Canada, Series V39079; and the Federal Reserve Board: www.federalreserve.gov /releases/h15/data/Monthly/H15_FF_O.txt

■ Lags and the Rules-versus-Discretion Debate

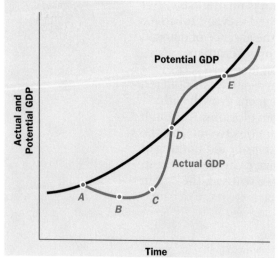

FIGURE 7

A Typical Business Cycle

Lags lead to a fundamental difficulty for stabilization policy—a difficulty so formidable that it has prompted some economists to conclude that attempts to stabilize economic activity are likely to do more harm than good. To see why, refer to Figure 7, which charts the behaviour of both actual and potential GDP over the course of a business cycle in a hypothetical economy with no stabilization policy. At point *A*, the economy begins to slip into a recession and does not recover to full employment until point *D*. Then, between points *D* and *E*, it overshoots potential GDP and enters an inflationary boom.

The argument in favour of stabilization policy runs something like this: Policy makers recognize that the recession is a serious problem at point *B*, and they take appropriate actions. These actions have their major effects around point *C* and therefore limit both the depth and the length of the recession.

But suppose the lags are really longer and less predictable than those just described. Suppose, for example, that actions do not come until point *C* and that stimulative policies do not have their major effects until after point *D*. Then policy will be of little help during the recession and will actually do harm by overstimulating the economy during the ensuing boom. Thus:

In the presence of long lags, attempts at stabilizing the economy may actually succeed in destabilizing it.

For this reason, some economists argue that we are better off leaving the economy alone and relying on its natural self-corrective forces to cure recessions and inflations. Instead of embarking on periodic programs of monetary and fiscal stimulus or restraint, they advise policy makers to stick to fixed rules that ignore current economic events.

For monetary policy, we have already mentioned the monetarist policy rule: The Bank of Canada should keep the money supply growing at a constant rate. For fiscal policy, proponents of rules often recommend that government resist the temptation to manage aggregate demand actively. Within the European community, for instance, national governments that run public deficits that represent more than 3 percent of GDP are liable to financial penalties from the European government.

■ DIMENSIONS OF THE RULES-VERSUS-DISCRETION DEBATE

Are the critics right? Should we forget about discretionary policy and put the economy on autopilot—relying on automatic stabilizers and the economy's natural, self-correcting mechanisms? As usual, the answer depends on many factors.

■ How Fast Does the Economy's Self-Correcting Mechanism Work— If Such a Mechanism Exists?

One of the most crucial debates among economists is whether the economy, when taken at the macroeconomic level and in contrast to microeconomic markets, has adequate self-correcting mechanisms. While some economists argue that these mechanisms are rather weak and even not functioning at all, other economists believe that self-correcting mechanisms are powerful and would be even more powerful if it were not for the presence of all the impediments to market mechanisms—such as labour-protecting laws, government regulations, and other rigidities associated with imperfect competition.

If recessions and inflations will disappear quickly by themselves, the case for intervention is weak. That is, if such problems typically last only a short time, then lags in discretionary stabilization policy mean that the medicine will often have its major effects only after the disease has run its course. In fact, a distinct minority of economists used precisely this reasoning to argue against a fiscal stimulus after the September 11, 2001, terrorist attacks. In terms of Figure 7, this is a case in which point *D* comes very close to point *A*.

Although extreme advocates of rules argue that this is indeed what happens, most economists would probably agree that the economy's self-correcting mechanism is slow and not terribly reliable, even when supplemented by the automatic stabilizers. To sum this up, let us recall the results of a 2000 survey of American economists.[3] One-third of them believed that there are efficient and quick self-correcting mechanisms in macroeconomics; slightly more than one-third thought that these self-correcting mechanisms were slow and unreliable; and slightly less than one-third claimed that these self-correcting forces did not exist at all.

■ How Long Are the Lags in Stabilization Policy?

We just explained why long and unpredictable lags in monetary and fiscal policy make it hard for stabilization policy to do much good. Short, reliable lags point in just the opposite direction. Thus advocates of fixed rules emphasize the length of lags while proponents of discretion tend to discount them.

---

[3] See Dan Fuller and Doris Geide-Stevenson, "Consensus among Economists: Revisited," *Journal of Economic Education*, Fall 2003, pp. 369–384.

Who is right depends on the circumstances. Sometimes policy makers take action promptly, and the economy receives at least some stimulus from expansionary policy within a year after slipping into a recession. Although far from perfect, the effects of such timely actions are felt soon enough to do some good. But, as we have seen, very slow policy responses may actually prove destabilizing. Because history offers examples of each type, we can draw no general conclusion.

How Accurate Are Economic Forecasts?

One way to compress the policy-making lag dramatically is to forecast economic events accurately. If we could see a recession coming a full year ahead of time (which we certainly *cannot* do), even a rather sluggish policy response would still be timely. In terms of Figure 7, this would be a case in which the recession is predicted well before point *A*.

Over the years, economists in universities, government agencies, and private businesses have developed a number of techniques to assist them in predicting what the economy will do. Unfortunately, none of these methods is terribly accurate. To give a rough idea of magnitudes, forecasts of either the inflation rate or the real GDP growth rate for the year ahead typically err by ± ¾ to 1 percentage point. But, in a bad year for forecasters, errors of 2 or 3 percentage points are common.

Is this record good enough? That depends on how the forecasts are used. It is certainly not good enough to support *fine-tuning*—that is, attempts to keep the economy always within a hair's breadth of full employment. But it probably is good enough for policy makers interested in using discretionary stabilization policy to close persistent and sizable gaps between actual and potential GDP.

The Size of Government

One bogus argument that is nonetheless sometimes heard is that active fiscal policy must inevitably lead to a growing public sector. Because proponents of fixed rules tend also to oppose big government, they view this growth as undesirable. Of course, others think that a larger public sector is just what society needs.

This argument, however, is completely beside the point because, as we pointed out in Chapter 11: *One's opinion about the proper size of government should have nothing to do with one's view on stabilization policy.* For example, George W. Bush, the twice-elected president of the United States, belongs to the Republican Party and is extremely conservative. Bush was devoted to shrinking the size of the public sector, as are Stephen Harper and the Conservative Party in Canada—but both expanded the size of the federal government, in part because of national security concerns. Still, the tax-cutting initiatives of Bush in 2001–2003 and in 2008 constituted an extremely activist fiscal policy to spur the economy. Furthermore, most stabilization policy these days consists of monetary policy, which neither increases nor decreases the size of government (although, ironically, because of debt servicing, government transfer payments increase when interest rates rise, thus also increasing disposable income).

Uncertainties Caused by Government Policy

Advocates of rules are on stronger ground when they argue that frequent changes in tax laws, government spending programs, or monetary conditions make it difficult for firms and consumers to formulate and carry out rational plans. They argue that the authorities can provide a more stable environment for the private sector by adhering to fixed rules, so that businesses and consumers will know exactly what to expect.

No one disputes that a more stable environment is better for private planning. Even so, supporters of discretionary policy emphasize that *stability in the economy* is more important than *stability in the government budget* (or in Bank of Canada operations). The whole idea of stabilization policy is to *prevent* gyrations in the pace of economic activity by *causing* timely gyrations in the government budget (or in monetary policy). Which atmosphere is better for business, they ask: one in which fiscal and monetary rules keep things peaceful in Parliament and at the Bank of Canada while recessions and inflations wrack the economy, or one in which government changes its policy abruptly on occasion but the economy grows more steadily? They think the answer is self-evident. The question, of course, is whether stabilization policy can succeed in practice.

A Political Business Cycle?

A final argument put forth by advocates of rules is political rather than economic. Fiscal policy decisions are made by elected politicians: the prime minister and the Cabinet ministers, along with members of the House of Commons. When elections are on the horizon (and in the case of minority governments, they nearly *always* are), these politicians may be as concerned with keeping their jobs as with doing what is right for the economy. This situation leaves fiscal policy subject to "political manipulation"—lawmakers may take inappropriate actions to attain short-run political goals. A system of purely automatic stabilization, its proponents argue, would eliminate this peril.

It is certainly *possible* that politicians could deliberately *cause* economic instability to help their own reelection. Indeed, some observers of these "political business cycles" have claimed that several American presidents have taken full advantage of the opportunity. Furthermore, even without any insidious intent, politicians may take the wrong actions for perfectly honourable reasons. Decisions in the political arena are never clear-cut, and it certainly is easy to find examples of grievous errors in the history of Canadian fiscal policy.

Taken as a whole, then, the political argument against discretionary fiscal policy seems to have a great deal of merit. But what are we to do about it? It is unrealistic to believe that fiscal decisions could or should be made by a group of objective and nonpartisan technicians. Tax and budget policies require inherently *political* decisions that, in a democracy, should be made by elected officials.

This fact may seem worrisome in view of the possibilities for political chicanery. But it should not bother us any more (or any less) than similar manoeuvering in other areas of policy making. After all, the same problem besets international relations, national defence, formulation and enforcement of the law, and so on. Politicians make all these decisions, subject only to sporadic accountability at elections. Is there really any reason why fiscal decisions should be different?

But monetary policy *is* different. Because politicians have always shown some concern that elected officials focus too much on the short run and are tempted to pursue inflationary monetary policies, the day-to-day decision-making authority over monetary policy was given to unelected technocrats. As we pointed out in Chapter 13, the Bank of Canada is relatively independent.

BETWEEN RULES AND DISCRETION: INFLATION TARGETING

As discussed on page 312, the debate about monetary and fiscal policy has evolved considerably over the last 15 years. Although many economists still advocate the necessity of countercyclical fiscal policy, most of the attention has turned to monetary policy, which is now considered to be the main instrument of stabilization.

In recent years, a number of economists and policy makers have sought a middle ground between saddling monetary policy makers with rigid rules and giving them complete discretion. Inflation targeting is considered by many to be a reasonable compromise between rules and discretion. On the one hand, the minister of Finance, an elected politician, and the governor of the Bank of Canada, an unelected bureaucrat, jointly decide on a numerical target for the inflation rate—currently 2 percent based on the CPI. The Bank of Canada must then do its best to reach the target. In that sense, the system functions like a *rule*. However, monetary policy makers are given complete *discretion* as to how they go about trying to achieve this goal. Neither the minister of Finance nor Parliament interferes with day-to-day monetary policy decisions. A very similar situation exists in other countries that have inflation targeting, such as the United Kingdom.

Benefits of Inflation Targeting

Many economists think that inflation targeting offers the better of two worlds. In particular, officials at the Bank of Canada believe that the inflation-targeting framework that was set up in February 1991 has delivered all of the benefits that it was supposed to—and perhaps even more! Still, some countries, like the United States, do not have inflation targeting, on the grounds that it would limit the range of its policy response when faced with unexpected circumstances. In addition, the United States Congress recently reaffirmed that the Federal Reserve has a dual mandate: price stability and full employment. Still, this may change in the future, since the current chairman of the Federal Reserve, Ben Bernanke, as well as the new vice chairman, Frederic Mishkin, have been vocal advocates of inflation targeting; both have written several books and articles on the subject.

A very obvious benefit of inflation targeting is that CPI inflation has averaged only 2 percent since 1991—precisely the midpoint value of the target inflation band, and has remained within the inflation band more than 80 percent of the time. Thus, as argued by Bank of Canada officials, the inflation-targeting framework has delivered lower and more stable inflation. For instance, between 1975 and 1990, the inflation rate was 7 percent and the variability of inflation (measured by a statistical tool called the *standard deviation*) was about two times greater than it was between 1991 and 2005 and three times greater than it was between 1996 and 2006. So, according to the Bank of Canada, not only is inflation lower, it also fluctuates much less, even if you measure these fluctuations as a ratio of the inflation level. In addition, the Canadian economy has performed relatively well over most of the target inflation period, with unemployment rates reaching historically low levels.

So why don't all countries adopt inflation targeting? One reason is that all developed countries in the world, including those that do not have an inflation-targeting framework, had lower and more stable inflation in the 1990s and 2000s. Success in taming inflation, therefore, may be due to something other than inflation targeting, such as a series of years with high unemployment and low commodity prices in the 1980s and early 1990s, or it may have been caused by changes brought about by globalization, which threatens the jobs of workers who refuse to grant salary concessions. With the rising oil prices that the world experienced in 2008, it will be interesting to see whether inflation-targeting central banks will succeed in keeping inflation under control.

In addition, while there is no doubt that inflation has been lower in Canada during the inflation-targeting period, it is not so clear that inflation has been more stable during this period. It all depends on the period of comparison. Researchers at the Bank of Canada take the 1975–1990 period as a basis of comparison, but this period includes the years during which the Bank of Canada was experimenting with monetarism, when both inflation and output varied considerably. If the basis of comparison is instead the 1983–1990 period, when the Bank of Canada had abandoned monetarism and was still searching for an alternative monetary policy framework, it then turns out that inflation *before* inflation targeting was no less stable than inflation *with* inflation targeting!

What Inflation Target?

Still, officials at the Bank of Canada don't question the relevance of inflation targeting. Rather, the issue being discussed is whether the inflation target should remain at 2 percent or whether it should be brought down to 1 or 0 percent, in the belief that lower inflation rates would bring even more benefits to the Canadian economy. There are even discussions about targeting a price level (targeting a constant Consumer Price Index) instead of an inflation rate. Bank of Canada officials have long been tempted to reduce the inflation target and the inflation band, but their enthusiasm for such a move has been tempered by the Japanese experience mentioned in Chapter 10.

Japan faced persistent price deflation and very weak output growth during the second half of the 1990s and the first half of the 2000s. The CPI fell for five years in a row and the GDP deflator

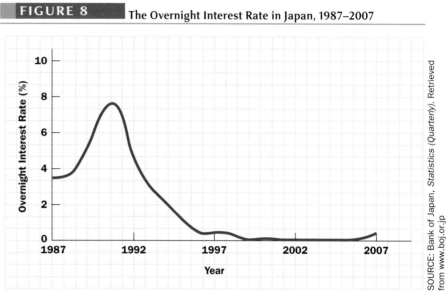

FIGURE 8　The Overnight Interest Rate in Japan, 1987–2007

SOURCE: Bank of Japan, *Statistics (Quarterly).* Retrieved from www.boj.or.jp

decreased for nearly ten years running. Monetary policy, despite the help of the stabilizers associated with fiscal policy, was powerless to stop negative inflation from occurring or to get the Japanese economy back on track. As can be seen from Figure 8, the Bank of Japan pushed down the overnight interest rate and kept it below 0.50 percent for over 10 years, including 7 years at exactly 0 percent! But even this extraordinary interest-setting behaviour was not enough, because even when the overnight rate is 0 percent, the *real* interest rate remains positive at 1 percent as long as the rate of price deflation is at 1 percent, in other words, as long as there is negative inflation. This is called the problem of the **zero lower bound on nominal interest rates**. With price deflation, it is very difficult for monetary policy to be expansionary, because nominal interest rates cannot fall any lower than 0 percent. By contrast, when the rate of inflation is at 2 percent, it is much easier to implement stimulating monetary policies: The *real* interest rate can be brought down to –2 percent by bringing down the *nominal* overnight interest rate to its lowest possible level of 0 percent.

It is mainly these considerations—the zero lower bound on nominal interest rates and the fear of replicating the Japanese experience—that, so far, have led the Bank of Canada to forgo a zero inflation target. If the target inflation band is set between 1 and 3 percent, instead of –1 and +1 percent, it is less likely that inflation will ever be negative and that the central bank will be constrained by the zero lower bound on nominal interest rates. The difficulty in bringing down real interest rates was pointed out by Keynes in another context long ago, and is also known as the *liquidity trap.*

Some critics of inflation targeting argue that inflation targets that are too low may have additional negative impacts on the economy because inflation, as some economists phrase it, "greases the wheels of adjustment" in the labour market. Companies that are facing pressure to reduce the real wages of their workers because of unprofitable conditions (say, in the forestry industry) may succeed in inducing their workers to accept such *real* wage reductions without labour disruptions as long as such reductions do not imply a reduction in *nominal* wages.

Other critics claim that the focus on low-inflation targeting leads to unnecessary reductions in aggregate demand. These critics often compare the situation in Europe with that of the United States. Low rates of unemployment in the United States are attributed to the degree of discretion that the Federal Reserve has in choosing between inflation and unemployment. By contrast, the sole goal of the European Central Bank is price stability, and thus the lack of concern for achieving high levels of aggregate demand is said by many (but certainly not by all) to be the main cause of high unemployment in most of Europe.

The problem of the **zero lower bound on nominal interest rates** is the fact that, when deflation occurs, central banks cannot set negative real interest rates and hence impose a truly expansionary monetary policy, because nominal interest rates cannot go any lower than 0 percent.

ISSUE REVISITED: *What Should Be Done?*

So where do we come out on the question posed at the start of this chapter? On balance, is it better to pursue the best discretionary policy we can, knowing full well that we will never achieve perfection? Or is it wiser to rely on fixed rules and the automatic stabilizers?

In weighing the pros and cons, your basic view of the economy is crucial. Some economists believe that the economy, if left unmanaged, would generate a series of ups and downs that would be difficult to predict, but that it would correct each of them by itself in a relatively short time. They conclude that, because of long lags and poor forecasts, our ability to anticipate whether the economy will need stimulus or restraint by the time policy actions have their effects is quite limited. Consequently, they advocate fixed rules.

Other economists liken the economy to a giant glacier with a great deal of inertia. Under this view, if we observe an inflationary or recessionary gap today, it will likely still be there a year or two from now because the self-correcting mechanism works slowly. In such a world, accurate forecasting is not imperative, even if policy lags are long. If we base policy on a forecast of a 4 percent gap between actual and potential GDP a year from now, and the gap turns out to be only 2 percent, we still will have done the right thing despite the inaccurate forecast. So holders of this view of the economy tend to support discretionary policy.

There is certainly no consensus on this issue, either among economists or politicians. After all, the question touches on political ideology as well as economics, and left-of-centre economists often look to government to solve social problems, whereas conservatives consistently point out that many efforts of government fail despite the best intentions. A prudent view of the matter might be that:

> The case for active discretionary policy is strong when the economy has a serious deficiency or excess of aggregate demand. However, advocates of fixed rules are right that it is unwise to try to iron out every little wiggle in the growth path of GDP.

But one thing seems certain: The rules-versus-discretion debate is likely to go on for quite some time.

A Nobel Prize for the Rules-versus-Discretion Debate

In 2004, economists Finn Kydland of Carnegie-Mellon University and Edward Prescott of Arizona State University were awarded the Nobel Prize for a fascinating contribution to the rules-versus-discretion debate. They called attention to a general problem that they labelled "time inconsistency," and their analysis of this problem led them to conclude that the Fed should follow a rule.

A close-to-home example will illustrate the basic time inconsistency problem. Your instructor announces in September that a final exam will be given in December. The main purpose of the exam is to ensure that students study and learn the course materials, and the exam itself represents work for the faculty and stress for the students. So, when December rolls around, it may appear "optimal" to call off the exam at the last moment.

SOURCE: © AFP/Getty Images

Of course, if that started happening regularly, students would soon stop studying for exams. So actually giving the exam is the better long-run policy. One way to solve this time inconsistency problem is to adopt a simple *rule* stating that announced exams will always be given, rather than allowing individual faculty members to cancel exams at their *discretion*.

Kydland and Prescott argued that monetary policy makers face a similar time inconsistency problem. They first announce a stern anti-inflation policy (giving an exam). But then, when the moment of truth (December) arrives, they may relent because they don't want to cause unemployment (all that work and stress). Their suggested solution: Central banks should adopt *rules* that remove period-by-period *discretion*.

SUMMARY

1. **Velocity** (V) is the ratio of nominal GDP to the stock of money (M). It indicates how quickly money circulates.

2. One important determinant of velocity is the rate of interest (r). At higher interest rates, people find it less attractive to hold money because money pays zero or little interest. Thus, when r rises, money circulates faster, and V rises.

3. **Monetarism** is a type of analysis that focuses attention on velocity and the money supply (M). Although monetarists realize that V is not constant, they believe that it is predictable enough to make it a useful tool for policy analysis and forecasting.

4. Monetarists believe that inflation is always and everywhere caused by excessive growth rates of the money supply. By contrast, the **banking view** holds that the growth rate of the money stock is caused by the growth rate of nominal GDP.

5. Monetarists emphasize the importance of stabilizing the growth path of the money supply, whereas the predominant Keynesian view puts more emphasis on keeping interest rates on target.

6. The stock of base money is the sum of currency plus the deposits of banks at the Bank of Canada (their *reserves*, as they used to be called). Monetarists and other economists thought that the relationship between the money supply and base money, the **money multiplier**, is fairly stable. Monetarists have therefore advised central banks to use base money as their operational target in their efforts to stabilize the growth path of the money supply—the intermediate target. Bank of Canada officials, however, have always been reluctant to follow such advice, even in the heyday of monetarism.

7. Monetarism was abandoned by the Bank of Canada in 1982 because velocity proved to be too unstable.

8. Because fiscal policy actions affect aggregate demand either directly through G or indirectly through C, the expenditure lags between fiscal actions and their effects on aggregate demand are probably fairly short. By contrast, monetary policy operates mainly on investment, I, which responds slowly to changes in interest rates.

9. However, the policy-making lag normally is much longer for fiscal policy than for monetary policy. Hence, when the two lags are combined, it is not clear which type of policy acts more quickly.

10. Because it cannot control the demand curve for money, the Bank of Canada cannot control both M and r. If the demand for money changes, the Bank must decide whether it wants to hold M steady, hold r steady, or adopt some compromise position.

11. When the aggregate supply curve is very flat, changes in aggregate demand will have large effects on the nation's real output but small effects on the price level. Under those circumstances, stabilization policy works well as an antirecession device, but it has little power to combat inflation.

12. When the aggregate supply curve is steep, changes in aggregate demand have small effects on real output but large effects on the price level. In such a case, stabilization policy can do much to fight inflation but is not a very effective way to cure unemployment.

13. There is still considerable debate about the best way to view the aggregate supply curve. The consensus so far is that the curve is relatively flat in the short run but vertical in the long run. The implication of this is that stabilization policy affects mainly output in the short run but mainly prices in the long run.

14. When the lags in the operation of fiscal and monetary policy are long and unpredictable, attempts to stabilize economic activity may actually destabilize it.

15. Some economists believe that our imperfect knowledge of the channels through which stabilization policy works, the long lags involved, and the inaccuracy of forecasts make it unlikely that discretionary stabilization policy can succeed.

16. Other economists recognize these difficulties but do not believe they are quite as serious. They also place much less faith in the economy's ability to cure recessions and inflations on its own. They therefore think that discretionary policy is not only advisable, but essential.

17. Stabilizing the economy by fiscal policy need not imply a tendency toward "big government."

18. Inflation targeting can be considered as a compromise between rules and discretion, since central banks have to achieve a given rate of inflation, but through the means that they choose.

19. Although inflation targeting has been successful in keeping inflation low and steady, other countries have achieved the same results without inflation targeting. Thus, it is not clear what has been the actual role of inflation targeting in this respect.

20. Critics of inflation targeting say that it focuses too much attention on inflation and not enough on economic growth and employment.

21. The Bank of Canada has repeatedly considered the possibility of lowering the target inflation rate (perhaps to 0 percent). This move, however, has been hindered by the disastrous Japanese experience, where monetary policy was made powerless by the impossibility of achieving negative real interest rates, even with nominal interest rates set at 0 percent. This is called the problem of the **zero lower bound on nominal interest rates**.

KEY TERMS

Velocity   305

Equation of exchange   305

Quantity theory of money   305

Effect of interest rate on velocity   307

Monetarism   307

Banking view   308

Money multiplier   310

Lags in stabilization policy   312

Rules versus discretionary policy   316

Zero lower bound on nominal interest rates   321

TEST YOURSELF

1. How much money by the M1+ definition (cash plus chequable deposits) do you typically have at any particular moment? Divide this amount into your total income over the past 12 months to obtain your own personal velocity. Are you typical of the nation as a whole?

2. The following table provides data on nominal gross domestic product and the money supply (M1+ definition) in recent selected years. Compute velocity in each year. Can you see any trend? How does it compare with the trend that prevailed from 1982–2003?

Year	End-of-Year Money Supply (M1+)	Nominal GDP, Fourth Quarter
2003	$314	$1,229
2004	343	1,319
2005	366	1,414
2006	406	1,453

Note: Amounts are in billions.

3. Use a supply and demand diagram similar to that of Figure 3, with a nearly vertical demand curve, to show the choices open to the Bank of Canada following a large *decline* in the demand for base money. If a strict monetarist policy was being enforced, what would happen to the overnight interest rate?

4. Which of the following events would strengthen the argument for the use of discretionary policy, and which would strengthen the argument for rules?

   a. Structural changes make the economy's self-correcting mechanism work more quickly and reliably than before.

   b. New statistical methods are found that improve the accuracy of economic forecasts.

   c. A minority government has been elected and it might hesitate to make quick decisions for fear of being defeated on a major issue.

5. The money supply is the sum of currency plus deposits at banks. Base money is defined as currency plus bank reserves (or banks' deposits at the Bank of Canada). With the money multiplier equal to 10, base money at $50 billion, and currency at $40 billion, what is the amount of deposits at banks?

DISCUSSION QUESTIONS

1. Use the concept of opportunity cost to explain why velocity is higher at higher interest rates.

2. How does monetarism differ from the quantity theory of money?

3. Given the behaviour of velocity shown in Figure 1, would it make more sense for the Bank of Canada to formulate targets for M1+ or M2+?

4. Distinguish between the expenditure lag and the policy lag in stabilization policy. Does monetary or fiscal policy have the shorter expenditure lag? What about the policy lag?

5. Explain why their contrasting views on the shape of the aggregate supply curve lead some economists to argue much more strongly for stabilization policies to fight unemployment and other economists to argue much more strongly for stabilization policies to fight inflation.

6. Explain why lags make it possible that policy actions intended to stabilize the economy will actually destabilize it.

7. Monetarists assume that base money determines (or causes) the money supply and that the money supply stock is a multiple of the stock of base money, so that the ratio of the first to the second aggregate is called the *money multiplier* (as in Test Yourself Question 5). In Chapter 13, we explained that the Bank of Canada supplies the currency that is demanded by banks on behalf of their clients, and that the deposits of banks at the Bank of Canada are virtually zero. Can it then still be said that the money supply is determined by the amount of base money?

15

BUDGET DEFICITS IN THE SHORT AND LONG RUN

National debt is not a burden on posterity because if posterity pays the debt it will be paying it to the same posterity that will be alive at the time when the payment is made.

ABBA P. LERNER (1903–1982), *THE ECONOMICS OF CONTROL*, 1944

Few fields in economics have seen more swings in expert opinion than has fiscal policy.

EDMUND S. PHELPS (1933–), RECIPIENT OF THE 2006 BANK OF SWEDEN PRIZE IN ECONOMIC SCIENCES IN MEMORY OF ALFRED NOBEL, *INCOME TAX CUTS WITHOUT SPENDING CUTS: HAZARDS TO EFFICIENCY, EQUITY, EMPLOYMENT AND GROWTH*, 2002

Monetary policy and fiscal policy are typically thought of as tools for short-run economic *stabilization*—that is, as ways to combat either inflation or unemployment. Debates over the Bank of Canada's next interest rate decision, or over this year's federal budget, are normally dominated by short-run considerations such as: Does the economy need to be stimulated or restrained *right now?*

But the monetary and fiscal choices the government makes today also have profound effects on our economy's ability to produce goods and services *in the future*. We began Part II by emphasizing long-run growth, and especially the role of capital formation (see Chapters 6 and 7). But for most of Part III, we have been preoccupied with the shorter-run issues of inflation, unemployment, and recession. This chapter integrates the two perspectives by considering both the long-run and short-run implications of fiscal and monetary policy decisions. What differences does it make if we stimulate (or restrain) the economy with fiscal or monetary policy? Should we strive to balance the budget? What are the economic virtues and vices of large budget deficits, both now and in the future?

CONTENTS

ISSUE: *Did the U.S. September 2001 Terrorist Attacks Warrant Fiscal Stimulus in Canada?*

The question of the appropriate reaction of policy makers to shocks to the economy was brought into sharp relief by the Canadian debate over the proper macroeconomic response directly following the terrorist attacks of September 11, 2001. Almost immediately, many economists and politicians in Canada, fearing the negative consequences on Canada's growth rate of a recession in the United States, began calling for a fiscal stimulus that would boost spending right away. For instance, during October and November 2001, New Democratic Party politicians and policy analysts at the Canadian Centre for Policy Alternatives issued press releases in support of a fiscal stimulus in the form of increased public spending. The reasoning was that the Canadian economy, which was already showing signs of weakness in late 2000 and early 2001, would be pushed over the brink by a blow to consumer and investor confidence here and by a decline in our exports to the United States. Indeed, even some analysts in the traditional fiscally conservative banking sector had expressed some support for a fiscal stimulus, once signs of a decline in real GDP growth during the third quarter of 2001 began to point to the severity of the slowdown (see the decline in the annual real GDP growth rate in 2001 in Table 1).

But others disagreed. Looking at the evidence, some claimed that the economy needed no further stimulus, since tax cuts from previous budgets were now kicking in. Others argued that monetary policy was better suited to the task than fiscal policy, which should be devoted to maintaining budget surpluses. Even some supporters of fiscal stimulus worried that the federal government would use the banner of "short-run stimulus" to enact deep tax cuts and introduce major new spending programs that would damage the commitment of Jean Chrétien's Liberal government to budget surpluses and bringing down the public debt.

TABLE 1
Selected Statistics on the Economic Performance of the Canadian Economy, 1998–2005

Year	Real GDP Growth Rate	Unemployment Rate	Inflation Rate
1998	3.3	8.3	0.9
1999	5.1	7.6	1.7
2000	4.5	6.8	2.7
2001	1.9	7.2	2.6
2002	3.4	7.7	2.2
2003	2.0	7.6	2.8
2004	3.3	7.2	1.9
2005	2.9	6.8	2.2

SOURCE: Finance Canada. Retrieved from www.fin.gc.ca/access/ecfisce.html

In keeping with the Liberal tradition of pursuing the "middle road," in December of 2001, Finance Minister Paul Martin offered something to everyone while staying the course of targeting a fiscal surplus. Martin recognized that the policy of fiscal consolidation and debt reduction that he had initiated in the mid-1990s provided room for the continued easing of tax burdens; modest discretionary spending measures, mostly in the areas of increased security and related infrastructure investment; and the working of the automatic stabilizers. But the big job of preventing a recession was left to monetary policy.

Was this a sufficient stimulus? By the end of this chapter, you will be in a good position to answer this important question. Could the fact that, by the fourth quarter of 2001, the Canadian economy did turn around somewhat attest to the appropriateness of the fiscal/monetary policy mix? Despite very little easing of fiscal tightness, Canada did not officially suffer a recession in 2001, thanks largely to the indomitable Canadian consumer who, spurred on by low interest rates, kept on spending.

SHOULD THE BUDGET BE BALANCED? THE SHORT RUN

Canada has not witnessed the strong political movements that, in both the United States and the European Union, have sought a constitutional commitment to ensuring balanced public sector budgets. Perhaps some who would defend such an idea would say that raising the spectre of a constitutional change would be unnecessary in Canada since, as the federal minister of Finance reminds us in his annual budget speeches, Canada is the only country of the G7 industrialized nations that has continued to run not only a balanced budget but an annual budget surplus—that is, it has taken in more revenue than it spends, year after year. Indeed, what is striking to many observers internationally is that the federal government has now been running these surpluses for over a decade, regardless of whether the Canadian economy was going through a period of high growth, as in 1999–2000, or through a period of slowdown, as in 2001 and 2008. On the other hand, on the European continent, where the Stability and Growth Pact has been in place since before the launching of the euro in 1999, governments (such as those of France and Germany) have found themselves running budget deficits even in excess of the norm established by the European Economic and Monetary Union. You might be tempted to ask: Why would you want to adopt explicit rules that could place a government in an uncomfortable fiscal straitjacket if you cannot really abide by them?

Let us begin our examination of balancing the government budget by reviewing the basic principles of fiscal policy that we have learned so far (especially in Chapter 11) to see what these principles say about the goal of balancing the budget. These principles certainly do *not* imply that we should always maintain a balanced budget, much as that notion may appeal to our intuitive sense of good financial management. Rather, they instruct fiscal policy makers to focus on balancing the *supply of output and aggregate demand*. They point to the desirability of budget *deficits* when private demand, $C + I + (X - IM)$, is too weak and of budget *surpluses* when private demand is too strong. The budget should be balanced, according to these principles, only when $C + I + G + (X - IM)$ approximately equals full-employment levels of output. This situation may sometimes occur, but it will not necessarily be the norm.

The reason why a balanced budget is not always advisable should be clear from our earlier discussion of stabilization policy. Consider the fiscal policy that the government would follow if its goal were to maintain a balanced budget every year. Suppose the budget was initially balanced and private spending sagged for some reason, as it did during the 1990–1991 recession. The multiplier would pull GDP down. Because personal and corporate tax receipts fall sharply when GDP declines, the budget would automatically swing into the red. To restore budget balance, the government would then have to cut spending or raise taxes—exactly the opposite of the appropriate fiscal-policy response. Thus:

> Attempts to balance the budget during recessions—as was done, say, during the Great Depression—will prolong and deepen slumps.

This is precisely what many observers feel happened to Japan when the government raised consumption taxes and other government revenues in a weak economy in 1997. The fiscal restraint did initially lead to a slight reduction in the deficit, but just to make the overall deficit situation even worse, during the following year, as consumption spending and housing investment declined, there was a fall in real GDP growth. In fact, Ryutaro Hashimoto, Japan's prime minister from 1996 to 1998, was disparagingly called the "Herbert Hoover of Japan" by some analysts because he sought to reduce the public sector budget deficit despite Japan's sinking economy, just as U.S. president Herbert Hoover did during the Great Depression. The Japanese economy was slowly able to recover, primarily because of significant doses of fiscal stimulus by Prime Minister Keizo Obuchi's administration from 1998 to 2000.

Budget balancing also can lead to inappropriate fiscal policy during boom conditions. If rising tax receipts from an overheated economy nearing potential output induce a budget-balancing government to spend more or to cut taxes, then fiscal policy will "boom the boom"—with unfortunate inflationary consequences. This possibility is one important reason why, for instance, no Western government during World War II was lowering taxes, since the compounding effect of greater military spending and lower taxes in the context of a fully employed economy would have led to an explosive inflation environment, as was experienced during World War I.

■ The Importance of the Policy Mix

Actually, the issue is even more complicated than we have indicated so far. As we know, fiscal policy is not the only way the government affects aggregate demand. It also influences aggregate demand through its *monetary policy*. For this reason:

> The appropriate fiscal policy depends, among other things, on the current stance of monetary policy. Although a balanced budget may be appropriate under one monetary policy, a deficit or a surplus may be appropriate under another monetary policy.

An example will illustrate the point. Suppose the government, through its minister of Finance believes that the aggregate supply and demand curves will intersect approximately at full employment if the budget is balanced. Then a balanced budget would seem to be the appropriate fiscal policy.

Now, suppose monetary policy turns contractionary as fears of inflation by the central bank push up interest rates, pulling the aggregate demand curve inward to the left, as shown by the blue arrow in Figure 1, thereby creating a recessionary gap. If the fiscal authorities wish to restore GDP to its initial level, Y_0, they must shift the aggregate demand curve back to its original position, D_0D_0, as indicated by the red arrow. To do so, they must either raise spending or cut taxes, thereby opening up a budget deficit. Thus, the tightening of *monetary* policy changes the appropriate *fiscal* policy from a balanced budget to a deficit, because both monetary and fiscal policies affect aggregate demand.

By the same token, a given target for aggregate demand implies that any change in *fiscal* policy will alter the appropriate *monetary* policy. For example, we can reinterpret Figure 1 as indicating the effects of reducing the budget deficit by cutting government spending. Then, if the Bank of Canada does not want real GDP to fall, it must reduce interest rates sufficiently to restore the aggregate demand curve to D_0D_0.

It is precisely this change in the *mix of monetary and fiscal policy*—smaller budget deficits (and eventually, growing budget surpluses) balanced by loose monetary policy—that the federal government has managed to engineer with considerable success since the mid-1990s. The Bank of Canada was able to pursue a sufficiently expansionist policy to return the "lost" aggregate demand to the economy through fiscal restraint by keeping interest rates low.

So, we should not expect a balanced budget to be the norm. If the objective is to achieve high employment, various policy mixes could be designed. As shown in Figure 2, as we move clockwise, four general policy mixes are available to the government authorities. If the economy finds itself at potential output as in Figure 1, combinations II and IV would be appropriate. If it is stuck at less than potential output, combination III ought to be considered. If the economy is already overheating at potential output, then combination I may even be considered in the arsenal of policy mixes. How, then, can we tell whether any particular budget deficit or surplus is too large or too small? From the discussion so far, it would appear that the answer depends on the strength of private sector aggregate demand and the stance of monetary policy. But those are not the only considerations.

FIGURE 1

The Interaction of Monetary and Fiscal Policy

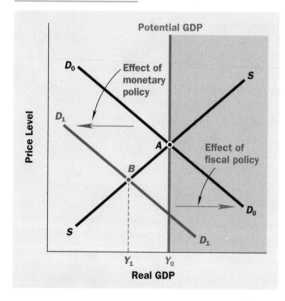

FIGURE 2

Typology of Fiscal and Monetary Policy Mixes

I	II
Restrictive fiscal policy combined with tight monetary policy	Expansionary fiscal policy combined with tight monetary policy
IV	III
Restrictive fiscal policy combined with loose monetary policy	Expansionary fiscal policy combined with loose monetary policy

SURPLUSES AND DEFICITS: THE LONG RUN

One implication of what we have just said is that various *combinations* of fiscal and monetary policy can lead to the *same* level of aggregate demand, and hence to the same real GDP and price level, in the short run. For example, the government could reduce aggregate demand by raising taxes, but the Bank of Canada could make up for it by cutting interest rates. Or the reverse could happen: The government could cut taxes while the Bank of Canada raises interest rates, leaving aggregate demand unchanged. The long-run consequences of these alternative mixes of monetary and fiscal policy may be quite different, however.

In previous chapters, we learned that tighter monetary policy is associated with higher real interest rates. In Figure 2, we could see, for instance, that combination II produces *higher* real interest rates and therefore *lower* private investment. Thus, such a policy mix should shift the composition of total expenditure, $C + I + G + (X − IM)$, toward more G, possibly more C (if from tax cuts), and less I.[1] The expected result is less capital formation and therefore slower growth of potential GDP. Indeed, it was a variant of this policy mix—tight monetary policy to combat inflation with a looser fiscal policy of budget deficits—that the Canadian government inadvertently chose in the early 1980s. However, as will be analyzed later in this chapter, the "looser" fiscal policy pursued during that era was not altogether of a discretionary nature, since a large part of the growth of government expenditures that pushed up public sector deficits was merely the result of higher servicing costs of the public debt due to the tight monetary policy.

But the opposite policy mix—looser monetary policy with tighter budgets—should produce the opposite outcomes: lower real interest rates; more private sector spending, especially investment spending; and hence faster growth of potential GDP. That was, in fact, the general direction Canadian macroeconomic policy took after the recession of 1990–1991. The looser monetary policy of lower interest rates stimulated private sector spending, reduced the servicing cost of the public debt, and therefore turned budget deficits into surpluses. Some of the growth in private spending did translate into higher business investment, with the investment share of GDP increasing from 15.3 percent in 1993 to 18.9 percent by 2006. However, an increasing portion took the form of higher household investment in housing, as well as increased consumption expenditures associated with plummeting household saving rates. The general point is this:

> The composition of aggregate demand is a major determinant of the rate of economic growth. If a larger fraction of GDP is devoted to investment, the nation's capital stock will grow faster and the aggregate supply schedule will shift more quickly to the right, accelerating growth.

International data likewise show a positive relationship between growth and the share of GDP invested. Figure 3 on the next page displays, for a set of 24 countries on four continents, both investment as a share of GDP and growth in per-capita output over two decades (the 1970s and 1980s). Countries with higher investment rates clearly experienced higher growth, on average.

While increasing productive capacity through investment is important to the growth process, an increase in overall demand, regardless of whether it is for consumption or investment purposes, can also lead to an increase of per-capita real GDP through the workings of what is commonly referred to as Verdoorn's Law—whereby higher levels of output generate higher productivity because of the importance of increasing returns in industry—as discussed in Chapter 7, page 150.

So it appears that when we ask whether the budget should be balanced, in deficit, or in surplus, we have posed a good but complicated question. Before attempting to answer it, we need to get some facts straight.

---

[1] We will deal with the consequences of fiscal and monetary policy on $X − IM$ in Chapter 19.

SOURCE: *Economic Report of the President* (Washington, D.C.: U.S. Government Printing Office, 1995), p. 28.

FIGURE 3

Growth and Investment
in 24 Countries

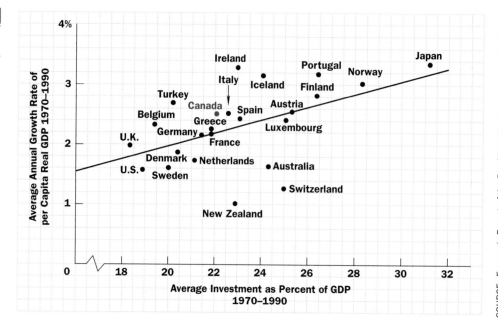

DEFICITS AND DEBT: TERMINOLOGY AND FACTS

First, some critical terminology. People frequently confuse two terms that have different meanings: *budget deficits* and the *national debt*. We must learn to distinguish between the two.

The budget deficit is the amount by which the government's expenditures exceed its receipts during some specified period of time, usually a year. If, instead, receipts exceed expenditures, we have a **budget surplus**. For example, according to the federal public accounts, during the fiscal year 2007–2008 the federal government raised roughly $242 billion in taxes and spent about $230 billion, resulting in a budgetary surplus of about $12 billion.[2] The budget deficit or surplus is a flow.

The **national debt**, also called the *public debt*, is the total value of the government's indebtedness at a moment in time. Thus, for example, Canada's federal gross debt at the end of fiscal year 2007–2008 was $513 billion, reflecting at that point in time the accumulated deficits since Confederation in 1867. However, when you deduct the financial assets of the federal government, Canada's net debt was $456 billion at the end of the 2007–2008 fiscal year. The national debt is a stock.

These two concepts—deficit and debt—are closely related because the government accumulates *debt* by running *deficits* or reduces its debt by running *surpluses*. The relationship between the debt and the deficit or surplus can be explained by a simple analogy. As you run water into a bathtub ("run a deficit"), the accumulated volume of water in the tub ("the debt") rises. Alternatively, if you let water out of the tub ("run a surplus"), the level of the water ("the debt") falls. Analogously, budget deficits raise the national debt, whereas budget surpluses lower it. But, of course, getting rid of the deficit (shutting off the flow of water) does not eliminate the accumulated debt (drain the tub).

Some Facts about the National Debt

Now that we have made this distinction, let us look at the size and nature of the accumulated public debt and then at the annual budget deficit. How large a public debt do we have? How did we get it? Who owes it? Is it growing or shrinking?

The **budget deficit** is the amount by which the government's expenditures exceed its receipts during a specified period of time, usually a year. If receipts exceed expenditures, it is called a **budget surplus** instead.

The **national debt** is the federal government's total indebtedness at a moment in time. It is the result of previous budget deficits.

---

[2] The fiscal year of the Government of Canada ends on March 31. Thus, the fiscal year 2007–2008 ran from April 1, 2007, to March 31, 2008.

To begin with the simplest question, the public debt is enormous. At the end of the fiscal year 2006–2007, it amounted to about $19,000 for every man, woman, and child in Canada. However, a little less than a quarter of this gross debt was countered by financial assets held by the government. If we deduct this portion, the net national debt was a bit over $15,000 per person.

Furthermore, when we compare the debt with the gross domestic product—the volume of goods and services our economy produces in a year—it does not seem so large after all. With a GDP close to $1.5 trillion in 2007, the net debt was only about one-third of the nation's yearly income. By contrast, many families who own homes owe *several years'* worth of income to the banks that granted them mortgages. Many Canadian corporations also owe their bondholders much more than 33 percent of a year's sales.

But before these analogies make you feel too comfortable, we should point out that simple analogies between public and private debt are almost always misleading. A family with a large mortgage debt also owns a home with a value that presumably exceeds the mortgage. A solvent business firm has assets (factories, machinery, inventories, and so forth) that far exceed its outstanding debt in value.

Is the same thing true of the Canadian government? No one knows for sure. How much is the building that houses Canada's Parliament worth? Or the national museums? And what about the national parks? Simply because these government assets are not sold on markets, no one really knows their true market value.

Figure 4 charts the path of the *net* federal debt from 1870 to 2007, expressing each year's net debt as a fraction of that year's nominal GDP. Looking at the debt *relative to GDP* is important for two reasons. First, we must remember that everything grows in a growing economy. Given that private debt has also expanded greatly since the nineteenth century, it would be surprising indeed if the public debt had not grown as well.

Second, the debt is measured in dollars and, as long as there is any inflation, the amount of purchasing power that each dollar represents declines each year. Dividing the debt by nominal GDP, as is done in Figure 4, adjusts for both real growth and inflation, and so puts the debt numbers in better perspective.

Figure 4 shows us how and when the federal government acquired all this debt. Notice the sharp increases in the percentage ratio of debt to GDP during periods of

SOURCES: Statistics Canada, CANSIM I Series D11473 and CANSIM II Series V151548 and V646937; and M. C. Urquhart, *Gross National Product, Canada, 1870–1926: The Derivation of Estimates* (Kingston and Montreal: McGill-Queen's University Press, 1993).

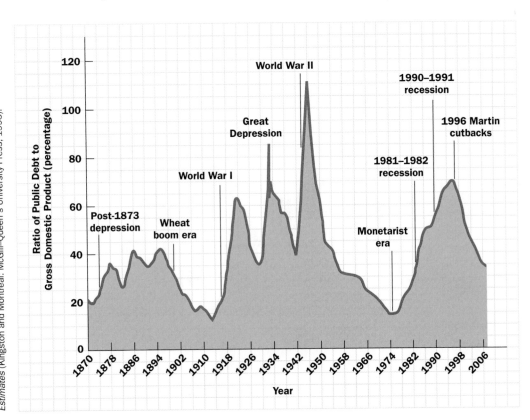

FIGURE 4

The Canadian National Debt Relative to GDP, 1870–2007

depression as, for example, just before the Wheat Boom era in the nineteenth century and during the Great Depression in the 1930s, as well as during periods of war—World Wars I and II. On the other hand, the ratio declined during periods of relative prosperity, such as during the Wheat Boom period at the beginning of the twentieth century and after World War II until the mid-1970s. In 1945, the national debt was the equivalent of 13 months' national income. By 1974, this figure had been whittled down to just two month's worth.

So, until the 1970s, the federal government had acquired most of its debt either from financing wars or during recessions. As we will see later, the *cause* of the debt is quite germane to the question of whether the debt is a burden. So, it is important to remember that:

> Until the mid-1970s, almost all of Canada's federal debt stemmed from financing wars and from the losses of tax revenues that accompany recessions.

But then things changed. For about 20 years, until the mid 1990s, the federal debt grew faster than nominal GDP, reversing the pattern that had prevailed since 1945. This growth spurt did not involve any wars, but there were two major recessions. By 1995, the debt exceeded six months' GDP—over triple its value in 1974. This disturbing development alarmed many economists and public figures.

At that point, supported by loose monetary policy, the federal government took drastic actions to reduce the budget deficit. Since then, the ratio of debt to GDP has continued to fall.

■ INTERPRETING THE BUDGET DEFICIT OR SURPLUS

We have observed that the federal government began to run major fiscal deficits during the mid-1970s, coinciding with the 1975 slump that resulted from the first oil price shock of 1973–1974. The year 1975 is also when the Bank of Canada began to implement a hybrid monetarist policy of targeting the growth rate of a monetary aggregate by raising real interest rates to combat the double-digit inflation. As Figure 5 shows, the budget deficit ballooned from about $2 billion in fiscal year 1974–1975

FIGURE 5

Fiscal Year Federal Budget Surplus or Deficit, 1962–2007

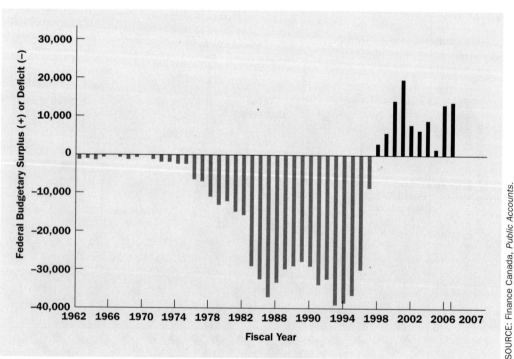

Note: Observations are for the fiscal years, ending on March 31 in each case.

SOURCE: Finance Canada, *Public Accounts.* Retrieved from www.fin.gc.ca/purl/afr-e.html

to a peak of roughly $37 billion a decade later in 1984–1985. That figure was to be eclipsed just twice after the 1990–1991 recession by a deficit of about $39 billion in both fiscal years 1992–1993 and 1993–1994. As late as fiscal year 1995–1996, the deficit was still about $30 billion, which then turned into a $3 billion surplus just two years later in 1997–1998. These are enormous, even mind-boggling, numbers. But what do they mean? How should we interpret them?

The Structural Deficit or Surplus

First, it is important to understand that the same fiscal program can lead to a deficit or a surplus, depending on the state of the economy. Failure to appreciate this point has led many people to assume that a larger deficit always signifies a more expansionary fiscal policy—which is not the case.

Think, for example, about what happens to the budget during a recession. As GDP falls, the government's major sources of tax revenue—income taxes, corporate taxes, and payroll taxes—all shrink because firms and people pay lower taxes when they earn less. Similarly, some types of government spending, notably transfer payments such as unemployment benefits, rise when GDP falls, because more people are out of work.

Recall that the deficit is the difference between government expenditures, which are either purchases or transfer payments, and tax receipts:

$$\text{Deficit} = G + \text{Transfers} - \text{Taxes} = G - (\text{Taxes} - \text{Transfers}) = G - T$$

Because a falling GDP leads to higher expenditures and lower tax receipts:

> The deficit rises in a recession and falls in a boom, even with no change in fiscal policy.

Figure 6 depicts the relationship between GDP and the budget deficit. The government's fiscal program is summarized by the blue and red lines. The horizontal red line labelled G indicates that federal purchases of goods and services are approximately unaffected by GDP. The rising blue line labelled T (for taxes minus transfers) indicates that taxes rise and transfer payments fall as GDP rises. Notice that the same fiscal policy (that is, the same two lines) leads to a large deficit if GDP is Y_1, a balanced budget if GDP is Y_2, or a surplus if GDP is as high as Y_3. Clearly, the deficit itself is not a good measure of the government's fiscal policy.

FIGURE 6

The Effect of the Economy on the Budget

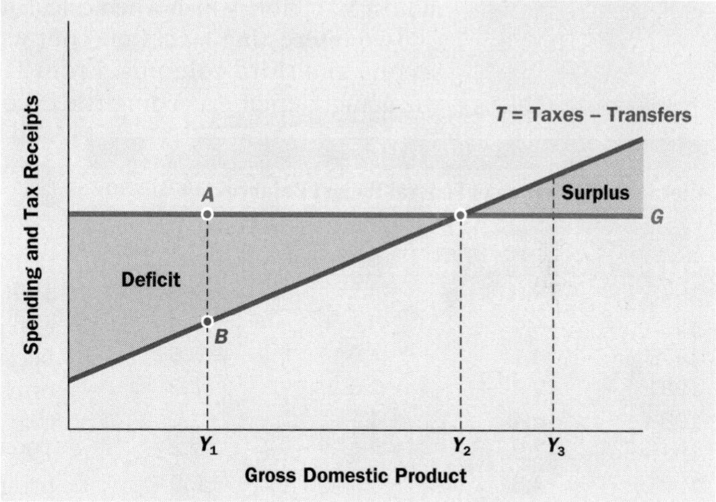

To seek a better measure, economists pay more attention to what is called the **structural** or **cyclically adjusted budget deficit or surplus**. This hypothetical measure replaces both the spending and taxes in the *actual* budget by estimates of how much the government *would be* spending and receiving, given current tax rates and expenditure rules, if the economy was operating at some fixed, high-employment level. For example, if the high-employment benchmark in Figure 6 was Y_2, although actual GDP was only Y_1, the structural deficit would be zero even though the actual deficit would be AB.

Because it is based on the spending and taxing the government *would be* doing at some fixed level of GDP, rather than on *actual* expenditures and receipts, the structural deficit does not depend on the state of the economy. It changes *only* when policy changes, *not* when GDP changes. That is why most economists view it as a better measure of the thrust of fiscal policy than the actual deficit.

In addition, we could rewrite our above definition of a deficit in a somewhat different way to highlight the difference between overall spending on programs and the

> The structural or cyclically adjusted budget deficit is the hypothetical deficit we *would* have under current fiscal policies if the economy was operating at its high-employment level.

servicing cost of the public debt. Remember that *T* is the sum of taxes less all transfers. These transfers include the interest payments (or transfers) to the holders of the public debt, which are labelled *In*. The **primary deficit** is defined as merely the actual deficit less *In*; that is:

> The **primary budget deficit** is the actual deficit less the interest payments on the public debt.

$$\text{Primary deficit} = \text{Deficit} - In = G - T - In$$

Policy makers at the federal Department of Finance have traditionally referred to the primary budget balance and, more precisely, the cyclically adjusted primary balance, as one of the most appropriate indicators of the federal fiscal stimulus to the Canadian economy. We have already seen why the structural or cyclically adjusted budget balance is a better measure of the discretionary actions of the fiscal authorities, but why the primary balance? The answer has to do with the actions of the monetary authorities. What if the monetary authorities choose to raise interest rates in order to slow down the inflation rate? As the Treasury refinances the public debt over time, it will be facing higher servicing costs, *In*. Hence, everything else constant, higher interest rates would result in a larger deficit—a deficit that is not necessarily wanted by the fiscal authorities but is simply an undesired outcome of the action of the Bank of Canada in implementing its interest rate policy. To avoid confusing the discretionary actions of the fiscal authorities from the direct effects of monetary policy on the budgetary balance, a more appropriate indicator of the fiscal position of the government is the cyclically adjusted primary balance.

These new concepts help us understand the changing nature of the large budget deficits of the 1980s and the stunning turn to surpluses in the mid- to late 1990s. These measures are presented in Table 2. To avoid being somewhat mesmerized by the numbers in billions of dollars, we have presented them as a percentage of Canada's GDP. Hence, in 2005, when measured on a national accounting basis,[3] the actual surplus was almost $2 billion, which when calculated as a proportion of GDP, was a mere 0.1 percent.

Two interesting facts stand out when we examine Table 2. First, let's compare the second and third columns. From 1975 to 1995 there were persistent deficits, with the actual deficit exceeding the cyclically adjusted (or structural) deficit only during and immediately following the 1981–1982 and the 1990–1991 recessions. Since 1997, both the actual and the cyclically adjusted budget balances turned into persistent surpluses that continue today. The continuance of budget deficits until the first half of the 1990s can be explained either by the fact that the federal government was not raking in enough revenues or because it was spending too much even when the economy was close to potential output. However, the fact that the Mulroney Conservatives between 1984 and 1993 did attempt to raise taxes and cut discretionary program spending might suggest that another factor that was somewhat outside of the control of the fiscal authorities could have been pushing the government into deficit.

Indeed, the last column may help to explain this shift from deficits to surpluses by the 1990s, as the primary cyclically adjusted balance became positive as early as 1991. During the 1990–1991 recession, the Bank of Canada brought down interest rates significantly and maintained them at a low level throughout the 1990s, thereby ensuring that the federal government moved from a primary deficit to a primary surplus. As interest payments on the federal public debt slowly declined, the actual and structural

TABLE 2

Alternative Measures of Federal Budget Balances, 1975–2007

Year	Actual	Cyclically Adjusted	Primary Cyclically Adjusted
1975	−3.0	−3.2	−1.8
1977	−4.4	−5.0	−3.4
1979	−4.1	−4.9	−2.6
1981	−2.8	−3.0	0.2
1983	−6.4	−4.6	−1.0
1985	−7.9	−8.0	−3.4
1987	−4.8	−5.6	−0.9
1989	−4.4	−5.9	−0.2
1991	−5.3	−4.2	1.4
1993	−5.2	−3.9	1.1
1995	−3.8	−3.2	2.2
1997	0.7	1.4	6.0
1999	0.9	0.8	5.0
2001	1.1	1.1	4.6
2003	0.3	0.6	3.2
2005	0.1	0.1	2.3
2007	1.0	1.0	2.8

Note: Measured on a national accounting basis as a percentage of potential GDP.

SOURCE: Department of Finance, *Fiscal Reference Tables*, Table 46 (Ottawa: September 2008). Reproduced with the permission of the Minister of Public Works and Government Services Canada, 2008.

[3] See the appendix to this chapter for a brief discussion of the difference between the public accounting and the national accounting approaches to measuring the federal budgetary balance.

POLICY DEBATE

Balance the Budget? By What Definition?

Debates over the balanced budget amendment in the United States and the budget of the European Union, which is subject to a strict annual balanced budget rule, have raised the question: What do we mean by a balanced budget? When we first introduced the concept in connection with fiscal policy in the previous chapter, it seemed easy enough to define—it merely meant that government expenditures equalled government revenues. But now we know that there are several measures of the public sector balance. Which, if any, of these measures should guide policy makers? Is it the actual, cyclically adjusted, or primary balance?

If this isn't difficult enough, there is a still more serious accounting problem that was first raised by Richard A. Musgrave (1910–2007) in the late 1930s and John Maynard Keynes in a series of articles in the early 1940s—the issue of how to deal appropriately with budgetary matters. It is a long-established business accounting practice to distinguish between current (or operating) expenditures and capital expenditures. Paying employee salaries for the current operation of a firm should not be confused with the purchases of long-lived assets such as plant and equipment that provide a return over many years. Hence, in treating a business investment, you should include only capital depreciation in the current operating budget and not the full value of the capital expenditure in the year of purchase. This is because a capital asset purchased today provides revenue over a number a years, which should be balanced with the cost of replacing it (its depreciation) over its useful life as a productive asset.

Following Musgrave and Keynes, a number of contemporary economists have argued that a similar division should be applied to

public accounting where such confusion between the current and capital accounts exists. For instance, investment in public infrastructure—for example, building a road in a remote community—could lead to a stream of increased future tax revenues by enhancing private sector productivity and raising incomes in the community. Should policy makers be balancing both their capital and their current operating accounts annually? Some economists have argued that a policy of balanced budgets, which does not differentiate current from capital expenditures, could lead to substantial underinvestment in public capital, while, for instance, an alternative policy rule that focuses only on balancing the operating account would not. Once again, the question arises: Which, if any, measure of the budget balance should policy makers in Canada be monitoring?

SOURCE: Colin McConnell/Torstar Syndication Services

balances ultimately followed, with a lag, the positive trend in the primary balance. This further reinforces the point made earlier that the high interest rate policy of the 1980s was a major factor behind the persistent deficits of the period. In that sense, it can be said that, with the help of a much looser monetary policy, the Martin cutbacks of the mid-1990s further strengthened a trend toward primary surpluses that had begun to take shape toward the end of the Mulroney years.

◾ Conclusion: What Was Behind Canada's Public Finance Disturbances over the Last Three Decades?

A look back at Figures 4 and 5 would suggest that something happened during the 1970s to move Canada from being an economy that saw the budget balance being mildly in deficit, hovering close to zero and associated with a declining ratio of debt-to-GDP during the 1960s to one that, by the late 1970s, displayed chronic budgetary deficits and a growing public debt in relation to GDP, a situation that lasted until the mid- to late 1990s. Throughout that period, successive governments repeatedly blamed the previous administration for mismanaging the federal finances. For instance, in 1984, the Mulroney government blamed the previous "spendthrift" Trudeau administration for having mismanaged the economy and plunging the government into debt. Yet, despite the Conservatives' attempt to balance the finances, the deficit persisted, even though the Conservative administration had generated a primary surplus as early as 1987–1988. When the Liberals returned to power under the leadership of Jean Chrétien in 1993, they in turn blamed the Conservatives for having brought the federal government to the brink of bankruptcy with a ratio of federal debt-to-GDP that had not been reached since

World War II, and that apparently was even alarming to some bureaucrats of the International Monetary Fund (IMF). So, given the state of the federal finances, early in their first mandate, the Chrétien Liberals cut deep into federal expenditures, especially transfers to the provinces, and suddenly by the late 1990s there was a dramatic turnaround.

What caused these two sharp breaks in the evolution of Canada's public finances? Was it the lavish spending of the Trudeau Liberals on social programs that moved the finances into chronic deficits, as the Mulroney government suggested? And was it the strength of Paul Martin as Finance minister, who was quoted as saying that he would combat the deficit "come hell or high water," that finally moved the federal finances out of the red? We would like to argue that, while these factors may have contributed toward moving the public finances in the directions that they actually took, these sharp deviations were mostly dictated by the evolution of monetary policy.[4] In combating the double-digit inflation of the 1970s, it was the blunt instrument of high real interest rates that initially destabilized the public (and private) finances and it was the return to lower real interest rates that finally stabilized them during the 1990s.

WHY IS THE NATIONAL DEBT CONSIDERED A BURDEN?

Now that we have gained some perspective on the facts, let us consider the charge that budget deficits place intolerable burdens on future generations. Perhaps the most frequently heard reason is that *future generations of Canadians will be burdened by heavy interest payments*, which will necessitate higher taxes. But think about who will receive those interest payments—mostly the future Canadians who own the bonds. Thus, as Abba P. Lerner asserted in the quotation at the beginning of this chapter, one group of future Canadians will be making interest payments to another group of future Canadians—which cannot be a burden on Canada as a whole.

But there *is* a future burden to the extent that the debt is held by foreigners. The share of Canada's unmatured federal debt held by nonresidents started from a low point of about 2.5 percent in the early 1970s, rose rapidly throughout the late 1970s and during the 1980s as interest rates rose in Canada, reached a peak of almost 28 percent in the early 1990s and fell back to 13.7 percent in the fiscal year 2005–2006. Paying interest on this share of the public debt is a real burden on future generations and represents sheer leakage for the Canadian economy, as a portion of Canada's GDP will be sent abroad to pay interest on the debts that were incurred during the late 1970s, the 1980s, and the early 1990s. Unlike our American neighbours, whose share of the U.S. federal debt held by nonresidents has continued to rise and has reached over 45 percent, this share has been declining in Canada. We can thus conclude:

> If the national debt is owned by Canadian residents, future interest payments will just transfer funds from one group of Canada's residents to another. But the portion of the national debt owned by nonresidents does constitute a burden on the nation as a whole.

Many people also worry that every nation has a limited capacity to borrow, just like every family and every business. If it exceeds this limit, it is in danger of being unable to pay its creditors and may go bankrupt—with calamitous consequences for everyone. For some countries, this concern is indeed valid and serious. Debt crises have done major damage to many countries in Latin America, Asia, and Africa over the years.

But the Canadian government need not worry about defaulting on its debt for one simple reason: *Canada's federal debt is an obligation to pay Canadian dollars*. Each debt certificate obligates the federal Treasury to pay the holder so many Canadian dollars on a prescribed date. But the Canadian government is the source of these dollars. It prints them! *No sovereign nation need default on debts that call for repayment in its own currency.* If worse comes to worse, it can always print whatever money it needs to pay off any creditors that might want to liquidate their holdings of federal government securities.[5]

---

[4] Admittedly, the mid-1990s turnaround was also aided by other factors (see Chapter 11, page 254).

[5] However, Russia astounded the financial world in 1998 by defaulting on its ruble-denominated debt.

The problem arises when a government has incurred debt that is in a foreign currency. With Canada as an important world trader and member of the G7 industrialized countries, a market exists for Canadian dollars. Canada is therefore in a privileged position to have foreigners who are willing to hold both public and private debts in our national currency. For instance, debt in foreign currency as a percentage of total unmatured federal debt was a mere 0.1 percent in 2006; this share has been declining over the long term since the 1960s and the early 1970s, when it used to be closer to 1 percent. The Canadian government hardly faces the danger of default when 99.9 percent of its debt is in its own currency. However, a number of developing countries in the world economy are not in this privileged position and the vast majority of their debt calls for payment in a foreign currency, for example, in U.S. dollars. The economic crises for countries that find themselves unable to meet financial obligations of this type can be shattering, as was the case in Southeast Asia in 1997 and Argentina in 2001. To conclude:

> There is a fundamental difference between nations that borrow in their own currency (such as Canada and other members of the G7 countries) and nations that borrow in some other currency (which is normally the U.S. dollar internationally). The former need never default; the latter might have to.

■ BUDGET DEFICITS AND INFLATION

We now turn to the effects of deficits on macroeconomic outcomes. It often is said that deficit spending is a cause of inflation—a view that was often articulated by famous Austrian economist Friedrich A. von Hayek (1899–1992) in his deep opposition to Keynesian deficit spending. Let us consider the argument with the aid of Figure 7, our standard aggregate supply and demand diagram.

Initially, equilibrium is at point A, where demand curve $D_0 D_0$ and supply curve SS intersect. Output is $7,000 billion, and the price index is 100. In the diagram, the aggregate demand and supply curves intersect precisely at potential GDP, indicating that the economy is operating at full employment. Let us also assume that the budget is initially balanced.

Suppose the government now raises spending or cuts taxes enough to shift the aggregate demand schedule outward from $D_0 D_0$ to $D_1 D_1$. Equilibrium shifts from point A to point B, and the graph shows the price level rising from 100 to 106, or 6 percent. But that is not the end of the story, because point B represents an inflationary gap. We know from previous chapters that inflation will continue until the aggregate supply curve shifts far enough inward that it passes through point C, at which point the inflationary gap is gone. In this example, deficit spending will eventually raise the price level 12 percent.

Thus, the cries that budget deficits are inflationary have a ring of truth. How much truth they hold depends on several factors. One is the slope of the aggregate supply curve. Figure 7 clearly shows that a steep supply curve would lead to more inflation than a flat one. A second factor is the degree of resource utilization. Deficit spending is more inflationary in a fully employed economy (such as that depicted in Figure 7) than in an economy with lots of slack.

FIGURE 7

The Inflationary Effects of Deficit Spending

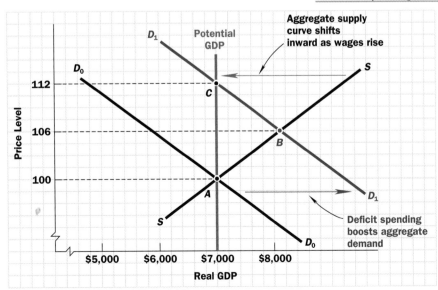

Note: Real GDP amounts are in billions of dollars.

Finally, we must remember that the Bank of Canada's monetary policy can always cancel out the potential inflationary effects of deficit spending by pulling the aggregate demand curve back to its original position. Once again, the *policy mix* is crucial.

■ The Monetization Issue

But will the Bank of Canada always neutralize the expansionary effect of a higher budget deficit? This question brings up another reason why some people worry about the inflationary consequences of deficits. They fear that the central bank may feel compelled to "monetize" part of the deficit by purchasing some of the newly issued government debt. Let us explain, first, the nature of the central bank purchases, and, second, why these purchases are called **monetizing the deficit**.

The central bank is said to **monetize the deficit** when it purchases bonds issued by the government.

Deficit spending, as we have just noted, could drive up both real GDP and inflation. Such economic expansion could shift the demand curve for base money (or cash). However, as was shown in Chapter 13, an increased demand for base money has no effect on the target overnight rate of the Bank of Canada unless the economic expansion is accompanied by a rise in the inflation rate. But the question of how the increased government spending is financed is highly controversial. There are those, inspired by the quantity theory tradition or monetarism (as discussed in Chapter 14), who argue that deficit financing, via central bank purchases of government securities, could have dire inflationary consequences since it entails monetizing the deficit.

But why is this process called *monetizing* the deficit? When the central bank purchases government securities, such as treasury bills, which the government requires to finance its expenditures in excess of its revenues, it increases the net amount of settlement balances in the system—what traditionally were referred to as *excess bank reserves*. It is assumed that when the government spends the newly created base money, banks will find themselves as a group with *positive* settlement balances. As profit maximizers, banks will then try to lend out these funds to the public and therefore bring about an increase in the quantity of money by means of the money multiplier mentioned in Chapter 14. In accordance with the monetarist tradition, a rise in the quantity of money will eventually lead to inflation in the long run.

While this has long been the traditionally accepted view, there are other economists who would question these monetarist implications. A budget deficit financed through central bank purchases of government securities will indeed have the effect of pushing the banking sector into a positive settlement-balance position. However, for these economists and followers of the banking view, to whom we referred in Chapter 14, the increase in base money does not lead to an increase in the money stock, as suggested by the monetarists. Instead, they point out that a banking sector that is awash in liquidity would quickly push the overnight rate down to the lowest end of the target range (that is, the rate on deposits held by the banks at the Bank of Canada, as discussed in Chapter 13), thereby frustrating the central bank's desire to keep the overnight interest rate at its target level. To avoid this, the central bank will conduct neutralizing operations, such as transferring government deposits away from the banking sector, thus bringing settlement balances back to zero. Since it is the *raison d'être* of central banks to control interest rates, Canadian monetary authorities always conduct these offsetting operations. In this case, the link between central bank purchases of government securities and increases in the money supply that is so important to those partial to the quantity theory view cannot materialize.

To summarize:

According to the traditional monetarist view, central bank financing of public sector deficits leads first to an increase in base money, then to an increase in the overall money supply via the money multiplier, and finally to inflation.

Critics of this approach reject the postulated causal link between changes in base money and changes in the money supply, as well as the relationship between the latter and inflation. The appearance of positive settlement balances in the banking system, arising from budget deficits, would have to be met with offsetting operations from the central bank so that the Bank of Canada can keep the overnight interest rate at its target level.

Supporters of the monetarist view often refer to countries with runaway inflation in Latin America and elsewhere as obvious confirmation of the significance of deficit monetization on inflation. However, when the theory is put through more rigorous empirical testing, the evidence is very weak and inconclusive. Indeed, throughout the 1980s and until the early 1990s, Canada was plagued with persistently high and even growing deficits, and yet the inflation rate actually declined.

◼ DEBT, INTEREST RATES, AND CROWDING OUT

So far, we have looked for possible problems that increases in the national debt can cause on the *demand* side of the economy, in terms of its possible inflationary consequences. But perhaps the most frequently cited consideration for cutting the deficit comes on the *supply* side—sometimes dubbed the orthodox "Treasury view," going back to controversies over deficit spending in Great Britain during the 1930s. In brief, the view is that large budget deficits discourage investment and therefore retard the growth of the nation's capital stock.

The mechanism is easy to understand just by looking once again at Figure 7. We can see that deficit spending could push up prices and fuel inflation and, accompanying the latter, a higher rate of interest. To the extent that higher deficits will ultimately be associated with a higher rate of interest, we know from earlier chapters that the rate of interest (r) is a major determinant of investment spending (I). In particular, higher r leads to less I, and lower r leads to more I. This, according to many economists, is the true sense in which a larger national debt may burden future generations, that is, by reducing the amount of productive capital available in the future because of a lower rate of investment today. Hence, in summary this view can be stated:

> A larger national debt *may* lead a nation to bequeath less physical capital to future generations. If they inherit less plant and equipment, these generations will be burdened by a smaller productive capacity—a lower potential GDP. By stifling private capital formation, large public deficits may retard economic growth.

Phrasing this point of view another way explains why this result is often called the **crowding-out** effect. Consider what is presumed to happen in financial markets when government engages in deficit spending. When it spends more than it takes in, the government must borrow the rest. Barring the possibility of the so-called monetizing of the deficit (where the overnight interest rate would instead tend to be pushed down!), the government must borrow funds from the public. It does so by selling bonds, which compete with corporate bonds and other financial instruments for the "available" supply of funds. As some savers decide to buy government bonds, the remaining investment funds will have to shrink. Thus, some private borrowers get "crowded out" of the financial markets as the government claims an increasing share of the economy's total saving.

Crowding out occurs when deficit spending by the government forces private investment spending to contract.

Because of this underlying belief of a fixed fund of available savings, some critics of deficit spending have taken this position to its illogical extreme. Some argue that each $1 of government spending crowds out exactly $1 of private spending, leaving "expansionary" fiscal policy with no effect whatsoever on total demand. In their view, when G rises, I falls by an equal amount, leaving the total of $C + I + G + (X - IM)$ unchanged.

Under what conditions would we expect this to occur? This extreme result would occur only under very exceptional circumstances. It is only when the economy has reached potential output (or full employment) that this full crowding out could arise. This is because if the real claim of government on a *fixed* output goes up, this increase could occur only at the expense of the private sector claim on that given output. The ensuing higher interest rate associated with the higher inflation rate would bring about a lower level of those private sector real expenditures that are moderately interest-elastic, such as business investment, household investment on housing, and household consumption of consumer durables. However, in all other circumstances where the economy is performing at less than its potential output, an increase in G would result in an *increase* in overall real GDP and, thus, would not necessarily entail a decline in I (or C) since all components of real aggregate expenditures could rise somewhat.

Indeed, in times of economic slack, a counterforce arises that we might call the **crowding-in** effect. Deficit spending presumably quickens the pace of economic activity. That, at least, is its purpose. As the economy expands, businesses find it more profitable to add to their capacity so as to meet the greater consumer demands. Because of this *induced investment* (or accelerating effect), as we called it in earlier chapters, any increase in G may *increase* investment, rather than *decrease* it as the crowding-out hypothesis predicts.

The strength of the crowding-in effect depends on how much additional real GDP is stimulated by government spending (that is, on the size of the multiplier) and on how sensitive investment spending is to the improved business opportunities that accompany rapid growth. Since private spending is only moderately sensitive to interest rate changes, it is highly conceivable that the crowding-in effect can dominate the crowding-out effect, so that I rises, on balance, when G rises.

But how can this be true in view of the crowding-out argument? Certainly, if the government borrows more *and the total volume of private saving is fixed*, then presumably private industry must borrow less. Isn't that just arithmetic? The fallacy in the strict crowding-out argument is of a twofold nature. As we discussed in Chapter 12, since banks are creators of money, credit advances from the banking sector are *not* constrained by the available savings. Therefore, *both* government and industry can borrow without facing a saving constraint. Moreover, the fallacy in the strict crowding-out argument also lies in supposing that the economy's flow of saving is really fixed. If government deficits succeed in raising output, we will have more income and therefore more saving. Remember from Chapter 9 that, at the macroeconomic level, it is investment that generates saving and *not* the other way round.

Which effect dominates—crowding out or crowding in? Crowding *out* stems from the increases in interest rates caused by the possible inflationary consequences of higher aggregate demand arising from public deficits, whereas crowding *in* derives from the faster real economic growth that deficits sometimes produce. The farther away the economy is from full employment, the more powerful would be the crowding-in effect. The strength of the crowding-out vis-à-vis the crowding-in effect also depends on the degree to which the central bank responds to inflation by raising interest rates; that is, it depends on the weight of inflation in the central bank's reaction function. Higher interest rates are not the necessary consequence of greater aggregate demand. They are higher only because central banks often fight the inflation that ensues from economic expansion by raising the central bank-administered overnight rate. But that may not always be so, since the decision is taken at the discretion of the monetary authorities.

Finally, another difficulty with the crowding-out hypothesis is the underlying assumption that government spending is purely for public consumption, such as the government purchases of all types of services that it renders to the public, from repairing our highways to paying for the services of the Canadian Armed Forces overseas. In reality, governments also engage in public investment—that is, investment in public infrastructures, such as building new roads, schools, and hospitals. Often these capital expenditures from government are highly complementary with private sector investment expenditures. Hence, taking an example already discussed earlier, building a public road cannot be seen as a drain on the productive potential of a community but rather a complementary input that enhances private sector economic performance. In the long run, just like private investment bequeaths higher productive capacity and generates higher productivity growth, so does public investment in social capital.

Crowding in occurs when government spending, by raising real GDP, induces increases in private investment spending.

◾ The Bottom Line

Let us summarize what we have learned so far about the crowding-out controversy.

- The basic argument of the crowding-out hypothesis rests on the premise that public sector deficits will push up interest rates. These higher interest costs will discourage investment spending and cancel out some of the expansionary effects of higher government spending. This view is predicated on a key assumption that interest rates rise as the economy expands. This is true only if the economy is nearing potential output and the central bank sets higher real interest rates as inflation accelerates.

- Unless the economy is at or is situated very close to its potential output, crowding out is rarely strong enough to cancel out the *entire* expansionary thrust of government spending. Some net stimulus to the economy remains.

- If deficit spending induces substantial GDP growth, the crowding-in effect would be strong and would normally offset any crowding-out effect caused by the higher interest rates.

- When evaluating the long-run effects of deficit spending, you must also consider the complementary nature of public investment and the latter's contribution to enhancing per-capita output over time.

◾ THE BURDEN OF THE NATIONAL DEBT

This analysis of crowding out versus crowding in helps us understand whether or not the national debt imposes a burden on future generations:

> When government budget deficits take place in a high-employment economy, the crowding-out effect probably dominates. So deficits exact a toll by leaving a smaller capital stock, and hence lower potential GDP to future generations. However, deficits in an economy with high unemployment may well lead to more investment rather than less. In this case, in which the crowding-in effect dominates, deficit spending increases growth and the new debt is a blessing rather than a burden.

Which case applies to federal and provincial debt? To answer this question, let us go back to the historical facts and recall how we accumulated all that debt prior to the 1980s. The first cause was the financing of wars, especially World War II. Because this debt was contracted in a fully employed economy, it undoubtedly constituted a burden in the formal sense of the term. After all, the bombs, ships, and planes that it financed were used up in the war, not bequeathed as capital to future generations.

Yet today's Canadians may not feel terribly burdened by the decisions of those in power in 1939 if they consider the alternatives. Instead of incurring huge deficits to finance the war, government could have raised taxes and thus placed the burden on consumption rather than on investment. However, that choice would truly have been ruinous and probably impossible, given the colossal wartime expenditures. Instead, the government chose to run large deficits, both by selling wartime bonds to the public and some to the central bank (thereby "monetizing" part of the deficit) and by ensuring that all of the debt was incurred at very low interest rates. Moreover, the inflationary effects of these huge deficits in a truly fully employed economy were somewhat mitigated by the imposition of wartime price controls. Finally, the government could have spent much less money and perhaps not have helped the Allied forces in Europe and elsewhere to ensure victory in 1945. Compared to these alternatives, Canadians living in the 1950s and 1960s did not feel burdened by the massive deficit spending undertaken in the 1940s. Neither did this massive debt prevent them from undertaking huge public investment during the first two decades of the post-war years, whose share of total government outlays grew throughout and peaked by the mid-1960s.

A second major contributor to the national debt prior to 1983 was a series of recessions, as in 1970, 1975 and 1981–1982, largely because of the workings of the automatic stabilizers. But these are precisely the circumstances under which budget deficits might prove to be a blessing rather than a burden. It was during the 1980s and the first half of the 1990s that Canada began to have the type of structural deficits that had become truly burdensome because they were incurred not to increase public investment or even public consumption but largely to service the public debt resulting from the high interest rate policy of the Bank of Canada. As we saw earlier in Table 2 in this chapter, once those interest rates fell and the Bank of Canada began to implement expansionary monetary policy, the ballooning deficits of the 1980s became primary surpluses by the early 1990s and then actual overall surpluses after the mid-1990s.

Despite the tax cuts of the Chrétien, Martin, and Harper years, Canada has continued to generate budget surpluses for over a decade. Indeed, the concern for some economists is that, by choosing to focus on tax cuts and reducing the public debt during a period of historically low interest rates, we are not bequeathing to future generations an equivalent amount of public capital that the generation of your grandparents and great-grandparents opted for during the 1950s and 1960s via massive public investment. As mentioned earlier, public capital is often complementary and not competitive with private capital, and the high public investment of the early post-World War II years was an important determinant of the overall macroeconomic performance of the economy of that generation.

On the other hand, there are economists who see merit in the federal government priority of getting Canada's debt-to-GDP ratio down to a target level of 25 percent by 2015. With an aging population that will be making greater demands on public health care, there are those who argue that it is important not to burden future generations with the high servicing costs of a large public debt. High servicing costs would, however, favour the older generation, who would normally be on the receiving end of the interest payments on the public debt. Placing a cap on the size of the public debt in relation to GDP would ensure that the burden of the debt in terms of interest payments would not grow out of proportion. While the redistributive effect of servicing the debt is a significant problem, there are critics of such tight federal fiscal policy who argue that there are other ways of dealing with this distributional matter; for instance, through tax policy instead of imposing global constraints on the size of the public debt in relation to GDP.

Let us now summarize our evaluation of the actual burden of Canada's public debt:

- Canada's national debt has been slowly declining since we began running budget surpluses in the mid-1990s. But the existence of a national debt will not lead a nation into bankruptcy. It could, however, impose a burden on future generations when the debt is sold to foreigners or contracted in a fully employed economy where crowding-out effects could dominate.

- Budget deficits are appropriate for stabilization policy purposes.

- The structural deficits of the 1980s were in part the result of the restrictive monetary policy stance of the Bank of Canada, which pushed up the servicing costs of the public debt and slowed the growth of interest-sensitive components of aggregate expenditures. Once interest rates began to fall in the 1990s because of the low-inflation environment, those deficits turned into structural surpluses, as lower interest rates stimulated the growth of the interest-elastic components of consumer spending.

? ISSUE REVISITED: *Was Fiscal Stimulus Warranted in 2001?*

We are now in a better position to answer the question posed at the beginning of this chapter: Was there sufficient fiscal stimulus immediately after September 11, 2001, to prevent a recession in Canada? We do know that, during the third quarter of 2001, real GDP did decline but then rebounded somewhat during the fourth quarter, although it did not again reach the high annual growth rates witnessed in 1999 and 2000. From Table 1, we could see that the overall annual growth rate went down to less than half of what it was in the previous two years of remarkable growth, and the unemployment rate did move up somewhat from its low point in 2000, only to return again to the level reached in 2000 some four years later. Moreover, the fiscal authorities could not claim that there was insufficient time to react. They were already well aware that both the Canadian and U.S. economies were slowing down even before the 9/11 attacks, mainly because of the dramatic slump in the high-tech sector that began in 2000.

Given the context, there were economists who argued that this was exactly the time when a strong fiscal stimulus in the form of a budget deficit was needed. Surely, with growing unemployment, concerns over either inflationary or crowding-out effects would have seemed unfounded. Because of the continued economic uncertainties caused by the terrorist attacks, public opinion would most likely have supported, for instance, greater public investment in infrastructure. There were others, instead, who advised the Finance minister to stay the course. A lower burden of debt was viewed as essential to long-term growth and the latter was seen as more desirable politically to a short-term fiscal stimulus.

What actually did happen? The cyclically adjusted primary budget surplus did fall mildly from 1.3 percent of GDP in 2000 to 1.0 percent in 2001, thereby suggesting that in addition to the triggering of automatic stabilizers, fiscal policy had become a bit less restrictive structurally, but not enough to entirely amortize the shock to the Canadian economy. Sticking to his commitment of targeting budget surpluses to bring down the public debt, the minister of Finance, Paul Martin, left it primarily to monetary policy to continue to stimulate the economy. Low interest rates did have a stabilizing effect and probably prevented the economy from slumping deeper into a recession, owing largely to the continued spending of consumers. But, in the context, some have argued that an added fiscal stimulus could probably have helped in preventing a slowdown.

As Canadian-born 1996 Bank of Sweden Nobel Memorial Prize laureate William S. Vickrey (1914–1996) would have advised, what was needed was a policy mix that would have looked more like that depicted in quadrant III of Figure 2, instead of that in quadrant IV. At the time, the fiscal authorities had a choice and they opted for a continued fiscal surplus because of its favourable long-term consequences in reducing the burden of federal debt. Indeed, the public debt did fall by some $8 billion in the fiscal year 2001–2002, but real GDP growth also declined by 2.6 percentage points (from 4.5 to 1.9 percent) and the unemployment rate rose by almost half of a percentage point (going from 6.8 to 7.2 percent) from the previous year.

If you had been in the position of the federal Finance minister, what policy mix would you have chosen?

SUMMARY

1. Rigid adherence to budget balancing would make the economy less stable, by reducing aggregate demand (via tax increases and reductions in government spending) when private spending is low and by raising aggregate demand when private spending is high.

2. Because both monetary and fiscal policy influence aggregate demand, the appropriate **budget deficit or surplus** depends on monetary policy. Similarly, the appropriate monetary policy depends on budget policy.

3. The same level of aggregate demand can be generated by different **mixes of monetary and fiscal policy**. But the composition of GDP will be different in each case. Tighter monetary policy coupled with larger deficits is associated with higher interest rates that could produce a smaller share of investment in GDP. Looser monetary policy accompanied by smaller deficits could lead to a larger investment share. High investment shares would normally be associated with faster growth.

4. One major reason for the large budget deficits of the early to mid-1980s and the early 1990s was the fact that the economy operated well below full employment. In those years, the **structural** or **cyclically adjusted deficit**, which uses estimates of what the government's receipts and outlays would be at high employment to correct for business cycle fluctuations, was much smaller than the official deficit.

5. For more than a decade, from the early 1980s to the mid-1990s, the economy continued to generate huge budget deficits but, since the early 1990s, primary surpluses have been generated. This would suggest that a crucial factor behind these deficits was the high interest rate policy pursued by the central bank.

6. The argument that a large **national debt** can bankrupt a country like Canada ignores the fact that our national debt consists almost entirely of obligations to pay Canadian dollars—a currency that the government can raise by increasing taxes or create by printing money.

7. Budget deficits can be inflationary because they expand aggregate demand when an economy is near or at full employment. If deficits are **monetized**—that is, if the central bank buys some of the newly issued government debt in the open market—the effect would be to thwart the ability of the central bank to set the overnight rate.

8. Depending on the economy's proximity to full employment, deficit spending can generate higher inflation that would be accompanied by higher interest rates. If the higher interest rates discourage private investment, this process is called **crowding out**.

9. Government deficits, by increasing aggregate demand and, hence, business sales and profits, may also have a favourable impact on private investment, a phenomenon known as **crowding in**.

10. Whether crowding out or crowding in dominates largely depends on whether or not the economy is close to or far from full employment. When unemployment is high, crowding in is the stronger force, so that higher *G* does not cause lower investment. On the other hand, when the economy is near full employment, higher government spending will displace private investment (and probably also consumption). In this case, the crowding-out effect dominates.

11. Whether or not deficits create a burden depends on how and why the government incurred the deficits in the first place. If the government runs deficits to fight recessions, more investment may be crowded in by rising output than is crowded out by rising interest rates. If, instead, a government decides to run deficits to fight a war in a high-employment economy (as during World War II), then these deficits certainly would impair the future capital stock of a nation, although they might not be considered a burden for noneconomic reasons.

KEY TERMS

Mix of monetary and fiscal policy 328

Budget deficit 330

Budget surplus 330

National debt 330

Structural or cyclically adjusted deficit or surplus 333

Primary budget deficit   334

Monetization of deficits 338

Crowding out 339

Crowding in 340

Burden of the national debt 341

TEST YOURSELF

1. Explain the difference between the budget deficit and the national debt. If the deficit gets turned into a surplus, what happens to the debt?

2. Explain in words why the *structural* budget might show a surplus while the *actual* budget is in deficit. Illustrate your answer with a diagram like Figure 6 (page 333).

3. If the Bank of Canada begins to raise interest rates, what will happen to the government budget deficit? (*Hint:* What will happen to tax receipts and interest expenses?) If the government wants to offset the effects of the Bank's actions on aggregate demand, what might it do? How will this action affect the deficit?

DISCUSSION QUESTIONS

1. Explain how Canada's federal government managed to accumulate a debt of almost $500 billion between the mid-1970s and the mid-1990s, after which the budget balance began to move into surplus territory. To whom does it owe this debt? Is the debt a burden on future generations?

2. Comment on the following: "Deficit spending paves the road to ruin. If we keep it up, the whole nation will go bankrupt. Even if things do not go this far, what right have we to burden our children and grandchildren with these debts while we live high on the hog?"

3. What links do you see between the crowding-out effects that were presented in this chapter and the anti-Keynesian episodes that were discussed in Chapter 11, page 254?

4. Explain the difference between crowding out and crowding in. Given the current state of the economy, which effect would you expect to dominate today?

5. Given the current state of the economy, what sort of fiscal-monetary policy mix seems most appropriate to you now? (*Note:* There is no one correct answer to this question. It is a good question to discuss in class.)

APPENDIX *Distinguishing the Public Accounting and the National Accounting Measures of Budgetary Balance*

There are two broad systems of accounting Canada's public sector: the Public Accounts, which are audited by the auditor general of Canada based on standard accounting techniques (see the data in Figures 4 and 5 in this chapter), and the System of National Accounts, which are established by Statistics Canada and treat the government sector on the same basis as other sectors of the economy, that is, based on measures of current production and income (as discussed in Chapter 8). While differences between the Public Accounts budgetary balance and the National Accounts balance have narrowed over time, the two techniques do not produce exactly the same result.

This is not only because the measure from the Public Accounts covers the fiscal year ending on March 31, while the National Accounts data pertains to the actual calendar year ending on December 31. According to the Department of Finance, the differences between the two measures pertain primarily to "the universe covered by each measure and timing issues." For instance, the Public Accounts include all departments, agencies, and Crown corporations, while the National Accounts include only a subset. Moreover, in the National Accounts, liability provisions are not registered until received by the ultimate recipient, while in the Public Accounts, a liability is entered in the year in which it is incurred, no matter when the payments are made.

Although the levels of the measured budget balances differ between the two accounting procedures, their trends are very similar, so if the budget balance changes, it will usually be in the same direction, regardless of the accounting method. However, this is not always so. For instance, the federal budgetary surplus from the Public Accounts went up from $1.5 billion to $13.2 billion between fiscal years 2004–2005 and 2005–2006, but it went down from $5.7 billion to $1.9 billion between the calendar years 2004 and 2005 according to the National Accounts.

For further details, go to the Department of Finance's website at www.fin.gc.ca/budget04/bp/bpa4e.htm

THE TRADE-OFF BETWEEN INFLATION AND UNEMPLOYMENT

The economists are at this moment called upon to say how to extricate the free world from the serious threat of accelerating inflation which, it must be admitted, has been brought about by policies which the majority of economists recommended and even urged governments to pursue.

FRIEDRICH VON HAYEK, 1974 CO-RECIPIENT OF THE BANK OF SWEDEN PRIZE IN ECONOMIC SCIENCES IN MEMORY OF ALFRED NOBEL, 1975

From our analysis in some of the preceding chapters, we have slowly come to recognize that there is a bothersome *trade-off between inflation and unemployment:* High-growth policies that reduce unemployment may tend to raise inflation, and slow-growth policies that reduce inflation tend to raise unemployment. We also observed, in Chapter 14, that the trade-off looks rather different in the short run than in the long run because the aggregate supply curve can be considered fairly flat in the short run but quite steep (perhaps even vertical) in the long run. A statistical relationship developed by economists, historically called the *Phillips curve,* seeks to summarize the quantitative dimensions of the trade-off between inflation and unemployment in both the short and long runs. In this chapter, we will discuss the nature of the Phillips curve, the debates surrounding the apparent lack of trade-off between inflation and unemployment, and the implications for public policy.

CONTENTS

ISSUE: *Is the Trade-Off between Inflation and Unemployment a Relic of the Past?*

In the late 1990s, unemployment in Canada and the United States fell to relatively low levels. Yet, in stark contrast to prior experience, inflation did not rise. In fact, it fell slightly. This pleasant conjunction of events, which was nearly unprecedented in Canadian and American history, set many people talking about a glorious "New Economy" in which there was no longer any trade-off between inflation and unemployment. The soaring stock market, especially for technology stocks, added to the euphoria. Record low rates of unemployment without rising inflation also blessed Canada from 2005 to 2007.

Is the long-feared trade-off really just a memory now? Can the modern economy speed along without fear of rising inflation? Or does faster growth eventually have inflationary consequences? These are the central questions for this chapter.

◼ DEMAND-SIDE INFLATION VERSUS SUPPLY-SIDE INFLATION: A REVIEW

We begin by reviewing some of what we learned about inflation in earlier chapters. One major cause of inflation, although certainly not the only one, is *excessive growth of aggregate demand*. We know that any autonomous increase in spending—whether by consumers, investors, the government, or foreigners—will have a multiplier effect on aggregate demand. So each additional \$1 of C or I or G or $(X - IM)$ will lead to more than \$1 of additional demand. We also know that firms normally find it profitable to supply additional output only at higher prices. Hence, a stimulus to aggregate demand will normally pull up both real output and prices.

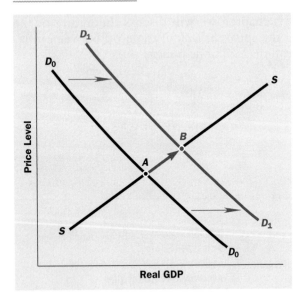

FIGURE 1

Inflation from the Demand Side

Figure 1, which is familiar from earlier chapters, reviews this conclusion. Initially, the economy is at point A, where aggregate demand curve D_0D_0 intersects aggregate supply curve SS. Then something happens to increase spending, and the aggregate demand curve shifts horizontally to D_1D_1. The new equilibrium is at point B, where both prices and output are higher than they were at A. Thus, the economy experiences both inflation and increased output. The slope of the aggregate supply curve measures the amount of inflation that accompanies any specified rise in output and therefore encapsulates the trade-off between inflation and economic growth.

But we also have learned in this book (especially in Chapter 10) that inflation does not always originate from the demand side. Anything that retards the growth of aggregate supply—for example, an increase in the price of foreign oil—can shift the economy's aggregate supply curve inward. This sort of inflation is illustrated in Figure 2, where the aggregate supply curve shifts inward from S_0S_0 to S_1S_1, and the economy's equilibrium consequently moves from point A to point B. Prices rise as output falls. We have *stagflation*.

Demand–side inflation is a rise in the price level caused by rapid growth of aggregate demand.

Supply-side inflation is a rise in the price level caused by slow growth (or decline) of aggregate supply.

Thus, although inflation can emanate from either the demand side or the supply side of the economy, a crucial difference arises between the two sources. **Demand-side inflation** is normally accompanied by rapid growth of real GDP (as in Figure 1), whereas **supply-side inflation** is normally accompanied by stagnant or even falling GDP (as in Figure 2). This distinction has major practical importance, as we will see in this chapter.

ORIGINS OF THE PHILLIPS CURVE

Let us begin by supposing that most economic fluctuations are driven by gyrations in *aggregate demand*. In that case, we have just seen that GDP growth and inflation should rise and fall together. Is this what the data show?

We will see shortly, but first let us translate the prediction into a corresponding statement about the relationship between inflation and unemployment. Faster growth of real output naturally means faster growth in the number of jobs and, hence, lower unemployment. Conversely, slower growth of real output means slower growth in the number of jobs and, hence, higher unemployment. Indeed, at extremely high levels of unemployment accompanied by lots of unused industrial capacity, as during the Great Depression, the economy may even experience a significant deflation. So we may conclude that, if business fluctuations emanate from the demand side, unemployment and inflation should move in opposite directions, thereby giving, at least, some loose inverse relationship between the unemployment rate and the inflation rate. In particular, unemployment should be low when inflation is high, and inflation should be low when unemployment is high.

Figure 3 illustrates the idea. The unemployment rate in Canada and the United States in 2006 averaged 6.0 percent, and the inflation rate was about 2 percent. Point *B* in Figure 3 records these two numbers. Had aggregate demand grown faster, inflation would have been higher and unemployment would have been lower. For the sake of concreteness, we suppose that unemployment would have been 5 percent and inflation would have been 3 percent—as shown by point *A* in Figure 3. By contrast, had aggregate demand grown more slowly than it actually did, unemployment would have been higher and inflation lower. In Figure 3, we suppose that unemployment would have been 7 percent and inflation would have been just 1 percent (point *C*). This figure displays the principal empirical implication of our theoretical model:

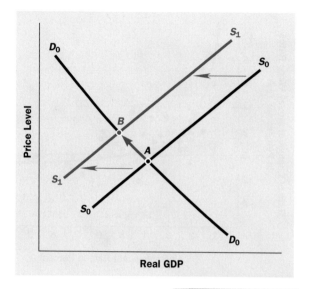

FIGURE 2

Inflation from the Supply Side

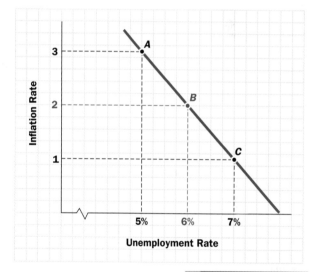

FIGURE 3

Origins of the Phillips Curve

> If fluctuations in economic activity are primarily caused by variations in the rate at which the aggregate demand curve shifts outward from year to year, then the data should show an inverse relationship between unemployment and inflation.

This relationship that links inflation to unemployment is none other than the celebrated **Phillips curve**, named after Alban William Phillips (1914–1975), a New Zealand-born British economist, who taught at the London School of Economics during most of his academic career. A half-century ago, in 1958, Phillips published a famous empirical study of the relationship between wage inflation and unemployment in the United Kingdom for the period 1861–1957. Phillips plotted data on unemployment and the rate of change of money *wages* (not prices) for several extended periods of British history on a series of scatter diagrams, one of which is reproduced as Figure 4. He then sketched in a curve that seemed to "fit" the data well. The data illustrated a trade-off between wage inflation and unemployment from which he inferred that one could reduce unemployment only at the cost of additional wage inflation. Phillips'

A **Phillips curve** is a graph depicting the rate of unemployment on the horizontal axis and either the rate of inflation or the rate of change of money wages on the vertical axis. Phillips curves are normally downward sloping, indicating that higher inflation rates are associated with lower unemployment rates.

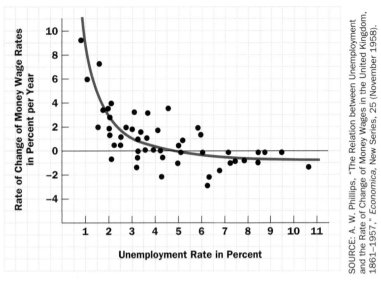

SOURCE: A. W. Phillips, "The Relation between Unemployment and the Rate of Change of Money Wages in the United Kingdom, 1861–1957," *Economica*, New Series, 25 (November 1958).

FIGURE 4

The Original Phillips Curve

Unit labour cost is the wage rate divided by average labour productivity—the average cost of a unit of output per unit of labour.

empirical relationship was of seminal importance. However, it was only in 1961, when well-known Canadian economist Richard G. Lipsey (1928–) provided theoretical foundations for the Phillips curve, that the curve attained immediate success and entered the vocabulary of professional economists and policy makers.

While the original Phillips curve formulation linked wage inflation and the unemployment rate, Phillips curves are more commonly constructed for price inflation; Figure 5 shows a Phillips-type diagram for early post-World War II Canada. The curve appears to fit the data reasonably well. The link between the two curves—the Phillips curve with wage inflation on the vertical axis (in Figure 4) and the Phillips curve with price inflation (as in Figure 5)—should be obvious. After all, as unit labour costs rise, so should prices. However, the degree to which prices rise *proportionally* with changes in nominal wages would depend on a number of factors, the most important of which is probably the link between wage growth and productivity growth. This is because the difference between wage change and growth in labour productivity defines the growth in **unit labour costs**—the latter being the variable on which firms would normally mark up their respective prices. As a simple rule, therefore, we can say that:

Price inflation *equals* wage inflation *less* the growth rate in labour productivity.

Hence, if nominal wages are increasing by, say, 3 percent and productivity is growing by 1 percent, all other things equal, prices would be rising on average by about 2 percent. Naturally, in this case, if firms are able to increase their profit margins, price inflation will exceed 2 percent (or if firms must reduce their profit margins, perhaps because of foreign competition, price inflation will be below 2 percent). However, over time, we may take the above equation as a fair approximation of the wage–price nexus.

During the 1960s and early 1970s, economists often thought of the Phillips curve as a "menu" of choices available to policy makers. In this view, policy makers could opt for low unemployment and high inflation—as in 1969, or for high unemployment coupled with low inflation—as in 1961. The Phillips curve, it was thought, described the quantitative trade-off between inflation and unemployment. And for a number of years it seemed to work.

Then something happened. The economy in the 1970s and early 1980s behaved far worse than the Phillips curve had led economists to expect. In particular, given the unemployment rates in each of those years, inflation was astonishingly high by historical standards. This fact is shown clearly by Figure 6, which compares the pre-1970 era with the post 1970-period. Undeniably, something went wrong with the old view of the Phillips curve as a menu for policy choices. But what?

FIGURE 5

A Phillips Curve for Canada, 1946–1969

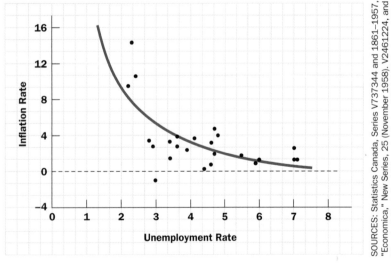

SOURCES: Statistics Canada, Series V737344 and 1861–1957, "Economica," New Series, 25 (November 1958), V2461224, and Historical Statistics of Canada, Series D223-235 (before 1976).

SOURCES: Statistics Canada, Series V737344 and V2461224, and *Historical Statistics of Canada*, Series D223-235 (before 1976).

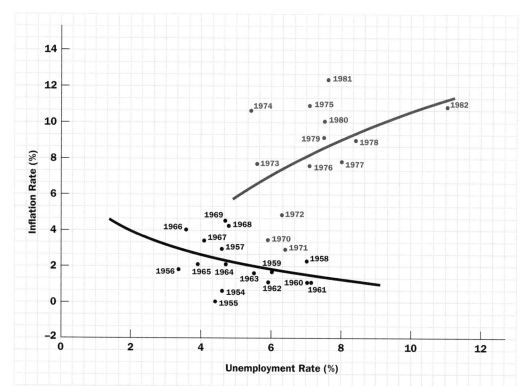

FIGURE 6

The Collapse of the
Canadian Phillips Curve

THE COLLAPSE OF THE PHILLIPS CURVE AND ADVERSE SUPPLY SHOCKS

There are two major answers to this question, and a full explanation contains elements of each. We begin with the simpler answer, which is that much of the inflation in the years from 1970 to 1982 did not emanate from the demand side. Instead, the 1970s and early 1980s were full of adverse "supply shocks"—events such as the oil price increases of 1973–1974 and 1979–1980. These events pushed the economy's aggregate supply curve inward to the left, as was shown in Figure 2 (page 349). What kind of "Phillips curve" will be generated when economic fluctuations come from the supply side?

Figure 2 reminds us that output will decline (or at least grow more slowly) and prices will rise when the economy is hit by an adverse supply shock. Now, in a growing population with more people looking for jobs each year, a stagnant economy that does not generate enough new jobs will suffer a rise in unemployment. Thus, inflation and unemployment will increase at the same time:

> If fluctuations in economic activity emanate from the supply side, higher rates of inflation will be associated with higher rates of unemployment, and lower rates of inflation will be associated with lower rates of unemployment.

The major supply shocks of the 1970s stand out clearly in Figure 6. (Remember—these are actual data, not textbook examples.) Food prices soared from 1972 to 1975, and again in 1978. Energy prices skyrocketed in 1973–1974, and again in 1979–1980. Clearly, the inflation and unemployment data generated by the Canadian economy in 1972–1975 and in 1978–1980 are consistent with our model of supply-side inflation. Many economists believe that supply shocks, rather than abrupt changes in aggregate demand, made the Phillips curve shift. As we can see from Figure 6, if we attempt to draw a Phillips curve through the points denoting the 1970–1982 years (the red curve), we uncover a *positive* relationship between inflation and unemployment. This is exactly what would be predicted when fluctuations in economic activity emanate mainly from the supply side.

Explaining the Fabulous Late 1990s

Now let's stand this analysis of supply shocks on its head. Suppose the economy experiences a *favourable* supply shock, rather than an adverse one, so that the aggregate supply curve shifts *outward* at an unusually rapid rate. Any number of factors—such as a drop in oil prices, bountiful harvests, or exceptionally rapid technological advance—can have this effect.

Whatever the cause, Figure 7—which duplicates Figure 14 of Chapter 10—depicts the consequences. The aggregate demand curve shifts outward as usual, but the aggregate supply curve shifts out more than it would in a "normal" year. So the economy's equilibrium winds up at point *B* rather than at point *C*, meaning that economic growth is *faster* (*B* is to the right of *C*) and inflation is *lower* (*B* is below *C*). Thus, inflation falls while rapid growth reduces unemployment.

Figure 7 more or less characterizes the experience of the Canadian economy in the late 1990s. Oil prices plummeted, lowering costs to Canadian businesses and households. Stunning advances in technology made computer prices drop even more rapidly than usual. Thus, we benefitted from a series of favourable supply shocks, and the effects were just as depicted in Figure 7. The Canadian economy grew rapidly, and both inflation and unemployment fell at the same time.

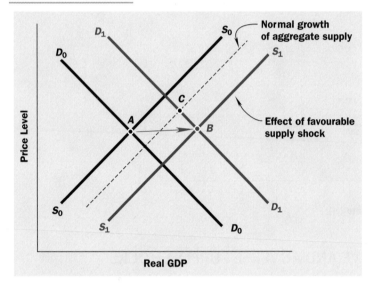

FIGURE 7

The Effects of a Favourable Supply Shock

? ISSUE RESOLVED: *Why Inflation and Unemployment Both Declined*

We now have the answer to the question posed at the start of this chapter. We need nothing particularly new or mysterious to explain the marvellous economic performance of the second half of the 1990s. According to the basic macroeconomic theory taught in this book, favourable supply shocks should produce rapid economic growth without rising inflation. The Canadian economy did so well, in part, because we were so fortunate.

THE VERTICAL LONG-RUN PHILLIPS CURVE

So one view is that adverse supply shocks caused the stagflation of the 1970s and 1980s. But there is another view of what went wrong with the Phillips curve. It holds that policy makers misinterpreted the Phillips curve and tried to pick combinations of inflation and unemployment that were simply unsustainable.

This second view was expounded nearly simultaneously by Milton Friedman and Edmund S. Phelps, who both received the Nobel Prize in part for their explanation. Just as there was a Keynesian revolution following the publication of John Maynard Keynes's *General Theory* in 1936, there was a *monetarist* revolution in the 1970s, following an article by Phelps in 1967 and the presidential address by Milton Friedman at the annual meeting of the American Economic Association, in December 1967. This revolution nearly swept away Keynesian ideas from academic discussion for about two decades, giving rise to a set of macroeconomic theories known as **new classical economics**. Many policy implications of the new classical economics have already been discussed in Chapter 14, when we presented several arguments against government stabilization policies.

The followers of **new classical economics** believe that there are economic mechanisms that quickly bring back the economy toward full employment and full use of capacity; many also argue that shocks to the economy arise mainly from the supply side.

■ The NAIRU

We have already explained in Chapter 14 how monetarism was associated with the quantity theory of money. But the most enduring contribution of monetarism is that Friedman (and Phelps) provided a convincing explanation of why the statistical relationship between inflation and unemployment—the Phillips curve—had apparently broken down and why some combinations of output and employment could not be maintained indefinitely. Friedman's model led to a complete reappraisal of the apparent trade-off between inflation and unemployment. This trade-off is now seen as a trade-off that arises only in the short-run; in the long run, there is no such trade-off. In the long run, the Phillips curve is vertical, as shown in Figure 8, so that there is a **vertical long-run Phillips curve**. According to Friedman, there is only one level of unemployment that is sustainable; in other words, there can be only a single rate of unemployment without the inflation rate eventually moving up or down. Friedman dubbed this rate the *natural rate of unemployment*, because he believed that unemployment would settle at this rate if market forces were left on their own. It is also often described as the **nonaccelerating inflation rate of unemployment (NAIRU)**— the rate of unemployment consistent with a nonaccelerating or steady inflation rate—and this is the term that we will use from now on.

■ FROM THE INFLATION–UNEMPLOYMENT RELATIONSHIP TO THE INFLATION–OUTPUT PHILLIPS CURVE

We have seen that the short-run Phillips curve is a relationship between inflation and unemployment; thus, the curve can be used to trace the ups and downs of the business cycle. If aggregate expenditures are rising, unemployment falls and inflation begins slowly to pick up and increase as the economy moves closer toward potential output. Hence, during a period of economic expansion, the economy would move leftward and upward along the short-run Phillips curve, and, during a period of contraction, it would move downward and rightward. Indeed, if the slump in demand is sufficiently strong to create a deep recession or depression, you could imagine the curve actually crossing the horizontal axis as the economy plunges farther and farther into deflation at excessively high levels of unemployment.

We could just as easily describe all of these analytics of the standard inflation–unemployment Phillips curve in terms of a relationship between inflation and real GDP—which can be defined as the **inflation–output Phillips curve** or simply the IO curve. On the assumption of a given state of technology and labour force behaviour, we could obtain such a short-run Phillips curve in inflation–output space resembling the upward-sloping relationship of the type represented in Figure 9.[1]

The **vertical long-run Phillips curve** shows the menu of inflation/unemployment choices available to society in the long run. It is a vertical straight line at the NAIRU.

The **nonaccelerating inflation rate of unemployment (NAIRU)** is the rate of unemployment at which inflation will neither rise nor fall over the long run.

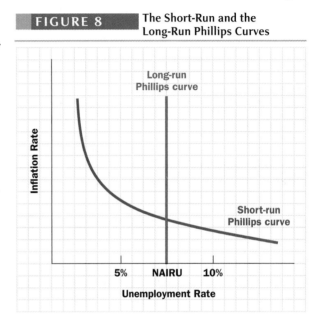

| FIGURE 8 | The Short-Run and the Long-Run Phillips Curves |

The **inflation–output Phillips relationship** is merely a diagrammatic representation of the traditional inflation–unemployment Phillips curve in inflation–real output space.

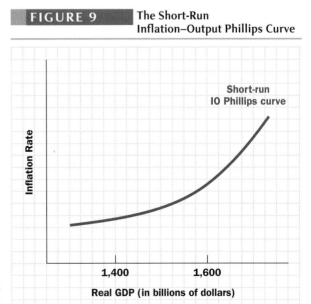

| FIGURE 9 | The Short-Run Inflation–Output Phillips Curve |

---

[1] For instance, an upward jump in productivity, all other things equal, would bring about a downward shift in the IO Phillips curve, while a decline in productivity would shift the curve upward and to the left.

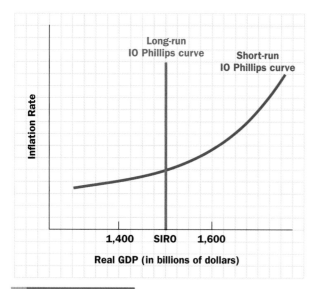

FIGURE 10

The Long-Run Inflation–Output Phillips Curve and the SIRO

The **steady inflation rate of output (SIRO)** is the level of output that would keep the rate of inflation constant. It is potential output as measured by the Bank of Canada, and it is the counterpart of the NAIRU in inflation–real output space.

The SIRO

We now need to explain why the long-run Phillips curve is vertical. To do so, we revert to the framework that we have just introduced: the Phillips relationship in the inflation and output space, on which we will now focus our attention. The explanation that we provide is not quite the one offered by Milton Friedman, but it is consistent with how officials in central banks, notably those at the Bank of Canada, view the inflationary process and decide on monetary policy.

Corresponding to the NAIRU and the vertical long-run Phillips curve in the inflation/unemployment space are the **steady inflation rate of output (SIRO)** and a vertical inflation–output long-run Phillips curve in the inflation and output space, as shown in Figure 10. Keeping the inflation rate low and steady is the goal of the Bank of Canada, as discussed in Chapter 13. The SIRO is the rate of output that keeps the inflation rate steady, moving neither up nor down, so it is the output equivalent of the NAIRU.

Why Is the Long-Run Inflation-Output Phillips Curve Vertical?

But why is the long-run IO Phillips curve vertical? Recall the shape of the short-run inflation–output Phillips curve, as depicted in Figure 10. This curve tells us that there is a positive relationship between the level of output, or the rate of capacity utilization, and the rate of inflation. The higher the rate of output or the rate of capacity utilization, the higher the rate of inflation. Formally, we can write this as:

Inflation = Various factors + *g* (Real output)

This simply says that the inflation rate depends on various unknown or imprecise factors plus a function of the rate of output. The letter *g* represents the slope of the relationship or how steep the inflation–output Phillips curve is. The larger *g* is, the steeper the IO Phillips curve is (in Figure 10, *g* is larger when real GDP is high). We can however make this formal relationship more precise, by saying that the relationship depends on the output gap, defined on page 288 as the discrepancy between real output and potential output or, in other words, the difference between actual real GDP and the steady inflation rate of output. We thus write the above equation in the following form:

Inflation = Various factors + *g* (% Output gap)

The inflation–output Phillips curve is not changed in any way by this new formulation. It just makes it more convenient to write it explicitly in terms of the output gap, as defined by the Bank of Canada, that is, in terms of the *percentage* difference between actual real GDP and the SIRO (this is why we use the letter *g* to characterize the strength of the effect of the output *gap* on inflation).

But what are the various other factors that enter the above two equations? What Friedman and Phelps had emphasized in the late 1960s, along with most economists ever since, is that among these other factors one should certainly include *inflation expectations*. If workers and their union representatives expect the inflation rate to be high, they will certainly ask for higher wage increases; and if their employers believe that the prices of their rivals and those of other goods will rise at the expected inflation rate, the employers will certainly be more likely to grant these wage increases and set higher prices accordingly. Thus, our formalized inflation equation becomes:

Inflation = Expected inflation + *g* (% Output gap) + Remaining factors

This addition is crucial, as it says that there will be a different inflation–output Phillips curve for each level of expected inflation. Thus, as shown in Figure 11, if workers and their employers expect high inflation rates, the inflation–output Phillips curve will be higher than if they expect a low inflation rate. The actual rate of inflation will thus be higher, for any given level of real GDP. This helps to solve the puzzle of the 1970s and early 1980s, as shown in Figure 6. When expectations of inflation rates rise, as they must have toward the end of the 1960s when actual inflation rates crept up, the Phillips curve shifts upward. At similar rates of unemployment, or with similar output gaps, inflation rates are higher than before. In Figure 11 for instance, it is shown that when real GDP is $1,600 billion, the actual inflation rate will be 2 percent, 5 percent, or 8 percent, depending on whether economic agents—workers and businesses—expect low, medium, or high inflation rates.

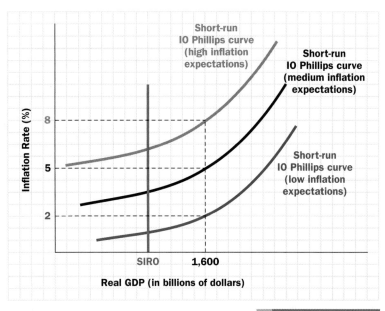

The Short-Run Inflation–Output Phillips Curve and Inflation Expectations

Adaptive expectations of inflation are expectations that economic agents formulate about the future inflation rate on the basis of the *past* values of inflation.

Indexing refers to provisions in a law or a contract whereby monetary payments are automatically adjusted whenever a specified price index changes. Wage rates, pensions, interest payments on bonds, income taxes, and many other things can be indexed in this way, and have been. Sometimes such contractual provisions are called *escalator clauses*.

■ Changes in Inflation Rates and the Output Gap

A key issue is how expectations of the inflation rate are formed. Economists have entertained several possibilities, but certainly the most simple one, which is both naive but at the same time probably realistic, is to assume that the expected inflation rate for this year is the inflation rate of the previous year, or some combination of past inflation rates. This is a variant of what are sometimes described as simple extrapolative or **adaptive expectations of inflation**. This term implies that when workers and their unions negotiate salary increases, they try to catch up with the purchasing power that they have lost during the previous year. As a result, wage agreements may contain an **indexing** clause that provides for an automatic increase in wages tied to the percentage increase of prices during the previous year. Our formalization of the inflation process now becomes:

Inflation = Previous inflation rate + *g* (% Output gap) + Remaining factors

But now we have arrived at a fundamental insight. If we omit for now the "Remaining factors," we can see immediately that the inflation rate will remain constant (that is, equal to the inflation rate of the previous period) only if real output is precisely equal to the SIRO. Otherwise, for instance, if real GDP is higher than potential output (the SIRO), the inflation rate this period will equal the previous inflation rate plus something positive. Symmetrically, if real output is lower than the SIRO, the inflation this period will equal the inflation rate of the previous period minus something.

Table 1 provides an example of what could occur under these circumstances. If the previous rate of inflation was 3 percent, only when real output is exactly equal to the SIRO will the new rate of inflation remain steady at 3 percent. Otherwise, the new inflation rate will either rise or fall, depending on the value taken by the output gap. For instance, as shown in Table 1, if real GDP is $1,050 billion while the SIRO is $1,000, the output gap is $50 billion and in percentage terms, therefore, it represents 5 percent ($50 billion/$1,000 billion) of potential output. If we assume that *g* = 0.2, it implies that this 5 percent

TABLE 1

The Inflation–Output Phillips Relationship and the New Inflation Rate

Previous Inflation Rate (%)	Real GDP*	SIRO*	Output Gap (%)	New Inflation Rate (%)
3%	$900	$1,000	−10%	1%
3	950	1,000	−5	2
3	1,000	1,000	0	3
3	**1,050**	**1,000**	**+5**	**4**
3	1,100	1,000	+10	5
3	1,150	1,000	+15	6

* Numbers are in billions of dollars; *g* = 0.20.

output gap will add 1 percent to the previous inflation rate. Thus, the new inflation rate ought to be 4 percent. Similarly, if there is a 5 percent *negative* output gap, the inflation rate will diminish by 1 percent, and the new inflation rate will be 2 percent. These various possibilities are also illustrated in Figure 12. Note that the short-run inflation–output Phillips curve crosses the SIRO when the inflation rate is at 3 percent because the inflation rate will remain at its previous level, 3 percent, precisely when real GDP is equal to the SIRO (unless the "Remaining factors" play a role in dislodging the economy from its steady path).

So, suppose that real GDP is equal to $1,050 in 2009 and that the inflation rate was 3 percent in 2008. The inflation rate in 2009 will thus move up to 4 percent. But suppose further that real GDP remains at $1,050 in 2010, and that the SIRO still stands at $1,000. The output gap is still positive at 5 percent and therefore will propel forward the inflation rate by a further 1 percent. The inflation rate in 2010 should thus rise to 5 percent. And if real GDP remains at $1,050 billion in 2011 as well, the inflation rate will move up by another 1 percent, to 6 percent, as shown in Figure 13. In other words, the inflation rate accelerates and keeps moving up. The short-run inflation–output curve is not stable. It shifts from I_0O_0 to I_1O_1, and then to I_2O_2. This will occur as long as real GDP is not brought back to the SIRO.

Analogously, starting once more from a 2008 inflation rate set at 3 percent, assume that real output is only $950 billion. The negative output gap will bring the inflation rate down to 2 percent in 2009. If real output remains at $950 billion, the inflation rate will fall by a further 1 percent, reaching 1 percent in 2010.

A fundamental lesson can be drawn from all of this: The Phillips curve is not just a static relationship. It is a dynamic relationship that shifts through time, as economic agents revise their expectations about inflation while taking into account changes in past inflation rates.

When real output is above the steady state rate of output (the SIRO), that is, when there is a positive output gap, the short-term inflation–output Phillips curve shifts up and there is a tendency for the inflation rate to rise.

When real output is below the steady state rate of output (the SIRO), that is, when there is a negative output gap, the short-term inflation–output Phillips curve shifts down and there is a tendency for the inflation rate to drop.

These dynamics were captured in Figure 13, and they are summarized in Figure 14. Whenever the economy finds itself on the right-hand side of the SIRO, the short-run Phillips curve eventually shifts up, as shown by the

FIGURE 12 The Inflation–Output Phillips Curve When the Previous Inflation Rate Is at 3 Percent

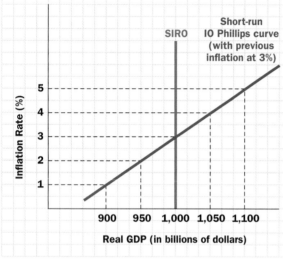

FIGURE 13 The Instability of the Short-Run Inflation–Output Phillips Curve

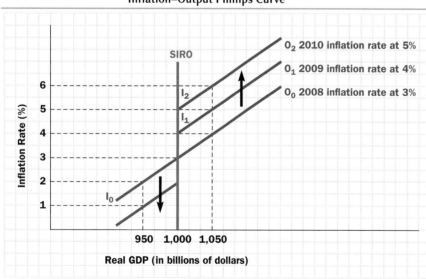

arrow pointing upward, and the inflation rate tends to rise. And whenever the economy is situated on the left-hand side of the SIRO, the short-run Phillips curve shifts down and the inflation rate tends to decrease, as reflected by the arrow pointing downward. Only when real output equals the SIRO will the inflation rate tend to remain where it is. In the case illustrated by Figure 13, this SIRO is a real GDP of $1,000 billion. Until the real GDP is brought back to $1,000 billion, the rate of inflation will tend to rise or to decrease over time.

Because ever-rising inflation rates or ever-falling inflation rates are not sustainable economic states, to many economists there is thus a single rate of output that is sustainable in the long run, and that is the SIRO. This is why most economists today consider that long-run Phillips curves, here more specifically the long-run inflation–output Phillips curve, are best represented by a vertical line. Eventually, the economy has to be at the SIRO or near the SIRO. Thus, in the long run, the only sustainable real output level is the SIRO.

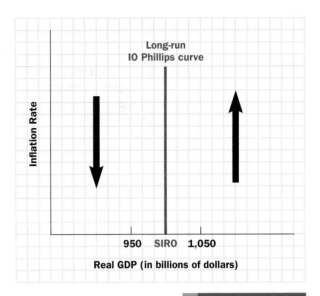

In this framework, the economy will return, in the long run, to the potential level of output (the SIRO). Thus, in the long run, the unemployment rate will be back to the NAIRU.

FIGURE 14

The Inflation Rate Decreases below the SIRO and Increases beyond the SIRO

We believe that this is the consensus view among central bank economists and even among many Keynesian economists. However, there is a fundamental difference in the actual mechanisms that are assumed to bring the economy back to the SIRO. Monetarists and new classical economists believe that the self-correcting mechanism is the result of natural long-run tendencies in the private economy that would take place regardless of the actions of the central bank. Many Keynesian economists argue, instead, that this mechanism is slow or may not materialize at all (as described in Chapter 10). In this case, it is the policy actions of the central bank that ensure that the economy would tend towards the SIRO. As discussed in Chapter 13, the above conclusions are predicated on a specific assumption regarding the reaction function of the central bank—to raise real (not just nominal) interest rates whenever inflation increases, and to reduce real interest rates when inflation subsides. If the central bank were to adopt some alternative monetary policy rule, the self-correcting mechanism that would bring the economy back to the SIRO would be disabled.

A MOVING NAIRU OR SIRO

It should now be understood that the SIRO is not the maximum output that could be produced if all factors of production were fully employed; rather, it is the maximum output that is compatible with steady inflation. Thus, if some means could be devised to restrain the forces of inflation, the SIRO could be augmented, real GDP could be higher without inflation accelerating, more workers would be hired, and hence the rate of unemployment would be lower. So, looking at the problem from a labour employment angle, might it not be possible to reduce the NAIRU—the rate of unemployment for which the long-run Phillips curve is vertical—by modifying some variables or institutional features of the economy? In this section we focus our attention on the rate of unemployment instead of real GDP; we stay within the confines of the traditional framework of the Phillips curve, in inflation/unemployment space.

The unpleasant consequences of the macroeconomic theoretical framework offered by the long-run vertical Phillips curve has led a number of economists and public officials to search for a way out of the limits imposed by the NAIRU. Because the traditional monetary and fiscal stabilization policies are demand-led, they affect

A Flat Inflation–Output Phillips Curve?

We saw on page 223 of Chapter 10 that some Keynesian economists believe that the aggregate supply curve is flat or at least has a large horizontal segment. In terms of the Phillips curve, this could be translated as a horizontal Phillips curve segment, where higher output would not induce faster wage and price inflation. If this is so, why is it that rates of output or higher rates of capacity utilization do not drive up the inflation rate, as we had assumed up until now? One possible reason is that many firms, especially in oligopolistic industries, face constant or slightly decreasing unit costs. As many oligopolistic price leaders set prices on the basis of unit costs, an increase in sales or in the rate of capacity utilization does not induce firms to raise prices any faster, as long as firms feel that they are operating not too far from what they consider to be their normal rate of capacity utilization. This gives rise to the flat segment of the inflation–output short-run Phillips curve. When firms operate much below, or much above, the normal rate of capacity utilization, they behave as was assumed until now.

There is some empirical evidence that the short-run inflation–output Phillips curve has the shape of a stylized puppy, as shown in the left-hand side of the accompanying figure. The middle segment is shown to be flat at a 2 percent inflation rate when rates of capacity utilization are between 80 and 86 percent. This corresponds to the flat range that has been estimated on the basis of Canadian data. Similar results, with a flat middle range, have been found on the basis of American data or the data of other countries. Some researchers attribute this to the success of inflation-targeting policies, which keep inflation rates around the target whatever the level of economic activity; flat ranges have however been observed before the advent of inflation targeting and in countries that do not target inflation.

With a flat segment, the long-run inflation–output Phillips curve would look as depicted on the right-hand side of the figure shown here. The implications are substantial: There are multiple SIROs, rather than a *unique* one, all to be found on the flat segment. In a sense, the SIRO is not a single value but ought to be more appropriately considered to be a *range* of values. In the figure, any real GDP between $1,490 and $1,565 billion is a SIRO. However, if officials at the Bank of Canada prudently estimate that the SIRO is at $1,500 billion, they will tighten monetary policy whenever they see GDP exceeding $1,500 billion (say, when it reaches $1,530 billion), arguing that there is a positive output gap that should lead to future increases in the inflation rate. Interest rates will be hiked up and real output will be brought back to the estimated SIRO at $1,500 billion, with the inflation rate still at 2 percent.

Will this induce the Bank of Canada to change its view of the long-run Phillips curve? It will not. While inflation remains steady at two different real GDP levels, Bank officials will argue that inflationary pressures were defeated at the higher–than-estimated SIRO output level precisely because the Bank took appropriate restrictive measures in a timely manner. The Bank will also argue that inflation targeting has helped to keep the inflation expectations of workers and firms around the 2 percent inflation rate. Thus, Bank officials will contend that the flat segment of the Phillips curve is a purely statistical phenomenon that must be attributed to the successful control of inflationary forces through a forward-looking monetary policy strategy. In the meantime, the Canadian economy is losing $65 billion worth of goods and services, as well as the jobs that would accompany the production of these goods and services.

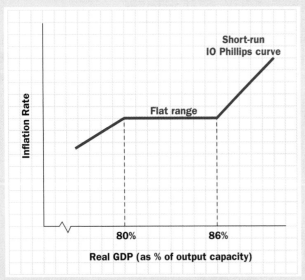

A Short-Run Inflation–Output Phillips Curve with a Flat Segment

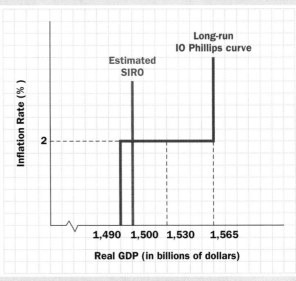

A Long-Run Inflation–Output Phillips Curve with a Flat Segment

only the aggregate demand curve. To utilize the various definitions of unemployment that we presented on page 122 of Chapter 6, these demand-led policies can affect only cyclical unemployment; they cannot affect the frictional and structural components of unemployment. Thus, in the long run, they can change only the inflation rate; they are unable to decrease the NAIRU (or increase the SIRO). In other words, they are unable to shift the long-run Phillips curve to a more favourable position. But what if other policies, so-called supply-side policies, were able to accomplish that task?

◼ OECD Labour Market Reforms

The Organisation for Economic Co-operation and Development (OECD), an agency that has 30 member countries (most of Europe, plus Canada, the United States, Mexico, Australia, New Zealand, Japan, South Korea, and Turkey) and is devoted to monitoring, analyzing, and forecasting statistical data and recommending economic policies, has been at the vanguard of those economists proposing supply-side policies to reduce the NAIRU. OECD economists argue that labour market rigidities are the main cause of a high NAIRU. Thus, because over the long run actual rates of unemployment ought to be around the NAIRU, these labour market rigidities explain the high rates of unemployment that have plagued many OECD countries, in particular those in the European Union. OECD economists thus argue that the best that governments can do is to introduce labour market reforms. By doing so, they say, we could enjoy lower unemployment without higher inflation.

But what are these labour market rigidities? At least five such rigidities are usually listed: minimum wage laws, strong unions, employment insurance programs, laws protecting workers, and the "tax wedge."

Minimum Wage Laws   High minimum wages relative to average wages, following the usual laws of supply and demand, would be conducive to higher unemployment rates, especially among young workers (but see the boxed feature "Does the Minimum Wage Cause Unemployment?" in Chapter 6, page 123, for an alternative point of view).

Strong Unions   Strong unions are said to restrain flexibility in work organization and in wage bargaining, thus leading to higher frictional and structural unemployment.

Employment Insurance Programs   There was an extensive description of our Employment Insurance system in Canada in Chapter 6. The duration of the unemployment benefits and the coverage ratio, that is, the ratio of weekly benefits to weekly wages, are said to be two major factors that favour frictional unemployment by encouraging workers to extend the duration of their search for job vacancies.

Laws Protecting Workers   Laws protecting workers or their jobs are also said to induce a higher NAIRU. It is said that such protection has the unintended effect of inducing companies not to hire more workers, as they fear they will be forced to keep these additional workers even when they don't need them any more, or because they fear that they will have to pay a large severance pay to workers that they have to lay off.

The "Tax Wedge"   The tax wedge is the percentage difference between the after-tax take-home pay of the worker and the cost of labour for the firm. This percentage difference can be substantial, as firms must pay all sorts of payroll taxes, while workers must contribute to various compulsory schemes such as the Employment Insurance program and public pension funds, on top of the usual income tax. The cost of one hour of labour may then be much higher than the net income of the employee for one hour of work. The larger the tax wedge is, the less attractive the salary offer for a given wage cost to the entrepreneur is, and hence the more difficult it is for workers and firms to achieve a wage bargaining position that is agreeable to both; this all results in the NAIRU being higher.

The OECD approach to the supply-side NAIRU consists of reducing all of the five elements identified above. This approach has been highly influential, especially in Europe, where unemployment rates have remained stubbornly high in several countries, and where the labour market is said to encompass many more rigidities than the American or even the Canadian labour markets. Many other labour market reforms have been implemented in Europe, but too often without any notable effect on unemployment rates, leading critics to argue that supply-side factors were not the problem, while OECD reform advocates conclude that the reforms have not yet gone far enough. But even in Canada, where unemployment rates have come down in a dramatic way—from about 12 percent in November 1992 to about 6 percent in 2006—the OECD view of the NAIRU is highly regarded by many Canadian economists. Here, as in Europe, most economists ask for more flexibility in all markets, but particularly in the labour market, pressuring government officials to reduce the labour market rigidities listed above.

A definite advantage of dealing with these supply-side factors is that they allow us to explain a puzzle regarding the behaviour of the NAIRU. Whereas the economists that first endorsed the NAIRU framework assumed the existence of a constant unique NAIRU (or of a unique natural rate of unemployment, as Friedman first called it), it soon became apparent that the NAIRU itself was not constant. It was certainly changing through time, because economists in various countries could observe periods of steady inflation even when unemployment rates were falling or rising (see the boxed feature "Measuring and Assessing the NAIRU"). Within the framework of the long-run Phillips curve, if the inflation rate is steady, it must be because the economy is at the NAIRU; under these circumstances, it follows that if the actual rate of unemployment is rising, it must be because it is tracking a rising NAIRU. The hypothesis of a unique NAIRU thus had to be forsaken, replaced by a NAIRU that varies over time.

But while all of the listed factors may appear to be reasonable determinants of the NAIRU, serious studies that have attempted to rely on these factors to explain both the evolution over time of the NAIRU within a country as well as comparisons of NAIRU values between countries have performed rather poorly. The evolution of the NAIRU may thus need to be explained by factors other than the supply-side ones.

Rather than wishing for reduced labour protection and work benefits, some economists, still convinced by the OECD flexible labour market approach, have proposed instead to take a positive outlook, focusing on more education, training, and job placement. The data clearly show that more educated workers become unemployed less frequently than the less educated. Vocational training and retraining programs, if successful, help unemployed workers with obsolete skills to acquire abilities that are currently in demand. By so doing, they both raise employment and help alleviate upward pressures on wages in jobs where qualified workers are in short supply, thus contributing to reduction of the NAIRU. Government and private job placement and counselling services play a similar role. Such programs try to better match workers to jobs by funnelling information from prospective employers to prospective employees.

These ideas sound sensible and promising. But besides the issue of whether financial resources should be taken away from employment insurance programs and transferred to these education and training programs, one major problem arises in the implementation of such programs: Training and placement programs often look better on paper than they do in practice, where they achieve only moderate success. Too often, people are trained for jobs that do not exist by the time they finish their training—if, indeed, the jobs ever existed. As Canadian-born economist John Kenneth Galbraith said, "Education, training is, indeed, central to a good society . . . but . . . a call for better-prepared workers as a remedy for recession-induced unemployment is the last resort of a vacant liberal mind."[2]

---

[2] John Kenneth Galbraith, *The Good Society* (Boston: Houghton Mifflin, 1996), p. 41.

Measuring and Assessing the NAIRU

In 1995, most economists in the United States believed that the NAIRU was about 6 percent in their country. If unemployment fell below this critical rate, they said, inflation would take off. Experience in the late 1990s belied that view. By the end of 1998, the unemployment rate was below 4.5 percent and it even dipped below 4 percent for a few months in 2001, without any signs of rising inflation.

In Canada in the mid-1980s, NAIRU estimates by various economists ranged from 6.2 percent to 11.5 percent! The Bank of Canada provided an estimate of 8 percent in 1988. This may explain why the Bank of Canada hiked up interest rates a year later, when unemployment rates settled at around 7.5 percent. Still, Canadian unemployment rates exceeded 9 percent throughout the entire 1993–1996 period, without any drop in the inflation rate. And they have been below 8 percent nearly every month since 2000, even reaching 5.8 percent in some months of 2007 and 2008, with no signs of rising inflation.

It follows that either NAIRU estimates are mistaken or that NAIRU values change quickly through time, so quickly perhaps that their estimates become useless for policy makers.

◼ Persistence and Hysteresis

That the NAIRU seems to vary over time brings up the issue of aggregate demand and its possible influence on the NAIRU. As we said before, it has become quite obvious that if the NAIRU exists, it has been changing over time. There have been periods of rising NAIRU and periods of falling NAIRU. While some of these movements can be attributed to changes in supply-side factors underlined by OECD and new classical economists, some Keynesian economists argue instead that the NAIRU is itself mainly influenced by past realized rates of unemployment. Two self-correcting mechanisms would therefore be at work. On the one hand, the actual rate of unemployment tends to move toward the NAIRU, possibly as a result of the monetary policy of the central bank. On the other hand, the NAIRU itself would tend to move toward past realized rates of unemployment. This is what we now examine.

Why would the NAIRU tend toward past recorded rates of unemployment instead of being unresponsive to them? Two main explanations have been offered. The first explanation rests on the observation that unemployed workers gradually lose some of the skills needed to be productive and efficient in the labour market. For instance, they may be unable to use current or new software needed at work, or they may lose the habit of getting up early in the morning to get to work on time. Human capital is thus being "scrapped." As a result, with higher unemployment rates, especially when these are associated with long unemployment spells, fewer workers will be able to meet job requirements, and hence inflationary pressures will take off when entrepreneurs start looking for new hires. The NAIRU has risen. Obviously this explanation ties in well with the need to have more worker education and retraining.

The other main explanation is tied to the scrapping of physical capital. With high unemployment, sales are low and hence firms make fewer profits. They may thus lose their incentives to invest in productive capacity, leaving their machinery to rust. Investment in new machines may be so low that it is insufficient to keep up the existing stock of capital, since part of the capital stock is being used up every year. As a result, the economy is left with less productive capacity and hence a lower potential output or SIRO, in which case inflationary pressures will arise much sooner. Again, since employment is tied to output capacity, this will drive up the NAIRU. In this case, retraining of workers and OECD strictures will be of little use.

Of course, the opposite of these two explanations is also true. When employment rates are high, a greater proportion of the labour force can be easily hired by entrepreneurs, thus lowering the NAIRU. Also, when employment rates and sales are high, profits of firms are high, and they tend to speed up investment, increase capacity, and thus potential output and the SIRO. The NAIRU falls.

A third explanation, which is mostly found among Marxist and left-leaning Keynesian economists, is that prolonged weak labour markets, as occurred in the early 1980s and early 1990s in Canada, have left workers and labour organizations powerless and more docile, even after labour markets have come back to a more normal situation. The implication would be that this drives down the unemployment rate that is compatible with a constant inflation rate.

A key question among economists is whether these three phenomena change the NAIRU in a temporary way or in a permanent way. Keynesian economists who still believe in the relevance of the NAIRU and SIRO analyses tend to argue that these changes in the NAIRU are only transitory in nature. Eventually, the NAIRU comes back to its long-run value, determined by the kind of supply-side factors emphasized, for instance, by OECD economists. The fact that steady inflation rates can, for a while, accompany unemployment rates that are much higher or lower than this long-run NAIRU is called **persistence**.

There is however a second group of Keynesian economists that argues that demand-led factors change the NAIRU in a permanent way, and that the NAIRU never returns to any long-run value determined exclusively by supply-side factors. This second interpretation of the data is called **hysteresis**. These staunch Keynesian economists believe that the NAIRU trundles along after the actual rate of unemployment. The NAIRU depends essentially on past values of the actual rate of unemployment. Supply-side factors have only a temporary effect on the NAIRU. The NAIRU, while being an attractor, is mostly an attractee, gravitating around past actual rates of unemployment determined by aggregate demand. With hysteresis, in the case of unemployment, the NAIRU depends on the path taken during the transition process, and hence will depend on past aggregate demand.

The proponents of hysteresis note that in Europe and in North America, unemployment rates have varied considerably between 1980 and now. They add that, according to the NAIRU framework, this should have led to substantial variations in inflation rates, with inflation rates either accelerating or decelerating, whereas exactly the opposite has occurred. For instance, in Canada, as we already pointed out in Chapter 14, page 320, inflation rates were quite steady between 1983 and 1990, and they were steady again after the deep recession of 1991–1992. Still during the first period of steady inflation rates, unemployment rates moved from 12 to 7 percent, while during the second period of steady inflation rates, unemployment rates plummeted from 11 percent to 6 percent.

The difference between persistence and hysteresis is represented in Figures 15 and 16. In both figures, it is assumed that supply-side factors such as those identified by OECD economists remain unchanged, and that the NAIRU is initially at 7 percent. In both figures, we assume that the central bank decides to impose a highly restrictive monetary policy with high real interest rates, in a drastic attempt to reduce the inflation rate. This leads, however, to high actual rates of unemployment, which rise as high as 12 percent. With persistence, as shown in Figure 15, the NAIRU rises temporarily, because of human capital or physical capital scrapping as explained earlier, but eventually the NAIRU returns to its equilibrium value at 7 percent, a value entirely determined by supply-side factors. By contrast, with hysteresis, the NAIRU, even after many years, remains influenced by past values of the actual rates of unemployment and does not return to its initial value (it could do so, but only if there was a positive shock to aggregate demand that would lead to a large decrease in the actual rate of unemployment). There are thus multiple possible long-run NAIRUs, and the realized one depends on past actual rates of unemployment.

Persistence means that a variable, such as the NAIRU, may stray from its defined long-run equilibrium value for a long time, but will eventually return to it.

The word **hysteresis** was introduced into economics by Edmund Phelps to mean a situation in which effects remain even after the initial causes have been removed, as in electromagnetics.

FIGURE 15

Persistence: The NAIRU Returns to Its Initial Value in the Long Run

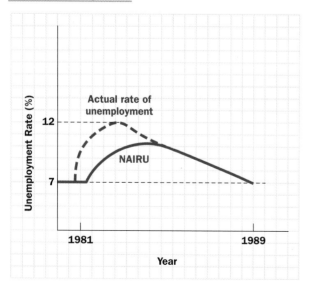

The unemployment hysteresis hypothesis is a radical modification of the NAIRU framework because, ultimately, the policy implications of NAIRU analysis become meaningless. Expansionary policies can keep the rate of unemployment at a low level, even in the long run, without leading to accelerating inflation. Expansionary fiscal policies, usually favoured by Keynesian economists, will thus have positive long-run effects. Similarly, the hysteresis hypothesis implies that the restrictive monetary policies pursued by central banks in their efforts to combat inflation will have negative long-run effects on the economy. It therefore becomes impossible for central banks such as the Bank of Canada to claim that because they have no long-run impact on employment, the best they can do is control inflation. With hysteresis, the Bank of Canada can improve economic activity and the rate of unemployment by being less keen on fighting inflation. This explains why Bank of Canada researchers have very vigorously denied the empirical relevance of the unemployment hysteresis hypothesis in Canada.

Unfortunately, it is very difficult to distinguish in statistical studies between hysteresis and persistence. As a result, the empirical evidence on this is mixed, and supporters of either explanation of the variability of the NAIRU over time can hold on to their beliefs.

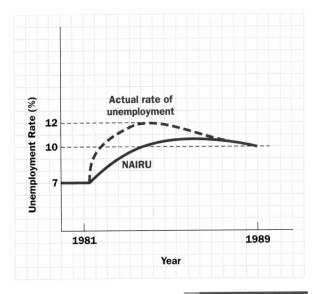

FIGURE 16

Hysteresis: The NAIRU Does Not Return to Its Initial Value in the Long Run

WHY ECONOMISTS (AND POLITICIANS) DISAGREE

This chapter has now taught us some of the reasons why economists may disagree about the proper conduct of stabilization policy. It also helps us understand some of the related political debates. One crucial issue has been the shape of the long-run Phillips curves, and the determinants of the NAIRU and the SIRO, with the various positions with regards to the relevance of the NAIRU framework, being described in Table 2.

TABLE 2					
Different Views of the Long-Run Phillips Curve					
School of Thought	Type of NAIRU	Short-Run Determinants	Long-Run Determinants	Long-Run Trade-Off between Inflation and Unemployment (or Output)	Long-Run Policy Implications
Old Keynesians	None			Trade-off	There is a menu between inflation and unemployment.
Earlier monetarists	Unique	Supply-side factors	Supply-side factors	No trade-off	No menu; a single unemployment rate can be sustained.
New classical and OECD economists	Varies over time	Supply-side factors	Supply-side factors	No trade-off	No menu; lower sustainable rates of unemployment require appropriate supply-side policies.
Persistence Keynesians	Varies over time	Supply-side factors and aggregate demand	Supply-side factors	No trade-off	No menu, but actual rates of unemployment may wander away from their long-run equilibrium value for a long time; lower sustainable rates of unemployment require appropriate supply-side policies.
Hysteresis Keynesians	Varies over time	Supply-side factors and aggregate demand	Past aggregate demand	Trade-off (NAIRU or SIRO irrelevant)	There is a menu of choices between inflation and unemployment.

Should the government take strong action to prevent or reduce inflation? You will say yes if you believe that (1) inflation is more costly than unemployment, (2) the short-run Phillips curve is steep, (3) expectations react quickly to past inflation rates or to policy announcements such as inflation targets, (4) the NAIRU is essentially determined by supply-side factors, and (5) the economy's self-correcting mechanism works smoothly and rapidly. These views on the economy tend to be held by monetarists and new classical economists.

But you will say no if you believe that (1) unemployment is more costly than inflation, (2) the short-run Phillips curve is not steep, (3) expectations react sluggishly to past values or to announcements, (4) the NAIRU is strongly influenced by demand-led factors in both the short run and the long run, and (5) the self-correcting mechanism is slow and unreliable. These views are held by many Keynesian economists, so it is not surprising that these economists often oppose the use of recessions to fight inflation.

The tables are turned, however, when the question becomes whether to use demand management to bring a recession to a rapid end. The Keynesian view of the world leads to the conclusion that the benefits of fighting unemployment are high and that the costs are low. Keynesians are eager to fight recessions. The monetarist and new classical views are precisely the reverse. They believe that the NAIRU or the SIRO are the ultimate supply-side determined barriers to economic activity, and hence that demand management will do more harm than good in the long run.

It would be nice to be able to provide a single and simple answer to the fundamental question of the long-run trade-off, or lack thereof, between inflation and unemployment or between inflation and real output growth. Unfortunately, models and theories are hard to disprove. And because value judgments and political opinions have some influence on every step of scientific research, economic theories that have quite opposed policy implications can be held and promoted concurrently by various groups of economists on the basis of legitimate evidence. It is important to be aware of these different theories and implications.

SUMMARY

1. Inflation can be caused either by rapid growth of aggregate demand or by the sluggish growth of potential output—the supply side.

2. The inverse relationship between unemployment and inflation is called the **Phillips curve**. Data internationally for the 1950s and 1960s display a clear Phillips curve relationship, but data for the post-1970s do not.

3. The Phillips curve collapsed in the early 1970s. The first explanation of this collapse relies on adverse supply shocks that led to higher rates of inflation and reduced economic activity, accompanied by higher unemployment.

4. The second explanation relies on the **vertical long-run Phillips curve**, a theoretical construct advocated by Milton Friedman and endorsed by monetarists, **new classical economists**, and many Keynesians.

5. The long-run Phillips curve incorporates the fact that workers and firms revise their expectations of future inflation and take those into account when bargaining for wages and setting prices.

6. In the short run, the economy can move up or down along the short-run Phillips curve. Temporary reductions in

unemployment can be achieved at the cost of higher inflation, and temporary increases in unemployment can be used to fight inflation.

7. In the long run, however, the economy's choices lie along the vertical Phillips curve, at the **NAIRU**, the only unemployment rate that can persist indefinitely since it is the only rate where inflation can remain steady. Looking at things in the inflation–output plane, there is a unique **SIRO**—a unique steady inflation rate of output.

8. The economy converges toward the NAIRU (or the SIRO), provided the central bank sets interest rates in an appropriate way.

9. There is an overwhelming amount of evidence that shows that the NAIRU, if it exists, varies considerably over time. This has led economists to consider the determinants of the NAIRU and even to question its existence or relevance.

10. Highly influential OECD studies assert that the NAIRU moves according to supply-side factors that affect mainly the labour market. Less rigidity in the labour market (for instance, reductions in the benefits of the Employment Insurance program) ought to help in reducing the NAIRU.

11. Keynesians have found that the NAIRU tends to vary with changes in the actual rates of unemployment and hence is influenced by demand-led factors. **Persistence** Keynesians believe that this effect is restricted to the short run, and that only supply-side factors affect the NAIRU in the long run.

12. **Hysteresis** Keynesians come to the opposite conclusion: They believe that the long-run NAIRU is essentially determined by aggregate demand, and that there is a trade-off between inflation and unemployment in the long run as well as in the short run.

KEY TERMS

Demand-side inflation 348

Supply-side inflation 348

Phillips curve 349

Unit labour cost 350

New classical economics 352

Vertical long-run Phillips curve 353

Nonaccelerating inflation rate of unemployment (NAIRU) 353

Inflation–output Phillips curve 353

Steady inflation rate of output (SIRO) 354

Adaptive expectations of inflation 355

Indexing 355

Persistence 362

Hysteresis 362

TEST YOURSELF

1. Show that, if the economy's inflation–output Phillips curve is vertical, fluctuations in aggregate demand produce only fluctuations in inflation, with no effect on output. Show what happens if the economy is in the flat range of the long-run inflation–output Phillips curve.

2. Explain the similarities and the differences between the concepts of persistence and hysteresis. Why is the latter concept associated more with Keynesian economists?

DISCUSSION QUESTIONS

1. When inflation and unemployment fell together in the 1990s, some observers claimed that policy makers no longer faced a trade-off between inflation and unemployment. Were they correct?

2. "There is no sense in trying to shorten recessions through fiscal and monetary policy because the effects of these policies on the unemployment rate are sure to be temporary." Comment on both the truth of this statement and its relevance for policy formulation.

3. Why is it said that decisions on fiscal and monetary policy are, at least in part, political decisions that cannot be made on "objective" economic criteria?

4. What is a Phillips curve? Why did it seem to work so much better in the period from 1954 to 1969 than it did in the 1970s?

5. Explain why expectations of inflation affect the wages that result from labour-management bargaining.

6. What advantage is there, from the standpoint of the Bank of Canada, to being a credible central bank? How does that tie in with the hypothesis of the vertical Phillips curves?

7. Discuss the reasons that would lead the Bank of Canada to deny adamantly the possibility of unemployment hysteresis in Canada?

8. Why is it so important to know the true shape of the inflation–output Phillips curve?

9. Check the current unemployment rate, the rate of growth of real GDP, and the inflation rate.

   a. Give one or more arguments for engaging in expansionary monetary or fiscal policies under the current circumstances.

   b. Give one or more arguments for engaging in contractionary monetary or fiscal policies.

   c. Which arguments do you find more convincing?

10. What possible link do you see between the existence of a Phillips curve that incorporates a flat segment and the arguments based on persistence and hysteresis?

CANADA IN THE WORLD ECONOMY

"Globalization" became a buzzword in the 1990s—and it remains one today. Given the growing interest in this phenomenon, many Canadian universities nowadays have even put in place interdisciplinary programs in the field of globalization and international studies that train an ever-growing number of students in this broad area of public policy. Some analysts extol the virtues of globalization in rescuing poor countries from poverty, and view it as something to be encouraged. Others deplore its costs and seek to stop globalization. But, love it or hate it, one thing is clear: As an open economy (discussed in Chapter 2), Canada is thoroughly integrated into a broader world economic system.

What happens in one country influences other countries, and events abroad reverberate back here. Trillions of dollars' worth of goods and services—Canadian auto parts, American computers, Chinese toys, Japanese cars—are traded across international borders each year. A vastly larger dollar volume of financial transactions—trade in stocks, bonds, bank deposits, and even international currencies themselves, for example—takes place in the global economy at lightening speed.

Although we have mentioned these subjects before, we have not emphasized them. Part IV brings international factors from the wings to centre stage. Chapter 17 studies the factors that underlie *international trade*, and Chapter 18 takes up the determination of *exchange rates*—the prices at which the world's currencies are bought and sold. Then Chapter 19 integrates these international influences fully into our model of the macroeconomy.

If you want to understand why so many Canadians are concerned about how international trade impacts on their livelihood, why many thoughtful observers think we need to overhaul the international monetary system, including some of its most important institutions, or why there has been so much economic and financial turmoil in Southeast Asia, Russia, and Latin America during the last decade, as well as understand the international reverberations resulting from the financial woes of our closest neighbour in recent years, read these three chapters carefully.

CHAPTER 17
International Trade and
Comparative Advantage

CHAPTER 18
The International Monetary System:
Order or Disorder?

CHAPTER 19
Exchange Rates and the Macroeconomy

INTERNATIONAL TRADE AND COMPARATIVE ADVANTAGE

Why are economists free-traders? It is hard not to suspect that our professional commitment to free trade is a sociological phenomenon as well as an intellectual conviction. . . . By emphasizing the virtues of free trade, we also emphasize our intellectual superiority over the unenlightened who do not understand comparative advantage.

PAUL R. KRUGMAN (1953–), 1993

Economists emphasize international trade as the source of many of the benefits of "globalization"—a loosely defined term that indicates a closer knitting together of the world's major economies. Of course, nations have always been linked in various ways. The Vikings, after all, landed in North America—not to mention Christopher Columbus, John Cabot and Jacques Cartier. In recent decades, however, dramatic improvements in transportation, telecommunications, and international relations have drawn the nations of the world ever closer together economically. This process of globalization is often portrayed as something new. But in fact, it is not, as the boxed feature "Is Globalization Something New?" on the next page points out.

Economic events in other countries affect Canada for both macroeconomic and microeconomic reasons. For example, we learned in Parts II and III that the level of net exports is an important determinant of a nation's output and employment. But we did not delve very deeply into the factors that determine a nation's exports and imports. Chapters 18 and 19 will take up these *macroeconomic* linkages in greater detail. First, however, this chapter studies some of the *microeconomic* linkages among nations: How are patterns and prices of world trade determined? How and why do governments interfere with foreign trade? The central idea of this chapter is one we have encountered before (in Chapter 3): the *principle of comparative advantage*.

CONTENTS

Is Globalization Something New?

Few people realize that the industrialized world was, in fact, highly globalized prior to World War I, before the ravages of two world wars and the Great Depression severed many international linkages. In the middle of the nineteenth century, under *Pax Britannica*, when Great Britain unilaterally became an advocate of free trade, cross-border trading of goods was perhaps more liberalized than it is today. It was only as a number of Western countries, such as Canada and Germany, sought to industrialize by the late nineteenth century that tariff barriers became progressively an important instrument of economic policy.

Furthermore, until World War I, international capital flows faced very few impediments. For instance, as shown in a study by Gerald Epstein published in 1998, the net flows of capital as a percentage of GDP among both the industrialized and industrializing countries at the end of the nineteenth century were much larger than they were at the end of the twentieth century. It was under the post-World War II Bretton Woods system that financial capital movements became subject to severe restrictions not seen previously.

The pace of globalization in the nineteenth century was driven by essentially the same factors that saw the expansion of globalization since the 1970s: the rate of technological change in transport and communications and the tempo of government policy changes favouring the reduction of barriers to international trade and capital mobility.

SOURCE: Bettmann/Corbis

SOURCES: "Schools Brief: One World?" *The Economist*, October 18, 1997, and Gerald Epstein, "L'intégration financière à l'échelle internationale et la politique monétaire de plein emploi," in Pierre Paquette and Mario Seccareccia (Eds.), *Vers le plein emploi, Pour un renouvellement des politiques publiques* (Montreal: Presses de l'Université de Montréal, 1998), p. 49.

ISSUE: *How Can Canadians Compete with "Cheap Foreign Labour"?*

Canadians (and the citizens of many other nations) often want their government to limit or prevent import competition. Why? One major reason is the common belief that imports take bread out of Canadian workers' mouths. According to this view, "cheap foreign labour" steals jobs from Canadians and pressures Canadian businesses to lower wages. Such worries were prominently voiced, for example, by Canadian labour organizations when the North American Free Trade Agreement (NAFTA)—the free trade pact between Canada, the United States, and Mexico—came into effect in January 1994.

Oddly enough, the facts are somewhat inconsistent with this story. For one thing, wages in most countries that export to Canada have risen dramatically in recent decades—much faster than wages here. The biggest merchandise exporters to Canada are the United States, China, Mexico, Japan, Germany, and the United Kingdom. Norway, France, Italy, South Korea, Taiwan, and Algeria (because of oil) are also large exporters to Canada. Table 1 shows hourly compensation rates in nine of these countries, each expressed as a percentage of hourly compensation in Canada, in 1975 and 2006. Only workers in Mexico, one of our NAFTA partners, lost ground to Canadian workers over this 30-year period. Labour in Europe gained substantially on its Canadian counterparts—rising in Britain, for example, from just above half the Canadian standard to near parity. And the wage gains in Asian countries were nothing short of spectacular. Labour compensation in South Korea, for example, soared from just 5 percent of Canadian levels to more than half.[1] Yet, while all this was going on, Canadian imports of automobiles from Japan, electronics from Taiwan, and textiles from Korea expanded rapidly.

---

[1] China would surely be an even more extreme example, but we lack Chinese and German data dating back to 1975.

Ironically, then, Canada's position in the international marketplace would have *deteriorated* just as wage levels in Europe and Asia were rising closer to our own. Clearly, something other than exploiting cheap foreign labour must be driving international trade—in contrast to what the "commonsense" view of the matter suggests. In this chapter, we will see precisely what is wrong with this "commonsense" view.

■ WHY TRADE?

The earth's resources are not equally distributed across the planet. Although Canada produces its own coal and wheat, it depends almost *entirely* on the rest of the world for such basic items as rubber and coffee. Similarly, the Persian Gulf states have little land that is suitable for farming but sit atop huge pools of oil—something we are constantly reminded of by geopolitical events. Because of the seemingly whimsical distribution of the earth's resources, every nation must trade with others to acquire what it lacks.

Even if countries had all the resources they needed, other differences in natural endowments such as climate, terrain, and so on would lead them to engage in trade. Canadians *could*, with great difficulty, grow their own bananas and coffee in hothouses. But these crops are grown much more efficiently in Honduras and Brazil, where the climates are appropriate.

The skills of a nation's labour force also play a role. If New Zealand has a large group of efficient farmers and few workers with industrial experience, while the opposite is true in Japan, it makes sense for New Zealand to specialize in agriculture and let Japan concentrate on manufacturing.

Finally, a small country that tried to produce every product would end up with many industries that are simply too small to utilize modern mass-production techniques or to take advantage of other economies of large-scale operations. For example, some countries operate their own international airlines for reasons that can only be described as political, not economic.

To summarize, the main reason why nations trade with one another is to exploit the many advantages of **specialization**, some of which were discussed in Chapter 3. International trade greatly enhances living standards for all parties involved because:

1. Every country lacks some vital resources that it can get only by trading with others.

2. Each country's climate, labour force, and other endowments make it a relatively efficient producer of some goods and an inefficient producer of other goods.

3. Specialization permits larger outputs and can therefore offer economies of large-scale production.

TABLE 1		
Labour Costs in Industrialized Countries as a Percentage of Canadian Labour Costs, 1975–2006		
Country	1975	2006
United States	101%	93%
Mexico	24	11
Japan	48	79
United Kingdom	55	105
Norway	113	159
France	74	97
Italy	76	97
South Korea	5	57
Taiwan	6	25

Note: Data are compensation estimates per hour, converted at exchange rates, and relate to production workers in the manufacturing sector.

SOURCE: U.S. Bureau of Labor Statistics, *International Comparisons of Hourly Compensation Costs for Production Workers in Manufacturing, Supplementary Tables*, Table 1. Retrieved from www.bls.gov/fls/hcpwsupptabtoc.htm

Specialization means that a country devotes its energies and resources to only a small proportion of the world's productive activities.

■ Mutual Gains from Trade

Many people have long believed that one nation gains from trade only at the expense of another. After all, nothing new is produced by the mere act of trading. So if one country gains from a swap, it is argued, the other country must necessarily lose. One consequence of this mistaken belief was and continues to be a policy prescription calling for each country to try to take advantage of its trading partners on the (fallacious) grounds that one nation's gain must be another's loss.

Yet, as Adam Smith emphasized, and as we learned in Chapter 3, both parties must expect to gain something from any *voluntary exchange*. Otherwise, why would they agree to trade?

But how can mere exchange of goods leave both parties better off? The answer is that although trade does not increase the total output of goods, it does allow each party to acquire items better suited to its tastes. Suppose Levi has four cookies and nothing to drink, while Malcolm has two glasses of milk and nothing to eat. A trade of two of Levi's cookies for one of Malcolm's glasses of milk will not increase the total supply of either milk or cookies, but it almost certainly will make both boys better off.

By exactly the same logic, both Canada and Mexico must reap gains when Mexico voluntarily ships tomatoes to Canada in return for pharmaceutical products. In general:

> Both parties must expect to gain from any *voluntary exchange*. Trade brings about mutual gains by redistributing products so that both parties end up holding more preferred combinations of goods than they held before.

A key issue will be whether this principle applies to nations just as it does to individuals. Those who believe strongly in the principle of comparative advantage assert that it must be so. Those who express doubts about this principle question this analogy. Voluntary trade that involves two nations may not provide mutual benefits.

INTERNATIONAL VERSUS INTRANATIONAL TRADE

Canada's ten provinces and three territories are an eloquent testimony of the gains that can be realized from specialization and free trade. Ontario specializes in growing grapes for wine and manufactures cars, Quebec produces jet airplanes and pork, Alberta extracts oil and produces beef, Saskatchewan grows wheat, the Maritime provinces harvest fish. All of these provinces trade freely with one another and enjoy great prosperity. Try to imagine how much lower your standard of living would be if you consumed only items produced in your own province.

The essential logic behind international trade is no different from that underlying trade among different provinces; the basic reasons for trade are equally applicable within a country or among countries. Why, then, do we study international trade as a special subject? There are at least three reasons.

Political Factors in International Trade

First, domestic trade takes place under a single national government, whereas foreign trade always involves at least two governments. But a nation's government is normally much less concerned about the welfare of other countries' citizens than it is about its own. In Canada, the federal government may intervene to prevent some provinces from taking steps that would be detrimental to the residents of other provinces. It is not so clear that it would also intervene if such steps were detrimental to people in the rest of the world. One major issue in the economic analysis of international trade is the use and misuse of political impediments to international trade.

The Many Currencies Involved in International Trade

Second, all trade within the borders of Canada is carried out in Canadian dollars, whereas trade across borders always involves at least two currencies. Rates of exchange between different currencies can and do change. In the early 1960s, one Canadian dollar was traded at close to par with the American dollar. But in January 2002, the value of the Canadian dollar fell as low as 62 American cents. At the time of writing, the Canadian dollar was back to parity with the American dollar. Variations in relation to the euro have also been spectacular since its creation in 2002. Variability in exchange rates brings with it a host of complications and policy problems.

Impediments to Mobility of Labour and Capital

Third, it is much easier for labour and capital to move about within a country than to move from one nation to another. If jobs are plentiful in Alberta but scarce in the Maritimes, workers can move freely to follow the job opportunities. Of course, personal costs such as the financial burden of moving and the psychological burden of leaving friends and familiar surroundings may discourage mobility. But such relocations are not inhibited by immigration quotas or by laws restricting the employment of foreigners.

There are also greater impediments to the transfer of capital across national boundaries than to its movement within a country. For example, many countries have rules limiting foreign ownership. Canada has limits and rules on the acquisition by foreigners of businesses in finance, transportation, cultural industries, and uranium production. Foreign investment is also subject to special political risks, such as the danger of outright expropriation or nationalization after a change in government.

But even if nothing as extreme as expropriation occurs, capital invested abroad faces significant risks from exchange rate variations. An investment valued at 140 million yen is worth $2 million to Canadian investors when the dollar is worth 70 yen, but it is worth only $1.4 million when it takes 100 yen to buy a dollar.

■ THE PRINCIPLE OF COMPARATIVE ADVANTAGE

The gains from international specialization and trade are clear and intuitive when one country is better at producing one item and its trading partner is better at producing another. For example, no one finds it surprising that Brazil sells coffee to Canada and Canada exports software to Brazil. We know that coffee can be produced using less labour and other inputs in Brazil than in Canada. Likewise, Canada can produce software at a lower resource cost than can Brazil.

In such a situation, we say that Brazil has an **absolute advantage** in coffee production, and Canada has an absolute advantage in software production. In such cases, it is obvious that both countries can gain by producing the item in which they have an absolute advantage and then trading with one another.

What is much less obvious, but equally true, is that, under certain conditions, these gains from international trade still exist *even if one country is more efficient than the other in producing everything*. This lesson, the principle of **comparative advantage**, is one we first learned in Chapter 3. It is the crucial concept that sustains the claims made by advocates of trade liberalization and free trade.

Even if one country is at an absolute *dis*advantage relative to another country in the production of every good, it is said to have a *comparative advantage* in making the good at which it is *least inefficient* (compared with the other country).

The great classical economist David Ricardo (1772–1823) discovered about 200 years ago that two countries can still gain from trade, even if one is more efficient than the other in *every* industry—that is, even if one has an absolute advantage in producing every commodity.

In determining the most efficient patterns of production, it is *comparative* advantage, not *absolute* advantage, that matters. Thus a country can gain by importing a good even if that good can be produced more efficiently at home. Such imports make sense if they enable the country to specialize in producing goods at which it is *even more* efficient.

One country is said to have an **absolute advantage** over another in the production of a particular good if it can produce that good using smaller quantities of resources than can the other country.

One country is said to have a **comparative advantage** over another in the production of a particular good relative to other goods if it produces that good less inefficiently as compared with the other country.

■ The Arithmetic of Comparative Advantage

Let's see precisely how comparative advantage works using a hypothetical example. Table 2 gives the trading positions of Canada and China. We imagine that labour is the only input used to produce computers and television sets in the two countries and that Canada has an absolute advantage in manufacturing both goods. In this example, one year's worth of labour can produce either 50 computers or 50 TV sets in Canada but only 10 computers or 40 televisions in China. So Canada is the more efficient producer of both goods. Nonetheless, as we will now show, it pays for Canada to specialize in producing computers and trade with China to get the TV sets it wants.

TABLE 2		
Alternative Outputs from One Year of Labour Input		
	In Canada	In China
Computers	50	10
Televisions	50	40

To demonstrate this point, we begin by noting that Canada has a comparative advantage in *computers*, whereas China has a comparative advantage in producing *televisions*. Specifically, the numbers in Table 2 show that Canada can produce 50 televisions with one year's labour whereas China can produce only 40; so Canada is 25 percent more efficient than China in producing TV sets. However, Canada is five times as efficient as China in producing computers: It can produce 50 per year of labour rather than 10. Because Canada's competitive edge is far greater in computers than in televisions, we say that Canada has a *comparative advantage* in computers.

From the Chinese perspective, these same numbers indicate that China is only slightly less efficient than Canada in TV production but drastically less efficient in computer production. So China's comparative advantage is in the television industry. According to Ricardo's principle of comparative advantage, then, the two countries can gain if Canada specializes in producing computers, China specializes in producing TVs, and the two countries trade.

Let's verify that this conclusion is true. Suppose China transfers 1,000 years of labour out of the computer industry and into TV manufacturing. According to the figures in Table 2, its computer output will fall by 10,000 units, while its TV output will rise by 40,000 units. This information is recorded in the middle column of Table 3. Suppose, at the same time, Canada transfers 500 years of labour out of television manufacturing (thereby losing 25,000 TVs) and into computer making (thereby gaining 25,000 computers). Table 3 shows us that these transfers of resources between the two countries increase the world's production of both outputs. Together, the two countries now have 15,000 additional TVs and 15,000 additional computers—a nice outcome.

TABLE 3			
Example of the Gains from Trade			
	Canada	China	Total
Computers	+25,000	−10,000	**+15,000**
Televisions	−25,000	+40,000	**+15,000**

Was there some sleight of hand here? How did *both* Canada *and* China gain *both* computers *and* TVs? The explanation is that the process we have just described involves more than just a swap of a fixed bundle of commodities, as in our earlier cookies-and-milk example. It also involves *a change in the production arrangements.* Some of China's inefficient computer production is taken over by more efficient Canadian manufacturers. And some of Canada's TV production is taken over by Chinese television companies, which are *less inefficient* at making TVs than Chinese computer manufacturers are at making computers. In this way, *world productivity* is increased. The underlying principle is both simple and fundamental:

> When every country does what it can do best, all countries can benefit because more of every commodity can be produced without increasing the amounts of labour and other resources used.

The Graphics of Comparative Advantage

The gains from trade also can be displayed graphically, and doing so helps us understand whether such gains are large or small.

The lines *CA* and *HN* in Figure 1 are closely related to the production possibilities frontiers of the two countries, but they differ in that they pretend that each country has the same amount of labour available.[2] In this case, we assume that each has 1 million person-years of labour. For example, Table 2 tells us that for each 1 million years of labour, Canada can produce 50 million TVs and no computers (point *C* in Figure 1), 50 million computers and no TVs (point *A*), or any combination between (the line *CA*). Similar reasoning leads to line *HN* for China.

Because the size of the workforce in China is about 40 times that of Canada, the *actual* production possibilities frontier are not those shown in Figure 1. The Chinese frontier

---

[2] To review the concept of the production possibilities frontier, see Chapter 3.

would lie above that of Canada. But Figure 1 is useful because it highlights the differences in *efficiency* (rather than in mere size) that determine both absolute and comparative advantage. Let's see how.

The fact that line *CA* lies *above* line *HN* means that Canada can manufacture more televisions and more computers than China *with the same amount of labour*. This difference reflects our assumption that Canada has an *absolute* advantage in both commodities.

Canada's *comparative* advantage in computer production and China's comparative advantage in TV production are shown in a different way: by the relative *slopes* of the two lines. Look back to Table 2, which shows that Canada can acquire a computer on its own by giving up one TV. Thus, the *opportunity cost* of a computer in Canada is one television set. This opportunity cost is depicted graphically by the slope of the Canadian production possibilities frontier in Figure 1, which is $0U/0A = 50/50 = 1$.

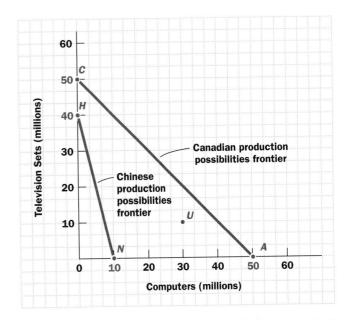

FIGURE 1

Production Possibilities Frontiers for Two Countries (per million years of labour)

Table 2 also tells us that the opportunity cost of a computer in China is four TVs. This relationship is depicted in Figure 1 by the slope of China's production possibilities frontier, which is $0H/0N = 40/10 = 4$.

A country's *absolute* advantage in production over another country is shown by its having a higher per-capita production possibilities frontier. The difference in the *comparative* advantages between the two countries is shown by the difference in the slopes of their frontiers.

Because opportunity costs differ in the two countries, gains are possible if the two countries specialize and trade with one another. Specifically, it is cheaper, in terms of real resources forgone, for *either* country to acquire its computers in Canada. By a similar line of reasoning, the opportunity cost of TVs is higher in Canada than in China, so it makes sense for both countries to acquire their televisions in China.[3]

Notice that if the slopes of the two production possibilities frontiers, *HN* and *CA*, were equal, then opportunity costs would be the same in each country. In that case, no potential gains would arise from trade. Gains from trade arise from *differences* across countries, not from similarities. This is an important point about which people are often confused. It is often argued that two very different countries, such as Canada and Mexico, cannot gain much by trading with one another. The fact is just the opposite:

Two very similar countries may gain little from trade. Large gains from trade are most likely when countries are very different.

How the two countries divide the gains from trade depends on the prices that emerge from world trade—a complicated topic taken up in the appendix to this chapter. But we already know enough to see that world trade must, in our example, leave a computer costing more than one TV and less than four. Why? Because, if a computer bought less than one TV (its opportunity cost in Canada) on the world market, Canada would produce its own TVs rather than buying them from China. And if a computer cost more than four TVs (its opportunity cost in China), China would prefer to produce its own computers rather than buy them from Canada.

We therefore conclude that, if both countries are to trade, the rate of exchange between TVs and computers must end up somewhere between 4:1 and 1:1. Generalizing:

If two countries voluntarily trade two goods with one another, the rate of exchange between the goods must fall in between the price ratios that would prevail in the two countries in the absence of trade.

---

[3] As an exercise, provide this line of reasoning.

To illustrate the gains from trade in our concrete example, suppose the world price ratio settles at 2:1—meaning that one computer costs as much as two televisions. How much, precisely, do Canada and China gain from world trade in this case?

Figure 2 is designed to help us visualize the answers. The red production possibilities frontiers, *CA* in Panel (b) and *HN* in Panel (a), are the same as in Figure 1. But Canada can do better than line *CA*. Specifically, with a world price ratio of 2:1, Canada can buy two TVs for each computer it gives up, rather than just one (which is the opportunity cost of a computer in Canada). Hence, if Canada produces only computers—point *A* in Figure 2(b)—and buys its TVs from China, Canada's *consumption possibilities* will be as indicated by the blue line that begins at point *A* and has a slope of 2—that is, each computer sold brings Canada two television sets. (It ends at point *B* because 40 million TV sets is the most that China can produce.) Because trade allows Canada to choose a point on *BA* rather than on *CA*, trade opens up consumption possibilities that were simply not available before.

A similar story applies to China. If the Chinese produce only television sets—point *H* in Figure 2(a)—they can acquire a computer from Canada for every two TVs they give up as they move along the blue line *HP* (whose slope is 2). This result is better than they can achieve on their own, because a sacrifice of two TVs in China yields only one-half of a computer. Hence, world trade enlarges China 's consumption possibilities from *HN* to *HP*.

Figure 2 shows graphically that gains from trade arise to the extent that world prices (2:1 in our example) differ from domestic opportunity costs (4:1 and 1:1 in our example). How the two countries share the gains from trade depends on the exact prices that emerge from world trade. As explained in the appendix, that in turn depends on relative supplies and demands in the two countries. Because world prices should be most influenced by the supply and demand conditions ruling in the countries with the largest economies, one should expect the smaller countries to receive relatively higher gains from international trade.

FIGURE 2   **The Gains from Trade**

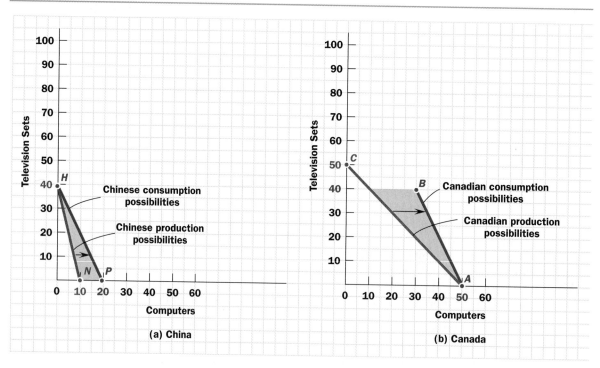

(a) China

(b) Canada

Note: Quantities are in millions.

? ISSUE RESOLVED: *Comparative Advantage Exposes the "Cheap Foreign Labour" Fallacy*

The principle of comparative advantage takes us a long way toward understanding the fallacy in the "cheap foreign labour" argument described at the beginning of this chapter. Given the assumed productive efficiency of Canadian labour, and the inefficiency of Chinese labour, we would expect wages to be much higher in Canada.

In these circumstances, one might expect Canadian workers to be apprehensive about an agreement to permit open trade between the two countries: "How can we hope to meet the unfair competition of those underpaid Chinese workers?" Chinese labourers might also be concerned: "How can we hope to meet the competition of those Canadians, who are so efficient in producing everything?"

The principle of comparative advantage shows us that both fears are unjustified, at least in theory (see the boxed feature "Objections to the Conclusions Drawn from the Principle of Comparative Advantage"). As we have just seen, when trade opens up between China and Canada, *workers in both countries will be able to earn higher real wages than before* because of the increased productivity that comes through specialization.

As Figure 2 shows, once trade opens up, Chinese workers should be able to acquire more TVs and more computers than they did before. As a consequence, their living standards should rise, even though they have been left vulnerable to competition from the super-efficient Canadians. Workers in Canada should also end up with more TVs and more computers, so their living standards should also rise even though they have been exposed to competition from cheap Chinese labour.

These higher standards of living, of course, reflect the higher real wages earned by workers in both countries. The lesson to be learned here is elementary:

Nothing helps raise living standards more than a greater abundance of goods.

■ TARIFFS, QUOTAS, AND OTHER INTERFERENCES WITH TRADE

Despite the large mutual gains from international trade, nations often interfere with the free movement of goods and services across national borders. In fact, until the rise of the free-trade movement about 200 years ago (with Adam Smith and David Ricardo as its vanguard), it was taken for granted that one of the essential tasks of government was to *impede* trade, presumably in the national interest.

Many argued then (and many still argue today) that the proper aim of government policy was to promote exports and discourage imports, for doing so would increase the amount of money foreigners owed the nation. According to this so-called **mercantilist** view, a nation's wealth consists of the amount of gold or other monies at its command.

Obviously, governments can pursue such a policy only within certain limits. A country *must* import vital foodstuffs and critical raw materials that it cannot supply for itself. Moreover, mercantilists ignore a simple piece of arithmetic: It is mathematically impossible for *every* country to sell more than it buys, because one country's exports must be some other country's imports. If everyone competes in this game by cutting imports to the bone, then exports must go the same way. The result is that everyone will be deprived of the mutual gains from trade. Indeed, that is precisely what happens in a trade war.

The worst example of a trade war occurred during the Great Depression of the 1930s and illustrates well the dangers of protectionism. Every country tried to "export its unemployment abroad" by imposing trade restrictions and manipulating its exchange rate in relation to gold. After World War II, in 1947, various countries, including Canada, joined forces to forge a General Agreement on Tariffs and Trade (GATT), the purpose of which was to gradually reduce trade restrictions by conceding to all countries the import conditions that had previously been granted to the most

Mercantilism is a doctrine that holds that exports are good for a country, whereas imports are harmful.

Objections to the Conclusions Drawn from the Principle of Comparative Advantage

The belief that the principle of comparative advantage, sometimes called the *law* of comparative advantage, rules international trade and makes it advantageous to all countries is nearly an article of faith among economists. In fact, the competency of an economist has long been judged on whether or not that economist accepts the principle of comparative advantage. As was noted in Chapter 1, a very small percentage of economists do not support free trade and disagree with the proposition that trade restrictions reduce economic welfare. Still, the doubts of these economists, which now include 2001 Nobel Prize winner Joseph Stiglitz, reflect the concerns of a lot of workers and young activists in relation to the detrimental effects of globalization on the poorer parts of the world.

While the principle of comparative advantage is unassailable *on its own grounds,* its critics question the *assumptions* that underlie the conclusions that are drawn from it. In other words, *if* international trade was conducted according to the principle of comparative advantage, with all nations always operating on their production possibilities frontier, at full employment and full capacity, free trade would be beneficial to all countries. What the critics say is that economies usually operate *inside* the production possibilities frontier, at less than full employment and full capacity, and that actual trade is ruled not by the principle of comparative advantage but instead by the principle of absolute advantage.

Criticisms of standard international trade theory are based on the following three arguments. First, the critics argue that international trade does not occur between nations but between firms. International trade is not some kind of barter between two nations, analogous to barter between two friends, as was represented in the previous section. Firms compete for shares on world markets just as they compete for shares on domestic markets.

Second, firms make decisions on the basis of absolute advantage, not comparative advantage. If production costs of lighting equipment in Ontario are lower than they are at similar Nova Scotian firms, because Ontario firms are better equipped than Nova Scotian ones, Ontario firms will be able to take over the lighting market in Nova Scotia because Nova Scotian lighting retailers will prefer to purchase the less costly Ontario products. The same will occur with Ontario wine, as long as it is cheaper to produce good wine there than it is to do so in Nova Scotia. The fact that Ontario has a comparative advantage in the production of wine and Nova Scotia has a comparative advantage in the production of lighting equipment will change nothing in this situation. Company decisions will be made on the basis of absolute advantage—the lower Ontario cost. Trade will go only one way: Ontario will export both its wine and its lighting equipment.

The third criticism of the principle of comparative advantage and its application to free trade is that, as long as most Ontario firms have an absolute cost advantage over Nova Scotian firms, the sales of Ontario firms will rise while those of Nova Scotian firms will decrease when interprovincial free trade is implemented. This means that employment in Ontario will rise and employment in Nova Scotia will be lowered. Thus, while employed Nova Scotian workers will indeed benefit from the lower prices of imported Ontario goods, thus gaining higher real wages and higher living standards, the number of unemployed Nova Scotian workers will rise and *their*

standard of living will plunge. On the Ontario side, more people will be able to find jobs and so family incomes will rise.

The application of the principle of comparative advantage assumes the existence of full employment in the two regions or the two countries that are trading. It assumes that Ontario is unable to produce, simultaneously, more wine and more lighting equipment. In other words, it assumes that economies are always on their production possibilities frontiers. But in general, say the critics, more could be produced because there are excess capacity and unemployed workers (Canada is at point *U* in Figure 1, and not somewhere on the *CA* line). Full employment is not the usual situation, neither in industrialized nations nor in less developed countries where there are many unemployed or underemployed workers.

Is it correct to make an analogy between interprovincial trade and international trade? The critics of comparative advantage say that it is. They argue, both on theoretical and historical grounds, that the mechanisms that are meant to transform some of the absolute advantages into merely comparative ones do not exist, or else do not function properly and may take too long to produce their favourable effects. The critics claim that those countries that suffer from absolute disadvantage will face persistent trade deficits. Free trade advocates would argue that these deficits lead to falling exchange rates or to falling domestic prices that transform the weaker country into a competitive one, by lowering its costs relative to those of its foreign competitors. The critics deny this. They say that the trade deficits will be compensated for by capital inflows, with foreign companies purchasing the domestic assets of the weaker countries, thus hindering the exchange rate from adjusting to the trade deficit. Thus, rich industrialized countries or successful exporting nations reap most of the benefits of free trade: They improve the employment situation of their workers at home, and their capitalists make more profits and acquire foreign assets at bargain prices.

Critics of free trade also argue that the modern giants of international trade did not industrialize by following the precepts of free trade. The evolution of world trade has been one of fierce rivalry, as countries jockeyed for technological superiority with accompanying protectionist measures, thereby conferring an absolute advantage to some nations at the expense of others during certain historical periods. Western European countries and the United States, along with Canada and the more recent Asian Tigers (Taiwan, Singapore, Hong Kong, and South Korea), moved up the ladder by exporting more while pursuing trade protection and state support to industry. They did not play by the rules that are now advocated by the United States and international organizations (such as the World Trade Organization, the International Monetary Fund, and the World Bank) and that are now imposed on the developing countries that are attempting to industrialize. It is said that rich countries are kicking away the ladder when they pressure developing countries to adopt free trade and the elimination of all trade impediments. There is some irony in noting that China is doing extremely well despite following none of the precepts advocated by international experts.

SOURCE: Anwar Shaikh, "Globalization and the Myths of Free Trade," in A. Shaikh (Ed.), *Globalization and the Myths of Free Trade: History, Theory, and Empirical Evidence* (London: Routledge, 2007).

favoured nations. The GATT meetings took years of negotiation in succeeding rounds, each one longer than the previous one. The last round, the so-called Uruguay Round, from 1986 to 1994, led to the creation of the World Trade Organization (WTO), in 1995. The WTO administers existing trade agreements, monitors national trade agreements, handles trade disputes, and organizes new trade negotiations.

In the meantime, Canada and the United States arranged for their own free trade agreement (the Canada–U.S. Free Trade Agreement), which took effect in 1989, when Canadian politicians began to fear the protectionist tendencies of their giant southern neighbour. The Canada–U.S. agreement was soon followed by the North American Free Trade Agreement (NAFTA) in 1994, which includes Mexico. Protectionism is not restricted to foreign trade, however. In 1994, the Canadian provinces signed the Agreement on Interprovincial Trade in an effort to reduce and eliminate barriers to interprovincial trade and to prevent the erection of new barriers. It is sometimes asserted that it is harder to trade between provinces than between a Canadian province and an American state, although few instances of such impediments have been documented, other than Quebec's prohibition of butter-coloured margarine, which was finally lifted in 2008!

Most of the world's trading nations are now engaged in a new multiyear round of trade talks under guidelines adopted at an important meeting in Doha, Qatar, in 2001 (see "Liberalizing World Trade: The Doha Round").

Modern governments use three main devices when seeking to control trade: tariffs, quotas, and export subsidies.

A **tariff** is simply a tax on imports. An importer of cars, for example, may be charged $2,000 for each auto brought into the country. Such a tax will, of course,

A **tariff** is a tax on imports.

Liberalizing World Trade: The Doha Round

The time and place were not auspicious: an international gathering in the Persian Gulf just two months after the September 11, 2001, terrorist attacks. Nerves were frayed, security was extremely tight, and memories of a failed trade meeting in Seattle in 1999 lingered on. Yet representatives of more than 140 nations, meeting in Doha, Qatar, in November 2001, managed to agree on the outlines of a new round of comprehensive trade negotiations—one that may take years to complete.

The so-called Doha Round focuses on bringing down tariffs, subsidies, and other restrictions on world trade in agriculture, services, and a variety of manufactured goods. It also seeks greater protection for intellectual property rights, while making sure that poor countries have access to modern pharmaceuticals at prices they can afford. Reform of the World Trade Organization's own rules and procedures is also on the agenda. Perhaps most surprisingly, the United States has even promised to consider changes in its antidumping laws, which are used to keep many foreign goods out of U.S. markets. (Dumping is explained at the end of this chapter.)

Large-scale trade negotiations such as this one, involving more than 100 countries and many different issues, take years to complete. After years of trade liberalization that seemed to have been beneficial to large exporting firms, the Doha Round was supposed to provide results helpful to the developing countries by making trade rules fairer to these countries and thus contributing to reducing world poverty. However, in Mexico in 2003, the talks collapsed, as participants from the developing countries found that the Europeans and the Americans were unwilling to concede large enough reductions in their farm government subsidies (while Canadians were unwilling to let go of their agricultural supply management system)—a theme that we touched on in Chapter 4. Further talks in Paris, Hong Kong, Geneva, and Potsdam brought little improvement, with farm subsidies still remaining the major sticking point.

Developing countries could not be blamed for having the impression that the Doha Round, despite the declarations of the main traders, is more intent on satisfying the lobbying efforts of the rich nations' exporters than in improving the economic conditions of developing countries. There is also the realization that, for most of the developing countries, globalization and free trade did not generate the gains that were predicted by their advocates. As of now, the Doha Round is a failure, as it has reached a deadlock.

SOURCE: © Patrick Baz/AFP/Getty Images

make automobiles more expensive and favour domestic models over imports. It will also raise revenue for the government. In fact, tariffs were a major source of tax revenue for the Canadian government during the nineteenth century—and also a major source of political controversy. But nowadays Canada is a low-tariff country, with only a few exceptions, notably in the farming sector. However, many other countries rely on heavy tariffs to protect their industries. Indeed, tariff rates of 100 percent or more are not uncommon in some countries.

A **quota** is a legal limit on the amount of a good that may be imported. For example, the government might allow no more than five million foreign cars to be imported in a year. In some cases, governments ban the importation of certain goods outright—a quota of zero. Because of its supply management program for some agricultural products such as dairy products, poultry, and eggs, Canada has a *de facto* quota system for these products. Until 2005, Canada also had a sophisticated quota system for textiles and clothing, as well as voluntary export restrictions, whereby foreign countries themselves agreed to place limits on the amounts of goods being exported to Canada. These textile and clothing quotas have now been removed for all practical purposes.

A **quota** specifies the maximum amount of a good that is permitted into the country from abroad per unit of time.

An **export subsidy** is a government payment to an exporter. By reducing the exporter's costs, such subsidies permit exporters to lower their selling prices and compete more effectively in world trade. Canada is considered to be a minor user of export subsidy although, over the last few years, Brazil has complained about Bombardier being subsidized to compete on the small aircraft international market. Also, the Americans have long been complaining about unfair competition brought about by the overly low fees being paid by Canadian softwood lumber companies to cut trees on government lands. An agreement on this was finally reached in the fall of 2006, thus putting an end to the countervailing duties that were being imposed by the U.S. government on Canadian softwood.

An **export subsidy** is a payment by the government to exporters to permit them to reduce the selling prices of their goods so they can compete more effectively in foreign markets.

■ Tariffs versus Quotas

Although both tariffs and quotas reduce international trade and increase the prices of domestically produced goods, there are some important differences using tariffs and quotas to protect domestic industries.

First, under a quota, profits from the higher price in the importing country usually go into the pockets of the foreign and domestic sellers of the products. Limitations on supply (from abroad) mean that customers in the importing country must pay more for the product and that suppliers, whether foreign or domestic, receive more for every unit they sell. For example, the right to sell sugar in the United States under the tight sugar quota that exists there has been extremely valuable for decades. The price of sugar in the United States is much higher than in Canada. Privileged foreign and domestic firms can make a lot of money from quota rights.

By contrast, when trade is restricted by a tariff instead, some of the "profits" go as tax revenues to the government of the importing country. (Domestic producers also benefit, because they are exempt from the tariff.) In this respect, a tariff is certainly a better proposition than a quota from the viewpoint of the country that enacts it.

Another important distinction between the two measures arises from their different implications for productive efficiency. Because a tariff handicaps all foreign suppliers equally, it awards sales to those firms and nations that can supply the goods most cheaply—presumably because they are more efficient. A quota, by contrast, necessarily awards its import licences more or less capriciously—perhaps in proportion to past sales or even based on political favouritism. There is no reason to expect the most efficient suppliers to get the import permits. For example, the U.S. sugar quota was for years suspected of being a major source of corruption in the Caribbean.

If a country must inhibit imports, two important reasons support a preference for tariffs over quotas:

1. Some of the revenues resulting from tariffs go to the government of the importing country rather than to foreign and domestic producers.

2. Unlike quotas, tariffs offer special benefits to more efficient exporters.

■ WHY INHIBIT TRADE?

To state that tariffs provide a better way to inhibit international trade than quotas leaves open a far more basic question: Why limit trade in the first place? Before NAFTA was put into place, it was estimated that trade restrictions cost Canadian consumers about 0.8 percent of GDP, or some $12 billion per year in the form of higher prices. Why should they be asked to pay these higher prices? A number of answers have been given. Let's examine each in turn.

■ Gaining a Price Advantage for Domestic Firms

A tariff forces foreign exporters to sell more cheaply by restricting their market access. If they do not cut their prices, they will be left with unsold goods. So in effect, the tariff amounts to government intervention to rig prices in favour of domestic producers.[4]

Not bad, you say. However, this technique works only as long as foreigners accept the tariff exploitation passively—which they rarely do. More often, they retaliate by imposing tariffs or quotas of their own on imports from the country that began the tariff game. For instance, when the United States imposed a special tariff on Canadian cedar shingles back in the 1980s, Canada retaliated by imposing duties on a variety of U.S. products. Such tit-for-tat behaviour can easily lead to a trade war in which no one gains more favourable prices but everyone loses through the resulting reductions in trade. Something like this, in fact, happened to the world economy in the 1930s, and it helped prolong the worldwide depression. Preventing such trade wars is one main reason why nations that belong to the World Trade Organization (WTO) pledge not to raise tariffs.

> Tariffs or quotas can benefit particular domestic industries in a country that is able to impose them without fear of retaliation. But when every country uses them, everyone is likely to lose in the long run.

■ Protecting Particular Industries

The second, and probably more frequent, reason why countries restrict trade is to protect particular industries from foreign competition. If foreigners can produce steel or shoes more cheaply, domestic businesses and unions in these industries are quick to demand protection. And their governments may be quite willing to grant it.

The "cheap foreign labour" argument is most likely to be invoked in this context. Protective tariffs and quotas are explicitly designed to rescue firms that are too inefficient to compete with foreign exporters in an open world market. But it is precisely this harsh competition that gives consumers the chief benefits of international specialization: better products at lower prices. So protection comes at a cost.

Thinking back to our numerical example of comparative advantage, we can well imagine the indignant complaints from Chinese computer makers, as the opening of trade with Canada leads to increased imports of Canadian-made computers. At the same time, Canadian TV manufacturers would probably express outrage over the flood of imported TVs from China. Yet Chinese specialization in televisions and Canadian specialization in computers is precisely what enables citizens of both countries to enjoy higher standards of living. If governments interfere with this process, consumers in both countries will lose out.

Industries threatened by foreign competition often argue that some form of protection against imports is needed to prevent job losses. For example, the Canadian steel

---

[4] For more details on this, see the appendix to this chapter.

industry has made exactly this argument time and time again—most recently in 2001, when world steel prices plummeted and imports surged. Indeed, the Canadian government has delivered some protection in response, as there are import quotas on steel. The softwood lumber trade dispute with the United States can also be seen in this light: American softwood producers have managed to get special tariff protection by complaining that Canadian softwood producers benefit from an unfair competitive advantage because they log trees on government lands at overly cheap fees. The U.S. producers contended that American jobs were unjustly being lost to their Canadian competitors.

A program that limits foreign competition will be more effective at preserving employment *in the particular protected industry*. But such job gains typically come at a high cost to consumers and to the economy. Some economists argue that the Canadian trade restrictions embedded in our farm product supply management system entail similar costs.

Nevertheless, complaints over proposals to reduce tariffs or quotas may be justified unless something is done to ease the cost to individual workers of switching to the product lines that trade makes profitable.

> The argument for free trade between countries cannot be considered airtight if governments do not assist the citizens in each country who are harmed whenever patterns of production change drastically—as would happen, for example, if governments suddenly reduced tariff and quota barriers.

Owners of television factories in Canada and of computer factories in China may see large investments suddenly rendered unprofitable. Workers in those industries may see their special skills and training devalued in the marketplace. Displaced workers also pay heavy intangible costs—they may need to move to new locations and/or new industries, uprooting their families, losing old friends and neighbours, and so on. Although the *majority* of citizens undoubtedly gain from free trade, that is no consolation to those who are its victims.

To mitigate these problems, there are two basic approaches. First, even WTO rules allow country participants to offer temporary protection from sudden surges of imports, on the grounds that unexpected changes in trade patterns do not give businesses and workers enough time to adjust.

Trade adjustment assistance provides special unemployment benefits, loans, retraining programs, and other aid to workers and firms that are harmed by foreign competition.

Second, the government can set up **trade adjustment assistance** programs to help workers and businesses that lose their jobs or their markets to imports. Firms may be eligible for technical assistance, government loans or loan guarantees, and permission to delay tax payments. Workers may qualify for retraining programs, longer periods of unemployment compensation, and funds to defray moving costs. Each form of assistance can be designed to ease the burden on the victims of free trade so that the rest of us can enjoy its considerable benefits. Indeed, unlike former Prime Minister Brian Mulroney, who promised special worker adjustment assistance at the time of the Canada–U.S. Free Trade Agreement in 1989 but did not deliver, the Clinton administration in the United States did attach a Transitional Adjustment Assistance program for displaced workers when the United States signed the NAFTA in 1993.

National Defence and Other Noneconomic Considerations

A third rationale for trade protection is the need to maintain national defence. For example, the National Defence staff could argue that Canada ought to produce its own military jets so that no foreign government could ever cut off supplies of this important product for the air force.

The national defence argument is fine as far as it goes, but it poses a clear danger: Even industries with the most peripheral relationship to defence are likely to invoke this argument on their behalf. For instance, for years the U.S. watchmaking industry argued for protection on the grounds that its skilled craftsmen would be invaluable in wartime!

Similarly, Canada has occasionally banned either exports to or imports from nations such as Cuba, Iran, and Iraq on political grounds. Such actions may have

How Popular Is Protectionism?

Although the world has been moving gradually toward freer trade, its citizens are not entirely persuaded that this trend is desirable. In 1998, a Canadian polling company asked almost 13,000 people in 22 countries the following question: "Which of the following two broad approaches do you think would be the best way to improve the economic and employment situation in this country—protecting our local industries by restricting imports, or removing import restrictions to increase our international trade?" By this measure, protectionists outnumbered free traders by a narrow margin—47 percent to 42 percent, with the rest undecided. Protectionist sentiment was even stronger in Canada, where the margin was 56 percent to 37 percent.

Indeed, more recent surveys show that this tendency toward protectionism may have become even more widespread. Canadian exporters in 2004 were asked whether they felt that protectionism in the United States was growing or receding. No less than 71 percent of the respondents thought that it was somewhat increasing, 24 percent that it was strongly increasing, and only 5 percent thought that it was decreasing. Note however that this survey was conducted in the middle of the softwood lumber dispute.

SOURCES: "How Popular Is Protectionism?" *The Economist*, January 2, 1999; Fred McMahon and Matthew Curtis, "Growing Concern about Protectionist Sentiment in the United States," *Fraser Alert*, October 2004. Retrieved from www.fraserinstitute.ca

Meanwhile, during the 2008 race for the presidential nomination, both Democratic Party candidates, Hillary Clinton and Barack Obama, vowed to renegotiate the NAFTA or else to withdraw from it. Most likely, this will not happen. Before he was elected Canadian prime minister in 1993, Jean Chrétien also promised to shred the NAFTA!

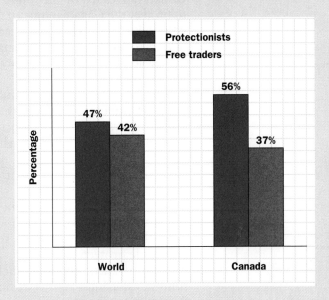

important economic effects, creating either bonanzas or disasters for particular industries. But they are justified by politics, not by economics. Canada has also suffered from such decisions, as, for instance, when the European Union decided to ban imports of seal furs and when asbestos was banned in the United Kingdom.

■ Strategic Trade Policy

A fourth argument for (temporary) protection has substantially influenced trade policy internationally. Proponents of this line of thinking agree that free trade for all is the best system, but they point out that we live in an imperfect world in which many nations refuse to play by the rules of the free trade game. And they fear that a nation that pursues free trade in a protectionist world is likely to lose out. It therefore makes sense, they argue, to *threaten* to protect your markets unless other nations agree to open theirs.

The United States has followed this strategy in trade negotiations with several countries in recent years. In one prominent case, the U.S. government threatened to impose high tariffs on several European luxury goods unless Europe opened its markets to imported bananas from the Americas. A few years later, the European Union turned the tables, threatening to increase tariffs on a variety of U.S. goods unless the Americans changed a tax provision that amounted to a subsidy to exports. In each case, a dangerous trade war was narrowly averted when an agreement was struck at the eleventh hour.

The strategic argument for protection is a difficult one for economists to counter. Although it recognizes the superiority of free trade, it argues that *threatening* protectionism is the best way to achieve that end. Such a strategy might work, but it clearly involves great risks. If threats that the United States will turn protectionist induce other countries to scrap their existing protectionist policies, then the gamble will have succeeded. But if the gamble fails, protectionism increases. In the case of Canada, such threats are not very credible, and hence they constitute a weak argument in favour of tariffs.

The Infant-Industry Argument

Yet a fifth common rationale for protectionism is the so-called *infant-industry argument*, which had been prominent in Canada since the adoption of the National Policy by the Conservatives led by Sir John A. MacDonald, back in 1879, the purpose of which was to protect the Canadian manufacturing industry with the help of high tariffs. Promising new industries often need breathing room to flourish and grow. If we expose these infants to the rigours of international competition too soon, the argument goes, they may never develop to the point where they can survive on their own in the international marketplace.

This argument, although valid in certain instances, is less defensible than it seems at first. Protecting an infant industry is justifiable only if the prospective future gains are sufficient to repay the up-front costs of protectionism. But if the industry is likely to be so profitable in the future, why doesn't private capital rush in to take advantage of the prospective net profits? After all, the annals of business are full of cases in which a new product or a new firm lost money at first but profited handsomely later on.

The infant-industry argument for protection stands up to scrutiny only if private funds are unavailable for some reason, despite an industry's glowing profit prospects. Even then it may make more sense to provide a government loan rather than to provide trade protection.

In an advanced economy such as ours, with fairly well-developed capital markets to fund new businesses, it is difficult to think of legitimate examples where the infant-industry argument would apply.

The Infant-Economy Argument

Whereas the infant-industry argument is difficult to fathom for a modern country such as Canada, the idea is certainly appealing to developing countries. In these countries, capital markets are not well developed and government help may be needed. This has now become known as the *infant-economy argument*. Instead of protecting specific industries, trade restrictions are designed to protect entire subsets of an economy, for instance the whole manufacturing sector. This helps to avoid pressures from special interests.

The rationale behind the infant-economy argument is not much different from that behind the argument for sustaining the existence of patents. As with research and development, the development of a strong manufacturing sector has spillover effects in all sectors. The potential short-run inefficiency effects of protection can be offset by the possible long-run dynamic gains associated with increasing returns to scale in manufacturing and the advances that can apply to other sectors. In other words, an expansion of the manufacturing sector generates a beneficial externality, which would not be taken into account by private market forces.[5] Moreover, advocates of infant-economy policies, like critics of the principle of comparative advantage, believe that unrestricted competition and free trade are more likely to be detrimental than useful to developing countries that do not have all of the institutions and knowledge that rich Western countries have.

---

[5] Increasing returns to scale imply that, as the scale of operations rises, unit costs of production fall. Beneficial externalities are positive spillover effects of some activity, which are unintended by those directly involved in the activity. See *Microeconomics: Principles and Policy*, Chapter 7 page 154–155 for information on increasing returns to scale, and Chapter 15, page 344 for a discussion of beneficial externalities.

Decreasing Average Costs

Further evidence has been advanced recently in favour of the infant-industry and the infant-economy arguments. In the case of many products, comparative advantage is not given anymore, as in the case of fruits and maple syrup; rather the comparative advantage is *created*, as is the case with many high-tech products. While the average costs of individual firms may be approximately constant, the average costs of the national industry could be decreasing. This downward-sloping shape of the domestic supply curve can occur as a result of spillover effects, whereby, for instance, the expansion of the industry generates better knowledge and improved technology for all of the industry participants—effects that are sometimes called *agglomeration effects*. The presence of increasing returns to scale at the industry level has implications for the optimality of unrestricted free trade.

FIGURE 3

Average Unit Costs for a High-Tech Gadget in Two Countries

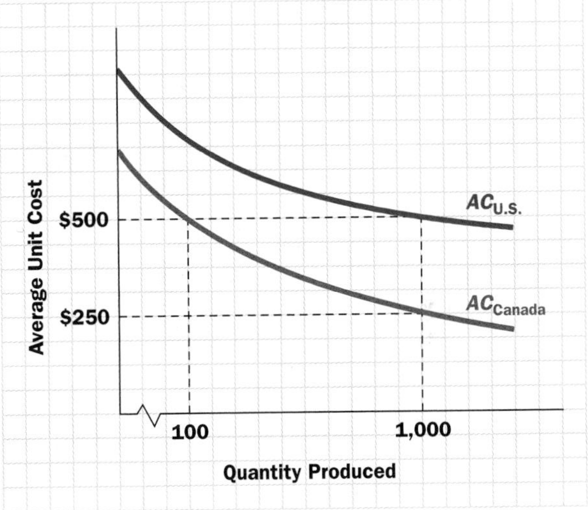

Take two countries such as Canada and the United States. Suppose that for some reason, the long-run average cost curve of producing some specific high-tech gadget in the United States, given by $AC_{U.S.}$ in Figure 3, lies above the average cost curve of the same product in Canada, given by AC_{Canada}. Suppose that this absolute advantage for Canada also translates into a comparative advantage so that, assuming that these two economies are on their production possibilities frontiers, it would be best for that product to be made in Canada. Suppose, however, that American companies start to produce and market the gadget ahead of Canadian companies, so that the U.S. industry output stands at 1,000, taking over the entire market. Canadian companies that try to enter later will be unable to compete unless they produce more than 100 units, because at any lower sale level, their average cost will be higher than that of the American industry. If the Canadian industry was protected, it could reach this level of output by operating on the Canadian market. Without protection, it will never achieve this level, and the North American gadget market will remain cornered by the American companies. As a consequence, whereas it would be best for North America as a whole to have Canadian companies produce this high-tech gadget at a cost of $250 per unit, American companies will retain the whole market, at $500 per unit.

Environmental Concerns

Those who object to free trade and globalization have now found a new argument. Trade of merchandise implies the transportation of goods. Energy—various kinds of fuel—is required to move merchandise from the producer to the consumer. The farther away from each other that the consumer and the producer are, the greater the amount of energy that must be expended for transportation. In addition, the production and use of this energy generates greenhouse gas emissions, which contribute to global warming. Some environmentalists and antiglobalization advocates now argue that the consumption of local products should be encouraged, as this will reduce the overall amount of greenhouse gas emissions. Campaigns based on "buy local, save the environment" are now being launched. On the basis of this argument, international trade should be hindered rather than favoured, because the market system does not take into account the environmental costs associated with international trade or even with interprovincial trade.

A possible answer to this objection to free trade is the imposition of an adequate worldwide carbon tax, in which case, the environmental costs would be incorporated into the transportation costs. Its effect would be to reduce international trade, but within an international context in which free trade would still be the norm.

The Effects of the NAFTA on the Canadian Economy: An Alternative View

Many economists believe that the NAFTA has allowed Canadian businesses to increase their export sales and the size of their firms, with Canadian consumers benefitting from lower prices for the reasons outlined in this chapter. But some economists and political scientists view free trade agreements as a ploy to Americanize our economy or to transform it from a moderate mixed-market economy into a closer approximation of the ideal free market economy, with low tax rates, low wages for blue-collar workers, and less-generous social programs. The following is an example of this point of view.

It is impossible to examine NAFTA in isolation from the broad anti-government and pro-deregulation policy agenda that has for the last two decades been transforming national economies and restructuring the roles and relationships among governments,

SOURCE: CP PHOTO/Chuck Stoody

markets, and citizens in the push to create an integrated global market economy. As a cornerstone of this well-known neoliberal family of policies—privatization, deregulation, investment and trade liberalization, public sector cutbacks, tax cuts, and monetary austerity—NAFTA has made it easier for Canadian policy makers to bring about a "structural adjustment" of the economy in line with the dominant U.S. model. Advancing and entrenching these policies in a treaty has secured investor rights, reined in interventionist government impulses and bargaining table demands of labor, and provided insurance against future governments' backsliding. . . . Have the FTA and NAFTA delivered the goods that were promised? The answer depends on who you ask.

SOURCE: Excerpt from Bruce Campbell, "False Promise: Canada in the Free Trade Era," *NAFTA at Seven: Its Impact on Workers in All Three Nations* (Washington: Economic Policy Institute, 2001). Retrieved from www.policyalternatives.ca

■ CAN CHEAP IMPORTS HURT A COUNTRY?

Dumping means selling goods in a foreign market at lower prices than those charged in the home market.

One of the most curious—and illogical—features of the protectionist position is the fear of low import prices. Countries that subsidize their exports are accused of **dumping**—of getting rid of their goods at unjustifiably low prices.

Many economists find this argument strange. As a nation of consumers, we should be indignant when foreigners charge us *high* prices, not *low* ones. That commonsense rule guides every consumer's daily life. Only from the topsy-turvy viewpoint of an industry seeking protection are low prices seen as being against the public interest.

Ultimately, the best interests of any country are served when its imports are as cheap as possible. It would be ideal for Canada if the rest of the world were willing to provide us with goods at no charge. We could then live in luxury at the expense of other countries. Indeed, along the same lines, many Canadian economists have long argued that it would be beneficial for Canada to remove entirely all of its tariffs and quotas, without negotiating any reciprocal reduction in return.

But, of course, benefits to Canada as a whole do not necessarily benefit every single Canadian. If quotas on, say, steel imports were dropped, Canadian consumers and industries that purchase steel or products made of steel would gain from lower prices. At the same time, however, owners of steel plants and their employees would suffer serious losses in the form of lower profits, lower wages, and lost jobs—losses they would fight fiercely to prevent. For this reason, politics often leads to the adoption of protectionist measures that we would likely reject on strictly economic criteria.

? ISSUE REDUX: *A Last Look at the "Cheap Foreign Labour" Argument*

The preceding discussion reveals the fundamental fallacy in the argument that Canada *as a whole* should fear cheap foreign labour. The average Canadian worker's living standard must *rise*, not fall, if other countries willingly supply their products to us more cheaply. *As long as the government's monetary and fiscal policies succeed in maintaining high levels of employment*, how can we possibly lose by getting world products at bargain prices? This is precisely what happened to the Canadian economy in the late 1990s and in the 2000s: Even though imports poured in at low prices, unemployment in Canada was at its lowest rate in a generation.

We must add some important qualifications, however. First, our macroeconomic policy may not always be effective. If workers displaced by foreign competition cannot find new jobs, they will indeed suffer from international trade. But high unemployment reflects a shortcoming of the government's monetary and fiscal policies, not of its international trade policies, although it must be recognized that, under certain circumstances, free international capital movements will restrict the ability of the federal government to conduct appropriate macroeconomic policies.

Second, we have noted that an abrupt stiffening of foreign competition can hurt Canadian workers by not allowing them adequate time to adapt to the new conditions. If change occurs fairly gradually, workers can be retrained and move on to the industries that now require their services. Indeed, if the change is slow enough, normal attrition may suffice. But competition that inflicts its damage overnight is certain to impose real costs on the affected workers—costs that are no less painful for being temporary. That is why our trade laws make provisions for people and industries damaged by import surges.

In fact, the economic world is constantly changing. The recent emergence of China and other formerly third-world countries, for example, has created new competition for workers in Canada and other rich nations—competition they never imagined when they signed up for jobs that may now be imperilled by international trade. It is not irrational, and it is certainly not protectionist, for countries like Canada to use trade adjustment assistance and other tools to cushion the blow for these workers.

But these are, after all, only qualifications to an overwhelming argument. They call for intelligent monetary and fiscal policies and for transitional assistance to

Unfair Foreign Competition

Satire and ridicule are often more persuasive than logic and statistics. Exasperated by the spread of protectionism under the prevailing mercantilist philosophy, the French economist Frédéric Bastiat decided to take the protectionist argument to its illogical conclusion. The fictitious petition of the French candlemakers to the Chamber of Deputies, written in 1845 and excerpted below, has become a classic in the battle for free trade.

We are subject to the intolerable competition of a foreign rival, who enjoys, it would seem, such superior facilities for the production of light, that he is enabled to inundate our national market at so exceedingly reduced a price, that, the moment he makes his appearance, he draws off all custom for us; and thus an important branch of French industry, with all its innumerable ramifications, is suddenly reduced to a state of complete stagnation. This rival is no other than the sun.

Our petition is, that it would please your honorable body to pass a law whereby shall be directed the shutting up of all windows, dormers, skylights, shutters, curtains, in a word, all openings, holes, chinks, and fissures through which the light of the sun is used to penetrate our dwellings, to the prejudice of the profitable manufactures which we flatter ourselves we have been enabled to bestow upon the country. . . .

We foresee your objections, gentlemen; but there is not one that you can oppose to us . . . which is not equally opposed to your own practice and the principle which guides your policy. . . . Labour and nature concur in different proportions, according to country and climate, in every article of production. . . . If a Lisbon orange can be sold at half the price of a Parisian one, it is because a natural and gratuitous heat does for the one what the other only obtains from an artificial and consequently expensive one. . . .

Does it not argue the greatest inconsistency to check as you do the importation of coal, iron, cheese, and goods of foreign manufacture, merely because and even in proportion as their price approaches zero, while at the same time you freely admit, and without limitation, the light of the sun, whose price is during the whole day at zero?

SOURCE: F. Bastiat, *Economic Sophisms* (New York: G. P. Putnam's Sons, 1922).

SOURCE: © Culver Pictures

unemployed workers, not for abandonment of free trade. In general, the nation as a whole need not fear competition from cheap foreign labour.

> In the long run, labour will be "cheap" only where it is not very productive. Wages will be high in countries with high labour productivity, and this high productivity will enable those countries to compete effectively in international trade despite high wages. It is thus misleading to say that Canada held its own in the international marketplace until recently *despite* high wages. Rather, it is much more accurate to note that the higher wages of Canadian workers were a result of higher worker productivity, which gave Canada a major competitive edge.

Remember, in this matter it is *absolute* advantage, not *comparative* advantage, that counts. The country that is most efficient in producing every output can pay its workers more in every industry.

■ CONCLUSION: A KNIFE EDGE

Thus, to sum up our discussion of this issue: Nearly all economists would agree that free trade and globalization have the potential to improve the productivity and living standards of all countries by drawing on the benefits of international specialization. However, the advocates of free trade have pushed too far by claiming that trade liberalization brings about these effects under all circumstances and by denying that it can lead, for some countries, to an overall reduction of output and employment, instead of reductions in specific industries that are being fully compensated by increases in others.

In many countries, the move toward trade liberalization has been accompanied by austerity policies, both at the microeconomic and macroeconomic levels, that were designed to make the domestic economy more competitive (with more absolute advantages), and thus more likely to benefit from trade liberalization, sometimes at the instigation of international institutions such as the International Monetary Fund. The flip side of these policies, however, is that the beneficial effects of free trade have been overwhelmed in some cases by the negative consequences of these austerity policies, with higher income shares going to capital and lower ones to labour. In a free trade open economy, governments are on a knife edge: They must endorse rules and regulations that will keep domestic businesses competitive on the international scene while providing proper social protection and income distribution to their citizens, and at the same time they must pursue macroeconomic policies that help generate full employment.

SUMMARY

1. Countries trade for many reasons. Two of the most important are that differences in their natural resources and other inputs create discrepancies in the efficiency with which they can produce different goods, and that specialization offers greater economies of large-scale production.

2. Voluntary trade will generally be advantageous to both parties in an exchange.

3. International trade is more complicated than trade within a nation because of political factors, differing national currencies, and impediments to the movement of labour and capital across national borders.

4. Two countries will gain from trade with each other if each nation exports goods in which it has a **comparative advantage**. Through this **specialization** even a country that is inefficient across the board will benefit by exporting the goods in whose production it is *least inefficient*.

5. When countries specialize and trade, each can enjoy consumption possibilities that exceed its production possibilities.

6. The "cheap foreign labour" argument ignores the fact that countries with low wages are also countries with low labour productivity, so that countries such as Canada, with high wages and high productivity, can compete with these "cheap labour" countries.

7. Critics of free trade believe that trade *actually* occurs on the basis of **absolute advantage** and that economies usually operate inside their production possibilities frontiers, so that the positive implications of the principle of comparative advantage do not necessarily arise. This would explain why the current trend toward globalization and liberalized trade seems to have had detrimental effects for a number of countries.

8. **Tariffs** and **quotas** aim to protect a country's industries from foreign competition. Such protection may sometimes be advantageous to that country, but not if foreign countries adopt tariffs and quotas of their own in retaliation.

9. From the point of view of the country that imposes them, tariffs offer at least two advantages over quotas: Some of the

gains go to the government rather than to foreign producers, and they provide greater incentive for efficient production.

10. When a nation eliminates protection in favour of free trade, some industries and their workers will lose out. Equity then demands that these people and firms be compensated in some way. The government should offer protection from import surges and various forms of **trade adjustment assistance** to help those workers and industries adapt to the new conditions.

11. Several arguments for protectionism can, under the right circumstances, have validity. They include the national defence argument, the use of trade restrictions for strategic purposes, environmental concerns, the infant-industry argument, and most importantly, the infant-economy argument. But each of these arguments can be abused.

12. **Dumping** will hurt certain domestic producers, but it benefits domestic consumers.

KEY TERMS

"Cheap foreign labour" argument 370

Specialization 371

Mutual gains from trade 371

Absolute advantage 373

Comparative advantage 373

Mercantilism 377

Tariff 379

Quota 380

Export subsidy 380

Trade adjustment assistance 382

Strategic trade policy 383

Infant-industry argument 384

Infant-economy argument 384

Dumping 386

TEST YOURSELF

1. The following table, based on an example taken from *Principles of Political Economy and Taxation* by David Ricardo (1817), describes the number of yards of cloth and barrels of wine that can be produced with a week's worth of labour in England and Portugal. Assume that no other inputs are needed.

	In England	In Portugal
Cloth	8 yards	12 yards
Wine	2 barrels	6 barrels

a. If there is no trade, what is the price of wine in terms of cloth in England?

b. If there is no trade, what is the price of wine in terms of cloth in Portugal?

c. Suppose each country has 1 million weeks of labour available per year. Draw the production possibilities frontier for each country.

d. Which country has an absolute advantage in the production of which good(s)? Which country has a comparative advantage in the production of which good(s)?

e. If the countries start trading with each other, which country will specialize and export which good?

f. What can be said about the price at which trade will take place?

2. Suppose that Canada and Mexico are the only two countries in the world and that labour is the only productive input. In Canada, a worker can produce 12 bushels of wheat *or* 2 barrels of oil in a day. In Mexico, a worker can produce 2 bushels of wheat *or* 4 barrels of oil per day.

a. What will be the price ratio between the two commodities (that is, the price of oil in terms of wheat) in each country if there is no trade?

b. If free trade is allowed and there are no transportation costs, which commodity would Canada import? What about Mexico?

c. In what range would the price ratio have to fall under free trade? Why?

d. Picking one possible post-trade price ratio, show clearly how it is possible for both countries to benefit from free trade.

DISCUSSION QUESTIONS

1. You have a dozen shirts and your roommate has six pairs of shoes worth roughly the same amount of money. You decide to swap six shirts for three pairs of shoes. In financial terms, neither of you gains anything. Explain why you are nevertheless both likely to be better off.

2. In the eighteenth century, some writers argued that one person in a trade could be made better off only by gaining at the expense of the other. Explain the fallacy in this argument.

3. Country A has a cold climate with a short growing season, but a highly skilled labour force. (Think of Canada!) What sorts of products do you think it is likely to produce? What are the characteristics of the countries with which you would expect it to trade?

4. After the removal of a quota on textiles, many Canadian textile producers go bankrupt. Discuss the pros and cons of removing the quota in the short and long runs.

5. Country A has a mercantilist government that believes it is always best to export more than it imports. As a consequence, it exports more to Country B every year than it imports from Country B. After 100 years of this arrangement, both countries are destroyed in an earthquake. What were the advantages or disadvantages of the surplus to Country A? To Country B?

6. Suppose the United States finds Country C guilty of unfair trade practices and penalizes it with import quotas. So U.S. imports from Country C fall. Suppose, further, that Country C does not alter its trade practices in any way. Is the United States better or worse off? What about Country C?

7. Why are labour unions generally hostile to free trade agreements such as the one that was signed by Canada, the United States, and Mexico?

APPENDIX *Supply, Demand, and Pricing in World Trade*

As noted in the text, price determination in a world market with free trade depends on supply and demand conditions in each of the countries participating in the market. This appendix works out some of the details in a two-country example.

When applied to international trade, the usual supply–demand model must deal with (at least) *two demand curves:* that of the exporting country and that of the importing country. In addition, it may also involve *two supply curves,* because the importing country may produce part of its own consumption. (For example, Canada, which is a big importer of oil, nonetheless produces quite a bit of domestic oil.) Furthermore, equilibrium does *not* take place at the intersection point of *either* pair of supply–demand curves. Why? Because if the two countries trade at all, the exporting nation must supply more than it demands while the importing nation demands more than it supplies.

All three of these complications are illustrated in Figure 4, which shows the supply and demand curves of a country that *exports* wheat in Panel (a) and of a country that *imports* wheat in Panel (b). For simplicity, we assume that these countries do not deal with anyone else. Where will the two-country wheat market reach equilibrium?

Under free trade, the equilibrium price must satisfy two requirements:

1. The quantity of wheat *exported* by one country must equal the quantity of wheat *imported* by the other country, for that is how *world* supply and demand balance.

2. The price of wheat must be the same in both countries.[6]

In Figure 4, these two conditions are met at a price of $2.50 per bushel. At that price, the distance *AB* between what the exporting country produces and what it consumes equals the distance *CD* between what the importing country consumes and what it produces. This means that the amount the exporting country wants to sell at $2.50 per bushel exactly equals the amount the importing country wants to buy at that price.

At any higher price, producers in both countries would want to sell more and consumers in both countries would want to buy less. For example, if the price rose to $3.25 per bushel, the exporter's quantity supplied would rise from *B* to *F* and its quantity demanded would fall from *A* to *E*, as shown in Panel (a). As a result, more wheat would be available for export—*EF* rather than *AB*. For exactly the same reason, the price increase would cause higher production and lower sales in the importing country, leading to a reduction in imports from *CD* to *GH* in Panel (b).

FIGURE 4   Supply–Demand Equilibrium in the International Wheat Trade

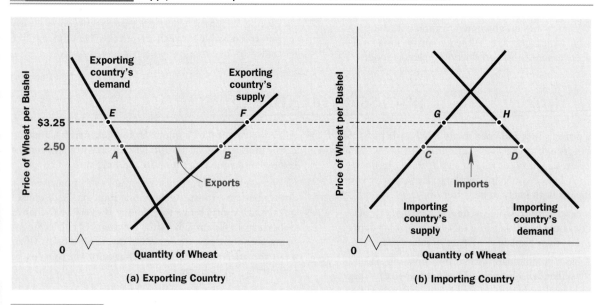

(a) Exporting Country
(b) Importing Country

---

[6] To keep things simple, we ignore such details as the costs of shipping wheat from one country to the other.

But this means that the higher price, $3.25 per bushel, cannot be sustained in a free and competitive international market. With export supply EF far greater than import demand GH, there would be pressure on price to fall back toward the $2.50 equilibrium price. Similar reasoning shows that no price below $2.50 can be sustained. Thus:

In international trade, the equilibrium price is the one that makes the exporting country want to export exactly the amount that the importing country wants to import. Equilibrium will thus occur at a price at which the horizontal distance AB in Figure 4(a) (the excess of the exporter's quantity supplied over its quantity demanded) is equal to the horizontal distance CD in Figure 4(b) (the excess of the importer's quantity demanded over its quantity supplied). At this price, the world's quantity demanded equals the world's quantity supplied.

HOW TARIFFS AND QUOTAS WORK

However, as noted in the text, nations do not always let free markets operate. Sometimes they intervene with quotas that limit imports or with tariffs that make imports more expensive. Although both tariffs and quotas restrict supplies coming from abroad and drive up prices, they operate slightly differently. A tariff works by raising prices, which in turn cuts the quantity of imports demanded. The sequence associated with a quota is just the reverse—a restriction in supply forces prices to rise.

The supply and demand curves in Figure 5 illustrate how tariffs and quotas work. Just as in Figure 4, the equilibrium price of wheat under free trade is $2.50 per bushel (in both countries). At this price, the exporting country produces 125 million bushels—point B in Panel

(a)—and consumes 80 million (point A). So its exports are 45 million bushels—the distance AB. Similarly, the importing country consumes 95 million bushels—point D in Panel (b)—and produces only 50 million (point C), so its imports are also 45 million bushels—the distance CD.

Now suppose the government of the importing nation imposes a *quota* limiting imports to 30 million bushels. The free trade equilibrium with imports of 45 million bushels is now illegal. Instead, the market must equilibrate at a point where both exports and imports are only 30 million bushels. As Figure 5 indicates, this requirement leads to different prices in the two countries.

Imports in Panel (b) will be 30 million bushels—the distance QT—only when the price of wheat in the importing nation is $3.25 per bushel, because only at this price will quantity demanded exceed domestic quantity supplied by 30 million bushels. Similarly, exports in Panel (a) will be 30 million bushels—the distance RS—only when the price in the exporting country is $2.00 per bushel. At this price, quantity supplied exceeds quantity demanded in the exporting country by 30 million bushels. Thus, the quota *raises* the price in the importing country to $3.25 and *lowers* the price in the exporting country to $2.00. In general:

An import quota on a product normally reduces the volume of that product traded, raises the price in the importing country, and reduces the price in the exporting country.

A tariff can accomplish exactly the same restriction of trade. In our example, a quota of 30 million bushels led to a price that was $1.25 higher in the importing country than in the exporting country ($3.25 versus $2.00). Suppose that, instead of a quota, the importing nation imposes

FIGURE 5   Quotas and Tariffs in International Trade

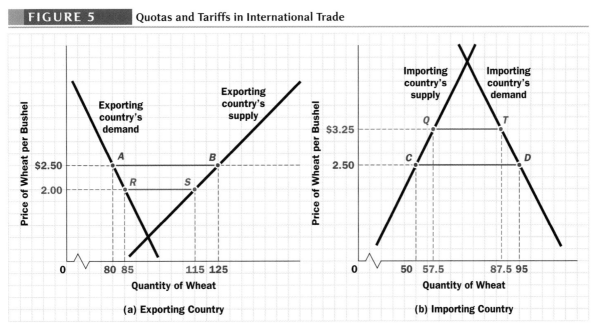

Note: Quantities are in millions of bushels.

a $1.25 per bushel *tariff*. International trade equilibrium then must satisfy the following two requirements:

1. The quantity of wheat *exported* by one country must equal the quantity of wheat *imported* by the other, just as before.
2. The price that consumers in the importing country pay for wheat must *exceed* the price that suppliers in the exporting country receive by the amount of the *tariff* ($1.25 in this example).

By consulting the graphs in Figure 5, you can see exactly where these two requirements are met. If the exporter produces at *S* and consumes at *R*, while the importer produces at *Q* and consumes at *T*, then exports and imports are equal (at 30 million bushels), and the two domestic prices differ by exactly $1.25. (They are $3.25 and $2.00.) What we have just discovered is a general result of international trade theory:

Any restriction of imports that is accomplished by a quota normally can also be accomplished by a tariff.

In this case, the tariff corresponding to an import quota of 30 million bushels is $1.25 per bushel.

We mentioned in the text that a tariff (or a quota) forces foreign producers to sell more cheaply. Figure 5 shows how this works. Suppose, as in Panel (b), that a $1.25 tariff on wheat raises the price in the importing country from $2.50 to $3.25 per bushel. This higher price drives down imports from an amount represented by the length of the red line *CD* to the smaller amount represented by the blue line *QT*. In the exporting country, this change means an equal reduction in exports, as illustrated by the change from *AB* to *RS* in Panel (a).

As a result, the price at which the exporting country can sell its wheat is driven down—from $2.50 to $2.00 in the example. Meanwhile, producers in the importing country, which are exempt from the tariff, can charge $3.25 per bushel. Thus, as noted in the text, a tariff (or a quota) can be thought of as a way to "rig" the domestic market in favour of domestic firms.

SUMMARY

1. The prices of goods traded between countries are determined by supply and demand, but one must consider explicitly the demand curve and the supply curve of *each* country involved. Thus the equilibrium price must make the excess of quantity supplied over quantity demanded in the exporting country equal to the excess of quantity demanded over quantity supplied in the importing country.

2. When trade is restricted, the combinations of prices and quantities in the various countries that are achieved by a quota can also be achieved by a tariff.

3. Tariffs or quotas favour domestic producers over foreign producers.

TEST YOURSELF

1. The following table presents the demand and supply curves for microcomputers in China and Canada.

Price per Computer	Quantity Demanded in Canada	Quantity Supplied in Canada	Quantity Demanded in China	Quantity Supplied in China
1	90	30	50	50
2	80	35	40	55
3	70	40	30	60
4	60	45	20	65
5	50	50	10	70
6	40	55	0	75

Note: Price and quantity are in thousands.

a. Draw the demand and supply curves for Canada on one diagram and those for China on another one.

b. If Canada and China do not trade, what are the equilibrium price and quantity in the computer market in Canada? In China?

c. Now suppose trade is opened up between the two countries. What will be the equilibrium price in the world market for computers? What has happened to the price of computers in Canada? In China?

d. Which country will export computers? How many?

e. When trade opens, what happens to the quantity of computers produced, and therefore employment, in the computer industry in Canada? In China? Who benefits and who loses *initially* from free trade?

18

THE INTERNATIONAL MONETARY SYSTEM: ORDER OR DISORDER?

Cecily, you will read your Political Economy in my absence.
The chapter on the Fall of the Rupee you may omit.
It is somewhat too sensational.

MISS PRISM IN OSCAR WILDE'S *THE IMPORTANCE OF BEING EARNEST*

Miss Prism, the Victorian tutor, may have had a better point than she knew. In the summer of 1997, the Indonesian rupiah (not the Indian rupee) fell and economic disaster quickly followed. The International Monetary Fund rushed to the rescue with billions of dollars and pages of advice. But its plan failed, and some say it may even have helped precipitate the bloody riots that led to the fall of the Indonesian government.

This chapter does not concentrate on such sensational political upheavals. Rather, it focuses on a seemingly mundane topic: how the market determines rates of exchange among different national currencies. Nevertheless, events in Southeast Asia in 1997–1998, in Brazil and Russia in 1998–1999, and in Turkey and Argentina in 2001–2002 have amply demonstrated that dramatic exchange rate movements can have severe human as well as financial consequences. This chapter and the next will help us understand why.

CONTENTS

PUZZLE: *What Was Behind the Spectacular Rise of the Canadian Dollar?*

Unlike most Americans who seem to pay little attention to the international value of their currency, Canadians watch the fluctuations of the Canadian dollar almost as closely as they watch the weather forecast. Few Canadians have missed the fact that, as recently as February 2002, the Canadian dollar was worth a mere 61.8 cents in U.S. funds. Then, just two years later, in 2004, Canadian Press, in its survey of news directors and editors, chose the meteoric *rise* of the Canadian dollar as the top business story of the year. Indeed, at the time of writing (early 2008), the Canadian dollar has reached parity with the U.S. dollar (one Canadian dollar being worth one American dollar), and continues to make headline news. It is easy to understand why there is so much interest in the movement of the Canadian dollar. Most of Canada's largest cities are within driving distance to the Canada–U.S. border. Also, close to one out of every three dollars' worth of goods that we produce in Canada is exported to the United States. What happens to the value of our currency could impact directly on our livelihood.

A 60 percent rise in the value of the Canadian dollar over a five-year period is a significant jump. What caused this? We will learn some of the answers to this and related questions in this chapter. But to do that, we first need to understand what determines exchange rates.

■ WHAT ARE EXCHANGE RATES?

We noted in the previous chapter that international trade is more complicated than domestic trade. There are no national borders to be crossed when, say, Alberta beef is shipped to Ontario. The consumer in Toronto pays with *Canadian dollars*, just the currency that the farmer in Lethbridge wants. If the same farmer ships her beef to Japan, however, consumers there will have only Japanese yen with which to pay, rather than the Canadian dollars the farmer in Alberta wants. So, for international trade to take place, there must be some way to convert one currency into another. The rates at which such conversions are made are called **exchange rates**.

> The **exchange rate** states the price, in terms of one currency, at which another currency can be bought.

There is an exchange rate between every pair of currencies. For example, in January 2008, the Canadian dollar was worth about 0.67 euro (or €0.67, with € being the euro symbol)—the single currency of several European countries. This meant that it cost 0.67 of a euro to purchase a Canadian dollar. But we can also express this the other way around. We can say that the euro then was worth about CDN$1.49, meaning that it cost CDN$1.49 to purchase a euro.

Figure 1 shows the evolution of a key exchange rate for Canadians—the Canada–U.S. dollar exchange rate over the last century, here expressed as the value of the Canadian dollar in U.S. funds. Interestingly, this key exchange rate showed remarkable stability for a very long historical period until the mid-1970s, with the Canadian dollar hovering close to par with the U.S. dollar (at around a mean of US$0.97 for the pre-1970s era). Since the mid-1970s, the Canadian dollar has been on a roller coaster. In particular, it declined sharply throughout most of the 1990s, experienced a trough in 2001, and then realized a dramatic turnaround beginning in early

---

FIGURE 1

Evolution of the Exchange Rate of the Canadian Dollar in U.S. Funds, Annual Averages, 1913–2008

SOURCES: Statistics Canada, *Historical Statistics of Canada*, 2nd ed. (Ottawa: Statistics Canada, 1983); CANSIM II Series V37426.

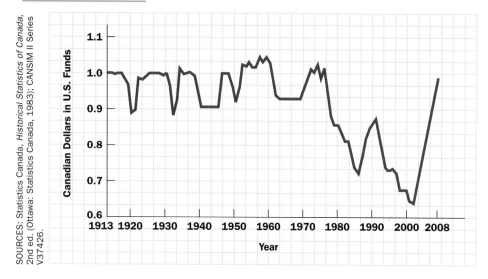

2002, reaching ever closer to parity with the U.S. dollar on average during 2007 and the first half of 2008. This chapter seeks to explain such currency movements.

Under our present system, currency rates change frequently. When other currencies become more expensive in terms of dollars, we say that they have **appreciated** relative to the dollar. Alternatively, we can look at this same event as the dollar buying less foreign currency, meaning that the dollar has **depreciated** relative to another currency.

What is a depreciation to one country must be an appreciation to the other.

For example, if the price of a British pound *rises* from $2.15 to $2.50, the price of a Canadian dollar in terms of pounds simultaneously *falls* from 47 pence to 40 pence. The United Kingdom has experienced a currency *appreciation*, while Canada has experienced a currency *depreciation*. In fact, the two mean more or less the same thing. As you may have noticed, these two ways of viewing the exchange rate are reciprocals of one another, that is, $1/2.15 = 0.47$ and $1/2.50 = 0.40$. And of course, when a number goes up, by definition its reciprocal goes down.

When many currencies are changing in value at the same time, the Canadian dollar may be appreciating with respect to one currency (say, the British pound) but depreciating with respect to another (say, the U.S. dollar). Table 1 offers a selection of exchange rates prevailing in January 1982, and then every five years until January 2008, showing how many Canadian dollars or cents it cost at each of those times to buy each unit of foreign currency. Between 1982 and 2002, the Canadian dollar *depreciated* sharply relative to the Japanese yen, the German mark (and then the euro after 1999), and the U.S. dollar. But it *appreciated* with respect to such currencies as the Australian dollar. Since 2002, the Canadian dollar appreciated with respect to both the U.S. dollar and the Japanese yen, remained stable with respect to certain European currencies, and depreciated in relation to the euro.

Although the terms "appreciation" and "depreciation" are used to describe movements of exchange rates in free markets, a different set of terms is employed to describe decreases and increases in currency values that are set by government decree. When an officially set exchange rate is altered so that a unit of a nation's currency can buy fewer units of foreign currency, we say that a **devaluation** of that currency has occurred. When the exchange rate is altered so that the currency can buy more units of foreign currency, we say that a **revaluation** has taken place. We will say more about devaluation and revaluation shortly, but first let's look at how unfettered market forces determine exchange rates.

> A nation's currency is said to **appreciate** when exchange rates change so that a unit of its currency can buy more units of foreign currency.
>
> A nation's currency is said to **depreciate** when exchange rates change so that a unit of its currency can buy fewer units of foreign currency.
>
> A **devaluation** is a reduction in the official value of a currency.
>
> A **revaluation** is an increase in the official value of a currency.

TABLE 1
Canadian Dollar Exchange Rates

Country	Currency	Symbol	Cost of CDN$1 in Foreign Currency					
			January 1982	January 1987	January 1992	January 1997	January 2002	January 2008
Australia	Dollar	$	0.75	1.11	1.15	0.95	1.2	1.12
France	Franc	FF	5	4.55	4.76	4	*	*
Germany	Mark	DM	1.92	1.37	1.37	1.19	*	*
Italy	Lira	L	1,030.93	970.87	1,030.93	1,162.79	*	*
Japan	Yen	¥	188.68	113.64	108.7	87.72	82.64	106.53
Mexico	New peso	$	0.022	0.68	2.63	5.88	5.88	10.79
Sweden	Krona	Kr	4.76	4.76	5	5.26	6.66	6.34
Switzerland	Franc	S.Fr.	1.54	1.15	1.22	1.03	1.04	1.09
United Kingdom	Pound	£	0.45	0.49	0.48	0.45	0.47	0.50
United States	Dollar	$	0.75	0.74	0.86	0.74	0.65	0.99
Euro countries	Euro	€	–	–	–	–	0.71	0.67

* These exchange rates were locked together when the euro was adopted in January 1999.

SOURCES: Statistics Canada, CANSIM Series V37426, V37428, V37429, V37430, V37444, V37450, V37453, V37454, V37455, V37456, and V21570998.

EXCHANGE RATE DETERMINATION IN A FREELY COMPETITIVE MARKET

Floating exchange rates are rates determined in free markets by the law of supply and demand.

In January 1999, 11 European countries adopted a new single currency, the euro. At the time of its official launching, only 0.71 euro could be purchased with one Canadian dollar, but at the time of writing, some nine years later, each Canadian dollar was worth about 0.63 euro. Why is this so? Also, why was the Canadian dollar worth about US$1.00 in the spring of 2008, whereas it was worth only US$0.65 in January 2002?

In a world of **floating exchange rates**, with no government intervention and no other major player controlling the purchases or sales of any one currency, the answer would be straightforward. Exchange rates would be determined by the forces of supply and demand, just like the prices of apples, computers, and haircuts would be in a freely competitive market.

In a leap of abstraction, imagine that the Canadian dollar and the American dollar are the only currencies on earth, so the market need determine only one exchange rate. Figure 2 depicts the determination of this exchange rate at the point (denoted *E* in the figure) where demand curve *DD* crosses supply curve *SS*. At this price (US$0.85 per Canadian dollar), the number of Canadian dollars demanded is equal to the number of Canadian dollars supplied on the foreign exchange market.

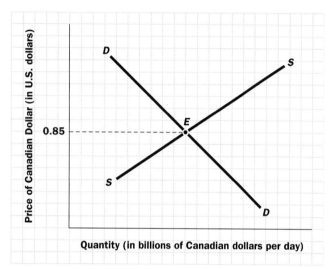

Quantity (in billions of Canadian dollars per day)

FIGURE 2

The Foreign Exchange Market with Floating Exchange Rates

In a free market, exchange rates are determined by supply and demand. At a rate below the equilibrium level, the number of Canadian dollars demanded on the foreign exchange market would exceed the number supplied, and the price of the Canadian dollar would be bid up. At a rate above the equilibrium level, quantity supplied would exceed quantity demanded, and the price of a Canadian dollar would fall. Only at the equilibrium exchange rate is there no tendency for the exchange rate to change.

As usual, supply and demand determine price. But in this case, we must ask: Where do the supply and demand come from? Why does anyone demand Canadian dollars? The answer comes in three parts:

1. *International trade in goods and services.* This factor was the subject of the previous chapter. If, for example, Jane Doe, the manager of a large grocery store chain in Las Vegas, wants to buy Canadian maple syrup, she will first have to buy Canadian dollars with which to pay the maple syrup distributor in Montreal.[1] Thus, the demand for Canadian maple syrup leads to a demand for Canadian currency. In general, *demand for a country's exports leads to demand for its currency.*[2]

2. *Purchases of physical assets such as factories and machinery overseas.* If IBM in the United States wants to buy a small Canadian computer manufacturer in Nova Scotia, the owners are most likely to be paid in Canadian dollars. So IBM will first have to acquire Canadian currency. In general, *direct foreign investment leads to demand for a country's currency.*

3. *International trade in financial instruments such as stocks and bonds.* If American pension funds want to purchase stocks on the Toronto Stock Exchange, they will first have to acquire the Canadian dollars that the sellers will insist on for payment. In this way, the demand for European financial assets leads to a demand for Canadian currency. Thus, *demand for a country's financial assets leads to demand for its currency.* In fact, nowadays the volume of international trade in financial assets among the major countries of the world is so large that it swamps the other two sources of demand.

---

[1] Actually, she will not do so because banks generally handle foreign exchange transactions for consumers. An American bank probably will buy the Canadian dollars for her. Even so, the effect is exactly the same as if Jane had done it herself.

[2] See Discussion Question 2 at the end of this chapter.

Now, where does the supply come from? To answer this question, just turn all of these transactions around. Canadians who want to buy U.S. goods and services, make direct investments in the United States, or purchase U.S. financial assets will have to offer Canadian dollars in the foreign exchange market (which is mainly run through banks) to acquire the needed American dollars. To summarize:

The *demand* for a country's currency is derived from the demands of foreigners for its export goods and services and for its assets—including financial assets, such as stocks and bonds, and real assets, such as factories and machinery. The *supply* of a country's currency arises from its imports, and from foreign investment by its own citizens.

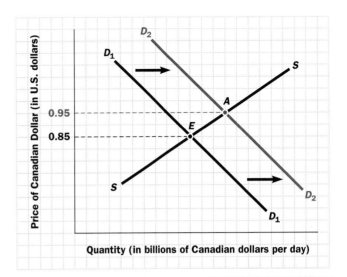

FIGURE 3

The Effect of a Canadian Stock Market Boom on the Exchange Rate

To illustrate the usefulness of even this simple supply and demand analysis, think about how the Canada–U.S. dollar exchange rate would change if Americans become attracted by the prospects of large gains on the Canadian stock market, perhaps because of the rising prices of oil and other primary commodities. To purchase Canadian shares, foreigners will first have to purchase Canadian dollars. In terms of the supply–demand diagram in Figure 3, the increased desire of Americans to acquire Canadian shares would shift the demand curve for Canadian dollars out from D_1D_1 (the black line in the figure) to D_2D_2 (the red line). Equilibrium would shift from point E to point A, and the exchange rate value of the Canadian dollar would rise from US$0.85 to US$0.95. Thus, the increased demand for Canadian dollars by Americans would cause the Canadian dollar to *appreciate* relative to the American dollar.

A summary list of some of the possible outcomes of such changes is provided in Table 2.

TABLE 2			
Summary of Outcomes on the Canadian Dollar in the Short Run			
	Impact on Demand for Canadian Dollars	Impact on Supply of Canadian Dollars	Exchange Rate Change of Canadian Dollar
Increase in Canadian Imports from the U.S.	No change	Rightward shift	Depreciation
Increase in Canadian Exports to the U.S.	Rightward shift	No change	Appreciation
Increase in Interest Payments to the U.S.	No change	Rightward shift	Depreciation
Increase in Interest Payments from the U.S.	Rightward shift	No change	Appreciation
Canadians Invest in the U.S.	No change	Rightward shift	Depreciation
Americans Invest in Canada	Rightward shift	No change	Appreciation

EXERCISE Test your understanding of the supply and demand analysis of exchange rates by showing why each of the following events would lead to a depreciation of the Canadian dollar on the foreign exchange market:

1. Canadian investors are attracted by prospects for profit on the New York Stock Exchange.
2. A recession in the United States cuts American purchases of Canadian goods.
3. Interest rates on government bonds rise in the United States but are stable in Canada.

To say that supply and demand determine exchange rates in a freely competitive market is to say everything and nothing at once. If we are to understand the reasons why some currencies appreciate whereas others depreciate, we must look into the factors that move the supply and demand curves. Economists believe that the principal determinants of exchange rate movements differ significantly in the short, medium, and long runs. So in the next three sections, we turn to the analysis of exchange rate movements over these three "runs," beginning with the short run.

Interest Rates and Exchange Rates: The Short Run

Most experts in international finance agree that interest rates and financial flows are the major determinants of exchange rates—certainly in the short run, and probably in the medium run as well. Specifically, one variable that often seems to call the tune in the short run is *interest rate differentials*. A multitrillion-dollar pool of so-called *hot money*—owned by banks, investment funds, multinational corporations, and wealthy individuals of all nations—travels rapidly around the globe in search of the highest interest rates.

As an example, suppose American government bonds pay a 5 percent rate of interest when yields on equally safe Canadian government securities rise to 7 percent. American investors will be attracted by the higher interest rates in Canada and will demand Canadian dollars, planning to use these Canadian dollars to buy Canadian securities. At the same time, Canadian investors will find it more attractive to keep their money at home, so fewer Canadian dollars will be offered by Canadians.

When the demand schedule for Canadian dollars shifts outward and the supply curve shifts inward, the effect on price is predictable: The Canadian dollar will appreciate, as Figure 4 shows. In the figure, the demand curve for Canadian dollars shifts outward from D_1D_1 to D_2D_2 when American investors seek to purchase Canadian dollars in order to buy Canadian securities. At the same time, Canadian investors want to buy fewer U.S. dollars because they no longer want to invest as much in U.S. securities, thus selling fewer Canadian dollars on the foreign exchange market. So the supply curve shifts inward from S_1S_1 to S_2S_2. The result in our example is an appreciation of the Canadian dollar from US\$0.90 to US\$1.05. In general:

> Other things equal, countries that offer investors higher rates of return attract more capital than countries that offer lower rates. Thus, a rise in interest rates often will lead to an appreciation of the currency, and a drop in interest rates will lead to a depreciation.

FIGURE 4

The Effect of a Rise in Canadian Interest Rates

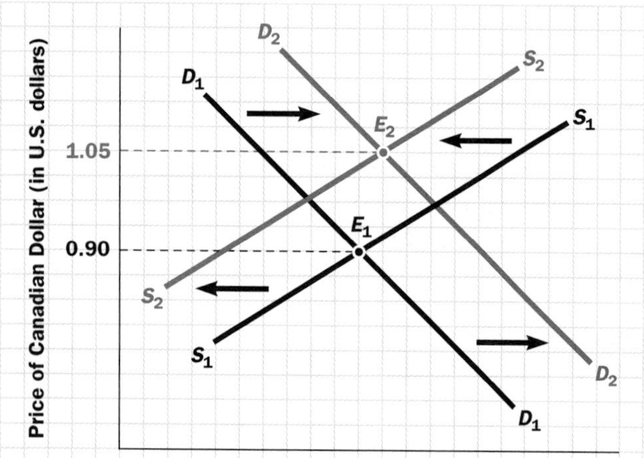

Think of interest differentials, in this context, as representing the differences in the relative returns on all sorts of financial assets in the two countries. With inflation abating following the deep recession of 1990–1991, interest rates in Canada fell in comparison to other countries—especially the United States. As a consequence, mobile foreign and even domestic financial capital started to move out of Canada and, accompanying this movement, the Canadian dollar depreciated. At the same time, the strong growth and the high return on equity resulting from the high-tech boom of the Clinton years attracted foreign capital and led to a soaring U.S. dollar during the 1990s, thereby further weakening the Canadian dollar in relation to its U.S. counterpart.

It should be emphasized, however, that it is not just fluctuations in actual returns that affect investors' decisions. It is the *expectations* of higher monetary returns on both financial and physical assets that often trigger cross-border movement of funds and lead investors to transfer funds from a low-return to a high-return country. For instance, nowadays there is often much fanfare from the Canadian media when forecasts of core inflation are above the target range fixed by the Bank of Canada. Such forecasts could set off a hike in the Canadian dollar merely on the basis of the expected higher future interest rates that would result from the central bank's policy of combating inflation.

Economic Activity and Exchange Rates: The Medium Run

The medium run is where the theory of exchange rate determination is most unsettled. Economists once reasoned as follows: Because consumer spending increases when income rises and decreases when income falls, the same thing is likely to happen to spending on imported goods. So *a country's imports will rise quickly when its economy booms and rise only slowly when its economy stagnates*.

For the reasons illustrated in Figure 5, then, a boom in Canada should shift the *supply* curve of Canadian dollars *outward* as Canadians sell Canadian currency to acquire more U.S. dollars to purchase more U.S. goods. And that, in turn, should lead to a *depreciation* of the Canadian dollar. In the figure, the Canadian dollar falls in value from US$0.95 to US$0.85.

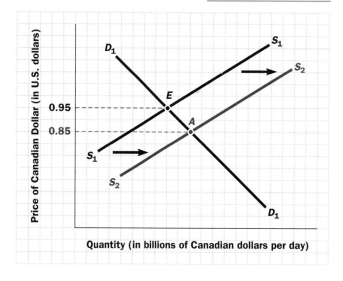

FIGURE 5

The Effect on the Exchange Rate of an Economic Boom in Canada

However, if the U.S. economy was booming at the same time, Americans would be buying more Canadian exports, which would shift *outward* the *demand* curve for Canadian dollars. On balance, the value of the Canadian dollar might rise or fall. It appears that what matters is whether exports are growing faster than imports.

> A country whose aggregate demand grows faster than that of the rest of the world normally finds its imports growing faster than its exports. Thus, the supply curve for its domestic currency on foreign exchange markets will shift outward more rapidly than its demand curve. *Other things equal*, that will make its currency depreciate.

This reasoning is sound—as far as it goes. And it leads to the conclusion that a "strong economy" might produce a "weak currency." But the three most important words in the preceding paragraph are "other things equal." Usually, they are not. Specifically, a booming economy will normally offer more attractive prospects to investors than a stagnating one—higher interest rates, rising stock market values, and so on. This difference in prospective investment returns, as we noted earlier, should attract capital and boost its currency value.

So there appears to be a kind of tug of war. Thinking about trade in goods and services leads to the conclusion that faster growth should *weaken* the currency. But thinking about trade in financial assets (such as stocks and bonds) leads to precisely the opposite conclusion: Faster growth should *strengthen* the currency. Which side wins this tug of war?

As we have suggested, it is usually no contest—at least among the major currencies of the world. In the modern world, the evidence seems to say that trade in financial assets is the dominant factor. For example, rapid growth in Canada in the mid-2000s was accompanied by a sharply *appreciating* Canadian dollar, even though Canadian imports soared as interest rates inched upward and expected returns, especially in energy-related industries, rose. We conclude that:

> Stronger economic performance often leads to currency *appreciation* because it improves prospects for investing in the country.

◼ The Purchasing-Power Parity Theory: The Long Run

We come at last to the so-called long run, where an apparently simple principle ought to govern exchange rates. As long as goods can move freely across national borders, exchange rates should eventually adjust so that the same product costs the same amount of money, whether measured in dollars in Canada , euros in Germany, or yen in Japan—except for differences in transportation costs and the like. This simple statement forms the basis of the major theory of exchange rate determination in the long run:

> The *purchasing-power parity theory of exchange rate determination* holds that the exchange rate between any two national currencies adjusts to reflect differences in the price levels in the two countries.

An example will illustrate the basic principle and also suggest some of its limitations. Suppose German and Canadian steel is identical and that these two nations are the only producers of steel for the world market. Suppose further that steel is the only tradable good that either country produces.

Question: If Canadian steel costs CDN$180 per ton and German steel costs 144 euros per ton, what must be the exchange rate between the Canadian dollar and the euro?

Answer: Because 144 euros and $180 each buy a ton of steel, the two sums of money must be of equal value. Hence, each euro must be worth $1.25. Why? Any higher price for a euro, such as $1.50, would mean that steel would cost $216 per ton (144 euros at $1.50 each) in Germany but only $180 per ton in Canada. In that case, all foreign customers would shop for their steel in Canada—which would increase the demand for dollars and decrease the demand for euros. Similarly, any exchange rate below $1.25 per euro would send all the steel business to Germany, driving the value of the euro up toward its purchasing-power parity level.

EXERCISE Show why an exchange rate of $1 per euro is too low to lead to an equilibrium in the international steel market.

The purchasing-power parity theory is used to make long-run predictions about the effects of inflation on exchange rates. To continue our example, suppose that steel (and other) prices in Canada rise while prices in Europe remain constant. The purchasing-power parity theory predicts that the euro will appreciate relative to the dollar. It also predicts the amount of the appreciation. After the Canadian inflation, suppose that the price of Canadian steel is $216 per ton, while German steel still costs 144 euros per ton. For these two prices to be equivalent, 144 euros must be worth $216, or one euro must be worth $1.50. The euro, therefore, must have risen from $1.25 to $1.50.

> According to the purchasing-power parity theory, differences in domestic inflation rates are a major cause of exchange rate movements. If one country has higher inflation than another, its exchange rate should be depreciating.

The theory is highly appealing because of its clear logic and relative simplicity. This strong appeal to logic notwithstanding, precise numerical predictions based on purchasing-power parity calculations have never been very accurate. At best, the theory could predict the direction of the change in the exchange rate, whereby nations with higher inflation have tended to experience depreciating currencies (see "Purchasing Power Parity and the Big Mac"). But even that does not always work well. For instance, throughout the 1990s, Canada's inflation rate tended to be close but consistently lower than the U.S. rate; yet the Canadian dollar persistently fell throughout the decade. Similarly, Canada–U.S. inflation rates have not differed much since 2001, but the Canadian dollar has been appreciating for most of the period since then. Clearly, the theory is missing something. What?

Many things. But perhaps the principal failing of the purchasing-power parity theory is, once again, that it focuses too much on trade in goods and services. Financial assets such as stocks and bonds are also traded actively across national borders—and

Purchasing-Power Parity and the Big Mac

Since 1986, *The Economist* magazine has been using a well-known international commodity—the Big Mac—to assess the purchasing-power parity theory of exchange rates, or as the magazine once put it, "to make exchange-rate theory more digestible."

Here's how it works. In theory, the local price of a Big Mac, when translated into U.S. dollars by the exchange rate, should be the same everywhere in the world. The following numbers show that the theory does not work terribly well.

For example, in February 2007, although the Big Mac cost an average of $3.22 in the United States, it sold for about 11.0 yuan in China. Using the official exchange rate of about 7.66 yuan to the U.S. dollar, that amounted to just US$1.44. Thus, according to the hamburger parity theory, the yuan was grossly undervalued.

By how much? The price in China was just 45 percent of the price in the United States ($1.44/$3.22). So the yuan was 55 percent below its Big Mac parity—and, therefore, should appreciate. Some of these undervalued or overvalued currencies are listed in the accompanying table in the "February 2007" column.

True Big Mac aficionados may find these data helpful when planning international travel. But can deviations from Big Mac parity predict exchange rate movements? Supposedly, they can.

When the economist Robert Cumby studied Big Mac prices and exchange rates in 14 countries over a 10-year period, he found that deviations from hamburger parity were transitory. Their "half-life" was

SOURCE: © lucky studio/Shutterstock

just a year, meaning that 50 percent of the deviation tended to disappear within a year. Thus the undervalued currencies in the accompanying table would be predicted to appreciate during 2008, whereas the overvalued currencies would be expected to depreciate.

Moreover, can convergence of Big Mac prices over time when adjusting for exchange rate differences be predicted? The last column of the table shows the percentage rate of change between April 2002 and February 2007. Did prices move in accordance with Big Mac parity over this five-year period? In the United States, the price of a Big Mac went up by 29 percent during the five years. However, prices in countries such as China, Japan, and Mexico moved in a direction that clearly conflicted with what the theory would have predicted. These prices in U.S. dollars grew less quickly than those in the United States, despite the fact that the currencies in these countries were undervalued in 2002. On the other hand, countries such as Brazil, Canada, the Euro area, and Russia moved in the predicted direction. This would suggest that, when there is adjustment toward Big Mac parity, it was mainly in those countries whose exchange rates were somewhat more freely floating vis-à-vis the U.S. dollar. Furthermore, this evidence indicates that the adjustment is primarily through changes in the exchange rate and not through competitive market pressures on the domestic price of the commodity.

	Deviations from Big Mac Purchasing-Power Parity				
	February 2007		April 2002		
Country	Big Mac Prices (converted to U.S. dollars)	Percent Over (+) or Under (−) Valuation Against U.S. Dollar	Big Mac Prices (converted to U.S. dollars)	Percent Over (+) or Under (−) Valuation Against U.S. Dollar	Rate of Change of Big Mac Prices between 2002 and 2007 in U.S. Dollars
United States	**$3.22**	—	**$2.49**	—	**29%**
Switzerland	5.12	+59%	3.81	+53%	34%
Euro area	3.96	+22	2.37	−5	67
Great Britain	3.93	+22	2.88	+16	36
Canada	3.34	+4	2.12	−15	58
Brazil	3.30	+2	1.55	−38	113
Mexico	2.69	−16	2.37	−5	14
Japan	2.30	−28	2.01	−19	14
Russia	1.89	−41	1.25	−50	51
China	1.44	−55	1.27	−49	13

SOURCES: OANDA Corporation (retrieved from www.oanda.com/products/bigmac/bigmac.shtml); and Robert Cumby, "Forecasting Exchange Rates and Relative Prices with the Hamburger Standard: Is What You Want What You Get with McParity?" Georgetown University, May 1997.

in vastly greater dollar volumes than goods and services. In fact, the astounding *daily* volume of foreign exchange transactions exceeds $1.5 trillion, which is more than an entire *month's* worth of world trade in goods and services. The vast majority of these transactions are financial. If investors decide that, say, Canadian assets are a better bet than Japanese assets, the dollar will rise, even if our inflation rate is well above Japan's. For this and other reasons:

> Most economists believe that other factors are much more important than relative price levels for exchange rate determination in the short run. But in the long run, purchasing-power parity could play a more important role.

◾ Market Determination of Exchange Rates: Summary

You have probably noticed a theme here: International trade in financial assets certainly dominates short-run exchange rate changes, may dominate medium-run changes, and also influences long-run changes. We can summarize this discussion of exchange rate determination in freely competitive markets as follows:

1. We expect to find *appreciating* currencies in countries that offer investors *higher rates of return* because these countries will attract capital from all over the world.

2. To some extent, these are the countries that are *growing faster* than average because strong growth tends to produce attractive investment prospects. However, such fast-growing countries will also be importing relatively more than other countries, which tends to pull their currencies *down*.

3. Currency values generally will appreciate in countries with *lower inflation rates* than the rest of the world's, because buyers in foreign countries will demand their goods and thus drive up their currencies.

Reversing each of these arguments, we expect to find *depreciating* currencies in countries with relatively high inflation rates, low interest rates, and poor growth prospects.

◾ WHEN GOVERNMENTS FIX EXCHANGE RATES: THE BALANCE OF PAYMENTS

Some exchange rates today, including the Canadian dollar exchange rate, are as close as one gets to a pure floating rate, since they are essentially left to be determined by the forces of supply and demand without any direct intervention by the country's central bank. Many other exchange rates are not. Indeed, while celebrated economists (such as 1976 Bank of Sweden Nobel Memorial Prize laureate Milton Friedman [1912–2006] of the United States and Harry G. Johnson [1923–1977] of Canada) long emphasized the benefits of floating rates in their capacity to absorb shocks emanating from the international economy, some other well-known economists (such as Canadian-born 1999 Bank of Sweden Nobel Memorial Prize laureate Robert A. Mundell [1932–]) claim that exchange rate fluctuations are so troublesome and destabilizing that the world would be better off with **fixed exchange rates** (if not a single world currency).

Fixed exchange rates are rates set by government decisions and maintained by government actions.

Governments, through their central banks, could intervene in the foreign exchange markets to fix their exchange rates. To do this, the authorities must closely monitor a country's *balance of international payments* to gauge movements in the supply and demand for a currency (see the appendix to this chapter, "Canada's Balance of International Payments," for details about the accounting framework).

To understand what the balance of payments is, look at Figure 6, which depicts a situation that might represent, say, Argentina in the winter of 2001–2002 A well-known example of an overvalued currency, the Argentine peso had been set at par with the U.S. dollar (at $1.00 U.S.) in the early 1990s and was supported at that level by the Argentine government for a decade. Although the supply and demand curves for pesos indicate an equilibrium exchange rate of US$0.50 to the peso (point *E*), the Argentine government held the rate at US$1.00. Notice that, at US$1.00 per peso, more people supply pesos than demand them. In this example, suppliers offer to sell 8 billion pesos per year, but purchasers want to buy only 4 billion.

This gap between the 8 billion pesos that some people wish to sell and the 4 billion pesos that others wish to buy is what we mean by Argentina's **balance of payments deficit**—4 billion pesos (or US$4 billion) per year in this hypothetical case. It appears as the horizontal distance between points *A* and *B* in Figure 6.

How can governments flout market forces in this way? Because sales and purchases on any market must be equal, the excess of quantity supplied over quantity demanded—or 4 billion pesos per year in this example—must be bought by the Argentine government. To purchase these pesos, it must give up some of the foreign currency that it holds as reserves. Thus, the Bank of Argentina would be losing about US$4 billion in reserves per year as the cost of keeping the peso at US$1.

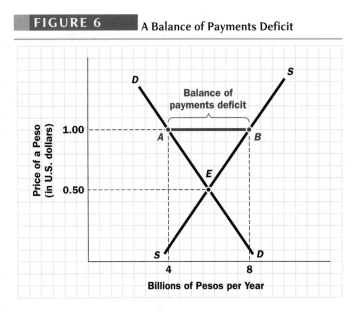

FIGURE 6   A Balance of Payments Deficit

Naturally, this situation cannot persist forever, as the reserves eventually will run out. This is the fatal flaw of a fixed exchange rate system. Once speculators become convinced that the exchange rate can be held for only a short while longer, they will sell the currency in massive amounts rather than hold on to money whose value they expect to fall. That is precisely what began to happen to Argentina in 2001. Lacking sufficient reserves, the Argentine government succumbed to market forces and let the peso float in early 2002. It promptly depreciated.

For a well-known international example of the reverse case, a severely undervalued currency, we can look at contemporary China. Figure 7 depicts demand and supply curves for Chinese yuan that intersect at an equilibrium price of 15 cents per yuan (point *E* in the diagram). Yet, in the example, we suppose that the Chinese authorities are holding the rate at 12 cents. At this rate, the quantity of yuan demanded (1,000 billion) greatly exceeds the quantity supplied (600 billion). The difference is China's **balance of payments surplus**, shown by the horizontal distance *AB*.

China can keep the rate at 12 cents only by selling all the additional yuan that foreigners want to buy—400 billion yuan per year in this example. In return, the country must buy the equivalent amount of U.S. dollars ($48 billion). All of this activity serves to increase China's reserves of U.S. dollars. But notice one important difference between this case and the overvalued peso:

The **balance of payments deficit** is the amount by which the quantity supplied of a country's currency (per year) exceeds the quantity demanded. Balance of payments deficits arise whenever the exchange rate is pegged at an artificially high level.

The **balance of payments surplus** is the amount by which the quantity demanded of a country's currency (per year) exceeds the quantity supplied. Balance of payments surpluses arise whenever the exchange rate is pegged at an artificially low level.

The accumulation of reserves rarely will force a central bank to revalue in the way that losses of reserves can force a devaluation.

This asymmetry is a clear weakness in a fixed exchange rate system. In principle, an exchange rate disequilibrium can be cured either by a *devaluation* by the country with a balance of payments deficit or by an upward *revaluation* by the country with a balance of payments surplus. In practice, though, only deficit countries are forced to act.

Why do surplus countries refuse to revalue? One reason is often a stubborn refusal to recognize some basic economic realities. They tend to view the disequilibrium as a problem only for the deficit countries and, therefore, believe that the deficit countries should take the corrective steps. This view, of course, is nonsense in a worldwide system

FIGURE 7   A Balance of Payments Surplus

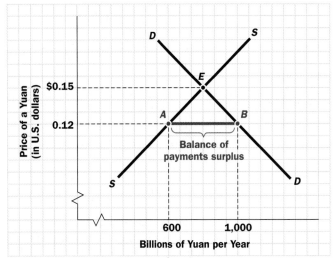

of fixed exchange rates. Some currencies are overvalued *because* some other currencies are undervalued. In fact, the two statements mean exactly the same thing.

The other reason why surplus countries resist upward revaluations is that such actions would make their products more expensive to foreigners and thus cut into their export sales. This, in fact, is presumed to be the main reason why China maintains an undervalued currency despite the protestations of many other nations. China's leaders believe that vibrant export industries are the key to growth and development.

The balance of payments comes in two main parts. The **current account** totes up exports and imports of goods and services, cross-border payments of interest and dividends, and cross-border gifts. It is close, both conceptually and numerically, to what we have called net exports ($X - IM$) in previous chapters. Unlike the United States that has been running large current account deficits for years, largely because of its negative commodity trade balance, Canada's current account balance has been positive in recent years, essentially because of its strong positive commodity trade balance.

> The **current account** balance includes international purchases and sales of goods and services, cross-border interest and dividend payments, and cross-border gifts to and from both private individuals and governments. It is approximately the same as net exports.

But that represents only one part of our balance of payments, for it leaves out all purchases and sales of assets. Purchases of Canadian assets by foreigners bring foreign currency to Canada, and purchases of foreign assets cost us foreign currency. Netting the capital flows in each direction gives us our surplus or deficit on **capital account**. Traditionally, Canada has registered a capital account surplus as a net receiver of foreign investment, which has led, especially in the 1960s and 1970s, to acrimonious debates over the issue of foreign ownership of Canadian industries. While foreign takeovers continue to make the news and raise concerns, since the late 1990s, the net outflow of Canadian capital to foreign countries (that is, a capital account deficit) has become more commonplace.

> The **capital account** balance includes purchases and sales of financial assets to and from citizens and companies of other countries.

In what sense, then, does the overall balance of payments balance? There are two possibilities. If the exchange rate is *floating*, all private transactions—current account plus capital account—must add up to zero because dollars purchased = dollars sold. But if, instead, the exchange rate is *fixed*, as shown in Figures 6 and 7, the two accounts need not balance one another. Government purchases or sales of foreign currency make up the surplus or deficit in the overall balance of payments.

A BRIEF HISTORICAL DIGRESSION: THE GOLD STANDARD AND THE BRETTON WOODS SYSTEM

It is difficult to find examples of strictly fixed exchange rates in historical records. About the only time exchange rates were truly fixed was under the gold standard, at least when it was practised in its ideal form.[3] Officially, it lasted from the nineteenth century until its final collapse during the Great Depression.

The Classical Gold Standard

> The **gold standard** is a way to fix exchange rates by defining each participating currency in terms of gold and allowing holders of each participating currency to convert that currency into gold.

Under the **gold standard**, governments maintained fixed exchange rates by pegging the price of a fixed weight of gold in terms of their domestic currencies and guaranteed convertibility by redeeming notes on demand that had been issued on the basis of gold reserves. As long as each national government set and maintained the price of gold unchanged, the result would be a fixed exchange rate system.

The gold standard posed many problems. Domestic economies were at the mercy of autonomous gold movements and therefore governments could not pursue independent monetary policy. Countries faced with balance of payments difficulties were under continual pressure to deflate their economies. Moreover, since domestic currency was issued on the basis of the amount of domestic gold reserves, the gold standard caused a deflationary bias internationally, since the supply of gold could not keep pace with the long-run growth of the world economy.

---

[3] As a matter of fact, although the gold standard lasted (on and off) for hundreds of years, it was rarely practised in its ideal form. Except for a brief period of fixed exchange rates in the late nineteenth and early twentieth centuries, governments periodically adjusted exchange rates even under the gold standard.

■ The Bretton Woods System

Following the financial chaos of the Great Depression and World War II, representatives of the industrial nations, including John Maynard Keynes of Great Britain, Harry Dexter White of the United States, and Canada's Louis Rasminsky (later to become governor of the Bank of Canada, 1961–1973), met at a hotel in Bretton Woods, New Hampshire, in 1944 to devise a new international monetary environment. The outcome was a hybrid system sometimes referred to as the *gold exchange standard* or, simply, the Bretton Woods system.

Unlike the previous gold standard, under the Bretton Woods system, countries would no longer be obliged to convert their domestic currencies into gold. This convertibility would be limited only to exchanges among central banks. In place of gold, the U.S. dollar was established as the reserve currency, with all other countries agreeing to fix their exchange rates in relation to the U.S. dollar. The final feature of the Bretton Woods system was that the U.S. Federal Reserve System agreed to set the U.S. dollar value to a fixed weight in gold by agreeing to buy and sell gold to maintain the US$35 per ounce price that President Franklin Roosevelt had originally established in 1933. Predictably, as the United States accumulated an ever-growing current account deficit, especially during the 1960s and early 1970s, the overvalued dollar finally triggered the collapse of the Bretton Woods system, when President Richard Nixon announced in 1971 that the United States would no longer buy or sell gold at US$35 per ounce.

Interestingly, Canada was somewhat of a maverick during the Bretton Woods era. As it is shown in Table 3, Canada did not join the international fixed exchange rate system until quite late in 1962 and, moreover, returned to a floating rate in May of 1970, somewhat before the official collapse of the Bretton Woods system in the early 1970s.

TABLE 3							
Successive Canadian Foreign Exchange Rate Regimes Since before Confederation							
Period	1854–1914	1914–1926	1926–1931	1931–1939	1939–1950	1950–1962	1962–1970	1970–present
Regime Type	Fixed (gold standard)	Floating	Fixed (gold standard)	Floating	Fixed, with periodic adjustment	Floating	Fixed	Floating

■ ADJUSTMENT MECHANISMS UNDER FIXED EXCHANGE RATES

Under the Bretton Woods system, devaluation was viewed as a last resort, to be used only after other methods of adjusting to payments imbalances had failed. What were these other methods?

We encountered most of them in our earlier discussion of exchange rate determination in freely competitive markets. Any factor that *increases the demand* for, say, Argentine pesos or that *reduces the supply* will push the value of the peso upward—if it is free to adjust. But if the exchange rate is pegged, the balance of payments deficit will shrink instead. (Try this for yourself using Figure 6 on page 403.)

Recalling our earlier discussion of the factors that underlie the demand and supply curves, we see that one way a nation can shrink its balance of payments deficit is to *reduce its aggregate demand*, thereby discouraging imports and cutting down its demand for foreign currency. Another is to *lower its rate of inflation*, thereby encouraging exports and discouraging imports. Finally, it can *raise its interest rates* to attract more foreign capital.

In other words, deficit nations are expected to follow restrictive monetary and fiscal policies *voluntarily*, just as they would have done more or less *automatically* under the classical gold standard. However, just as under the gold standard, this medicine is often unpalatable.

A surplus nation could, of course, take the opposite measures: pursuing *expansionary* monetary and fiscal policies to increase economic growth and *lower* interest rates. By increasing the supply of the country's currency and reducing the demand for it, such actions would reduce that nation's balance of payments surplus. But surplus countries often do not relish the inflation that accompanies expansionary policies, and so, once again, they leave the burden of adjustment to the deficit nations. The general point about fixed exchange rates is that:

> Under a system of fixed exchange rates, a country's government loses some control over its domestic economy. Sometimes balance of payments considerations may force it to contract its economy in order to cut down its demand for foreign currency, even though domestic needs call for expansion. At other times, the domestic economy may need to be reined in, but balance of payments considerations suggest expansion.

That was certainly the case in Argentina in 2002, when interest rates soared to attract foreign capital, and the government pursued contractionary fiscal policies to curb the country's appetite for imports. Both contributed to a long and deep recession. Argentina took the bitter medicine needed to defend its fixed exchange rate for quite a while. But high unemployment eventually led to riots in the streets, toppled the government, and persuaded the Argentine authorities to abandon the fixed exchange rate.

■ WHY TRY TO FIX EXCHANGE RATES?

In view of these and other problems with fixed exchange rates, why did the international financial community work so hard to maintain them for so many years? And why do some nations today still fix their exchange rates? The answer is that floating exchange rates also pose problems.

Chief among these worries is the possibility that freely floating rates might prove to be highly variable rates, thereby adding an unwanted element of risk to foreign trade. For example, if the exchange rate is $1.50 to the euro, then a Parisian dress priced at 200 euros will cost $300. But if the euro appreciates to $1.60, that same dress would cost $320. A Canadian department store thinking of buying the dress may need to place the order far in advance and will want to know the cost *in dollars*. It may be worried about the possibility that the value of the euro will rise, making the dress cost more than $300. And such worries brought about by exchange rate risk might inhibit trade.

There are two responses to this concern. First, freely floating rates might prove to be fairly stable in practice. Prices of most ordinary goods and services, for example, are determined by supply and demand in free markets and do not fluctuate unduly. Unfortunately, experience since 1973 has dashed this hope (see Figure 1 on page 394). Exchange rates have proved to be extremely volatile, which is why some observers now favour greater fixity in exchange rates.

A second possibility is that business firms can find means to evade exchange rate risks. Consider the department store example. If each euro costs $1.50 today, the department store manager can assure herself of paying exactly $300 for the dress several months from now, say six months later, by making the following simple arrangement. All she needs to do is borrow $300 now from a Canadian bank, use the $300 to purchase, at the going $1.50 to the euro exchange rate, the 200 euros needed to buy the Parisian dress, and deposit the 200 euros in a safe bank in Paris until the payment comes due six months later. The department manager will need to pay the going lending interest rate on the dollars being borrowed but, on the other hand, she will be earning the going deposit interest rate on the euros that are being held. The department store manager ends up paying just a bit more than $300 if the lending interest rate on Canadian dollars is higher than the deposit rate on euros, and she might even pay slightly less than $300 if the deposit rate on euros is higher than the lending rate on Canadian dollars. The manager has hedged against foreign exchange risk.

In reality, things are even less complicated for the department store manager. For a small fee, her bank can do all these operations on her behalf, through a device called the **forward foreign exchange market**. Her bank will borrow the Canadian dollars on the Canadian money market for six months, purchase the euros right away, and have the counterpart bank in Europe lend the euros on the money market there until the end of the six months. When the payment of the dress is due, six months later, her bank will deliver the promised 200 euros.

> It is possible for business firms to protect themselves from the risks of fluctuating currencies, for as long as a year in advance, through the forward foreign exchange market.

Still, firms can do little to protect themselves from exchange rate changes that could arise many years in the future. Few contracts on foreign currencies, such as forward contracts, last more than a year, and only for the better-known currencies. In particular, businesses cannot protect themselves against speculators who get carried away from time to time, moving currency rates in ways that are difficult to understand, that frustrate the intentions of governments, and that devastate both businesses and households—as happened in Mexico in 1995 and in Southeast Asia in 1997.

Indeed, there are widespread fears that speculators can generate wild gyrations in foreign exchange rates. The fears that speculative activity in freely competitive markets can completely destabilize markets, although occasionally valid, are often unfounded. The reason is simple.

> To make profits, international currency speculators must *buy* a currency when its value is low (thus helping to support the currency by pushing up its demand curve) and *sell* it when its value is high (thus holding down the price by adding to the supply curve). This means that successful speculators must come into the market as *buyers* when demand is weak (or when supply is strong) and come in as *sellers* when demand is strong (or when supply is scant). In doing so, they help limit price fluctuations. Looked at the other way around, speculators can *destabilize* prices only if they are systematically willing to lose money.[4]

Notice the stark—and ironic—contrast to the system of fixed exchange rates in which speculation often leads to the wild "runs" on currencies that are on the verge of devaluation—as happened in Mexico in 1995, several Southeast Asian countries in 1997–1998, Brazil in 1999, and Argentina in 2001. Speculative activity, which may well be *destabilizing* under fixed rates, is more likely to be *stabilizing* under floating rates.[5]

Despite all of the problems, international trade has flourished under floating exchange rates. So perhaps exchange rate risk is not as burdensome as some people think.

The margin note: *Forward foreign exchange markets allow business firms to avoid the risk of fluctuations in foreign exchange rates for as long as one year for a small fee.*

■ THE CURRENT "NONSYSTEM"

The international financial system today is an eclectic blend of fixed and floating exchange rates, with no grand organizing principle. Indeed, it is so diverse that it is often called a "nonsystem."

Some currencies are still pegged in the old Bretton Woods manner. One prominent example is China, which maintains a nearly fixed value for its currency by standing ready to buy or sell U.S. dollars as necessary. (In recent years, it has been buying steadily.) A few small countries, such as Panama and Ecuador, have taken the more extreme step of actually adopting the U.S. dollar as their domestic currencies. Other nations tie their currencies to a hypothetical "basket" of several currencies, rather than to a single currency.

More nations, however, let their exchange rates float, although not always freely. Such floating rates change slightly on a day-to-day basis, and market forces determine the basic trends, up or down. But governments do not hesitate to intervene to moderate exchange movements whenever they feel such actions are appropriate.

---

[4] See Test Yourself Question 4 at the end of the chapter.
[5] After their respective currency crises in 1995 and 1999, both Mexico and Brazil floated their currencies. Each weathered the subsequent international financial storms rather nicely. But Argentina, with its fixed exchange rate, struggled.

The stated purpose of the Bank of Canada is to intervene in the foreign exchange markets on behalf of the federal government to ensure orderly foreign exchange markets. Prior to September 1998, interventions were typically aimed at ironing out what were deemed to be transitory fluctuations. Hence, the Bank of Canada would intervene systematically in the foreign exchange markets to smooth out exchange rate movements, thereby seeking to reduce volatility. For example, during the turbulent period between January 1995 to September 1998 (with currency crises in Mexico, Asia, and Russia), the Bank of Canada intervened on more than 150 days both to smooth out the fluctuations *and* to change the direction of the exchange rate movement. The problem, however, was that one cannot easily distinguish in advance movements caused by so-called "fundamental" factors behind the exchange rate from movements due to supposed "transitory" elements.

Because of this, since 1998, policy changed from intervening systematically to mitigate exchange rate fluctuations to one of intervening on a discretionary basis only in what the monetary authorities now deem to be "the most exceptional of circumstances." Since 1998, however, the Bank of Canada has not intervened at all (not even when the Canadian dollar reached US$1.07 in August 2007), thereby making the Canadian dollar one of the most freely fluctuating exchange rates in the world today. Indeed, in contrast to the Canadian dollar, most floating exchange rates are not *pure* floats. Most countries that have adopted floating rate regimes since the breakdown of the Bretton Woods system of fixed exchange rates have adopted hybrid forms. The terms *managed float* or *dirty float* have been coined to describe this mongrel system, in which the central banking authorities intervene systematically to manage the movement of the exchange rate.

The Role of the IMF

During the 1930s, countries experienced economic instabilities that could not be managed by any one national government. Some of the most serious problems were the exchange rate instabilities caused particularly by short-term capital movement, as well as the lack of adjusting mechanisms to overcome liquidity problems when a country faced a balance-of-payments crisis. The International Monetary Fund (IMF), which was established at Bretton Woods in 1944, was set up to deal with these difficulties. Instead of engaging in competitive currency devaluations that would spread the crisis to other trading countries, a country that ran into serious financial trouble would get loans from the IMF.

By the 1980s, following the demise of Bretton Woods, the rise of monetarism and the growing popularity of more conservative economic policies in the advanced market economies of North America and Western Europe, the role of the IMF began to change. As before, the IMF kept making loans to countries facing financial difficulties, but now with significantly more strings attached. Loans were conditional on countries pursuing policies of "structural adjustment." For example, if the country had a large current account deficit—as is normally the case when countries come to the IMF—the IMF would typically insist on contractionary fiscal and monetary policies to curb the country's appetite for imports. Such austerity measures would often be coupled with the abandonment of price support programs and the privatization of public assets, so as to make the economy more price-competitive and attractive for foreign investment. These sweeping policies of "structural adjustments" often spelled a domestic recession.

During the 1990s, the IMF found itself at the epicentre of a series of very visible economic crises: in Mexico in 1995, in Southeast Asia in 1997, in Russia in 1998, and in Brazil in 1999. In 2001, Turkey and Argentina ran into trouble and appealed to the IMF for help. Although each case was different, they shared some common elements.

Most of these crises were precipitated by the collapse of a fixed exchange rate pegged to the U.S. dollar. In each case, the currency plummeted, with ruinous consequences. Questions were raised about the country's ability to pay its bills. In each case, the IMF arrived on the scene with both money and lots of advice, determined to stave off default. In the end, each country suffered through a severe recession—or worse.

The IMF's increased visibility with its well-advertised regime of austerity measures imposed on numerous countries in Latin America, Eastern Europe, and Southeast Asia naturally brought it increased criticism. Some critics complained that the IMF sets excessively strict conditions on its client-states, requiring them, for example, to cut their government budgets and raise interest rates during recessions—which makes bad economic situations even worse. One of the most celebrated of these critics is none other than the former chief economist of the World Bank and the 2001 co-recipient of the Bank of Sweden Prize in Economics, Joseph E. Stiglitz (1943–). For instance, during the Asian financial crisis, the IMF imposed high interest rates and fiscal prudence on Asian countries that already had balanced public budgets—in an attempt to stop capital outflows. But capital outflow did not stop and debt service rose because of the higher interest rates! Stiglitz has argued quite forcefully that, instead, the IMF should have encouraged these countries to follow Keynesian policies and reflate their economies.

Other critics worried that the IMF was serving as a bill collector for banks and other financial institutions from the United States and other rich countries. Because the banks loaned money irresponsibly, these critics argued, they deserved to lose some of it. By bailing them out of their losses, the IMF simply encouraged more reckless behaviour in the future.

Suggestions for reform are everywhere and some minor changes have been made in the IMF's procedures. But the debate rages on.

The Volatile Canadian Dollar: Is It Both a Commodity and Energy Currency?

As mentioned earlier, floating exchange rates have not proved to be stable exchange rates. No currency illustrates this point better than the experience of the Canadian dollar vis-à-vis the U.S. dollar since the 1970s.

As shown in Figure 1 at the beginning of this chapter, the Canadian dollar was roughly at par with the U.S. dollar at the end of the Bretton Woods era. Since the mid-1970s, the Canadian dollar went through two successive waves of depreciation until it hit bottom at the beginning of 2002. The first wave was associated with the oil price shocks of the 1970s, followed by the major recession of the early 1980s. Being the only country of the G7 industrialized nations that is a major exporter of primary products (with the latter constituting somewhat less than one-third of our overall commodity exports), Canada was hit badly, not only by the oil price hikes that caused havoc in Canada's industrial heartland, but also by the accompanying slump in primary commodity prices, as industrial economies faced slower growth and descended into recession.

Things did turn around to some degree during the late 1980s, as strong economic growth throughout the world pushed primary commodity prices upward and, with this, the value of the Canadian dollar. However, following the 1990–1991 recession, the Canadian dollar once more continued its downward trend. Low primary commodity prices in the 1990s, coupled with strong economic growth during the Clinton era in the United States, led to a soaring U.S. dollar vis-à-vis the anemic Canadian dollar. The latter hit bottom only after the American economy slipped into recession, particularly after 2001. Some analysts, especially in the media, have attributed the decline of the Canadian dollar in the 1990s to the political instabilities caused by the constitutional wrangling over the Charlottetown Accord in 1992 and the Quebec referendum of 1995, but we would argue that these political factors were, at best, of secondary importance. In any case, since then, despite the continued constitutional stalemate, we have witnessed an unprecedented reversal of the fate of the Canadian dollar, with it reaching heights not seen in three decades.

Despite Canada's importance as an exporter of manufactured products, the value of the Canadian dollar still remains strongly tied to the volatile behaviour of primary commodity prices. Indeed, much like the currencies of Australia and New Zealand, the Canadian dollar is still viewed as a "commodity currency"—a currency whose international exchange value mirrors mainly the movement of commodity prices. This fact is

POLICY DEBATE

Should Canada Join a North American Monetary Union?

As mentioned earlier, in 1999, several members of the European Union established a single currency—the euro—in the hope of creating a large unified market like that of the United States. This was the culminating step in moving toward a full European monetary union. The 15 countries of the European Union that, at the time of writing, have adopted the euro as their home currency constitute the *euro zone*. Their move from fixed exchange rates to a single currency is a great economic experience, which was followed closely by economic and financial observers in other countries.

In Canada, opinion about the desirability of greater North American monetary integration seems to have followed the ebbs and flows of the Canadian dollar. With the international value of the Canadian dollar hitting unprecedented lows and with our trade with the United States peaking under NAFTA during the late 1990s and the early 2000s, a growing number of academics, pundits, and politicians in Canada began to propose greater monetary integration with the United States. This reached a crescendo just after the launching of the euro in 1999 when, among other things, a motion to study the possibility of a currency union in North America, especially along the lines of the European Economic and Monetary Union (EMU), was proposed by the political opposition and defeated in the federal House of Commons . However, several alternatives to the current floating rate have been proposed, including a fixed exchange rate, the abandonment of our national currency in favour of the unilateral adoption of the U.S. dollar (commonly described as "dollarization"), as well as a North American Monetary Union (NAMU) to launch a new, single currency in this hemisphere.

Interest in greater monetary integration appears to be strongest in those commodities and services sectors of the Canadian economy that are involved in foreign trade. Firms in the foreign sector often view the Canadian dollar as a "nuisance cost," largely because their revenues are in U.S. funds but their costs are in Canadian dollars. A rising value of the Canadian dollar puts a squeeze on firms engaged in the export sector. Hence, as we discussed earlier, industries with a certain degree of exchange rate exposure must engage in exchange rate risk-management strategies. Exchange rate hedging is commonplace, but hedging can occur for only about one year ahead, so long-term projections of sale revenues are rendered more uncertain because of possible exchange rate fluctuations.

Those partial to greater monetary integration have at times referred to at least one other important benefit of a NAMU that is often connected with the name of a famous Canadian-born econo-

mist and Nobel Memorial Prize laureate, Robert A. Mundell. Mundell has argued that the regional configuration of a currency area is very important. Take Canada, where there is sufficient industrial diversity across regions with, say, manufacturing in Ontario (whose growth depends on low energy costs) and oil in Alberta (whose growth depends on high energy costs). A common external shock to these regions, such as a major jump in the international price of oil, would naturally hurt Ontario and benefit Alberta. However, the existence of a floating exchange rate would compound the negative effect on Ontario, since Canada's exchange rate would also be rising with the increase in the price of oil. In this case, both Ontario and Alberta would be better off either with a fixed exchange rate vis-à-vis the principal importer of Canada's exports—the United States—or an outright monetary union. Canada's floating exchange rate becomes a negative externality, the removal of which would be beneficial to the Canadian economy.

While the above can be considered tangible benefits, there are also associated costs of abandoning our national currency. Indeed, these are more than merely the psychic cost of losing a national symbol. Despite the problems raised by Mundell and others, opponents of a NAMU, such as Canadian economist David E. W. Laidler (1938–), point out that Canada's current floating rate normally does serve well as a shock absorber in times of crisis in the global economy, as when commodity prices fell during the Asian crisis. The disappearance of the Canadian dollar would mean that we would have one less instrument of macroeconomic stabilization.

Moreover, the elimination of the Canadian dollar would take away other important instruments of macroeconomic policy. With a "one size fits all" for monetary policy within the NAMU, a North American central bank would not cater sufficiently to Canada's regional needs. Moreover, if we were to adopt the EMU blueprint, Keynesian critics of NAMU argue that fiscal policy would also be heavily constrained, so that a more active fiscal policy would no longer be possible in any one region of the NAMU. Much like provinces in a federation, financial markets would probably prevent "excessive" borrowing for any one regional government to pursue active fiscal policy unless all regions within the NAMU moved in tandem.

Given these conflicting positions, it is no wonder that most Canadians remain wedded to the status quo of an independent, floating Canadian dollar. However, public opinion can always change, especially if the Canadian dollar were to sink to even lower depths than those reached during the 1990s and early in the 2000s.

reflected in a seminal equation developed by researchers at the Bank of Canada to forecast the evolution of the Canada–U.S. exchange rate. Changes in a specific measure of the Canada–U.S. exchange rate depended on three key market "fundamentals:" a primary commodity price index (excluding energy), an energy price index (mainly oil, natural gas, and electricity), and a measure of the Canada–U.S. short-term interest rates differential (the difference in the Canada–U.S. 90-day commercial paper rate).

According to recent empirical research at the Bank of Canada, an *increase* in international commodity prices and an *increase* in Canadian short-term interest rates vis-à-vis

U.S. rates still seem generally to lead to an *appreciation* of the Canadian dollar, as expected. However, the role of energy prices in influencing Canada's exchange rate seems to have changed over time. In the original formula developed at the Bank of Canada based on the experience of the pre-1990s era, an *increase* in world energy prices, all other things equal, would tend to lead to *depreciation* in the international value of the Canadian dollar. Hence, during the period when Canada had not yet become an important energy net exporter, an increase in, say, the international price of oil would have slowed down the world economy and would have reduced demand for Canadian exports, thereby putting downward pressure on Canada's exchange rate, as occurred during the late 1970s and early 1980s.

Since the 1990s, Canada has become a very significant energy net exporter in the context of the North American energy market, whose development was first facilitated by the Canada–U.S. Free Trade Agreement and subsequently reinforced under the North American Free Trade Agreement. Because of Canada's vast oil sands reserves and the new continental energy environment, when the price of oil goes up, this now pushes up the demand for Canadian dollars and therefore leads to an appreciation in the international value of Canada's currency. Some would suggest that, given the growing importance of our energy exports, Canadian industry is now ailing from the so-called **Dutch disease**—a jump in the international price of oil puts upward pressure on our exchange rate and bleeds our manufacturing exports. Thus, the continued rise in Canada's exchange rate accompanying the climbing price of oil in recent years spells difficult times ahead for Canada's manufacturing exports.

The term **Dutch disease** refers to the Netherlands' experience in the 1960s, when the discovery of North Sea gas pushed the exchange rate so high that Holland's manufacturing sector became less competitive and the country experienced some deindustrialization.

PUZZLE RESOLVED: *What Drove Up the Canadian Dollar in Recent Years?*

We have learned in this chapter that the Canadian dollar not only remains as a commodity currency, reflecting Canada's traditional position as exporter of natural resources, but also, since the 1990s, it has also become what we can describe as an "energy" currency or a petrodollar moving somewhat in tandem with oil prices as Canada assumes an ever-increasing role as an important exporter of oil and gas to the United States. The sustained growth of the domestic economy since 2001, accelerated by consumer spending, with both profit and interest rates inching upward, has also contributed to a spectacular rise in the international value of Canada's currency. Moreover, the large U.S. current account deficit that continues to weaken the international value of the U.S. dollar feeds expectations of a still higher Canadian dollar.

Whether this rising Canadian dollar will be sustainable over time will depend on the dynamism of the Canadian manufacturing sector, whose exports to the United States rose tremendously during the 1990s partly because of the opening up of the U.S. market under freer trade but mostly because of a weak Canadian dollar. Anecdotal evidence was often put forth by critics of a floating Canadian dollar that our undervalued currency of the 1990s discouraged entrepreneurial dynamism—the so-called "lazy manufacturer hypothesis"—and had slowed the growth in investment and productivity in Canadian manufacturing. If that hypothesis is indeed true, it remains to be seen whether Canadian manufacturing will rise to the challenge imposed by the rising value of our currency. Since firms in the export sector can no longer rely on a low exchange rate, will the Canadian manufacturing sector be sufficiently dynamic to improve its competitiveness by investing more and taking advantage of the low cost of imported robotized machinery? Or, will it succumb to the infamous Dutch disease and plunge Canada back into its traditional role of "hewer of wood and drawer of water"? That is the challenge of the decade.

SUMMARY

1. **Exchange rates** state the value of one currency in terms of other currencies, and thus translate one country's prices into the currencies of other nations. Exchange rates therefore influence patterns of world trade.

2. If governments do not interfere by buying or selling their currencies, exchange rates will be determined in freely competitive markets by the usual laws of supply and demand. Such a system is said to be based on **floating exchange rates**.

3. Demand for a nation's currency is derived from foreigners' desires to purchase that country's goods and services or to invest in its assets. Under floating rates, anything that increases the demand for a nation's currency will cause its exchange rate to **appreciate**.

4. Supply of a nation's currency is derived from the desire of that country's citizens to purchase foreign goods and services or to invest in foreign assets. Under floating rates, anything that increases the supply of a nation's currency will cause its exchange rate to **depreciate**.

5. Purchasing-power parity plays a major role in very-long-run exchange rate movements. The **purchasing-power parity theory** states that relative price levels in any two countries determine the exchange rate between their currencies. Therefore, countries with relatively low inflation rates normally will have appreciating currencies.

6. Over shorter periods, however, purchasing-power parity has little influence over exchange rate movements. The pace of economic activity and, especially, the level of interest rates exert greater influences.

7. Capital movements are typically the dominant factor in exchange rate determination in the short and medium runs. A nation that offers international investors higher interest rates, or better prospective returns on investments, will typically see its currency appreciate.

8. An exchange rate can be fixed at a nonequilibrium level if the government is willing and able to mop up any excess of quantity supplied over quantity demanded, or provide any excess of quantity demanded over quantity supplied. In the first case, the country is suffering from a **balance of payments deficit** because of its overvalued currency. In the second case, an undervalued currency has given it a **balance of payments surplus**.

9. The **gold standard** was a system of **fixed exchange rates** in which the value of every nation's currency was set in terms of gold. The system created problems because a nation could not pursue an independant monetary policy and would impose harsh conditions of deflation on countries with a balance-of-payments deficit.

10. After World War II, the gold standard was replaced by the **Bretton Woods system**, in which exchange rates were fixed in terms of U.S. dollars, and the dollar was in turn tied to gold. The system broke up officially by 1973, partly as a result of the U.S. dollar abandoning its link with gold in 1971, as the U.S. dollar had become chronically overvalued.

11. Since 1971, the world has moved toward a system of relatively free exchange rates, but with plenty of exceptions. We now have a thoroughly mixed system of **"dirty" or "managed" float**, which continues to evolve and adapt.

12. Floating rates are not without their problems. For example, importers and exporters justifiably worry about fluctuations in exchange rates.

13. Under floating exchange rates, normally, speculators stabilize rather than destabilize exchange rates, because that is how they make profits.

14. The Canadian dollar fell dramatically from the mid-1970s to the mid-1980s. It then rose somewhat during the late 1980s, only to fall to even lower depths during the 1990s. It hit bottom early in 2002 and has since shown a spectacular rise in the Canada–U.S. exchange rate, recouping all of its losses of the last three decades.

15. The Bank of Canada equation says that the Canadian dollar vis-à-vis the U.S. dollar goes up when interest rates in Canada rise relative to those in the U.S., and when the prices of energy and primary commodities tend to move up.

KEY TERMS

Exchange rate 394

Appreciation 395

Depreciation 395

Devaluation 395

Revaluation 395

Floating exchange rates 396

Purchasing-power parity theory 400

Fixed exchange rates 402

Balance of payments deficit and surplus 403

Current account 404

Capital account 404

Gold standard 404

Bretton Woods system 405

Forward foreign exchange market 407

International Monetary Fund (IMF) 408

"Managed" or "dirty" float 408

"Dutch disease" 411

TEST YOURSELF

1. Use supply and demand diagrams to analyze the effect of the following actions on the exchange rate between the Canadian and U.S. dollars:

   a. The United States closes its domestic market to foreign competition and abrogates NAFTA.

   b. Investors come to believe that the values on the New York Stock Exchange will fall.

   c. The Federal Reserve cuts interest rates in the United States.

   d. To help solve problems in Afghanistan, the Canadian government offers the country massive foreign aid.

   e. The United States has a recession, while Canada booms.

   f. Inflation in the United States exceeds that in Canada.

2. For each of the following transactions, indicate how it would affect the Canadian balance of payments if exchange rates were fixed:

   a. You spent the summer travelling in Europe.

   b. Your uncle in the United States sent you $20 as a birthday present.

   c. You bought a new Honda, made in Japan.

   d. You bought a new Honda, made in Ontario.

   e. You sold some stock you own on the Tokyo Stock Exchange.

3. Suppose each of the transactions listed in Test Yourself Question 2 was done by many Canadians. Indicate how each would affect the international value of the dollar if exchange rates were floating.

4. We learned in this chapter that successful speculators buy a currency when demand is weak and sell it when demand is strong. Use supply and demand diagrams for two different periods (one with weak demand, the other with strong demand) to show why this activity will limit price fluctuations.

DISCUSSION QUESTIONS

1. What items do you own or routinely consume that are produced abroad? From what countries do these items come? Suppose Canadians decided to buy fewer of these things. How would that affect the exchange rates between the dollar and these currencies?

2. If the dollar appreciates relative to the euro, will the German camera you have wanted become more or less expensive? What effect do you imagine this change will have on Canadian demand for German cameras? Does the Canadian demand curve for euros, therefore, slope upward or downward? Explain.

3. During the first half of the 1980s, inflation in (West) Germany was consistently lower than that in Canada. What, then, does the purchasing-power parity theory predict should have happened to the exchange rate between the mark and the dollar between 1982 and 1987? (Look back at Table 1 to see what actually happened.)

4. How are the problems of a country faced with a balance of payments deficit similar to those posed by a government regulation that holds the price of milk above the equilibrium level? (*Hint:* Think of each in terms of a supply–demand diagram.)

5. Under the old gold standard, what do you think happened to world prices when a huge gold strike occurred in California in 1849? What do you think happened when the world went without any important new gold strikes for 20 years or so?

6. Explain why the members of the Bretton Woods conference in 1944 wanted to establish a system of fixed exchange rates. What flaw led to the ultimate breakdown of the system in 1973?

7. Suppose you want to reserve a hotel room in London for the coming summer but are worried that the value of the pound may rise between now and then, making the room too expensive for your budget. Explain how a bank could relieve you of this worry. (Don't actually try it. In this case, banks deal only in large sums!)

8. In 2003 and 2004, market forces raised the international value of the Japanese yen. Why do you think the government of Japan was unhappy about this currency appreciation? (*Hint:* Japan was trying to emerge from a recession at the time.) If they wanted to stop the yen's appreciation, what actions could the Bank of Japan (Japan's central bank) and the U.S. Federal Reserve have taken? Why might the central banks have failed in this attempt?

APPENDIX *Canada's Balance of International Payments*

In this appendix, we provide some additional information about Canada's balance of payments and national accounting.

As pointed out on page 404, the balance of payments (*BP*) is made up of two accounts—the current account balance (*CAB*) and the capital account balance (*KAB*), which in Canada is called the *capital and financial account.* In a world of floating exchange rates, the balance of payments is zero or close to zero, but whenever the central bank makes an intervention on the foreign exchange market, the balance of payments is positive or negative and equal to the change in the official foreign reserves position of the government (ΔOR). We thus have:

$$BP = CAB + KAB = \Delta OR$$

But whereas Statistics Canada is able to monitor receipts and payments on the current account, it is much more difficult to record with precision the acquisition or sale of foreign assets by Canadians or the acquisition and sale of domestic assets by foreigners. As a result, there are errors and omissions, mostly attributed to the capital account measures, such that the balance of payments is brought back to the known change in official foreign reserves only by the addition of this statistical discrepancy (*ERR*):

$$BP = CAB + KAB + ERR = \Delta OR$$

From a national accounting point of view, all of these elements must sum to zero, so that the *accounting* balance of payments (*ABP*) is such that:

$$ABP = CAB + KAB + ERR - \Delta OR = 0$$

In the case where there is no error term, and with no change in official foreign reserves (as it should be in a floating exchange rate regime, as pointed out page 404), whenever the current account is in surplus, the capital account must be in deficit, with identical absolute numbers, and vice versa, because then:

$$CAB + KAB = 0$$

The Canadian balance of payments for 2007 is shown in Table 4. An entry with a positive sign (+) represents receipts of funds by the domestic economy, an inflow of funds, and thus a demand for Canadian dollars; these transactions tend to raise the value of the Canadian dollar (expressed in foreign currencies, say, in American dollars). Entries with a negative sign (−) represent payments abroad, that is an outflow of funds, and thus a supply of Canadian dollars; these transactions tend to diminish the value of the Canadian dollar.

For instance, looking first at the current account, Canadian exports of goods result in receipts of funds, whereas Canadian imports result in payments. Money spent by foreign tourists in Canada is included in

TABLE 4				
Canada's Balance of Payments Accounts, 2007				
	Receipts, Inflows	Payments, Outflows	Balance	Balance
A. Current Account Lines, 12 + 34, *CAB*				**+14**
1. Goods	+465	−415	+50	
2. Services	+67	−87	−20	
12. *Trade balance, X − IM,* Lines 1 + 2			**+30**	
3. Investment income	+63	−79	−16	
4. Current transfers	+10	−10	0	
34. *NFY,* Lines 3 + 4	**−16**			
B. Capital Account, *KAB*				**−13**
Increase in claims on nonresidents (excluding increase in official foreign reserves)		−159		
Increase in liabilities to non-residents	+146			
C. Statistical discrepancy, *ERR*				**+4**
Balance of Payments, *BP,* Lines A + B + C				**+5**
D. Increase in official foreign reserves		−5		**−5**
***ABP,* Lines A + B + C + D**	0			

Note: Numbers are in billions of dollars. A minus sign denotes a payment, an outflow of capital resulting from an increase in claims on nonresidents, an increase in official reserves, or a decrease in liabilities to nonresidents.

SOURCE: Statistics Canada, *Canada's Balance of International Payments,* Catalogue No. 67-001-XIE.

receipts and is part of services. Travel expenditures of Canadians when they are abroad represent payments. Similarly, looking now at the investment income section of the current account balance, when Canadians receive investment income from abroad, such as profits, interests, or dividends, these are receipts. By contrast, when Canadian companies pay interests and dividends to foreign businesses, these are payments made abroad.

Looking now at the capital account, when Canadians purchase foreign companies, foreign bonds, or foreign shares, or when they establish deposits abroad, there is a capital outflow. There is an increase in Canadian assets held abroad, or an increase in the claims on nonresidents. Canadians are supplying Canadian dollars to acquire foreign currency. Such transactions thus carry a negative sign, and these transactions tend to diminish the value of the Canadian dollar.

Reciprocally, when foreigners purchase Canadian companies, Canadian bonds, or Canadian shares, or when they establish deposits in Canadian banks, there is a capital inflow. Such transactions carry a positive sign. There is an increase in Canadian liabilities to nonresidents, or an increase in the claims of nonresidents on the Canadian economy. Foreigners demand Canadian dollars to purchase Canadian assets, and these transactions tend to increase the value of the Canadian dollar. Thus, when foreigners purchase Canadian assets, this tends to raise the value of the Canadian dollar (but it tends to reduce its value later, when investment income is being paid abroad).

Looking at the data for 2007, we see that Canada has a large positive trade balance in goods and services, which in previous chapters we identified as net exports, $X - IM$, and which amounts to $30 billion (line 12). This is however partially compensated for by large *net* interest and dividend payments to the rest of world, to the tune of $16 billion. In other words, net foreign income, which we called *NFY* in Appendix B of Chapter 9, is negative, and equal to –$16 billion (line 34). This negative number arises because Canada is still an international net debtor, with foreigners having more claims on the Canadian economy than Canadians have claims on nonresidents. Adding the trade balance and net foreign income yields a current account surplus, with the current account balance, *CAB*, being positive and equal to +$14 billion (line A).

The capital account balance, *KAB*, is in deficit, and that deficit is equal to –$13 billion (line B), meaning that Canadians have spent more funds to acquire foreign assets than foreigners have invested in Canada. However, the Bank of Canada has declared that the value of the change in its official foreign reserves (ΔOR) has been +$5 billion (line D, but this increase in official foreign reserves is an increase of claims on nonresidents—acquired by supplying Canadian dollars—and hence it carries a negative sign, as shown).[6] This implies that there has been a statistical discrepancy of +$4 billion, and that most likely the true capital account balance is instead –$9 billion.

If things continue at this pace, Canada soon will not be an international debtor anymore; instead, it will become an international creditor. Its stock of claims on nonresidents will soon be larger than its stock of liabilities to the rest of the world.

---

[6] Even if the Bank of Canada does not intervene on foreign exchange markets (a pure floating exchange regime), official foreign reserves will usually rise because interest income on foreign assets, earned in foreign currency, will be added to existing reserves. Thus, despite floating exchange rates, the Canadian balance of payments, *BP*, is close to but not equal to zero.

19

EXCHANGE RATES AND THE MACROECONOMY

Canada hasn't intervened to influence the Canadian dollar since 1998.

DAVID DODGE, 2001–2008 GOVERNOR OF THE BANK OF CANADA, MAY 2007

The nations of the world are locked together in an uneasy economic union. Fluctuations in foreign growth, inflation, and interest rates profoundly affect the Canadian economy. Fluctuations in world commodity prices or energy prices also have a dramatic impact on the different regions of Canada. Stock market crashes abroad and financial and banking panics in foreign countries can also have strong implications for the Canadian economy. Economic events that originate in our country—and even more so those that originate in the United States—reverberate around the globe. Anyone who ignores these international linkages cannot hope to understand how the world economy works.

The macroeconomic model we developed in earlier chapters does not go far enough because it only alluded to such crucial influences as exchange rates and international financial movements. The previous chapter showed how major macroeconomic variables such as gross domestic product (GDP), domestic prices, world commodity prices, and interest rates affect exchange rates. In this chapter, we complete the circle by studying how changes in the exchange rate affect the domestic economy. Then we bring international capital flows into the picture and learn how monetary and fiscal policy work in an **open economy**. In particular, we build a model suitable for a *medium-sized open* economy with *substantial capital flows* and a *floating exchange rate*—in short, a model meant to resemble Canada.

> An **open economy** is one that trades with other nations in goods and services, and perhaps also trades in financial assets.

CONTENTS

ISSUE: *Should the Canadian Government Try to Stop the Canadian Dollar from Rising?*

The United States is Canada's major trading partner. As we already observed in the previous chapter, the Canadian dollar reached its lowest value ever relative to the U.S. dollar in February 2002, when one Canadian dollar was worth only US$0.618. At the time of writing this book, the Canadian dollar is trading nearly at par with the U.S. dollar—an appreciation of about 60 percent over five years. While most Canadian snowbirds who spend their winters in the southern regions of the United States welcome the rise of the Canadian dollar, Canadian manufacturers and producers of wood, paper, and pulp products have been complaining that such rapid changes in the exchange rate have damaged their businesses; they have lost export and domestic markets to their American rivals, and they are unable to adapt to the overly rapid appreciation of our domestic currency.

Some of the affected trade organizations have urged the Canadian government and the Bank of Canada to stop, or at least to slow down, the rise of the Canadian dollar. But the Bank of Canada has not intervened on foreign exchange markets to affect the value of the Canadian dollar since September 1998, and it has repeatedly insisted that currency values should be "flexible," that they should be determined in the world markets by the forces of supply and demand that we studied in the previous chapter.

Who is right? We will examine this question as the chapter progresses.

INTERNATIONAL TRADE, EXCHANGE RATES, AND AGGREGATE DEMAND

We know from earlier chapters that a country's net exports, $(X - IM)$, are one component of its aggregate demand, $C + I + G + (X - IM)$. It follows that an autonomous increase in exports or decrease in imports has a multiplier effect on the economy, just like an increase in consumption, investment, or government purchases.[1] Figure 1 depicts this conclusion in an aggregate demand and supply diagram. A rise in net exports shifts the aggregate demand curve outward to the right, pushing equilibrium from point A to point B. Both GDP and the price level therefore rise.

But what increases net exports? One factor mentioned in Chapter 8 was a rise in foreign incomes. If foreign economies boom, their citizens are likely to spend more on a wide variety of products, some of which will be Canadian exports. Thus, Figure 1 illustrates the effect on the Canadian economy of more rapid growth in foreign countries.

Similarly, a recession abroad would reduce Canadian exports and shift the Canadian aggregate demand curve inward. Thus, as we learned in Chapter 9:

> Booms or recessions in one country tend to be transmitted to other countries through international trade in goods and services.

Another important determinant of net exports was mentioned in the previous chapter: According to the exchange rate equation developed at the Bank of Canada, a rise in the world prices of both energy and non-energy commodities now tends to lead to an appreciation of the Canadian dollar. The Canadian dollar rises because there is a stronger demand for Canadian exports in commodities, oil, and gas. Thus, the increase in world commodity prices also tends to shift the aggregate demand curve outward to the right, as shown in Figure 1.

FIGURE 1

The Effects of Higher Net Exports

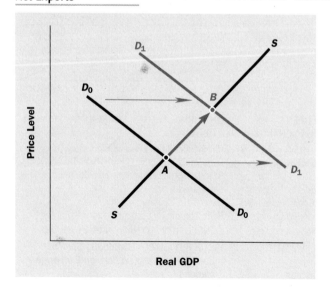

---

[1] Appendix D to Chapter 9 showed that international trade lowers the numerical value of the multiplier. Autonomous changes in *C, I, G,* and $(X - IM)$ all have the same multiplier.

One final important determinant of net exports was mentioned in Chapter 8, but not discussed in depth: the relative prices of foreign and domestic goods. This idea involves a simple application of the law of demand. Namely, if the prices of the goods of Country X rise, people everywhere will tend to buy fewer of them—and more of the goods of Country Y. As we will see next, this simple idea holds the key to understanding how exchange rates affect international trade.

Relative Prices, Exports, and Imports

First assume—just for this short section—that exchange rates are *fixed*. What happens if the prices of Canadian goods fall while, say, Japanese prices are constant? With Canadian products now less expensive *relative to Japanese products*, both Japanese and Canadian consumers will buy more Canadian goods and fewer Japanese goods. As a result, Canada's exports will rise and its imports will fall, adding to aggregate demand in this country. Conversely, a rise in Canadian prices (relative to Japanese prices) will *decrease* Canadian net exports and aggregate demand. Thus:

> A *fall* in the relative prices of a country's exports tends to *increase* that country's net exports and hence to raise its real GDP. Analogously, a *rise* in the relative prices of a country's exports will *decrease* that country's net exports and GDP.

Precisely the same logic applies to changes in Japanese prices. If Japanese prices rise, Canadians will export more and import less. So $X - IM$ will rise, boosting GDP in Canada. Figure 1 applies to this case without change. By similar reasoning, falling Japanese prices decrease Canadian net exports and depress our economy. Thus:

> Price increases for foreign products raise a country's net exports and hence its GDP. Price decreases for foreign products have the opposite effects.

The Effects of Changes in Exchange Rates

From here it is a simple matter to figure out how changes in exchange rates affect a country's net exports, because *currency appreciations or depreciations change international relative prices.*

Recall that the basic role of an exchange rate is to convert one country's prices into another country's currency. Table 1 uses two examples of Canadian–Japanese trade to remind us of this role. Suppose the dollar depreciates from 120 yen to 100 yen. Then, from the Canadian consumer's viewpoint, a television set that costs ¥30,000 in Japan goes up in price from $250 (that is, 30,000/120) to $300. To Canadians, it is just as if Japanese manufacturers had raised TV prices by 20 percent. Naturally, Canadians will react by purchasing fewer Japanese products, so Canadian imports will decline.

TABLE 1				
Exchange Rates and Home Currency Prices				
	¥30,000 Japanese TV Set		$1,000 Canadian Home Computer	
Exchange Rate	Price in Japan	Price in Canada	Price in Canada	Price in Japan
$1 = 120 yen	¥30,000	$250	$1,000	¥120,000
$1 = 100 yen	¥30,000	$300	$1,000	¥100,000

Now consider the implications for Japanese consumers interested in buying Canadian personal computers that cost $1,000. When the dollar falls from 120 yen to 100 yen, they see the price of these computers falling from ¥120,000 to ¥100,000. To them, it is just as if Canadian producers had offered a 16.7 percent markdown. Under such circumstances, we expect Canadian sales to the Japanese to rise, so Canadian exports should increase. Putting these two findings together, we conclude that:

> A currency *depreciation* should *raise* net exports and therefore *increase* aggregate demand. Conversely, a currency *appreciation* should *reduce* net exports and therefore *decrease* aggregate demand.

The aggregate supply and demand diagram in Figure 2 illustrates this conclusion. If the currency depreciates, net exports rise and the aggregate demand curve shifts outward

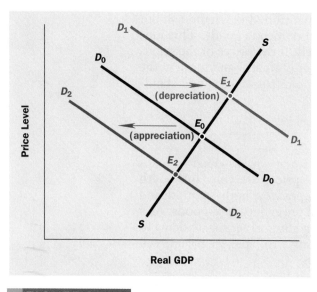

FIGURE 2

The Effects of Exchange
Rate Changes on
Aggregate Demand

from D_0D_0 to D_1D_1. Both prices and output rise as the economy's equilibrium moves from E_0 to E_1. If the currency appreciates, everything operates in reverse: Net exports fall, the aggregate demand curve shifts inward to D_2D_2, and both prices and output decline.

This simple analysis helps us understand why the GDP contribution of net exports, $X - IM$, has dropped so much in Canada since 2002. We learned in the previous chapter that the value of the Canadian dollar vis-à-vis the currency of our major trading partner, the United States, rose more or less steadily between 2002 and 2007. According to the reasoning we have just completed, within a few years, such an appreciation of the Canadian dollar should have boosted our imports and damaged Canadian exports. That is precisely what happened. In *constant* dollars, between 2002 and 2007, Canadian imports (most of them from the United States) soared by over 34 percent. By contrast, Canadian exports (most of them to the United States) rose by only 6 percent during the same time period, despite the recovery of the American economy from the 9/11 aftermath.

AGGREGATE SUPPLY IN AN OPEN ECONOMY

So far we have concluded that a currency depreciation increases aggregate demand and that a currency appreciation decreases it. To complete our model of macroeconomics in an open economy, we turn now to the implications of international trade for *aggregate supply.*

Part of the story is already familiar to us. As we know from previous chapters, the Canadian economy, like all economies, purchases some of its productive inputs from abroad. In particular, Canadian firms often purchase machinery from foreign countries. Canadian consumers also purchase plenty of fruits and other agricultural products from the south of the United States and from many other countries with warm climates. When the Canadian dollar depreciates, these imported inputs and consumer goods should cost more in Canadian dollars—just as if foreign prices had risen.

FIGURE 3

The Effects of Exchange
Rate Changes on
Aggregate Supply

The consequence is clear: With imported goods being more expensive, it is very likely that, at any given level of output, Canadian firms will charge higher prices and that foreign consumer goods will be sold at a higher price on Canadian markets. Graphically, this means that the *aggregate supply curve will shift upward* (or inward to the left). The Canadian economy is said to face an *adverse supply shock*, as discussed in Chapter 10.

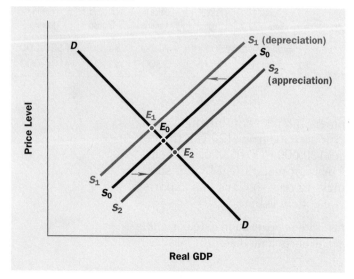

When the Canadian dollar *depreciates*, the prices of imported inputs and imported goods rise. This is an adverse supply shock. The Canadian aggregate supply curve therefore shifts *upward*. By exactly analogous reasoning, an *appreciation* of the Canadian dollar makes imported goods cheaper and shifts the Canadian aggregate supply curve *downward*. This is a favourable supply shock. (See Figure 3.)

The Exchange Rate Pass-Through

Now, how important are those possible adverse or favourable supply shocks that could arise from the depreciation or the appreciation of the local currency? This has been the subject of considerable attention from economists over the last decade. From now on, we focus on the case of currency depreciation, because of its possible adverse effect on the inflation rate.

We should start by saying that the views of the officials at the Bank of Canada have completely changed on this issue. In the 1980s, the Bank of Canada was deeply concerned with the inflationary impact of the depreciation of the Canadian dollar, as it was illustrated in Figure 3. In those years, when the Bank of Canada was still intervening regularly in foreign exchange markets, researchers at the central bank thought that a 10 percent depreciation would be accompanied by a 10 percent increase in import prices within a few quarters, and that this would induce increases in unit labour costs that would quickly feed into consumer prices. It was then estimated that a 10 percent depreciation would raise the CPI inflation rate by 2 or 3 percentage points in the first year following the decline in the exchange rate, and even more thereafter. The inflationary consequences of depreciation thus help us to understand why the Bank of Canada attempted then to have some control over the value of the Canadian dollar on foreign exchange markets.

The view of the Bank of Canada on this matter is completely different now, because several studies have questioned the importance of the inflationary effects of depreciation. Take the case of the Japanese TV sets that we presented in Table 1. As the value of the Canadian dollar drops from 120 yen to 100 yen, we would expect the price of a Japanese television set to rise by 20 percent, from $250 to $300. If this is indeed what happens, there is a full, 100 percent **exchange rate pass-through**, because the retail prices of imported TV sets on the Canadian market have risen by the full amount of the depreciation. However recent studies have shown that the exchange rate pass-through is often only partial. Instead of being sold at $300, the price of the Japanese TV set may rise to only $255. In this case the pass-through is only 10 percent (the increase has been $5 instead of $50).

Why is this? Japanese producers and Canadian importers of Japanese TV sets may fear a loss of their share of the Canadian TV set market if their products are retailed at $300. As a result, they both may decide to absorb part of the depreciation by diminishing their profit margins.

There is considerable empirical evidence that the exchange rate pass-through in G7 countries (which include Canada) is much lower now than it was before. This is particularly the case for countries that have low and stable inflation rates. What possibly happens is that in countries such as Canada that have credible anti-inflationary policies, inflation expectations are solidly anchored to the target rate of inflation, so that firms are reluctant to impose price increases that exceed the target inflation rate even when these increases could be justified by the depreciation of the local currency.

The exchange rate pass-through effect on the inflation rate as measured by the Consumer Price Index is particularly low in Canada. Some studies show that there is no pass-through at all when *core* inflation is taken as the measuring rod (as defined on page 288 of Chapter 13). This would imply that the aggregate supply curve in Figure 3 does not shift at all, or shifts only a little, and hence that the inflationary consequences of a depreciation of the Canadian dollar are now very weak in Canada. This would explain why the Bank of Canada and Canadian economists at large are now less concerned about the possible inflationary effects of a depreciation of the Canadian dollar.

There is a drawback to this, however. With a weak exchange rate pass-through, prices do not fall as much as Canadians would expect when the Canadian dollar appreciates. This was notably the case in 2007, when, after a brisk climb, the Canadian dollar reached parity with the American dollar and remains close to par there as this book is being written. Consumer associations are complaining that imported

The **exchange rate pass-through** measures the extent to which depreciation (appreciation) of the local currency is passed to higher (lower) import prices and consumer prices.

products, most notably cars and trucks, are still more expensive in Canada than they are in the United States. But this situation is not surprising—foreign producers and Canadian importers are attempting to recover normal profit margins, which they felt compelled to cut when the Canadian dollar was low.

THE MACROECONOMIC EFFECTS OF EXCHANGE RATES

Let us now put aggregate demand and aggregate supply together and think through the macroeconomic effects of changes in exchange rates.

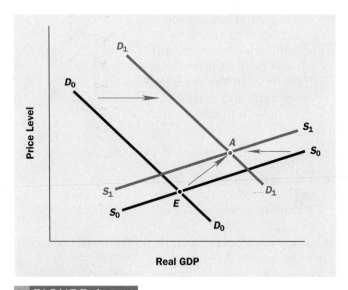

FIGURE 4

The Effects of Currency Depreciation in Canada

First, suppose that the international value of the Canadian dollar falls. Referring back to the red lines in Figures 2 and 3, we see that this depreciation will shift the aggregate demand curve *upward* (or *outward*), from D_0D_0 to D_1D_1 and the aggregate supply curve *upward* as well (or *inward*), from S_0S_0 to S_1S_1. The result, as Figure 4 shows, is that the inflation rate certainly rises. But whether real GDP rises or falls depends on whether the demand shift is the dominant influence. The evidence, for Canada, the United States, and many other industrialized countries, strongly suggests that aggregate demand shifts are usually much larger, as illustrated in Figure 4, because of the weak exchange rate pass-through on consumer prices, so we expect real GDP to rise. Hence:

A depreciation of the Canadian dollar has slight inflationary effects on the Canadian economy and is expansionary.

The intuitive explanation for this result is clear. When the Canadian dollar falls, foreign goods become more expensive to Canadians. The effect is directly inflationary but only mildly so because of the partial exchange rate pass-through. At the same time, aggregate demand in Canada is stimulated by rising net exports. As long as the expansion of aggregate demand outweighs the adverse shock on the aggregate supply curve brought on by currency depreciation, real GDP should rise.

Let's now reverse direction and look at what happens when the currency *appreciates*. In this case, net exports *fall*, so the aggregate demand curve shifts *downward* (or *inward*). At the same time, imported inputs and goods tend to become cheaper, so the aggregate supply curve also shifts *downward* (or *outward*), but only moderately so.

FIGURE 5

The Effects of Currency Appreciation in Canada

Both of these shifts are shown in Figure 5, with the equilibrium moving from point *E* to point *B*. Once again, as the diagram shows, we can be sure of the movement of the inflation rate: it falls. Output also falls as long as the aggregate demand shift is relatively larger, as is likely and as is assumed here. Thus:

An appreciation of the Canadian dollar has disinflationary effects on the Canadian economy and is contractionary.

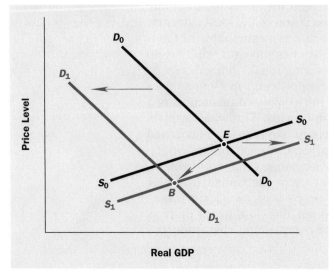

This analysis explains why many economists and financial experts groaned when the Japanese yen appreciated relative to the U.S. dollar in 2002–2004. Japan, as we pointed out on a number of occasions, was then experiencing price deflation and very slow real GDP growth. The last thing it needed, they argued, was an appreciation of the yen, as this would worsen deflation and stall real GDP growth.

The Impact of Currency Depreciation in Emerging Countries

We have argued that currency depreciation has only minor inflationary effects on advanced economies such as G7 countries (the United States, Japan, the United Kingdom, France, Germany, Italy, and Canada), and that real GDP should rise following depreciation. Still, many emerging economies prefer to remain on a fixed exchange rate regime precisely because they fear currency depreciation. Isn't this contradictory to what we have just learned?

What happens is that emerging countries face conditions that are different from those of advanced economies. In emerging countries, there is an almost immediate and full exchange rate pass-through. Thus, any local currency depreciation is quickly reflected in higher import prices and faster inflation rates in consumer prices. Because some of these countries, especially South American countries, have long been experiencing high inflation rates, they often have well-organized *indexing* provisions, in particular, clauses that provide for automatic increases in money wages whenever prices rise. Currency depreciation thus produces large upward shifts of the aggregate supply curve, which overcome the expansionary effects of increased net exports, as shown in the accompanying diagram. As a result, depreciation of the local currency generates a move from point *E* to point *A;* that is, both higher inflation and lower real GDP—the worst-case scenario!

An additional feedback effect may also worsen things. We saw in the previous chapter that the long-run evolution of the value of one currency relative to another is determined by differences in domestic inflation rates. The country that has the highest inflation rate should see its currency depreciate. When inflation rates rise in an emerging country because of the initial depreciation or devaluation of the local currency, it is likely that foreign exchange market participants will start to expect further depreciation, thus putting downward pressure on the exchange rate of the emerging country. A vicious circle results, with depreciation and inflation feeding on each other. This explains why central banks in emerging countries are reluctant to let their currency float, fearing the occurrence of this vicious circle when their currency happens to depreciate.

A further dramatic and important phenomenon has not yet been considered. Recall the massive depreciations of several Southeast Asian currencies in 1997 and 1998. These, if Figure 4 was relevant to their case, should have given these economies a tremendous boost. Instead, the so-called Asian Tigers suffered horrific

slumps, as did Mexico when the peso tumbled in 1995. Why? The answer is that our simple analysis omits a detail that, although unimportant for Canada, is critical in many developed countries.

Countries that borrow in foreign currency—most often U.S. dollars—will see their debts increase whenever their currencies fall in value. For instance, an Indonesian business that borrowed US$1,000 in July 1997, when one U.S. dollar was worth 2,500 rupiah, thought it owed 2.5 million rupiah. But when the U.S. dollar suddenly became worth 10,000 rupiah, the company's debt skyrocketed to 10 million rupiah. Many businesses found themselves unable to cope with their crushing debt burdens and simply went bankrupt. In terms of our simple graphics, this can be represented as an additional inward shift of the aggregate supply curve, as potential output falls and less can be produced. In addition, as bankrupt or near-bankrupt companies cannot or do not want to invest anymore, the positive impact of the lower value of the domestic currency on net exports is likely to be nearly wiped out, so that the aggregate demand curve will barely shift upward.

All of this clearly shows that while depreciation is most certainly expansionary in Canada and in other advanced economies, it is likely to be sharply contractionary in most emerging economies.

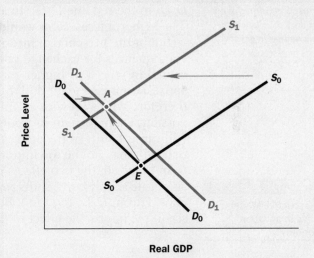

The Effects of Currency Depreciation in an Emerging Economy

■ INTEREST RATES AND INTERNATIONAL CAPITAL FLOWS

One important piece of our international economic puzzle is still missing. We have analyzed international trade in goods and services in some detail, but we have ignored international movements of *capital*.

For some nations, this omission is inconsequential because they rarely receive or lend international capital. But things are quite different for Canada. Although capital flows involving Canadians or Canadian assets are not as important as they are for the United States and the U.S. dollar, they are still substantial, with assets denominated in Canadian dollars being bought and sold internationally. In addition, we cannot hope to understand the origins of the various international financial crises since the 1990s without incorporating capital flows into our analysis. Fortunately, given what we have just learned about the effects of exchange rates, this omission is easily rectified.

Recall from the previous chapter that interest rate differentials, differentials in expected rates of return, and capital flows are typically the most important determinants of exchange rate movements. Specifically, suppose interest rates in Canada rise while foreign interest rates are unchanged. We learned in the previous chapter that this change in relative interest rates will attract capital to Canada and cause the dollar to appreciate. This chapter has just taught us that an appreciating dollar will, in turn, reduce net exports, prices, and output in Canada—as indicated in Figure 5. Thus:

> A rise in interest rates tends to contract the economy by appreciating the currency and reducing net exports.

Notice that this conclusion has a familiar ring. When we studied monetary policy in Chapter 13, we observed that the monetary policy transmission mechanism described by the Bank of Canada relied precisely on this relationship. In its attempt to reduce the inflation rate, the Bank of Canada raises the target overnight rate in order to raise both nominal and real interest rates in general. The higher real rates deter investment spending. In studying an open economy with **international capital flows**, we see that higher interest rates also reduce the net export component of aggregate spending.

International capital flows are purchases and sales of financial assets across national borders.

How can we represent this in our standard graphical framework? Let us consider a *tightening* of monetary policy in an open economy with floating exchange rates and international capital mobility, which is the case in Canada. As we just pointed out, contractionary monetary policy *reduces* aggregate demand, which lowers both real GDP and the inflation rate. This situation is shown in Figure 6 by the shift from D_0D_0 to the red line D_1D_1. In a **closed economy**, that would be the end of the story. The higher interest rates would move the economy from point A to point B.

A **closed economy** is one that does not trade with other nations in either goods or assets.

But in the presence of international capital flows, we must also think through the consequences for exchange rates. The higher Canadian interest rates attract foreign capital in search of higher rates of return. The exchange rate therefore *rises*. The appreciating Canadian dollar encourages imports and discourages exports. Canada therefore winds up with an inflow of capital and a decrease in its trade surplus (or, possibly, an increase in its trade deficit). In addition, the appreciating Canadian dollar will cause a shift of the aggregate supply curve, as we pointed out earlier, although that shift may not be too important.

In Figure 6, the two effects of the exchange rate appreciation appear in blue: The aggregate supply curve shifts *outward* (to S_1S_1) and the aggregate demand shifts further *inward* (from D_1D_1 to D_2D_2). Both effects tend to reduce the inflation rate. As you can see in the figure, the effect of monetary policy is enhanced in an open economy, with the economy being pushed all the way to point C.

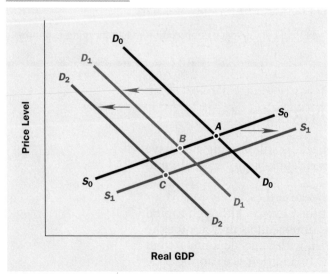

FIGURE 6

A Restrictive Monetary Policy in an Open Economy

> International capital flows increase the ability of monetary policy to reduce economic activity and inflation rates.

Many economists argue that this is exactly what happened during the 1990–1991 recession, which was partly planned by the Bank of Canada when it decided to reduce briskly inflation rates. Interest rates remained quite high for more than two years, beginning in January 1989, thus keeping the Canadian dollar at a high value relative to the U.S. dollar. The combined domestic effects of high real interest rates and external effects attributed to the strong Canadian dollar led to a reduction in real GDP and in inflation rates.

If interest rates fall in Canada, everything we have just said is turned in the opposite direction.

The conclusions are:

A decline in interest rates tends to expand the economy by depreciating the currency and raising net exports.

International capital flows increase the ability of monetary policy to increase economic activity and inflation rates.

EXERCISE Provide the reasoning behind these conclusions.

■ MONETARY POLICIES IN AN OPEN ECONOMY WITH FLOATING EXCHANGE RATES

We have seen the impact that changes in interest rates, induced by a more restrictive monetary policy, have on the exchange rate of the Canadian dollar, net exports, and aggregate demand. But should the Bank of Canada make its monetary policy more restrictive or more expansionary when there are fluctuations in the international value of the Canadian dollar? This question gets us back, somewhat, to the issue that we raised at the beginning of the chapter: Should the Bank of Canada do anything when, for instance, the Canadian dollar is quickly rising relative to the U.S. dollar—the currency of our major trading partner—as happened between 2003 and 2007? Or should the Bank of Canada have done anything when the international value of the Canadian dollar fell nearly continuously between 1992 and 2002?

Let us consider the situation where the Bank of Canada takes as an article of faith that exchange rates ought to be floating and left to market forces. What we want to argue is that the response of the Bank of Canada to a rising or a falling Canadian dollar depends on the *causes* of the movement in the exchange rate or of the pressures being applied to the exchange rate.

■ Changes in Exchange Rates Caused by Increases in the Demand for Canadian Goods and Services

We stated in Chapter 18 that different factors, which for reasons of convenience we subdivided into short-run, medium-run, and long-run factors, can determine the exchange rate of the Canadian dollar. We also explained that, in the case of the Canadian economy, the value of the Canadian dollar can be relatively well explained by the fluctuations of world commodity prices, both energy and non-energy commodity prices. This, it was pointed out, arose because the Canadian economy, despite being a modern advanced economy, is still an important net exporter of commodities, such as iron ore, uranium, and nickel. Hence, when the world prices of these commodities rise, the higher prices reflect a strong demand for these products and hence for the mineral products that Canada exports in relatively large quantities. A similar argument can be put forth about energy products, such as oil and natural gas. Because the oil and natural gas markets were liberalized under the original Canada–U.S. Free Trade Agreement in 1989, Canada has become a large net exporter of these commodities since the early 1990s.

Put simply, when world primary commodity prices and the world demand for commodities rise, this implies a rise in the demand for Canadian goods and services. This will generate two effects. First, as we would expect, net exports will rise. Secondly, it is very likely that firms in the primary commodity sectors will be induced to invest more, to respond to the growing world demand and hence to the future demand for their products. But even if this second effect does not materialize, the initial impact of the increase in world commodity prices is that there will be an increase in aggregate demand. This, as reflected in Figure 7, will cause an outward shift of the aggregate demand curve, from D_0D_0 to the red line D_1D_1.

If the Canadian economy was on a fixed exchange rate regime, things would end there. The short-run position of the economy would move from point A to point B. Real GDP would be higher and the inflation rate would be higher. Floating exchange rates, however, provide a stabilization mechanism. With floating exchange rates, the higher

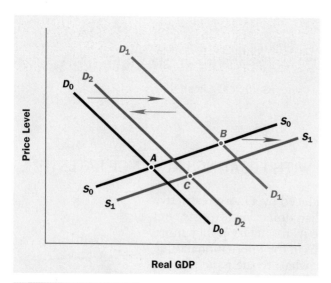

FIGURE 7

The Effects of an
Increase in the World
Demand for
Commodities

demand for Canadian products generates an appreciation of the Canadian dollar. This, as we have observed before, leads to an inward shift of the aggregate demand curve in Figure 7, from the red line D_1D_1 to the blue line D_2D_2, as well as a downward shift of the aggregate supply curve, from S_0S_0 to the blue line S_1S_1. The Canadian economy would then end up in a position such as point C, where real GDP is slightly higher than it was, and where the inflation rate is little different from its starting value.

The floating exchange rate thus acts like an automatic shock absorber. Assuming that real GDP is initially equal to potential output, the positive demand shock on the economy is negated by the appreciation of the Canadian dollar, with real output being brought back next to potential output. The inflationary effects of the positive demand shock are also automatically neutralized. With rising world commodity prices, the resources of the Canadian economy need to be shifted toward the commodity-producing sector so that this sector can respond to rising demand. This is accomplished (in part) with the help of the exchange rate. As the Canadian dollar appreciates, it becomes harder for Canadian manufacturers and producers of services to sell abroad. As a result, their output is reduced, and the human and financial resources of the manufacturing and service sectors become available for use by the commodity producers. This is certainly the situation that has prevailed since about 2003, with world commodity prices increasing presumably due to the strong demand arising from large and fast-growing countries such as India and China.

Changes in Exchange Rates Caused by Decreases in the Demand for Canadian Goods and Services

The exchange rate plays a symmetrical role when world commodity prices are falling and hence when the demand for Canadian primary products is falling. This case is illustrated with the help of Figure 8. As net exports of commodities fall, aggregate demand initially falls from D_0D_0 to the red line D_1D_1. This, however, is accompanied by a depreciation of the Canadian dollar, which in turn leads to a shift of aggregate demand back toward D_0D_0, say, to the blue line D_2D_2, as noncommodity sectors find it easier to compete with foreign producers. The depreciation also induces an inward shift of the aggregate supply curve, from S_0S_0 to the blue line S_1S_1. The Canadian

Floating Exchange Rates as an Automatic, Fully Offsetting Demand Shock Absorber

According to some estimates made by the Bank of Canada, the aggregate demand curve D_2D_2 shifts in such a way that real GDP at the end of the appreciation process turns out to be exactly equal to what it was before the increase in commodity prices. In other words, point C would be right next to point A in Figure 7—a remarkable coincidence.

At the Bank of Canada, [we have] estimates that include foreign GDP growth and the growth of real commodity prices as well as interest rates and exchange rates. The estimated effect of a 10 percent increase in the price of commodities would ultimately be a 0.7 percent increase in the growth of real GDP. In addition, our exchange rate model predicts that the same commodity price increase would lead to an appreciation of the Canadian dollar of 4.8 percent. According to our . . . estimates, an appreciation of this magnitude would reduce the growth rate of GDP by 0.7 percent, fully offsetting the effect of the commodity price increase.

SOURCE: Mark Kruger, "Discussion," in Bank of Canada Conference, *Revisiting the Case for Flexible Exchange Rates*, November 2000, p. 363. Retrieved from www.bankofcanada.ca/en/res/wp/2000/reinhart.pdf. Copyright © 1995–2007, Bank of Canada. Permission is granted to reproduce or cite portions herein, if attribution is given to the Bank of Canada.

The Dutch Disease

In Figure 7, we suggested that the overall effect of the increase in world commodity prices, followed by the appreciation of the Canadian dollar, was an increase in real GDP. And we pointed out in the previous boxed feature, "Floating Exchange Rates as an Automatic, Fully Offsetting Demand Shock Absorber," some estimates at the Bank of Canada indicate that the overall effect may even be neutral. But what if commodity-sensitive exchange rates are *too* sensitive to increases in commodity prices? What if the negative effect of appreciation on aggregate demand is greater than the positive effect of larger commodity exports? This case is reproduced in the accompanying diagram, where final real GDP, at point *C*, is smaller than its starting value at point *A*.

This case illustrates the *Dutch disease*, which we mentioned in Chapter 18, on page 411. When the Netherlands made huge discoveries of natural gas and started exporting it, observers noted a large decline in the Dutch manufacturing sector. This was apparently caused by the appreciation of the Dutch guilder due to the large exports of natural gas. A similar phenomenon seems to have arisen in the case of many other countries when they started exporting large quantities of oil, for instance Norway and Mexico in the 1970s and 1980s, African countries such as Nigeria, and more recently Russia and Azerbaijan. Some economists fear that Canada may also be subjected to the Dutch disease, and that the fate of the Canadian manu-

facturing industry may be in danger, as rising and future rising oil exports tend to raise the international value of the Canadian dollar.

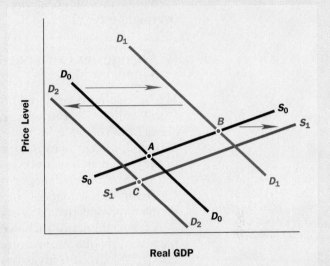

Real GDP

The Dutch Disease: Real Output Declines Following an Increase in Commodity Prices and the Exchange Rate

economy would then end up in a position such as point *C*, where once more real GDP and the inflation rate are not too far away from their starting values. The flexibility of the exchange rate allows the manufacturing and service industries to hire the labour and financial resources that are not being used by the commodity producers, since they are facing a lower demand for their products.

This set of events happened in particular during the aftermath of the Asian and Russian crises of 1997 and 1998, when global demand for primary commodities became very weak. Canadian commodity producers were hit very hard by the dramatic fall in commodity prices that occurred in the middle of 1998. The currencies of countries that export raw materials, such as Canada and Australia, were then subjected to sharp depreciation. The depreciation of the Canadian dollar helped the manufacturing and service sectors to increase their exports and pick up the slack left by commodity producers, who had reduced their activity, thus keeping both real GDP and inflation rates on track.

Fluctuations in exchange rates also help the Canadian economy to mitigate fluctuations in revenues arising from changes in world prices. These prices are usually expressed in U.S. dollars. When world commodity prices fall in U.S. dollars, Canadian producers do not fully feel the brunt of the price drop if the Canadian dollar depreciates at the same time. The same $10 in American currency could be worth $12 in Canadian currency before the depreciation, but $14 after the depreciation.

FIGURE 8

The Effects of a Decrease in the World Demand for Commodities

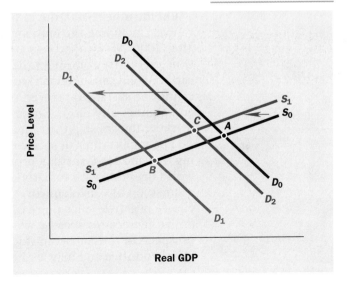

Real GDP

Thus, if the unit price of some commodity falls from US$10 to US$8, the Canadian commodity producer will recover as much as $11.20 (US$8 × 1.40) per unit in Canadian currency, a loss of only $0.80 per unit (relative to the previous $12 per unit).

To sum up, with the kind of demand shocks that we have outlined, the Bank of Canada needs to do little as long as exchange rates are freely floating and continue to operate as a buffer. Most of the stabilization will occur through the fluctuations of the exchange rate. Hence, the Bank of Canada does not need to change the target overnight interest rate.

Changes in Exchange Rates Caused by Changes in International Financial Markets

We have so far considered demand shocks that affect the *current account*, as we called it in Chapter 18. But what if the cause of the appreciation of the Canadian dollar arises from the *capital account*? What if changes in the international value of the Canadian dollar occur because of turmoil in world financial markets? What if fluctuations of the Canadian dollar versus the U.S. dollar are caused mainly by changes in investor sentiment and rebalancing of portfolios? As we said in Chapter 18, page 398, the short-run movements of the exchange rate are probably dominated by the reassessments of prospective rates of return on financial assets.

A few examples of such events can be given. In 1994 and 1995, one of our NAFTA partners, Mexico, came quite close to default on its foreign debt, dubbed the "Peso Crisis." As a result, investors started to beware (for only a short time, however!) of governments that were heavily in debt, as was the Canadian government at the time. These investors moved their claims away from these countries and into countries, such as the United States, that were then considered to be a safe heaven for financial investments. The capital funds flowing into the United States explain in part the sharp depreciation of the Canadian dollar during that time period.

The Canadian dollar also suffered during the two-year stint that preceded the stock market crash in the United States in 2000, when investors all over the world became increasingly optimistic about the future prospects of the American economy, even showing signs of "irrational exuberance." This drove up the value of the U.S. dollar vis-à-vis all major currencies, including the newly created euro, the yen, and the Canadian dollar. Indeed, the efforts of the European Central Bank to crank up the value of the euro relative to the U.S. dollar, by raising the target interest rate in the euro zone, were completely in vain, as each increase in European interest rates strengthened further the conviction of world investors that the future prospects of the American economy were much better than those of Europe. Each increase in the euro interest rate then led to a depreciation of the euro, thus contradicting economic theory!

On the other hand, the value of the U.S. dollar fell in relation to many major currencies, including the euro and the Canadian dollar, over the 2003–2004 period and after 2006. Many observers attribute the weakness of the U.S. dollar to the growing concern of investors about the large trade and current account deficits of the American economy, about which we will say more later. They believe that such imbalances cannot be sustained forever, so they are not placing their funds in American bonds and equities any more. Some of these funds flow instead to the Canadian financial markets, thus raising the value of Canadian dollar relative to the U.S. dollar.

The implications of such capital flows are different from those arising from growing demand for Canadian products. When the Canadian dollar appreciates because world investors wish to harbour their funds in Canadian bonds and equities or in the acquisition of Canadian corporations, the effect on aggregate demand in Canada is clearly negative, since there is no compensating factor. Similarly, when the Canadian dollar depreciates because world investors become overenthusiastic about the future prospects of the American stock market, the effect on aggregate demand in Canada is clearly positive and may create inflationary pressures without any dampening effect.

FIGURE 9

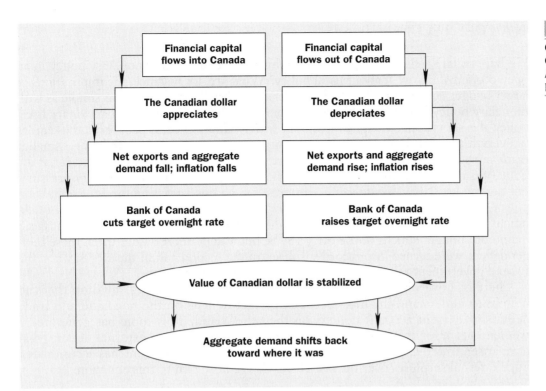

Capital Flows, the
Canadian Dollar,
Aggregate Demand, and
Monetary Policy

Thus, when international capital flows disrupt the value of the Canadian dollar, the Bank of Canada needs to intervene. How?

We have already developed all of the tools that allow us to provide an answer. When the Canadian dollar appreciates and the cause can clearly be attributed to the capital account, the effect on aggregate demand will be negative, thus putting downward pressure on both inflation and real GDP, so the Bank of Canada needs to decrease the target overnight rate. This should raise aggregate demand back to its previous level, and it should put downward pressure on the Canadian dollar, stabilizing the value of the Canadian dollar. The Bank of Canada thus kills two birds with one stone (see the left-hand side of Figure 9).

In a symmetrical way, when the cause of the depreciating Canadian dollar is the shift in portfolio allocation, aggregate demand in Canada will be shifted upward, so the Bank of Canada will need to raise the target overnight rate, as shown on the right-hand side of Figure 9. This will put upward pressure on the Canadian dollar, helping to stabilize it, and it will eventually reduce aggregate demand back to its neutral position.

While monetary policy in an open economy looks straightforward in the framework presented here, things are never that simple. It is not always easy for Bank of Canada officials to find out whether the Canadian dollar is appreciating because of demand-led factors, such as rising world commodity prices, or because of the weakness of the U.S. dollar and changes in the mood of portfolio holders. For instance, in the first half of 2004, Bank officials attributed much of the appreciation during 2003 to rising international capital inflows and decided to cut the target overnight rate to as low as 2 percent; they changed their mind during the course of the year, however, raising the target rate back to 2.5 percent when it appeared that net exports had made a positive rather than a negative contribution to GDP growth.

Whether the central bank is acting in a closed or in an open economy, there is always a great deal of uncertainty surrounding its monetary strategy. Potential output, the output gap, the risk of inflationary pressures, and the causes of the depreciation or the appreciation of the Canadian dollar must all be assessed, but there is never any certainty about them.

FISCAL POLICY IN AN OPEN ECONOMY

We have so far spent a considerable amount of space discussing monetary policy in an open economy. But what about fiscal policy? What are, for instance, the implications of larger budget deficits for the Canadian exchange rate? Things are not as simple as with monetary policy. If the Canadian government decides to pursue an expansionary fiscal policy, this should lead to higher economic activity and, hence, as people purchase more of everything, this should lead to rising imports, a higher **trade deficit** (or a smaller **trade surplus**), and resulting downward pressure on the exchange rate. However, if the Bank of Canada is unhappy about the higher real GDP, fearing inflationary pressure, our central bank may decide to raise interest rates, thus attracting foreign capital and putting upward pressure on the exchange rate. Looking at statistical data does not help much: The Canadian dollar depreciated when the Canadian federal government faced mammoth budget deficits in the early 1990s, but it kept depreciating when these budget deficits were turned into record surpluses in the second half of the 1990s, when the Liberal government raised taxes and cut government expenditures.

> A country's **trade deficit** is the excess of its imports over its exports. If, instead, exports exceed imports, the country has a **trade surplus**.

There is, however, a fundamental and highly useful *accounting* equation that can help us to understand the links between budget deficits on the one hand and trade deficits or current account deficits on the other hand. This topic has generated a tremendous amount of interest and concern due to the large external deficits that have arisen in the United States since the early 1990s, while China has accumulated huge external surpluses over the last 10 years. We now turn to this equation.

A Fundamental Accounting Equation

It can easily be shown (see the appendix to this chapter, page 439) that the following **fundamental accounting equation** must hold at all times:

$$-CAB = (I - S) + (G - T)$$

> There is a **fundamental accounting equation** that says that the current account deficit of a country must be equal to the financial deficit of the private sector plus the government budget deficit.

The negative of the current account balance, CAB, is none other than the current account deficit. Remembering that $G - T$ is the government budget deficit, while $I - S$ is the excess of investment over private domestic saving, that is, the financial deficit of the private sector, the above fundamental accounting equation may thus be rewritten in words as:

Current account deficit = Private financial deficit + Government budget deficit

There is nothing mysterious about this equation. It simply says that when the private and public sectors cannot finance their own expenditures (both are running deficits), they must resort to foreign lending. Why is that? As we already know from Chapter 18, when an economy is running a current account deficit, it must have a capital account surplus of the same size. This implies that this economy is borrowing from abroad, and hence that foreign residents lend funds to this economy.

If we take the two terms on the right-hand side of our fundamental equation and move them to the left-hand side, we get another version of the fundamental equation, which is:

$$(S - I) + (T - G) - CAB = 0$$

Or, in words:

Domestic private net lending + Domestic public net lending + Foreign net lending = 0

Notice that the various forms of the fundamental equation are a matter of national *accounting*, not economics. They must hold in *all* countries simultaneously and at *all* times. They have nothing to do with any particular economic theory.

A particularly simple application of the above fundamental accounting equations is to *assume* that investment is exactly equal to domestic private saving ($I = S$). It then becomes obvious from the first version of the fundamental equation that any increase in government deficits will be accompanied by an increase in the current account deficit or, vice versa, that any current account deficit must be associated with an identical government budget deficit. This is called the **twin-deficit problem**. This relationship is at the heart of the "structural adjustment" programs that the IMF imposes on countries (often less developed ones or emerging economies) that have large current account deficits and ask for help from the IMF. By insisting on contractionary fiscal policies, the IMF believes that the reductions in government budget deficits will lead to reductions in current account deficits.

The **twin-deficit problem** is the recognition that *if* private saving and investment are equal, the current account deficit and the government budget deficit must rise or fall together.

The Fundamental Equation Applied to the United States and Canada

The United States   The U.S. economy has also been subjected to a twin-deficit problem for a long time, and this has generated some concern throughout the world. Figure 10 illustrates the evolution of the three components of the second form of our fundamental accounting identity, from 1970 to 2006, as percentages of GDP: nonresident lending (the current account deficit), government sector lending (the budget surplus, $T - G$), and private sector financial lending (its financial surplus, $S - I$). The twin-deficit problem became an issue in the 1980s, vanished for a while, and reappeared after the stock market crash of 2000.

It is interesting to note however that the link between the government budget deficit and the current account deficit appears to be rather loose. For instance, when the Democrats and President Bill Clinton took over in 1993, the government budget moved quickly from a large deficit to a balanced position. Other things equal, that should have led to a substantial *reduction* in the current account deficit. But other things were not equal. The equation reminds us that the balance between saving and investment matters, too. As shares of GDP, business investment boomed while household saving declined from 1992 to 2000. So $S - I$ moved sharply in the negative direction. And that change, as our equation shows, should *raise* the current account deficit, reducing net exports.

Indeed, an examination of Figure 10 reveals another relationship that seems more systematic than that of the twin-deficit, at least if we consider the years after 1980. You can observe a negative relationship between private net lending and public net lending. In other words, when the private sector tends to save more than it is investing, the government sector tends to go into a deficit position (as in the 1989–1993 and 2000–2004 periods). Reciprocally, when the private sector tends to invest more than it is saving, the government sector tends to move toward a surplus position (as in the 1993–2000 period).

SOURCE: Data provided by Wynne Godley, Dimitri B. Papadimitriou, and Gennaro Zezza, "The U.S. Economy; What's Next?" *Strategic Analysis*, April 2007 (Annandale-on-Hudson, NY: The Levy Economics Institute of Bard College).

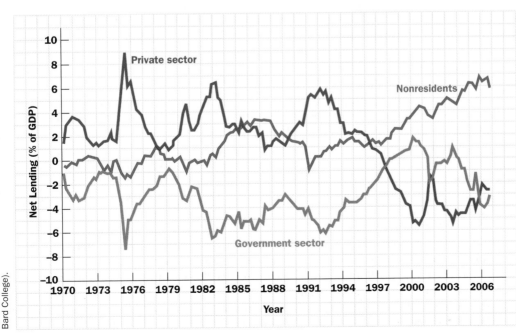

FIGURE 10

The Three Components of the Fundamental Equation, United States, 1970–2006

SOURCE: Statistics Canada, Series V31751 (persons and unincorporated business), V33016 (corporations and government business), V33360 (government), V32967 (nonresidents), all from Table 378-0001, and V498074 (GDP at current prices).

FIGURE 11

Four Components of the Fundamental Identity Equation, Canada, 1970–2007

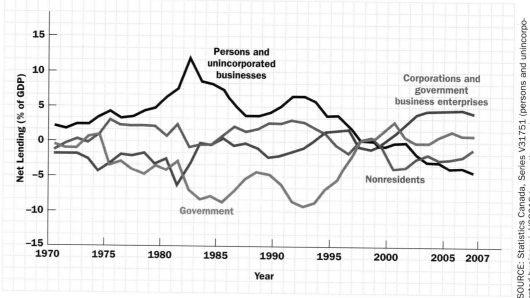

Two explanations of this new relationship can be provided. The first one is typically Keynesian and claims that when aggregate demand and real GDP are low (due to feeble investment and consumption), the government deficit tends to be high, either automatically (as shown in Figure 6 in Chapter 15, page 333) or because governments try to pursue countercyclical fiscal policies. The second explanation reverses the causality and claims that when government deficits are high, firms are being crowded out in the financial markets and cannot borrow funds to invest, so that investment is low relative to private saving (as argued on page 339). Given our modern financial systems, this second explanation seems less convincing.

Canada   What about Canada? Figure 11 gives measures of the three components of the second fundamental equation as applied to the Canadian economy between 1970 and 2007, as percentages of Canadian GDP. We have split domestic private net lending $(S - I)$ into two subcomponents: corporate net lending, which includes both financial and nonfinancial corporations (as well as government business enterprises), and personal net lending, which includes households and unincorporated businesses. Clearly, Canada does not suffer from a twin-deficit problem; rather, Canada has had a twin surplus for a number of years. The government sector runs a surplus, and net lending to Canadians by nonresidents is positive as well, meaning that foreign saving is negative (as shown in Figure 11, via nonresidents lending) and hence that the current account balance is positive. This implies that Canadian government debt and foreign debt are both diminishing over time.

What is most remarkable, however, is the evolution of the personal sector. As in the United States, there tends to be a negative relationship between the financial surplus of the personal sector and that of the government sector. But, in addition, net lending by households has become negative since 2001, instead of being positive as one would expect. This does not mean that households do not save at all, although their propensity to save is indeed very low, as was pointed out in Chapter 8. What happens is that Canadian households increased their purchases of new residential dwellings by nearly 100 percent between 2001 and 2007. They thus had no funds left to lend to the corporate sector. In fact, quite the opposite has been happening since 2002. The retained earnings of the corporate sector—profits net of dividend payments and taxes on corporate profits—are so large that corporations lend to households a large chunk of their retained earnings, in the form of consumer credit and mortgages. Thus, currently, households are not helping to finance the investment expenditures of companies; rather, Canadian corporations are financing consumer credit and the purchases of residential dwellings! And they are also lending abroad.

■ IS THE U.S. CURRENT ACCOUNT DEFICIT A PROBLEM?

The preceding explanation suggests that the United States' large trade and current account deficits over the past decade are a symptom of a deeper problem: The nation as a whole—including both the government and the private sector—has been consuming more than it has been producing for years. The United States has therefore been forced to borrow the difference from foreigners. The current account deficit is just the mirror image of the required capital inflows.

Those who worry about trade deficits point out that these capital inflows create debts on which interest and principal payments must be made in the future. In this view, Americans have been mortgaging their futures to finance higher consumer spending.

But another, quite different, interpretation of the trade deficit is possible. Suppose foreign investors come to see the United States as an especially attractive place to invest their funds. Then capital will flow there, not because Americans need to *borrow* it, but because foreigners are eager to *lend* it. The desire of foreigners to acquire American assets should push the value of the dollar up, which should in turn push U.S. net exports down. In that case, the current account deficit would still be the mirror image of the capital inflows. But it would signify the economic *strength* of the U.S. economy, not its weakness.

Each view holds elements of truth, but the second raises a critical question: How long can it go on? As long as the United States continues to run large trade deficits, foreigners will have to continue to accumulate large amounts of U.S. assets—one way or another. Starting in 2002, however, private investors abroad began concluding that they had acquired about all the American assets they wanted. That would have marked the day of reckoning for the United States but for one important fact: The governments of Japan and China decided to buy hundreds of billions of American dollars (selling equivalent amounts of their own currencies), adding them to the foreign reserves of their central banks, rather than let the yen and the yuan appreciate. These large *government* capital inflows allowed the United States to continue to run mammoth trade deficits.

■ ON CURING THE U.S. CURRENT ACCOUNT DEFICIT

How can Americans cure their foreign trade problem and end their addiction to foreign borrowing? There are five basic ways.

■ Change the Mix of Fiscal and Monetary Policy

The fundamental equation

$$-CAB = (I - S) + (G - T)$$

suggests that an increase in the budget surplus or *a decrease in the budget deficit* (that is, shrinking $G - T$) would be a good way to reduce the trade deficit. A reduction in G or an increase in T would reduce aggregate demand and hence would reduce the demand for imported goods, leading to a smaller trade deficit and hence to a smaller current account deficit.

When the government curtails its spending or raises taxes, aggregate demand falls. If Americans do not want the shrinking budget deficit to slow economic growth, they must therefore compensate for it by providing monetary stimulus. Lower interest rates depreciate the dollar and should therefore help reduce the trade deficit. So the policy recommendation actually amounts to tightening *fiscal* policy and loosening *monetary* policy.

Both the Canadian and the American governments changed the policy mix decisively in this direction in the 1990s, tightening fiscal policy and reducing real interest rates. But the American trade deficit rose anyway because private investment spending soared while private saving stagnated. Then, starting in 2001, the federal budget turned rapidly from a substantial surplus to a record-high deficit, which pushed the trade deficit up further. What else might work?

◼ More Rapid Economic Growth Abroad

One factor behind the growing U.S. trade deficit is that the economies of many foreign nations—the customers for American exports—have grown more slowly than the U.S. economy. If foreign economies would grow faster, the U.S. government has frequently argued, they would buy more American goods, thereby raising U.S. exports and reducing the trade deficit. So the Americans have regularly urged their major trading partners to stimulate their economies—but with only modest success. Alternatively, the U.S. economy could enter into a recession or grow more slowly than its trade partners, as happened after the stock market crashes of 2000 and in 2008, as a consequence of the subprime financial crisis. The trade deficit would recede. But no one thinks that this is a very good remedy.

◼ Raise Domestic Saving or Reduce Domestic Investment

Our fundamental equation calls attention to two other routes to a smaller current account deficit: more saving or less investment.

The U.S. personal saving rate (saving as a share of disposable income) has hit postwar lows in recent years. If Americans would simply save more, they would need to borrow less from abroad. This solution, too, would lead to a cheaper dollar and a smaller trade deficit, once again by reducing aggregate demand and the demand for imported goods.

The trouble is that no one has yet found a reliable way to induce Americans to save more. The government has implemented a variety of tax incentives for saving, and more are suggested every year. But little evidence suggests that any of them has worked. Instead, large increases in stock market wealth in the second half of the 1990s, and then in housing wealth in the early 2000s, convinced Americans that it was prudent to save *even less* than they used to. A similar phenomenon is happening in Canada: Personal saving rates, which were in the 4 to 5 percent range in 2000, were as low as 2.3 and 1.5 percent in 2006 and 2007.

If the other cures for the U.S. trade deficit fail to work, the deficit may cure itself in a particularly unpleasant way: by reducing U.S. domestic investment. The 2001 recession accomplished this to some extent, reducing the share of investment in real GDP. That effect was only temporary, however, and the longer-run problem mentioned above remains: If their trade deficit persists, Americans will have to borrow more and more from foreigners. Some economists, using the laws of demand and supply, argue that foreigners, at some point, will start demanding higher interest rates. Skyrocketing interest rates would then lead to lower investment in the United States and possibly to a severe recession.

You have seen, however, that (short-term) interest rates in countries such as Canada and the United States are essentially under the control of the central banks, so the Federal Reserve could keep American interest rates where they are. Thus, if foreigners were to refuse to make any new loans to the United States, or if central banks—such as the Bank of Japan and the People's Bank of China—decided not to accumulate U.S. dollars anymore, the more likely scenario would be a quickly depreciating U.S. dollar, which would eventually improve the current account balance of the United States. A large depreciation of the U.S. dollar would however decrease the value of the foreign reserves of foreign central banks—including the People's Bank of China and the Bank of Canada—and this makes unlikely a sudden change of attitude among central banks.

◼ Generalized Floating Exchange Rates

American economists often argue that a possible solution to the current world imbalances, with the huge American current account deficit, is for countries that contribute to these imbalances to move on to a floating exchange rate regime. Indeed the trade deficit of the European Union vis-à-vis China in 2007 was just as large as that of the United States vis-à-vis China. In addition to China, even Japan is often accused of not letting its currency float freely. Floating exchange rates in these countries would allow the U.S. dollar to depreciate in relation to Asian currencies, helping the American economy to recover a smaller current account deficit. But Communist China is highly reluctant to let its currency float and be subjected to market forces and speculation, so this solution may have to await the coming of a more prosperous and liberalized China. In any case, the U.S. economy runs a trade deficit with every region of the globe, including Canada, Mexico, Europe, and Africa, whatever their exchange rate regime. Thus, generalized floating exchange rates could provide a partial solution at best.

◼ Protectionism

We have saved for last what is most likely the worst remedy. One seemingly obvious way to cure the American trade and current account deficits is for Americans to limit imports by imposing stiff tariffs, quotas, and other protectionist devices. We discussed protectionism, and the reasons why most economists oppose it, in Chapter 17. Despite the economic arguments against it, protectionism has an undeniable political allure. It conveniently shifts the blame onto foreigners. Canadians know that this can be powerful rhetoric, with all of the ongoing disputes over Canadian exports of softwood lumber. Indeed, it was the rising American current account deficit in the 1980s that led Canadian politicians to look for a free trade agreement with the United States, as they feared that the Americans would resort to protectionism to improve their trade balance. Canada has a huge trade account surplus with the United States, around $80 or $90 billion in the 2000s, so Canadians would have much to lose if Americans were to revert to protectionism.

But the U.S. trade deficit with Canada, despite Canada being its main trading partner, represents only about 10 percent of the overall trade deficit of the United States. This explains why most proposals there for tariffs and quotas are targeting the Asian countries that run large trade surpluses with the United States. Another issue is that Asian exporters are often large American companies that have decided to move their production to these low-wage countries.

◼ CONCLUSION: NO NATION IS AN ISLAND

The poet John Donne wrote that "no man is an island." Similarly, no nation is isolated from economic developments elsewhere on the globe. Instead, we live in a world economy in which the fates of nations are intertwined. The major trading countries are linked by exports and imports, by capital flows, and by exchange rates. What happens to national income, prices, and interest rates in one country affects other nations. No events make this point clearer than the international financial crises that erupt from time to time (see the previous chapter).

As we noted in Chapter 18, one root cause of almost all of these crises was the countries' decisions to fix their exchange rates to the U.S. dollar. Unfortunately for nations such as Thailand, Indonesia, and South Korea, the U.S. dollar rose spectacularly from 1995 to 1997. With their exchange rates tied to the dollar, the Thai baht, the Indonesian rupiah, and the Korean won automatically appreciated relative to most other currencies—making their exports more costly. Soon these one-time export powerhouses found themselves in an unaccustomed position: running large trade deficits.

Then the crisis hit, and all three of these countries watched their currencies tumble in value. The sharp depreciations restored their international competitiveness, but it also impoverished many of their citizens. The shrinking Asian economies curbed their appetite for American and other foreign goods, and that had a negative impact on economic activity in the rest of the world. The currencies of many countries, including the Canadian dollar, suffered a depreciation relative to the U.S. dollar, as investors moved their financial capital to what they considered to be the safest haven—the United States.

Thus, a primarily American development (the rise of the U.S. dollar) harmed the Asian economies, and then an Asian development (deep recessions in the Asian Tigers) hurt the world economy. The nations of the world are indeed linked economically.

ISSUE REVISITED: *Should the Bank of Canada Intervene on Foreign Exchange Markets?*

Recall the question with which we began this chapter: Should the Canadian government try to stop the Canadian dollar from rising? Remember that a rising Canadian dollar slows down exports and growth in Canada. Some economists say that businesses would face less uncertainty if the Canadian dollar was on a fixed exchange rate with the U.S. dollar; a few have asked the Bank of Canada to intervene on foreign exchange markets, asking it to purchase U.S. dollars so as to stop the U.S. dollar from falling relative to the Canadian dollar.

The point of view of the Bank of Canada is that the flexibility of the exchange rate provides an efficient stabilizing mechanism when fluctuations in the exchange rate are caused by briskly increasing or diminishing international demand for Canadian products. The floating exchange rate helps the Bank of Canada to control inflation by stabilizing real GDP, which is why the Bank of Canada does not want to move back to the fixed exchange rate regime that prevailed in Canada between 1962 and 1970. If the appreciating Canadian dollar does have strong detrimental effects on the overall Canadian economy, the Bank believes that it holds the instrument—a reduced target overnight rate—that can put the Canadian economy back on track. By cutting into real interest rates, the Bank of Canada believes it can raise domestic aggregate demand, stop the Canadian dollar from appreciating, and hence help Canadian producers and exporters. But the Bank of Canada will be willing to do this only when it feels that the Canadian economy is, or is likely to be, running below potential output.

In Canada, the situation is further complicated by the fact that commodity producers and manufacturers are not all located in the same provinces or in the same regions. In 2007, the number of manufacturing jobs in Ontario and Quebec decreased by 6.5 and 7.5 percent. During the same time period, employment in the natural resource industries of Alberta (which include oil and gas) grew by 8.5 percent. In early 2008, the Canadian inflation rate (the price change over 12 months) was about 2 percent, but it was well below 2 percent in central Canada and in British Columbia. Inflation was running high only in Alberta and Saskatchewan (at around 3.5 percent). Should the Bank of Canada stay put, or should it crank up interest rates because of high inflation rates in these two provinces? Or should interest rates be lowered to help central Canada manufacturers?

As long as the Canadian dollar appreciates as a result of rising world commodity prices, notably oil and gas prices, the Bank of Canada is unlikely to make any move. This will not hurt Alberta, but it will be detrimental to the areas where most of the manufacturing occurs—Quebec and southern Ontario, where many manufacturing jobs were lost in 2006 and 2007. Since the Bank of Canada raised interest rates in 2006 and essentially made them stay put in 2007, it must believe that the appreciation of the Canadian dollar is a demand-led phenomenon that requires no counteraction from the central bank. Indeed, interest rates did fall in 2008, but only as a response to the dangers brought about by the subprime financial crisis in the United States.

SUMMARY

1. The nations of the world are linked together economically because national income, prices, and interest rates in one country affect those in other countries. They are thus **open economies**.

2. Because one country's imports are another country's exports, rapid (or sluggish) economic growth in one country contributes to rapid (or sluggish) growth in other countries.

3. A country's net exports depend on whether its prices are high or low relative to those of other countries. Because exchange rates translate one country's prices into the currencies of other countries, the exchange rate is a key determinant of net exports.

4. If the currency depreciates, net exports rise and aggregate demand increases, thereby raising both real GDP and the price level. A depreciating currency also reduces aggregate supply by making imported inputs more costly (an adverse supply shock).

5. If the currency appreciates, net exports fall and aggregate demand, real GDP, and the price level all decrease. An appreciating currency also increases aggregate supply by making imported inputs cheaper (a favourable supply shock).

6. When the home currency depreciates, import prices and consumer prices do not rise by the full extent of the depreciation. There is a partial **foreign exchange pass-through**. Similarly, with appreciation, import and consumer prices do not decrease by the full extent of appreciation.

7. **International capital flows** respond strongly to rates of return on investments in different countries. For example, higher domestic interest rates lead to currency appreciations, and lower interest rates lead to depreciations.

8. Contractionary monetary policies raise interest rates and therefore make the currency appreciate. Both the higher interest rates and the stronger currency reduce aggregate demand. Hence, international capital flows make monetary policy more powerful than it would be in a closed economy.

9. The floating exchange rate acts as a shock absorber when the Canadian economy is subjected to demand shocks. For instance, when world commodity prices rise, there is a boom in the sectors producing raw materials and energy. But the Canadian dollar then appreciates, reducing export sales in the manufacturing and service industries, thus contributing to stabilization of the Canadian economy. There is no need for an intervention by the Bank of Canada. By contrast, when the Canadian dollar appreciates because of changes in the sentiments of portfolio holders, the central bank may need to lower interest rates to compensate for the deflationary impact of the appreciation.

10. A fundamental accounting identity links the government budget balance $(T - G)$ and the current account balance (CAB) that depends largely on the trade balance $(X - IM)$. In a floating exchange rate regime, the capital account balance is the negative of the current account balance. This means that when the economy is running a current account deficit, it has a positive capital account balance, and hence is borrowing from abroad. This occurs when domestic private saving is insufficient to finance domestic investment and the government budget deficit. The **fundamental accounting equation** thus says that the current account deficit must be equal to the government budget deficit, plus the excess of investment over private saving, and can be written as:

$$-CAB = (G - T) + (I - S)$$

11. In contrast to Canada, which has both a budget surplus and a current account surplus, the United States has faced a **twin-deficit problem** for a number of years, running both a budget deficit and a large current account deficit. It follows from the above equation that the American current account deficit, which is a growing concern for a number of economists and investors, could be cured by some combination of lower budget deficits, higher saving, and lower investment.

12. Ideally, the American current account deficit could be reduced through expansionary policies in the rest of the world, including Canada, which would lead to a reduction of the American **trade deficit**. It would also help if Asian countries that still control their foreign exchange rates and that run huge trade surpluses with the United States were to move toward more flexible exchange rates.

13. The Bank of Canada does not intervene in foreign exchange markets, even when the appreciation of the Canadian dollar drives manufacturers out of business, because it believes that floating exchange rates help to stabilize inflation rates. Also, the central bank believes that it can use the target overnight interest rate to generate more aggregate demand and compensate for the deflationary effects of the appreciation of the Canadian currency, if needed.

KEY TERMS

Open economy 417

Net exports 418

Exchange rate 419

Appreciation 420

Exchange rate pass-through 421

Depreciation 422

International capital flows 424

Closed economy 424

Trade deficit 430

Trade surplus 430

Fundamental accounting equation 430

Twin-deficit problem 431

$-CAB = (G - T) + (I - S)$ 433

TEST YOURSELF

1. Use the diagrams in this chapter to analyze the likely effects of a currency appreciation on the Canadian economy. Show that currency appreciation could lead to a different impact in the case of economies that react differently to exchange rate fluctuations.

2. Assume that net foreign income (*NFY*), that is, the difference between investment income that Canadians receive from abroad and the investment income that Canadians pay abroad, is zero, so that the current account balance is just equal to the trade balance. Explain why $X - IM = (S - I) - (G - T)$. Now multiply both sides of this equation by –1 to get

$$IM - X = (I - S) + (G - T)$$

and remember that the trade deficit, $IM - X$, is the amount we have to borrow from foreigners to get

$$\text{Borrowing from foreigners} = (I - S) + (G - T)$$

Explain the common sense behind this version of the fundamental equation.

3. **(More difficult)** Suppose consumption and investment are described by the following:

$$C = 150 + 0.75DI$$

$$I = 300 + 0.2Y - 50r$$

Here *DI* is disposable income, *Y* is GDP, and *r*, the interest rate, is measured in percentage points. (For example, a 5 percent interest rate is $r = 5$.) Exports and imports are as follows:

$$X = 300$$
$$IM = 250 + 0.2Y$$

Government purchases are $G = 800$, and taxes are 20 percent of income. The price level is fixed and the central bank uses its monetary policy to peg the interest rate at $r = 8$.

a. Find equilibrium GDP, the budget deficit or surplus, and the trade deficit or surplus.

b. Suppose the currency appreciates and, as a result, exports and imports change to

$$X = 250$$
$$IM = 0.2Y$$

Now find equilibrium GDP, the budget deficit or surplus, and the trade deficit or surplus.

DISCUSSION QUESTIONS

1. For years, the U.S. government has been trying to get Japan and the European Union to expand their economies faster. Explain how more rapid growth in Japan would affect the U.S. economy.

2. If inflation is lower in Germany than in Spain (as it is), and the exchange rate between the two countries is fixed (as it is, because of the monetary union), what is likely to happen to the balance of trade between the two countries?

3. Explain why a currency depreciation leads to an improvement in a country's trade balance.

4. Explain why Canadian monetary policy is more powerful in an open economy than in a closed economy.

5. Given what you now know, do you think it was a good idea for Canada to adopt a policy mix of high interest rates and large government budget deficits in both the early 1980s and early 1990s? What were the benefits and costs of reversing that policy mix in the 1990s?

6. Suppose the Canadian government decides to grant substantial tax cuts to the Canadian taxpayers. What effect is this likely to have on the Canadian current account balance?

7. Despite a strong appreciation of the Canadian dollar, the Bank of Canada decided to raise interest rates in 2006 and to keep them constant in 2007. Retrospectively, from the information that you can now gather on current employment and inflation rates, how do you assess such decisions? Were they the proper ones to make, given the state of the Canadian economy?

8. Suppose that your parents own a large beach property in Florida, but to finance this property, they took a mortgage with a Canadian bank in Canadian dollars. Would you say that their net wealth is being reduced or increased when the Canadian dollar appreciates relative to the U.S. dollar? What if the Canadian dollar were to depreciate?

9. In 2004, the international value of the yen rose somewhat. This development was viewed with alarm in Japan. Why?

10. What would you advise if you were asked to find ways to increase the Canadian current account surplus?

APPENDIX   *Deriving the Fundamental Accounting Equations*

Let's explore the connection between the budget deficit and the current account deficit in more detail. To do so, we start out with the mathematical relationship that we derived in Appendix B of Chapter 9, which defined the generalized macroeconomic identity linking investment to saving.

$$I = S + (T - G) + (IM - X - NFY)$$

This is the first form of our fundamental equation. All of the terms of the equation are familiar to us, except for *NFY*, which we encountered only in the appendixes of Chapters 9 and 18. *NFY* represents the net foreign income of Canadians, that is, the amount of investment income that Canadian residents receive from abroad less the amount of investment income that Canadian residents pay to nonresidents. This version of the fundamental equation tells us that investment is equal to saving, where saving is decomposed into three components: domestic private saving (S), which includes both household and corporate saving; domestic public saving, that is the saving of the government sector, ($T - G$); and nonresident saving, ($IM - X - NFY$).

As surprising as it may be, nonresident saving entering the Canadian economy turns out to be the *negative* of the current account balance *CAB*, as we defined it in Chapter 18, page 404, which is equal to:

$$CAB = (X - IM) + NFY$$

The current account balance is usually pretty close to the trade balance, or what we have called net exports, $X - IM$, with net foreign income usually accounting for a small difference in a country such as Canada. But why is nonresident saving the negative of the current account balance? Recall from Chapter 18 that under floating exchange rates, it is almost always true that:

Current account balance + Capital account balance = 0

Thus, when the current account balance is negative, that is, when the current account is in deficit, the capital account balance must be positive—the capital account is in surplus—and vice versa. Whenever the Canadian economy runs a current account deficit, it has to finance part of its imports and investment income payments abroad by selling domestic assets to the rest of the world. In other words, it has to borrow from the rest of the world (there is a capital account surplus), with nonresidents providing saving (lending funds) to the Canadian economy. The expression ($IM - X - NFY$)—the current account deficit—thus truly represents foreign saving entering the Canadian economy.

By moving the I term to the other side of the first form of the fundamental equation, we obtain a second form:

$$(S - I) + (T - G) + (IM - X - NFY) = 0$$

Remembering that the savings that are not invested in tangible assets must be placed in financial assets, this equation can be interpreted in two ways, which gave rise to Figures 10 and 11 in the main text:

Domestic private net lending + Domestic public net lending + Foreign net lending = 0

or

Private financial surplus + Government surplus + Current account deficit = 0

Rewriting the equation by moving the first two terms to the other side gives us the third form of the fundamental equation, the one from which we started in the main text:

$$(IM - X - NFY) = (I - S) + (G - T)$$

In words, this means that:

Current account deficit = Private financial deficit + Government deficit

This last form of the fundamental equation is the algebraic link that facilitates discussion of the issue of the twin deficits—the current account deficit (nearly the trade account deficit) and the government budget deficit.

TEST YOURSELF

1. Suppose that net lending by the private sector represents 2 percent of GDP, while the public sector budget is in balance. What is the current account balance as a percentage of GDP? Is it a current account deficit or a current account surplus?

2. You have been told that Spendonia has net lending by its private sector equal to −5 percent of GDP, with a public sector budget surplus representing 1 percent of GDP. What is the current account balance as a percentage of GDP? Is it a deficit or a surplus?

3. Thriftonia has a current account surplus equal to 4 percent of GDP. The budget of its public sector is balanced. Is the private sector of Thriftonia showing positive or negative net lending? How much as a percentage of GDP? Is the private sector saving more than it is investing?

GLOSSARY

Absolute advantage One country is said to have an absolute advantage over another in the production of a particular good if it can produce that good using smaller quantities of resources than can the other country. (p. 373)

Abstraction Abstraction means ignoring many details so as to focus on the most important elements of a problem. (p. 8)

Adaptive expectations of inflation These are expectations that economic agents formulate about the future inflation rate on the basis of the *past* values of inflation. (p. 355)

Aggregate demand Aggregate demand is the total amount that all consumers, business firms, and government agencies want to spend on final goods and services. (p. 168)

Aggregate demand curve The aggregate demand curve shows the quantity of domestic product that is being demanded and the overall price level. (pp. 95, 196)

Aggregate supply curve The aggregate supply curve shows the relationship between the quantity of domestic product that is being supplied and the overall price level. (p. 95)

Aggregation Aggregation means combining many individual markets into one overall market. (p. 93)

Allocation of resources Allocation of resources refers to society's decisions on how to divide up its scarce input resources among the different outputs produced in the economy and among the different firms or other organizations that produce those outputs. (p. 53)

Amortization The value of the portion of the nation's capital equipment that is used up within the year is described as *amortization*. It tells us how much output is needed just to maintain the economy's capital stock. (p. 186)

Appreciate A nation's currency is said to appreciate when exchange rates change so that a unit of its currency can buy more units of foreign currency. (p. 395)

Asset An asset of an individual or business firm is an item of value that the individual or firm owns. (p. 269)

Automatic stabilizer An automatic stabilizer is a feature of the economy that reduces its sensitivity to shocks, such as sharp increases or decreases in spending. (p. 247)

Autonomous increase in consumption An autonomous increase in consumption is an increase in consumer spending without any increase in consumer incomes. It is represented on a graph as a shift of the entire consumption function. (p. 205)

Balance of payments deficit The balance of payments deficit is the amount by which the quantity supplied of a country's currency (per year) exceeds the quantity demanded. Balance of payments deficits arise whenever the exchange rate is pegged at an artificially high level. (p. 403)

Balance of payments surplus The balance of payments surplus is the amount by which the quantity demanded of a country's currency (per year) exceeds the quantity supplied. Balance of payments surpluses arise whenever the exchange rate is pegged at an artificially low level. (p. 403)

Balance sheet A balance sheet is an accounting statement listing the values of all assets on the left side and the values of all liabilities and net worth on the right side. (p. 269)

Banking view The banking view holds that changes in nominal GDP cause changes in the stock of money, thus reversing the causality generally endorsed by adherents to the quantity theory of money. (p. 308)

Bank rate The bank rate is the interest rate charged to banks that still have negative large-value transfer system (LVTS) balances at the end of the day and hence must take advances (borrow funds) for one night from the Bank of Canada in order to settle with the LVTS. (p. 292)

Bank run A bank run (also called a run on a bank) occurs when many depositors withdraw cash from their accounts all at once. (p. 260)

Barter Barter is a system of exchange in which people directly trade one good for another, without using money as an intermediate step. (p. 261)

Base money The stock of base money is the sum of currency plus the deposits of banks at the Bank of Canada. (p. 298)

Budget deficit The budget deficit is the amount by which the government's expenditures exceed its receipts during a specified period of time, usually a year. If receipts exceed expenditures, it is called a budget surplus instead. (p. 330)

Budget surplus The budget surplus is the amount by which the government's receipts exceed its expenditures during a specified period of time, usually a year. If expenditures exceed receipts, it is called a budget deficit instead. (p. 330)

Buyback operations Buyback operations are sales of securities that are accompanied by promises to repurchase the securities at a predetermined price on a specific day, usually the next day. They occur on a segment of the overnight market, called the *repo market*. (p. 299)

Capital A nation's capital is its available supply of plant, equipment, and software. It is the result of past decisions to make *investments* in these items. (p. 148)

Capital account The capital account balance includes purchases and sales of financial assets to and from citizens and companies of other countries. (p. 404)

Capital adequacy requirements To meet capital adequacy requirements, a bank's capital must be large enough relative to the size of its assets, most notably the size of its loans. (p. 270)

Capital consumption allowances The value of the portion of the nation's capital equipment that is used up within the year is called the *capital consumption allowance*. It tells us how much output is needed just to maintain the economy's capital stock. (p. 186)

Capital formation Capital formation is synonymous with investment. It refers to the process of building up the capital stock. (p. 148)

Capital gain A capital gain is the difference between the price at which an asset is sold and the price at which it was bought. (p. 132)

Central bank A central bank is a bank for banks. Canada's central bank is the *Bank of Canada*, which acts as Canada's monetary authority. (p. 282)

Central bank independence Central bank independence refers to the central bank's ability to make decisions without political interference. (p. 283)

Closed economy A closed economy is one that does not trade with other nations in either goods or assets. (pp. 29, 424)

Collateral Collateral is property (e.g., car, house, business inventory, government securities) that is pledged by the borrower as security for a loan. (p. 270)

Commodity money Commodity money is an object in use as a medium of exchange, but which also has a substantial value in alternative (nonmonetary) uses. (p. 264)

Comparative advantage One country is said to have a comparative advantage over another in the production of a particular good *relative to other goods* if it produces that good less inefficiently as compared with the other country. (pp. 55, 373)

Consumer expenditure Consumer expenditure (*C*) is the total amount spent by consumers on newly produced goods and services (excluding purchases of new homes, which are considered investment goods). (p. 169)

Consumer Price Index (CPI) The Consumer Price Index (CPI) is measured by pricing the items on a list representative of a typical household budget. (p. 137)

Consumption function The consumption function shows the relationship between total consumer expenditures and total disposable income in the economy, holding all other determinants of consumer spending constant. (p. 174)

Convergence hypothesis The convergence hypothesis holds that nations with low levels of productivity tend to have high productivity growth rates, so that international productivity differences shrink over time. (p. 147)

Coordination failure A coordination failure occurs when party A would like to change his behaviour if party B would change hers, and vice versa, and yet the two changes do not take place because the decisions of A and B are not coordinated. (p. 200)

Core inflation This is the rate of change of a modified Consumer Price Index that excludes certain items whose prices are the most volatile, such as food and energy. It is considered to be a useful guide for estimating inflationary pressures. (p. 288)

Correlated Two variables are said to be correlated if they tend to go up or down together. Correlation need not imply causation. (p. 10)

Corridor system The corridor system is the operating framework adopted by the Bank of Canada that forces the overnight interest rate to remain within the operating band and close to the midpoint of the band, as defined by the target overnight rate. (p. 292)

Cost disease of the personal services The cost disease of the personal services is the tendency of the costs and prices of these services to rise persistently faster than those of the average output in the economy. (p. 160)

Creditworthiness Creditworthiness is at the core of the bank lending system. It can be demonstrated by providing collateral or by demonstrating the ability to fulfill loan obligations. (p. 270)

Crowding in Crowding in occurs when government spending, by raising real GDP, induces increases in private investment spending. (p. 340)

Crowding out Crowding out occurs when deficit spending by the government forces private investment spending to contract. (p. 339)

Currency The sum of coins and paper money is called *currency*. (p. 265)

Current account The current account balance includes international purchases and sales of goods and services, cross-border interest and dividend payments, and cross-border gifts to and from both private individuals and governments. It is approximately the same as net exports. (p. 404)

Cyclical unemployment Cyclical unemployment is the portion of unemployment that is attributable to a decline in the economy's total production. Cyclical unemployment rises during recessions and falls as prosperity is restored. (p. 124)

Deflating Deflating is the process of finding the real value of some monetary magnitude by dividing by some appropriate price index. (p. 138)

Deflation Deflation refers to a sustained decrease in the general price level. (p. 103)

Demand curve A demand curve is a graphical depiction of a demand schedule. It shows how the quantity demanded of some product will change as the price of that product changes during a specified period of time, holding all other determinants of quantity demanded constant. (p. 63)

Demand schedule A demand schedule is a table showing how the quantity demanded of some product during a specified period of time changes as the price of that product changes, holding all other determinants of quantity demanded constant. (p. 63)

Demand-side inflation Demand-side inflation is a rise in the price level caused by rapid growth of aggregate demand. (p. 348)

Deposit insurance Deposit insurance is a system that guarantees that depositors will not lose money even if their bank goes bankrupt. (p. 268)

Depreciate A nation's currency is said to depreciate when exchange rates change so that a unit of its currency can buy fewer units of foreign currency. (p. 395)

Devaluation A devaluation is a reduction in the official value of a currency. (p. 395)

Development assistance Development assistance ("foreign aid") refers to outright grants and low-interest loans to poor countries from both rich countries and multinational institutions like the World Bank. The purpose is to spur economic development. (p. 161)

Discouraged worker A discouraged worker is an unemployed person who gives up looking for work and is therefore no longer counted as part of the labour force. (p. 122)

Disposable income Disposable income (*DI*) is the sum of the incomes of all individuals in the economy after all taxes have been deducted and all transfer payments have been added. (p. 169)

Division of labour Division of labour means breaking up a task into a number of smaller, more *specialized* tasks so that each worker can become more adept at a particular job. (p. 54)

Dumping Dumping means selling goods in a foreign market at lower prices than those charged in the home market. (p. 386)

Dutch disease The term *Dutch disease* refers to the Netherlands' experience in the 1960s when the discovery of North Sea gas pushed the exchange rate so high that Holland's manufacturing sector became less competitive and the country experienced some deindustrialization. (p. 411)

Economic model An economic model is a simplified, small-scale version of some aspect of the economy. Economic models are often expressed in equations, by graphs, or in words. (p. 12)

Efficiency A set of outputs is said to be produced efficiently if, given current technological knowledge, there is no way one can produce larger amounts of any output without using larger input amounts or giving up some quantity of another output. (p. 53)

Employment Insurance Employment Insurance is a government program that replaces some of the wages lost by eligible workers who lose their jobs. (p. 125)

Equation of exchange The equation of exchange states that the money value of GDP transactions must be equal to the product of the average stock of money times velocity. That is: $M \times V = P \times Y$ (p. 305)

Equilibrium An equilibrium is a situation in which there are no inherent forces that

produce change. Changes away from an equilibrium position will occur only as a result of "outside events" that disturb the status quo. (pp. 71, 192)

Exchange rate The exchange rate states the price, in terms of one currency, at which another currency can be bought. (p. 394)

Exchange rate pass-through The exchange rate pass-through measures the extent to which depreciation (appreciation) of the local currency is passed to higher (lower) import prices and consumer prices. When prices rise by the extent of the depreciation, there is a full exchange rate pass-through; otherwise, the pass-through is only partial. (p. 421)

Expenditure schedule An expenditure schedule shows the relationship between national income (GDP) and total spending. (p. 194)

Export subsidy An export subsidy is a payment by the government to exporters to permit them to reduce the selling prices of their goods so they can compete more effectively in foreign markets. (p. 380)

45° line Rays through the origin with a slope of 1 are called 45° lines because they form an angle of 45° with the horizontal axis. A 45° line marks off points where the variables measured on each axis have equal values. (p. 22)

45° line diagram An income–expenditure diagram, or 45° line diagram, plots total real expenditure (on the vertical axis) against real income (on the horizontal axis). The 45° line marks off points where income and expenditure are equal. (p. 195)

Factors of production Inputs or factors of production are the labour, machinery, buildings, and natural resources used to make outputs. (p. 26)

Fiat money Fiat money is money that is decreed as such by the government. It is of little value as a commodity, but it maintains its value as a medium of exchange because people have faith that the issuer will stand behind the pieces of printed paper and limit their production. (p. 264)

Final goods and services Final goods and services are those that are purchased by their ultimate users. (p. 97)

Fiscal policy The government's fiscal policy is its plan for spending and taxation. It can be used to steer aggregate demand in the desired direction. (p. 105)

Fisher debt effect The Fisher debt effect is the negative effect that lower output prices have on real spending, as the real value of the money-fixed liabilities of households and firms rise when prices are lower. (p. 230)

Fixed exchange rates Fixed exchange rates are rates set by government decisions and maintained by government actions. (p. 402)

Fixed taxes Fixed taxes are taxes that do not vary with the level of GDP. (p. 256)

Floating exchange rates Floating exchange rates are rates determined in free markets by the law of supply and demand. (p. 396)

Foreign direct investment Foreign direct investment is the purchase or construction of real business assets—such as factories, offices, and machinery—in a foreign country. (p. 162)

Forward foreign exchange markets Forward foreign exchange markets are markets that, for a small fee, allow business firms to avoid the risk of fluctuations in foreign exchange rates for as long as one year. (p. 407)

Frictional unemployment Frictional unemployment is unemployment that is due to normal turnover in the labour market. It includes people who are temporarily between jobs because they are moving or changing occupations, or are unemployed for similar reasons. (p. 122)

Full employment Full employment is a situation in which everyone who is willing and able to work can find a job. At full employment, the measured unemployment rate is still positive. (p. 124)

Fundamental accounting equation There is a fundamental accounting equation that says that the current account deficit of a country must be equal to the financial deficit of the private sector plus the government budget deficit. (p. 430)

GDP deflator The price index used to deflate nominal GDP is called the *GDP deflator*. It is a broad measure of economy-wide inflation; it includes the prices of all goods and services in the economy. (p. 139)

Gold standard The gold standard is a way to fix exchange rates by defining each participating currency in terms of gold and allowing holders of each participating currency to convert that currency into gold. (p. 404)

Government purchases Government purchases (G) refer to the goods (such as airplanes and paper clips) and services (such as school teaching and police protection) purchased by all levels of government. (p. 169)

Gross domestic income Gross domestic income is a measure of gross output seen from the income side. Because it is valued at market prices, it incorporates all wages, interest, and profits, as well as all taxes on factors of production and sales taxes. It excludes transfer payments from the government, in particular interest paid on public debt. (p. 170)

Gross domestic product (GDP) Gross domestic product (GDP) is the sum of the money values of all final goods and services produced in the domestic economy and sold on organized markets during a specified period of time, usually a year. (pp. 28, 96, 183)

Gross national product (GNP) Gross national product is the sum of the money values of all final goods and services produced by the factors of production owned by the *nationals* of a country, during a specified period of time, usually a year. (p. 188)

Gross private domestic investment (I_{na}) Gross private domestic investmentincludes business investment in plant, equipment, and software; residential construction; and inventory investment. (p. 184)

Growth policy Growth policy refers to government policies intended to make the economy grow faster in the long run. (p. 114)

Human capital Human capital is the amount of skill embodied in the workforce. It is most commonly measured by the amount of education and training. (p. 146)

Hysteresis The word *hysteresis* was introduced into economics by Edmund Phelps to mean a situation in which effects remain even after the initial causes have been removed, as in electromagnetics. (p. 362)

Income–expenditure diagram An income–expenditure diagram, or 45° line diagram, plots total real expenditure (on the vertical axis) against real income (on the horizontal axis). The 45° line marks off points where income and expenditure are equal. (p. 195)

Indexing Indexing refers to provisions in a law or a contract whereby monetary payments are automatically adjusted whenever a specified price index changes. Wage rates, pensions, interest payments on bonds, income taxes, and many other things can be indexed in this way, and have been. Sometimes such contractual provisions are called *escalator clauses*. (p. 355)

Index number An index number expresses the cost of a market basket of goods relative to its cost in some "base" period, which is simply the year used as a basis of comparison. (p. 137)

Index number problem When relative prices are changing, there is no such thing as a "perfect price index" that is correct for every consumer. Any statistical index will understate the increase in the cost of living for some families and overstate it for others. At best, the index can represent the situation of an "average" family. (p. 137)

Induced increase in consumption An induced increase in consumption is an increase in consumer spending that stems from an increase in consumer incomes. It is represented on a graph as a movement along a fixed consumption function. (p. 205)

Induced investment Induced investment is the part of investment spending that rises when GDP rises and falls when GDP falls. (p. 195)

Inflation Inflation refers to a sustained increase in the general price level. Inflation occurs when prices in an economy rise rapidly. The rate of inflation is calculated by averaging the percentage growth rate of the prices of a selected sample of commodities. (p. 96)

Inflationary gap The inflationary gap is the amount by which equilibrium real GDP exceeds the full-employment level of GDP. (pp. 199, 226)

Inflation–output Phillips relationship The inflation–output Phillips relationship is merely a diagrammatic representation of the traditional inflation–unemployment Phillips curve in inflation–real output space. (p. 353)

Inflation targeting The goal of inflation targeting by the Bank of Canada is to keep the inflation rate at a particular level; currently, 2 percent is the target. (p. 286)

Innovation Innovation is the process that begins with invention and includes improvement to prepare the invention for practical use and marketing of the invention or its products. (p. 154)

Inputs Inputs or factors of production are the labour, machinery, buildings, and natural resources used to make outputs. (pp. 26, 48, 113)

Insolvent bank An insolvent bank has negative net worth—its liabilities are greater than its assets. (p. 273)

Interest rate on deposits at the central bank The interest rate on deposits at the central bank is the rate of interest that banks receive on their deposits at the Bank of Canada as a result of the operation of the large-value transfer system (LVTS). Banks with positive LVTS balances must deposit them in their accounts at the Bank of Canada when settlement occurs at the end of the day. (p. 292)

Intermediate good An intermediate good is a good purchased for resale or for use in producing another good. (p. 97)

International capital flows International capital flows are purchases and sales of financial assets across national borders. (p. 424)

Invention Invention is the act of discovering new products or new ways of making products. (p. 154)

Investment Investment is the *flow* of resources into the production of new capital. It is the labour, steel, and other inputs devoted to the *construction* of factories, warehouses, railroads, and other pieces of capital during some period of time. (p. 148)

Investment spending Investment spending (I) is the sum of the expenditures of business firms on new plant and equipment and households on new homes. Financial "investments" are not included, nor are resales of existing physical assets. (p. 169)

Invisible hand *Invisible hand* is a term used by Adam Smith to describe how, by pursuing their own self-interests, people in a market system are "led by an invisible hand" to promote the well-being of the community. (p. 62)

Labour force The labour force is the number of people holding or seeking jobs. (p. 116)

Labour productivity Labour productivity is the amount of output a worker turns out in an hour (or a week, or a year) of labour. If output is measured by GDP, it is GDP per hour of work. (p. 116)

Large-value transfer system (LVTS) The large-value transfer system is the main Canadian clearing and settlement system, where banks exchange and deposit payment items for their clients, determine the net amounts owed to each, and settle their accounts at the end of the day. (p. 274)

Large-value transfer system (LVTS) balance This is the multilateral clearing position that a bank has accumulated within the large-value transfer system in the course of the day. When the bank is in a net credit position, the balance is positive; when it is in a net debit position, the balance is negative. (p. 274)

Law of supply and demand The law of supply and demand states that in a free market the forces of supply and demand generally push the price toward the level at which quantity supplied and quantity demanded are equal. (p. 72)

Liability A liability of an individual or business firm is an item of value that the individual or firm owes. Many liabilities are known as *debts*. (p. 269)

Liquidity An asset's liquidity refers to the ease with which it can be converted into cash. (p. 267)

M1+ The narrowly defined money supply, usually abbreviated M1+, is the sum of currency held by the public and all chequable deposits at banks, credit unions, caisses populaires, and trust and mortgage loan companies. (p. 265)

M2+ The broadly defined money supply, usually abbreviated M2+, is the sum of currency held by the public, plus all types of chequable deposits, plus savings deposits, plus shares in money market mutual funds and life insurance annuities. (p. 265)

Marginal propensity to consume (MPC) The marginal propensity to consume (MPC) is the ratio of changes in consumption relative to changes in disposable income that produce the change in consumption. On a graph, it appears as the slope of the consumption function. (p. 174)

Marginal propensity to save The marginal propensity to save is the ratio of changes in saving relative to changes in disposable income that produce the change in saving. (p. 207)

Market system A market system is a form of economic organization in which resource allocation decisions are left to individual producers and consumers acting in their own best interests without central direction. (p. 57)

Medium of exchange Money is the standard object used in exchanging goods and services. In short, money is the medium of exchange. (p. 262)

Mercantilism Mercantilism is a doctrine that holds that exports are good for a country, whereas imports are harmful. (p. 377)

Metallist or commodity concept of money This is a concept that views money primarily as a commodity possessing an intrinsic value that emerged spontaneously to facilitate the exchange of goods and services and to overcome the problem of double coincidence related to barter exchange. (p. 261)

Mixed economy A mixed economy is one with some public influence over the workings of free markets. There may also be some public ownership mixed in with private property. (p. 42)

Monetarism Monetarism is a mode of analysis that uses the equation of exchange to organize and analyze macroeconomic data. (p. 307)

Monetary policy This term refers to actions that the Bank of Canada takes to affect the macroeconomic performance of the economy. (p. 106)

Monetary policy implementation Monetary policy implementation is the set of rules, instruments, and day-to-day actions that allow the central bank to achieve its operational target. (p. 284)

Monetary policy strategy Monetary policy strategy comprises the decisions that the central bank makes about the level of the target overnight rate of interest to try to influence or achieve, for example, a target inflation rate. (p. 285)

Monetize the deficit The central bank is said to monetize the deficit when it purchases bonds issued by the government. (p. 338)

Money Money is the standard object used in exchanging goods and services. In short, money is the medium of exchange. (p. 262)

Money-fixed asset A money-fixed asset is an asset whose value is a fixed number of dollars. (p. 176)

Money-fixed liability An example of a money-fixed liability is a mortgage taken to purchase a house, the value of which is a fixed number of dollars. (p. 176)

Money multiplier The money multiplier is the ratio of some broad money aggregate to base money. (p. 310)

Moral hazard Moral hazard refers to the tendency of insurance to discourage policyholders from protecting themselves from risk. (p. 269)

Multinational corporations Multinational corporations are corporations, generally large ones, that do business in many countries. Most, but not all, of these corporations have their headquarters in developed countries. (p. 162)

Multiplier The multiplier is the ratio of the change in equilibrium GDP (Y) divided by the original change in spending that causes the change in GDP. (p. 200)

National debt The national debt is the federal government's total indebtedness at a moment in time. It is the result of previous budget deficits. (p. 330)

National income accounting The system of measurement devised for collecting and expressing macroeconomic data is called *national income accounting*. (p. 183)

Near moneys Near moneys are liquid assets that are close substitutes for money. (p. 266)

Net domestic product at basic prices The net domestic product at basic prices is simply net domestic product less all of the various sales taxes. (p. 186)

Net domestic product at market prices The net domestic product at market prices is simply gross domestic product less amortization. (p. 186)

Net exports Net exports, or $X - IM$, is the difference between exports (X) and imports (IM). It indicates the difference between what we sell to foreigners and what we buy from them. (p. 169)

Net worth Net worth is the value of all assets minus the value of all liabilities. (p. 269)

New classical economics Now the main rival of Keynesian economics, followers of new classical economics believe that there are economic mechanisms that quickly bring back the economy toward full employment and full use of capacity. Most of them further argue that shocks to the economy arise mainly from the supply side. (p. 352)

Nominal GDP Nominal GDP, also called GDP at current prices, is calculated by valuing all outputs at current prices. (p. 96)

Nominal rate of interest The nominal rate of interest is the percentage by which the money the borrower pays back exceeds the money that she borrowed, making no adjustment for any decline in the purchasing power of this money that results from inflation. (p. 131)

Nonaccelerating inflation rate of unemployment (NAIRU) NAIRU is the rate of unemployment at which inflation will neither rise nor fall over the long run. (p. 353)

On-the-job training On-the-job training refers to skills that workers acquire while at work, rather than in school or in formal vocational training programs. (p. 153)

Open economy An open economy is one that trades with other nations in goods and services, and perhaps also trades in financial assets. (pp. 29, 417)

Open-market operations Open-market operations refer to the Bank of Canada's purchase or sale of government securities through transactions in the open market. (p. 298)

Operating band The operating band is the zone of overnight rates between the bank rate and the interest rate on bank deposits at the central bank. (p. 292)

Opportunity cost The opportunity cost of some decision is the value of the next best alternative that must be given up because of that decision (for example, working instead of going to school). (p. 47)

Optimal decision An optimal decision is one that best serves the objectives of the decision maker, whatever those objectives may be. It is selected by explicit or implicit comparison with the possible alternative choices. The term *optimal* connotes neither approval nor disapproval of the objective itself. (p. 48)

Origin (of a graph) The "0" point in the lower-left corner of a graph where the axes meet is called the *origin*. Both variables are equal to zero at the origin. (p. 19)

Output gap The output gap is a measure of the inflationary tensions that exist in the economy, based on the discrepancy between actual real GDP and potential GDP, as defined by the Bank of Canada. (p. 288)

Outputs The outputs of a firm or an economy are the goods and services it produces. (pp. 26, 48, 113)

Overnight interest rate The overnight interest rate is the interest rate that banks and other financial market participants pay and receive when they borrow and lend surplus funds among themselves for one night; in particular, when banks borrow and lend LVTS balances among themselves. (p. 285)

Overnight market The overnight market is the financial market where banks and other financial market participants lend and borrow surplus funds among themselves for one night. (p. 276)

Paradox of thrift The paradox of thrift is the surprising fact that individual efforts to save more will ultimately be unsuccessful at the aggregate level, leading instead to lower equilibrium income and output levels, and failing to raise aggregate saving. (p. 208)

Persistence This means that a variable, such as the NAIRU, may stray from its defined long-run equilibrium value for a long time, but will eventually return to it. (p. 362)

Phillips curve A Phillips curve is a graph depicting the rate of unemployment on the horizontal axis and either the rate of inflation or the rate of change of money wages on the vertical axis. Phillips curves are normally downward-sloping, indicating that higher inflation rates are associated with lower unemployment rates. (p. 349)

Potential GDP Potential GDP is the real GDP that the economy would produce if its labour and other resources were fully employed. (p. 116)

Price ceiling A price ceiling is a maximum that the price charged for a commodity cannot legally exceed. (p. 78)

Price floor A price floor is a legal minimum below which the price charged for a commodity is not permitted to fall. (p. 80)

Primary budget deficit The primary budget deficit is the actual deficit less the interest payments on the public debt. (p. 334)

Principle of increasing costs The principle of increasing costs states that as the production of a good expands, the opportunity cost of producing another unit generally increases. (p. 50)

Production function The economy's production function shows the volume of output that can be produced from given inputs (such as labour and capital), given the available technology. (p. 117)

Production indifference map A production indifference map is a graph whose axes show the quantities of two inputs that are used to produce some output. A curve in the graph corresponds to some given quantity of that output, and the different points on that curve show the different quantities of the two inputs that are just enough to produce the given output. (p. 23)

Production possibilities frontier The production possibilities frontier is a curve that shows the maximum quantities of outputs it is possible to produce with the available resource quantities and the current state of technological knowledge. (p. 49)

Productivity Productivity is the amount of output produced by a unit of input. (p. 224)

Progressive tax A progressive tax is one in which the average tax rate paid by an individual rises as income rises. (p. 42)

Property rights Property rights are laws and/or conventions that assign owners the rights to use their property as they see fit (within the law)—for example, to sell the property and to reap the benefits (such as rents or dividends) while they own it. (p. 151)

Purchasing power The purchasing power of a given sum of money is the volume of goods and services that it will buy. (p. 127)

Quantity demanded The quantity demanded is the number of units of a good that consumers are willing and can afford to buy over a specified period of time. (p. 63)

Quantity supplied The quantity supplied is the number of units that sellers want to sell over a specified period of time. (p. 67)

Quantity theory of money The quantity theory of money assumes that velocity is (approximately) constant. In that case, nominal GDP is proportional to the money stock. (p. 305)

Quota A quota specifies the maximum amount of a good that is permitted into the country from abroad per unit of time. (p. 380)

Ray through the origin (or ray) Lines whose Y-intercept is zero have so many special uses in economics and other disciplines that they have been given a special name: a ray through the origin, or a ray. (p. 22)

Real GDP Real GDP, also called GDP at constant prices, is calculated by valuing outputs of different years at constant prices. Therefore, real GDP is a far better measure than nominal GDP of changes in total production. (p. 96)

Real GDP per capita Real GDP per capita is the ratio of real GDP divided by population. (p. 101)

Real rate of interest The real rate of interest is the percentage increase in purchasing power that the borrower pays to the lender for the privilege of borrowing. It indicates the increased ability to purchase goods and services that the lender earns. (p. 131)

Real wage rate The real wage rate is the wage rate adjusted for inflation. Specifically, it is the nominal wage divided by the price index. The real wage thus indicates the volume of goods and services that the nominal wages will buy. (p. 127)

Recession A recession is a period of time during which the total output of the economy declines. (pp. 31, 96)

Recessionary gap The recessionary gap is the amount by which the equilibrium level of real GDP falls short of potential GDP. (pp. 199, 226)

Relative price An item's relative price is its price in terms of some other item rather than in terms of dollars. (p. 129)

Research and development (R&D) Research and development (R&D) is the activity of firms, universities, and government agencies that seeks to invent new products and processes and to improve those inventions so that they are ready for the market or other users. (p. 154)

Resources Resources are the instruments provided by nature or by people that are used to create goods and services. Natural resources include minerals, soil, water, and air. Labour is a scarce resource, because of time limitations (the day has only 24 hours) and because the number of skilled workers is limited. Factories and machines are resources made by people. These three types of resources are often referred to as *land*, *labour*, and *capital*. They are also called *inputs* or *factors of production*. (p. 46)

Retained earnings Retained earnings are the portion of a corporation's profits that management decides to keep and reinvest in the firm's operations rather than paying it out as dividends to shareholders. (p. 171)

Revaluation A revaluation is an increase in the official value of a currency. (p. 395)

Scatter diagram A scatter diagram is a graph showing the relationship between two variables (such as consumer spending and disposable income). Each year is represented by a point in the diagram, and the coordinates of each year's point show the values of the two variables in that year. (p. 172)

Self-correcting mechanism The economy's self-correcting mechanism refers to the way changes in wages brought about by competitive forces will drive the economy back to potential output, thus eliminating the inflationary gap or the recessionary gap. (p. 230)

Settlement-balance management Settlement-balance management is the action that the Bank of Canada takes to neutralize the impact of government transactions, thus bringing back the supply of settlement balances to their desired level, usually zero. It is carried by shifting government deposits between the central bank and banks. (p. 295)

Settlement balances Settlement balances are the *net* aggregate amount of LVTS balances held by *banks*, that is, the sum of the positive and negative LVTS balances of all of the banks. (p. 295)

Shift in a demand curve A shift in a demand curve occurs when any relevant variable other than price changes. If consumers want to buy *more* at any and all given prices than they wanted previously, the demand curve shifts to the right (or outward). If they desire *less* at any given price, the demand curve shifts to the left (or inward). (p. 64)

Shortage A shortage is an excess of quantity demanded over quantity supplied. When there is a shortage, buyers cannot purchase the quantities they desire at the current price. (p. 71)

Slope of a curved line The slope of a curved line at a particular point is defined as the slope of the straight line that is tangent to the curve at that point. (p. 20)

Slope of a straight line The slope of a straight line is the ratio of the vertical change to the corresponding horizontal change as we move to the right along the line or, as it is often said, the ratio of the "rise" over the "run." (p. 20)

Solvent bank A solvent bank is a bank that has positive net worth. The bank's capital is positive, so its assets are larger than its liabilities. An **insolvent bank** has negative net worth. (p. 273)

Specialization Specialization means that a country devotes its energies and resources to only a small proportion of the world's productive activities. (p. 371)

Stabilization policy Stabilization policy is the name given to government programs designed to prevent or shorten recessions and to counteract inflation (that is, to *stabilize* prices). (p. 109)

Stagflation Stagflation is inflation that occurs while the economy is growing slowly ("stagnating") or in a recession. (pp. 106, 232)

Standing facilities Standing facilities are routine monetary operations involving the central bank that banks can use *at their discretion at any moment*. Standing facilities include *borrowing* facilities and *deposit* facilities. (p. 293)

State or **chartalist concept of money** A theory about the origin of money that identifies money as primarily a unit of account created by the state to permit individuals to discharge their obligations to the state; it also evolved as a medium of exchange in market transactions. (p. 262)

Steady inflation rate of output (SIRO) The steady inflation rate of output is the level of output that would keep the rate of inflation constant. It is potential output as measured by the Bank of Canada, and it is the counterpart of the NAIRU in inflation–real output space. (p. 354)

Store of value A store of value is an item used to store wealth from one point in time to another. (p. 262)

Structural (or cyclically adjusted) budget deficit The structural or cyclically adjusted budget deficit is the hypothetical deficit we *would* have under current fiscal policies if the economy was operating at its high-employment level. (p. 333)

Structural unemployment Structural unemployment refers to workers who have lost their jobs because they have been displaced by automation, because their skills are no longer in demand, or because of similar reasons. (p. 122)

Supply curve A supply curve is a graphical depiction of a supply schedule. It shows how the quantity supplied of some product will change as the price of that product changes during a specified period of time, holding all other determinants of quantity supplied constant. (p. 68)

Supply–demand diagram A supply–demand diagram graphs the supply and demand curves together. It also determines the equilibrium price and quantity. (p. 71)

Supply schedule A supply schedule is a table showing how the quantity supplied of some product changes as the price of that product changes during a specified period of time, holding all other determinants of quantity supplied constant. (p. 68)

Supply-side inflation Supply-side inflation is a rise in the price level caused by slow growth (or decline) of aggregate supply. (p. 348)

Surplus A surplus is an excess of quantity supplied over quantity demanded. When there is a surplus, sellers cannot sell the quantities they desire to supply at the current price. (p. 71)

Systemic risk There is systemic risk in a payment system when the failure of one bank to meet its obligations could lead to the failure of other banks to meet their obligations, thus jeopardizing the functioning of the entire payment system. (p. 275)

Tangent A tangent to the curve is a *straight* line that *touches*, but does not *cut*, the curve at a particular point. (p. 20)

Target overnight interest rate The target overnight interest rate is the operational target of the Bank of Canada; it is the overnight rate that the central bank would like to see realized. (p. 285)

Tariff A tariff is a tax on imports. (p. 379)

Theory A theory is a deliberate simplification of relationships used to explain how those relationships work. (p. 10)

Trade adjustment assistance Trade adjustment assistance provides special unemployment benefits, loans, retraining programs, and other aid to workers and firms that are harmed by foreign competition. (p. 382)

Trade deficit A country's trade deficit is the excess of its imports over its exports. If, instead, exports exceed imports, the country has a trade surplus. (p. 430)

Trade surplus A country's trade surplus is the excess of its exports over its imports. If, instead, imports exceed exports, the country has a trade deficit. (p. 430)

Transfer payments Transfer payments are sums of money that the government gives certain individuals as outright grants rather than as payments for services rendered to employers. Some common examples are social assistance and unemployment benefits. (pp. 42, 171)

Twin-deficit problem The twin-deficit problem is the recognition that *if* private saving and investment are equal, the current account deficit and the government budget deficit must rise or fall together. (p. 433)

Unemployment rate The unemployment rate is the number of unemployed people, expressed as a percentage of the labour force. (p. 119)

Unit labour cost The unit labour cost is simply the wage rate divided by average labour productivity. It is the average cost of a unit of output per unit of labour. If wage rates rise with labour productivity remaining unchanged, unit labour costs rise. If labour productivity rises with wage rates remaining unchanged, unit labour costs fall. (p. 350)

Unit of account The unit of account is the standard unit for quoting prices. (p. 262)

Value added The value added by a firm is its revenue from selling a product minus the amount paid for goods and services purchased from other firms. (p. 186)

Variable A variable is something measured by a number; it is used to analyze what happens to other things when the size of that number changes (varies). (p. 19)

Variable taxes Variable taxes are taxes that vary with the level of GDP. (p. 256)

Velocity Velocity indicates the number of times per year that an "average dollar" is spent on goods and services. It is the ratio of nominal gross domestic product (GDP) to the number of dollars in the money stock. That is:

$$\text{Velocity} = \frac{\text{Nominal GDP}}{\text{Money stock}} \quad \text{(p. 305)}$$

Vertical long-run Phillips curve The vertical long-run Phillips curve shows the menu of inflation/unemployment choices available to society in the long run. It is a vertical straight line at the nonaccelerating inflation rate of unemployment (NAIRU). (p. 353)

Wealth effect The wealth effect is the negative effect that higher output prices have on real consumer spending, as the real value of the money-fixed assets of households fall when prices are higher. (p. 176)

_Y_-intercept The Y-intercept of a line or a curve is the point at which it touches the vertical axis (the Y-axis). The X-intercept is defined similarly. (p. 22)

Zero lower bound on nominal interest rates The problem of the zero lower bound on nominal interest rates is the fact that, when deflation occurs, central banks cannot set negative real interest rates and hence impose a truly expansionary monetary policy, because nominal interest rates cannot go any lower than 0 percent. (p. 321)

INDEX